Comparative Education
The Dialectic of the Global and the Local

FIFTH EDITION

■ ■ ■

Edited by

Carlos Alberto Torres
UCLA

Robert F. Arnove
Indiana University

Lauren Ila Misiaszek
Beijing Normal University

ROWMAN & LITTLEFIELD
Lanham • Boulder • New York • London

Acquisitions Editor: Mark Kerr
Acquisitions Assistant: Sarah Rinehart
Sales and Marketing Inquiries: textbooks@rowman.com

Credits and acknowledgments for material borrowed from other sources, and reproduced with permission, appear on the appropriate pages within the text.

Published in cooperation with the Association for Conflict Resolution

Published by Rowman & Littlefield
An imprint of The Rowman & Littlefield Publishing Group, Inc.
4501 Forbes Boulevard, Suite 200, Lanham, Maryland 20706
www.rowman.com

86-90 Paul Street, London EC2A 4NE

Copyright © 2023 by The Rowman & Littlefield Publishing Group, Inc.
Second edition 2003. Third edition 2007. Fourth edition 2013.

All rights reserved. No part of this book may be reproduced in any form or by any electronic or mechanical means, including information storage and retrieval systems, without written permission from the publisher, except by a reviewer who may quote passages in a review.

British Library Cataloguing in Publication Information Available

Library of Congress Cataloging-in-Publication Data
Names: Torres, Carlos Alberto, editor. | Arnove, Robert F., editor. | Misiaszek, Lauren Ila, editor.
Title: Comparative education : the dialectic of the global and the local / Carlos Alberto Torres, Robert F. Arnove, Lauren Ila Misiaszek.
Other titles: Comparative education (Rowman and Littlefield, Inc.)
Description: Fifth edition. | Lanham, Maryland : Rowman & Littlefield, 2022. | Includes bibliographical references and index.
Identifiers: LCCN 2022002464 (print) | LCCN 2022002465 (ebook) | ISBN 9781538145548 (cloth) | ISBN 9781538145555 (paperback) | ISBN 9781538145562 (epub)
Subjects: LCSH: Comparative education—Philosophy. | Education and globalization.
Classification: LCC LB43 .C68 2022 (print) | LCC LB43 (ebook) | DDC 370.9—dc23/eng/20220125
LC record available at https://lccn.loc.gov/2022002464
LC ebook record available at https://lccn.loc.gov/2022002465

Brief Contents

Introduction: Reframing Comparative Education: The Dialectic of the Global and the Local by Robert F. Arnove — 1

1. **Institutionalizing International Influence** by Joel Samoff — 29
2. **Economics, Education, and Society: Myths and Possibilities** by Steven J. Klees — 71
3. **The State, Social Movements, and Education: Between Reform and Transformation** by Raymond Morrow and Carlos Alberto Torres — 87
4. **Culture and Education** by Vandra Lea Masemann — 125
5. **The Question of Identity from a Comparative Education Perspective** by Christine Fox — 147
6. **Equality of Education: Six Decades of Comparative Evidence Seen from a New Millennium** by Joseph P. Farrell (posthumous) — 163
7. **Women's Education in the 21st Century** by Nelly P. Stromquist — 187
8. **Control of Education: Issues and Tensions in Centralization and Decentralization** by Mark Bray — 221
9. **Transforming Adult and Community Education: A Theory of Literacies for Analyzing Change in Grenada's Revolution and After** by Anne Hickling-Hudson — 243
10. **Between the State, Society, and Global Markets: Three Roles of Higher Education** by Susan Wiksten & Daniel Schugurensky — 273
11. **Education for All in Africa—Not Remediation but Transformation and Innovation** by Joel Samoff & Bidemi Carrol — 297
12. **Education in Latin America: From Dependency and Neoliberalism to Alternative Paths to Development** by Robert F. Arnove, Stephen Franz, Carlos Ornelas & Carlos Alberto Torres — 343
13. **The Education of Youngsters in Conflict-Ridden Regions of the Middle East: Challenges and Opportunities** by Muzna Awayed-Bishara — 377

14 Education in the Asia-Pacific Region: Achievements and Challenges *by John Hawkins (posthumous) & Anthony Welch*   395

15 Living Well Together as Educators in Our Oceanic "Sea of Islands": Epistemology and Ontology of Comparative Education *by Kabini Sanga, David Fa'avae & Martyn Reynolds*   433

16 The Political Construction of European Education *by António Teodoro*   455

17 Education in Eastern and Central Europe: Rethinking Postsocialism in the Context of Globalization *by Ben Eklof & Iveta Silova*   473

18 Technocracy, Uncertainty, and Ethics: Contemporary Challenges Facing Comparative Education *by Anthony Welch*   499

19 Comparative Education: The Dialectics of Globalization and Its Discontents *by Carlos Alberto Torres*   527

Index   565
About the Contributors   587

Contents

■ ■ ■

**Introduction: Reframing Comparative Education:
The Dialectic of the Global and the Local** *by Robert F. Arnove* 1
    Globalization 2
    Evolution of the Field 4
    The Dimensions of Comparative Education 5
    About the Book 13
    Current Trends and New Directions 14
    Conclusion 19
    Notes 21
    References 21

1 Institutionalizing International Influence *by Joel Samoff* 29
    Context 30
    Organizations 36
    Aid and Education 42
    Pathways of Influence 45
    The Role(s) of Research 51
    Continuities and Challenges 59
    Education and Development 60
    Notes 62
    References 64

2 Economics, Education, and Society: Myths and Possibilities
by Steven J. Klees 71
    The Dominant Story 72
    Myth #1: Unfettered Free Markets Are the Best Policies for Economic Growth and Development 73
    Myth #2: Unfettered Free Markets Are the Most Efficient Way to Organize an Economy 74
    Myth #3: Evidence-Based Policy Is Central to Improving Education 75
    Myth #4: Human Capital Theory and Practice Offers Useful Guidance on Investing in Education 76
    Myth #5: The World Bank Has Been an Impartial Advocate for Improving Education 78

	An Alternative Story	80
	Notes	82
	References	82
3	**The State, Social Movements, and Education: Between Reform and Transformation** by Raymond Morrow and Carlos Alberto Torres	87
	Theories of Social Movements: American Versus European Perspectives	90
	Educational Change and Social Movements: Sociocultural Reproduction and Transformation	97
	The Relationship Between Education and Social Movements: An Agenda of Issues	103
	Concluding Pandemic Reflections on Our Global Risk Society: Social Movements, Global Citizenship Education, and Cosmopolitanization	116
	Note	118
	References	118
4	**Culture and Education** by Vandra Lea Masemann	125
	The Concept of Culture	126
	Cultural Values	128
	Culture and Educational Philosophy	129
	Evolutionism and Colonialism	131
	Functionalism and Scientism	134
	School Ethnography	136
	Conclusion	141
	Note	142
	References	142
5	**The Question of Identity from a Comparative Education Perspective** by Christine Fox	147
	Colonizers and Colonized: A Brief Foray into the Literature of Intercultural Interaction	150
	Comparative Education and the Intersectionalization of Identity	153
	Conclusion: Tackling the Issue of Identity as a Social Justice Issue	159
	Notes	160
	References	160
6	**Equality of Education: Six Decades of Comparative Evidence Seen from a New Millennium** by Joseph P. Farrell (posthumous)	163
	Background: The Optimistic Reforms of the 1960s	163
	Results: Much Less Than Anticipated	165
	Theoretical Accounts of Reform Failure	167
	Changing Meanings of Educational Equality	168
	Categories of Differentiation	168
	From Opportunity to Results	169

	Equality as Similarity or Equality as Valuation of Difference	170
	Equity or Equality?	170
	A Review	171
	A "Model" of Educational Inequality	171
	What Do We Know?	172
	Equality of Access	173
	Equality of Survival	174
	Equality of Output	176
	Equality of Outcome	179
	Conclusion	180
	Note	183
	References	184
7	**Women's Education in the 21st Century** *by Nelly P. Stromquist*	187
	The Contribution of Feminist Theory to the Understanding of Educational Institutions	189
	The Conditions of Women's Schooling	193
	Primary and Secondary Education	197
	The Content of Knowledge and the Experience of Schooling	198
	Nonformal Education Programs for Primary Schoolchildren	201
	Higher Education	202
	The Education of Adult Women	204
	The State and Women's Education	206
	Donor Agencies and Their Support for Education	207
	The Juncture of Actors Behind Education Policy Formation	211
	Challenges in Developing Countries	213
	References	216
8	**Control of Education: Issues and Tensions in Centralization and Decentralization** *by Mark Bray*	221
	Meanings, Motives, Models, and Measurements	222
	Themes and Variations	228
	Conclusion	237
	References	238
9	**Transforming Adult and Community Education: A Theory of Literacies for Analyzing Change in Grenada's Revolution and After** *by Anne Hickling-Hudson*	243
	Postcolonialism, Literacies, and Comparisons	244
	Coloniality, the Postcolonial Space, and Grenada's Revolution	245
	A Theory of Literacies for Analyzing Educational Change	248
	Adult Basic Education: Challenges in Developing Epistemic and Technical Literacies	251
	Community Education: Challenges in Developing Humanist and Public Literacies	255

      Ways Forward for Adult Education: Global Experiments   262

      Conclusion: Literacies and Educational Change in the Postcolonial Space   266

      Notes   267

      References   268

10 Between the State, Society, and Global Markets: Three Roles of Higher Education *by Susan Wiksten & Daniel Schugurensky*   273

      International Policy Framework for Higher Education   276

      Comparative Data on Participation in Higher Education   277

      Three Roles of Higher Education   281

      Discussion   287

      Conclusion   289

      References   291

11 Education for All in Africa—Not Remediation but Transformation and Innovation *by Joel Samoff & Bidemi Carrol*   297

      Education for All in Africa: From Crisis to Renewed Hope   298

      Challenges, Issues, and Initiatives   313

      The Broader Context   326

      From Education as Social Transformation to Education as (and for) Production   333

      Notes   336

      References   338

12 Education in Latin America: From Dependency and Neoliberalism to Alternative Paths to Development *by Robert F. Arnove, Stephen Franz, Carlos Ornelas & Carlos Alberto Torres*   343

      Defining the State and Its Relationship to Education   345

      The "Conditioned" State   346

      Privatization   354

      Decentralization   357

      Counterhegemonic State Initiatives   358

      Popular Education and Other Innovations   359

      Promising Comparative Research   365

      Reflections on the Region in the Time of COVID-19   367

      Conclusion   367

      Notes   370

      References   370

13 The Education of Youngsters in Conflict-Ridden Regions of the Middle East: Challenges and Opportunities *by Muzna Awayed-Bishara*   377

      The Intersection Between Global Categories and Local Structures in the Middle East   380

      Challenges at Local and Global Levels   382

Opportunities Emerge From Youth and Women Agency	390
Conclusion	391
Note	391
References	391

14 Education in the Asia-Pacific Region: Achievements and Challenges *by John Hawkins (posthumous) & Anthony Welch* — 395

Access and Equity	401
Quality Assurance	404
Mobility and Migration	414
Regionalism and Higher Education	417
Conclusion	423
Notes	425
References	425

15 Living Well Together as Educators in Our Oceanic "Sea of Islands": Epistemology and Ontology of Comparative Education *by Kabini Sanga, David Fa'avae, & Martyn Reynolds* — 433

A Sketch of Oceania	435
A Relational Approach	437
The Colonial as Relational	438
(Re)negotiated Relationships	439
Case Studies	440
Weaving the Strands	445
An Existential Threat	446
Conclusion: Living Well Together	447
References	448

16 The Political Construction of European Education *by António Teodoro* — 455

The Political Construction of Europe	456
The European Dimension of Education	458
Education at the Center of the Lisbon Strategy	459
The Open Method of Coordination	460
Fabricating Europe Through Education	462
The Education and Training EU Targets to 2025	464
Final Remarks	468
Notes	469
References	470

17 Education in Eastern and Central Europe: Rethinking Postsocialism in the Context of Globalization *by Ben Eklof & Iveta Silova* — 473

Diverse Historical Legacies	476
Postsocialist Transformations	483
Conclusion	493

		Notes	494
		References	495
18	**Technocracy, Uncertainty, and Ethics: Contemporary Challenges Facing Comparative Education** *by Anthony Welch*		499
		From History to Science?	499
		Dominance of Western Culture	504
		Alternatives to Western Frameworks	504
		Nation-State as Unit of Analysis	505
		Tributaries	506
		Things Fall Apart	509
		Globalization and Changes in the State	509
		From Positivism to Post-ism	511
		Postmodern, Postcolonial, and the "Other"?	514
		New Comparative Education, New Millennium?	515
		Notes	520
		References	521
19	**Comparative Education: The Dialectics of Globalization and Its Discontents** *by Carlos Alberto Torres*		527
		Afterthought for the Second Edition	527
		How Might These Changes Affect Educational Priorities?	531
		The Outstanding Debts of Comparative Education	533
		Afterthought for the Third Edition: The Future of Comparative Education	539
		Afterthought for the Fourth Edition: Another Globalization Is Possible	540
		Will the Economic Crisis Herald the End of the Market Democracy?	541
		How Can We Face the Challenges Ahead to Comparative Education: What Can Be Done?	545
		Anti-Hegemonic Globalization	545
		Afterthought to the Fifth Edition: The End of Globalization and the Crises of Democracy and Citizenship	548
		The End of Globalization? The Crises of Democracy and Citizenship	548
		New Actors, New Concepts, New Challenges	557
		Conclusion: COVID-19 and Our Circumstances	559
		Notes	560
		References	561
Index			565
About the Contributors			587

Introduction

Reframing Comparative Education: The Dialectic of the Global and the Local

Robert F. Arnove
Indiana University

ABSTRACT

The chapter begins with the central thesis of *Comparative Education* (fifth edition) that the workings of a global economy and the increasing interconnectedness of societies pose common problems concerning the goals, governance, financing, provision, content, and outcomes of mass education. Simultaneously, regional, national, and local responses vary. A dialectic is at work between the global and the local. Understanding this interactive process, the tensions, and contradictions is central to recasting or "reframing" the field of comparative and international education. After exploring the various manifestations of globalization, the chapter traces the institutionalization of comparative education as a field of study and research in universities as a phenomenon of the post–World War II period. The chapter then proposes studying who pays and benefits from education along three dimensions: the scientific, the pragmatic, and international understanding and peace. Then follows a description of the content of the various chapters in the book. The concluding section of Reframing Comparative Education reviews promising current trends and new directions. Woven throughout the chapter, attention is given to the challenges posed by COVID-19 for historically disadvantaged populations.

■ ■ ■

This book reflects the forces shaping comparative education in the third decade of the 21st century. These forces are internal as well as external to the field of comparative education. Within the discipline, theories and methods for studying school-society relations change following advances in knowledge, shifts in paradigms, and increases in capacity to process and analyze large data sets in more sophisticated ways. Conceptual and methodological frameworks, in turn, are constantly being reshaped by events on the world stage and corresponding changes in economic, social, and educational policies.

At the outset of 2020, these events include a global pandemic that has inflicted inequitable harm on the world's most vulnerable populations, wreaked havoc on fragile national economies, and aroused mass-scale protests against historical and institutional injustice. These protests have joined grassroots progressive organizations across national borders. At the same time, counter-progressive movements have mobilized and been reinforced by an emergent spate of nationalist/authoritarian governments, reactionary and racist. These conflictive transnational forces necessarily have had a profound impact on education systems.

A central thesis of this book is that the workings of a global economy and the increasing interconnectedness of societies pose common problems for education systems around the world. These problems relate to the goals, governance, financing, and provision of mass education; they relate to issues of equality of educational opportunities and outcomes for differently situated social groups, especially those who historically have been most discriminated against—women, ethnic minorities, immigrants, rural populations, the working class, and LGBTQ individuals. Although there are common problems—and what would appear to be increasingly similar education agendas—regional, national, and local responses also vary. As the title of this book indicates, a dialectic is at work between the global and the local. Understanding this interactive process, the tensions, and the contradictions is central to recasting or "reframing" the field of comparative and international education. I believe that the adoption of a focus on globalization contributes to a greater understanding of the dynamics of school-society relations as well as the potential and limitations of education systems to contribute to individual and societal advancement.

GLOBALIZATION

Globalization can be defined as "the intensification of worldwide social relations which link distant localities in such a way that local happenings are shaped by events occurring many miles away and vice versa" (Carney, 2009; Giddens, 1991; Sassen, 2007a; 2007b). Various adjectives may be used to describe the different dimensions of this process. Certainly, economic and cultural globalization are foremost among the descriptors used for the processes by which societies are increasingly linked in real and virtual time (King, 1997; Väyrynen, 1997; Waters, 1995). Economic globalization, the result of major transformations in the processes of producing and distributing goods and services, is integrally related to changes in the international division of labor.

One of the central characteristics of this highly globalized capitalism is that the factors of production are not located in close geographic proximity. At the same time, however, national economies are increasingly integrating into regional ones. "Just-in-time Toyotism" since the early 1970s has replaced the era of "Fordist" mass-scale production within national boundaries (Dowbor et al., 1998; Wilms, 1996). This very term suggests not only the interconnectedness of the global capitalist system but its vulnerability to disruptions caused, for example, by the 2020/2022 COVID-19 pandemic.

The fragmentation and reintegration of economies are facilitated by concurrent revolutionary improvements in telecommunications and computerization, all made possible by quantum leaps in the production of scientific and technological knowledge. The ease with which individuals can communicate via satellite and the internet, and by which products can be assembled and disseminated, has its cultural and social counterparts (Barber, 1995). They involve not only iconic goods to consume and places to shop, movies and television programs to view, and music to download, but, increasingly so, the linkages between peoples and movements via interactive social media, most evident in current grassroots movements of various political stripes. While these linkages can reinforce various forms of domination, they also can unite progressive forces transnationally to challenge various forms of hegemony and bring about democratic reforms (For the further discussion of the various forms globalization may take, including "globalization from below," see Carlos Torres's Chapter 19, especially the section Afterthought to the Fifth Edition, in this volume).

In the realm of education, as the various authors in this book point out, globalization also refers to the closely intertwined economic and education agendas promoted by the major international donor, technical assistance, and policy-setting agencies—namely, the World Bank (formerly, the International Bank for Reconstruction and Development), the International Monetary Fund (IMF), and the Organization for Economic Cooperation and Development (OECD)—as well as national overseas aid agencies such as the United States Agency for International Aid (USAID), the Canadian International Development Agency (CIDA), and the Japan International Cooperation Agency (JICA). Similar prescriptions are being offered by these powerful agencies for enhancing the equality, efficiency, and quality of education systems (Collins & Wiseman, 2012; Klees et al., 2012; Mundy, 2007).[1] Reforms are being implemented by education policymakers who often have little choice but to do so in exchange for access to needed funds.

Common prescriptions and transnational forces, however, are not uniformly implemented or unquestioningly received. As the title of this book suggests, a dialectic is at work by which these global processes interact with national and local actors and contexts to be modified and, in some cases, transformed. There is a process of give-and-take, an exchange by which international trends are reshaped to local as well as regional ends. Just as scholars from the Global South have challenged dominant research paradigms and conceptual frameworks of the industrialized north to propose more relevant theories related to dependency as well as education for critical consciousness and liberation (Cardoso, 1977; Cardoso & Faletto, 1969; Freire, 1970; Rodney, 1981; Santos, 1970a; 1970b), so have local people appropriated and transformed the language of the former colonizers. For example, Hickling-Hudson (1998) illustrates how the English language is received and reshaped by Creole-speaking Jamaicans into something beautifully and poetically different.

In the previous edition of *Comparative Education*, I discussed how hegemonic forces were refracted and opposed by the emergence of counterhegemonic blocs, such as ALBA (*Alianza Bolivariana de los Pueblos de América*, the Bolivarian Alliance of the Peoples of America). The regional alliance, with its economic, education, cultural, and security elements, promotes alternative values of cooperation and mutual solidarity, meeting the needs of the most vulnerable while respecting the environment (Hart-Landsberg, 2009). Yet, as described in Chapter 12 in this volume on Latin America, governments change as do relations among countries, and the bloc's chances to improve significantly the well-being of its most disadvantaged populations have been significantly diminished.

Similarly, the 2013 edition of *Comparative Education*, perhaps too optimistically called attention to how extra-territoriality units, such as the European Union (EU), contributed to the erosion of national boundaries that impeded the flow of people, capital, and goods. I noted how the various treaties and accords that are by-products of the union involved agreements to integrate education systems by establishing the equivalence of course offerings and degrees. As such, the international conventions opened education opportunities, previously closed by state borders—but they also involved the imposition of standards not reflective of national differences that accommodate the needs of nontraditional students—for example, those who are working, and cannot go through a lockstep curriculum. Furthermore, while the December 31, 2020, exit of Great Britain from the EU might offer a measure of greater national determination in certain areas, it also has reimposed a national barrier to freer commerce across the English Channel in matters both economic and educational. Moreover, increasingly nationalist authoritarian regimes in Poland and Hungary have challenged the ability of EU governing authorities located in Brussels to enforce democratic norms throughout the bloc (see Chapter 16).

The impact of globalization on education systems has significant and manifold implications that are studied in this volume. They include questions such as: Who has access to what levels of education and with what outcomes? What types of jobs will be available for whom? (Aronowitz & Cutler, 1998; Drucker, 1993; Reich, 1991; 2010). Will decentralization and privatization of education—promoted by international donor agencies as well as by national elites—lead to greater equality, efficiency, and quality? What will be taught and in what language? These various transnational forces raise significant questions about the viability of the nation-state and the role of public education systems in creating citizens.

As the loci of economic production, political decision-making, and group identity are transformed, so, too, do our understandings of the nature of public education in contributing to citizenship formation and economic development come under challenge. Changes on the world stage call for new ways of viewing education-society relations. Comparative education, which traditionally has taken as its subject matter the macro- and micro-level forces shaping education systems around the world, is a field ideally situated to study the dynamic interactions between global trends and responses. This volume represents an attempt to "reframe," or shift the foci of, the field to this interplay between the global and the local, as well as the regional. It seeks to provide generalizable propositions and useful insights into the forces shaping the origins, workings, and outcomes of education systems.

EVOLUTION OF THE FIELD

Although the origins of the field of international and comparative education are frequently traced to the pioneering work of Marc-Antoine Jullien and César August Basset in the first half of the 19th century, its institutionalization as a field of study and research in universities is largely a phenomenon of the post–World War II period (Altbach & Tan, 1995; Manzon, 2011; Sobe, 2018).

Closely tied to major shifts in geopolitical realities and changing views of education's role in advancing personal enlightenment and social progress, the comparative study of education systems initially attempted to explain, in the words of Watson (1998, p. 6), the "beginning of a new world order in Europe" in the aftermath of the Napoleonic War, or according to N'Dri Thérèse Assié-Lumumba and Yusef Waghid (2023), early 19th-century European colonial expansion into Africa and elsewhere (Epstein, 1994). Since then, the comparative study of education has been concerned with attempting to explain the role of education in contributing to nation-state building as well as to totalitarian or democratic forms of government. Major expansion in the field occurred in the 1960s, when, according to Altbach and Tan (1995), "higher education in the industrialized nations was expanding rapidly, and . . . the major powers were preoccupied not only with Cold War rivalries, but with understanding the newly emerging nations of what came to be called the Third World" (p. ix). The emergence and widespread acceptance of notions of education's contribution to human capital formation and the economic growth of nations further fueled interest in comparative education. More recently, the belief that there is a causal relationship between the "excellence" of a school system, as measured by national standardized examinations, and the economic success of a country in global competition, has revived the interest in the relationship between education systems and national productivity. Furthermore, these significant topics and issues have contributed to renewed interest in the relationship of education to political stability and development: the end of the Cold War, the breakup of the former Soviet Union with the emergence of newly independent republics, often microstates, and the outbreak of ethnic conflict in various regions of the world with massive movements of displaced individuals and their communities nationally and internationally.

THE DIMENSIONS OF COMPARATIVE EDUCATION

Historically, the field of comparative and international education has comprehended three principal dimensions or thrusts, which I call the scientific/theoretical, pragmatic/ameliorative, and international understanding and peace/globalization. These dimensions are closely related and,[2] as I shall argue, are converging to an even greater extent (Arnove, 2001; Habermas, 1971).

The Scientific Dimension

The term "scientific" dimension of the field is most frequently associated with the work of Noah and Eckstein (1969). One major goal of comparative education has been to contribute to theory building: to the formulation of generalizable propositions about the workings of school systems and their interactions with their surrounding economies, polities, cultures, and social orders. As Farrell (1979) noted, all sciences are comparative. The goal of science is not only to establish that relationships between variables exist but also to determine the range over which they exist (Farrell, 1979). As Bray and Thomas (1995) further pointed out, comparison enables researchers to look at the entire world as a natural laboratory to view the multiple ways in which societal factors, educational policies, and practices may vary and interact in otherwise unpredictable and unimaginable ways.

The COVID-19 pandemic offers an excellent example of how different countries pursued different responses to it and how their policies have affected not only morbidity and mortality rates in comparable countries—take the case of Sweden's "herd immunity" approach versus more restrictive measures by neighboring Scandinavian countries—but also how education systems were affected about staying open or closed and how student populations were affected in which ways.

It is the range of experiences that come to light through comparison that enables us to question taken-for-granted assumptions about school-society relations and the generalizability of major social science studies conducted in North America and Europe. In my 2001 Comparative and International Education Society (CIES) presidential address, I illustrated the theory-building contributions of our field by referring to the lyrics of George Gershwin's song, "It Ain't Necessarily So." That's right. It ain't necessarily so that family background is more important than the adequacy and quality of school resources, or that investments in higher education as compared with those in primary education do not have a high social rate of return or utility, or that teachers and schools are responsible for supposedly lagging achievement scores and stagnant economies, or that school systems are the primary determinants of equitable life chances and economic equality, or that schools necessarily reproduce social inequalities (Arnove, 2001; Buchmann & Hannum, 2001; Coleman et al., 1966; Farrell & Schiefelbein, 1985; Heyneman, 1976; Jencks et al., 1972; Plowden, 1967).

The value of comparative cross-national as well as longitudinal data, for example, is illustrated in calculating social rates of return to investments in education. Leading rate-of-return economists, such as Psacharopoulos (1990) argued that the best education investment for a country is at the primary school level, followed by secondary, and last by higher education (Psacharopoulos & Patrinos, 2018). Such conclusions by prominent economists working for the World Bank led this lender agency, as well as other bilateral aid agencies such as USAID, to propose that higher education institutions charge tuition fees to comprise a more substantial share of costs. The policies favored by these agencies also led to a greater emphasis on the privatization of education. Yet the social rate of return is usually higher for primary education because the costs are minimal relative to secondary and tertiary levels of schooling. The important point is that a diminishing social rate of return to primary education occurs as access becomes nearly universal.

Over time, assessments of what levels of education have what impact on the academic careers and life chances of individuals change markedly. Comparative studies by Carnoy (1995) and Heyneman (1995), for example, suggest that in some countries secondary education, including vocational education, as well as tertiary education could have a higher rate of return than primary education in countries as diverse as Botswana and Brazil. James Wolfensohn, then president of the World Bank, admitted in March 2000 that the bank had seriously miscalculated the social rate of return to higher education, and therefore there are valid reasons for adequately funding this level of education, in countries as diverse as Botswana and Brazil (Task Force on Higher Education and Society, 2000). Since then, economists such as McMahon (2009) and Shafiq (2010; 2015) have presented comparative evidence from industrialized and developing countries on the nonmonetary social benefits of higher education such as increased support for democratic advancement and reduced support for terrorism and corruption. To highlight both the quantity and quality of higher education, higher education leaders in developing countries have argued that what these societies need are not poorly funded universities but well-endowed, first-rate institutions capable of conducting the type of scientific research that helps them overcome their dependency on the metropolitan centers of the North, whose technologies often are inappropriate for them (Gorostiaga, 1993). (For political economy critiques of "human capital" and, more generally, "neoclassical economic" approaches to the study of education, see Chapter 2 by Stephen Klees in this volume; Richard Desjardins [2023]).

Meyer and Baker (1996) offer another example of the need for longitudinal comparative studies that have policy relevance. Cross-national studies, as they point out, can provide important lessons and enrich our understanding of how various organizational arrangements improve school outcomes, especially those other than enrollment figures and achievement scores, and the trade-offs involved in reform efforts to increase national achievement levels. One such trade-off they discuss concerning the United States is between the lowering of standards and "the short-term costs of the achievement of particular students" with the long-term benefits of "enhanced attitudes towards education on the part of school leavers towards learning even decades after they leave school" (Meyer & Baker, 1996, p. 121).

Comparative data also provide the basis for critiquing the validity of the common assertion that schools are the main culprit for lagging economic performance, whether in the United States or abroad. While the association between levels of educational attainment and lifetime earning streams is substantial, especially in industrialized countries, much more problematic is the relationship between national levels of education per se and overall measures of an economy's growth and productivity in developing countries (Pritchett, 2001). And while the gap between the rich and the poor is getting greater within and across countries, comparative data (from Germany, the Netherlands, Switzerland, and the United Kingdom) also point out that wage policies and efforts made to provide high-level skills to those not receiving a higher education can lead to more equitable systems of income distribution (Nickell & Bell, 1996).

Comparative data further indicate that income inequality and poverty rates in a country significantly influence the academic achievement and attainment of children by social class. The 2018 Program for International Student Assessment (PISA) results show that the United States scored 13th out of 79 education systems in reading measures. Summarizing the test results, Fred Hechinger observed: "As with math, U.S. performance hasn't changed much since the first PISA tests in 2000" (Barshay, 2019; Komatsu & Rappleye, 2017). In an earlier review of PISA test results, Ladd and Fiske (2011) found that generally, higher income and status students in the United States consistently did better on PISA tests. They then queried: "Can anyone credibly believe that the mediocre overall performance of American students on international tests is unrelated to the fact that one-fifth of American children live in poverty?" (Ladd & Fiske, 2011, para. 3). Since then, socioeconomic factors driving performance on international assessments of educational achievement have not changed and, have worsened in the wake of the

COVID-19 pandemic and a faltering economy in a highly inequitable society—in January 2021 approximately one-fourth of children in the United States were facing food insecurity. (For further discussion of research on international testing regimes, see David and Leslie Rutkowski [2023].)

The value of gathering comparative data guided by theory to reach reasonable propositions about the workings and outcomes of education systems concerning their social and historical contexts is particularly pertinent to a consideration of the second dimension of the discipline.

The Pragmatic Dimension
Another reason for studying other societies' education systems is to discover what can be learned that will contribute to improved policy and practice at home. Altbach (1981) has referred to the processes involved in the study and transfer of educational practices among countries as *lending* and *borrowing* (Alexander et al., 1999; Steiner-Khamsi, 2004; 2010). Countries may alternately or simultaneously be involved in both processes, as evidenced by the cases of Japan, China, and the United States over time. One of the earliest examples of educational borrowing occurred in CE 607 when the Japanese court sent a mission to China to study the empire's education system. According to Kobayashi (1990), one outcome of this visit was the establishment of Japan's first national school system. At the turn of the 20th century, Japanese education authorities looked to the West for guidance as they attempted to modernize their school system. In turn, countries such as China and Thailand found the Japanese model to be appropriate in their attempts to develop economically without abandoning their cultural traditions.

The United States, similarly, has undergone various phases of borrowing and lending. In the 19th century, the country was a borrower. Academics from the United States studied the higher education systems of other European countries (for example, that of Prussia), as a basis for establishing research-oriented graduate schools (Johns Hopkins University being the first such institution). Many U.S. postbaccalaureate students completed their graduate studies in Europe. Today, the flow of students and scholars has been reversed, with the United States being a principal destination for advanced scholarly studies in major research universities.

At the same time, hundreds, if not thousands, of U.S. educators have been involved in the process of lending, if not transplanting (whether appropriate or not) educational policies and practices to other countries.

Conversely, since the 1970s, the United States has been fascinated with the high rankings of many Asian countries (first Japan, and, more recently, Singapore, Taiwan, and South Korea, among others), on various international assessments of educational achievement. This fascination with Asian school systems, which have a much longer academic year, led to increases in the number of days of schooling across the United States and sometimes to longer school days. These modifications of the school calendar were based on the problematic assumption that extending the time involved in learning would necessarily lead to improved scores on standardized achievement instruments, regardless of how that time was used or the quality of the teaching. While the United States attempted to instill elements of the more rigorous and standardized Asian curricula and school systems, reform-minded Asian educators were looking at the more child-centered and progressive elements of the U.S. system (Feinberg,

1993; Russell, 1997). In other words, previously very distinctive education systems have been enviously eyeing one another's education systems and attempting to borrow elements from them.

The problem is that education policymakers cannot simply uproot elements of one society and expect them to flourish in the soil of another society (Noah, 1984). But, as Cogan (1984) notes, certain principles may be deduced from the study of school systems in other societies that may apply to another country. These principles, however, are very general ones, such as the greater the status accorded to a teacher, the shorter the time or obstacles required to obtain a teaching license; and the more opportunities for in-service professional development, the greater the likelihood that highly competent individuals will be motivated to select a teaching career and stick with it (Cummings, 1994; Ohanian, 1987; Tobin et al., 1987; Willis & Yamamura, 2002).

Finland, for example, is currently viewed by many as perhaps the most successful education system because of its excellent results on international assessments of academic achievement and because of its highly equitable nature—there is very little difference between the quality of schools and their students' achievement. Finland, however, differs significantly from other countries with high-performing schools: The academic calendar has fewer days and hours of schooling, and high-stakes examinations have been largely eliminated. Clearly, important factors distinguishing Finland are that it is a small and fairly homogenous country with a low immigrant population, a strong egalitarian and democratic ethos, and a comprehensive social safety net. A succession of social democratic governments has invested heavily in early childhood education and public health for all. This context is important, but also important is their vision of what makes for an excellent education system. Finland places a high value on the professionalization of teaching. This means that all teachers are required to have a master's degree and their autonomy as professionals is respected. Schools and teachers have significant input into national policy decisions. At the heart of the Finnish vision of education is the belief that all children, from day one, are prepared to learn. The goal of the school system is to find out how to meet the needs of each student. These are principles that can be extracted and tested in other settings (Sahlberg, 2011).

Moreover, the most important principle to be derived from studying the history of educational borrowing and lending is that there is no one best system, that all systems have strengths as well as weaknesses. Also, education systems, as I noted earlier, reflect their societies—their many tensions and contradictions. Perhaps more can be learned from lessons of failure—what not to do—than from stories of success. However, I do not believe that it is necessary to experience failure to succeed. If understanding is to be advanced as to what works and what does not work in a country, then such study must be guided by knowledge of that country, by familiarity with its history and unique qualities, as well as by recognition of what it shares in common with other societies (Watson, 1998).

The role of the systematic accumulation of knowledge or guiding principles and theories (i.e., the scientific dimension) of comparative education is central to the pragmatic and ameliorative thrust of the discipline: to improve educational policy and practice. However, there has often been a separation or tension between these two components. Reviews of pioneering work in the field commonly trace two different approaches to the field—one more scientific and one more historical. In the early 19th century, French scholar Marc-Antoine Jullien called for the development of "detailed research guidelines and checklists for foreign studies in education" (Fraser, 1964). As Crossley and Vulliamy (1997) note, Jullien's initiative is seen as the "inspiration for the twentieth century development of international databases for education" and as the beginnings of an attempt at establishing a scientific basis for identifying "the one best policy and practice for all contexts." They further point out that an alternative path was marked by Sir Michael Sadler, who drew "attention to the dangers and dilemmas of international transfer, and to the importance of contextual factors in the analysis and development of education" (Crossley & Broadfoot, 1992; Fraser, 1964). In his study of 19th-century Germany, Sadler (1912) noted:

> In the educational policy of a nation are focused its spiritual aspirations, its philosophical ideals, its economic ambitions, its military purpose, its social conflicts. For a German or for an Englishman to speak of his own country's educational aims is to speak of its ideal, of its hope and fears, of its weakness as well as of its strength. To attempt even this is not an easy task, but to speak of another country's education system from the standpoint of a foreign observer is to hazard more and to risk misunderstanding. (p. 125)

Following in the footsteps of Sadler (1912), Kandel (1933), a leading figure in the field of comparative education during the first half of the 20th century, observed, "In order to understand, appreciate and evaluate the real meaning of the education system of a nation, it is essential to know something of the history and traditions, of the forces and attitudes governing its social organizations, of the political and economic conditions that determine its development" (Crossley & Vulliamy, 1997, p. 8).

Kandel's research itself has been placed in historical context by Keita Takayama (2018) who notes that his scholarship and policy engagements, while a professor at Teachers College, Columbia University, derived from "colonial logics" and "gained legitimacy" through the Cold War geopolitical context in which the field was established.

In later sections of this chapter, I further discuss the evolution and permutations of these different approaches to the comparative study of education systems. At this point, I indicate how these two paths relate to the third dimension of the field: education for international understanding and peace (Wilson, 1994).

International Education: The Global Dimension

A third and significant (but previously underemphasized) dimension of the discipline is that of contributing to international understanding and peace. In recent years, this dimension has become a more important feature of comparative education as processes of globalization increasingly require people to recognize how forces from areas of the world previously considered distant and remote impinge on their daily lives. The study of cross-national currents and interactions is closely linked to notions of global education and, in many ways, to world-systems analysis. In 1980, I called for increased emphasis on the international dimensions of our field. As I noted, studies of the ecology of educational institutions and processes often failed to take into account an international context of transactions. Most macro studies of education accepted the nation-state as the basic unit of analysis. But I argued that an examination of the international forces impinging on education systems was no less essential than an examination of the international economic order would be to an understanding of the dynamics of economic development or underdevelopment in any one set of countries (Arnove, 1980; McGinn, 1996; Torres, 1998).

For those attempting to introduce international perspectives not only into scholarly research but also into teaching at all levels of education (i.e., suffuse curricula with content and activities that enable oncoming generations as well as adults to understand the increasingly interconnected world in which they live), a global set of lenses is essential. Global education, as defined by Alger and Harf (1986), is differentiated from international education. They contrast international education, which they view as large area studies or descriptive accounts of discrete countries and regions of the world, with global education, which they distinguish as emphasizing values, transactions, actors, mechanisms, procedures, and issues (Epstein, 1992).

Briefly, values education teaches that people across the globe have different ways of viewing the world, ways that are equally valid and reflective of their life circumstances, which they call " perspective consciousness" (Hanvey, 1976). It also recommends seeking out and building upon what interests people have in common. An example of this is Piscitelli's (1997) use of art to point out the common concerns of children all around the world—their fears and hopes—and also their differing societal contexts—why a Vietnamese eight-year-old might draw a picture of children working on a tea plantation as something very natural. Assié-Lumumba and Yusef Waghid (2023) have further described this process of "acting with discernment and an appreciation of the ways of others that might be incommensurable with one's own ways of being and acting."

In pointing out the importance of actors and transactions, Alger and Harf (1986) call attention to the multiplicity of actors (at all levels from the international to the local, governmental as well as nongovernmental) involved in diverse interactions across national boundaries in areas including telecommunications, meteorology, emergency relief, health, and education. The study of the mechanisms and procedures provides insights into what, for example, an international agency like the IMF, an important transnational actor, does when it enters a country experiencing debt and currency crises and attempts to stabilize the economic situation. Issues are those that face all of humanity—environmental destruction, the spread of disease, the proliferation of weapons of mass destruction, as well as the increasing impoverishment of populations and the growing disparity of wealth among regions and within nations (Alger & Harf, 1986).

In the third edition of *Comparative Education* (Arnove & Torres, 2007), I used the case of the 1997 economic crisis in the four Asian nations of Indonesia, Korea, Malaysia, and Thailand to illustrate very concretely the value of a global perspective (as outlined by Alger and Harf). In the fourth edition (Arnove et al., 2013), I described the worldwide economic crisis that first erupted in 2007/2008 in the United States and Europe dramatically demonstrated how the bursting of various bubbles (e.g., housing) and the indebtedness of not only central, but seemingly peripheral, economies negatively affected the entire global system. Austerity measures that were imposed by governments seriously reduced funding for education and other social sectors at the same time that more oversight was imposed on school systems at all levels. Moreover, the economic downturn and the growing unemployment and impoverishment of those once considered middle class negatively affected the opportunities for many to continue with their education.

This edition points out the impact of the 2020/2022 COVID-19 pandemic on societies, their economies and their education systems, in ways even more dramatic. While our text describes and analyzes the varying crises engendered by it, the disruption in the ways things normally are viewed and managed, the current situation also provides, according to Indian novelist and activist Roy (2020), a "portal" to various possible futures with greater potential for fulfilling human needs and aspirations.

The contributors to this volume contend that teachers, at all levels of formal as well as nonformal education, need to educate their students about the causes, dynamics, and outcomes of these transnational forces and actors and that comparative and international education, for example, can play a vital role in teacher education. Although past CIES presidential addresses by Brembeck (1975) and Heyneman (1993) warned about the dangers of our field distancing itself from teacher education or becoming a marginalized field irrelevant to the knowledge needs of policymakers, we believe that comparative education will become even more relevant within colleges of education and decision-making circles. Complementing these concerns, Tatto (2011) underscored the value of collaborative, reflective, capacity-building international and comparative education research that contributes to better informed and more enlightened education policy. Furthermore, Theisen (1997) suggested that the knowledge-building dimension of the field could contribute to resolving pressing educational problems by studying how various institutions (nongovernmental as well as governmental technical assistance agencies) could better coordinate their efforts while incorporating grassroots organizations.

These problems relate to the need to expand access to education to all groups in society, promote effective learning, and, simultaneously, achieve greater efficiency in the running of school systems. Systems all around the world confront these problems as well as more significant issues related to achieving more equitable education systems and just societies.

At the same time, the prescriptions proposed by powerful transnational actors such as the World Bank may not always be the correct medicine (Collins & Wiseman, 2012; Klees et al., 2012). The application of market mechanisms—including privatization, charging user fees for services previously offered free of charge, and decentralizing highly centralized state bureaucracies—to resolve problems of equality of educational opportunity may lead to inequitable consequences and may be counterproductive as various chapters in the fifth edition of *Comparative Education* point out.

In 2022, these issues are even more obvious as the impact of the coronavirus pandemic has closed schools around the world. By the end of 2020, more than 1.6 billion children were either not attending classes or doing so on an infrequent basis with questionable quality. In 14 countries, nine of them in Latin America and the Caribbean, schools remained largely shut (UN News, 2020, 2021). Furthermore, the United Nations Children Fund (UNICEF) estimates that as many as 10 million female students who no longer have regular access to schooling are at risk of becoming child brides (defined as being under 18 years of age) (Sharma & Gettleman, 2021). For many children from low-income and marginalized populations, schools are the one place where children might have their only nutritious meal of the day, or where basic health services and amenities are available. Tragically, developing countries are falling further behind in their ability to provide these services as their economies shrink, their external debt burden to the lending countries of the North increase, and their prospects of obtaining vaccines to immunize their populations against the deadly COVID-19 virus lag behind those of the wealthier countries of North America, Europe, and East Asia. In the face of these crises, what role can education systems play in addressing the extent to which they have helped perpetuate inequitable social and economic systems and what they can now do to prepare students to understand and take action to correct social ills and existential problems ranging from the local to the global, among them, for example, climate change? (For further discussion, see chapter by Greg Misiaszlek [2023]).

Does a sense of international obligation to amend the past enrichment of the north at the expense of the south fuel any desire to do so? Do education systems develop a sense of commitment to more vulnerable populations within and across national borders? These are central questions for those who are working in the area of international education.

ABOUT THE BOOK

This chapter (as well as this book) is a call for efforts to unite the three strands of comparative and international education so that all work together to contribute to improved theory, policy, and practice, and the conditions for greater equity in schooling and society that contribute to global peace and justice. The initial chapters in this book address topics pertinent to (1) what theoretical and methodological frameworks promise to offer more effective ways to study education systems cross-nationally and cross-culturally (Chapter 18 by Anthony Welch); (2) the importance of examining the assumptions, workings, and outcomes of major international financial and technical assistance agencies (Chapter 1 by Joel Samoff); (3). The value of political economy approaches to the study of education systems (Chapter 2 by Stephen Klees.); the need to reconceptualize the role of the nation-state as the basic unit of collective identity and educational provision as well as the importance of studying social movements concerning education for social change (Chapter 3 by Raymond Morrow and Carlos Alberto Torres); and (4) the relevance of the study of culture and personal identity formation to continued inquiry in the field of comparative education that contributes to theory building and improved educational policy and practice (Chapter 4 by Vandra Lea Masemann and Chapter 5 by Christine Fox).

The various chapters in the middle section of the book examine current challenges to education systems around the world and offer new ways to study the limitations as well as the emancipatory potential of different reform efforts. This section includes chapters on changing notions of equality of educational opportunity and outcomes (Chapter 6 by Joseph P. Farrell), the significance of studying gender and social movements (Chapter 7 by Nelly P. Stromquist), different ways of conceptualizing centralization and decentralization of education systems (Chapter 8 by Mark Bray), the role of nonformal education and literacy programs in fostering social change (Chapter 9 by Anne Hickling-Hudson), and how neoliberal and neoconservative agendas are reshaping higher education internationally (Chapter 10 by Susan Wiksten and Daniel Schugurensky).

Then follows a section examining how global economic currents and convergence in educational reform proposals play out in specific world regions—namely, Africa (Chapter 11 by Joel Samoff and Bidemi Carrol), Latin America (Chapter 12 by Robert F. Arnove, Stephen Franz, Carlos Ornelas, and Carlos Alberto Torres), the Middle East (Chapter 13 by Muzna Awayed-Bishara), Asia-Pacific (Chapter 14 by John Hawkins and Anthony Welch), Oceania (Chapter 15 by Kabini Sanga, David Fa'ave, and Martyn Reynolds), the EU (Chapter 16 by António Teodero), and Eastern and Central Europe (Chapter 17 by Ben Eklof and Iveta Silova).

In a concluding chapter, Carlos Alberto Torres reviews major events that have transpired internationally since the publication of the first edition of this text. He reflects on ways in which the field of comparative education can contribute to advances in knowledge and more informed and progressive educational policy and practice.

CURRENT TRENDS AND NEW DIRECTIONS

A review of educational change in the previously mentioned regions indicates that the field of comparative education is particularly pertinent to an understanding of the common issues and regional, national, and local differences that education policymakers and practitioners face. Familiarity with developments in the field further suggests that higher education institutions are offering courses and instituting programs in recognition of the relevance of our field. Although comparative programs may have been cut back or integrated into larger policy studies units of schools of education in various countries, evidence of its continued vitality and growth is found in several countries, especially in Asia, Africa, and Latin America (Bray, 2003). In 2020, there were 45 constituent members of the World Council of Comparative Education Societies (WCCES), with some serving several countries.[3]

A central issue in the formation of the newly independent states of Eastern and Central Europe and Asia is the language of government and instruction. This issue is attracting a general interest in comparative education on the part of policymakers and scholars. The growing interest in English as an international language of communication represents a complementary, fascinating subject of study for the field of comparative and international education.

The dominance of English as the language of scholarly communication and publication is both a fact and a point of contention. Although many scholars recognize that English most likely will continue to be the primary language for scholarly research, dissemination, and exchange for the foreseeable future, there is also remarkable recent growth in Chinese language usage. Concerning language usage on the internet, in 2020 English represented 25.9%, and Chinese, 19.4%, followed by Spanish at 7.9%, Arabic at 5.2%, and Bahasa Indonesia/Malaysia at 4.3% (Johnson, 2021). A challenge to the field will be to find ways to provide adequate outlets for articles in major scholarly journals in languages other than English or abstracts of such articles, at the very least.

The growing body of literature from different regions of the world, whether in English or not, will continue to expand the existing theoretical and conceptual framework of comparative international education, eventually transforming the very boundaries of the field. Just as Latin American scholarship has contributed dependency theory and Freirean notions of education for critical consciousness and liberation, the literature of Asia and Africa will help offset the hegemony of European and North American scholarship (Akkari & Perez, 1998; Bray & Gui, 2001; Masemann, 1997; Swing, 1997). What do teaching and learning mean in societies imbued with Confucian, Taoist, and Zen notions? How, for example, can North American and European art educators learn from traditional Japanese and Chinese forms of instruction? And, conversely, what can Asian educators learn from new curricular approaches to art education in the West? (Davenport, 1998; Hayhoe, 2000; Mackinnon, 1996; Paine, 1990; Tremmel, 1993). At the level of current trends in higher education around the world, Hayhoe and Pan (2001), for example, have called for "a dialogue among civilizations," which would enable education policymakers to build on the strengths of different cultural traditions in meeting the challenge of providing a humanistic education that accords with global realities and more internationally minded citizens.

Furthermore, what can North American universities attempting to achieve greater diversity in education, as well as inclusion of minority students, learn from the example of historically white higher education institutions in South Africa as they attempt to incorporate students of color, especially Black South Africans, who constitute a majority population? Are the experiences of North American universities attempting to desegregate their institutions pertinent to South African higher education institutions (King, 1998; Mabokela & King, 2001)?

What is being advocated here is not only the need for different perspectives, based on different cultural traditions, to be infused into the literature but also, ultimately, a multidirectional flow of scholarship and ideas to improve not only educational policy and practice but also our ability to generalize about education-society interactions. Willis and Rappleye (2011), in their coedited volume *Reimaging Japanese Education*, argue for comparative educators to critically assess the different transnational forces that shape their research traditions to obtain more comprehensive and appropriate concepts and methodological tools for understanding the workings of education systems (Helfenbein & Mason, 2012; Tatto, 2011). (For further discussion of how sociocultural traditions influence Japanese and Anglophone comparative education research see chapter by Shoko Yamada [2023].)

In his chapter, Anthony Welch asks whether comparative education is more science or more history. Similarly, the theoretical and pragmatic thrusts of education, at various times, have gone their separate ways or have been at odds with each other (Epstein, 1994; Watson, 1998). The answer to Welch's question is that comparative and international education, at its best, should be both science and history, contributing to theory building and to more informed and enlightened educational policy and practice. Although eclecticism may be viewed as "a disease that can be cured by taking a stand,"[4] the contributors to this volume believe in the value of a variety of epistemologies, paradigms, methods, and approaches to studying education systems across national boundaries and at various levels—from the global to the local.

Bray and Thomas (1995), as previously discussed, provide useful frameworks for attempting to link different geographic/locational levels, nonlocational demographic groups, and aspects of education and society as well as the processes by which policies are transformed as they move from the international to the local levels over time and space. They noted that comparative education typically focused on countries as the locational unit of analysis, but that the units could range from that of the world/regions/continents to that of schools/classrooms/individuals. The nonlocational demographic groups could range from ethnic/age/religious/gender groups to entire populations. The aspects of education typically studied could comprehend curriculum, teaching methods, educational finance, and management structures, as well as others. Their article recommended that comparativists could make their greatest contribution to improve theory and policy by attempting to introduce as many levels of analysis as possible to portray the complex interplay of different social forces and how individual and local units of analysis are embedded in multiple layered contexts (Bray & Thomas, 1995). Subsequently, Vavrus and Bartlett (2009) elaborated on these recommendations, in seminal publications involving "vertical case studies." Their comprehensive approach to elucidating the trajectory of education policy initiatives and outcomes includes not only a scalar axis of macro-, meso, and micro-levels of analysis, but also a horizontal geographical axis of the spaces in which policy plays out with attention to issues of power differentials and contestation, and a "transversal" axis that analyzes policy processes over time (Bartlett, 2014; Bartlett & Vavrus, 2016).

I believe that the vitality of our field depends on strengthening dialogue with one another and welcoming diverse approaches to gathering and analyzing data on education-society relations. These approaches are qualitative and quantitative, case oriented, and variable oriented. Theory-building depends on attempts to generalize from case studies while also building on and contextualizing large-scale cross-national studies (Preston, 1997; Ragin, 1987; Steiner-Khamsi et al., 2002; Rust et al., 1999; Torney-Purta et al., 1999; Yin, 1981).

Case studies are likely to continue to be the most commonly used approach to studying education-society relations. Given the limited resources of most researchers working in the academy, individual scholars tend to study familiar areas. More than just a convenience, Ragin (1987) argues, the comparative method is essentially a case-oriented strategy of comparative research. In case studies "outcomes are analyzed in terms of intersections of conditions, and it is usually assumed that any of several combinations might produce a certain outcome" (Ragin, 1987). Bartlett and Vavrus (2016), furthermore, have found critical comparative case study research to be especially promising in remedying the deficiencies of research that fails to "attend simultaneously to global, national, and local dimensions of case-based research" (p. 1).

By contrast, quantitative cross-national studies sometimes have an unreal quality to them—countries become organisms with systemic distress, for example—and the data examined have little meaningful connection to actual empirical processes. More concrete questions—relevant to the social bases and origins of specific phenomena in similarly situated countries and regions—do not receive the attention they deserve (Ragin, 1987).

Ragin's orientation is toward macro-level comparative studies and causal analysis. Others, such as Bradshaw and Wallace (1991), view the value of case studies as residing in their contribution to the refinement and modification of extant theory, and ultimately to the creation of new theory when existing explanatory frameworks are not applicable. They find much of the existing social science theory, formulated in a few select countries of the north, to be inappropriate to much of the world. Their concern is not so much with achieving generalizable propositions concerning causal relationships as with understanding, much in the tradition of Weber (1964), the patterning of relationships in different types of historical and social configurations.

Examples of promising studies according to the lines suggested by Bradshaw and Wallace (1991) and Bartlett and Vavrus (2016) include those by Heidi Ross et al.(2011), Iveta Silova and colleagues (2017), Bjorn Nordtveit (2010), and Antoni Verger, Xavier Bonal, and Adrián Zancajo (2016).

Ross (2000) in her case studies of girls' education in rural areas of China employs ethnographic methods, life narratives, and a longitudinal perspective to illuminate human agency in overcoming various barriers to self-fulfillment and contributions to society. As she documents, the very process of interviewing female students enhanced their self-image and served to empower them. Her research focus on social interactions in the formation of self-identities and life trajectories accords with the theme of her 2002 CIES presidential address on the importance of relational theory to the field of comparative and international education (Ross, 2002; Ross et al., 2011).

While Ross's (2000) case studies operate at the level of individual interviews, much of the research of Silva takes place at national and regional levels in postsocialist societies formerly under the domination of the Soviet (2010). Her work, much in the spirit of the writings of Robert Cowen on "transitology" (Larsen, 2010), focuses on nonlinear processes of change in society and education where outcomes are never certain. Her conceptual framework further overcomes dichotomies and static categories. The various case studies in her edited volumes further illustrate how the transformations in various stages and forms of socialism can only be comprehended within specific historical and sociocultural context; and more recent writings by Silova et al. (2017) involve imagining possible utopian and nonutopian futures for education (Larsen, 2010; Silova & Niyozov, 2020; Silova et al., 2017). (For further discussion of her writings on postsocialism, see Chapter 18 with Ben Eklof in this volume.)

Another promising line of research is provided by Nordtveit's (2010) "compressed ethnographic" methods (short visits to various sites) with complexity theory to study programs designed to serve youth living under conditions of extreme hardship. Complexity theory leads researchers to understand the multiple sources and interactions of education reform initiatives that may lead to unanticipated and often conflicting results. Avoiding simplistic and often misguided categorizations based on dualities or binaries (such as developed and undeveloped countries, childhood and adulthood, and the worlds of school and work), researchers, instead, find continua and interactions that enable them to more accurately delineate the realities that families face in deciding whether or not their children should study, help at home, or engage in some form of paid work. Grounded in an understanding of village life, for example, in Namibia, Swaziland, and Benin, he recommend to policymakers ways in which schools may contribute to protecting children from the most exploitive forms of labor while serving as a resource for community development (Nordtveit, 2010).

A remarkable conceptual framework is provided by Verger et al. (2016) in their case study of the heavily market-based Chilean education systems. Briefly, the researchers employ "A realist evaluation perspective" to study "Public-private partnerships (PPPs) in education . . . as a cost-effect policy solution to the access and quality problems that many education systems, especially in developing countries face" (Verger et al., 2016, p. 223). According to Verger et al. (2016), the advantages of this perspective over more conventional evaluation methods is this: "It is especially appropriate for analyzing education policies whose implementation depends so decisively on the strategic behavior, 'logics of action' (Ball & Maroy, 2009) and preferences of the intended beneficiaries of the intervention—clearly the case for PPPs in education" (p. 225).

These studies illustrate how different levels of government, the relationship between the state and the private sector, and the interplay of the global and the local impacted the various dimensions of education systems. The most promising studies employ multilevel analysis (ranging from the individual to the international), situate individuals and their groups within specific contexts with a variety of intervening factors shaping actions and outcomes. Furthermore, they examine not only the limitations but also the potential of education policies and practices to bring about more equitable school systems and just societies.

Case studies, however, have their limitations and pitfalls. There is a danger in attempting to generalize from one case to other instances that are not appropriate and to view the world only from the lens of that which is most familiar. Major funding agencies for international research also tend to favor quicker, quantitative studies that meet the exigencies of immediate decision-making and present the façade of being more scientific (Crossley & Bennett, 1997).

Large-scale variable-oriented studies, whatever their limitations, also have great value in contributing to theory building as well as more informed and enlightened policymaking. We see great utility in studies such as those conducted as part of the International Evaluation of Educational Achievement (IEA) or PISA. As Husén (1987) and others (Kamens & McNeely, 2010; Meyer & Baker, 1996) have pointed out, the great range of examples provided by such studies enables researchers and policymakers to examine the effects of introducing different subject matter (e.g., foreign languages) at certain points in the curriculum, of permitting early specialization in certain disciplines (e.g., mathematics and sciences), or of taking different pedagogical approaches to instruction (e.g., inquiry-oriented vs. more didactic science education).[5] Large-scale research can reveal, for example, what conditions favor the educational careers and life chances of females (Stewart & Winter, 1977) or successful literacy and adult basic education programs (Elley, 1997). Although such studies are useful in illuminating general patterns, we also believe the general tendencies revealed by them need to be studied in greater detail through individual cases of educational institutions and programs within their unique contexts (Postlethwaite, 1999; Theisen et al., 1983).[6]

A promising line of inquiry is found in combining randomized trials with qualitative studies to draw upon the strengths of the experimental method of studying various education and social interventions with more ethnographic approaches to revealing why things work the way they do. Although relatively new to the field of comparative and international education, this mixed-method approach is illustrated by Burde (2012) who studies the various factors influencing access to education and learning outcomes, especially for rural children living in situations of internal conflict and war—with their numbers, unfortunately, increasing significantly.[7]

CONCLUSION

In previous editions I cited the promotional brochure of the June 1998 Western Region meeting of the CIES titled "Dance on the Edge." It was organized to "celebrate comparative and international education at the cusp of the 21st century." I quoted at length from the brochure because I believed it so cogently (and delightfully) captures the state of our field in the early decades of the 21st century:

> Comparative and international education is enjoying a renaissance. Globalization has infused the ever-present need to learn about each other with an urgency and emphasis like no other in history. At the same time, the postmodern attack on metanarratives and totalizing discourses has infused our scholarship and practice with doubt about much orthodox wisdom. Even the meaning of "comparative" and "international" is in question, accompanied by vigorous contests over who will control "education." For some, education is an instrument of social justice and bulwark against cultural hegemony. For others it is a commodity to be bought and sold on a "free market."[8]

Yes, indeed. Vigorous debate continues within our field. I also would question a central point made in the conference's announcement. As the various chapters in this volume underscore, "metanarratives and totalizing discourses," although under attack, continue to be alive and well; rumors of their demise (to paraphrase the American humorist Mark Twain) are much exaggerated. Moreover, if they are to be challenged, their continued prevalence, workings, and implications need to be understood.

If there is a constant in the field of comparative education, it is its constantly changing nature. Since its institutionalization in the academy, our field has undergone marked shifts in paradigms and approaches to the field—from modernization theory and structural functionalism combined with attempts to create a science of education based on the rigorous gathering of comparative data to test theoretically based hypotheses, to neo-Marxist, world systems, and dependency theories of school-society relations, to ethnomethodological and ethnographic approaches, to a variety of isms—poststructuralism, postmodernism, and postcolonialism coupled with feminist perspectives (Altbach et al., 1982; Kelly, 1992). New developments in comparative education include the incorporation of theories of multiculturalism, social movements, and the state as well as critical race theory and critical modernism (Torres & Mitchell, 1998). The field has undergone a shift from a macro focus on the role of schooling in contributing to such outcomes as social mobility and stability, political development, economic growth, cultural continuity, and change to a microcosm on the inner workings of schools and on what is learned and taught in school. Increasingly, attention is given to human agency, to how individuals and their collectivities interact with educational and other societal institutions to make sense of the world and leave their mark on it. As I pointed out in my 2001 CIES presidential address, there is a need to study the lived and often contested reality of individual schools and education programs: how the interactions of students, teachers, staff, parents, and various nonschool agencies affect how the world is interpreted, meanings are negotiated, decisions are made, and academic and occupational careers are constructed (Arnove, 2001).

These shifts do not have demarcated dates. The trends have tended to overlap. At times, advocates of these different approaches have been at odds with one another, sometimes in dialogue with one another. Now more than ever, there is a need to learn from one another, to view the strengths and limitations of different theoretical and methodological approaches to the study of education. Small-scale case studies and large-scale research demonstrate increasing sophistication in attempting to combine different levels of analysis (from the world system to the local context), quantitative and qualitative data to reach more precise conclusions about the nature of what is being studied and what may be generalized. If a discipline is based on systematic, cumulative increases in knowledge, with studies building on previous research to refine and expand our understanding of the social world, comparative education is indeed becoming more of a discipline that can contribute to improved policy and practice.

The continued growth of a systematic, codified body of theory and knowledge, however, does not mean homogeneity or even a consensus about the boundaries of the field or the best way to go about studying education across countries and cultures. In a predecessor to this text, Kelly (1992) noted that:

> Research in the field has been and will in the future be diverse, focusing on a range of topics which at times seem tenuously connected, like school finance, illiteracy among women, textbook publishing practices, colonial schools . . . and so forth. The field has no center—rather, it is an amalgam of multidisciplinary studies, informed by a number of theoretical frameworks. Debates in the field will likely over time shift as educational policies and practices and needs change and the trust placed in particular theories, social systems, or reforms prove themselves valid or lacking in validity. The fact that the field has not resolved these debates about culture, method, and theory may well be a strength, rather than a weakness and point to the viability of the field and its continued growth. (pp. 21–22)

In the same text, Arnove et al. (1992) maintain that although comparative education was a loosely bounded field, it was held together by a "fundamental belief that education can be improved and can serve to bring about change for the better of all nations" (p. 1). In this chapter and text, the various authors state the belief that our field can contribute to positive change efforts in education and society. One way in which comparative education can help effect change is by contributing to a more realistic and comprehensive understanding of the transnational forces influencing all societies and education systems—both their potentially deleterious as well as beneficial features. Also, members of our field can become more directly involved in teacher education and educational reform initiatives—infusing programs and efforts with international/global perspectives (Ginsburg et al., 1992; Mundy et al., 2010). We believe that comparative education can—and should—play a significant role in contributing to the possibility that coming generations will use their talents on behalf of international peace and social justice in an increasingly interconnected and interdependent world.

NOTES

The author wishes to acknowledge the invaluable assistance of Li Yan in formatting and verifying the references in the chapter and to Najeeb Shafique and Carlos Alberto Torres for substantive contributions. Stephen Franz also provided valuable editorial advice. I wish to dedicate this chapter to the memory of my late beloved wife and colleague Toby, who inspired and assisted in so many ways my scholarship and writing in the field of education.

1. UNESCO (the United Nations Educational Scientific, and Cultural Organization) and UNICEF are important international technical assistance agencies working in the field of education, but they are not following the neoliberal economic agenda similar to that of the World Bank and the IMF, and their educational goals often differ in a number of respects from the World Bank and IMF. More recently, OECD and the World Trade Organization have been major agencies determining international trends in educational change and relations among countries.

2. The three knowledge interests are the empirical-technical, the historical-hermeneutic, and the emancipatory.

3. For example, among the more recent regional members to join the WCCES are the Gulf Comparative Education Society; the Indiana Ocean Comparative Education Society; and the Africa for Research in Comparative Education Society.

4. This is a quip from Jerome Harste, Emeritus Professor of the Language Education Department of the Indiana University School of Education, Bloomington. Harste, a leading proponent of whole-language education, has difficulty with people who claim to be eclectic in their approaches to teaching reading and writing.

5. Excellent data on various independent and dependent variables related to academic achievement and other school outcomes are found in the PISA website linked to the National Center for Educational Statistics, www.nces.edu.gov/surveys/pisa.

6. See the November 2006 issue of the *Comparative Education Review* containing the 2006 CIES presidential address of Martin Carnoy and commentary by others, in which the value of large-scale quantitative studies for purposes of establishing verifiable propositions within the field of comparative education is contrasted with the contributions of small-scale qualitative studies to theory-building.

7. Recent United Nations data on 19 million displaced within their own countries in 2019, and making them at risk to contract and spread COVID-19 is found at "Internal displacement": https://news.un.org/en/story/2020/05/1063162.

8. Brochure presented at the 1998 CIES Western Region Conference, Department of Educational Studies, University of British Columbia, Vancouver, B.C., Canada.

REFERENCES

Akkari, A., & Perez, S. (1998). Educational research in Latin America. *Education Policy Analysis Archives*, 6(7). doi:10.14507/epaa.v6n7.1998

Alexander, R., Broadfoot, P., & Phillips, D. (Eds.). (1999). *Learning from comparing: New directions in comparative education research. Contexts, classrooms and outcomes.* (Vol. 1). Symposium Books.

Alger, C. F., & Harf, J. E. (1986). Global education: Why? For whom? About what? In R. E. Freeman (Ed.), *Promising practices in global education: A handbook with case studies* (pp. 1–13). National Council on Foreign Language and International Studies.

Altbach, P. G. (1981). The university as center and periphery. *Teachers College Record*, 82(4), 601–621.

Altbach, P. G., & Tan, E. T. J. (1995). *Programs and centers in comparative and international education: A global inventory*. State University of New York Press.

Altbach, P. G., Arnove, R. F., & Kelly, G. P. (1982). Trends in comparative education: A critical analysis. In P. G. Altbach, R. F. Arnove, & G. P. Kelly (Eds.), *Comparative education* (pp. 505–533). Macmillan.

Arnove, R. F. (1980). Comparative education and world-systems analysis. *Comparative Education Review*, 24(1), 48–62. doi:10.1086/446090

Arnove, R. F. (2001). Comparative and International Education Society (CIES) facing the twenty-first century: Challenges and contributions. *Comparative Education Review*, 45(4), 477–503. doi:10.1086/447689

Arnove, R. F., Altbach, P. G., & Kelly, G. P. (Eds.). (1992). *Emergent issues in education: Comparative perspectives*. State University of New York Press.

Arnove, R. F. & Torres, C. A. (Eds.). (2007). *Comparative education: The dialectic of the global and the local* (3rd Ed.). Rowman & Littlefield.

Arnove, R. F., Torres, C. A., & Franz. S. (Eds.), (2013). *Comparative education: The dialectic of the global and the local.* Rowman & Littlefield.

Aronowitz, S., & Cutler, J. (Eds.). (1998). *Post-work: The wages of cybernation*. Routledge.

Assié-Lumumba, N'D. T., & Waghid, Y. (2023). Comparative education as an act of *uBuntu*: human encounters reconsidered. In L. I. Misiaszek et al. (Eds.), *Emergent trends in comparative education: The dialectic of the global and the local.* Rowman & Littlefield.

Ball, S. J., & Maroy, C. (2009). School's logics of action as mediation and compromise between internal dynamics and external constraints and pressures. *Compare*, 39(1), 99–112. doi:10.1080/03057920701825544

Barber, B. R. (1995). *Jihad vs. McWorld*. Times Books.

Barshay, J. (2019). *What 2018 PISA international rankings tell us about U.S. schools*. Retrieved from https://hechingerreport.org/what-2018-pisa-international-rankings-tell-us-about-u-s-schools/

Bartlett, L. (2014). Vertical case studies and the challenges of culture, context and comparison. *Current Issues in Comparative Education*, 16(2), 30–33.

Bartlett, L., & Vavrus, F. (2016). *Rethinking case study research: A comparative approach.* Routledge.

Bradshaw, Y., & Wallace, M. (1991). Informing generality and explaining uniqueness: The place of case studies in comparative research. *International Journal of Comparative Sociology*, 32(1–2), 154–171. doi:10.1177/002071529103200108

Bray, M. (2003). Editorial introduction: Tradition, change, and the role of the World Council of Comparative Education Societies. *International Review of Education*, 49(1–2), 1–13.

Bray, M., & Thomas, R. M. (1995). Levels of comparison in educational studies: Different insights from different literatures and the value of multilevel analyses. *Harvard Educational Review*, 65(3), 472–491. doi:10.17763/haer.65.3.g3228437224v4877

Bray, M., & Gui, Q. (2001), Comparative education in greater China: Contexts, characteristics, contrasts, and contributions. *Comparative Education*, 37(4), 451–473.

Brembeck, C. S. (1975). The future of comparative and international education. *Comparative Education Review*, 19(3), 369–374. doi:10.1086/445844

Buchmann, C., & Hannum, E. (2001). Education and stratification in developing countries: A review of theories and research. *Annual Review of Sociology*, 27(1), 77–102. doi:10.1146/annurev.soc.27.1.77

Burde, D. (2012). Assessing impact and bridging methodological divides: Randomized trials in countries affected by conflict. *Comparative Education Review*, 56(3), 448–473. doi:10.1086/664991

Cardoso, F. H. (1977). The consumption of dependency theory in the United States. *Latin American Research Review*, 12(3), 7–24.

Cardoso, F. H., & Faletto, E. (1969). *Dependencia y desarrollo en América Latina* [Dependency and development in Latin America]. Siglo XXI Editores.

Carney, S. (2009). Negotiating policy in an age of globalization: Exploring educational "policyscapes" in Denmark, Nepal, and China. *Comparative Education Review*, 53(1), 63–88. doi:10.1086/593152

Carnoy, M. (1995). Rates of return to education. In M. Carnoy (Ed.), *International encyclopedia of economics of education* (2nd ed., pp. 364–369). Pergamon Press.

Cogan, J. J. (1984). Should the US mimic Japanese education? Let's look before we leap. *Phi Delta Kappan*, 65(7), 463–468.

Coleman, J. S., Campbell, E. Q., Hobson, C. J., McPartland, J., Mood, A. M., Weinfeld, F. D., & York, R. L. (1966). *Equality of educational opportunity*. U.S. Government Printing Office.

Collins, C. S., & Wiseman, A. W. (Eds.). (2012). *Education strategy in the developing world: Understanding the World Bank's education policy revision*. Emerald Group Publishing Limited.

Crossley, M., & Bennett, J. A. (1997). Planning for case study evaluation in Belize, Central America. In M. Crossley & G. Vulliamy (Eds.), *Qualitative educational research in developing countries* (pp. 221–243). Garland.

Crossley, M., & Broadfoot, P. (1992). Comparative and international research in education: Scope, problems and potential. *British Educational Research Journal*, 18(2), 99–112. doi:10.1080/0141192920180201

Crossley, M., & Vulliamy, G. (Eds.). (1997). *Qualitative educational research in developing countries: Current perspectives*. Garland.

Cummings, W. K. (1994). From knowledge seeking to knowledge creation: The Japanese university's challenge. *Higher Education*, 27(4), 399–415. doi:10.1007/BF01384901

Davenport, M. (1998). *Asian conceptions of the teacher internship: Implications for American art education*. Indiana University, School of Education.

Desjardins, R. (2023). Alternative approaches to the political economy of education and some of their implications. In L. I. Misiaszek et al. (Eds.), *Emergent trends in comparative education: The dialectic of the global and the local*. Rowman & Littlefield.

Dowbor, L., Ianni, O., & Resende, P. E. (1998). *Desafios da globalização* [Challenges of globalization]. Editora Vozes.

Drucker, P. F. (1993). *Post-capitalist society*. Harper Business.

Elley, W. B. (Ed.). (1997). *The IEA study of reading literacy: Achievement and instruction in thirty-two school systems*. Pergamon Press.

Epstein, E. H. (1992). Editorial. *Comparative Education Review*, 36(3), 409–416. doi:10.1086/447096

Epstein, E. H. (1994). Comparative and international education: Overview and historical development. In T. Husén & T. N. Postlethwaite (Eds.), *The international encyclopedia of education* (pp. 918–923). Pergamon Press.

Farrell, J. P. (1979). The necessity of comparisons in the study of education: The salience of science and the problem of comparability. *Comparative Education Review*, 23(1), 3–16. doi:10.1086/446010

Farrell, J. P., & Schiefelbein, E. (1985). Education and status attainment in Chile: A comparative challenge to the Wisconsin model of status attainment. *Comparative Education Review, 29*(4), 490–506. doi:10.1086/446545

Feinberg, W. (1993). *Japan and the pursuit of a new American identity: Work and education in a multicultural age*. Routledge.

Fraser, S. (1964). *Jullien's plan for comparative education, 1816–1817*. Bureau of Publications, Teachers College, Columbia University.

Freire, P. (1970). *Pedagogy of the oppressed*. Continuum.

Giddens, A. (1991). *The consequences of modernity*. Stanford University Press.

Ginsburg, M. B., Kamat, S., Raghu, R., & Weaver, J. (1992). Educators/politics. *Comparative Education Review, 36*(4), 417–445. doi:10.1086/447144

Gorostiaga, X. (1993). New times, new role for universities of the South. *Envio: The Monthly Magazine of Analysis on Central America, 12*(144), 29–40.

Habermas, J. (1971). *Knowledge and human interests* (J. J. Shapiro, Trans.). Beacon Press.

Hanvey, R. (1976). *An attainable global perspective*. Center for Global Perspectives.

Hart-Landsberg, M. (2009). Learning from ALBA and the Bank of the South: Challenges and possibilities. *Monthly Review, 61*(4), 1–18. doi:10.14452/MR-061-04-2009-08_1

Hayhoe, R. (2000). Redeeming modernity. *Comparative Education Review, 44*(4), 423–439. doi:10.1086/447628

Hayhoe, R., & Pan, J. (2001). *Knowledge across cultures: A contribution to dialogue among civilizations*. Comparative Education Research Centre, Hong Kong University.

Helfenbein, R. J., & Mason, T. C. (Eds.). (2012). *Ethics and international curriculum work: The challenges of culture and context*. Information Age Publishing.

Heyneman, S. P. (1976). Influences on academic achievement: A comparison of results from Uganda and more industrialized societies. *Sociology of Education, 49*(3), 200–211. doi:10.2307/2112231

Heyneman, S. P. (1993). Quantity, quality, and source. *Comparative Education Review, 37*(4), 372–388. doi:10.1086/447205

Heyneman, S. P. (1995). Economics of education: Disappointments and potential. *Prospects, 25*(4), 557–583. doi:10.1007/BF02334136

Hickling-Hudson, A. (1998). When Marxist and postmodern theories won't do: The potential of postcolonial theory for educational analysis. *Discourse: Studies in the Cultural Politics of Education, 19*(3), 327–339. doi:10.1080/0159630980190306

Husén, T. (1987). Policy impact of IEA research. *Comparative Education Review, 31*(1), 29–46. doi:10.1086/446654

Jencks, C., Smith, M., Acland, H., Bane, M. J., Cohen, D., Gintis, H., . . . & Michelson, S. (1972). *Inequality: A reassessment of the effect of family and schooling in America*. Basic Books.

Johnson, J. (2021). *Most common languages used on the internet 2020*. Retrieved from https://www.statista.com/statistics/262946/share-of-the-most-common-languages-on-the-internet/

Kamens, D. H., & McNeely, C. L. (2010). Globalization and the growth of international educational testing and national assessment. *Comparative Education Review, 54*(1), 5–25. doi:10.1086/648471

Kandel, I. L. (1933). *Studies in comparative education*. Houghton and Mifflin.

Kelly, G. P. (1992). Debates and trends in comparative education. In R. Arnove, P. Altbach, & G. Kelly (Eds.), *Emergent issues in education: Comparative perspectives* (pp. 13–24). State University of New York Press.

King, A. D. (Ed.). (1997). *Culture, globalization and the world system: Contemporary conditions for the representation of identity*. University of Minnesota Press.

King, K. L. (1998). *From exclusion to inclusion: A case study of black South Africans at the University of Witwatersrand* (Unpublished doctoral dissertation). Indiana University, Bloomington.

Klees, S. J., Samoff, J., & Stromquist, N. P. (Eds.). (2012). *The World Bank and education: Critiques and alternatives*. Sense Publishers.

Kobayashi, T. (1990). China, India, Japan and Korea. In W. D. Halls (Ed.), *Comparative education: Contemporary issues and trends* (pp. 200–226). UNESCO.

Komatsu, H., & Rappleye, J. (2017). A new global policy regime founded on invalid statistics? Hanushek, Woessmann, PISA, and economic growth. *Comparative Education*, 53(2), 166–191. doi:10.1080/03050068.2017.1300008

Ladd, H. F., & Fiske, E. B. (2011, December 12). Class matters. Why won't we admit it? *New York Times*, p. A3.

Larsen, M. A. (Ed.). (2010). *New thinking in comparative education: Honouring Robert Cowen*. Sense Publisher.

Mabokela, R. O., & King, K. L. (Eds.). (2001). *Apartheid no more: Case studies of Southern African universities in the process of transformation*. Bergin & Garvey.

Mackinnon, A. (1996). Learning to teach at the elbows: The Tao of teaching. *Teaching and Teacher Education*, 12(6), 653–664. doi:10.1016/S0742-051X(96)00009-1

Manzon, M. (2011). *Comparative education: The construction of a field*. Comparative Education Research Centre, University of Hong Kong.

Masemann, V. (1997). *Recent directions in comparative education*. Paper presented at the Annual Conference of the Comparative and International Education Society, Mexico City.

McGinn, N. F. (1996). Education, democratization, and globalization: A challenge for comparative education. *Comparative Education Review*, 40(4), 341–357. doi:10.1086/447398

McMahon, W. W. (2009). *Higher learning, greater good: The private and social benefits of higher education*. Johns Hopkins University Press.

Meyer, J. W., & Baker, D. P. (1996). Forming American educational policy with international data: Lessons from the sociology of education. *Sociology of Education*, 69, 123–130. doi:10.2307/3108459

Misiaszek, G. W. (2023). Contested terrains of environmental pedagogies: Comparing ecopedagogy, education for sustainable development and environmental education. In L. I. Misiaszek et al. (Eds.), *Emergent trends in comparative education: The dialectic of the global and the local*. Rowman & Littlefield.

Mundy, K. (2007). Educational multilateralism: Origins and indications for global governance. In K. Martens, A. Rusconi, & K. Leuze (Eds.), *New arenas of education governance* (pp. 19–39). Palgrave Macmillan.

Mundy, K., Bickmore, K., Hayhoe, R., Madden, M., & Madjidi, K. (Eds.). (2010). *Comparative and international education: Issues for teachers* (2nd ed.). Teachers College Press.

Nickell, S., & Bell, B. (1996). Changes in the distribution of wages and unemployment in OECD countries. *American Economic Review*, 86(2), 302–308.

Noah, H. J. (1984). The use and abuse of comparative education. *Comparative Education Review*, 28(4), 550–562. doi:10.1086/446467

Noah, H. J., & Eckstein, M. A. (1969). Towards a science of comparative education. *British Journal of Educational Studies*, 17(3), 334–334. doi:10.2307/3119655

Nordtveit, B. H. (2010). Development as a complex process of change: Conception and analysis of projects, programs and policies. *International Journal of Educational Development*, 30(1), 110–117. doi:10.1016/j.ijedudev.2009.06.004

Ohanian, S. (1987). Notes on Japan from an American schoolteacher. *Phi Delta Kappan*, 68(5), 360–367.

Paine, L. (1990). The teacher as virtuoso: A Chinese model for teaching. *Teachers College Record*, 92(1), 49–81.

Piscitelli, B. (1997). Culture, curriculum and young children's art: Directions for further research. *Journal of Cognitive Education*, 6(1), 27–37.

Plowden, B. (Ed.). (1967). *Children and their primary schools: A report of the Central Advisory Council for Education (England)*. Her Majesty's Stationery Office.

Postlethwaite, T. N. (1999). *International studies of educational achievement: Methodological issues*. Comparative Education Research Centre, Hong Kong University.

Preston, R. (1997). Integrating paradigms in educational research: Issues of quantity and quality in poor countries. In M. Crossley & G. Vulliamy (Eds.), *Qualitative educational research in developing countries* (pp. 31–64). Garland.

Pritchett, L. (2001). Where has all the education gone? *The World Bank Economic Review*, 15(3), 367–391. doi:10.1093/wber/15.3.367

Psacharopoulos, G. (1990). Comparative education: From theory to practice, or are you A:\neo.* or B:*.ist?. *Comparative Education Review*, 34(3), 369–380. doi:10.1086/446952

Psacharopoulos, G., & Patrinos, H. A. (2018). Returns to investment in education: A decennial review of the global literature. *Education Economics*, 26(5), 445–458. doi:10.1080/09645292.2018.1484426

Ragin, C. C. (1987). *The comparative method: Moving beyond qualitative and quantitative strategies*. University of California Press.

Reich, R. B. (1991). *The work of nations: Preparing ourselves for 21st-century capitalism*. Vintage Books.

Reich, R. B. (2010). *Aftershock: The next economy and America's future*. Alfred A. Knopf.

Rodney, W. (1981). *How Europe underdeveloped Africa*. Howard University Press.

Ross, H. (2002). The space between us: The relevance of relational theories to comparative and international education. *Comparative Education Review*, 46(4), 407–432. doi:10.1086/345417

Ross, H. A. (2000). In the moment—discourses of power, narratives of relationship: Framing ethnography of Chinese schooling, 1981–1997. In J. Liu, H. A. Ross, & D. P. Kelly (Eds.), *The ethnographic eye: Interpretive studies of education in China* (pp. 123–152). Falmer Press.

Ross, H. A., Shah, P. P., & Wang, L. (2011). Situating empowerment for millennial schoolgirls in Gujarat, India and Shaanxi, China. *Feminist Formations*, 23(3), 23–47.

Roy, A. (2020, April 3). The pandemic is a portal. *Financial Times*. Retrieved from https://www.ft.com/content/10d8f5e8-74eb-11ea-95fe-fcd274e920ca

Russell, N. U. (1997). Lessons from Japanese cram schools. In W. K. Cummings & P. G. Altbach (Eds.), *Education in Eastern Asia: Implications for America* (pp. 153–170). State University of New York Press.

Rust, V. D., Soumaré, A., Pescador, O., & Shibuyu, M. (1999). Research strategies in comparative education. *Comparative Education Review*, 43(1), 86–109. https://www.jstor.org/stable/1189215

Rutkowski, D., & Rutkowski, L. (2023). The promise and methodological limits of international. In L. I. Misiaszek et al. (Eds.), *Emergent trends in comparative education: The dialectic of the global and the local*. Rowman & Littlefield.

Sadler, M. E. (1912). The history of education. In J. H. Rose, C. H. Herford, E. C. K. Gooner, & M. E. Sadler (Eds.), *Germany in the nineteenth century: Five lectures* (pp. 103–127). Manchester University Press

Sahlberg, P. (2011). *Finnish lessons: What can the world learn from educational change in Finland?* Teachers College Press.

Santos, T. (1970a). *Dependencia económica y cambio revolucionario en América Latina* [Economic dependency and revolutionary change in Latin America]. Editorial Nueva Izquierda.

Santos, T. (1970b). The structure of dependence. *American Economic Review, 60*(2), 231–236.

Sassen, S. (2007a). *A sociology of globalization*. W. W. Norton.

Sassen, S. (Ed.). (2007b). *Deciphering the global: Its scales, spaces and subjects*. Routledge.

Shafiq, M. N. (2010). Do education and income affect support for democracy in Muslim countries? Evidence from the Pew Global Attitudes Project. *Economics of Education Review, 29*(3), 461–469. doi:10.1016/j.econedurev.2009.05.001

Shafiq, M. N. (2015). Aspects of moral change in India, 1990–2006: Evidence from public attitudes toward tax evasion and bribery. *World Development, 68*, 136–148. doi:10.1016/j.worlddev.2014.11.017

Sharma, B., & Gettleman, J. (2021, March 9). Child marriages soar in pandemic, curbing global dreams. *New York Times*, p. A9.

Silova, I., & Niyozov, S. (Eds.). (2020). *Globalization on the margins: Education and post-socialist transformations in Central Asia*. Information Age Publishing.

Silova, I., Sobe, N. W., Korzh, A., & Kovalchuk, S. (Eds.). (2017). *Reimagining utopias: Theory and method for educational research in post-socialist contexts*. Springer.

Sobe, N. W. (2018). Problematizing comparison in a post-exploration age: Big data, educational knowledge, and the art of criss-crossing. *Comparative Education Review, 62*(3), 325–343. doi:10.1086/698348

Steiner-Khamsi, G. (Ed.). (2004). *The global politics of educational borrowing and lending*. Teachers College Press.

Steiner-Khamsi, G. (2010). The politics and economics of comparison. *Comparative Education Review, 54*(3), 323–342. doi:10.1086/653047

Steiner-Khamsi, G., Torney-Purta, J., & Schwille, J. (Eds.). (2002). *New paradigms and recurring paradoxes in education for citizenship: An international comparison*. JAI Press.

Stewart, A. J., & Winter, D. G. (1977). The nature and causes of female suppression. *Signs: Journal of Women in Culture and Society, 2*(3), 531–553. doi:10.1086/493386

Swing, E. S. (1997). *From Eurocentrism to post-colonialism: A bibliographic perspective*. Paper presented at the Annual Conference of the Comparative & International Education Society, Mexico City.

Takayama, K., (2018). Beyond comforting histories. The colonial/imperial entanglements of the International Institute, Paul Monroe. and Isaac L. Kandel at Teachers College, Columbia University. *Comparative Education Review, 62*(4), 453–481. 0010-4086/2018/6204-0027$10.00

Task Force on Higher Education and Society. (2000). *Higher education in developing countries: Peril and promise*. World Bank.

Tatto, M. T. (2011). Reimagining the education of teachers: The role of comparative and international research. *Comparative Education Review, 55*(4), 495–516. doi:10.1086/661769

Theisen, G. (1997). The new ABCs of comparative and international education. *Comparative Education Review, 41*(4), 397–412. doi:10.1086/447462

Theisen, G. L., Achola, P. P. W., & Boakari, F. M. (1983). The underachievement of cross-national studies of achievement. *Comparative Education Review, 27*(1), 46–68. doi:10.1086/446345

Tobin, J. J., Wu, D. Y. H., & Davidson, D. H. (1987). Class size and student/teacher ratios in the Japanese preschool. *Comparative Education Review, 31*(4), 533–549. doi:10.1086/446715

Torney-Purta, J., Schwille, J., & Amadeo, J. A. (1999). *Civic education across countries: Twenty-four national case studies from the IEA civic education project*. IEA.

Torres, C. A. (1998). Democracy, education, and multiculturalism: Dilemmas of citizenship in a global world. *Comparative Education Review*, 42(4), 421–447. doi:10.1086/447522

Torres, C. A., & Mitchell, T. R. (Eds.). (1998). *Sociology of education: Emerging perspectives*. State University of New York Press.

Tremmel, R. (1993). Zen and the art of reflective practice in teacher education. *Harvard Educational Review*, 63(4), 434–459. doi:10.17763/haer.63.4.m42704n778561176

UN News. (2020). *Record child displacement figures due to conflict and violence in 2019: UNICEF*. Retrieved from https://news.un.org/en/story/2020/05/1063162

UN News. (2021). *Over 168 million children miss nearly a year of schooling, UNICEF says*. Retrieved from https://news.un.org/en/story/2021/03/1086232

Vavrus, F., & Bartlett, L. (Eds.). (2009). *Critical approaches to comparative education: Vertical case studies from Africa, Europe, the Middle East, and the Americas*. Palgrave Macmillan.

Väyrynen, R. (1997). *Global transformation: Economics, politics, and culture*. Sitra.

Verger, A., Bonal, X., & Zancajo, A. (2016). What are the role and impact of public-private partnerships in education? A realist evaluation of the Chilean education quasi-market. *Comparative Education Review*, 60(2), 223–248. doi:10.1086/685557

Waters, M. (1995). *Globalization*. Routledge.

Watson, K. (1998). Memories, models and mapping: The impact of geopolitical changes on comparative studies in education. *Compare: A Journal of Comparative and International Education*, 28(1), 5–31. doi:10.1080/0305792980280102

Weber, M. (1964). The fundamental concepts of sociology. In T. Parsons (Ed.), *The theory of social and economic organization* (pp. 105–124). Free Press.

Willis, D. B., & Rappleye, J. (Eds.). (2011). *Reimagining Japanese education: Borders, transfers, circulations, and the comparative*. Symposium Books.

Willis, D. B., & Yamamura, S. (2002). Japanese education in transition 2001: Radical perspectives on cultural and political transformation. *International Education Journal*, 3(5), 1–4.

Wilms, W. W. (1996). *Restoring prosperity: How workers and managers are forging a new culture of cooperation*. Times Business.

Wilson, D. N. (1994). Comparative and international education: Fraternal or Siamese twins? A preliminary genealogy of our twin fields. *Comparative Education Review*, 38(4), 449–486. doi:10.1086/447271

Yamada, S. (2023). Synchrony and diachrony of multiple comparative educations: Japanese language publications in a global academic field. In L. I. Misiaszek et al. (Eds.), *Emergent trends in comparative education: The dialectic of the global and the local*. Rowman & Littlefield.

Yin, R. K. (1981). The case study as a serious research strategy. *Knowledge*, 3(1), 97–114. doi:10.1177/107554708100300106

1

Institutionalizing International Influence

Joel Samoff
*Stanford University and
University of Johannesburg*

ABSTRACT

Education for all. There has been progress on this objective with global support. In at least some settings, international assistance has increased enrollment. In many, education innovation and reform depend on external support. In a few, textbooks, chalk, and teachers' salaries depend on foreign funding. That support does not travel unaccompanied. Even where the progress is clear, the values, expectations, approaches, and analytic constructs that have become the global standard may in practice burden education development and impede education change well into the future. A broad review of experiences in the world's poorest countries does not find the globalization of responsibility for assuring access to education for all the world's learners but rather the localization and internalization of internationally promulgated perspectives on education even where education for all remains frustratingly beyond reach. The story here is a tale with several threads. Understanding international influences in education requires critical attention to the faith and enthusiasm of the evangelists of global goals, standards, and assessment, to the roles of foreign aid and empirical research, to the claims of research-supported policy priorities, and to the ways in which strategies intended to promote empowerment can become vehicles for undermining education reform and entrenching poverty.

■ ■ ■

Education for all. A global objective that must be accomplished locally. How to understand the Education for All (EFA) campaign, now decades-long and not expected to achieve universal basic education in this century? In practice, we find not the globalization of responsibility for assuring access to education for all the world's learners but rather the localization and internalization of internationally promulgated perspectives on education even where education for all remains frustratingly beyond reach. The story here is a tale with several threads. Understanding international influences in education requires critical attention to the faith and enthusiasm of the evangelists of global goals and standards, to the roles of research and foreign aid, and to the ways in which strategies intended to promote empowerment can become vehicles for undermining education reform and entrenching poverty.

To be sure, there has been important progress. In at least some settings, international support has increased the number of children in school and their teachers. In many, education innovation and reform depend on external support, and in a few, without that support, there would be no textbooks or chalk. That support does not travel unaccompanied. Even where the progress is clear, the values, expectations, approaches, and analytic constructs that have become the global standard may in practice burden education development and impede education change well into the future. Let us trace the evolution of that process, concerned especially with the experiences of the world's poorer countries, most in Africa, and particularly those that became independent during the second half of the 20th century. A brief overview of the international context and its principal institutions provides the foundation for an exploration of the forms and consequences of international influences and the roles of research.

CONTEXT

Exploring commonalities amid diversity is a powerful tool for examining both what is—education in different places—and how we know what is—research and the sociology of knowledge. The field of comparative education frets about its central concerns, sometimes focused on what appear to be universal patterns and sometimes oriented toward the unique and exotic. Its enduring challenge is to employ each perspective to illuminate the other.

Global Education Convergence

Throughout human history, societal interactions have involved both borrowing and conquest. Perhaps because educational achievement has often been associated with elite status, the organization and focus of education nearly everywhere in the modern era reflects international influences, some more forceful than others.

Higher education is one clear example. Instructors regularly employ what they term the Socratic method, more or less accurately seeking to capture the intellectual master-apprentice relationship associated with classical Greece. Students of education in Asia find persisting influences of Confucian patterns and ideas. As Altbach (1991) points out, universities nearly everywhere are modeled on institutions created in 13th-century France. Over time academics have secured significant institutional and individual independence and self-regulation, in part by imposing their own ideological and methodological orthodoxies. Professor-centered and relatively autonomous even when state-funded, that model has withstood academic, social, religious, and political challenges in diverse settings. There have, of course, been significant additions to the pattern. As institutions became advocates and enforcers of truths with universal validity, they came to be called universities. Notions of nation and nation-building have tightened the links between universities and the state and have nurtured the expectation that contributing to national development must be one of their priorities. Research is an increasingly important responsibility, commonly organized into a set of disciplines that are strikingly similar across the world. While the institutions themselves vary, the general point is clear. Notwithstanding diverse roots, different settings, and local variations, the commonalities stand out, from basic features of organization and governance to pedagogy to claims of autonomy and academic freedom. Approach and method rather than content have become the universal truth. Like their predecessors, though now generally detached from religious doctrine, more or less confidently they assert the universality of their ways of knowing—academic standards and scientific methods. Altbach (1991) concludes, "Regardless of political system, level of economic development, or educational ideology, the expansion of higher education has been the most important single postwar trend worldwide" (p. 44). We see in this example international influence as imposition and as emulation, with both coercion and rewards.

Colonial rule, another example, provided the setting for a particular sort of international influence: the implantation of metropolitan education institutions in the colonized world. Emulations, models, replicas, or overseas branches, these institutions often reproduced not only the curriculum, pedagogy, and hierarchical organization of their European models but even their architecture and staff and student codes of conduct. Both the intentions of the colonizers and the aspirations of the colonized elite they socialized insisted that the new education institutions resemble their models as closely as possible. Still, they remained distinctly colonial. Charged to equip a segment of the colonized society with the skills needed to administer the colonial enterprise, in practice, they were fully integrated into neither the local society nor the metropolitan education system. Even the special schools that served expatriates and an emerging national elite were generally truncated copies of their metropolitan counterparts.

Both borrowing and imposition have occurred. In the modern era, with few exceptions, the direction of influence is from the European core to the southern periphery. Institutional arrangements, disciplinary definitions and hierarchies, legitimizing publications, and instructional authority reside in that core, which periodically incorporates students and professors from the periphery, of whom many never return home. There are, to be sure, challenges to this dominance. Japan has a widely respected university system and institutions in China and across Asia attract and graduate outstanding students. Several middle-tier, rapidly industrializing countries have invested heavily in higher education, developing recognized centers of research and innovation. As in the perspective developed by Samir Amin (1974; 1976; 2014; 2019a), occasionally an academic debate initiated in the periphery (e.g., dependency in Latin American, oral history in Tanzania) becomes a critical concern for core institutions, perhaps supporting the view that the weakest links of the global system are those at the periphery. Intellectual challenges rooted in the core regularly include advocates from outside the core.[1]

Contemporary Education Reform

Contemporary education reform initiatives have roots in several different national settings. Early in the 20th century, U.S. education reformers sought to link schools more closely with their communities and to reinforce the organic connections among learning, schooling, and work. The Bolshevik Revolution provided an opening for reconceptualizing education's role, though in practice Soviet educators drew heavily on the thinking of the U.S. reformers as they emphasized technical education and sought to link schooling even more closely to employment needs and opportunities (Carnoy, 1990, p. 91*ff*, n. 12). The decolonization era following World War II saw experiments and ferment in education. For the newly decolonized countries of Africa and southern Asia, the transfer of sovereignty offered the hope and possibility of charting new directions. For parts of Latin America and China, regime transitions provided space for education innovators. The competition of capitalism and socialism, especially the efforts of the United States and the Soviet Union to extend their influence in the Global South, created space for experimentation. At the same time, the widespread student and worker militancy of May 1968 highlighted a parallel upheaval in the North Atlantic. Students asserted their political role, condemning their education and the societies whose expectations and values it transmitted. Although the national mobilizations generally fell short of their political objectives, education itself became both the focus of intense reform efforts and the vehicle for broader challenges to the political order.

Similarities

Still, it is the similarities across national settings that have most intrigued scholars of comparative education. Especially striking has been the relatively rapid movement in most countries from education as the privilege of a small elite to mass education as a responsibility of the state. Analysts have sought explanations for that transition within particular societies. In specific settings, scholars have attributed the national decision to develop mass education to the importance of schools as mechanisms of social control, to the role of education as a desired good able to win public support, to schooling as a common experience essential to developing social solidarity and national identity, to the perceived need to prepare the labor force for industrial society, and to the belief that education promotes national development. Other scholars (Carnoy 1984; 1992) have sought to elucidate the theories of the state embedded in national philosophies of education and to understand education in terms of the national and global political economy. Refining their earlier argument about the correspondence between state and school, Bowles and Gintis (1981) argue that education necessarily reflects, and simultaneously is in tension with, the structure of the national political economy.

Challenging that national orientation Boli, Ramirez, and Meyer (Boli et al., 1985; Boli & Ramirez, 1987) interpret the rapid implementation of compulsory schooling in diverse societies as the global consequence of a distinctly Western set of values and cultural practices. In their view, the 19th century produced revised understandings of the individual, the state, and social organization, which in turn required the transition from elite to mass education. Drawing on notions of modernization (Inkles & Smith, 1974) and world system (Wallerstein 1974; 1980; 1989), they argue that the widespread adoption of mass education reflected a global diffusion of Western cultural values, including a focus on an improved material standard of living, a sense of the individual as the fundamental social unit and the ultimate source of value and authority, and an expanded state responsible for social welfare.

Other authors focused on the agency of that diffusion in the postcolonial era. Arnove and Berman explored the critical roles of national commissions of inquiry and philanthropic foundations in specifying the organization of the social sciences—that is, the acceptable procedures for studying society, and thereby the organization of the education system (Arnove & Berman, 1984; Arnove, 1983; Arnove, 1980; Berman, 1983; see also Sutton, 2001; McGoey, 2016). Westernization did not mark inexorable and inevitable progress toward a universal modernity but rather reflected a conscious process of creating and shaping institutions, globally as well as locally. Born in the changing organization of production and accompanied by the expansion of monotheistic religions and the creation of the nation-state, the development of capitalist hegemony was not a conscious design with a master plan. Rather, its heterogeneity and diversity had powerful orienting and constraining currents, with key roles for particular individuals and institutions. Education was both cause and consequence.

My concern here is to build on this foundation, maintaining the notion that deeper structural relationships and pressures operate through and are thus visible in specific institutional arrangements. Within that context, I explore education and development in the Third World, especially Africa, in terms of the conjunction of international organizations, increased dependence on aid, and the development of a particular role for research.[2]

Development Requires Foreign Aid

Decolonization brought with it a notion of development. Thirty-five years after the 1884–1885 Berlin conference declaration of European authority over Africa, the Versailles Treaty ended German colonial rule in Africa. That treaty institutionalized a notion of development, or rather, lack of development. Colonies were deemed not ready for independence. After all, if the German colonies could become independent, why not those of England, France, Portugal, and Spain? The notion of development nurtured by decolonization envisioned a largely linear scale of progress on which countries could be located. That linkage was elaborated over the years between the wars and further institutionalized when the League of Nations Mandates became United Nations Trusteeships. While development has had many definitions, all include a core notion of progress from less developed to more developed. In the rationalism and empiricism of 20th-century social science, development was, and continues to be, addressed as a knowable set of stages and a knowable set of steps to close the development gap.

Modernization provided the theoretical underpinnings, interpreting human progress as more or less linear, characterized by a fundamental distinction between the more and the less modern. Talcott Parson's (1963) pattern variables provided a scientific legitimacy for that differentiation. Valentin Y. Mudimbe (1988; 1994) explores how those who saw themselves as modern required an "other" to define themselves, inventing it as necessary. Achille Mbembe (2001) and Jacques Depelchin (2005) have developed that perspective.

Critical to that was the asserted distinction between barbarian and civilized, which scholars refined into *traditional* and *modern*. That core idea and its associated stereotypes motivated and informed a good deal of the research on what were termed primitive societies. Modern and traditional, less offensive and more friendly than "primitive," became scientific terms, ostensibly detached from colonial motives, exploitation, and abuses. By clothing the traditional versus modern distinction in scientific language and credibility, social science provided a foundation for the notions that backward is a property of Africa—that is, a cause, not an effect, a condition not a process—and that the humane task of colonialism was to overcome that backwardness. Those ideas persist. Colonial rule crystallized the we/they, modern/primitive categorization and reached to notions of social obligation (colloquially, the "white man's burden") to justify the often harsh imposition of European rule and rules.

Continued European oversight—trusteeship—was thereby packaged as a development strategy. Following World War II, even as it became an arena for challenging and terminating colonial rule, the new United Nations system incorporated the idea of trusteeship.

At the same time, the link between development and aid was formally institutionalized in the creation of the International Bank for Reconstruction and Development. Charged with supporting the rebuilding of Europe, generally in alliance with the International Monetary Fund, the World Bank dispensed both funds and advice and by the 1970s had turned its attention to the former colonies.

Education was to be the development dynamo. If education was associated with economic progress, then surely it had to be a prominent component of development aid. As a large number of former colonies became independent, many of them very poor and with little investment or infrastructure to support autonomous development, it became commonplace that improving education required foreign assistance.

The understanding implicit in the assistance relationship thus begins with two related assumptions: education is essential for development, and education in poor countries, especially Africa, is in such disarray that it cannot fulfill its developmental role. From that starting point comes a third widely accepted proposition: foreign assistance is required to support new education initiatives, to rehabilitate education systems that have deteriorated, and for Africa, even to meet recurrent expenditures.

The initial promise, however, was not fulfilled. After a period of high expectations and apparently rapid progress, education in the poorest countries became a story of decay, crisis, and dependence instead of development and independence. Indeed, increasingly that has prompted a cry for the return of colonial rule—"some states are not yet fit to govern themselves"—a proposal that might be regarded as outrageous but seems sufficiently legitimate to warrant prominent attention (Johnson, 1993; see also Kaplan, 2000; Ignatieff, 2004).

To take us toward the major characters in this story of the localization of global patterns in education, aid, the funding and technical assistance agencies that manage the aid relationship, and the scholars and scholarship that have become essential to its operations and legitimacy, let us consider briefly major changes in the international system.

Socialist Disarray and U.S. Triumphalism

The precipitous dissolution of communist rule is widely interpreted as the inevitable victory of the United States over the Soviet Union, capitalism over socialism, the market over planning, indeed, good over evil. Capitalism prevailed because it is inherently better. What better proof could there be than its unequivocal victory? Everything that can be linked to socialism, however tenuous the link, is presumed flawed, precisely because of that link.

The arrogance of U.S. triumphalism is palpable and unceasing: "We're the only country complicated enough, sophisticated enough, big enough to lead the human race."[3]

There is a grand—and instructive—irony in a triumphalism that is politically and ideologically centered in the United States. As Przeworski (1992) put it:

> Neoliberal ideology, emanating from the United States and various multinational agencies, claims that the choice is obvious: there is only one path to development, and it must be followed. . . . Yet if a Martian were asked to pick the most efficient and humane economic systems on earth, it would certainly not choose the countries that rely most on markets. The United States is a stagnant economy in which real wages have been constant for more than a decade and the real income of the poorer 40 percent of the population has declined. It is an inhumane society in which 11.5 percent of the population—some 28 million people, including 20 percent of the children—lives in poverty. It is the oldest democracy on earth, but has one of the lowest voter-participation rates in the democratic world, and the highest per capita prison population in the world. (p. 46)

Inequality in the United States has increased, likely compounded by the COVID-19 pandemic.

Where socialism can provide neither useful ideas nor instructive experiences and where only one strategy of development is worth considering, the lessons are clear. Third World poverty is a Third World phenomenon. Where poverty is a long-standing condition worsened by poor policies, policy reform—structural adjustment became the descriptive terminology—is the essential remedy. The prescription follows from the diagnosis: "getting macroeconomic policies right" (especially reducing budget deficits, increasing tax revenues, eliminating price and exchange controls, encouraging foreign investment); "taxing agriculture less"; "putting exporters first" ("rationalizing import barriers," "privatizing public enterprises," and "financial reform"—especially "reducing financial repression, restoring bank solvency, and improving financial infrastructure").[4]

This triumphalism has (at least) two powerful consequences for the relationship between aid and policymaking. Those who have triumphed need no longer listen. Since they know what is correct and since it is their power (rather than negotiation) that secures their interests, they can instruct rather than listen and learn. As well, since the triumph, they believe, proves the correctness of their perspective, they need not feel reticent or guilty about telling others what to do.

Like its 1960s incarnation, contemporary developmentalism takes the global political economy as given, rather like a complex weather pattern. Monsoon rains and droughts are simply beyond human control. So, too, the world system—imposing, inexorable, and largely out of reach. That understanding itself fosters impotence. Consciously and forcefully, contemporary developmentalism directs attention away from efforts to conceive of the world system as a web of nation-states and corporations linked in complex but understandable and modifiable ways. Countries and companies, after all, are organized and managed by people and can be changed by people, sometimes even the lowest-level laborers and poorest citizens. At issue here is not a contest between external/foreign and internal/national explanations for the Third World's problems. Rather, it is the internalization within the Third World of the relationships and understandings of that larger environment, the internationalization even of ways of knowing, that has largely been excluded from the analytic and policy agendas.

Resuscitation of Modernization
Contemporary developmentalism also reflects the resuscitation of modernization theory, which insists now, as it did more than a half-century ago, that the causes of the Third World's problems are to be found within the Third World: its people, resources, capital, skills, psychological orientation, child-rearing practices, and more. That analytic framework is seductive and often assumed uncritically. Just as poverty is to be explained by the characteristics and (in)abilities of the poor, so the problems of Third World education are to be explained in Third World schools. Institutionalized in the centers of financial, industrial, and academic authority, this fundamental misunderstanding is sheltered from the challenge that the primary sources of contemporary problems are to be found in the process by which most Third World countries have been incorporated into the global economy. The international relationships are acknowledged and are at the same time treated as fixed features of the policy environment. They are the furniture, the paint on the walls, the air in the room—a part of the setting and thereby not a principal concern for policy attention. As normal and largely unexceptional features of the structure of international interactions, those relationships are assigned a low priority in the search for explanations and strategies for change. In this way, what may matter most receives little explicit attention. Notwithstanding the fascination with globalization, the explanatory framework and research agenda that dominate the aid relationship and scholarship on the Third World more generally largely exclude from active consideration the analytic perspective that emphasizes global integration, its forms, and its consequences. Studies of Third World education rarely mention, and even less frequently address critically the sources and consequences for education of the Washington development consensus and its sequels. The powerful critique developed by the dependency and world-systems literature—that explaining poverty in the contemporary Third World requires attention to the role of particular countries in a world system and the institutionalization of global connections within poor countries—is widely noted and, except in its broadest sweep and most superficial form, commonly ignored. The international order is a background condition. Not a set of relationships to be understood and challenged. Not a process to be analyzed and modified. To take as given what are potentially primary causes is to exclude them from the policy (and research) discourse. What is unseen and undiscussed cannot be the focus of policy attention or public action.

ORGANIZATIONS

This brief review of decolonization, developmentalism, and the broader political environment leads us to more differentiated attention to the global political economy and the institutions important to education in the Third World. At first glance, studying the conjunction between foreign aid and research requires attention to aid providers and aid recipients. Focusing solely or primarily on aid providers and recipients, however, would decontextualize their interactions, leading to limited understanding and superficial explanations. The aid relationship is embedded in a dense web of organizations of different sizes, scales, forms and roles, each with its own interests and strategies. While it is beyond the scope of this analysis to explore systematically the visible features and dark corners of that web, it is useful to note briefly the range of organizations and institutional forms.

The Constellation of Organizations

While it is reasonable to refer to the international system, and while indeed the United Nations is structured as a system, many organizations, both larger and smaller, have international reach. Their loose connections, overlapping terrains, and periodic tensions are important, but must not obscure the common assumptions and supportive patterns of behavior that are directive and influential in the third world.

Generally termed "multilaterals," some organizations are juridically international, especially those that constitute the United Nations system. Commonly the members of those organizations are countries, though there are important variations. The International Labor Organization, for example, includes countries, unions, and employers' groups. Governance rules also vary: majority rule in the United Nations General Assembly and United Nations Educational, Scientific and Cultural Organization (UNESCO), permanent members' vetoes in the Security Council, votes proportional to member countries' investment in the World Bank.

Frequently and somewhat misleadingly termed "bilateral," some organizations are distinctly *national*, with a primary mandate to serve national interests, for example, the U.S. Agency for International Development and the Canadian International Development Agency.

International and national agencies have initiated and supported continental, regional, national, and local organizations that assume particular education responsibilities. The World Bank, for example, has spawned the Capacity Building Foundation, the African Economic Research Consortium, the African Virtual University, Donors to African Education that became the Association for the Development of Education in Africa, and the global Development Gateway. Organizations of that sort may reflect a conflicted identity. Born with the values, orientations, and objectives of their parent or foster agencies, they also seek to establish their independent existence and legitimacy.

The term "nongovernmental organization" (NGO) has come to refer to a very wide range of groups, including some that operate within countries or even small local areas, others that are national in origin and operate international programs, and still others that have an international constitution. Many have education programs. Some NGOs depend so heavily on contracts with national governments and international organizations that functionally they might reasonably be regarded as quasi-governmental organizations.

Education researchers have created several regional networks, grouping scholars in Latin America, eastern and southern Africa, western and central Africa, and Southeast Asia, as well as education researchers in the industrialized north concerned with education, aid, and development (McGinn, 1996). Often still dependent on external funding and constituted by scholars themselves dependent on contracts with external agencies, those networks find it difficult to assert an effective autonomous voice and play a strong independent role.

Several foundations, most but not all with headquarters in the United States, have also played important roles in education and development. The Carnegie, Ford, and Rockefeller Foundations have all explicitly sought to influence the development of the social sciences at home and abroad. That process continues. In 2000, Carnegie Corporation, Ford Foundation, Rockefeller Foundation, and MacArthur Foundation combined to support African universities. With additional partners, that effort was extended and doubled in 2005 (Grant Lewis et al., 2010). Among the non-U.S. foundations with education activities in the third world are the Gulbenkian Foundation and the Aga Khan Foundation.

Of course, companies are prominent in this web. Especially visible have been the technology companies, several with direct investments in education and a few, for example, Cisco and Microsoft, with their own academies. Most recently, chains of private schools have emerged, claiming to fill gaps in the public education system, with relatively low fees and centrally developed prepacked instruction managed by instructional staff with little or no professional education.

At the larger and smaller scale, community organizations have challenged education systems in the Global South. I shall return to their efforts to create space for transformation initiatives below.

Increasingly, international academic organizations have sought to influence the development of their disciplines globally. As the International Political Science Association, for example, functions to propagate the fundamental assumptions and orientations of the U.S. political science mainstream, notwithstanding periodic challenges it plays a role in promoting a global convergence of understandings and ways of knowing. Similarly, a small set of internationally recognized journals in each discipline functions to impose standards and set the terms through which Third World scholars must establish their legitimacy (Fuenzaldia, 1983; see also Mamdani, 2008; Zeleza, 2002

These are all rich stories that warrant detailed analysis. The general observation is that international influences follow multiple pathways. Especially striking is how few of these organizations have sought to transform the organization and role of education in the Third World.

Changing Roles in the United Nations System

In the post–World War II mood of reconstruction, education was widely understood as the principal vehicle for remaking the world. Education had to be central to rebuilding and social transformation, whether in the countries shattered by war, in those recently decolonized, or in countries in which socialism was to become the ideal to be achieved and the engine of development. In many minds, there was no alternative. Education was an essential antidote to the horrors of the recent past, the Holocaust, trench warfare, and nuclear devastation. The optimism was nearly unbounded.

In that understanding, countries were the policymaking domains and educators were to be the critical education policymakers. The newly fashioned international system had a distinctly developmental thrust. International financial organizations were to stabilize currency flows (and thus both international trade and national growth) and to support the reconstruction and development of Europe. Special UN councils were charged with economic and social development and with overseeing the final days of the colonial system. For education, science, and culture, UNESCO was to provide technical expertise and assistance. Structured to be responsive to its member states, it was to be less constrained by the major power vetoes of the Security Council and the rich country dominance of the financial organizations.

That structure regularly obscured the locus of power and authority. Earlier, powerful nations imposed the will of the international system on former colonies. By the 1990s the international financial institutions had become the principal enforcers of global dictates.

Surprisingly rapidly, structural adjustment became both the description and the content of the imposition of that external control. Effectively, structural adjustment offered access to capital in exchange for the adoption of externally specified national policies and the surrender of some national autonomy. Although the mix of policies termed structural adjustment varied from one setting to another, the general strategy was similar across diverse countries. Aid not linked to projects and increased foreign assistance in general became available, on the condition that the recipient government adopt a series of economic policies (often termed liberalization). Nearly everywhere that required new or increased fees for social services and increased prices for consumers. For impoverished countries and dysfunctional economies, structural adjustment was stick as well as carrot.

Although their rhetoric seemed to call for a sharply curtailed role for the state, structural adjustment programs required a state sufficiently strong to implement highly unpopular measures, especially austerity and reduced price supports for basic food and other staples. Conditionalities—providing debt relief, currency support, and aid only when explicit conditions were met—meant that their own governments assumed major responsibility for the dependent integration of poor countries into the global political economy. "Effective governance" became the preferred terminology, with emphasis on administration, management, and appropriate technology.

The terminology evolves. The umbrella construct became "poverty reduction," an objective everyone can support. Recipient countries are required to develop an inclusive and complex poverty reduction strategy, ostensibly to guide both national and foreigners' behavior. On examination, though, we find the same thinking about the requisites for development and many of the same imposed conditions. Subtly insinuated in a rhetoric of partnership and development cooperation, these precepts for progress become difficult to discern and even more difficult to challenge. Wearing the cloak of science and resting on the staff of research, this orientation dismisses alternative perspectives on development as political and nonscientific, especially those that emphasize raised consciousness of inequality and exploitation, mass mobilization, and citizen participation.

In that context, international financial institutions increasingly characterized themselves as development advisory services. Human capital theory legitimized their direct involvement in education. The end of the Cold War, accompanied by renewed attention to the globally destabilizing consequences of persisting poverty, created maneuvering room for humanitarian and other NGOs, and ironically made it easier for the United States and its allies to reduce UNESCO's role.

Especially striking has been the reorientation of education roles and responsibilities among the organizations of the United Nations system. In its 1980 Education Sector Policy Paper, the World Bank highlighted UNESCO's role, crediting it for what became the World Bank's major focus on primary education (World Bank, 1980, p. 79). By 1995, the World Bank's education sector overview barely mentioned UNESCO and certainly did not indicate that it or anyone else would rely on UNESCO for technical assistance and expertise in education, science, and culture, a clear reflection of changed roles in the international system (World Bank, 1995; 1999; 2011).

By the 1990s the World Bank had effectively eclipsed UNESCO's education influence. Reviewing the evolution of UNESCO is beyond the scope of this discussion (Mundy, 1999; Mundy & Verger, 2015). It is important to note, however, that the UN organization institutionally most directly responsive to the majority of its members (no major power veto, no votes weighted by affluence) has lost much of its advisory role to the World Bank.

The institutionalization of this relationship, and particularly of the World Bank's role, takes several forms, in part because there is a fundamental tension between international control and national implementation. Having analyzed the problems and prescribed the solutions, the international agencies commonly assume they must direct events. At the same time, education reform is the responsibility of national authorities. Where they perceive the recommendations to be imposed and perhaps inimical to their interests, national leaders are unlikely to pursue energetically the prescribed reforms. Where they see innovations and reforms as externally initiated and managed, national education communities are unlikely to invest the energy and resources required to sustain changes. Widely proclaimed to be critical for the success of education reforms, "national ownership" often becomes the rhetorical fig leaf that permits avoiding discussion of the barely obscured international influences that nearly everyone, foreign and local, prefers not to address (Samoff, 1999; 2004). For the international agencies, the challenge is to exercise influence while encouraging national commitment to and implementation of the recommended reform strategy.

A major international conference, little known outside the circle of those most directly involved in Third World education but a point of reference and legitimacy ever since, was one response to that challenge. With appropriate ceremony, a distinguished group of educators and political leaders met in Jomtien, Thailand, in March 1990 to declare their support for making education available to everyone on the planet. Initiated and guided by the World Bank, the World Conference on Education for All had several formal sponsors: United Nations Development Programme (UNDP), UNESCO, United Nations Children's Fund (UNICEF), and the World Bank. Amid formal ceremonies, official statements, and research reports, some 1,500 participants from 155 governments, 20 intergovernmental bodies, and 150 NGOs adopted by acclamation "A World Declaration on Education for All" and "A Framework for Action" (Inter-Agency Commission, World Conference on Education for All, 1990). Other resolutions adopted by acclamation reflected the conference title. All people must have access to basic education, both because (basic) education should now be considered a right of citizenship and because development, however conceived, requires an educated populace.

It is far from clear, however, that the Jomtien conference and the follow-up efforts have dramatically altered priorities for basic education among aid recipients. When the major participants met again in the World Education Forum in

Dakar, Senegal, a decade later, none of the major targets had been met.[5] Though promised, the massive increase in global aid estimated to be necessary to achieve education for all has not been delivered.[6] Access has increased, but for many students there is little learning. The world renewed its commitment to universal basic education, resetting the achievement date to 2015. Yet, as the education community gathered in Incheon, South Korea, in 2015, the monitors' report noted important achievements and once again lamented persisting inequality and the failure to achieve the primary objective, universal access (UNESCO, 2015a, p. xv; Klees, 2017).

About the same time, a second strategy for exercising international influence within national responsibility for education emerged. Seeking to institutionalize its leadership position among the aid agencies active in Africa, by far the most aid-dependent continent, the World Bank supported the creation of Donors to African Education (DAE). Formally committed to promoting cooperation and coordination among the agencies and between the agencies and African education ministries, DAE became the umbrella for a series of focused working groups, with agency leadership and finance. To increase both impact and legitimacy, by the mid-1990s, its secretariat had moved out of the World Bank, with a more energetic and influential role for Africa's education ministers. Renamed, the Association for the Development of Education in Africa (ADEA) subsequently moved to Africa. Here we see a striking reflection of the power relationship. As ADEA grew more distant from its funders, its apparent legitimacy increased and its role diminished.

These two initiatives employed the language of collaboration as they institutionalized the leading role of international organizations, especially the World Bank. In practice, both reinforced particular understandings about education and development and thus institutionalized influence by making it unexceptional. Conventional wisdom on analyzing and understanding education came to reflect the perspectives of economists and bankers. That education ought to be considered an investment and that education funding should be analyzed with the tools used to assess investments become commonplace framework assumptions that were hardly noticed. Here, too, what otherwise might seem to be controversial issues that warrant extended discussion escape critical attention. Major assumptions that might be sharply contested if highlighted are embedded in ostensibly uncontroversial tools. The active debates focus on which investment yields a higher return rather than on the utility of the investment metaphor as an analytic construct for understanding education or setting education policy.

As well, both initiatives reflect education policy and practice as contested terrain. Influence is not unchallenged control. In some circumstances, institutions created for one purpose can be redirected toward another. Although the patterns of power and dominance are clear, it would be incorrect to presume that influence moves in only one direction or to ignore the ways in which how the ostensible victims of the global system assert initiatives and influence courses of action.

AID AND EDUCATION

Aid Critiques

Decolonization, notions of development and development gap, and the understanding that poor countries cannot fully fund their education systems have created space and leverage for foreign aid. Education policy and practice in the world's poorest countries, most in Africa, are framed by the aid relationship. Global meets local.

Among the numerous studies of foreign aid and its problems, including attention to the role of the International Monetary Fund and the World Bank,[7] there has been increasing attention to aid and education.[8] Still, empirical analysis of the links between the large-scale agenda and activities of the international and national aid agencies and the small-scale decisions and activities of education decision-makers and educators remains limited.

Advocates of aid argue that the situation would have been much worse in the absence of assistance and that education in particular settings has clearly benefited from foreign support. Critics argue equally passionately that although there have been some benefits; on balance, aid has been more harmful than helpful. They point to funds allocated to projects that have shown no significant benefit, to promising projects begun but not sustained long enough to bear fruit, to periodic and abrupt shifts in priorities among the aid agencies, and to a general preference for large-scale and high-tech efforts that are often situationally inappropriate. Their critique is also structural. In its very conception, foreign aid is fundamentally disempowering. Notwithstanding the widespread use of terms like cooperation, partnership, and empowerment, and notwithstanding periodic international efforts to develop guidelines and codes for the provision of external support, in practice, aid generally functions to undermine local authority and initiative. By substituting external decisions for local autonomy, it reduces rather than builds capacity. Notwithstanding periodic reform efforts, both in its conception and in its practice the aid relationship itself becomes a major obstacle to achieving its stated purposes. Yet, even as they criticize particular aid programs and insist on their national autonomy, most Third World governments are anxious to secure as much education assistance as they can get, generally accepting the accompanying conditions.

Aid Dependence

How do external events and forces influence what happens within particular countries? Notwithstanding the rhetoric of partnership and development cooperation, even modest aid can have a very loud voice. That is especially clear in Africa. Pulled by popular demand and pushed by the need for highly educated and skilled personnel, education in Africa quickly became an insatiable demand for resources. Especially as economic crises succeeded earlier developmental optimism and structural adjustment replaced rapid development as the realistic short-term objective in Third World countries, there was strong pressure to assign the highest priority for available funds to directly productive activities, which often did not include education. How, then, to educate the teachers, develop new textbooks, or equip the science laboratories? Or more commonly, how to fix the leaking school roof? The common recourse was to external funding. For many Third

World countries, aid has become the center of gravity for education and development initiatives. Over time, it has come to seem not only obvious but unexceptional that new initiatives and reform programs require external support, and therefore responsiveness to the agenda and preferences of the funding agencies.

Although foreign aid to Third World education is substantial, in most countries it represents a small portion of total education spending. Its influence, however, regularly far exceeds its volume. Where nearly all national education resources are committed to paying the teachers, the foreign support is critical for innovation and reform. Limited aid thus acquires substantial leverage. Aid dependence becomes endemic, even when the foreign funds pay a small portion of total costs.

Especially since the reaffirmation of the commitment to education for all in 2000, global pressure for more and more rapid aid has increased. Yet, the very strong commitment at the Dakar meeting—"no countries seriously committed to education for all will be thwarted in their achievement of this goal by a lack of resources"—has not led to significantly increased aid or to a clear and adequately funded strategy for financing education for all.[9] There has been debt relief—in some countries spending on debt service exceeded allocations to education—of several sorts, including a complex process for certifying and assisting Heavily Indebted Poor Countries (HIPC). Responding to complaints about the slow delivery of promised support, the funding agencies created the Fast Track Initiative (FTI), subsequently (after critical review) the Global Partnership for Education, which shares eligibility rules and certification with HIPC. Still, the EFA Global Monitoring Reports regularly show that external support continues to fall far short of the volume needed, jeopardizing the achievement of the EFA goals.[10] After a period of stagnating and declining education aid, its volume has increased, but unevenly, and most important, still falls far short of the need (UNESCO, 2020b).

In several countries, as funding agencies have shifted from supporting particular projects to contributing directly to the education or national budget, even recurrent expenditures have become increasingly dependent on external support. Though not directly and without saying so, the funding agencies are paying the teachers. Net Official Development Assistance received in 2018 accounted for over 60% of total government expenditure and thereby a substantial percentage of education spending in several African countries: Central African Republic (92%), Malawi (86%), Mali (71%), Rwanda (62%), Mozambique (62%), Ethiopia (54%), and Madagascar (51%).[11] Support of that magnitude may well help those countries achieve education for all. But surely it is not sustainable over the longer term. Even more important, it is difficult, perhaps impossible, for a national government and its education community to set priorities and directions for a core development activity so dependent on foreign funds.

As education's reliance on foreign funds increases, so does the influence of both the finance ministry and the external agencies. Representing the government in negotiations with those agencies, the finance ministry becomes much more directly involved in policy and programmatic details across all government departments. That increased role may well suit the external agencies, which are likely to see the finance ministry as their ally in reducing and managing spending.

The alliance between external agency and finance (and perhaps planning) ministry may be structured as a powerful lever for influencing national policy.

Case studies of national responses to economic crisis indicate both the forms of aid dependence and differences among countries. Heavily dependent on foreign assistance, Sénégal and Tanzania have repeatedly modified education and training policies and programs in ways that reflected the priorities and preferences of the funding agencies (Samoff, 1994a). By the end of the 1980s, for example, the planning director in Tanzania's education ministry characterized his work as "marketing" (Samoff & Sumra, 1994). His task, he said, was to advertise and market broad ideas and specific projects in the hope of finding a sponsor—an external assistance agency—to fund them. Over time priorities were set less by government and party leaders and more by what foreign governments and their aid organizations were willing to finance. The power brokers in education had once been those who could put together coalitions of people influential in Tanzania's public and private life. By the late 1980s, they had become those who were most successful in securing foreign funding.[12]

Marketing may be a reasonable and reasonably successful coping strategy in an adverse setting, yielding additional resources in times of economic distress and permitting national elites and their foreign partners to delay confronting major problems and avoid undertaking serious economic, political, and social transformation. At the same time, when marketing is the prevailing orientation, innovation is limited to whatever the funders are willing to finance.

National patterns of course vary. Aid dependence does not always secure compliance with external recommendations and expectations. "A small country has no choice." Asked why his relatively affluent Third World country had accepted the conditions attached to foreign assistance, the former Costa Rican president insisted he had no alternative (quoted in Carnoy & Torres, 1994, p. 92). Already deeply in debt, economically dependent on export sales to the countries that control most of its external aid, resisting with difficulty entanglement in efforts to overthrow a neighbor government, Costa Rica acquiesced to pressures to adopt structural adjustment policies and maintained that orientation through governments led by different political parties. What else could this small country do, its leaders argued. In practice, however, Costa Rica not only secured massive external assistance but also maintained a good deal of its agenda, protecting many of the social services, including education and training, targeted for reduction. A combination of its regional role, its history of stable democratic government and limited civil strife, its economic base and relative affluence, and the broad legitimacy of its national political system enabled Costa Rica to retain a good deal of policy autonomy even as it acceded to externally imposed conditions.

Teachers' unions and militant student organizations that allied to block staff reductions and other austerity measures in Senegal's structural adjustment program provide another example of effective local resistance (Carton & Diouf, 1994). Conflicts over the imposition of higher education fees in Ghana and Kenya show that countries can reject aid conditions and continue to receive support and that effective implementation of aid conditions requires the active cooperation of the recipient country's government (Samoff & Carrol, 2004: 20-23).

Dependence on external funds leads to both explicit conditions and more subtle influences. Sometimes that relationship is aggressively manipulative. The funding agency may condition the provision of support on the adoption of specific policies, priorities, or programs. Conditions can be direct (aid is contingent on the adoption of a specific policy or the implementation of specified institutional changes) or indirect (support for vocational schools may be contingent on the implementation of a strategy designed to increase female enrollment in the technical curriculum). Occasionally influence flows in the other direction. To secure resources for a preferred program, the national leadership may mobilize support and bring pressure to bear on the funding agency in its home.

PATHWAYS OF INFLUENCE

Aid's indirect influences are generally far less visible, more difficult to challenge, and often far more consequential. A brief overview of other pathways of influence is instructive.

Globalization by Conference

International conferences have become increasingly important vehicles for transmitting and implanting fundamental ideas about education and shaping how education is understood, organized, and managed. As I have noted, the 1990 EFA conference sought to pressure governments in poor countries to prioritize and fund basic education. Functionally that required an administrative apparatus, follow-up meetings, and monitoring and research.

Recognizing the failure to achieve the agreed objectives but reluctant to assign responsibility, the 2000 Dakar conference reaffirmed the commitment, rolled back the target dates, and rejuvenated the secretariat. Major Dakar goals were subsequently incorporated in the United Nations' Millennium Development Goals (2001). Increased pressures on governments included regional conferences and periodic progress reports to be prepared according to a specified format, itself a vehicle for imposing the constructs, categories, and terms to describe and analyze education. By the next international conference in Incheon in 2015, the education goals were fully integrated into the Sustainable Development Goals, and the target dates once again reset, to 2030.[13] Here, then, is an ongoing process for institutionalizing international influence, ostensibly collaborative and formally lodged at UNESCO but with an agenda and analytic constructs that clearly reflect World Bank influence.

Some countries charged that the preference for basic education was intended to undermine support for higher education and thereby confine poor countries in their poverty. Without the development of advanced skills and research capacity, poor countries are relegated to the intellectual periphery, perpetually dependent on ideas and technologies (and, more important, ways of understanding) developed elsewhere. Acknowledging that impoverishing universities, the principal institutions for educating teachers and teacher educators, eventually undermines even the commitment to basic education, funding agencies and foundations have moved to restore some support for higher education.[14] In the poorest countries, higher education institutions are beyond the reach of nearly all learners, and their limited funding and, often, even more limited political support, preclude their playing a significant development role.

Globalizing Standards

Calls in many countries for global education standards have spawned a series of cross-national efforts to measure and compare achievement at different levels.[15] Although they claim sensitivity to the unique characteristics of specific national and local settings, by design those assessments seek to use and thereby institutionalize internationally particular assumptions about both the content and the process of learning and teaching. Most problematic are the common assumptions that reading skill can be measured independent of context and language and, even more troubling, that score on a reading assessment is a reasonable proxy for education quality, indeed the quality of an entire education system. The results of the assessment measures may contribute to improving the quality of education in some settings, but their more powerful role is to undermine the education philosophy that associates effective learning with education objectives and measures that are debated and decided locally.

Managing Knowledge

"Information is power" has become a cliché. In the contemporary aid world, with triumphant capitalism as the context, economics as the dominating social science, and business as the appropriate model for public institutions, that understanding of information has been transformed into the claim that knowledge is development (Castells, 1997a; 1997b; 1998). In a knowledge economy, where information, it is claimed, becomes a more important factor of production than land, labor, or capital, eliminating poverty requires knowledge affluence. Generating, storing, managing, and disseminating knowledge thus becomes another path for institutionalizing international influence.

Funding and technical assistance agencies regularly reiterate that their advice is more important than their funds. Indeed, the World Bank goes a good deal further, proposing to develop and manage knowledge repositories and gateways.[16] "My goal is to make the World Bank the first port of call when people need knowledge about development," its former president asserted.[17] Ironically, the overdue and slow shift in attention from schooling to learning has compounded this problem, as external agencies assert their role in generating, organizing, and disseminating knowledge about learning (World Bank, 2017; Bashir et al., 2018).

While the potential problems here are numerous and well beyond the scope of this discussion (Samoff & Stromquist, 2001; see also Torres, 2001), in this review of pathways of influence, it is important to note briefly some of the risks of this combination of funds and advice. What is deemed valid and legitimate information (termed "knowledge") becomes increasingly centralized in the Global North. Information that is collected in the Global South is thereby shaped and framed by its interpreters—that is, those who create and manage the development of knowledge databases and information systems. That powerful role in determining what is and what is not knowledge is obscured by the mystique of science and scientific method. The centralization of the determination of what is knowledge entrenches the role of the elite education and research institutions in the world, nearly all located in the most affluent countries. What is regarded as the important knowledge is likely to become more technical and less humanistic and critical. The projection of broad, nearly universal and thus democratizing access to web-based information databases underestimates both current technical obstacles and cost and the likelihood that in the current global system, the technological gap will increase, not decrease. Overall, information databases created and maintained by authoritative institutions in the Global North with substantial economic leverage and ideological influence are most likely to reinforce existing power relations, both within and across countries.

Constraining Outcomes by Shaping Conceptions and Analytic Frameworks

We are exploring how influence is institutionalized. Recall the earlier discussion of decolonization. The postwar creation of international institutions, the League of Nations and the United Nations, embedded notions of traditional/modern, recast as development, into international agreements, legal frameworks, and organizations. Quickly, the discussions were not about the idea of trusteeship but rather about how to implement it. What had been a distinction between barbarian and civilized became relabeled, dressed up, and everyday practice, even the rationale for resource allocation.

Traditional versus modern marches on, deeply entrenched and mostly invisible, with occasional reminders. The 2020 South African National Arts Festival described a jazz musician as "Urban, erudite, international and skilled, but rooted in his culture." Not "and"—"but."

The most powerful pathways of influence are thus often the least visible. While the conditionalities of aid can be rigid and painful, they are clear and can be clearly challenged. Far more difficult to detect and resist are the influences embedded in the conceptions of education that seem so ordinary that they are taken for granted and in the analytic frameworks that seem so obvious that they avoid critical scrutiny. Let us consider briefly three such frameworks: education as investment, as production, and as delivery system.

Note that the notion of external influence has to do with context and content, not nationality. Rate-of-return analysis, for example, emerged as an analytic approach and technique in a specific setting and within a particular theoretical orientation. It reflects the interests of investors and allocators of resources, whether foreign or local, who seek to choose among alternate uses of their funds. While that approach may (or may not) prove useful to education researchers, decision-makers, and managers in poor countries, it was not the creation of those responsible for education in those countries. Its proponents may be citizens of the United States, England, Hungary, Japan, Chile, or Ghana. Characterizing it as "external," therefore, highlights not the nationality of its advocates but rather the particular setting, including assumptions, ideas, interests, theory, and ideology, in which it was developed and refined.

Education as Investment

Amid alternative perspectives on education, those of economics and finance have come to dominate the discourse on education and development. For the World Bank, the starting point is human capital theory: Education ought to be regarded as an investment in developing a country's human resources. In its 1995 education policy review, the assertion of its superiority is unqualified: "Human capital theory has no genuine rival of equal breadth and rigor."[18] The East Asian[19] experience proves the value of investing in education, the World Bank argues, since it is precisely that investment that differentiates the successes from the failures. Rate of return analysis then becomes the preferred approach to deciding among alternative education approaches. Education policy and practice are managed through the prism of investment banking and its tools.

Far from universally accepted, both human capital theory and rate of return analysis are intensely debated. Other funding agencies and the World Bank's staff are among the critics: "Traditional cost-benefit studies of education have tended to indicate the advantages of investment in education at various different levels, based on analyses of the social return which each produces. Recent studies have shown this method to be both fallacious and limiting."[20] Much of the concern with education as an investment self-consciously ignores the *process* of education. Adopting an economic systems approach, it focuses on inputs and outputs, leaving inside the opaque black box most of what those involved in education do every day. In education, however, process is itself an output.

Schools select and socialize. For both society and individuals, schooling frequently matters more than learning. Although specific circumstances vary, the education system everywhere is central to constructing and maintaining a particular sort of social order. Often it is equally central to challenging and transforming it. To ignore the ways in which curriculum entrenches and legitimizes inequality, examinations reinforce and justify patterns of social stratification, or textbooks privilege some perspectives over others is to render meaningless findings about the number of graduates and their subject specializations. Limiting the analysis to the relative values of alternative inputs and outputs permits proposing global solutions. But in practice, education is interactive, replete with discontinuities, and always locally contingent.

A second consequence of treating education primarily as a social investment is a disjunction between the issues deemed most important and the objectives articulated by Third World governments and educators, which commonly receive little attention: for example, fostering an inquiring and critical orientation, eliminating discrimination and reducing elitism, promoting national unity, preparing youth for the rights and obligations of citizenship, equipping them to work cooperatively and resolve conflicts nonviolently, and developing among learners a strong sense of individual and collective competence, self-reliance, and self-confidence. These objectives are of course more difficult to quantify and measure than, say, building classrooms or increasing the availability of instructional materials. Yet, to ignore these objectives entirely is to delete them from the education agenda.

Education as Production

A second metaphor commonly used to explain and reform schooling is education as production, which in turn leads to a focus on efficiency. Education policy and practice are managed through the prism of manufacturing and its tools. But what exactly is efficiency in education?

In manufacturing, efficiency seems clear: reduce the costs of production—less expensive raw materials, less waste and breakage, more skilled workers, improved machinery, low-cost energy, simplified maintenance, and expenditures on marketing that are exceeded by income from increased sales. Though the production metaphor is occasionally useful, education is fundamentally different from manufacturing. In an interactive process, the distinction between inputs and outputs is consciously blurred. Bottles do not contribute to their own manufacture. Students do contribute to their own education. Cars do not suggest improvements in the assembly process or reject the old way of doing things. Learners are active participants in their education, not only suggesting improvements and rejecting received wisdom but taking the initiative to chart new paths. At first glance, ever larger classes would increase an education system's efficiency by spreading teachers' salaries across more students. But of course the appropriate unit of education is not the student or the number of students per teacher but learning.

Beyond those problems, it is far from clear that efficiency, however defined, is or ought to be the primary goal to be maximized. Like those responsible for space travel, educators in poor countries may assign higher priority to self-reliance or redundancy. For example, economies of scale might favor centralized production of education materials. But the realities of power failures, equipment breakdowns, and the unavailability of supplies likely favor dispersed and redundant production, so that problems at one site do not disrupt all production. Whether efficiency, self-reliance, redundancy, or some other goal should have the highest priority cannot be assumed but must be determined in each setting.

Not only is efficiency problematic when applied to learning, but in three important ways the constructs common in this perspective, internal efficiency (roughly, increase pass rate and reduce repetition) and external efficiency (roughly, increase employment rate), misdirect policy attention. Concern with reducing the unit cost per student is likely to be far less fruitful than focusing on increasing the effectiveness of each unit of expenditure. Second, since pass and graduation rates are largely the consequences of general education and national policy and therefore not of either student or school achievement, it seems particularly obfuscating to characterize the decision to promote few students as internal inefficiency. Third, recognizing that the charter of schooling is far broader than (and may not even include) vocational preparation requires discarding efforts to assess education's external efficiency from rates and types of employment. The common use of efficiency as an analytic construct in education converts major issues of policy and pedagogy into ostensibly uncontroversial issues of management and administration amenable to technical solutions, effectively excluding them from both critical review and participatory decision-making.

A corollary to stress on efficiency is insistence on feasibility and practicality. Even as the aid agencies stress feasibility and practicality, however, their own studies are regularly criticized for their inattention to context and feasibility. The former functions to limit critique and innovation while the latter permits them to promote general recommendations across diverse settings. That apparently reasonable focus on feasibility and practicality functions in practice to constrain both education and development. Innovations are inherently risky. Attempts to change roles (e.g., teachers and students as curriculum developers), quality measures (the mix and weights of student portfolios, continuous assessment, and standardized examinations), pedagogy (mixed-ability groups, learner-centered instruction), and links with the world of work (education with production) may fail or interfere with other objectives. Since innovations are risky, funding and technical assistance agencies generally require using older, ostensibly proven and reliable approaches. If it were fully effective, that orientation would restrict creative departures to the affluent countries. Those who are poor scramble to catch up as they watch those who are more affluent discard the approaches and technologies they are told to use. In practice, poverty is deemed to preclude fundamental innovation, which in turn is likely to perpetuate poverty.

Education as Delivery System

Aid dependence entrenches policy and programmatic change as something done *to* rather than *by* Third World education. Often, learning is understood as information acquisition. The common construct is what Paulo Freire (1970) has termed the banking model of education. Learners are like empty bank accounts. More or less formally, teachers and others with the relevant capital, wisdom, make deposits into those accounts. Successful students save their resources and complete their education with heads full of knowledge on which they can subsequently draw. At least for younger learners, learning is understood largely as a passive process. Teachers give or provide or offer, and students receive. But what of the extensive thinking, experimentation, and research that regard learning as far larger than information acquisition? What of the notion that what learners do is not simply acquire but generate, master, develop, and create knowledge? Educators who understand learning as an active process, who situate learners at the center of that process, and for whom learning involves the appropriation, manipulation, and integration of information have little voice in the policies and programs developed using the education as delivery standard tool kit.

The terminology commonly used is both instructive and formative. Education reforms are regularly termed *interventions*—that is, insertions from outside rather than initiatives from within. Externally funded, externally guided, and often externally managed, specific reform projects are rarely directly responsible to the settings—whether teachers, students, or the local community—in which they function. How are Third World educators to become owners of those reforms when they are the objects of the surgery, not the surgeons?

Education policy and practice are managed through the prism of delivery service and its tools. That perspective displaces understanding education as an organic process in which learners are the doers rather than the receivers. In practice, this combination of a vantage point external to education (whether national or foreign), and very limited accountability generally proves fundamentally disempowering.

Specifying Constructs and Analytic Frameworks

These three conceptions of education carry with them frameworks for understanding education, for analyzing its problems, and for charting future paths. As people consider major education approaches and choices, rare is the recognition that they are doing so with the tools of investment banking, or of manufacturing, or of delivery systems. Even less common is the recognition that as these constructs frame policy and practice they displace other available frames, say, education as a right, or education as a public good.

Direct aid discussions are one carrier for these constructs and frameworks. Another is what has come to be an externally specified process for developing education objectives, priorities, and plans, and the studies undertaken to provide a foundation for that process. Concerned that aid funds be used appropriately, effectively, and efficiently, the funding and technical assistance agencies have long required that proposed projects make sense in terms of overall education objectives and policies. Especially for the world's poorest countries, most in Africa, that requirement has become increasingly complex and cumbersome. To be eligible for debt relief and accelerated support, countries must prepare a comprehensive development framework and detailed national strategy papers focused on reducing poverty, including an extensive analysis of the education sector and a statement of education policies.[21] At first glance, that seems quite reasonable. Concerned with high priority objectives and required to justify their allocations to their parent bodies, the funders seek reassurance that their support will be well used. Recipients are expected to have a comprehensive and inclusive planning process, based on solid research, that produces objectives, policies, and indicators to measure progress.

In practice, however, the required process has become more complex than many countries can manage, diverts attention and energy from the reform and management of the education system, and notwithstanding a formal commitment to broad participation effectively entrenches the expectations and frameworks of the funders, especially the World Bank. Overwhelmed education ministries engage consultants to prepare key documents. With a self-ascribed mandate to assure quality control and consistent planning, the funders thus both set the standards for acceptable plans and programs and judge which documents have met them. Open hearings that permit community groups to present their views function largely to legitimize recommended courses of action.

Most important, this process domesticates and institutionalizes key constructs and analytic perspectives. It is in this way that internal and external efficiency, rate of return analysis, and other precepts and tools of what might be termed the Washington education consensus are rendered invisible—so ordinary and normal that they require no attention—and thereby immune to critical assessment. As the key constructs and analytic frameworks are embedded in the instructions and format for required documents, and as policy and decision-makers take them for granted, institutionalizing the externally set agenda need no longer requires explicit external direction.

THE ROLE(S) OF RESEARCH

Though periodically castigated as too theoretical and irrelevant to education practice, researchers and research play an important role in this story. While comparative education research reaches in many directions, research on education and development regularly shares a common frame—the ways ideas, issues, and relationships are described and understood (Foster et al., 2012; Samoff, 2021). We have seen that the shared frame has its roots in decolonization, a generally linear notion of more and less developed, and the aid relationship. Understanding the role of research—including research not directly focused on development—requires exploring that framing and how it works.

That framing is particularly clear in Africa. Commissioned research abounds. Consider what are termed education sector studies. Education is perhaps the most visible and contested of public policies. The insistence on comprehensive development frameworks and poverty reduction strategies has increased the demand for studies of the education sector. Analyses of education in Africa, whether launched within Africa to improve education or required as necessary background by funding agencies, are most striking for their similarities, notwithstanding their diversity of country, commissioning agency, and specific subject.[22] With few exceptions, these studies have a common framework, a common approach, and a common methodology. Given their shared starting points, their common findings are not surprising: African education was and in many places continues to be in crisis. Most governments cope poorly. Quality has deteriorated, commonly attributed to expanded access. Funds are misallocated. Management is poor and administration is inefficient. More recently, more positive assessments, especially highlighting expanded enrollment and girls' participation, accompany the persisting critiques. From predominantly Islamic Mauritania in the western Sahara to the mixed cultural, colonial, and political heritage of Mauritius in the Indian Ocean, the recommendations too are similar, the Washington education consensus come to Africa: Reduce the central government role in providing education. Decentralize. Increase post-primary school fees. Expand private schooling. Reduce direct support to students, especially at the tertiary level. Introduce double shifts and multigrade classrooms. Assign high priority to instructional materials. Favor in-service over pre-service teacher education. The shared orientation of these studies reflects a medical metaphor. Study teams, often expatriate-led, are expert clinicians who diagnose and then prescribe. The patient (i.e., the country) must be encouraged, perhaps pressured, to swallow the bitter medicine. For the most part, learning disappears from view, buried by the focus on finance.

Though these studies are explicitly commissioned to guide policy decisions, they have very limited circulation. Designated "confidential" or "restricted," Africa's education sector studies are generally available only to the commissioning agency and a few government officials. Unpublished and inaccessible, they are not subjected to critical review, either by scholars with relevant expertise or by the affected communities, and they cannot contribute to the cumulation of knowledge.

The volume of these studies, their central role in the aid relationship, and thereby their influence on objectives and priorities in African education are a very powerful path for the institutionalization of international influence. Individually, none of these studies, or perhaps even the aid programs that spawned them, is likely to prove very consequential over the longer term. But as a group, these studies frame debate and orient policies, both international and national.

Let us return for a moment to the Jomtien, Dakar, and Incheon conferences and the apparent consensus on education for all. Few would disagree with this grand goal, even though many countries lack the resources to achieve it rapidly. But why? Why is universal mass education the highest priority? And if it is, why focus primarily on basic (primary) education in schools, rather than, say, adult and other education programs outside school settings?

There are many answers to those and related questions, but the answer that seems the most persuasive, especially to those who disburse education aid funds, is that *research shows* that investing in primary education yields the best return. Support for this focus on primary education rests on the claim that research has persuasively demonstrated that investing in primary education promises the greatest progress toward development (however defined).

It is not the specific conclusion that is most striking here. I have already noted problems with uncritical reliance on rate-of-return analysis. The history of public discourse on education suggests that every broadly accepted observation is eventually discarded as partial, misleading, incorrect, or all three. A successor truth will emerge, advocated just as ardently. Rather, what is remarkable here is the implicit consensus on research as the principal determinant, or legitimizer, of education policy. Here is but a single example of the privileged position of research (or, more accurately, claims about research and its findings) in debates on education policy. In practice, research may inform and guide policy, rationalize and justify policies adopted for other reasons, or be quite irrelevant to policy. But claims about what research shows constitute the core of the development discussion. Without the claim of research support, policy proposals lose credibility. Similarly, policy critiques that do not cite supporting research are easily ignored. Prospective participants in the policy debate must demonstrate an adequate supply of relevant research simply to have their voices heard (Samoff, 2012).

As "evidence-based policy" has become the mantra, the formulation "Research shows that . . ." and its synonyms are ubiquitous. Yet, notwithstanding the World Bank's reiterated insistence on the primacy of research, its 2020 Education Strategy is relentlessly self-referential (only its research matters) and makes no significant provision for the development of Third World research capacity.[23] The insistence that decisions be based on research seems eminently reasonable. But as applied, that insistence is profoundly problematic. First, it misunderstands the relationship between research and policy. Second, in practice it privileges—by assumption rather than by critical reflection—a particular sort of research, dismissing alternative research strategies. Third, by legitimizing the authority to determine what constitutes research it reinforces power relationships and dependence. The prominence and pervasiveness of the claim that "research shows" within the development arena reflects a powerful contemporary phenomenon: the emergence of a financial-intellectual complex spawned by the development business. It is important to recognize both the unique characteristics and the short- and long-term consequences of that combination of research and funding. That, in turn, requires understanding the ways in which the increasing importance of external assistance and the privileged position of research combine to condition and constrain education's substantive content.

Research and Policy

As I have noted, research has become the currency of development planners and decision-makers, used to assign value to alternative and often competing projects. Surely that is desirable. Research guides decisions. Expertise rather than politics prevails. Perhaps an attractive image but far from an accurate portrayal. This idealized model of the allocation and use of development assistance is deceptive in several ways.

First, the common view that competent policymakers base their decisions primarily on a careful review of relevant research is simply inaccurate. In development, as in most other policymaking arenas, research enters the decision-making process through multiple, often indirect routes. Decision-makers draw on their academic learning as well as their practical experience to formulate questions, select proposals, specify evaluative criteria, and make decisions. That indirect influence is often both subtle and may not be apparent to the decision-makers themselves.

Second, policymakers who are largely guided by research focused on the issue to be decided do not necessarily make better decisions. The research that is deemed relevant is generally instrumental and relatively narrowly gauged, taking as given existing economic, political, and social patterns. Yet effective and appropriate public policy cannot ignore interests, preferences, and politics. Making public policy is not an antiseptic, sheltered, apolitical process. Successfully implemented policies must confront and engage, not avoid, the conflict of interests and the tensions among the organization of production, the structure of power, and patterns of social differentiation.

Third, research regularly enters the policy process as justification for decisions already made. Especially in a bureaucratic environment where decision-makers are charged to emphasize evidence and rationality and deemphasize politics and favoritism, the claim that research supports a particular course of action is the most powerful defense against all challengers. Put crudely, in the policy shootout, the gunfighter quickest to draw the research pistol and best supplied with research ammunition is most likely to emerge victorious. Even a slow draw with few bullets may ensure survival.

Fourth, as I have argued, the conjunction of development assistance and research transforms both research and its role in the policy process, to the detriment of both. That research influences policy indirectly and that research is used to justify decisions are not necessarily problematic. In the contemporary development business, however, the same agencies are increasingly responsible for decisions, funding, and research. Just as their funds seat foreign aid organizations at the education policy table, so, too, do those funds secure powerful influence over research and the research process. Little anticipated and not yet well understood, this conjunction of external funding and education research is only beginning to be studied systematically.[24] The major outlines of this relationship have become sufficiently clear, however, to warrant concern among both researchers and policymakers. To put the issue sharply, research and policy are both at risk.

The Facade of Precision

Numbers are prominent in nearly all studies of education and development. Especially in those that are concerned with what works—that is, explorations of the effectiveness of alternative approaches to a larger or smaller development objective—numbers dominate. The assumption that quantification is essential for explanation and evaluation is another dimension in which foundation ideas seem so obvious and uncontroversial that they are not subjected to critical scrutiny. As well, while numbers suggest comparability and certainty—everyone knows that 4 is bigger than 2 and that it is reasonable to understand 4 as twice 2—in practice, numbers are often neither certain nor comparable.

Where much of education research yields results that are partial, ambiguous, and contingent, policy research is expected to generate clear and confident findings that are reliable and precise. Quantification is preferred. Yet the push for precision often overstates the precision that is possible and ignores the ways in which the pursuit of precision impedes interpretation and understanding (Samoff, 1991). When social scientists are constrained to construct mutually exclusive categories, the disadvantages of eliminating inconsistency and ambiguity may outweigh the value of the apparent resulting clarity. The variations in temporal and spatial context that go unrecorded because they are smaller than the units of measure employed may prove to be critical to inference and interpretation.

Even the most advanced techniques can at best provide only partial remedies for inaccuracies and inconsistencies in the original data. Many, perhaps most, reported national statistics for the Third World, for example, have a large margin of error.[25] As well, what are regularly taken to be basic data may reflect political decisions more than careful counting. Jerven (2013; 2015) provides compelling evidence that major increases in the reported gross domestic product (GDP), transforming a low-income country into middle income overnight, have resulted from revised calculation and reporting rather than from what appears to be substantial and rapid expansion of the national economy. As Jerven (2013) concludes, "the most basic metric of development, GDP, should not be treated as an objective number but rather as a number that is a product of a process in which a range of arbitrary and controversial assumptions are made" (p. 121).

Careful examination shows that available figures are often inaccurate, inconsistent, and not readily comparable. Schools, districts, and other sources provide incomplete and inaccurate information. Sources differ on periodization and on the specification of expenditure categories. Reports regularly fail to distinguish between budget and actual expenditure data and compare budget figures in one year with expenditure reports in another. Recurrent and development (capital) expenditures are treated inconsistently. Often the available data do not include individual, family, local government, and direct foreign spending. Discussions of the cost of education generally refer to government expenditures on education and sometimes only to education ministry spending. Inflation, deflation, and exchange rates are treated inconsistently. Data series are frequently too short to be sure that observed variation reflects significant change, and longer series are usually not comparable.

Addressing the numbers, then, requires recognizing that the margin of error may be large. Taking seriously that margin of error requires treating national statistics as rough approximations. Small and sometimes larger observed changes may be more apparent than real. Consequently, apparent changes that fall within a reasonable margin of error are a weak foundation for broad inferences and for public policy. Taking seriously that error margin requires both researchers and policymakers to reject statistics whose underlying assumptions require a level of precision, linearity, or continuity that the data do not reliably support. Although quantification may make findings more defensible, it does not automatically produce better understanding.

Widespread acknowledgment of the uncertainty in the available data notwithstanding, the canons of social science impel those who conduct research, those who support research, and those who rely on research to justify their actions to overstate the precision of their findings and to attach to them an unrealistically high level of confidence. A profusion of numbers neither makes a particular interpretation more valid nor renders a policy proposal more attractive. Indeed, the numeric shroud may well obscure far more than it reveals.

There are here two critiques. One focuses on the façade of precision. The second focuses on the insistence on quantification. When the pressure to quantify confronts the problems in measuring learning, it is learning that is ignored. What is at issue is not quantification or a particular research project that rests on quantified information. Rather, in this exploration of how particular ideas and perspectives are institutionalized we must recognize the largely uncritical dismissal of the alternative perspective captured in the quotation mistakenly attributed to Einstein: "Not everything that counts can be counted, and not everything that can be counted counts." To reiterate, it is not quantification that is problematic but the uncritical adoption of the assumption that quantification increases reliability. Problematic is the risk of trivializing important events, interactions, and relationships by limiting attention only to what can be counted. Problematic is the ready dismissal of insights from the small-scale observations and interviews, the synthetic review of texts, and the access available through personal contacts that are not amenable to, or worse, are distorted by quantification.

The assumption that to matter, evidence must be counted, the protocols for gathering and manipulating quantitative information that are developed in the elite universities of the Global North, and the technical requirements for managing the enormous data volumes that can now be collected combine to constitute a powerful channel for institutionalizing international influence.

Economics as Social Science

I have noted the pressure to quantify in research and evaluation. Reinforcing that orientation, the behavioral revolution in the social sciences, with its notion of the quasi-experiment as the appropriate model for research and recurring cries of "Falsifiability!" and "Reproducibility!" has pushed us toward the sort of information that can be recorded and stored in quantitative form. Accompanying and fueling the inclination to quantify has been the emergence of economics as the modal social science. This increasingly influential and powerful role for economics stands on two legs, one within and the other outside the academy.

In their ideal form, the methods taught in basic economics courses correspond well to dominant currents within social science. The focus is on causal relationships, established by drawing on lawlike statements about patterned regularities and exploring the connections among precisely defined factors. Whatever is deemed extraneous may be ignored. Factors that may affect the relationship being studied are either assumed not to vary ("other things being equal") or to vary randomly (thereby having no systematic influence). Or they are directly or indirectly controlled by the researchers. Then, the restricted set of factors to be examined (the "variables") can be studied. Ideally, those factors can be changed in some orderly way, either by careful choice of locations, times, or observations or by simulating the variation based on the information available. Expectations about causality (hypotheses) can then be rejected or supported. For many scholars, this orientation defines the social scientific method. The challenge is to approach the ideal, a controlled experiment in which the experimenter manipulates all of the factors, as closely as possible.

The current preeminence of economics also stems from its role as the social science deemed to have the most important practical consequences. That fits well with the claim that the market is the most efficient allocator of values and the powerful support for privatizing education and treating it as a commodity. The principal objective is what used to be called social engineering: how to make society function better. Technical displaces political in understanding social tensions and policy choices. Of course there are challenges and critics as well as variations and counter-currents within the mainstream. Still, the dominant perspective is reinforced by university recognition, high-status journal editors and reviewers, and research grant agencies. When educators consider how best to teach reading or prepare teachers, they are quick to consider inputs and outputs, costs and benefits, and returns on alternative allocations. Only rarely do they ask anthropologists to explore social organization or sociologists to analyze the intersection of class, race, and gender, or historians to trace the roots of current tensions. In this orientation, for research on education and development, economics serves well. Other disciplines fall short. As they do, their insights, their critiques, their voices become even more faint.

For many researchers, especially noneconomists, economics is social science.

When Research Becomes Consulting

Where public funding for education is inadequate, public funding for education research hardly exists. Just as third world education and training decision-makers and planners look overseas to fund innovation and development, so do scholars look abroad for support for their research. They quickly learn that unencumbered research grants are scarce and difficult to obtain. More readily available are contracts for research commissioned by external assistance agencies. With those commissions come specifications of appropriate approaches, methods, and analytic frameworks. Hence, education research too becomes part of the aid relationship, a process especially clear in Africa, with senior researchers regularly shuttling between cramped offices and empty libraries on the one hand, and on the other, the computers, cellular telephones, and substantial fees of client consulting.

With low basic salaries, individual researchers are highly motivated to become consultants to the external agencies. Unable to pay a living wage or to provide direct research funding, universities are inclined to tolerate, often encourage, that practice. Obliged to justify their programs and allocations and chastised for relying so heavily on expatriate researchers, the funding and technical assistance agencies eagerly recruit local education researchers. The interests converge. Research becomes consulting.

In some respects, that is a very positive outcome. Quite reasonably, the funding agencies seek expertise on the issues of concern. From their perspective, they do not set out to control or manipulate education research. Scholars retain their independence. This arrangement makes research possible. Senior scholars can provide fieldwork opportunities and experience with data interpretation and analysis for younger colleagues and selected students. Without that funding, African participation in international conferences, collaboration with overseas partners, and publication in the most respected journals would be even more limited.

Yet, the conversion of research into consulting has several problematic consequences.

First, generally, the contracting agency selects the topic to be studied and often the methodology to be used. Only rarely do the topics studied emerge organically from interactions among educators, teachers, learners, and the community. Nor do they emerge from debates among education decision-makers and researchers. Rarely does the methodology reflect researchers' experiences, local methodological debates, or locally developed critiques of dominant methodological orientations. Second, commissioned research generates reports with very restricted circulation and assessment.[26] Only very rarely are findings subjected to academic and practitioners' peer review. In the absence of the ordinary confrontation of ideas and perspectives that increases the credibility of research, untested observations become firm conclusions. As a result, what are taken as authoritative results and recommendations may be partial, seriously flawed, skewed, or all three. Third, since the reports of commissioned research rarely enter the academic literature. rather than the cumulation and sifting and winnowing that are central to the creation of knowledge, commissioned research produces largely disconnected lonely trees, some robust but many quite frail, scattered across the desolate plain of bookless schools and deskless classrooms.

Fourth, research as consulting transforms the academic reward system. Africa again provides the sharpest examples. For researchers with agency funding promotion in university rank becomes less important and far less remunerative than securing another consulting contract. Fifth, even as commissioned studies make research possible, their disconnectedness functions to undermine the research institutions. Effectively unable to set their agenda or to control the principal reward systems for their staff, research institutions are buffeted by the fickle winds of agency priorities and preferences. Sixth, the current penchant for reducing government functions reinforces the privatization of research. Beyond their individual consulting contracts, in many countries researchers have formed local consulting firms that market their services to foreign funding and technical assistance agencies. In itself, that is desirable, not problematic. As the privatization of research has developed, however, it leads more toward the multiplication of organizations entirely dependent on foreign patrons than toward the development of the institutional capacities and the autonomy that enable research centers to establish and sustain solidly grounded, high-quality research programs.

The creation of knowledge is always a complex and spasmodic process. The boundaries between the university and other knowledge-generating arenas are often productively ambiguous. And it is certainly not unique in human history to insist that knowledge creation be utilitarian or to find knowledge creators dependent on those with disposable funds. Yet, when research as consulting functions to determine how problems are specified and addressed (often with economics and its perspectives and assumptions privileged), national dependence is institutionalized well into the future.

Methodological Orthodoxy Stymies Critical Inquiry
That the external assistance agencies have influenced education policy is clear. Less discussed but equally troubling has been their influence on research. Notwithstanding the debates and disagreements among those involved in commissioned research, the conjunction of external funding and research fosters a methodological orthodoxy. Quite simply, some theories and methods are deemed acceptable—and justified by terming them "scientific." As local researchers develop their skills within that orthodoxy, their broader critical edge is dulled. The presumed universalism of the accepted research canons is reinforced by disciplinary codes and journal editors who become arbiters of quality. Dismissed as simply poor social science are efforts to depart from the mainstream to tune approach and method

to the local setting. For example, while quantified and detached education impact analysis is favored and funded, largely uncritically, participatory evaluation, ethnographic observation, and context-contingent assessment are regularly accorded low priority (Samoff et al., 2016).

In this way, the combination of foreign assistance and commissioned research functions to disseminate globally not only particular understandings of education and development but also how those understandings are created, revised, and refined. Effectively, even more powerfully than the foundations' efforts to mold Third World universities, financial crisis and structural adjustment have reinforced and entrenched the globalization of a particular sort of social science.

The Mystification of Knowledge and Power Relations

It is striking that individual scholars may orient their work very differently in the academic and financial-intellectual spheres of operation. In the former, the relevant audience is institutional and disciplinary, academic peers and university chairs and deans, whereas in the latter the officials of the employing agency constitute the audience that matters. They are more likely than the general body of academics to have shared preferences about method, approach, and findings. Much more easily than is possible at most universities and research institutes, funding agencies can readily terminate their relationship with a particular scholar.

As research becomes an increasingly proprietary endeavor, the process of knowledge creation is obscured, mystifying the power relations embedded in the research and thereby in the programs it supports. Power relations that might be regarded as profoundly problematic if they were seen clearly are so enmeshed in everyday practices that they become invisible. Perhaps not entirely aware of their own role, scholars become advocates not only for particular understandings of development and underdevelopment but also for a particular sort of global order.

CONTINUITIES AND CHALLENGES

We have seen that many of the understandings and orientations that guide education policy and practice in the postcolonial Third World reflect, directly and indirectly, the perspectives of a particular global economy. While learning is a local process and while sovereign countries have their unique characteristics, a cluster of assumptions, ideas, and understandings, termed neoliberalism in its current incarnation, are so deeply internalized that only occasionally are external guidance and pressure required to maintain them. Current practice, say the focus on cross-national testing or the generally unchallenged assumption that valid education evaluation requires quasi-experimental design and randomized control trials, refreshes that cluster. We have seen as well that notwithstanding the excitement of independence and sovereignty and the nonalignment of the Cold War, in practice a fundamental dependence remains prominent in education policy and practice. That dependence is not simply a legacy but is nurtured, updated, and reinforced with a combination of incentives and sanctions. Especially powerful is that much of that process is embedded in ideas and constructs rather than directives and conditions. Research plays a prominent role in that institutionalization, especially where it has itself become dependent on foreign funding. In that financial intellectual complex, most important is who specifies what is science and scientific methods: critics are dismissed not because they are critics or troublemakers but because they are, the verdict pronounces, nonscientific.

Powerful and often barely visible, that institutionalization is a relational process, not a linear march across an unreacting field or, with rare exceptions, not a brutal assault with crushed victims. That creates space for challenges and oppositions.

Communities and organizations have sought different outcomes. A few large-scale initiatives have sought to expand access by creating parallel schools, for example, BRAC in Bangladesh and Escuela Nueva, initially in Colombia.[27] Some have become education incubators and accelerators, for example, Council for the Development of Social Science Research in Africa (CODESRIA). Education activist organizations have navigated this web with varying success. Equal Education in South Africa has combined political and legal action to hold the government accountable for learners' constitutional right to education.[28] Tosten in Senegal has used its foundation of work on women's literacy to challenge genital cutting at the village level.[29] HakiElimu in Tanzania has been a public education conscience, encouraging local education activism and challenging the education ministry both to improve schooling and to report accurately.[30] Pratham in India and, adapting its approach, Uwezo in East Africa have sought to mobilize parents to press schools to improve education outcomes.[31] These and other organizations have challenged and innovated. With occasional local exceptions, however, they have not transformed their national education systems.

Other challenges emerge from the world system. The dissolution of the Soviet Union and the socialist bloc closed the innovation and transformation space created by Cold War competition. The current global challenger is China, with active outreach in the Third World. As Samir Amin (1990; 2019b) long argued, the world system is most vulnerable—for our concern here, the opportunities for fundamental transformation—in the center-periphery links.

The organization of power and authority is neither permanent nor invulnerable. Radical initiatives and critical challenges periodically emerge to confront education systems. Still, the current constellation of power has proved surprisingly resilient. For the present, schooling across the Third World maintains its conservative charter and notwithstanding occasional rhetorical appeals to resistance and change, resists transformation. In that, the internalization of external influences plays a prominent role. Just as anticolonial activists understood the necessity of decolonizing the colonial mind, contemporary education activists assert the importance of decolonizing education.

EDUCATION AND DEVELOPMENT

What progress, then, on the grand objective, universal access to education, over the past few decades? The World Bank regularly suggests that we know more about education and development, thanks to an improved and expanded research base. Schools, meanwhile, remain overpopulated and underequipped, and in many poor countries, education for all remains a distant dream. Many who make it to school learn little. International organizations and national authorities are apparently unable to translate greater knowledge systematically and reliably into useful and sustainable practices. Or rather, stated objectives are often misdirections, and differentiation and inequality are essential features of the contemporary global political economy, often so deeply embedded in its operating system that they are understood as givens of nature rather than products of people, power, and authority.

Cause and effect are very difficult to establish clearly in education, which is an intricate web of processes, some integrally related and others distantly connected. It is therefore not surprising that the relationships between aid-supported curricular and instructional reforms on the one hand and specific developmental outcomes on the other are complex and difficult to discern. The links between education and development more generally are still harder to establish. However daunting the challenge, though, it is essential to explore the consequences of education assistance programs, both positive and negative.

Real-world outcomes are both consequential and instructive. After decades of pronounced commitment to education for all, the current projection is that poor rural African girls will take nearly a century to get there. Poverty and limited national funding for education are insufficient explanations since from the outset EFA strategies have had to address those starting points. What must we infer? Perhaps the world's educators have been horribly incompetent. Or, more likely, EFA is a rhetorical objective, not a global goal, and education differentiation, not universal access, remains the working priority.

Similarly, if after years of efforts to close the development gap, inequality has increased, then maintaining inequality must be very important to powerful global forces. Put sharply, we must recognize that global inequality, both in education and more generally, is not accidental or inadvertent or simply slow progress, but rather the result of conscious actions by individuals and institutions. Rhetorically the aid relationship is about promoting development and reducing poverty. In practice, it functions as a major tool for setting the terms for Third World participation in the global political economy, with both rewards and sanctions. It functions as well to foster the institutionalization of its influence, including core understandings of education, of education's roles, and of how education should be funded, organized, and managed. Institutionalized influence makes direct controls, among them aid conditions, less important. Voices of authority are increasingly homegrown.

Note that in the debates about education aid, its actual value to recipients remains unclear. While foreign assistance is generally presented as a transfer of resources from more to less affluent countries, critics regularly charge that aid results in a net capital outflow. The actual transfer is less than the total amount of aid, since much of the aid received must be spent on products, services, and personnel from the granting country and since the uses of that aid may cause other outflows (e.g., expenditures on parts and fuel for aid-provided vehicles). Education aid's claimed benefits may be overwhelmed by education aid's direct and indirect costs. The apparently expanding gap between the most and least affluent countries, the rapidly increasing debt burden of many of the world's poorest countries, and the dramatic increase in aid dependence challenge claims about its essential role and value. Racing down the fast track to planned dependence is surely not a viable development strategy.

It seems clear that effective education reform requires agendas and initiatives with strong local roots and the broad participation of those with a stake in outcomes, including not only officials but also students, parents, teachers, and communities. Unless the beneficiaries of education reform become its bearers, it is likely to be stillborn.

Both providers and recipients of foreign aid must recognize that with some exceptions its primary role is to promote the development of the providing country. Within that, there can be room for genuine cooperation that is neither philanthropy nor determining direction.

Research matters here. Many studies of education and development and their recommendations function in practice not to foster and facilitate dialogue but to undermine and discourage it. Seeking to provide clear and firm findings, they announce and pronounce. They set terms. They declare. Sheltered by specialized language and the strictures of confidentiality, they remain largely inaccessible outside a very small circle. Though they talk about capacity building, far too often they are incapacitating.

NOTES

1. As, for example, the composition of the Gulbenkian Commission on the Restructuring of the Social Sciences, chaired by Immanuel Wallerstein. *Open the Social Sciences*, 1996.

2. A challenge here is to find terminology that captures what is common without losing sight of what is different. Initially used to designate countries not aligned with either the U.S./NATO or the U.S.S.R./Warsaw Pact, *Third World* is used to refer to countries that experienced colonial rule, that sit at the periphery in world system analyses that differentiate core and periphery, and that remain relatively and absolutely poor. Third World is thus a category whose intent and content are clear without precise specification and with recognition of the differences between, say, Paraguay and Brazil. More recently, *Global South* refers to that category, recognizing that even as some countries labeled "developing" are moving into the middle income group, there remains an important analytic and political distinction between core and periphery in the global political economy. I use Third World and Global South to refer to that conceptual periphery.

3. Newt Gingrich, Speaker of the U.S. House of Representatives, June 7, 1995, quoted in the *New York Times*, June 8, 1995. The U.S. triumphalism persists. In the 2008 presidential debates: John McCain, "But the fact is, America is the greatest force for good in the history of the world." Barack Obama, "Now, Senator McCain and I do agree, this is the greatest nation on earth. We are a force of good in the world." http://www.debates.org/index.php?page=october-7-2008-debate-transcrip.

4. World Bank 1994b, pp. 10–3, drawing on the full report, World Bank, 1994a, pp. 184–196.

5. World Education Forum, 2000. Based at UNESCO, the EFA global monitoring unit produces annual assessments of progress and problems, beginning with UNESCO, 2002. For the reports: https://en.unesco.org/gem-report/allreports. Rosa Maria Torres provides an insightful and critical perspective on the 1990 and 2000 conferences (2000a; 2000b).

6. The Education for All Global Monitoring Reports (since 2015, Global Education Monitoring Reports) provide data on aid flows to education and on the persisting gap between projected need and actual receipts, notwithstanding the affluent countries' promise that in countries with an effective EFA strategy, lack of funds should not preclude achieving EFA objectives. Earlier reviews of projected aid requirements for EFA include Bennell & Furlong, 1997; Colclough & Samarrai, 2000.

7. The literature on foreign aid has expanded rapidly. Among the sharpest critics are several former senior officials of the World Bank and the International Monetary Fund. Starting points: Berkman, 2008; Easterly, 2006; Ellerman, 2005; Marphatia & Archer, 2005; Moyo, 2009; Riddell, 2007; Menashy, 2019.

8. Among the focused critiques: Klees et al., 2012; Colclough, 1991; Collins & Wiseman, 2012; Heyneman, 2003; Jones, 2004; Samoff, 1993, 1996c.

9. World Education Forum, 2000, p. 9. On financing education for all, International Commission on Financing Global Education Opportunity, 2016; Samoff & Irving, 2014.

10. The 2015 EFA Global Monitoring Report calculated that even with optimistic assumptions about economic growth, efficient financial management, and increased domestic spending and foreign aid, achieving the 2030 goals would require annual supplemental funding of $39 billion. UNESCO. 2015b. A recent analysis suggests the gap may be as large as $45 billion per year (UNESCO, 2020).

11. The World Bank, "World Development Indicators | DataBank." https://databank.worldbank.org/reports.aspx?source=world-development-indicators#

12. I review the successive strategies for formulating education policy in Samoff, 1994b. Additional case studies of education policymaking in Africa are reported in Association for the Development of African Education, 1996.

13. For the Sustainable Development Goals: https://sdgs.un.org/goals. For Goal 4, Education, targets and indicators: https://sdgs.un.org/goals/goal4.

14. World Bank, 2002. For the foundation Partnership for Higher Education in Africa noted above (2000–2010), see http://www.foundation-partnership.org/linchpin/index.php.

15. Among the best known are: International Association for the Evaluation of Educational Achievement [IEA]; Latin American Laboratory for Assessment of the Quality of Education [LLECE]; Monitoring Learning Achievement [MLA] (UNESCO/UNICEF); Programme for International Student Assessment [PISA] (OECD); Programme d'analyse des systèmes éducatifs des pays de la CONFEMEN [PASEC] (Confemen); Southern African Consortium for Monitoring Educational Quality [SACMEQ]; Trends in International Mathematics and Science Study [TIMSS]; and Progress in International Reading Literacy Study [PIRLS]. For an overview, Meyer & Benavot, 2013.

16. World Bank, 1999. For a World Bank initiative that has become a separate organization, see also the Development Gateway (www.developmentgateway.org/). For an overview of the critiques, see Wilks, 2001. That paper and an ongoing lively debate are available at www.brettonwoodsproject.org.

17. Wolfensohn, 1997: 14. His successors have reiterated this perspective.

18. Quoting Mark Blaug, World Bank, 1995, p. 21. The citation attached to this sweeping claim (Blaug, 1976) is misleading, since Blaug's writing—for example, Blaug, 1985—rejects the unqualified accolade and many of the common uses of human capital theory. Human capital theory continues to underpin education analyses, for example, World Bank, 2017.

19. "East Asia" is a recurring reference in World Bank, 1995, presumably used to refer not to a geographic region but to the countries (and at the time colony) widely regarded to have experienced rapid economic growth: Singapore, South Korea, Taiwan, and Hong Kong. Critical analyses that highlight the central state role in these countries and the more recent Asian recession and currency crisis have apparently not modified the thinking.

20. Overseas Development Authority, 1990, p. 7. For the use of rate-of-return analysis to reach the opposite conclusion—in Kenya, secondary, not primary, education has the higher rate of return—see Knight & Sabot, 1990.

21. For a HIPC overview, https://www.worldbank.org/en/topic/debt/brief/hipc. For Global Partnership for Education grants: https://www.globalpartnership.org/funding

/applying-for-grants. For the IMF Poverty Reduction and Growth Facility: https://www.imf.org/external/np/exr/facts/prgf.htm. The World Bank provides 1,300 pages of instructions for preparing Poverty Reduction Strategy papers.

22. For a detailed inventory and analytic overview of studies undertaken within the context of the aid relationship, see Samoff, 1996a. The ADEA Working Group on Education Sector Analysis supported several national reviews of these studies, including Burkina Faso, Ghana, Lesotho, and Zimbabwe.

23. World Bank, 2011. The research priorities and inattention to developing Third World research capacities are also prominent in the first of the World Bank's annual development reports to focus on education: World Bank, 2017.

24. For an overview, see Samoff, 1996b. Abhijit Banerjee et al. (2006) provide a detailed assessment that highlights the institutional pressures that can undermine research quality. I address the framing that emerges from this conjunction of funding and research in Samoff, 2019.

25. Problems with the reported data and their major causes are well known. The basic data deficiencies are often compounded by careless use of what is available (e.g., assuming that budgeted allocations are approximately the same as actual expenditures or comparing budget data in one year with expenditure data in another).

26. Here I conflate commissioned research (studies initiated and funded by an external agency) and consulting (individual and occasionally institutional contracts for services rendered) because that is the common usage among the practitioners. For the extent of uncirculated education research in Africa, see Maclure (2006).

27. BRAC: initially Bangladesh Rehabilitation Assistance Committee, subsequently Bangladesh Rural Advancement Committee and later as Building Resources Across Communities. See http://www.brac.net/. For Escuela Nueva: http://escuelanueva.org/portal1/es/.

28. https://equaleducation.org.za/
29. https://www.tostan.org/
30. https://www.hakielimu.or.tz/en/
31. Pratham: https://www.pratham.org/; Uwezo: https://www.uwezo.net/

REFERENCES

Altbach, P. G. (1991). Patterns in higher education development: Toward the year 2000. *The Review of Higher Education*, 14(3), 293–315.

Amin, S. (1974). *Accumulation on world scale: A critique of the theory of underdevelopment*. (Vol. 1). Monthly Review Press.

Amin, S. (1976). *Unequal development: An essay on the social formation of peripheral capital*. Monthly Review Press.

Amin, S. (1990). *Delinking: Towards a polycentric world*. Zed Press.

Amin, S. (2014). *Eurocentrism* (2nd ed.). Zed Books.

Amin, S. (2019a). *Only people make their own history: Writings on capitalism, imperialism, and revolution*. Monthly Review Press.

Amin, S. (2019b). *The long revolution of the Global South: Toward a new anti-imperialist international*. Monthly Review Press.

Arnove, R. F. (Ed.). (1980). *Philanthropy and cultural imperialism: The foundations at home and abroad*. Hall.

Arnove, R. F. (1983). The Ford Foundation and the transfer of knowledge: Convergence and divergence in the world–system. *Compare: A Journal of Comparative and International Education*, 13(1), 7-24.

Arnove, R. F., & Berman, E. H. (1984). *Neocolonial policies of North American philanthropic foundations*. World Congress of Comparative Education.

Association for the Development of African Education. (1996). *Formulating education policy: Lessons and experiences from sub-saharan Africa*. Association for the Development of African Education.

Banerjee, A. et al. (2006). *An evaluation of World Bank research, 1998–2005*. World Bank.

Bashir, S., Lockheed, M., Ninan, E., & Tang, J. P. (2018). *Facing forward: Schooling for learning in Africa*. World Bank.

Bennell, P. & Furlong, D. (1997). Has Jomtien made any difference? Trends in donor funding for education and basic education since the late 1980s. IDS Working Paper 51. Sussex.

Berkman, S. (2008). *The World Bank and the gods of lending*. Kumarian Press.

Berman, E. H. (1983). *The Ideology of philanthropy: The influence of the Carnegie, Ford, and Rockefeller foundations on American foreign policy*. State University of New York Press.

Blaug, M. (1976). The empirical status of human capital theory: A slightly jaundiced survey. *Journal of Economic Literature*, 14(3), 827–855.

Blaug. M. (1985). Where are we now in the economics of education? *Economics of Education Review*, 4(1): 17–28.

Boli, J. & Ramirez, F. O. (1987). The political construction of mass schooling: European origins and worldwide institutionalization. *Sociology of Education*, 2–17.

Boli, J., Ramirez, F. O., & Meyer, J. W. (1985). Explaining the origins and expansion of mass education. *Comparative Education Review*, 29(2), 145–170.

Bowles, S., & Gintis, H. (1981). Education as a site of contradictions in the reproduction of the capital-labor relationship: Second thoughts on the "correspondence principle." *Economic and Industrial Democracy*, 2(2), 223–242.

Carnoy, M. (1984). *The state and political theory*. Princeton University Press.

Carnoy, M. (1990). Education and the transition state. In M. Carnoy & J. Samoff (Eds.), *Education and social transition in the third world*. Princeton University Press.

Carnoy, M. (1992). Education and the state: From Adam Smith to perestroika. In R. F. Arnove, P. G. Altbach, & G. P. Kelly (Eds.), *Emergent issues in education: Comparative perspectives* (pp. 143–159). State University of New York Press.

Carnoy, M., & Torres, C. A. (1994). Educational change and structural adjustment: A case study of Costa Rica. In J. Samoff (Ed.), *Coping with crisis: Austerity, adjustment, and human resources*. Cassell/UNESCO.

Carton, M., & Diouf, P. N. (1994). Budget cuts in education and training in Sénégal: An analysis of reactions. In J. Samoff (Ed.), *Coping with crisis: Austerity, adjustment, and human resources* (pp. 121–133). Cassell/UNESCO.

Castells, M. (1997a). *The rise of the network society*. Wiley.

Castells, M. (1997b). *The power of identity*. Wiley.

Castells, M. (1998). *End of millennium*. Wiley.

Colclough, C. (1991). Who should learn to pay? An assessment of neo-liberal approaches to education policy. In Colclough, C. & Manor, J. (Eds.). *States or markets? Neo-Liberalism and the development policy debate* (pp. 197–213). Clarendon.

Colclough, C. & Manor, J. (Eds.). (1991). *States or markets? Neo-Liberalism and the development policy debate*. Clarendon.

Colclough, C. & Al-Samarrai, S. (2000). Achieving schooling for all: Budgetary expenditures on education in sub-saharan Africa and South Asia. *World Development*, 28(11), 1927–1944.

Collins, C. S. & Wiseman, A. W. (Eds.). (2012). *Education strategy in the developing world: Revising the World Bank's education policy*. Emerald Group Publishing,

Depelchin, Jacques. (2005). *Silences in African history: Between the syndromes of discovery and abolition*. Mkuki na Nyota Publishers.

Easterly, W. R. (2006). *The white man's burden: Why the West's efforts to aid the rest have done so much ill and so little good*. Penguin Press.

Ellerman, D. (2005). *Helping people help themselves: From the World Bank to an alternative philosophy of development assistance. Evolving values for a capitalist world*. University of Michigan Press.

Foster, J., Addy, N. A., & Samoff, J. (2012). Crossing borders: Research in comparative and international education. *International Journal of Educational Development*, 32(6), 711–732.

Freire, Pablo. (1970). *Pedagogy of the oppressed*. Herder and Herder.

Fuenzalida, E. F. (1983). The reception of "scientific sociology" in Chile. *Latin American Research Review*, 18(2), 95–112.

"Gingrich says English must be the 'common language'." (1995, June 8). *New York Times*, pp. A22.

Grant Lewis, S., Friedman, J., & Schoneboom, J. (2010). Accomplishments of the Partnership for Higher Education in Africa, 2000–2010. *Partnership for Higher Education*. Retrieved from April 23, 2013, www.foundation-partnership. org/pubs/pdf/accomplishments.pdf

Heyneman, S. P. (2003). The history and problems in the making of education policy at the World Bank 1960–2000. *International Journal of Educational Development*, 23, 315–337.

Ignatieff, M. (2004). *Empire lite*. Penguin.

Inkles, A., & Smith, D. (1974). *Becoming modern: Individual change in six developing countries*. Harvard University Press.

Inter-Agency Commission, World Conference on Education for All (UNDP, UNESCO, UNICEF, World Bank). (1990). *Final Report, World Conference on Education for All: Meeting Basic Learning Needs*. UNICEF.

International Commission on Financing Global Education Opportunity. (2016). *The learning generation: Investing in education for a changing world*. International Commission on Financing Global Education Opportunity.

Jerven, M. (2013). *Poor numbers: How we are misled by African development statistics and what to do about it*. Cornell University Press.

Jerven, M. (2015). *Africa: Why economists get it wrong*. Zed Books.

Johnson, P. (1993). Colonialism's back—and not a moment too soon. *New York Times Magazine*, 18, 22–24.

Jones, P. W. (2004). Taking the credit: Financing and policy linkages in the education portfolio of the World Bank. In Steiner-Khamsi, G. (Ed.). *The global politics of educational borrowing and lending* (pp. 188–200). Teachers College Press.

Kaplan, R. D. (2000). *The Coming Anarchy: Shattering the Dreams of the Post Cold War*. New York: Random House.

Klees, S. J. (2017). Will we achieve education for all and the education sustainable development goal? *Comparative Education Review*, 61(2), 425–440.

Klees, S. J., Samoff, J., and Stromquist, Nelly, eds. (2012). *The World Bank and Education: Critiques and Alternatives*. Sense Publishers.

Knight, J. B. & Sabot, R. H. (1990). *Education, productivity, and inequality: The East African natural experiment*. Oxford University Press/World Bank.

Maclure, R. (2006). No longer overlooked and undervalued? The evolving dynamics of endogenous educational research in sub-Saharan Africa. *Harvard Educational Review*, 76(1), 80–109.

Mamdani, M. (2008). *Scholars in the marketplace: The dilemmas of neo-liberal reform of Makerere University 1989–2005*. HSRC Press.

Marphatia, A. A., & Archer, D. (2005). *Contradicting commitments: How the achievement of education for all is being undermined by the International Monetary Fund*. ActionAid.

Mbembe, A. (2001). *On the postcolony*. University of California Press.

McGinn, N. F. (Ed.). (1996). *Crossing lines: Research and policy networks for developing country education*. Praeger.

McGoey, L. (2016). *No such thing as a free gift: The Gates Foundation and the price of philanthropy*. Verso.

Menashy, F. (2019). *International aid to education: Power dynamics in an era of partnership*. Teachers College Press.

Meyer, H-D., & Benavot, A. (Eds). (2013). *PISA, power, and Policy: The emergence of global education governance*. Symposium Books.

Moyo, D. (2009). *Dead aid: Why aid is not working and how there is a better way for Africa*. Farrar, Straus and Giroux.

Mudimbe, V. Y. (1988). *The invention of Africa: Gnosis, philosophy, and the order of knowledge*. Indiana University Press.

Mudimbe, V. Y. (1994). *The idea of Africa*. Indiana University Press.

Mundy, K. (1999). Educational multilateralism in a changing world order: UNESCO and the limits of the possible. *International Journal of Educational Development, 19*(1), 27–52.

Mundy, K., & Verger, A. (2015). The World Bank and the global governance of education in a changing world order. *International Journal of Educational Development, 40*, 9–18.

Open the Social Sciences: Report of the Gulbenkian Commission on the Restructuring of the Social Sciences. (1996). Stanford University Press.

Overseas Development Authority. (1990). *Into the nineties: An education policy for British aid*. Overseas Development Authority.

Parson, T. (1963). *Structure and process in modern societies*. Free Press.

Przeworski, A. (1992). The neoliberal fallacy. *Journal of Democracy, 3*(3), 45–59.

Riddell, R. (2007). *Does foreign aid really work?* Oxford University Press.

Samoff, J. (1991). The façade of precision in education data and statistics: A troubling example from Tanzania. *Journal of Modern African Studies, 29*(4), 669–689.

Samoff, J. (1993). The reconstruction of Schooling in Africa. *Comparative Education Review. 37*(2), 181–222.

Samoff, J. ed. (1994a). *Coping with crisis: Austerity, adjustment, and human resources*. Cassell/UNESCO.

Samoff, J. (1994b). Education policy formation in Tanzania: Self-reliance and dependence. In D. R. Evans (Ed.), *Education policy formation in Africa: A comparative study of five countries* (pp. 85–126). U.S. Agency for International Development.

Samoff, J., with Assié-Lumumba, N. T. (1996a). *Analyses, agendas, and priorities in African education: A Review of externally initiated, commissioned, and supported studies of education in Africa, 1990–1994*. UNESCO.

Samoff, J. (1996b). Chaos and certainty in development. *World Development, 24*(4), 611–633.

Samoff, J. (1996c). Which priorities and strategies for education? *International Journal of Educational Development, 16*(3), 249–271.

Samoff, J. (1999). Education sector analysis in Africa: limited national control and even less national ownership. *International Journal of Educational Development, 19*(4–5), 249–272.

Samoff, J. (2004). From funding projects to supporting sectors? Observation on the aid relationship in Burkina Faso. *International Journal of Educational Development, 24*(4), 397–427.

Samoff, J. (2012). "Research shows that . . . ": Creating the knowledge environment for learning for all. In S. J. Klees, J. Samoff, & N. P. Stromquist (Eds.), *The World Bank and education* (pp. 143–157). Brill Sense.

Samoff, J. (2019). *Higher education for self-reliance: Tanzania and Africa.* HakiElimu.

Samoff, J. (2021). Two tales, contending perspectives, and contested terrain. In *Comparative and international education* (pp. 183–198). Palgrave Macmillan, Cham.

Samoff, J., & Carrol, B. (2004). *From manpower planning to the knowledge era: World Bank policies on higher education in Africa.* UNESCO Forum on Higher Education, Research and Knowledge.

Samoff, J. & Irving, M. (2014). *Education for all: A global commitment without global funding.* Open Society Foundations. ESP Working Paper Series, 2014 No. 60.

Samoff, J., Leer, J., & Reddy, M. (2016). *Capturing complexity and context: Evaluating aid to education.* Expertguppen för biståndsanalys/Expert Group for Aid Studies, Rapport 2016.03.

Samoff, J., & Stromquist, N. P. (2001). Managing knowledge and storing wisdom? New forms of foreign aid?. *Development and Change, 32*(4), 631–656.

Samoff, J., & Sumra, S. (1994). From planning to marketing: Making education and training policy in Tanzania. In J. Samoff (Ed.), *Coping with crisis: Austerity, adjustment and human resource* (pp. 134–172). Cassell/UNESCO.

Steiner-Khamsi, G. (Ed.). (2004). *The global politics of educational borrowing and lending.* Teachers College Press.

Sutton, F. X. (2001). The Ford Foundation's transatlantic role and purposes, 1951–81. *Review* 24(1), 77–104.

Torres, R. M. (2000a). *One decade of education for all: The challenge ahead.* UNESCO. IIEP (Buenos Aires).

Torres, R. M. (2000b). *What happened at the World Education Forum?*

Torres, R. M. (2001). "Knowledge-based international aid": Do we want it, do we need it? In W. Gmelin et al. (Eds.), *Development Knowledge, National research and international cooperation* (pp. 103–124).

UNESCO. (2002). *Education for all: Is the world on track?* UNESCO.

UNESCO. (2015a). *Education for all 2000–2015: Achievements and challenges. EFA Global monitoring report 2015.* UNESCO.

UNESCO. (2015b). Global education monitoring report. *Pricing the right to education: The cost of reaching new targets by 2030.* Policy Paper 18. UNESCO.

UNESCO. (2020). Global Education Monitoring Report. *COVID-19 is a serious threat to aid to education recovery.* Policy Paper, 41. UNESCO.

United Nations General Assembly. (2001). Resolution A/56/326, (6 September).

Wallerstein, I. (1974). *The modern world-system; Capitalist agriculture and the origins of the European world-economy in the sixteenth century.* Academic Press.

Wallerstein, I. (1980). *The modern world-system II: mercantilism and the consolidation of the European world-economy, 1600–1750.* Academic Press.

Wallerstein, I. (1989). *The modern world system III: The second era of great expansion of the capitalist world-economy, 1730–1840s.* Academic Press.

Wilks, A. (2001). *A Tower of Babel on the internet? The World Bank's Development Gateway.* Bretton Woods Project.

Wolfensohn, J. D. (1997). *The challenge of inclusion: Address to the board of governors, Hong Kong, China, September 23, 1997.* World Bank.

World Bank. (1980). *Education: Sector policy paper.* World Bank.

World Bank. (1994a). *Adjustment in Africa: Reforms, results, and the road ahead.* Oxford University Press.

World Bank. (1994b). *Adjustment in Africa: Reforms, results, and the road ahead—Summary.* Oxford University Press.

World Bank. (1995). *Priorities and strategies for education: A World Bank review*. World Bank.

World Bank. (1999). *World development report 1998/1999: Knowledge for development*. Oxford University Press for the World Bank.

World Bank. (2002). *Constructing knowledge societies: New challenges for tertiary education*. World Bank.

World Bank. (2011). *Learning for All: Investing in People's Knowledge and Skills to Promote Development. World Bank Education Sector Strategy 2020*. World Bank.

World Bank. (2017). *Learning to realize education's promise. World development report 2018*. World Bank.

World Education Forum. (2000). *The Dakar framework for action*. UNESCO.

Zeleza, P. T. (2002). The politics of historical and social science research in Africa. *Journal of Southern African Studies*, 28(1), 9–23.

2

Economics, Education, and Society

Myths and Possibilities

Steven J. Klees
University of Maryland

ABSTRACT

Economics has long been central to the comparative and international education field. However, approaches to economics are debated. In this chapter, I argue that the dominant approach, called neoclassical economics, is based on five myths: that unfettered free markets are best for economic growth and development; that unfettered free markets are efficient; that the recommendations of these economists are based on empirical evidence; that human capital theory and practice are a good basis for deciding on investments in education; and that a bastion of neoclassical economists, the World Bank, has been an impartial advocate for improvements in education. I conclude by looking at an alternative approach to understanding education policy and practice offered by political economists.

■ ■ ■

Economics has been an integral part of the comparative education field since the 1960s when the idea of human capital became ubiquitous, used by neoclassical economists as a framework for planning and evaluating education and development programs and policies.[1] Yet, from the beginning, the meaning of and approaches to economics were contested. This chapter explores the conflicting views that economics continues to bring to education policy and practice. Overall, I argue that the dominant neoclassical economics perspective is based on an elaborately constructed mythology. This analysis has special relevance today as I am writing this with schools around the world closed and economies shut down due to the COVID-19 pandemic. The trajectory of the virus is unclear, but, to me, regardless, its exposure of the many fault lines of our societies should be a wake-up call that we can no longer engage in business as usual. Whether the virus is here for the short or long term, it is time to confront these myths and choose alternative paths.

I find it useful to think of three major widely held economic and political perspectives: conservative, liberal, and progressive. Briefly, the conservative perspective, also known as neoliberal, emphasizes the efficiency of a market system and the very limited role governments should play. The liberal perspective sees the need for more balance between state and market, arguing that the inefficiencies and inequities that can result from a market system may need corrective government action. Speaking somewhat simplistically, neoclassical economists can hold neoliberal or liberal views, although, since the 1980s, the neoliberal view has dominated much of the world. The third, progressive perspective, which I also refer to as a political economy perspective, focuses on the reproductive nature of both the market and the state under current world system structures like capitalism, patriarchy, and racism and emphasizes transformation from below through more participatory forms of democracy and collective action.

I hold a progressive political economy view, and this chapter offers an explanation and critique of neoclassical economics' views of education and development and a discussion of the alternatives to it. The meaning of the term "political economy" is contested. Historically, it was used to refer to all of what has come to be known as social science. Today, the right sometimes uses the term to refer to a neoliberal perspective and the left uses it in the progressive sense in which I will be using it in this chapter (Caporaso & Levine, 1992). I begin by briefly summarizing the dominant neoclassical perspective, with a little attention at the end to how liberals differ from neoliberals. The bulk of this chapter then examines five myths that underlie this story, concluding by summarizing an alternative political economy story.

THE DOMINANT STORY

Adam Smith wrote *The Wealth of Nations* at the end of the 18th century, examining how a competitive capitalist market system works and how it could operate in the interests of society as a whole. Classical economists, like Ricardo, Malthus, and Mill, examined aspects of this. At the end of the 19th century, Alfred Marshall (1890/1920) wrote about what he called the "neoclassical synthesis," and this underlying vision of economics has changed little since then. It tells the story of a "perfectly competitive" economic system that operates according to a few idealized assumptions. Firms and households, the two main private actors, strive to maximize profits and utility (i.e., happiness) respectively. So many of both are competing that none has any control over the market; they all just react to prices in the marketplace but cannot influence them. Moreover, both actors have perfect knowledge of production processes and product quality. Such a system is said to be "efficient" in the sense that production of all goods and services uses the best technologies to produce them, firms then sell them as cheaply as possible, and their distribution is directed and balanced by the preferences of sovereign consumers. It is recognized that consumers' demand for these goods and services is only effective to the extent that they have money to pay for them. To some extent, it is believed that workers' pay reflects their contribution to production; if society judges the results as inequitable, we can redistribute resources. In this scheme, the public sector's role is to correct inefficiencies when the real world doesn't operate according to the assumptions of perfect competition and when there are goals other than efficiency, such as greater equity (Friedman, 1984).

While some economists have paid attention to education over the centuries, it was not until the 1960s, with the advent of human capital theory, that education became an integral part of this neoclassical story. Education came to be seen as an investment, analogous to investment in physical capital, whose rate of return could be calculated by comparing the monetary costs of education to its monetary benefits of increasing income, productivity, and gross domestic product (GDP). Sometimes, innovative economists find other outcomes of education that can be measured in monetary terms (Haveman & Wolfe, 1984). When outcomes are not easily measurable in monetary terms, economists compare costs and effectiveness, with outcomes measured in other ways, such as learning gains, changes in attitudes, or dropout and graduation rates (Cohn & Geske, 1990).

A major issue for neoclassical economists has been the role of government in education. During the neoliberal era of the past four decades, it has become commonplace to argue that the private sector has a major role to play in providing educational services around the world. In addition, the logic of business is increasingly seen to apply to education decision-making, with test results often seen as the "bottom line" and business executives and leaders recruited for everything from managing schools to making policy (Klees, 2016a).

Most noneconomists think the main subject of economics applied to education must be financing. While this is not accurate—since, as noted earlier, their purview is much broader—how to pay for education has certainly been a concern. The neoclassical framework treats finance as a second-order problem. The first-order problem is determining what types of education investments are necessary to achieve efficiency and desired equity; after that, governments need to tax to the extent necessary to make sure that such investments are forthcoming (Levin, 1995).

Most of this brief story would be agreed upon by both liberal and neoliberal economists, but the differences are quite relevant. Liberals see that, in the real world, imperfections in competition and inequitable results make government intervention more necessary than for neoliberals who see the economic system as more efficient and equitable than liberals do. Moreover, neoliberals argue that even in the presence of inefficiencies and inequities, governments are so inept and self-interested that their interference in the market should be kept to a minimum. As stated earlier, a neoliberal perspective has dominated since the 1980s, and this has played out in education in a variety of ways. Neoliberals emphasize more the need for private sector competition with public schools and advocate for the expansion of private schooling. Also, while neoliberals sometimes recognize that more money is needed for education, they emphasize that as or more important is spending the money that is allocated more efficiently (Klees, 2016a). More details on the neoclassical story will be provided as we look at the myths that underlie it.

MYTH #1: UNFETTERED FREE MARKETS ARE THE BEST POLICIES FOR ECONOMIC GROWTH AND DEVELOPMENT

Contrary to this neoliberal dogma, there is considerable evidence that economic growth comes more from the ability to control and restrict markets than from any unfettered competition. Historically, the growth of the now-industrialized Northern countries took place under protectionist policies, often in exploitative colonial contexts (Rodrik, 2008). Yet now, these same countries are trying to sell the world on free markets as the best way to achieve economic progress. The success of capitalism has been heralded by holding up successful "miracle" countries, where free markets supposedly brought rapid growth: the Ivory Coast in the 1960s, Brazil in the 1970s, Chile in the 1980s, the "Asian Tigers" in the 1990s, and subsequently. None of these exemplars have remained miracles. Moreover, the success of some of the East Asian countries has other explanations: stable military or "strongmen" governments made them a safe place for foreign capital; all were gateways to doing business with China; and most used "industrial policies," anathema to free-market neoliberals (Chang, 2006). Industrial policies, recommended by many liberal neoclassical economists, are ones that have government leading or partnering with industries (can be in agriculture, too), thereby intervening in markets (infant industry protections are a type of industrial policy).

Until now, I have been talking about economic growth as opposed to a broader view of what development might mean. While neoliberals too often treat the two as synonymous, many liberal neoclassical economists take a broader view. Many would be concerned with the distribution of GDP and its equity. Some recognize that GDP is even a very flawed measure of economic growth and propose alternatives (Stiglitz et al., 2009). Amartya Sen (1999) has been very influential in trying to focus development on increasing what he calls individuals' capabilities and functionings. To attain most of these broader ideas of development requires placing limits on the market system.

While political economists might agree with some points made by liberal neoclassical economists, they would take debunking this neoliberal myth further. Political economists point out that free-market capitalism has yielded very deformed development. Billions of people in this world are living on the margins, many barely surviving. Neocolonial relations persist, and there is no reason to believe that we are on some progressive global path (Klees, 2020a; 2020b).

MYTH #2: UNFETTERED FREE MARKETS ARE THE MOST EFFICIENT WAY TO ORGANIZE AN ECONOMY

This claim may not seem much different than the previous one about economic growth, but to neoclassical economists, this is a different issue. Whether a country is growing a little or a lot is a different question than whether the economy is efficient in whatever it is doing. However, the whole neoclassical economics' concept of efficiency is problematic. It is based on having "perfect competition," but neoclassical economists' own "second-best" theory says if you have just one imperfection, say, one monopoly in what is otherwise a perfectly competitive system, the economy is inefficient; you can't even say whether it is close to efficient. Any imperfection sends ripples through the entire system of market prices so that the invisible hand of the marketplace no longer operates in the interest of some fictitious "society as a whole" (Friedman, 1984; Rakowski, 1980).

This great myth of neoclassical economists has rested on convincing people that there is an efficiency vantage point, separable from concerns with equity and distribution, from which you can say society as a whole is better off. But almost all policy decisions come down to tradeoffs between the welfare of different groups. If prices are not defined according to the exact dictates of perfect competition, then private profitability tells us nothing about the comparative worth—that is, "efficiency"—of producing, let's say, more yachts for rich people than more rice and beans for poor people. Thus, in practice, economic efficiency is really an empty concept.[2]

Liberals debate neoliberals on how much government intervention in markets is needed for an economy to be efficient, a debate I find irrelevant. Of course, we must regulate markets. The more serious question is not unfettered free markets versus regulation, but what kinds of goods and services do we want to supply to whom and what kind of organization, regulations, and incentives for markets can bring this about. To rely on market "efficiency" as accomplishing this through some sort of automatic, atomistic, modern miracle has been to reify self-interest and greed and to relegate any attention to economic alternatives to outside the realm of reason and possibility (Klees, 2016a).

Political economists generally argue that relying on markets for producing some goods and services may be practically useful, but would point out that, in practical terms, our capitalist world system is very inefficient. While markets are a convenience that future, saner, societies may continue to rely on for some purposes, they have at least two fundamental flaws that render them problematic. First, they contribute to an abrogation of social responsibility, as today, when market outcomes of horrendous income inequality, spiraling food prices and hunger, or environmental destruction are seen as natural, not anyone's fault. Second, markets are fragile. For example, millions of small decisions can contribute to economic or environmental crises. Albritton adds: "Markets are often thought to be highly efficient, but in the future, they will be seen as highly inefficient and costly. Markets not only fail to take account of social and environmental costs, but they also generate instability, insecurity, inequality, antisocial egotism, frenetic lifestyles, cultural impoverishment, beggar-thy-neighbor greed and oppression of difference" (quoted in Wall, 2015, p. 1).

How can you call a system efficient that relegates so many people to a marginal existence? Political economists also point out that equally important with what is produced is how we produce it. Free markets have produced so much environmental destruction that it threatens human existence. Also, neoclassical economics relegates the "how" of production to firms' decisions, ignoring our collective interest in providing good jobs and sustainable livelihoods for everyone (Klees, 2020b).

MYTH #3: EVIDENCE-BASED POLICY IS CENTRAL TO IMPROVING EDUCATION

This myth goes beyond education and economics, but it is essential to understand why we can't prove which perspectives are correct about which issues. Neoclassical economists, neoliberal or liberal, like many education researchers and social scientists, in general, argue that their policy recommendations are based primarily, if not exclusively, on what the empirical evidence tells them. Does investment in primary education have a higher rate of return than investment in higher education? Does an academic education have better results than a vocational education? Is phonics or a whole language approach more successful at teaching reading? Are free markets more conducive to economic growth than regulated ones? Do students learn more at private schools than public schools? The questions in education, economics, and elsewhere that can supposedly be settled by empirical evidence are endless. I, of course, don't want to argue that evidence is irrelevant to policy. But whose evidence and what kind of evidence counts? Over the last decade or two, the ubiquitous cry for "evidence-based policy" has become a fetish that masks the extent to which ideological choices affect findings. Here I want to focus on the quantitative approaches to impact evaluation that have dominated the discourse.

There are two ways to uncover the extent to which an intervention, or any variable, yields an outcome of interest—through statistical controls or physical controls. Regression analysis relies on the former by building a mathematical model of how "inputs" affect an outcome of interest. However, to trust the resulting impact measures, these models have to satisfy three conditions: all input variables have to be in the model; they have to be measured correctly; and their functional interrelationships have to be accurately specified (Angrist & Pischke, 2009). These conditions *never* hold, so it is no wonder that model specification is usually ad hoc and debatable (Edwards, 2018; Klees, 2016b; Leamer 1983). The result is that multiple studies investigating the same topic come to different conclusions, and the ideological underpinnings of liberal versus neoliberal versus political economists yield different policy recommendations that are never settled by empirical evidence, as illustrated in the previous myths and those later on in the chapter.

The other quantitative methodological approach to impact evaluation is randomized controlled trials (RCTs) (i.e., experiments), in which you usually have two groups, one subject to an intervention and the other not, and the difference in outcome is then attributed to the intervention. However, RCTs have fundamental problems, too. A principal one is that the results of an RCT may not tell you anything about what will happen when an intervention is implemented in a real-world, uncontrolled environment. Moreover, even the results in the experimental situation may be suspect, since control groups, in practice, often have systematic differences from treatment groups. While there are oft-used statistical methods for adjusting the findings, such methods run into the problems of specification in terms of which variables to control for and how to do so (Deaton & Cartwright, 2016; Edwards, 2018). When there are few RCTs on a topic, they may appear to give consistent answers, but when there are many RCTs on the same topic—such as the impact of performance pay for teachers or conditional cash transfers for students and their families—there are inconsistent results on which to base policy (Klees et al., 2020).

MYTH #4: HUMAN CAPITAL THEORY AND PRACTICE OFFERS USEFUL GUIDANCE ON INVESTING IN EDUCATION

Since the 1960s, neoclassical economists have applied human capital theory to education to offer advice on what policies and programs are efficient and equitable. In this section, I comment briefly on three major directions these economists have taken. Based on my analysis of the myths above, I see much of this work as flawed conceptually and empirically; conceptually because it is based on the bankrupt idea of efficiency, and empirically because the evidence used is easily contested.

First, much effort has been devoted to estimating the benefits of education in monetary terms—mostly, in terms of its effect on GDP and income—to compare it with the efficiency of other public and private investments. For GDP, the work of Hanushek and Woessman (2008; 2015) has received a lot of attention. Their regression analyses purportedly show that an improvement in the quality of education (as measured by a country's PISA scores) on GDP to be substantial; they argue that increasing "quality" by one standard deviation results in a two percentage point increase in the rate of growth of GDP/capita. However, their work has fundamental problems: their specification of what economists call an aggregate production function model (i.e., GDP as the dependent variable) was idiosyncratic and easily contested; the projection of very uncertain effects decades in the future is unwarranted; and there is the narrowness of equating PISA scores with education quality (Klees, 2016b).

Much more common than looking at the impact of education on GDP is studying the effect of education on earnings. This has led to many studies around the world of the rate of return (ROR) on investment in completing years or levels of education (Patrinos & Psacharopoulos, 2020). These studies also have many flaws: earnings is only of interest to economists as a good proxy for productivity, but it is not; they are usually missing essential economic data on what economists call externalities (i.e., impacts on people other than the buyer and seller of education);[3] and, as always, the earnings function regression models used are idiosyncratic and easily contestable. The whole idea that this type of ROR market proxy analysis can tell you anything about, let's say, the relative value of primary education compared to higher education, I find absurd on the face of it.[4] Therefore, using RORs in making education policy decisions makes no sense. Of course, the impact of education on income is important as one outcome among so many, but it has nothing to do with what is efficient or productive (Klees, 2016a).

A second major direction, followed when education outcomes cannot be measured in money terms, is when neoclassical economists use what they call education production functions to look at the impact of inputs on direct outcomes of schooling, usually test scores. Not surprisingly, these studies have not yielded consistent findings, so there is little agreement on what inputs affect what outcomes (Hanushek, 1986). There is some agreement that teachers are important, which, of course, is true, but finding this in an education production function only results from torturing the data (Klees, 2016b). Again, there are many fundamental flaws of these studies, including that test scores are poor measures of valued outcomes and the processes by which these outcomes are determined are too complex to be captured by these mathematical models (Klees, 2008; 2016b).

A third direction taken by neoclassical economists revolves around discussions of education finance and governance. Since the main question for an economist is to use ROR-type studies to tell policymakers where to invest, education finance, in theory, is about the best ways to tax to provide needed education investment (Bradley & Green, 2020; Cohn & Geske 1980; Levin, 1995). In practice, in these neoliberal times, taxation is hard to do politically, so there is much discussion of finding "innovative" financing. Innovative financing refers to things like impact investing by the private sector, which are always small in scale, focused on narrow outcomes, self-interested, and rarely aligned with public priorities. Alternatively, neoclassical economists argue that we needn't rely exclusively on public education; public financing may be less necessary if countries expand private schooling.

Neoliberal and liberal neoclassical economists generally agree on the first two directions of the field but have important disagreements regarding finance and governance. Liberals point out that the expansion of private schooling may well yield inequities and may even be inefficient as private schools only pay attention to consumer demand, ignoring the external benefits of education (Levin, 1998). In terms of education finance, neoliberals often argue that more money for schooling is not as important as finding and reallocating resources that are now wasted in inefficient provision. Liberals generally argue more strongly for the need for additional resources.

My point in this section is simply that it is a myth that we get good guidance from neoclassical economists on education policy. Conceptual flaws and disagreements and empirical difficulties yield an endless argument among them about what choices are best. Moreover, as political economists point out, the narrowness of a human capital framework has taken attention away from what is really needed (Apple, 2006; Samoff, Chapter 1 in this volume). Too often, social problems are seen as due to a lack of individual skills and education as the remedy. Contrary to this skills discourse, people are not poor because they have few skills, the dearth of decent jobs is not due to a lack of skills, and the horrendous inequality we see today is not because skills are not better distributed. Improving education's ability to impart skills will not do anything *by itself* to solve these challenges, which are structural. Full employment, decent jobs, and greater equality are neither features nor goals of capitalism, most especially in this neoliberal era (Klees, 2020a; 2020b).

MYTH #5: THE WORLD BANK HAS BEEN AN IMPARTIAL ADVOCATE FOR IMPROVING EDUCATION

The World Bank, an organization full of neoclassical economists, has played an outsized role in influencing developing country education policy and practice, most especially since the 1970s. The World Bank is a monopoly, which is rather contradictory for an institution that exalts competitive markets. There is no other institution like it. UNESCO used to have a more dominant role in education, but the withdrawal of the U.S. and U.K. contributions for several years forced it to play a much more minor role, and the World Bank became the true director of the Education for All (EFA) processes and more (Jones, 2007; Mundy, 2002). While the World Bank pretends everyone—countries, bilateral and multilateral organizations, civil society, and more—is in partnership with it, it is the World Bank that takes the lead on education policy. With its periodic strategy reports and a virtual juggernaut of research done internal to the World Bank or financed by it, it greatly influences the global directions for education policy, backed by conditional grant and loan money that ensures countries follow those directions (Klees et al., 2012).

In the 1960s and 1970s, liberal economists dominated the World Bank. It routinely argued that there were vast inequalities in education and that public education needed substantial additional resources that should be provided through expanded progressive taxes (Jallade, 1979). Starting in the 1980s, with little theoretical or empirical justification, the World Bank ideology was rapidly transformed to a neoliberal perspective and the privatization of education was strongly promoted. While the lack of sufficient resources was occasionally mentioned as an issue, it was always with a "yes, but"—where the "but" was that the main issue was seen as inefficient use of existing resources and neoliberal remedies would make resource use more efficient.[5]

For decades, the World Bank has downplayed its role in lending money, trying to position itself as the "Knowledge Bank," the repository of best practice. This is arrogant and frightening. The World Bank usually only looks at its own research and that of its adherents, basing its one-size-fits-all recommendations on ideology, not evidence (Klees et al., 2012). Even the idea of a central repository of "best practice" is frightening in a world where best practice is always contested. The World Bank as that repository is more frightening still.

The World Bank selects and interprets the research that fits with its neoliberal ideology (Klees et al., 2020). In this sense, it resembles right-wing ideological think tanks like the Cato Institute or the Heritage Foundation in the United States. However, it differs in two important ways. First, everyone realizes Cato and Heritage are partisan. The World Bank, on the other hand, makes a pretense of objectivity and inclusiveness. Second, Cato and Heritage are private institutions with limited influence. The World Bank is a public institution, financed by taxes, which gives grants, loans, and advice around the world, yielding a vast global influence.

There is no "Knowledge Bank," only an "Opinion Bank," and, worse still, an opinion bank with monopoly power. This Monopoly Opinion Bank (I cannot resist—it should be known as the MOB) may not be the only source of knowledge in education in developing countries, but it is the predominant producer and arbiter of what counts as knowledge. If there were applicable antitrust legislation, The MOB's research and advice enterprise would be broken up. The MOB's defense is that they try to incorporate all knowledge from all their partners, including countries, other aid agencies, nongovernmental organizations, other civil society organizations, indigenous people, and the poor of the world. This is neither possible nor sensible nor true in a world where knowledge is contested within and among all these groups. The MOB distills and disseminates the knowledge it wants to promulgate (Klees, 2012).

While loan officers in the World Bank are more pragmatic than the policy and research staff, internally and externally World Bank ideology pervades practice. Even some World Bank staff complain of the (neoliberal) "thought police" in the World Bank that force ideological conformity (Broad, 2006). And World Bank staff, in the world of international aid agencies, are royalty. They rarely must face serious criticism or challenges. I do not see the World Bank as responsible for neoliberalism, but they have taken it as gospel and have become its chief purveyor in education in developing countries.

AN ALTERNATIVE STORY

From a political economy perspective, a human capital framework today is seen as embedded in a neoliberal, market fundamentalist regime that reproduces and advances the prevailing social order. The central neoclassical idea of an efficient society is seen as problematic; "efficient for whom?" is the real question. For me, the essential problem with neoclassical economics is captured in a story that political economist Martin Carnoy tells. Milton Friedman was a professor of Martin's at the University of Chicago. When Friedman came to Stanford University 20 years later, Martin made an appointment to see him with no real agenda. Friedman, knowing of Martin's radical proclivities, started talking to him about the "seven sisters" oil companies. While this oligopoly is a clear violation of economists' notions of a competitive marketplace, Friedman proceeded to offer a detailed argument why they mirrored a perfectly competitive market. Martin left there astonished, partly because of the topic Friedman chose and partly because of Friedman's analysis. In the end, Martin says, he realized that his only chance of refuting Friedman's argument was if he had stopped him at the very beginning and questioned his starting assumptions. That's the fundamental problem with neoclassical economics. If you don't challenge their initial assumptions, neoclassical economists are off to the races, spinning yarns about the fictitious idea of the overall economic efficiency for society as a whole. I think that this is how neoclassical economics turns out so many economists uncritical of the framework. They begin the first few weeks of their doctoral coursework making a set of totally unrealistic assumptions and then spend the next four or five years assuming them to construct an amazing set of false implications and conclusions. By the time they get their PhD the assumptions are unquestioned.

Educational policies touted by neoclassical economists that promote, for example, vouchers, charters, and other forms of privatization and narrow approaches to testing, accountability, and standards are seen as furthering inequality and ignoring the realities of unequal power. While political economy perspectives previously focused on class and capitalism, they are now an intersection of contributions from "various neo-Marxist, feminist, postmodern, poststructural, postcolonial, queer, disability, environmental, and other communities" (Apple, 2006, p. 54). While these theories do not offer identical perspectives, there is often a common focus on marginalization. They see the world as composed of systems and structures that reproduce and legitimate existing inequalities. While reproduction is pervasive, there is agreement that there are spaces for progressive actions through exercising individual and collective human agency. I use the term "human agency" in the sense that political economists use it to refer to the capacity for individual and collective action to challenge oppressive structures like capitalism, patriarchy, racism, ableism, and heterosexism (Adams et al., 2013; Apple, 2006; 2013; Carnoy & Levin, 1985; Robertson & Dale, 2015).

From a political economy perspective, the most promising source for progressive change is through social movements—such as the women's movement, the civil rights movement, alter-globalization movement, landless movement, Dalit movement, the human rights movement, the children's rights movement, and others—which bring the power of collective action to confronting the unfairness and irrationality of pervasive marginalization. In terms of education, in Brazil, for example, where I have worked extensively, the Citizen School movement has built a sizeable democratic, participatory, Freirean-based education system (Fischman & Gandin, 2007). In Brazil also, there are the Landless Workers Movement schools, founded by some of the poorest people in all the world, often living off agricultural labor, now forming an organized and politically influential social movement, with a large system of very participatory, democratic, Freirean-based schools (McGowan, 2003; Tarlau, 2019). These schools teach—and exemplify by their very structure—the role of education in preparing people for a much more participatory and democratic economy and society (Edwards & Klees, 2012). So do many examples of alternative critical pedagogy practices from the United States and other countries (Apple & Beane, 2007; McLaren & Kincheloe, 2007; Picower, 2012).

Many people can imagine a world without racism, patriarchy, heterosexism, and ableism; imagining a world without capitalism is perhaps more difficult. In 1933, John Maynard Keynes wrote:

[Capitalism] is not a success. It is not intelligent, it is not beautiful, it is not just, it is not virtuous—and it doesn't deliver the goods. In short, we dislike it, and we are beginning to despise it. But when we wonder what to put in its place, we are extremely perplexed. (Quoted in Albert, 2014, p. xv)

Nevertheless, today, many people see alternatives. We live in a world that could provide a decent standard of living for everyone, but we have an economic system that offers no way of doing that. Margaret Thatcher uttered the famous TINA: There Is No Alternative (to neoliberal capitalism). To the contrary, as Bollier (2015) says, the relevant acronym should be TAPAS: There Are Plenty of Alternatives! There are lots of small-scale alternatives around the globe: cooperatives, worker-owned firms, alternative monetary systems, participatory budgeting, solidarity economies, and much more (Hahnel & Wright, 2016). And there are many countries that, although capitalist, offer social capitalism that is much fairer than the neoliberal capitalism that dominates. But to me, any form of capitalism is likely to exacerbate, not ameliorate, our global social problems. Despite creating wealth for some, capitalism is the most inefficient system in history, leaving billions of people at its margins, destroying our planet, and feeding a war machine.

While there are no blueprints for alternatives, a lot of people are thinking about and working on larger-scale alternatives. Nor should there be blueprints. Alternatives must be constructed on the ground in context. But there can be visions. As examples, look at the work of Michael Albert and Robin Hahnel on participatory economics. Search online for "Parecon." Or the organization started by Gar Alperovitz and Gus Speth—search online for the amazing "Next System Project." Or the 2018 initiative started by Yanis Varoufakis and Jane (wife of Bernie) Sanders to bring all of us together—"Progressive International." Or search the work of Gustavo Esteva—on what he and others are calling Crianza Mutua (Mutual Upbringing) in which representatives of the Zapatista community have been meeting with other alternative communities to flesh out principles and approaches to living very differently on this planet in what some call a radical pluralism. Finally, search online for the wonderful "Global Tapestry of Alternatives" that has taken this approach worldwide.

I see reasons for optimism. I see the struggle in electoral politics that brought a progressive left to power in a half dozen or more Latin American countries during the first two decades of the 21st century. Despite setbacks, change is possible. Even in the United States, while he didn't win the nomination, polls showed that Bernie Sanders, an avowed democratic socialist, would have had a close race with Trump in both 2016 and 2020. I am also optimistic because I was fortunate enough to twice attend the World Social Forum (WSF) in Brazil and march with 100,000 activists from all over the world and meet some of them who were struggling to change the world in areas like education, health, food, water, environment, or development generally. They go home from the Forum and interact with millions, building a global network. I am also optimistic because I have been fortunate to work in dozens of countries, and *everywhere* I found people who believed what is the slogan of the WSF—Another World Is Possible—and who were struggling for it. Naomi Klein (2014) called the climate crisis a civilizational wake-up call. So should the pandemic be. If we are to survive, let alone thrive, we cannot go back to business as usual.

NOTES

1. Terms like "development" and "developing" country are problematic but are used for wont of a good alternative. See Esteva et al. (2013).

2. If efficiency is taken in the much more limited practical sense that free markets do better in bringing goods and services to people with money (e.g., stores filled with merchandise) compared to a centralized State-run economy like the former Soviet Union, then markets do better.

3. Externalities are impacts of a market transaction other than on the buyer and seller. Automobile and other sources of pollution are a major negative example. Education is thought to have many positive externalities such as better health, democratic functioning, and societal productivity. If externalities are present, the invisible hand posited by Adam Smith is no longer efficient without governments stepping in to take account of them. Liberals and neoliberals differ over their extent. Recently, liberal Harvard University neoclassical economist Dani Rodrik has upset neoliberals (and some liberals) by his groundbreaking argument that job creation yields major societal externalities and therefore governments should be very actively involved in creating "good" jobs. This is anathema to most neoclassical economists who leave this key function to markets—which has resulted in a world where billions of people have few decent employment opportunities (see Rodrik & Stantcheva, 2020, and the related movement to democratize work: https://democratizingwork.org/).

4. Not all political economists would agree.

5. Its sister institution, the International Monetary Fund, has followed a neoliberal macroeconomic policy that has greatly affected education by recommending caps on the wage bill for public employees, thus severely limiting the number of teachers that countries could hire (Ambrose & Archer, 2020). Also, the OECD has been very influential in narrowly shaping education policy and practice from its early focus on the economics of education to its more recent related domination of global testing through PISA (Elfert, 2019; Ydesen, 2019).

REFERENCES

Adams, M., Blumenfeld, W., Castaneda, C., Hackman, H. W., Peters, M. L., & Zuniga, X. (Eds.). (2013). *Readings for diversity and social justice* (3rd ed.). Routledge.

Albert, M. (2014). *Realizing hope: Life beyond capitalism*. Zed.

Ambrose, S., & Archer, D. (2020). *Who cares for the future: Finance gender responsive public services*. ActionAid International. https://actionaid.org/sites/default/files/publications/final%20who%20cares%20report.pdf

Angrist, J. D., & Pischke, J-S. (2009). *Mostly harmless econometrics: An empiricist's guide.* Princeton University Press. Apple, M. W. (2006). *Educating the "right" way: Markets, standards, God, and inequality* (2nd ed.). Routledge.

Apple, M. W. (2013). *Can education change society?* Routledge.

Apple, M. W., & Beane, J. A. (2007). *Democratic schools: Lessons in powerful education* (2nd ed.). Heinemann.

Bollier, D. (2015). Foreword to the new edition. In D. Wall, *Economics after capitalism*. Pluto.

Bradley, S., & Green, C. (Eds.). (2020) *The economics of education* (2nd ed.). Academic Press.

Broad, R. (2006). Research, knowledge, and the art of "paradigm maintenance": The World Bank's development economics vice-presidency. *Review of International Political Economy, 13*(3), 387–419.

Caporaso, J. A., & Levine, D. P. (1992). *Theories of political economy*. Cambridge University Press.

Carnoy, M., & Levin, H. M. (1985). *Schooling and work in the democratic state*. Stanford University Press.

Chang, H-J. (2006). *The East Asian development experience*. Zed Books.

Cohn, E., & Geske, T. G. (1990). *The economics of education* (3rd ed.). Pergamon.

Deaton, A., & Cartwright, N. (2016). The limitations of ramdomised controlled trials. Vox. http://voxeu.org/article/limitations-randomised-controlled-trials

Edwards, D. B. (2018). *Global education policy, impact evaluations, and alternatives: The political economy of knowledge production*. Palgrave Macmillan.

Edwards Jr., D. B., & Klees, S. (2012). Participation in development and education governance. In A. Verger, M. Novelli, & H. Kosar-Altinyelken (Eds.)., *Global education policy and international development: New agendas, issues and programmes*. Continuum.

Elfert, M. (2019). The OECD, American power, and the rise of the "economics of education" in the 1960s. In C. Ydesen (Ed.), *The OECD's historical rise in education: The formation of a global governing complex* (pp. 39–61). Palgrave Macmillan.

Esteva, G., Babones, S., & Babcicky, P. (2013). *The future of development: A radical manifesto*. Policy Press.

Fischman, G., & Gandin, L. A. (2007). Escola cidade and critical discourses of educational hope. In P. McLaren & J. Kincheloe (Eds.), *Critical pedagogy: Where are we now?* Peter Lang.

Friedman, L. S. (1984). *Microeconomics policy analysis*. McGraw-Hill.

Hahnel, R., & Wright, E. O. (2016). *Alternatives to capitalism: Proposals for a democratic economy*. Verso.

Hanushek, E. (1986). The economics of schooling: Production and efficiency in public schools. *Journal of Economic Literature, 24*(3), 1141–1177.

Hanushek, E., & Woessmann, L. (2008). The role of cognitive skills in economic development. *Journal of Economic Literature, 46*(3), 607–668.

Hanushek, E., & Woessmann, L. (2015). *Universal basic skills: What countries stand to gain*. OECD.

Haveman, R. H., & Wolfe, B. L. (1984). Schooling and economic well-being: The role of nonmarket effects. *Journal of Human Resources, 19*(3), 377–407.

Jallade, J.-P. (1979, March). Financing education for income distribution. *Finance and Development*.

Jones, P. W. (2007). *World Bank financing of education: Lending, learning and development* (2nd ed.). Routledge.

Klees, S. (2008, August). Reflections on theory, method, and practice in comparative and international education. *Comparative Education Review, 52*(3), 301–328.

Klees, S. (2012). World Bank and education: Ideological premises and ideological conclusions. In S. Klees, J. Samoff, & N. Stromquist (Eds.), *World Bank and education: Critiques and alternatives*. Sense.

Klees, S. (2016a). Human capital and rates of return: Brilliant ideas or ideological dead ends? *Comparative Education Review, 60*(4), 644–672.

Klees, S. (2016b). Inferences from regression analysis: Are they valid? *Real World Economics Review, 74*, 85–97.

Klees, S. (2020a). Beyond neoliberalism: Reflections on capitalism and education. *Policy Futures in Education, 18*(1), 9–29.

Klees, S. (2020b). *The conscience of a progressive*. Zero Books.

Klees, S. (2021). Economics, development, and comparative and international education. In B. Lindsay (Ed.), *Comparative and international education: Leading perspectives from the field*. Palgrave Macmillan.

Klees, S., Ginsburg, M., Anwar, H., Baker, R., M., Bloom, H., Busacca, C., Corwith, A., DeCoster, B., Fiore, A., Gasior, S., Le, H. M., Primo, L. H., & Reedy, T. D. (2020, February). The World Bank's SABER: A critical analysis. *Comparative Education Review, 64*(1) 46–65.

Klees, S., Samoff, J., & Stromquist, N. (Eds.). (2012). *The World Bank and education: Critiques and alternatives*. Sense.

Klein, N. (2014). *This changes everything: Capitalism vs. the climate*. Simon & Schuster.

Leamer, E. E. (1983, March). Let's take the con out of econometrics. *American Economic Review, 73*, 31–43.

Levin, H. M. (1995). School finance. In M. Carnoy (Ed.), *International encyclopedia of education* (pp. 412–419). Elsevier.

Levin, H. M. (1998). Educational vouchers: Effectiveness, choice, and costs. *Journal of Policy Analysis and Management, 17*, 373–392.

Marshall, A. (1890/1920). *Principles of economics*. Macmillan.

McCowan, T. (2003). Participation and education in the landless people's movement of Brazil. *Journal for Critical Education Policy Studies, 1*(1).

McLaren, P., & Kincheloe, J. (Eds.). (2007). *Critical pedagogy: Where are we now?* Peter Lang.

Mundy, K. (2002). Retrospect and prospect: Education in a reforming World Bank. *International Journal of Educational Development, 22*, 483–508.

Patrinos, H., & Psacharopoulos, G. (2020). Returns to education in developing countries. In S. Bradley & C. Green (Eds.), *The economics of education* (2nd ed.). Academic Press.

Picower, B. (2012). *Practice what you teach: Social justice education in the classroom and the streets*. Routledge.

Rakowski, J. (1980). The theory of the second best and the competitive equilibrium model. *Journal of Economic Issues, 14*, 197–207.

Robertson, S. L., & Dale, R. (2015). Towards a "critical cultural political economy" account of the globalising of educaation. *Globalisation, Societies and Education, 13*(1), 149–170.

Rodrik, D. (2008). *One economics, many recipes: Globalization, institutions, and economic growth*. Princeton University Press.

Rodrik, D., & Stantcheva, S. (2020, June 17). We need to create more good jobs. The old easy answers won't work anymore. *Market Watch*. https://www.marketwatch.com/story/we-need-to-create-more-good-jobs-the-old-easy-answers-wont-work-any-more-2020-06-17

Sen, A. (1999). *Development as freedom*. Oxford University.

Stiglitz, J. E., Sen, A., & Fitoussi, J. (2009). Report of the Commission on the Measurement of Economic Performance and Social Progress, Paris, France. www.stiglitz-sen-fitoussi.fr

Tarlau, R. (2019). *Occupying schools, occupying land: How the landless worker's movement transformed Brazilian education*. Oxford University Press.

Wall, D. (2015). *Economics after capitalism*. Pluto.

Ydesen, C. (Ed.). (2019). *The OECD's historical rise in education: The formation of a global governing complex*. Palgrave Macmillan.

3

The State, Social Movements, and Education

Between Reform and Transformation

Raymond A. Morrow
University of Alberta

Carlos Alberto Torres
UCLA

ABSTRACT

This chapter develops an analysis of the relationship between the state, social movements, and education from a historical and comparative perspective informed by critical social theory. The first section contrasts the more empirical American tradition of social movement theory to the more theoretical post-Marxist European tradition concerned with democratization and a distinction between "old" social movements based on social class and "new" movements concerned with identity politics and the quality of life. The second section introduces theories of sociocultural reproduction and change in education, drawing upon the European tradition (Jürgen Habermas and Claus Offe) to sketch an analysis of the relationship between democratic legitimation crisis and education. The third reviews an agenda of issues as topics for research: education as a target of and resource for movements; the historical expansion of mass schooling; student movements; teacher activism and professional movements; critical pedagogy and democratization; Southern theory and subaltern movements in the Global South (especially Latin America); movements as sites of learning; and the spectrum of reform possibilities from neoliberal through radical democratic and revolutionary. The conclusion reflects on risk society theory (Ulrich Beck) and the global implications of education and social movements as a now well-established, if dispersed subfield of comparative education.

■ ■ ■

The task of this chapter is to consider the relationship between the state, social movements, and education from a historical and comparative perspective. When it was first conceived in the late 1990s, and even in its subsequent publication in four editions with revisions, the topic was not widely recognized as a research field in education. At first glance, this might be a surprising claim, given the extensive research on reform movements in education. But the social movement problematic needs to be differentiated from earlier histories of "reform movements" in education based on official accounts of "progressive" histories that are generally ideologically deceptive: they mask the continuing reproduction of power, as well as the interests of the cultural capital of the professional experts of reform who speak the language of scientific "social ameliorism" and progress (Popkewitz, 1991). Such initiatives in reforming education "from above," even when cultivating stakeholder and special interest support, represent a form of elitist democracy very different from one whose dynamic character is linked to social movements from below or even those of largely middle-class origin.

With these historical considerations in mind, our earlier title referring to "social movements and educational reform" can be criticized as ambiguous, since historically few examples of reform have been strongly influenced by social movements in the sociological and political sense. This question is further complicated because in the context of education the political dominance of neoliberalism since the 1980s has created in developed democratic societies—most dramatically in the United States—a technocratic "cult of reform" that is driven by the logic of neoliberalization (Scapp, 2016).

Consequently, we now prefer to title our chapter "The State, Social Movements, and Education: Between Reform and Transformation" to highlight reform as a spectrum of possibilities—cosmetic, technocratic, transformative, radical, revolutionary—with no inherent relation to the increasingly contentious notion of "progress" or right versus left ideological distinctions. Especially problematic is the assumption of a "progressive" convergence on a "world culture" of education (Carney et al., 2011). Moreover, the social origin of reform projects—whether more elitist or inspired by social movements outside of official politics—has no automatic relation to their "progressive" effects or having an enduring value for processes of democratization. Social movements are not necessarily progressive and ideas originating in elites, for example, the history of the philosophy of education, often represent important contributions to humanization.

Nevertheless, certain cases of social movements in education can stand as models of a profound process of democratization at work. One of the most remarkable and now well studied is the relation between the civil rights movement beginning in the 1960s and education in the United States. What is less well recognized is that there is a much longer historical social movement trajectory represented by the earlier struggles of Black educators going back to the antebellum period (Anderson & Kharem, 2009). What is also striking about this case, however, is that it stands in relative isolation from a more theoretical and comparative account of education and social movements as foundational for the understanding of European and global modernity.

An excellent recent review article by Tricia Niesz et al. (2018), however, provides instructive reference points for rethinking the state of scholarship on education and social movements, calling for a "united field of scholarship": "we argue that the issue is not a lack of research on social movements and education; the issue is that this scholarship emerges from myriad fields across the interdisciplinary landscape of educational research, and these fields and their social movement researchers are not in conversation with one another" (p. 41).

In light of these changes, we have completely revamped our earlier strategy of presentation, which was caught between a review of the meager literature available and attempting to introduce themes relating to an alternative approach from the perspective of critical social theory, especially legitimation crisis theory. Given the availability now of a systematic review of the literature in English, we have shifted our focus to highlight key issues that were to some extent introduced earlier, but in need of more coherent development concerning our critical social theory approach to education and social movements, as well as taking into account the subsequent expansion of the literature. Our points of departure are several problematic issues and absences that were implicit in the just cited comprehensive review of fragmented research on education and social movements. This should not be read as a criticism of what the authors accomplished, especially covering such a complex topic in limited space, as opposed to using their analysis as a starting point for further development of the issues.

- The lack of consideration of the issues at stake in competing theoretical approaches to social movements. The first section will address this question by contrasting the dominant, more empirically focused American approaches to social movements with European ones that are divided between Marxist and post-Marxist perspectives.
- No consistent consideration of the theories of society, state, and democracy that could frame and give normative and analytical direction to such inquiries. For this purpose, the second section will consider education and social movements from the perspective of critical theories of social and cultural reproduction and transformation. It will be argued that the understanding of the relation of social movements to transformative educational change can best be further developed through a revival of Jürgen Habermas's theory of democratic "legitimation crisis" in the context of neoliberalism and recognition of the centrality of social movements in collective learning in his theory of communicative action.
- The need to highlight a wider range of topics central to the construction of a more unified field of research. The third section frames the distinctive character of education as a site of social movements in terms of being both a "target of" and "resource for" movements, as well as introducing an agenda of issues relating to education and social movements that raise important questions requiring further development.
- Finally, the need to expand the scope of issues in comparative education to include the theory of a "global risk society," a topic whose importance has been highlighted by a pandemic that can potentially help reset the agenda of global citizenship education.

THEORIES OF SOCIAL MOVEMENTS: AMERICAN VERSUS EUROPEAN PERSPECTIVES

Before turning to the relations between the state, social movements, and social change and reform in contemporary democratic societies, it is necessary to begin with a closer look at theories of social movements. This will require addressing the question of defining social movements, as well as developing a broad contrast between the American and European social movement theoretical traditions. As we will see, a weakness of the otherwise comprehensive discussion of social movements and education by Niesz and her collaborators was only alluding to, without clarifying these and related issues. Moreover, such problems also reflect a more general tendency in the field of education: rather imprecise or misleading characterizations of the relations between the now ambiguous concept of "critical theory" and Marxism(s).

Defining and Situating Social Movement Theory

Social movements represent a distinctive form of collective behavior that needs to be differentiated from more or less spontaneous activities such as crowd outbursts, looting, soccer hooliganism, or even riots that are isolated responses to a particular situation, for example, prison riots. Social movements have an ongoing identity and an inherent political dimension, though this may be indirect, as in the case of cultural politics. Their political appeals cover the ideological spectrum from right to left, ranging from calls for moderate to radical reform, or more comprehensive revolutionary transformations, whether more political (e.g., Marxism, fascism) or religious (e.g., theological regimes, messianic cults). The following definition of social movements captures many of the key issues:

> A social movement is a collective actor constituted by individuals who understand themselves to have common interests and, for at least some significant part of their social existence, a common identity. Social movements are distinguished from other collective actors, such as political parties and pressure groups, in that they have mass mobilization, or the threat of mobilization, as their primary source of social sanction, and hence of power. They are further distinguished from other collectivities, such as voluntary associations or clubs, in being chiefly concerned with defending or changing society, or the relative position of the group in society. (Scott, 1990, p. 6)

Several points are necessary to qualify and clarify this definition. First, "mass mobilization" needs to be understood relatively. For example, a local environmental movement may be successful in mobilizing in that immediate context, but by gaining regional or national attention it can persuade changes by local authorities or be supported by threats of higher political levels. Second, the definition does not refer explicitly refer to social movements as collective actors within "civil society," hence as forms of voluntary association *independent of* both the market and the state. Social movements are part of civil society, just as are political parties, charitable associations, pressure groups, and religious organizations. As a form of a political association, however, social movements are distinctive because they stand in opposition to existing electoral institutions as failing to adequately address their issues of concern.

Third, despite the reference to "defending or changing society, or the relative position of the group in society," the definition does not highlight sufficiently the fact that a sense of political *exclusion* from formal institutions of democratic representation motivates collective mobilization. As a more recent, succinct formulation puts it: "A social movement is an excluded collectivity in sustained interaction with economic and political elites seeking social change" (Almeida, 2019, p. 6). As well, six basic levels of social movement activity can be differentiated: "(1) everyday forms of resistance, (2) local grassroots movements, (3) national social movements, (4) waves of protest, (5) revolutionary movements, and (6) transnational social movements" (Almeida, 2019, p. 21).

Though the field of social movement studies is fragmented, it has been argued that there is a basis for a broad distinction between two broad traditions with rather different objectives: the more empirically oriented American tradition that has focused in general theories of social movements as expressions of often irrational collective behavior or the decisions of strategic rational actors, as opposed to a European critical social theoretical tradition concerned primarily with analyzing social movements from the political sociological perspective of their relation to social change and democratization within modern societies (Crossley, 2002). These two traditions will be introduced as part of the argument that the European tradition provides the most productive foundation for a theory of education and social movements, whereas the American tradition is more useful for empirical studies of specific movements.

Origins: From Crowds to Collective Behavior

Psychological theories tended to characterize early approaches to social movements in the late 19th century. Theories focusing on the irrational dimensions and destructive effects were closely associated with explaining the behavior of "masses," whether following French theorist Le Bon's theory of the "crowd" in the late 19th century or Freud's theory of "mass psychology" in the early 20th. Le Bon's theory had a particular appeal to the manipulative imagination of potential authoritarian leaders (Mussolini was a fan of Le Bon). The sociological origins of social movement theory can be found in the tradition of collective behavior theory developed in the Chicago School of sociology beginning in the 1920s. Though also reflecting the 19th-century fascination with and fear of crowd behavior, the Chicago School reinterpreted these issues in terms of the social psychological research paradigm of symbolic interactionism grounded in the writings of pragmatist philosopher George Herbert Mead. A key assumption, based on the model of the crowd, was that collective behavior was characterized by spontaneity, hence distinct from and less rational than institutionalized behavior. The primary focus was on developing typologies of collective behavior along a continuum of degrees of irrationality, for example, mobs, crowds, masses, social movements, and the public.

From the perspective of the later, and now dominant American tradition, which is concerned primarily with social movements and their relation to the state and "contentious politics," the collective behavior tradition had a flawed understanding of the specificity of social movements for several reasons: the emergence of movements was reduced psychologically to difficulties arising from "structural strains" and "anomie" (normlessness); protests were characterized as tending to be irrational, as in the case of "mob hysteria"; members of movements were depicted as isolated individuals (e.g., as part of "masses") and not well integrated into society; and the distinctive nature of social movements was not recognized because of lumping them together with a range of different manifestations of collective action such as panics, crazes, and crowds (Crossley, 2002, p. 11).

The New Dominant American Synthesis: Bringing the State Back In

In earlier editions of this chapter, we cited an article from the mid-1990s whose point of departure is no longer valid: "Surprisingly little attention has been paid to the interaction between social movements and the state" (Jenkins & Klandermans, 1995, p. 5). As critics of the older collective behavior approach, the authors referred to were part of an emerging tradition of social movements that made the state of central importance. Unlike the earlier collective behavior tradition's emphasis on the irrational, the newer theories emphasized the rationality of movements in the narrow sense of "strategic rationality" oriented toward realizing the group's interests. Despite the fragmentation of social movement studies, claims for a dominant paradigm emerged in the mid-1990s on the part of collaborations between North American and European scholars concerned with integrating previously competing and often antagonistic perspectives into an "emerging consensus":

> Increasingly one finds movement scholars from various countries and nominally representing different theoretical traditions emphasizing the importance of the same three broad sets of factors in analyzing the emergence and development of social movements/revolutions. These three factors are (1) the structure of political opportunities and constraints confronting the movement; (2) the forms of organization (informal as well as formal), available to insurgents; and (3) the collective processes of interpretation, attribution, and social construction that mediate between opportunity and action. Or perhaps it will be easier to refer to these three factors by the conventional shorthand designations of *political opportunities*, *mobilizing structures*, and *framing processes*. (McAdam et al., 1996, p. 2)

The concept of "political opportunities" (or "political process") refers specifically to the state and its capabilities for responding. From this perspective, social movements can only emerge when states enable them to do so, whether to actively incorporate them into political debate or because too weak to suppress them. Charles Tilly's (2005) pioneering research on "repertoires of contention" suggests that social movements are historically specific and coincide with the emergence of modern democracy, transforming "claims-making" from premodern forms that are spontaneous and fleeing direct activism (vandalism, seizures of grain, banditry) to those based on organized, sustained protest based on inventing new strategies (p. xx). Second, mobilizing structures refers to the so-called resource mobilization theory that focuses on the development of organizational capacities and financing. Many movements with substantial ideological appeal and relative political opportunities fail because of a lack of capacity for resource mobilization. Finally, "framing processes" refers to the ideological discourse of movements and their ability to communicate with and appeal to their potential constituencies. The incorporation of framing theory, however, creates some problems for the assumption of strategic rationality, especially when framing assumes forms that are substantively irrational, as in the case of more extreme cultic or fascist movements.

Two key characteristics of this later American tradition need to be highlighted in anticipation of the contrast with the European tradition: the absence of any explicit normative basis for assessing social movements beyond the degree that their strategies are characterized by individualistic forms of "strategic" rationality in achieving their ends; and the lack of a specific theory of society and democracy which would ground the theory of the state presupposed by the analysis of political opportunities and ideological framing. Judgments of movements as "progressive" and "creative" have to be made primarily from rather arbitrary, personal points of view. In other words, the concepts of political opportunities, resource mobilization, and framing tend to be value-neutral, micro-sociological, and ambiguous for the theory of society that is presumed. Consequently, a critical normative stance has no intrinsic relationship to the theories themselves beyond the strategic rationality criterion. For example, though the late Charles Tilly (2007) is justifiably regarded as one of the most important contemporary American sociologists, his otherwise analytically admirable book on processes of democratization and de-democratization does not adequately address the question of the "quality" of democracy and even fails to refer to neoliberalism and the vast literature on the erosion of American democracy. These blind spots are built into the analytical framework: he was perfectly aware of the issues via his radical activist son, a professor of economics, earlier teaching at the New School, and being a colleague of Jean Cohen at Columbia University, a prominent proponent of critical European social movement theory.

Concerning the second question of the lack of a specific theory of society and the state, a critique of the American contentious politics social movement tradition has been articulated in terms of "the strange disappearance of capitalism from social movement studies," which is to say a more explicit macro-sociological theory of society and political sociology of power and the capitalist state (Hetland & Goodwin, 2013). That "disappearance" refers to the earlier centrality of capitalism in the 1970s, which was largely developed by researchers primarily interested in social movements as "progressive" political movements. Though such work has continued in other contexts (e.g., critical sociology, some approaches to identity politics, or identification with the European tradition of social movements), even then it was largely peripheral to the narrower, more generic project of a unified social movement "theory." To frame the question in terms of the "strange disappearance of capitalism" rather than "Marxism" has other implications, suggesting that such questions are not a monopoly of Marxism. For example, the earlier work of Charles Tilly (1978) made capitalism central but analyzed it from an eclectic, "Marxisant" sociological perspective that included Marx, without embracing "Marxism." Various approaches make capitalism central: non-Marxist political economy, neo-Weberian sociology, the new institutional economics, economic sociology, or the several forms of post-Marxist critical social theory of the European tradition of social movements.

The Post-Marxist European Tradition: Bringing Capitalism Back In

Aspects of the European tradition were clearly articulated some time ago in a book by Ron Eyerman and Andrew Jamison (1991). Significantly, their "cognitive approach" was also the primary theoretical reference point of the review by Tricia Niesz et al. (2018) on social movements of education cited in the introduction. But the authors made no effort to compare it with the many competing approaches, or justify it beyond confirming their sense of the importance of creative ideas in social movements relating to education:

> Eyerman and Jamison (1991) have argued convincingly that the "forms of consciousness that are articulated in social movements provide something crucial in the constitution of modern societies: public spaces for thinking new thoughts, activating new actors, generating new ideas." (p. 161)
>
> We take this to mean that before social movements can move people, institutions, and culture in their fight to shape the future, they must move ideas. The educational implications of this statement are immense. Our scholarship as educational researchers ought to reflect this, and a first step is establishing social movements and education as an interdisciplinary field of scholarship. (pp. 31–32)

Even if accepting that the educational implications of the perspective represented by Eyerman and Jamison (1991) are "immense," considerably more "reflection" is required to understand the theoretical tradition within which they were working. The central theme of the discussion that follows will be that it is of crucial importance to problematize the concept of "critical theory" and its relation to social movements by differentiating between Marxist and post-Marxist approaches. Though the call for unification in the field is promising, there is considerable vagueness concerning the theoretical foundations of such a prospect. Consider the following ambiguous discussion by Niesz et al. (2018) of the relation between "critical theory" and "social movement theory":

> Critical theory is perhaps equal in influence to social movement theory across both categories of literature, and is often combined with social movement theory perspectives. . . . More specifically, much social movement-oriented educational scholarship across varied fields is informed by the work of Freire and Gramsci, both of whom were not only theorists but also personally involved with education in social movements for significant periods of their lives. Freire's perspectives on conscientization and pedagogical methods linked to personal and social transformation, along with Gramsci's theories related to critical consciousness, organic intellectuals, counterhegemony, and the forming of hegemonic blocs, have been of great interest to educational researchers studying social movements across varied fields of inquiry . . . relevant work on synthesizing the theories of Gramsci and Freire as they relate to education for social action). (Niesz et al., 2018, p. 24)

Beyond eliding the question of the exact relationship to Marx and Marxism, this summary does not address the range of possible implications of being "informed by" Freire and Gramsci, the specific meaning of "critical theory" as a form of social movement theory, or how to engage the proliferation of theories of social movements. Above all, what is required is a more differentiated analysis of the fundamentally opposed positions involved in relating "critical theory" and "social movement theory." Whose Gramsci, whose Freire? Which social movement theory? Even such a wide-ranging critical theorist of adult education as Stephen Brookfield (2005) is similarly evasive: "Yet, though critical theory can be conceived as a constant conversation with Marx, it is not a simple replication of Marxism" (p. 19). His formulation begs the question of the wide range of critical theory "conversations" and the specific methodological implications of alternatives to "replication." These variations suggest the need for a sharp distinction between Marxist (or "neo-Marxist") and post-Marxist perspectives, which in turn calls into question the unqualified use of the term "critical theory." At one extreme, John Holst (2002) defends a neo-Marxist approach that incorporates readings of Gramsci and Freire that, while not being an exact replication, entails fidelity to Marx and his philosophy of history based on the revolutionary mission of the proletariat. His formulation concisely and helpfully differentiates between what he calls a "socialist" (in the narrow sense of "classical Marxist," excluding social democracy) and a "radical-pluralist" perspective for "the new paradigm":

> Throughout this study, I use a radical pluralist-socialist dichotomy to reflect the major division within the debate over this new paradigm. The radical pluralists, who also call themselves radical democrats or post-Marxists, advocate social movement and civil society politics as a fundamentally new and more authentic politics capable of significant social transformation in the contemporary era. The socialist perspective is generally skeptical of the political potential of social movements, arguing that on their own new social movements tend to be temporary, largely middle class and therefore reformist, and easily so-opted by capitalist democracy . . . if we are to operate from a Gramscian perspective, we must take seriously his insistence upon the political party (an old social movement) as the fundamental organizational form to unite all the manifestations of resistance that confront us in our daily work as radical adult educators. . . . I based my critique on what I consider to be a classical Marxist position, which sees Marxism as a living and ongoing effort to understand and transcend capitalist relations. (pp. 8–9)

Though Holst's basic distinction sharpens the issues at stake, his terminology does not. A "paradigm" in the context of the social sciences refers to a "community" of researchers that share a set of common background assumptions and conception of the "object" of inquiry. Holst's distinction suggests *two very different, rival paradigms* that only share a "conversation" with Marx, Gramsci, and Freire. Further, given the varieties of socialism (e.g., Marx himself differentiated between "utopian" and "scientific"), it would be better to refer to a revolutionary and humanistic "scientific socialism" as perhaps a way to avoid the pejorative implications of the alternative of "communist." But that in turn would raise the thorny question of what makes Marxism more "scientific" than post-Marxist approaches. Further, if one defends Gramsci (as does Holst) as remaining an orthodox, revolutionary Marxist to the end of his short life (a contentious issue), then it would be appropriate to mention that this entails a sophisticated form of Marxism-Leninism. Peter McLaren (2016) has no need for euphemisms: "It is important to expose those left liberals and radical reformists who have emasculated and vulgarized the political center of gravity that informs Gramsci's revolutionary theories, thereby distorting his legacy as a committed communist" (p. 312).

Finally, to refer to the opposing paradigm as "radical-pluralist" has some justification, as long as it is not confused with traditional liberal understandings of pluralism. There are several post-Marxist routes to radical pluralism and a post-Marxist, democratic "conversation" with Marx and Gramsci. One influential version, the poststructuralist approach of Ernest Laclau and Chantal Mouffe (1985), pioneered the use of the term post-Marxist in defining their radical democratic conception of "socialist politics." The other main route—which has various paths that are broadly convergent—could be called "sociological" because its proponents attempt to take into account the various social scientific critiques of Marx in both classical (Durkheim, Weber) and contemporary sociology (e.g., Anthony Giddens, Pierre Bourdieu, Jürgen Habermas, Ulrich Beck), or strategies that more directly engage his economic and sociological theory (what was once called "analytical Marxism") (Heath, 2009).

One of the more unfortunate characteristics of many of those returning to Marx in educational theory is that they attempt to revive Marx directly, most often via Gramsci, without addressing the issues raised by sociological and analytical Marxist critiques (Ball, 2007). Michael Apple, however, is an important exception: From the orthodox perspective, "Weberians" such as Michael Apple and Jean Anyon are not "really" Marxist, or at best, pejoratively described as "neo-Marxists," because of rejecting the bipolar class model. The later Peter McLaren (2016), for example, dismisses Weber as someone who "frames class more in terms of consumption habits and lifestyle than objective conditions of exploitation." Further, he laments, ignoring some more recent sociology of education texts, that the Weberian consumption approach is the only theory of class available to teacher education students (McLaren, 2015, pp. 378–379). Not unsurprisingly, such authors in their amateurish discussion of theories of social class seem to have never heard of the rigorous sociological work of the late Weberian Marxist Erik Ohlin Wright (2002).

Though they call for the resurrection of a binary class model—the working class versus the bourgeoisie—they are confronted with the dilemma that the proletariat seems less and less capable of recognizing itself and that the Communist parties of France and Italy were disbanded some time ago.

In short, it is necessary to situate the origins of Eyerman and Jamison's critical social theory approach as distinct from Marxism, as well as part of a critique of the lack of a normative perspective beyond "strategic rationality" in the social movement theories that dominate American research. Instead, they seek to identify creative movements that can effectively produce and diffuse new forms of knowledge ("ecological science" is Eyerman's favorite example) and contribute to democratic social transformation.

The contemporary European tradition of social movement theory stands in the shadow of the Paris revolts of the spring of 1968 and other student movements around the world. On the one hand, these events continue to be nostalgically celebrated by some as the "world-historical moment" of the New Left, and theorized in neo-Marcusean terms as the "Eros effect" and "spontaneous combustion" (Del Gandio & Thompson, 2017). On the other hand, most of the noted contemporary theorists who were also affected by the experience of 1968 share a rejection of this mythical revolutionary imagery ultimately based on the Marxist philosophy of history. In somewhat different ways, they suggest alternative strategies for addressing the crisis and the political options available to social movements in advanced capitalism, for example, Zygmunt Bauman, Anthony Giddens,

Pierre Bourdieu, Michel Foucault, Ulrich Beck, and Habermas, who will be the focus of attention here.

The European tradition is defined by several variants of critical social theory that "bring capitalism back in" (a theme neglected in the American tradition), but in a manner distinct from orthodox Marxism. Consequently, the American and European traditions cannot be directly compared because they are addressing completely different questions. The more empirical American tradition oriented toward "middle-range" theory is concerned with general theories that can be applied universally—whether historically or comparatively. Consequently, this does not preclude their use as a methodological resource for case studies of specific movements from the critical social theoretical perspective of the European tradition (della Porta, 2015; Rucht, 2016). Moreover, European critical social theory has been used and further developed outside of Europe, as in the case of research on civil society in the United States that also draws on the more empirical movement theories (Cohen & Arato, 1992).

The European critical social theory tradition represented by social theorists such as Alain Touraine, Alberto Melucci, and Jürgen Habermas has been primarily concerned with the social theoretical question of the changed relationship between social movements and social change in contemporary advanced capitalist liberal democracies (see Castells, 2015). In this respect, they "bring capitalism back in" but in ways that diverge from Marxism, both analytically and politically. These approaches have a political and normative dimension that takes the form of a post-Marxist strategy that shifts from a focus on a revolutionary working-class party (Lenin) or the revolutionary working-class dominance of an alliance of classes (Gramsci) to the relationship between social movements and radical democratization, a framework that potentially provides shareable and persuasive criteria for both analyzing and criticizing emerging forms of movements and their relation to education.

EDUCATIONAL CHANGE AND SOCIAL MOVEMENTS: SOCIOCULTURAL REPRODUCTION AND TRANSFORMATION

From Functionalism to Social and Cultural Reproduction

To understand the relationship between social movements, education, and democratization from the perspective of post-Marxist critical social theory, it is necessary to turn to the history of sociological theories of education and social change. The basic sequence can be described in terms of the early dominance of liberal functionalist theory followed by the emergence of more critical conflict theories of sociocultural reproduction and transformation (Morrow & Torres, 1995). Whereas functionalist theory viewed the 19th-century expansion of public education as a natural outcome of modernization and social differentiation, conflict theories viewed it as reflecting the democratic struggles related to the emergence of working classes, other social movements, and the capacity of economic elites to control education policies in ways that ensured the formation of a docile labor force.

The origins of conflict theories of education can be traced back to Karl Marx's conception of social reproduction based on the distinction between the cultural and political "superstructure" and the material or economic "base." As part of the superstructure, educational institutions in capitalism functioned primarily to reproduce the kinds of workers needed by capital. Though Marx did not give much attention to education, partly because mass public education was institutionalized only after his death, later authors came to recognize the centrality of education to social and cultural reproduction. By the end of the 1960s, neo-Marxist theories of cultural reproduction called into question functionalist theory, demonstrating that despite the cosmetic changes produced by educational reform and the expansion of educational opportunity, institutions of education continued to reproduce the dominant order of social classes (social reproduction of workers) and the hegemonic cultural system that legitimated it (cultural reproduction of the dominant ideology).

The neo-Marxist approaches to social and cultural reproduction in education that emerged in the 1970s took two influential forms. French philosopher Louis Althusser's (1971/2008) "structuralist" Marxist theory gave education a central role as an "ideological state apparatus" that had considerable functional autonomy, but was ultimately serving the economic interests of the capitalist class "in the last instance." The relation of social movements to education was thus reduced to the working class. From Althusser's Marxist-Leninist political perspective, meaningful educational change had to await a working-class revolution. In contrast, the American economists Samuel Bowles and Herbert Gintis (1976) proposed a more empirical approach to educational reproduction based on a "correspondence principle" that identified how the school served as a "factory" for producing docile workers for capital, especially for the lower classes and minorities. They proposed that only a radical democratic socialist movement could transform American education, without providing a persuasive analysis of how such a movement might form (Bowles & Gintis, 1986; 2002). Their important work should be assessed today, however, in light of significant revisions in their empirical argument (e.g., a theory of socialization that recognizes agency) and a clarification of the postliberal, radical democratic primacy of their approach to socialism. In England, Paul Willis's (1977/1981) pioneering and highly influential ethnographic study of teenage "lads" showed that schools were also sites of "resistance" against the school's reproduction of social classes, even though the "agency" evident in such resistance was counterproductive in not taking advantage of the few opportunities available and not having any significant political effects. In all these cases, educational reproduction theory took a more or less *deterministic* form: the prognosis for transforming education was pessimistic and the strategy of analysis provided little insight into the broader questions of resistance and transformative movements, hence of the dynamic relationships between social movements, education, and social change (Giroux, 1983).

In contrast, more sociological, post-Marxist approaches to social and cultural reproduction have been influenced by Max Weber's critique of Marx's theory of social class and the related deterministic theory of social reproduction. Rejecting Marx's reductionist, binary class model based on a polarization between the working class and capital, Weber attempted to take into account the emergence of the middle classes and the need to differentiate between three bases of power: social class as a structural relation to the economy; status as a form of prestige based on expertise and education (e.g., the middle classes and professions); and other noneconomic sources of power such as political parties and religious institutions. In other words, *class*, *status*, and *power* gained through politics had created a plurality of conflicts and social movements in society, through which the continuing tensions between capital and wage-labor were refracted in complex ways. Such neo-Weberian approaches have provided the basis for a rich literature in the historical sociology of education and a more balanced assessment of the contradictory achievements and continuing deficiencies of modern public education.

The most influential theory of cultural reproduction in education today was developed by French sociologist Pierre Bourdieu (Morrow, 2014). Introduced partly as a critique of Althusser's structuralist Marxism, Bourdieu's theory synthesized insights from Marx and the classical sociologists Émile Durkheim and Max Weber. His relational sociology of practice links agency and structure, focusing on the notion of "habitus" or the internalized dispositions that are formed by educational systems which generate unequal outcomes because of the advantage of the cultural capital provided by family backgrounds (Bourdieu & Passeron, 1970/1977). Though his early account of reproduction theory was rather determinist, and he gave only limited attention to educational change or social movements, later developments in his approach provided a rich sociological framework for exploring the changing dynamics of sociocultural reproduction in education that takes into account the complexity of class structure and its reproduction and potential for transformation (Schmitt, 2016). Similarly, though the poststructuralist theorist Michel Foucault has also been productively used to study in a more differentiated way of educational reproduction in terms of "discipline," his more individualistic account of strategies of "counter-conduct" provides limited insight into the formation of social movements.

For example, though criticizing past curricular movements and building upon the work of William Pinar, James Burns draws upon Foucault without any reference to the implications of the potential movement dimension of individual practice: if "reconceptualized as complicated conversation imbued with the agency of subjectivity and historicality," curriculum "is also a site through which students and teachers can embody counter-conduct and generate new counter-politics against punitive disciplinary power and reconstruct themselves and the social world" (Burns, 2018, p. vii).

Habermas and Offe: Education, Legitimation Crisis and Social Movements

From our perspective, a potentially important resource for envisioning the transformative, radical democratic potential of education's relation to social movements can be found in Jürgen Habermas's critical social theory, despite his limited attention to education (Morrow, 2022, in press). One of his central concerns as the leading second-generation representative of the Frankfurt School tradition of critical theory has been a fundamental critique of the theoretical approach of his mentors. Though the heterodox neo-Marxist Frankfurt School tradition represented by key figures such as Max Horkheimer, Theodor Adorno, and Hebert Marcuse developed a theory of sociocultural production focusing on the "culture industries" of the new mass media, it largely neglected education. Moreover, early critical theory suffered from problems similar to that of the structuralist reproduction theory of Althusser and the original version of Bowles and Gintis's correspondence theory, or even Bourdieu and Foucault: the inability to locate potential sources of democratic transformation in the relations between the state, education and social movements, especially given the decline of working-class social movements.

The second generation of critical theory led by Habermas attempted to overcome what he saw as the weaknesses of this earlier Frankfurt School tradition: its pessimism, a continuing reliance on the Marxist philosophy of history, and an inability to formulate a constructive democratic political program. As an alternative, he developed a theory of emancipatory knowledge interests, legitimation crisis, communicative action, and deliberative democracy. This social theoretical framework provided the structural basis for rethinking the role of social movements in contemporary societies based on a distinction between the "old" social movements of the working classes oriented toward economic redistribution and the "new" social movements concerned with identity politics and recognition, as well as quality of life issues relating to questions such as the environment and peace (Finlayson, 2005; Ingram, 2010). Of key importance is that his approach provides a framework for interpreting movement ideologies in terms of different forms of rationality and reasoning (e.g., relating to the quality of life and democratic values), not just the strategic rationality of interests that is the focus of resource mobilization and contentious politics theories (Tucker, 1989). The differences between these two strategies have contrasting implications for learning and education. Whereas strategic rationality takes for granted that social actors naturally and validly know their interests and needs, limiting learning to expanding "repertoires of contention," social or normative rationality as understood by Habermas requires problematizing self-understanding as possibly deformed by markets and administrative power (including the history of colonialism), as well as by cultural traditions in need of revision. In modern societies, only education systems, subcultures, and social movements provide the potential learning communities that enable such self and collective reflection.

In the present context of the problem of the relations between education and social movements, two theses will be briefly introduced relating aspects of Habermas's approach that are particularly worthy of further exploration: the revival of his theory of democratic legitimation crisis as a research question and the basis of a critique of neoliberal policies in education; and the potential contribution of his theory of communicative action to recognizing that the neglect of education has been a major weakness of social movement theory generally. The first thesis is that the revival of his legitimation crisis theory provides a potentially fruitful strategy for conceptualizing education as a crucial site of contestation against neoliberalism. An analysis of the "legitimation crisis" of the democratic welfare state was developed in the early 1970s at the more theoretical level by Habermas, and elaborated more empirically by his former student, political sociologist Claus Offe. The concept of crisis in social and political theory is based on a medical analogy: just as pathologies of the body can produce crisis symptoms (fever, pain), pathological and contradictory social processes can result in social crisis as evident in dysfunctional institutions at the level of society. Social crisis theory also has a psychological dimension that brings it closer to crisis in a psychoanalytic sense: feelings of alienation, anomie (normlessness), and hopelessness at the individual level (Cordero, 2017). A key expression of such dysfunctionalities are social movements that arise across the ideological spectrum because of the failure of official democratic political institutions to satisfy the expectations of large numbers of citizens.

Habermas's analysis of the welfare state was based on a distinction between the early, laissez-faire capitalism confronted by Marx and "late capitalism" in its more democratic form as welfare state capitalism. In the early 1970s, responding to the fiscal crisis of the welfare state and more conservative worries about increasing "ungovernability," he attempted to diagnose this situation in terms of what he called a potential democratic "legitimation crisis" (Habermas, 1975). Though the modern state had some success using Keynesian policies to stabilize economic cycles, they remained, but had been displaced to other spheres resulting in crises of *rationality*, *legitimation*, and *motivation*. The state's "functional" rationality crisis arose from two contradictory demands: the demand of business for the accumulation of capital *and* responding to democratic expectations relating to public goods such as health and education, as well as offsetting the effects of unemployment, inequality, and poverty. The failure of the state to fulfill such expectations was increasingly reflected in "stagflation" (the combination of inflation without growth) and the "fiscal crisis of the state" as evident in resistance to higher taxes and the accumulation of public debt. Habermas's hypothetical diagnosis was that to the extent that the state could not meet these contradictory demands, there was potential for a political "legitimation crisis" that might result in more radical demands and social movements that might challenge state policies and the dominance of capital. Finally, such a radical transformation was predicated on the development of a "motivation crisis" that might emerge in a younger generation that was increasingly disenchanted by the weak link between education and promises of occupational success and more general dissatisfaction and alienation from life in a consumer society. As evidence, Habermas could draw upon examples of the student revolts of 1968, the "hippie" counterculture, and new social movements.

Claus Offe's related political sociology of the state was directed, initially in the German context, against both neo-Marxist interpretations (e.g., the "derivationist school") that viewed the institutions of the state rather directly reflected the imperative of capital accumulation and the liberal and social democratic approaches (e.g., Ralf Dahrendorf) that viewed the welfare state as having successfully dealt with the crisis tendencies of capitalism. Offe's (1984; 1985) approach, based on what he referred to as a "cheerful eclecticism," attempted to draw upon a variety of conceptual resources, for example, Marxism, systems theory, empirical political science, Max Weber, and Habermas (Bochert & Lessenich, 2016). His relational approach attempted to view the state, capital, and democracy as entangled in a series of contradictory and continuous changing tendencies that resulted in the emergence and then eventual crisis of the welfare state. To confront this fundamental contradiction, the state was obliged to increase its institutional functions and interventions, a process especially evident in the field of education. Though the growth of public education had already begun before the welfare state, the postwar period resulted in an unprecedented expansion, especially higher education, which according to the functionalist sociology of education should have—but failed—to ensure equality of opportunity and high levels of social mobility.

Nevertheless, the crisis did not materialize as hypothetically projected, mainly because of the emergence of a new capitalist strategy in the 1980s that was initially labeled "post-Fordism" (referring to an alternative to Ford's pioneering strategy of encouraging workers to become consumers and the welfare state as safety nets providing security). By the end of the 1980s, this new model of state regulation was increasingly referred to as "neoliberalism" and neoliberal globalization by its critics, and was symbolized in the regimes of Margaret Thatcher in Britain and Ronald Reagan in the United States. Consequently, Offe and Habermas largely abandoned this line of investigation because the democratic crisis appeared to have been avoided, though Offe and many others returned to legitimation crisis theory after the major economic crisis of 2007–2008.

The earlier legitimation crisis theory of Habermas and Offe not only anticipated aspects of the later formulation of new social movement theory, but it also provided a foundation for an analysis of the neoliberal state. Whereas the postwar welfare state had created a "pact" with labor that undermined the lingering working-class threat to capitalism, it had neither eliminated economic crisis tendencies nor resolved the problems associated with the effects of continuing and deepening economic inequalities, the increasing cultural diversity of the population, and new expectations emerging from social movements concerned with the politics of recognition and awareness of questions relating to the quality of life (e.g., the environment). Though the advent of neoliberalism in the 1980s had simultaneously lowered expectations by reducing democratic accountability and enhanced capital accumulation sufficiently to stave off the legitimation crisis of the 1970s, it had at the same time set the stage for a *delayed* crisis, as well as a precipitating the further proliferation of new types of social movements, including right-wing populism (Streeck, 2013/2017).

As Offe (1985) had argued, anticipating later neoliberal strategies, there was a transformation in the political strategy of the state from reactive, "conjunctural" policies that responded to immediate demands as they are first identified, to an alternative "structural" form of political rationality that attempted to sustain economic efficiency by anticipating future problems, for example, the expansion of vocational education (Bonal, 2003; Morrow & Torres, 1995; Torres, 1989). A related strategy of neoliberalism, analyzed in terms of Foucault's theory of governmentality, was making individuals increasingly responsible as "entrepreneurial" agents of their own fate (Ball, 2013).

Neoliberalism has extensively used public education as a scapegoat for problems generated primarily by the market system and state, as well as part of a proactive strategy of de-democratization disguised as the technical imperatives of economic efficiency to avert problems of ungovernability—hence political instability—that might arise from the mobilization of social movements. The consequence, at least where such policies actually dominate, has been to increasingly submit education to the supposed needs of the economy and reduce resources and programs that might contribute to the forming of active citizens who might question the legitimacy of neoliberal globalization (Giroux, 2020; Torres, 2009). Critics have also attempted to articulate alternative strategies, despite the difficulties (Peters & Jandric, 2018; Rudd & Goodson, 2017). Not surprisingly, the potential for education to become an important context for legitimation crisis has also become a new focus of attention, especially in the context of neoliberal efforts to dismantle public education (Bonnano, 2017; Borman, 2011).

The second thesis is that Habermas's critical social theory provides a framework for identifying education in modern societies as playing a decisive role in mediating between social movements and transformative political and social change, a theme that is completely absent in the contentious politics and resource mobilization literature and only hinted at by Habermas himself. The basis of his theory of society is that contemporary liberal democratic societies are integrated at two levels: the "system" level by money (markets) and power (state administration) and at the level of the "lifeworld" of everyday life through communicative interaction and democratic participation. However, the contradictions and conflicts generated at the level of the market and state have led to a "colonization of the lifeworld" by money and administrative power and a resulting erosion of democracy culminating in neoliberalism. In the context of the resulting crisis, social movements represent the primary context for democratic revival. Klaus Eder, a former collaborator of Habermas, summarizes the complex implications as follows:

> The main argument in the theory of communicative action . . . is that social movements can be seen as mechanisms triggering collective learning processes in societies. Social movements on the one hand acted against the systemic decoupling of state and markets from the life-world while drawing upon the resources that only life-worlds can offer, that is, the reference to basic moral standards contained in the structure of communicative action among free and equal people. *Social movements are phenomena, situated between systems and the life-world and fostered by the capacity to reclaim the normative standards betrayed by the systemic decoupling of politics and economic exchange as executed in the modern state and in capitalism.* Such normative standards not only included universalist moral standards of justice, but also standards of equal recognition and standards of cognitive knowledge made available by modern science. (Eder, 2015, p. 5, emphasis added)

Even though social movements potentially trigger collective learning, to the extent that they do so depends crucially on the reflexivity, resilience and quality of the knowledge and pedagogical strategies produced by and informing the mediating institutions of education (Kilgore, 1999; Welton, 1995; 2005). As will become evident in the next section, the sites of such collective learning are widely dispersed and have enjoyed highly variable degrees of success.

THE RELATIONSHIP BETWEEN EDUCATION AND SOCIAL MOVEMENTS: AN AGENDA OF ISSUES

The task of this third section will be to rather briefly introduce a rather heterogeneous agenda of more specific issues that have been topics of research—ranging from the now well-studied to the as yet marginal—on education and social movements. Though the treatments will vary in terms of length and adapted to the history and nature of the topic, they share a concern with illustrating potential areas of research as part of developing a more integrated field of education and social movement studies.

Educational Institutions as a Target of and Resource for Social Movements

Beyond other limitations discussed earlier relating to the absence of a normative perspective, the contentious politics approach of Charles Tilly and his collaborators, given its narrow definition of social movements as claims-making protests against the state, does not lend itself to the complexities and historical importance of education as a site of social movement activity. One of the most distinctive features of education as a site related to social movements is the role of higher education in particular as both a *target of*, and *resource for*, social movement activity in modern democratic societies. This ambiguous location of education as both distinct from the state and a source and evaluator of movement ideas has contributed to its virtual absence in the social movement literature as a distinctive topic, aside from the case of student movements to be discussed later.

On the one hand, institutions of education are targets of social movements demanding educational reform, whether curricular or relating to access and opportunities, as keys to the longer-term realization of their ideals. This represents the most familiar theme in the education and social movements literature and can be traced back to the early 20th-century student movements influenced by the "old" social movements of the working class, and now with the various demands of new social movements for educational change. There is now extensive literature on how the new movements have more or less successfully targeted higher education, with related effects at lower levels, relating to both identity and multicultural politics (race, gender, sexual orientation, disability, etc.) and sustainability and quality of life issues (Crossley, 2017; Henry, 2017; Snow, et al., 2019).

Several relatively neglected topics can be identified this context. Little attention has been given to often conflicting *relations within and between movements* competing to influence education, a topic that is related work on alliances of movements and to broader discussions of intersectionality in feminist theory and queer studies (P. H. Collins, 2019). Also significant has been the emergence of countermovements that seek to overturn or transform changes in education resulting from new social movements. While some of these are traditionalist, reactionary, or racist, the case of often justifiable reactions against specific forms of affirmative action in education presents a case of competing conceptions of "equality" that present complex empirical, juridical, and philosophical issues (Rhoads et al., 2005). Another relatively unexplored issue is the nature of "parasitic" relationships with a broader movement. For example, teaching in bilingual education in the United States has been identified as an autonomous movement (Cortina et al., 2015), even though the multiple affiliations of the participants might suggest locating it as a spinoff from Latino identity politics.

New social movements that are not based on identity politics, however, have different characteristics and problems of mobilization that suggest new avenues of comparative research. Most importantly, they are not based directly on the standpoint of oppressed groups and the victims of violations of human rights. Instead, movements concerned with environmental issues speak "on behalf" of nature, whereas human rights, peace, and postconflict education claim to speak, "on behalf of" and "with" those who have been victims (see Bekerman & Zembylas, 2012; Misiaszek, 2017; Verma, 2017). In this respect, such educational activities resemble "professional" movements in working for the benefit of others, even if some participants have related personal experiences. Finally, they are political in the distinctive sense in calling for "transformative learning" that, beyond cognitive learning, involves embodied experiential practice oriented to forming what has been described in the case of the environment in Bourdieu's terms as an "ecological habitus" (Haluza-DeLay, 2008).

On the other hand, less attention has been given to higher education as providing *resources for* social movements, taking often conflicting forms such as the following: providing foundational and innovative ideas; research that may facilitate justification in the public sphere, especially when academics embrace roles as public intellectuals; and, conversely, research whose evaluative and critical implications might contribute to reflexivity and self-criticism within movements or have implications for their de-legitimation, whether more generally or to particular tendencies. The more constructive role of higher education in serving as a resource that actively promotes particular movements has been reasonably well-studied in the literature relating to new social movements in the contexts of identity politics and environmental, peace and reconciliation education, as previously noted.

Less often considered from the perspective of the sociology of knowledge, however, have been the more critical debates *within* particular standpoints (e.g., women's studies) or the primarily *negative or even exclusionary* reception of some movements. In the former case, for example, internal histories have suggested a series of "waves" of feminist theory that is generally viewed as a progressive development, similar to the "accumulation" of knowledge in the natural sciences. In this respect, higher education, given the relative autonomy of academic work, serves as a constructive resource given its capacity to sustain high-level forms of dialogue, hence reducing the factionalism so prevalent and divisive in the case of debates within the movements.

Though many cases in the past illustrate examples of higher education serving as a resource for social movements, the history of exclusion is equally significant. The fate of the pioneering Black American sociologist W. E. B. Du Bois provides a poignant example of the difficulties. Though the pragmatist sociological tradition in which he was trained had neglected the topic of racism, his early research reworked its concepts as the basis for pioneering critical sociology of race. Nevertheless, he was marginalized within the academy and eventually left it to help found the emerging civil rights movement (Itzigsohn & Brown, 2020).

The more general implication of the Du Bois example is that higher education generally and schools of education in particular have selective and critical relationships to social movements, for better or worse, which require further investigation. A significant transformation of higher education since the 1960s has been the gradual if contested legitimation of human rights and social justice concerns as topics of research and practice across the disciplines. But that, in turn, has other kinds of exclusionary consequences. Conservatives often complain that their views do not receive "equal" treatment in higher education and many of their speakers have been denied the right to "free speech" on campus. There are many "studies" programs relating to race, women, and indigenous peoples, but none on the atheist "oppression" of religious "creationism" or advocacy of the revival of militant nationalism. Conservative think tanks and private, fundamentalist religious postsecondary institutions reflect this sense of exclusion and marginalization. Nevertheless, on the revolutionary left, there are similar experiences of exclusion, even if greater toleration within academic communities: there are no "studies" programs on the "oppression" of the working class either, even if such issues are studied in specialized fields. An important research question that arises from issues relating to the criticism and delegitimation of "nonprogressive" or "revolutionary" movements is whether there are not more constructive dialogical approaches to reconciling differences through mutual learning. As well, these issues are a reminder of the long, uneven history of the role of higher education and research in contributing to the legitimation, delegitimization, and transformation of social movements.

Old Social Movements: Educational Expansion and Mass Schooling

Though there is significant historical literature on education and social movements relating to the origins of public education, it has not been adequately integrated into comparative education or discussions of the social movements and education literature. These historical and comparative approaches to the origins of public education can be contrasted to the single factor approaches (human capital theory, functionalist differentiation in modernization theory), as well as the "world culture" theory pioneered by John Meyer. Beyond the more well-studied case of the French Revolution (e.g., Mary & Amirault, 2020), there are also pioneering historical discussions that have given particular attention in British context to the Owenite and Chartist movement on the origins of public education, as well as efforts of working movements of developing their own, autonomous educational activities (Dobbs, 1969; Thompson 1968). Obviously, similar transformations that were taking place in other European societies would provide instructive comparative reference points which have been taken up in part in the rich literature on the comparative historical origins of educational expansion and mass schooling. As well, this work needs to be reread and further developed in terms of a more integrated and theoretically well-developed version of the field. A pioneering neo-Weberian contribution was Margaret Archer's (1982) comparative analysis of educational expansion in Europe that provided a comparative national analysis of the interplay of diverse class positions and politics, giving some attention to pressures from social movements. Another earlier neo-Weberian study by Randall Collins (R. Collins, 2019) developed a critique of functionalism by showing that its analysis of education had overestimated the ability of educational expansion demanded by the middle and lower classes to resolve problems of inequality, hence not taking into account how "credentialization" led to an oversupply of educated workers. One of the few explicit contemporary attempts to link the state, social movements, and education as part of a general theory can be found in Martin Carnoy and Henry Levin's (1985) "social-conflict" theory of the state, which "provides a framework for developing a dialectical analysis of education in capitalist society, because it views social movements as playing a vital role in affecting educational policy" (pp. 46–47). On this basis, an effort can be made to "predict" educational reforms and assess the potential and limits of struggles over schooling. Nevertheless, this approach remains largely within the framework of the class-based assumptions of "old" social movement theory, ignoring the peculiarities of the new social movements.

Student Movements

Student movements are historically the most visible and well-studied example of education and social movements. The focus of this literature, however, reflects that it was written by people who were affected by student movements in their youth. Consequently, student movements have been analyzed primarily as *political movements*, hence for the most part in isolation from their relation to educational change and transformation or the relation between educational institutions and social change. Another characteristic of the student movement literature is that it is rarely comparative, primarily taking the form of case studies focusing on national contexts of revolt, revolution, modernization, and democratization around the world (Choudry & Vally, 2020).

Student movements have had a periodic influence in modern industrial societies, for example, the revolutionary uprisings in Europe after World War I; confrontations in Europe involving fascists, socialists, and communists in the 1930s; and the worldwide student revolts of the late 1960s. In many underdeveloped contexts, student movements have continued to be a source of agitation against more or less authoritarian states that serve to reproduce vast inequality of income and opportunity. Or even in relatively well-consolidated new democracies such as South Africa, the issue of racial inequities has resulted in widespread student protest, including violence.

Student movements—primarily in universities and colleges, but sometimes secondary schools—represent the most important exception, if only partial, to the parasitic character of the relation of education to social movements. Student activism may be closely linked to existing social and political movements or be relatively independent, as in the case of more recent opposition to tuition levels, though embedded in larger issues. For example, the protest against neoliberalism in Quebec higher education in 2012 had a relatively narrow focus (Bégin-Cauette & Jones, 2014; Giroux, 2013), whereas more expansive political agendas have been evident in South Africa and Chile (Booysen, 2016). Though student activism in education has been for some time less evident in the United States than in many other countries, there have been more recent movements relating to opting out of standardized exams and demands for greater gun controls. Finally, the efforts of Swedish teenager Greta Thunberg to facilitate the international mobilization of more than a million students to protest against climate change suggest an unprecedented emergence of generational consciousness.

A characteristic of student movements is that they mobilize around a specific issue with much broader political implications, which in turn becomes an internal source of division between more "issue-focused" moderates and "radical" efforts to expand the agenda of demands. Student movements also typically have a dual inward and outward agenda, especially when influenced by existing social movements: one face is directed toward educational institutions as a prefigurative model for radical change, and the other the transformation of society. The great weakness of student movements, however, is that their life span tends to be generationally limited, hence episodic and with only limited continuity. The few exceptions, however, suggest important comparative research questions where intergenerational continuity is evident, for example, in Chile and South Africa.

Teacher Activism: From Professional Movements to Education as a Social Movement?

Though often overlapping with student movements, teacher movements have rather different characteristics given the ambivalent social location of teachers as a professional interest group and the particular characteristics of unions in education. Though the emergence of mass public education in the 19th century has been viewed as an outcome of various social movements, teachers have also often been active participants. An early example of teacher involvement in a social movement is the seemingly respectable, noncontroversial institution of the kindergarten. But if we listen to the voice of a 21-year-old woman—who later became an international leader in the international kindergarten movement—beginning her studies in the year of the Revolution of 1848 we hear a different story: "Finally, finally, I will feel free!" she confided to her diary. 'I will have a profession, which will give me the right to think, to develop my intellect'" (Allen, 2017, p. 1). Though her famous teacher Friedrich Fröbel (1782–1852) gave the concept its name, less well known is that the kindergarten movement "actually began as the radical creation of feminists, revolutionaries, and political exiles" (Allen, 2017, p. ix). The year before Fröbel's death, the fledgling kindergarten project was banned in Prussia and other German states as fostering "socialism and atheism." Only with the later lifting of the bans did the kindergarten movement expand as a transnational one that was primarily created by women: "the kindergarten became the center of a movement for educational and social reform—a movement that spread to many parts of the world but had its greatest success in North America" (Allen, 2017, p. 2). Though having national variations, the movement viewed itself as embodying the universal needs and interests of children everywhere.

Similarly, popular education as inspired by Paulo Frere in Latin America had an important dimension as a movement within education forming alliances with popular social movements, initially focusing on informal literacy education. Henry Giroux's (1992) critical pedagogy has attempted to generalize Freire's example by attempting to appeal to teachers and cultural workers to become agents of educational change by becoming public intellectuals. Nevertheless, critical pedagogy has remained more of a force within faculties of education than a grassroots movement mobilizing teachers. In an interesting and surprisingly neglected strategy of research, Tricia Niesz (2018) has investigated the question of "when teachers become activists" with distinctive characteristics as "professional" movements. Important questions include the extent to which teacher organization around unions also have a "new social movement" dimension directed toward radical educational reform and race and gender, hence better understood as forms of "professional" activism that cannot be reduced to the traditional unionism of "working-class" movements (Bascia, 2015; Blanc, 2019; Todd-Breland, 2018).

Though the concept of transformative "professional movements" is not well developed, a recent study in the field of public health, based in the international movement for health universalism, suggests that under the right political conditions, professionals have untapped potential for participating in policy transformation. Based on case studies of health professionals and lawyers in Thailand, Brazil, and South Africa, the following important thesis has been proposed:

Although conventional wisdom has emphasized the way in which democratization empowers the masses, this book draws out an underappreciated dynamic: *the extent to which democratization empowers elites*, who in turn can have a progressive impact on politics. As I show, these newly empowered (and public-minded) elites, in turn, often work on behalf of the poor and needy to institute important new social rights. (Harris, 2017, pp. 5–6, emphasis added)

These examples in the health field are the inverse of the more general tendency within education, where neoliberal "reform" has disempowered teachers, for example, in the United States where "as the influence of testing company lobbyists, billionaire philanthropists, and for-profit providers has grown, the strength of the unions (historically teachers' most powerful advocates) has declined" (Niesz, 2018, p. 25).

The more recent expansion of concern with global citizenship education has also opened interesting research questions relating to transnational movements—composed primarily of activist professionals—with pedagogical implications of various kinds. Transnational movements take many different forms that cannot be fully understood in terms of approaches designed for contention within the civil society and the public sphere of the nation-state. For example, Oxfam as an educational and antipoverty organization operating in a majority of the countries of the world views its mission in terms of a global civic education movement: "Towards Global Equity offers an invitation to the growing number of individuals, groups and organizations throughout the world who share Oxfam's belief that ending poverty requires *a global citizens' movement* for economic and social justice" (Spring, 2004, p. 37, emphasis added). And invoking a version of popular education in the Global South, Santiago Rincón-Gallardo (2019) has provocatively proposed the reframing of educational change itself as part of a social movement.

Critical Pedagogy: A Failed Unifying Social Movement?

Critical pedagogy can be viewed as originating in an attempt to sustain a relation between the older and newer social movements through a universalistic vision of radical democratization. The relation of mutual learning between Henry Giroux and Paulo Freire illustrates the rationale for such an open-ended "language of possibility" and its vision of "unity in diversity." On the one hand, Freire was forced by his dialogue with Giroux to confront the tensions between his earlier class-focused conception of popular education and the broader, multidimensional character of his concepts of oppression and dialogue. When viewed in this generalized, "progressive postmodern" way, resistance to oppression through the "language of possibility" could incorporate all of the issues of new social movements, thus linking redistribution, recognition, and their relation to cosmopolitan "border" issues such as decolonization, ecopedagogy, sustainability, and peace. In the context of the democratic transition in Brazil, this unifying agenda based on critical citizenship education and "unity in diversity" had a certain plausibility in the context of a radical democratic political party with a social movement dimension that eventually gained power.

In contrast, Giroux's conception of a universalizing critical pedagogy lacked an "addressee," hence was doomed to failure given the absence of a social movement or political party that could bring together issues of class, race, and gender. Despite a flirtation with postmodernism and partly because of wariness about the essentialist and fragmenting tendencies of identity politics, his approach never completely lost its connection with older social movement issues of redistribution, a point implicit also in his later slogan of "beyond modernism and postmodernism" (Giroux, 2011). His universalizing message was thus necessarily directed primarily to teachers and other cultural workers as potential "public intellectuals." Yet this was problematic because to the extent that they were receptive, they were already engaged with or being recruited by the various fragments of the new social movements and identity politics. From this perspective, his later shift to the theme of the neoliberal assault on youth can be viewed as part of longer-term hope for the emergence of a generationally based and more integrated radical democratic movement. Jean Anyon's (2014) more focused argument for a new democratic movement in the United States centered on radical reform in education suggests the possibility of an alliance of already existing movements, but there are few signs of this happening soon.

Latin America and the Global South: Southern Theory, Subaltern Social Movements, and Decolonization

The old versus new social movement distinction in its original form is largely specific to the context of Western Europe and other relatively affluent democratic societies. The Global South presents diverse situations that do not fit this model, even if overlapping in important respects, giving rise to a tradition of "southern theory" (Connell, 2007). On the hand, there are new social movements made up of largely middle-class members, largely urban, who have often become a significant voice in politics and public education, for example, relating to issues such as gender, sexuality, or the environment, where indigenous groups have also been prominent (Almeida & Ulate, 2015; Alvarez et al., 1998; Avritzer, 2002). The rise of identity and multicultural politics, however, has increasingly expanded the participation of indigenous and other rural and marginal groups (Eisenstadt et al., 2013). Consequently, a novel, hybrid configuration that retains important aspects of class-based "old" social movement theory is more characteristic of the Global South given that the majority remain relatively marginalized and in poverty. Given constraints of space and competence, we will focus on Latin America.

A pioneering example of an alternative postcolonial "southern theory" in education is the approach to "popular education" developed by Paulo Freire in Brazil (Morrow, 2013). Though developed before the old-new social movement distinction in the context of what was then called the "third world," Freire's approach was grounded in an explicit conception of "education as political" in the sense of providing the citizenship competence necessary for participation in social movements given exclusion from official politics (Morrow, 2021a). From the outset, despite identifying with Marxism by the end of the 1960s, he used the concept of "the oppressed" rather than "the proletariat," using plural terms such as "popular classes" or "working classes" to indicate the primacy given to local contextualization of pedagogical projects and resistance to the lingering effects of colonialism and economic dependency. Consequently, popular education from the beginning was inherently linked to diverse radical democratic social movements and open to the issues introduced by "new" social movements. A central objective was to facilitate, through the use of participatory methodologies, the formation of active citizens with competencies necessary for participation in the various kinds of social movements necessary to confront their exclusion from the more formal, official channels of participation in weak, unconsolidated democracies. By the 1980s, given that Freire had never been strongly class-reductionist in a Marxist sense, popular education began to incorporate a variety of influences from the "new social movements," thus engaging a broader agenda of "oppressions" relating to identity politics and the environment, without abandoning its concerns with social class and redistribution. After his return to Brazil, during his two years as head of the public school system of São Paulo, he introduced radical reforms that demonstrated the potential of his approach based on the principle of "unity in diversity" by attempting in practice to overcome the polarization between old and new social movements (O'Cadiz et al., 1998). The concept of popular education was also adapted to more affluent and democratic societies to engage various kinds of marginalized populations in fields such as education, health, and social work.

More recent developments in the Global South continue to suggest patterns of social conflict rather different than the classic European working-class model of movements. Though there are relatively weak urban working-class movements closer to what Marx had in mind, more significant, however, has been the mobilization of more militant, largely rural equivalents of his "lumpenproletariat" or what has been labeled as "subaltern social movements." Such movements remain very heterogeneous and tend to be fragmentary, local, and rural, suffering from dispossession driven by global "extractive" forms of investment capital. Nevertheless, "these formations include . . . increasing resilient Southern subaltern social movements (SSMs), sociopolitical formations market by their perennial political presence and obstinacy (refuse to disappear?) in face of these repeated colonizations" (Kapoor, 2009, p. 72). In the case of Latin America, a persuasive case has also been made, in a sympathetic critique of the new social movement approach, for the continuing importance of structural arguments for understanding both persisting working-class movements and the differentiation within the newer ones (Wickman-Crowley & Eckstein, 2015). The journal *Interface*, subtitled "A Journal for and About Social Movements," publishes both activist and more academic work oriented toward such movements around the world.

The central themes of social movement demands relating to education more generally have been given access and quality, though in response to postcolonial and decolonial theory (Andreotti, 2011), decolonization of Eurocentric and nationalistic curricula has also become an important issue, especially for indigenous groups in the context of bilingual intercultural education (Cortina, 2017; Smith et al., 2019). Indigenous movements thus present an exemplary case of the relation between new social movements and education given the primacy of cultural decolonization, despite the contested character of what that might or should mean. And as Regina Cortina (2011) emphasizes, such change was driven by grassroots movements:

> the empowerment of women and indigenous groups took place not because of state action but because of social movements contesting the restricted identity and incomplete citizenship provided for them through the capacity of the nation-state.

It is crucial to understand the "full social ends of education" to see the way forward in strengthening education, citizenship and social opportunity. (p. 1197)

In the case of Latin America, a variety of civil society organizations (CSOs) have also played an increasingly important role in education reform, often assuming advocacy roles that reflect a cooperative relationship with the social movements that originally put the new issues on the agenda of reform:

> Examples of CSOs—grassroots organizations, cooperatives, NGOs, unions, philanthropic foundations, mutual aid associations, religious organizations, community-based organizations, transnational advocacy networks, and student organizations—suggest their diverse structures, ideologies, and resources. (Cortina & Lafuente, 2018)

Some subaltern movements have tended to become self-determined sites of learning, especially where attempting to transform public education appears to be futile. Two of the most well-known examples of autonomous, counterhegemonic education projects are the Zapatistas in Mexico (Baronnet, 2008) and the Landless Workers Movement in Brazil (Tarlau, 2015). Not only do they attempt to produce knowledge "from below" that is resisted by the dominant educational system, they also publicize the illegal practices and abuses relating to policing, pollution, criminalization of protest, and the effects of poverty and oppression. Nevertheless, such extreme communitarian forms of collective self-isolation to gain self-determination can be criticized for seriously limiting the life chances of its youth, imposing a narrow conception of identity and autonomy that makes life outside the subaltern community a difficult and rare choice (Arnove & Bull, 2015).

Social Movements as Sites of Learning: History's Schools

As distinct from the preceding discussion of various examples of the dispersed literature on the relations between social movements and education, adult education has developed more coherent literature on education and learning "in" social movements. A central theme is the particular contribution of social movements as counter-publics and sites of learning is captured by their characterization as "history's schools," which is to say history as rewritten from the perspective of those whose perspectives had not been adequately addressed in the hegemonic system of public education (Choudry & Vally, 2018; Hall et al., 2012). Though that problematic has a longer history in adult education that was preoccupied with the traditional working class where it was pioneered, the theme of social movement learning now has become central to new social movements, as well as subaltern movements and popular education in the Global South. In this context, small-scale social experimentation and the expansion of the "social economy" are playing key *prefigurative* roles in both the Global North and South. As social movement theorist Geoffrey Pleyers (2018) has argued:

> Indigenous communities, small farmers, critical consumers, and "transition towns" have all contributed to renew the environmentalist movement by implementing alternative practices at the local scale and in their daily life. These actors

have focused most of their energy in building "spaces of experience" where alternative practices are experimented with and implemented. (n.p.)

Tricia Niesz and her collaborators (2018) have developed an instructive characterization of the five types of knowledge evident in social movement learning, ranging from the more instrumental to the more critical:

1. Scientific, expert, and movement-promoted knowledge about issues central to the social movement . . .
2. Skills and practices of organization, mobilization, and collective action . . .
3. The vision of the movement . . .
4. Individual and collective identity . . .
5. Social critique and agency . . . (pp. 14–15)

The Spectrum of Educational Transformation: Between Reform and Revolution

As awareness of the history of educational reform suggests, one of the most contentious issues has been the labeling of change efforts, whether as part of a discourse of public justification or more analytically as part of a typology of what might be called the "spectrum" of educational transformations. The use of the omnibus term "reform" obscures the issues at stake. As was recognized some time ago with the introduction of an epidemiological metaphor, educational policy reforms issues had increasingly become an elite level response to a perceived crisis that had the characteristics of an epidemic. Though ideally, this could involve a process of mutual learning, this appeared to be rarely the case (Levin, 1988). At the opposite extreme, efforts to identify approaches and policy in pedagogy and education as "revolutionary" introduce a rather different complex of semantic difficulties. Without pretending to provide a systematic response to these issues, several basic distinctions can clarify the issues at stake.

For the revolutionary end of the spectrum of labels, it is important to differentiate a revolution in scientific or disciplinary discourse (e.g., the Copernican revolution) from a social revolution. But even the category of social revolution has diverse implications, as when Marx himself speaks of the "bourgeois revolution" against feudalism. The reception of Paulo Freire's pedagogy has been plagued by such issues, given that his conception of critical literacy could be described as both a "revolutionary" methodology in the disciplinary sense relating to critical literacy in adult education, but one that lent itself—following Freire's example in Africa and his identification with Amilar Cabral's anticolonial revolution—to being instrumentalized as part of a social revolution.

As a response to these problems, it is important to differentiate more clearly between radical democratic revolutions and the Marxist-Leninist revolutions of the type found in the Russian Revolution, Mao's China, and Castro's Cuba. The educational revolutions carried out by Marxist-Leninist single-party regimes have generally suppressed the potential alternative "socialist" visions of education by typically labeling them as "anarchist." Nevertheless, anarchism as a cultural movement has been a rich source of a wide range of creative pedagogical ideas (e.g., the "free school movement") that constitute an educational philosophy that is distinct from both libertarian and child-centered education (Suissa, 2006).

Consequently, Marxist-Leninist revolutions need to be sharply differentiated from educational "revolutions" that were the product of more open democratic struggle involving multiple movements. In short, there are many intermediate possibilities of change in education between neoliberal technocratic reform and revolution carried out by a political party with a monopoly of power from above.

Three historical cases can be singled out to illustrate such possibilities, which are characterized by the intersection of competing social movements with more or less different conceptions of transformation: the Mexican Revolution; the so-called "Quiet Revolution" in Quebec in the 1960s; and the ongoing transformation of education in Chile. Other cases in Latin America merit attention, as well as South Africa as a laboratory of experimentation in democratic education. The Mexican Revolution, despite its elitist institutionalization and the eventual hegemonic dominance of a single party, nevertheless produced an educational revolution that was the outcome of the confluence of several types of social movements: Pancho Villa's northern movement appealing to small independent farmers and ranchers; Emiliano Zapata's peasant revolution composed of communally organized mestizos and indigenous peoples; small but intellectually and culturally significant anarchist and revolutionary Marxist groups; middle-class liberal democratic, anticlerical modernizing movements; and the emergence of defenders of women's rights in all these tendencies in an otherwise very patriarchal culture (Vaughan, 1997).

Though not well known outside of Canada, Quebec's "Quiet Revolution" resulted in a democratic educational "revolution" with important implications for any comparative sociology of education and social movements (Behiels, 1985). Until the late 1950s, Quebec had remained a traditionally conservative society with education under the control of the Catholic Church. Nevertheless, after World War II two social movements had emerged to challenge the traditional regime: a liberal and social democratic movement with links to unions and influenced by the "personalist" Catholic movement in France; and a neonationalist movement partly inspired by anticolonial movements in the third world and the American civil rights movement. The Liberal Party that gained power in 1960 established a provincial royal commission on education that orchestrated a reconciliation of conflicting demands, providing the framework for institutionalizing a completely new, secular educational system.

Finally, as the outcome of many years of student movements, Chile is in the process of reconstructing its educational system, as well as the writing of a new constitution to replace the one inherited from the Pinochet dictatorship. The outcome of these transformative movements has been described sociologically with a term that might be applied as well to the Mexican and Quebec cases: the idea of *"refundación,"* hence of a "re-founding" as a radical democratic transformative process that falls between the technocratic jargon of reform and the authoritarian rhetoric of revolution (Garretón, 2014).

The more conservative and technocratic end of the spectrum beginning with "reform" presents a rather different complex of issues that was obscured by our earlier vague use of the term "educational reform." The stricter meaning of social movements as a challenge to existing institutions should be differentiated from the quite different and "weaker" conventional understanding of *reform movements* in education, which for the most part have been elite-driven, of quite variable significance, and typically—unlike the civil rights movement in American education—have little to do with politically threatening mass mobilization outside normal political channels. For the most part, in short, they take the form of "professional" movements, some with small popular followings, that use more or less dramatic rhetoric about "transforming" education, for example, behaviorism, and later cognitive psychology; proponents of "phonics" in reading or "back to basics" in the curriculum; "creationist" demands for teaching "intelligent design" in science; or the "cultural literacy" movement inspired by E. D. Hirsch. Such "reform movements" need to be differentiated from those with links to social movements that reflect efforts to redemocratize education, or empowered by the spaces opened up by radical democratic initiatives.

Indeed, the very term "reform" has been appropriated in a manner that has been described satirically by Pasi Sahlberg's (2012) "Finnish lessons" with the acronym "GERM": Global Educational Reform Movement. The five key symptoms of infection by this pandemic are the following obsessions now associated with neoliberalism: standardization; a focus on core subjects; the search for a low-risk way to reach learning goals; the use of corporate management models; and test-based accountability policies. Though still claiming to provide a scientific, nonideological agenda for reform, this global elite "movement" is different than the older "ameliorist" traditions of educational reform movements because it tends to reduce its social scientific justifications to economic rationality, disregarding professional perspectives and the practical experience of teachers. Nevertheless, the earlier and more recent technocratic traditions share characteristics of an elitist reform movement led by "experts" without a radical democratic mandate, hence distinct from the mobilization of social movements outside of official electoral politics or democratic professional movements.

Another expression of the ambiguity of interpreting reform related to neoliberal "reform" are cases relating to the evaluation of expanding of school "choice," for example, through charter schools and the use of vouchers. An instructive version of these issues and their relation to critical social theory can be found in efforts of some in the "charter school" groups in the United States to justify themselves as creating educational "counter-publics" and authentic democratic pluralism. Nevertheless, empirical research has called these claims into question by showing that most charter schools create new forms of segregation (Wilson, 2011). Consequently, transformational and radical reform must be defined in terms of a "view of educational counterpublics as social and discursive spaces that can present radical challenges to our fundamental social and political ideas, over a view of counterpublics as making demands for educational access, provision, and content within, and on the terms of, the existing political system" (Suissa, 2016, p. 772). The choice movement in education, despite the good intentions of most participants, evades the challenges of investing in radical reform in education across the board and contributes to the undermining of community-based public education and eroding a sense of shared citizenship. As a detailed historical study of the use of vouchers in the United States concluded: "Perhaps more than any other education reform, school vouchers are an example of a social policy emanating from conservative circles" (Carl, 2011, p. 201).

CONCLUDING PANDEMIC REFLECTIONS ON OUR GLOBAL RISK SOCIETY: SOCIAL MOVEMENTS, GLOBAL CITIZENSHIP EDUCATION, AND COSMOPOLITANIZATION

As the preceding review of an agenda of issues relating to education and social movements has attempted to demonstrate, the topic has finally emerged as a central problematic in comparative education. To draw out the broader pedagogical implications, we will argue that such research should become central to civic education and its intrinsic relationship to global citizenship education and cosmopolitanism, or more precisely to *cosmopolitanization* (Torres, 2017). Understanding social movements should be central to civic education because it provides a historical laboratory for analyzing the relative success of democracies and their continuing failures. The very fact of the existence of social movements and their capacity to voice indignation on the margins of the public sphere and official electoral politics is a sign of the necessary tolerance and pluralism that defines democracy. In contrast, the official absence or relative marginality of movements—as in the cases respectively of the People's Republic of China and Putin's Russia—reflect the more or less effective criminalization of dissent.

Nevertheless, the proliferation of social movements is also indicative of the ongoing legitimation crisis of official electoral politics, given the failure to confront a variety of unmet needs relating to recognition and inequality, chronic abuses of power, and an incapacity to act in name of future generations and the earth as a sustainable habitat. Another manifestation of paralysis is the sense of powerlessness expressed in the general decline of political participation in liberal democracies and the difficulties of social movements in have significant effects on transforming policy outcomes.

Drafting this revised chapter in the wake of the COVID-19 pandemic has provided a context for further reflection on the crisis of democracy. The sociologist Manual Castells (2020) has described the pandemic as an opportunity for an epochal "reset": "The necessary reset is an entrance way toward another form of living, another culture, and another economy" in which the democratic "public" is given more priority in the organization of the economy and society (p. 103). Underlying this suggestion is the political adage "never let a good crisis go to waste." Setting aside the disputes about the origins of the phrase, its content can be traced back through Machiavelli and the history of power and politics. To speak of "good" here is of course ironic because a crisis is "all the better" to the extent that it is a source of fear and anxiety. Moreover, crises have been most often been taken advantage of by tyrants. But there have been episodes of history where they have been transformed into opportunities for "collective learning," a theme central to the more hopeful side of Habermas's conception of a democratic "legitimation crisis" and "normative revolutions." Though the pandemic has resulted in setbacks for social movements given the severe restrictions on assembly, it is also created conditions for a potential renewal of democratic politics.

The pandemic also serves as a reminder that what "was" postmodernism and its understanding of so-called postmodernity provided little guidance for such a "reset" and has inadvertently contributed to de-democratization. The exaggerated and overly dramatized postmodernist destabilization of scientific "truth" set the stage for "post-truth" acquiring a degree of populist legitimacy, undermining the very idea of democratic deliberation as a dialogic process. The epochal turn of events initiated by the pandemic can thus be read as a reconfirmation of an alternative to postmodernism: the late German sociologist Ulrich Beck's (1944–2015) theory of a "second modernity" in the form of a "reflexive modernity" as a more concrete, sociological elaboration of the implications of what Habermas called an "incomplete modernity." The resulting theory of the "risk society" is based on the thesis of a transition between an "industrial society" and a new form of modernity that questions its foundations (Mythen, 2020; Tooze, 2020). From this perspective, most of the epistemological questioning of modernity highlighted by postmodernism was prefigured in modernity itself in contexts such as romanticism, Dewey's critique of the "quest for certainty," the sociology of knowledge and the Frankfurt School, and historical and social studies of science. For Beck and others such as Anthony Giddens and Habermas, therefore, reflexive modernity is a radicalization of modernity. Though not normally considered as a theorist of social movements, Beck's concern with environmental movements locates his work within the trajectory of "new social movement theory" in ways that have not been adequately developed. Social movement research has tended to focus on progressive movements oriented toward social justice, often summarized in terms of the tensions between the politics of "recognition and redistribution." Nevertheless, Beck's approach suggests a third, cross-cutting theme of justice in the form of the "politics of risk" (Hudson, 2003). Though this concern is implicit in the concept of those "new social movements" oriented to the quality of life, the emphasis shifts in his work to future threats to well-being and life as such. Moreover, his approach anticipated more recent discussions of the "posthuman," even if providing a rather different and more sociologically grounded, decentered critical humanist interpretation of relations between humans and nature. As well, his strategy does not entail ignoring issues of economic inequality and social class, even if suggesting that greater economic equality by itself would not confront the risk of the potential "bads" that confront us all. Indeed, an obsessive, narrow focus on economic redistribution (or recognition) distracts attention from investing in the reduction and more equitable sharing of risk, which necessarily takes the form of "cosmopolitanization" as a process:

> More precisely, to ensure the survival of all a worldwide collective learning process in a very brief space of time ("fast learning") is required. All nations, all religions, all ethnic groups and the individuals belonging to them must work toward reducing national and religious conflicts and foe images so that they do not hinder the possibility of "saving cooperation." In other words: *Particularities yes, foe images no!* . . . Otherwise the crisis will turn into a catastrophe, the community of fate into a community of downfall. (Beck, 2011)

Nevertheless, in this epochal context the proliferation of social movements, whether on the right or left, has ambivalent implications for such possibilities. Paulo Freire summarized an earlier version of the problem of fragmentation in his typical, generalized way with the slogan "unity in diversity," without explaining more precisely how. The influential activist journalist Naomi Klein (2001) has reframed the question somewhat more concretely: "But I think it is more accurate to picture a movement of many movements-coalitions of coalitions" (p. 81). She means here "envisions" as a utopian idealization, not as a concrete historical fact. As she admits,

> The biggest challenge facing us is to distill all of this into a message that is widely accessible. . . . But to outsiders, the mere scope of modern protests can be a bit mystifying. If you eavesdrop on the movement from the outside, which is what most people do, you are liable to hear what seems to be a cacophony of disjointed slogans, a jumbled laundry list of disparate grievances without clear goals . . . slogans for everything everywhere, to the point of absurdity. (Klein, 2001, p. 86)

The communitarian fantasy of direct democracy as a vast constituent assembly cannot deal with the pluralism of risk societies or the fragmenting sectarianism inherent in social movements. Historically, it has been the task of political parties to aggregate and prioritize movement demands and grievances through intra-party and cross-party processes of dialogue and mutual learning. The key challenge for civic education in the context of postpandemic politics would thus be to create a curriculum that facilitates the formation of competencies that make possible a form of cosmopolitan citizenship that enables new generations of deliberative subjects to construct dialogues—at times inevitably agonistic—between the voices of social movements and official politics. That would entail critically questioning and appropriating the perspectives of social movements as part of constructing new cooperative agendas that need to be articulated in the larger public sphere as part of the transformation of electoral politics into deliberative democracy.

NOTE

The first version of this completely revised chapter was presented to the Comparative and International Education Society Conference, Mexico City, March 19–23, 1997. Thanks to Bob Arnove for some helpful last-minute suggestions.

REFERENCES

Allen, A. T. (2017). *The transatlantic kindergarten: Education and women's movements in Germany and the United States.* Oxford University Press.
Almeida, Paul. (2019). *Social movements: The structure of collective action.* University of California Press.
Almeida, P., & Cordero Ulate, A. (Eds.). (2015). *Handbook of social movements across Latin America.* Springer.
Althusser, L. (1971/2008). Ideology and ideological state apparatuses (notes toward an investigation) (B. Brewster, Trans.). In *On ideology* (pp. 1–60). Verso.
Alvarez, S. E., Dagnino, E., & Escobar, A. (Eds.). (1998). *Cultures of politics/politics of cultures: Re-visioning Latin American social movements.* Westview.
Anderson, N. S., & Kharem, H. (Eds.). (2009). *Education as freedom: African American educational thought and activism.* Lexington Books.
Andreotti, V. (2011). *Actionable postcolonial theory in education.* Palgrave Macmillan.
Anyon, J. (2014). *Radical possibilities: Public policy, urban education, and a new social movement* (2nd ed.). Routledge.

Archer, M. S. (1982). *The sociology of educational expansion: Take-off, growth and inflation in educational systems*. Sage.

Arnove, R., & Bull, B. L. (2015). Education as an ethical concern in the global era. *FIRE: Forum for International Research in Education, 2*(2), 6–87.

Avritzer, L. (2002). *Democracy and the public space in Latin America*. Princeton University Press.

Ball, S. J. (2007). Reading Michael Apple—The sociological imagination at work. *Theory and Research in Education, 5*(2), 153–159.

Ball, S. J. (2013). *Foucault, power and education*. Routledge.

Baronnet, B. (2008). Rebel youth and Zapatista autonomous education. *Latin American Perspectives, 35*(4), 112–124.

Bascia, N. (Ed.) (2015). *Teacher unions in public education: Politics, history, and the future*. Palgrave Macmillan.

Beck, U. (2011). Cosmopolitanism as imagined communities of global risk. *American Behavioral Scientist, 55*(10), 1341–1361.

Bégin-Cauette, O., & Jones, G. A. (2014). Student organizations in Canada and Quebec's "Maple Spring." *Studies in Higher Education, 39*(3), 412–425.

Behiels, M. D. (1985). *Prelude to Quebec's quiet revolution: Liberalism versus neo-nationalism 1945–1960*. McGill-Queens University Press.

Bekerman, Z., & Zembylas, M. (2012). *Teaching contested narratives: Identity, memory and reconciliation in peace education and beyond*. Cambridge University Press.

Blanc, E. (2019). *Red state revolt: The teachers' strike wave and working-class politics*. Verso.

Bonal, X. (2003). The neoliberal educational agenda and the legitimation crisis: Old and new state strategies. *British Journal of Sociology of Education, 24*(2), 159–175.

Bonanno, A. (2017). *The legitimation crisis of neoliberalism: The state, will-formation, and resistance*. Palgrave Macmillan.

Booysen, S. (Ed.). (2016). *Fees must fall: Student revolt, decolonisation and governance in South Africa*. Wits University Press.

Borchert, J., & Lessenich, S. (2016). *Claus Offe and the critical theory of the capitalist state*. Routledge.

Borman, D. (2011). *The idolatry of the actual: Habermas, socialization and the possibility of autonomy*. State University of New York Press.

Bourdieu, P., & Passeron, J.-C. (1970/1977). *Reproduction in education, society, and culture*. Sage.

Bowles, S., & Gintis, H. (1976). *Schooling in capitalist America: Educational reform and the contradictions of economic life*. Basic Books/Harper.

Bowles, S., & Gintis, H. (1986). *Democracy and capitalism: Property, community, and the contradictions of modern thought*. Basic Books.

Bowles, S., & Gintis, H. (2002). Schooling in capitalist America revisited. *Sociology of Education, 75*(1), 1–18.

Brookfield, S. D. (2005). *The power of critical theory for adult learning and teaching*. Open University Press.

Burns, J. P. (2018). *Power, curriculum, and embodiment: Re-thinking curriculum as counter-conduct and counter-politics*. Palgrave Macmillan.

Carl, J. (2011). *Freedom of choice: Vouchers in American education*. Praeger.

Carney, S., Rappleye, J., & Silova, I. (2011). Between faith and science: World culture theory and comparative education. *Comparative Education Review, 56*(3), 366–393.

Carnoy, M., & Levin, H. M. (1985). *Schooling and work in the democratic state*. Stanford University Press.

Castells, M. (2015). *Networks of outrage and hope: Social movements in the internet age*. Wiley.

Castells, M. (2020). Reset. In B. Bringel & G. Pleyers (Eds.), *Alerta global. Políticas, movimientos sociales y futuros en disputa en tiempos de pandemia* (pp. 101–103). CLACSO. Authors' translation.
Choudry, A., & Vally, S. (Eds.). (2018). *Reflections on knowledge, learning and social movements: History's schools*. Routledge.
Choudry, A., & Vally, S. (2020). *The university and social justice: Struggles across the globe*. Pluto Press.
Cohen, J. L., & Arato, A. (1992). *Civil society and political theory*. MIT Press.
Collins, P. H. (2019). *Intersectionality as critical social theory*. Duke University Press.
Collins, R. (2019 [1979]). *The credential society*. Columbia University Press.
Connell, R. (2007). *Southern theory*. Polity.
Cordero, R. (2017). *Crisis and critique: On the fragile foundations of social life*. Routledge.
Cortina, R. (2011). Globalization, social movements, and education. *Teachers College Record, 113*(6), 1196–1213.
Cortina, R., (Ed.). (2017). *Indigenous education policy, equity, and intercultural understanding in Latin America*. Palgrave Macmillan.
Cortina, R., & Lafuente, C. (Eds.). (2018). *Civil society organizations in Latin American Education: Case studies and perspectives on advocacy*. Routledge.
Cortina, R., Makar, C., & Mount-Cors, M. F. (2015). Dual language as a social movement: Putting languages on a level playing field. *Current Issues in Comparative Education, 17*(1), 5–16.
Crossley, A. D. (2017). Women's activism and education. In H. J. MacCammon, V. Taylor, J. Reger, & R. L. Einwohner (Eds.), *The Oxford handbook of U.S. women's social movement activism* (pp. 582–601). Oxford University Press.
Crossley, N. (2002). *Making sense of social movements*. Open University Press.
Del Gandio, J., & Thompson, A. (Eds.). (2017). *Spontaneous combustion: The Eros effect and global revolution*. State University of New York Press.
della Porta, D. (2015). *Social movements in times of austerity: Bringing capitalism back into protest analysis*. Polity.
Dobbs, A. E. (1969). *Education and social movements 1700–1850* (Reprint of 1919 ed.). Augustus M. Kelley.
Eder, K. (2015). Social movement in social theory. In D. Dalla Porta & M. Diani (Eds.), *The Oxford handbook of social movements* (pp. 1–21): Oxford Handbooks Online.
Eisenstadt, T., Danielson, M. S., Bailon Corres, M. J., & Sorroa Polo, C. (Eds.). (2013). *Latin America's multicultural movements: The struggle between communitarianism, autonomy, and human rights*. Oxford University Press.
Eyerman, R., & Jamison, A. (1991). *Social movements: A cognitive approach*. Polity.
Finlayson, J. G. (2005). *Habermas: A very short introduction*. Oxford University Press.
Garretón, M. A. M. (2014). Apéndice: por la refundación del sistema de educación. *Anales de la Universidad de Chile, 7*(7), 199–207. doi:10.5354/0717-8883.2015.35896
Giroux, H. (1983). Theories of reproduction and resistance in the new sociology of education: A critical analysis. *Harvard Educational Review, 53*(3), 257–293.
Giroux, H. (1992). *Border crossings: Cultural workers and the politics of education*. Routledge.
Giroux, H. (2011). *On critical pedagogy*. Continuum.
Giroux, H. (2013). The Quebec student protest movement in the age of neoliberal terror. *Social Identities, 19*, 515–535.
Giroux, H. (2020). *Neoliberalism's war on higher education* (2nd ed.). Haymarket Books.
Habermas, J. (1975). *Legitimation crisis* (T. McCarthy, Trans.). Beacon.
Hall, B. L., Clover, D. E., Crowther, J., & Scandrett, E. (Eds.). (2012). *Learning and education for a better world: The role of social movements*. Sense Publishers.

Haluza-DeLay, R. (2008). A theory of practice for social movements: Environmentalism and ecological habitus. *Mobilization: The International Quarterly, 13*(2), 205–218.

Harris, J. (2017). *Achieving access: Professional movements and the politics of health universalism.* Cornell University Press.

Heath, J. (2009). Habermas and analytical Marxism. *Philosophy & Social Criticism, 35*(8), 891–919.

Henry, C. P. (2017). *Black studies and the democratization of American higher education.* Palgrave Macmillan.

Hetland, G., & Goodwin, J. (2013). The strange disappearance of capitalism from social movement studies. In C. Barker, L. Cox, J. Krinsky, & A. G. Nilsen (Eds.), *Marxism and social movements* (pp. 83–102). Brill.

Holst, J. (2002). *Social movements, civil society, and radical adult education.* Bergin & Garvey.

Hudson, B. (2003). *Justice in the risk society: Challenging and re-affirming justice in late modernity.* Sage.

Ingram, D. (2010). *Habermas: An introduction and analysis.* Cornell University Press.

Itzigsohn, J., & Brown, K. L. (2020). *The sociology of W. E. B. Du Bois: Racialized modernity and the global color lines.* New York University Press.

Jenkins, J. C., & Klandermans, B. (1995). The politics of social protest. In J. C. Jenkins & B. Klandermans (Eds.), *The politics of social protest: Comparative perspectives on states and social movements* (pp. 3–13). University of Minnesota Press.

Kapoor, D. (2009). Globalization, dispossession, and subaltern social movement (SSM) learning in the South. In A. Abdi and D. Kapoor (Eds.), *Global perspectives on adult education* (pp. 71–92). Palgrave Macmillan.

Kilgore, D. H. (1999). Understanding learning in social movements: A theory of collective learning. *International Journal of Lifelong Education, 18*(3), 191–202.

Klein, N. (2001, May–June). Reclaiming the commons. *New Left Review, 9*, 81.

Laclau, E., & Mouffe, C. (1985). *Hegemony and socialist strategy: Towards a radical democratic politics* (W. M. a. P. Cammack, Trans.). Verso.

Levin, B. (1998). An epidemic of education policy: (What) can we learn from each other? *Comparative Education, 34*(2), 131–141.

Mary, O., & Amirault, R. J. (2020). *Nicholas de Condorcet: The revolution in higher education.* Springer.

McAdam, D., McCarthy, J. D., & Zald, M. N. (1996). Introduction: Opportunities, mobilizing structures, and framing processes—Toward a synthetic, comparative perspective on social movements. In D. McAdam, J. D. McCarthy, & M. N. Zald (Eds.), *Comparative perspectives on social movements: Political opportunities, mobilizing structures, and cultural framings* (pp. 1–20). Cambridge University Press.

McLaren, P. (2015). *Pedagogy of insurrection: From resurrection to revolution.* Peter Lang.

McLaren, P. (2016). *This fist called my heart: The Peter McLaren reader* (Vol. 1), Pruyn & L. Huerta-Charles (Eds.), Information Age Publishing.

Misiaszek, G. W. (2017). *Educating the global environmental citizen: Understanding ecopedagogy in local and global contexts.* Routledge.

Morrow, R. A. (2013). Rethinking Freire's "oppressed": A postcolonial route to Habermas's communicative turn and theory of deliberative democracy. In R. Lake & T. Kress (Eds.), *Paulo Freire's roots: Toward historicity in praxis* (pp. 65–87). Bloomsbury Academic.

Morrow, R. A. (2014). Reproduction theories. In D. C. Phillips (Ed.), *Encyclopedia of educational theory and philosophy* (pp. 706–711). Sage.

Morrow, R. A. (2021a). From deliberative to contestatory dialogue: Reconstructing Paulo Freire's approach to critical citizenship literacy. In S. Wiksten (Ed.), *Centering global citizenship education in the public sphere* (pp. 42–55). Routledge.

Morrow, R. A. (2022, in press). Habermas and civic education. In R. Desjardins & S. Wiksten (Eds.), *Handbook of civic engagement and education*. Edward Elgar.

Morrow, R. A., & Torres, C. A. (1995). *Social theory and education: A critique of theories of social and cultural reproduction*. State University of New York Press.

Mythen, G. (2020). Ulrich Beck: E-special introduction. *Theory, Culture & Society, 37*(7-8), 383–409.

Niesz, T. (2018). When teachers become activists. *Phi Delta Kappan, 99*(8), 25–29.

Niesz, T., Korora, A., Walkuski, C. B., & Foot, R. (2018). Social movements and educational research: Toward a united field of scholarship. *Teachers College Record, 120*(3), 1–41.

O'Cadiz, M. d. P., Wong, P. L., & Torres, C. A. (1998). *Education and democracy: Paulo Freire, social movements, and educational reform in São Paulo*. Westview.

Offe, Claus. (1984). *Contradictions of the welfare state* (J. Keane, Ed.). Hutchinson.

Offe, Claus. (1985). *Disorganized capitalism: Contemporary transformations of work and politics* (J. Keane, Trans.). MIT Press.

Peters, M. A., & Jandric, P. (2018). Neoliberalism and the university. In D. Cahill, M. Cooper, M. Konings, & D. Primrose (Eds.), *The Sage handbook of neoliberalism* (pp. 533–563). Sage.

Pleyers, G. (2018). Globalization and social movements: Human agency and mobilizations for change. In M. S. Schulz (Ed.), *Frontiers of global sociology: Research perspectives for the 21st century* (pp. 314–318). ISA Research, International Sociological Association.

Popkewitz, T. S. (1991). *A political sociology of educational reform: Power/knowledge in teaching, teacher education, and research*. Teachers College Press, Columbia University.

Rhoads, R. A., Saenz, V., & Carducci, R. (2005). Higher education reform as a social movement: The case of affirmative action. *The Review of Higher Education, 28*(2), 191–220.

Rincón-Gallardo, S. (2019). *Liberating learning: Educational change as social movement*. Routledge.

Rucht, D. (2016). Conclusions. Social movement studies in Europe: Achievements, gaps and challenges. In O. Fillieule & G. Accornero (Eds.), *Social movement studies in Europe: The state of the art*. Berghahn.

Rudd, T., & Goodson, I. (Eds.). (2017). *Negotiating neoliberalism: Developing alternative educational visions*. Sense Publishers.

Sahlberg, P. (2012). Global educational reform is here! Retrieved from https://pasisahlberg.com/global-educational-reform-movement-is-here/.

Scapp, R. (2016). *Reclaiming education: Moving beyond the culture of reform*. Palgrave Macmillan.

Schmitt, L. (2016). Bourdieu meets social movement. In J. Roose & H. Dietz (Eds.), *Social theory and social movements: Mutual inspirations* (pp. 57–74). Springer.

Scott, A. (1990). *Ideology and the new social movements*. Unwin Hyman.

Smith, L. T., Tuck, E., & Yang, K. W. (Eds.). (2019). *Indigenous and decolonizing studies in education: Mapping the long view*. Routledge.

Snow, D. A., Soule, S. A., Kriesei, H., & McCammon, H. J. (Eds.). (2019). *The Wiley Blackwell companion to social movements* (2nd ed.). Wiley.

Spring, J. (2004). *How Educational ideologies are shaping global society: Intergovernmental organizations, NGOs, and the decline of the nation-State*. Lawrence Erlbaum Associates.

Streeck, W. (2013/2017). *Buying time: The delayed crisis of democratic capitalism* (P. Camiller & D. Fernbach, Trans.; 2nd ed.). Verso.

Suissa, J. (2006). *Anarchism and education: A philosophical perspective*. Routledge.

Suissa, J. (2016). Reflections on the "counter" in educational counterpublics. *Educational Theory*, *66*(6), 769–786.
Tarlau, R. (2015). How do new critical pedagogies develop? Public education, social change, and landless workers in Brazil. *Teachers College Record*, *117*(11), 1–36.
Thompson, E. P. (1968). *The making of the English working class*. Penguin.
Tilly, C. (1978). *From mobilization to revolution*. Random House.
Tilly, C. (2005). *Popular contention in Great Britain, 1758–1834*. Paradigm Publishers.
Tilly, C. (2007). *Democracy*. Cambridge University Press.
Todd-Breland, E. (2018). *A political education: Black politics and education reform in Chicago since the 1960s*. University of North Carolina Press.
Tooze, A. (2020). The sociologist who could save us from coronavirus. *Foreign Policy*, *20*(10). https://foreignpolicy.com/2020/08/01/the-sociologist-who-could-save-us-from-coronavirus
Torres, C. A. (1989). The capitalist state and public policy formation: A framework for a political sociology of educational policy-making. *British Journal of Sociology of Education*, *10*(1), 81–102.
Torres, C. A. (2009). *Education and neoliberal globalization*. Routledge.
Torres, C. A. (2017). *Theoretical and empirical foundations of critical global citizenship education*. Routledge.
Tucker, K. J. (1989). Ideology and social movements: The contributions of Habermas. *Sociological Inquiry*, *59*(1), 30–47.
Vaughan, M. K. (1997). *Cultural politics in revolution: Teachers, peasants, and schools in Mexico 1930–1940*. University of Arizona Press.
Verma, R. (2017). *Critical peace education and global citizenship: Narratives from the unofficial curriculum*. Routledge.
Welton, M. (Ed.). (1995). *In defense of the lifeworld: Critical perspectives on adult learning*. State University of New York Press.
Welton, M. (2005). *Designing the just learning society: A critical inquiry*. National Institute of Adult Education.
Wickham-Crowley, T. P., & Eckstein, S. E. (2015). "There and back again": Latin American social movements and reasserting the powers of structural theories. In P. Almeida & A. Cordero Ulate (Eds.), *Handbook of social movements across Latin America* (pp. 25–42). Springer.
Willis, P. (1977/1981). *Learning to labor: How working class kids get working class jobs*. Columbia University Press.
Wilson, T. S. (2011). Civic fragmentation or voluntary association? Habermas, Fraser, and charter school segregation. *Educational Theory*, *60*(6).
Wright, E. O. (2002, December). The shadow of exploitation in Weber's class analysis. *American Sociological Review*, *67*, 832–838.

4

Culture and Education

Vandra Lea Masemann
OISE, University of Toronto

ABSTRACT

This chapter explores the possibilities that anthropological theory and method hold for research in comparative education and illustrates great changes that have taken place in the role of the researcher and the research subject since the first edition of this chapter in 1999. Beginning with fundamental concepts of the cultural approach to the study of comparative education, this chapter shows the links between education and culture and explores ways the anthropological perspective is useful in educational research. Then the history of anthropological theories of functional and evolutionism and their respective relationships to scientism and colonialism are discussed. I argue that a critical or neo-Marxist approach is necessary to delineate connections between the micro-level of the local school experiences and the macro-level of structural forces at the global level that shape the delivery and experiences of education. Recent studies in anthropological research in education are then summarized, referencing many current issues. I agree with Foley (2010) that a more nuanced class culture paradigm has emerged, superseding earlier cultural transmission and modernization paradigms, which I see as suitable for studies of both the local and the global aspects of schooling.

■ ■ ■

Exploring education using an anthropological lens provides perspectives that differ from those of other disciplines. The depth of field and focus are very different from those in large-scale comparative studies. The scope of studies and unit of analysis are usually much smaller and the findings less generalizable than in other kinds of comparative studies. The ethnographic methodology commonly used in an anthropological approach both constrains and liberates the researcher in the kinds of analysis and findings that are possible. Moreover, voices of marginalized or peripheral populations can be heard in ways that are muted or never even listened to in large-scale comparisons.

In this chapter, the possibilities that anthropological theory and method hold for comparative education are explored. This chapter outlines the fundamental concepts of the cultural approach to the study of comparative education, shows the links between education and culture, and explores ways the anthropological perspective is useful in educational research. The main thesis of the chapter is that although the ethnographic approach is necessary to explore the workings of culture in the classroom, school, and administrative system, it should not constrain the researcher mainly to phenomenological approaches or ones which focus only on the participants' subjective experiences. I argue that a critical or neo-Marxist approach is necessary to delineate connections between the micro-level of the local school experiences and the macro-level of structural forces at the global level that shape the delivery and experiences of education in every country. A cultural approach to the study of comparative education is important to counter some increasing trends in the economistic analysis of school effectiveness that rest on productivity-oriented criteria, an analysis used on every level of education from early childhood education to the tertiary level (Steiner-Khamsi et al., 2018; Winthrop et al., 2013; see also Chapter 2 in this volume).

This chapter opens with a brief summary of the central concepts used in the study of education and culture, followed by a discussion of the relationship of cultural values to education. Then the connections among culture, educational philosophy, and social class are examined. The role of evolutionism and colonialism and their relationship to the anthropological study of education are discussed, followed by an examination of the relationship of anthropology to functionalism and scientism. The contribution of neo-Marxist approaches is considered, and the rise of school ethnography and its contribution to comparative education are then presented. Finally, recent studies in anthropological research in education are summarized, with particular reference to migration and transmigration, global citizenship, indigenous education, education reform and innovation, policy linkages, and the world of big data. The COVID-19 pandemic is the setting for this 2022 revision for the fifth edition of this book.

THE CONCEPT OF CULTURE

The foundation stone of the anthropological approach is the concept of culture. While there are many different definitions of culture, the one I find most useful says that culture is "concerned with actions, ideas, and artifacts which individuals in the tradition concerned learn, share, and value" (Keesing, 1960, p. 25). Culture refers to all aspects of life, including the mental, social, linguistic, and physical forms of culture. It refers to ideas people have, the relationships they have with others in their families and with larger social institutions, the languages they speak, and the symbolic forms they share, such as written language and art/music forms. It refers to their relationship with their physical surroundings as well as the technology used in any society (Williams, 1972, p. 125). Considerable criticism has been leveled at earlier definitions of culture in their unquestioning assumption of homogeneity and seeming denial of plural perspectives within any one social group. However, Geertz (as cited in Barrett, 1996, p. 239) supported the idea that although groups of people may not exhibit identical forms of behavior, they may possess similar kinds of "control mechanisms—plans, recipes, rules, instructions . . . for the governing of behavior." Barrett (2011) wrote that in Geertz's later view "the fieldwork scene . . . resembled a literary text of meanings which the anthropologist attempted to interpret, as in a novel, rather than explain, as under a laboratory microscope" (p. 33).

Other related terms are *enculturation* and *socialization*. Enculturation refers to the process of learning how to be a competent member of a specific culture or group, and socialization is considered by some anthropologists to refer to the general process of learning human culture (Williams, 1972, p. 1). *Acculturation* refers to the process of cultural transfer from one group to another (Keesing, 1960, p. 28). These terms have relevance for the study of education because it is important to delineate which aspects of culture are being transmitted or transferred from one group to another, whether through cross-generational transmission or a cross-group transfer of knowledge, skills, values, or attitudes. The terms *intercultural* and *multicultural* also connote cross-group transfer and, in some cases, a political connotation of redrawing cultural lines to include a more pluralistic combination of what had previously been considered separate groups. All these terms rest on the fundamental assumption that education is not simply an information transfer but has a cultural component. The effectiveness of multicultural education policy rests on the willingness (or lack thereof) of members of various groups to identify as members of a single nation or identifiable group, or to share a common culture. The recent interest in the processes of colonialism, colonization, and coloniality, and in the intersectionality of race, class, and culture, have shifted the analysis away from hopes for societal harmony via attitude change to the unpacking of structures of oppression. One recent example is a study of the treatment of Acquired Immunodeficiency Syndrome (AIDS), children's well-being, and education in Malawi (Kendall et al., 2019).

Margaret Mead (1970) went so far as to define education as "the cultural process, the way in which each newborn human infant, born with a potentiality for learning greater than that of any other mammal, is transformed into a full member of a specific human society, sharing with the other members a specific human culture" (p. 1). She thus defined all the processes that a human undergoes as education (Mead, 1970), whereas Yehudi Cohen (1971) and many educators distinguish between the processes of socialization and formal education.

In Cohen's (1971) view, "socialization and education are two fundamentally different processes in the shaping of the mind—found in all societies, albeit in different proportions" (p. 21). He defines socialization as "the activities that are devoted to the inculcation and elicitation of basic motivational and cognitive patterns through ongoing and spontaneous interaction with parents, siblings, kinsmen, and other members of the community" and education as "the inculcation of standardized and stereotyped knowledge, skills, values, and attitudes by means of standardized and stereotyped procedures" (Cohen, 1971, p. 22). Cohen (1971) hypothesizes that "the quantitative role played by socialization in the development of the individual is in direct proportion to the extent to which the network of kin relations coincides with the network of personal relations" (p. 22). Thus he argues that it is the nature of the wider social structure that provides the setting in which socialization and education processes play out (Cohen, 1971). This perspective is at the heart of this chapter, for it provides the anthropological and ultimately philosophical justification for seeing educational processes of any kind as inextricably linked with the social structure that gives rise to them. Thus the process of an ethnographic study of education cannot be carried out without acknowledging the setting in which the educational processes are taking place and the cultural content of the forms of educational transmission. For example, recent studies by Varvus and Bartlett (2009) and Bartlett and Vavrus (2019) advocate for a vertical case study approach to comparative education, in which the local, regional, national, and international structures and their links are examined (Bartlett & Vavrus, 2019; Vavrus & Bartlett, 2009).

CULTURAL VALUES

Another fundamental characteristic of culture is that it expresses the value systems of a particular society or group. Florence Kluckhohn (1961), in her classic work on dominant and variant value orientations, states that "there is a systematic variation in the realm of cultural phenomena which is both as definite and as essential as the demonstrated systematic variation in physical and biological phenomena" (p. 3). She links her argument to a defense of the concept of cultural relativism and explores the range of value systems that answer the following five basic questions common to all human groups.

First, what is the character of innate human nature? It may be (1) evil—mutable or immutable, (2) neutral—mutable, (3) mixture of good and evil—immutable, and (4) good—mutable or immutable. In other words, human beings are seen as being born evil, neutral, or good and having the possibility of changing or not. Depending on the culture's prevailing value system, the goals of socialization or education will aim to enforce an orientation either considered unchangeable and/or to change the child into a better person (although changing the child for the worse is also theoretically possible in this schema). A third possibility is not to interfere at all with what is perceived to be the essential nature of the child or the person that the child will become.

Second, what is the relation of human beings to nature (and supernature)? They may be (1) subjugated to nature, (2) in harmony with nature, or (3) dominant over nature. These values are expressed in an emphasis on learning to accept whatever nature brings, to attempt some sort of collaboration with nature, or to want to triumph over nature.

Third, what is the temporal focus of human life—past, present, or future?

Fourth, what is the valued modality of human activity—being, being-in-becoming, or doing?

Fifth, what is the valued modality of people's relationship to other people—lineality, collateral, or individualism? (Kluckhohn, 1961, p. 12). In other words, do people value their ties to their ancestors, their relationships within their generation, or primarily themselves?

The answers to these five questions form the underlying assumptions of any system of socialization and/or education, formal or informal, in any society. The content of what is taught through socialization and/or education reflects the basic value orientations of any culture, mostly with variant value orientations that allow for a range of required and permitted variation within the system. For example, the emphasis on the practical value of education as an investment for the future in modern universities is counterbalanced (but not equally) by the aesthetic values of the arts curriculum or the humanistic contribution of the liberal arts. Moreover, the valuing of athletic superiority is also counterpoised to the valuing of more intellectual aspects of the university enterprise. It is interesting to note the shift of focus in the current early pandemic period when people had to stay home for several months. While in most countries science is considered to be the authority on curbing the spread of infections and the treatment of the disease, some people who are relatively privileged are finding comfort in the arts and humanities—music, art, drama, literature—and the homegrown skills in cooking, gardening, sewing, craftwork, and home renovation, with information from the internet. For athletic pursuits, people focused on individual activities such as walking, running, hiking, and yoga.

Kluckhohn (1961) argues that these dominant and variant value orientations could coexist, were complementary, and would shift under external pressure to varying degrees. Thus values are not the individual psychological attitudes of an individual but socially structured orientations patterned with the strictures of the society in which people play out their roles. Kluckhohn (1961) says that people could shift in their value orientations away from one set of values into another set of equally sanctioned or perhaps even preferable values, as in the case of socially mobile persons in American culture (p. 39). Although this schema can be applied to the analysis of culture as it was traditionally seen by anthropologists, it can also be applied to the analysis of the cultural foundations of education, to the study of formal curriculum and policy documents, and to the analysis of the classroom. This schema can also be applied to the study of the "hidden curriculum" of the school, which refers to the unintended cultural messages of the school experience (Pai & Adler, 1997). An ethnographic study of schools can reveal the cultural messages that the educational experience transmits, intentionally and unintentionally. To the educational anthropologist, all observed behavior in the classroom and school, as well as all printed and electronic information, carry their forms of cultural knowledge, whether overtly or covertly expressed and whether formally articulated or as part of the informal social life of the school (Spindler, 1982). Thus the link between what educators call curriculum and culture is clearly established.

CULTURE AND EDUCATIONAL PHILOSOPHY

Kluckhohn's (1961) schema can also be applied to the analysis of changes in educational philosophy in Europe and North America in the last two centuries (via Comenius, Rousseau, Pestalozzi, Froebel, Steiner, Montessori, and Dewey), in the shift from teacher-centered pedagogy to student-centered pedagogy as a result of changes in conceptualizing the child from evil to good and from a creature to be dominated to one who should be nurtured, or at least allowed to develop as naturally as possible (Ulich, 1965). There are also structural changes in the organization of society and work itself that have been concomitant with these changes in values. The perceived need for a more highly skilled workforce and the necessity for students to keep studying for many years make it necessary for the experience of schooling to be somewhat more endurable than in an era when most people's educational biographies were relatively short.

This change of paradigm has also had a profound effect on the education of adults globally, expressed most articulately by Paulo Freire (1974). He proposed a "pedagogy of the oppressed" that is forged with individuals or peoples in "the incessant struggle to regain their humanity" (Freire, 1974, p. 33). The philosophy of enabling adults to formulate their path of learning is that they can use their newly aroused consciousness to resist forms of external authority they find oppressive and that they "must perceive the reality of oppression not as a closed world from which there is no exit, but as a limiting situation which they can transform.... The oppressed can overcome the contradiction in which they are caught only when this perception enlists them in the struggle to free themselves" (Freire, 1974, p. 34).

This is quite different from the situation in a middle-class school where students are treated as if they were not being controlled while being socialized into believing that they have the freedom to control their lives and the lives of others. Basil Bernstein (1977) commented on this seeming contradiction, that student-centered pedagogy (which he designates as invisible) appears to be based on the assumption that there is no external form of control to which the child must succumb when it is mainly middle-class students in progressive primary schools who are spared the most oppressive forms of teacher-centered pedagogy. He states that changing the code (underlying principle) that controls education transmission involves changing the culture and its basis in privatized class relationships (Bernstein, 1977). In other words, it is not possible just to teach students a new form of speech and writing to change society, since that only results in the social mobility of an individual or group of individuals. It is instead necessary to change the structural basis of society in which certain dialects or speech patterns are associated with certain forms of privilege or social class status, which have their basis in the economic, not the linguistic, order of society.

However, because integrated codes (found in situations of invisible pedagogy) are integrated at the level of ideas, they do not involve integration at the level of institutions, such as school and work. Bernstein (1977) states that "there can be no such integration in Western societies (to mention only one group)" because the abstracting of education from work, such as in the tradition of liberal education, "masks the brutal fact that work and education cannot be integrated at the level of social principles in class societies" (pp. 145–146). However, class societies exist in all regions of the world.

Bernstein (1977) argues this position is derived from Emile Durkheim, and that the division of labor in society is the fundamental characteristic that determines the shift in the principles of social integration through schooling, as exemplified in "the movement away from the transmission of common values through a ritual order and control based upon position or status, to more personalized forms of control where teachers and taught confront each other as individuals" (p. 69). This is the classic shift from mechanical to organic solidarity, in Durkheim's terms, in the shift from an appeal to shared values, group loyalties, and ritual to the recognition of differences among individuals as they play out individualized, specialized, and independent social roles. However, it is a student's social class position that ultimately determines how she or he experiences any form of pedagogy. We conclude that the seeming variations in values are not only cultural but also class-based.

Thus the link is made between education, culture, and class in every society. The cultural foundations of every form of socialization and/or education are made explicit in all the multiplicity of admonitions and rewards that kinfolk bestow on children as they grow up and in the content of the curriculum as well as classroom and school practices that students experience within formal education systems worldwide. Students' experiences of and reactions to their education are not only grounded in culture and values perceived in the liberal tradition as unconnected to the material basis of their society (the world of work) but also fundamentally shaped by the economic basis of their neighborhood, community, region, country, and the global economy (Ilon, 1994). The relationship between education, culture, and economics is not simple, and the ethnographic study of education in various countries can illuminate its complex dimensions. I turn now to the colonial experience as an example of this complexity.

EVOLUTIONISM AND COLONIALISM

Early conceptualizations of society by anthropologists such as Edward Tylor (1871), Lewis Henry Morgan (1877), and Herbert Spencer (1896) were based on a theory of evolutionism, in which societies were described as progressing through a series of stages, based on increasing rationality, improved technology, or stages similar to those of biological organisms, from the simple to the complex (Barrett, 2011, pp. 49–54). Thus societies based on hunting and gathering, pastoral nomadism, agriculture, herding of domesticated animals, feudalism, and industrialism were no longer understood to be static entities (labeled and classified like butterflies in a museum case, interesting each in its own right and unrelated to the others), but as stages through which every society had to pass to progress further up the evolutionary ladder.

The rise of evolutionism in the 19th-century context of growing belief in rationality, human perfectibility, progress, and the promotion of technological advancement laid the foundations of the belief that development reached its apogee in the 20th century. Darwin's (1859) theory of biological evolution reinforced this theory of social evolution, with its attendant notions of "survival of the fittest" and the underlying assumption that all societies had to progress through the stages in the same order. Armchair anthropologists were no longer sitting in Europe simply applying labels to other cultures and groups; they were now proposing that all other peoples were evolving to more complex levels of society. Eventually, education was seen as the major means of forcing this evolutionary process to speed up.

Even though anthropological theorizing has become far more eclectic since those early days, and probably is characterized now by a willingness to study societies from a much more pluralistic perspective, education as a field has clung to this implicit evolutionary schema for a much longer period. As anthropologists were developing their "stages of society" schemata, educators were developing the beginnings of comparative education. These early comparativists were not searching for any kind of relativism, but for "borrowing from abroad useful educational devices for the improvement of education at home" (Noah & Eckstein, 1969, p. 112).

This implicit evolutionary schema has not persisted merely as a heuristic device or some lingering trace of a firmly entrenched tenet of teacher ideology. The foundations for the growth of the development idea were firmly laid during the last several hundred years of colonial education. The development idea has been held in place by the history of the colonial relationships between major European countries and the rest of the world: the newer neocolonial relationships that emerged after European countries "granted" independence to former colonies, and the creation of new forms of fiscal dependency of poor countries by major international lending agencies. Philip Altbach and Gail Kelly (1978) note that forms of internal colonialism still exist in the case of "populations still dominated by foreign nations existing within the same national boundaries" (p. 1) (such as the case of Indigenous peoples of the Americas and South Africa). There is also the case of populations still dominated by elites within their own national borders (such as women, racial, religious, and ethnocultural minorities, and the working classes everywhere). (See Chapter 1 by Samoff and Chapter 11 by Samoff and Carrol in this volume.)

In colonial contexts, education took on various forms. It was not just a simple matter of colonial powers establishing schools in the colonies to produce citizens who resembled their colonial masters. Kelly (1996) notes that colonial schools were sometimes quite removed from the metropolitan experience and were meant to produce subjugated people who could not function in the metropole. In other cases, colonial schools produced a distorted version of education in the metropole, particularly concerning gender roles. For example, Kelly (1996) describes vividly how, in the classes for teaching English to Vietnamese refugees in the United States, previously independent women, income-earning fisherwomen were taught gender-stereotyped phrases in English for performing domestic duties and passing their time in leisure pursuits.

This imposition of gender-stereotyped expectations is also reflected in curriculum materials in colonial (or formal colonial) countries. I give examples of a home economics curriculum in a West African girls' boarding school, in which the exercises were entirely based on the operation of a European-style household, with cooking and laundry activities being performed by a wife in a nuclear family (Masemann, 1974). In fact, in this West African country, the presence of domestic servants and various relatives, as well as a hired laundryman from the home village, usually meant that well-educated women were not expected to perform these duties. Thus even students' everyday life outside of school was distorted in its curriculum representation in school (Masemann, 1974).

Johann Galtung's (1973) work on center-periphery theory deals with colonial education as part of the dominant country's process to penetrate the countries to be dominated. He describes how "structural power really becomes operational when one nation gets under the skin of the other so that it is able to form and shape the inside of the nation" (Galtung, 1973, p. 43). Galtung (1973) distinguishes between processes of subversion (from the bottom or periphery) and supervision (from the top). In the latter process, the education system is a key institution used to produce elites. Through being educated either in elite schools in the colonized country or in the metropole itself, colonial elites have more in common with their colonizers than they do with populations in their own peripheral country. This process also fragments peripheral populations, as Galtung (1973) believes that the relative affluence of peripheral elites of the major colonial countries results in their having a greater political loyalty to their own national interest and to the international bourgeoisie than to the world proletariat of which they are a part.

He sees structural domination as made up of three processes—exploitation, fragmentation, and penetration. Galtung (1973) notes that structural domination is in place wherever the Western model of technical-economic development is accepted and the periphery depends on the center to supply something that the periphery thinks is indispensable and unavailable elsewhere. Moreover, "the Periphery thinks these things are indispensable because it has been taught to think so, because it has adopted and adapted to the culture of the Center" (Galtung, 1973, p. 46). While the direct colonial relationship has been altered since many countries have become politically independent, this form of domination continues. However, the metaphor of evolution has changed, and the metaphors of educational development have become increasingly technicized, as if new rationality had been invented that could make the old evolutionary processes speed up. Notions of social justice or equity are excluded from any politicized discourse. Within the new metaphors, the process of evolution is accelerated and the definition of time is understood to be linear and industrial. Christine Fox (1997) describes the dimensions of the new metaphors as being based on

> economic, structural images of building models, drawing analogies to the formulation of ground plans, making a blueprint for program implementation, delivery of materials, the sending "in" of a "team," the tight time line, inputs, and outputs, product flow, monitoring and so on. . . . The language used by consultants "in the field" is often particularly distorting, since they move within the "packaged" time frame, speaking of strategic planning and delivery, while their counterparts move within the more fluid and broader cultural framework of their ongoing educational context, speaking of people's lives. (p. 60)

Shen-Keng Yang (1991) makes a similar point in his analysis of the cultural assumptions underlying the passage of time in educational research and policy planning studies, and the way ordinary people experience or plan their lives. He refers to the concept of *time institutionalized* and points out that the railroad (in the past) and the development of information technology (in the present) are how ordinary people experience the speeding up of institutionalized time (Yang, 1991). In the preindustrial concept of time, the length of the task at hand and the repetitive cycle of the days, weeks, months, and seasons of the year formed the basis of a nonlinear sense of time that was incorporated into the rituals of the culture and the sense of the worth of an individual human life span. In the industrial concept of time, human actions are arranged and connected in a linear sequence with a purpose and goal. When imposing one concept on the other, planners become frustrated at the seeming lack of impact of their ideas while the people who are being planned for became baffled at the seeming impatience of such highly educated but apparently impractical people.

Arturo Escobar (1992) refers to development as

> a powerful and encompassing discourse which has ruled most social designs and actions of those [underdeveloped] countries since the early post–World War II period . . . [that has] shaped in significant ways the modes of existence of Third World societies, mediating in a profound sense the knowledge they seek about themselves and their peoples, mapping their social landscape, sculpting their economies, transforming their cultures. (pp. 411–412)

Writing from an anthropologist's perspective, Escobar (1992) states that "there is an acute need to assert the difference of cultures, the relativity of history, and the plurality of perceptions" (p. 412) to negate the view that more Development (his capitalization) is needed. He presents an analysis of the debacle of the development idea, in which grassroots and other social movements "are opening the way for the creation of a politics for an alternative Development anchored in the grassroots and . . . providing new possibilities for satisfying human needs (including foods, nutrition, and health)" (Escobar, 1992, p. 412). Escobar (1992) also points to the importance of local knowledge in this process and notes that "a new dialectic of micro-practice and macro-thinking seems to be emerging, one which is advanced by intellectuals and activists engaged in processes of social transformation" (p. 412).

Galtung (1973) explicates this relationship still further in his analysis of the education of the elites of the center and periphery countries. He notes that the interests of the elite in the center were well served by having the elite of the periphery educated either in elite colonial schools that were able to reproduce the social relations of the center in the peripheral country or in the elite schools of the center itself. Kelly's (1996) analysis fits in with Galtung's more in relation to the education of the peripheral populations of the periphery. She is mostly focusing on peripheral populations that have been colonized by representatives of the center, either by external colonizers (in the case of classical colonialism) or by internal colonizers (in the case of internal colonization) (Kelly, 1996).

Freire's (1974) analysis of mental colonialism takes the analysis further. He postulates that the main effect of colonial education was to produce a mindset so that the colonized took on the mentality of the colonizer and judged themselves and others from the viewpoint of the colonizer (Freire, 1974). This perception was the essence of the neocolonial mentality. African leaders such as Kwame Nkrumah used to fulminate against the neocolonial mentality in their public speeches, warning their citizens not to continue to think like their former colonial masters. Even West African schoolchildren in the 1960s were well aware of the dangers of having a neocolonial mentality (Masemann, personal recollection).

As Archie Mafeje (1976) points out, the dangers of the neocolonial mindset went far deeper than comparing one's appearance, art, or politics to those of Europeans. Positivist thought, the epistemology of European functionalists, became embedded in the pursuit of knowledge and was an insidious mechanism for depriving Africans of their birthright (Mafeje, 1976). Mafeje (1976) saw the major epistemological links as being between the bourgeois colonial mind, on one hand, and functionalism and scientism, on the other. (See also wa Thiong'o (1986) on the role of African literature on decolonizing the mind.)

FUNCTIONALISM AND SCIENTISM

Functionalism was a major strand in the development of anthropological and sociological thought. Bronislaw Malinowski and A. R. Radcliffe-Brown were two anthropologists most commonly associated with functionalism in anthropology. Malinowski's (1944) version of functionalism focused more on the cultural needs approach—societies had to have institutions that functioned to meet the various needs of human beings. He saw ethnographies as showing how any society was able to meet the needs of its members. Radcliffe-Brown's (1948) version of functionalism was more of an analogy that compared the social system with a functioning human body, with various social institutions playing their respective roles in the healthy functioning of the whole. In both these versions of functionalism, there was an underlying sense of harmoniousness; conflict and social change did not fit well in these models of societal function (Barrett, 2011, pp. 65–68; also see Chapter 18 in this volume).

Functionalism formed the foundation of quantitative social science in the twentieth century and became very popular as the foundation of research in the "applied" areas of social science such as education. It was also the foundational research paradigm for educational research and statistics. Therefore, functionalism has had an impact on educational research, which has perhaps been even stronger than on its original disciplines.

It is not possible to outline all the criticisms that have been leveled at the functionalist approach in anthropology in this chapter. Mafeje (1976) does an excellent job of this in his perspective from the Global South. He states primarily that anthropology, functionalism, and positivism were the handmaidens of colonialism and bourgeois social science in that they were an essential part of the imperialist enterprise:

> Their decision to leave their desks and disappear into the jungles of Africa, South America and Asia was not determined by love of unknown natives, but rather by the imperatives of European development, including intellectual curiosity and growing impatience with speculative theories of the nineteenth century evolutionists. (Mafeje, 1976, pp. 317–318)

He continues his argument by discussing the contradiction in many liberal anthropologists' position on subject-object relations and of their conception of knowledge itself:

> The harder the positivists insist on their conception of science as a guarantee for a closer and closer relation between knowledge and the real, the more they exacerbate the anomaly. In their belief that knowledge grows by secretion and that it is a result of specialized subjects (the scientists) who are able to extract knowledge from an object-world, they have overlooked the important principle of the reversibility of the subject-object relation in knowledge-formation.
>
> If at first it seemed that "positivist science" was making the world, it is now the same world that is forcing a crisis in positive science by throwing up contradictions and anomalies in real life. . . . As a consensus model, it is inherently incapable of dealing with contradiction and revolution except in negative terms. These terms are not a problem of syntax but of ideology which precedes and predetermines possible forms of knowledge. (Mafeje, 1976, p. 325)

He thus concludes that anthropology is

> generically a child of imperialism [which] has been a systematic extension of bourgeois economic, political, intellectual, and cultural forms. From the twenties onwards anthropologists became embroiled in colonial affairs with the best intentions but with identical results as those of their soldier-administrator brethren. (Mafeje, 1976, pp. 326–327)

The implications of Mafeje's arguments for the field of comparative education lie in the relationship between the forms of knowledge developed throughout the colonial and imperial experience and the spread of formal schooling in many countries, particularly after the Second World War. The comparison was implicitly between the kinds of school systems developed in the European context and all other forms of schooling. The rise of a scientific culture allied with evolutionary notions of development coincided with many countries becoming independent in the post–World War I period. Not surprisingly, the newly established education systems within these countries became linked with a world educational research enterprise firmly embedded in a functionalist framework. This research endeavor was primarily linked to European and North American publishing houses and later to the development of the computer. The implicit positivistic bias of the computer and the ability to analyze "more data" meant that emphasis shifted from anthropological interest in Indigenous cultures to a more sociological/economic preoccupation with collecting statistics on the new or expanding social institutions in newly developed states. The result has been the increasing homogenization of the culture of education on a worldwide scale, with educators' accompanying assumption that there is only one valid epistemology. From a functionalist perspective, it is assumed that the most scientifically reputable view has prevailed.

SCHOOL ETHNOGRAPHY

Following the logical implications of Mafeje's (1976) conclusions concerning the culture of positivism, the then "new" sociologists of education in the 1970s, such as Michael Young (1971) and others, rejected that culture and based their accounts of schooling on the experiences of those participating in the daily life of schools. This approach opened the way for the development of ethnographic approaches to educational research that harked back in a methodological sense to the heyday of anthropological fieldwork and that could be conducted effectively in schools at home or abroad. The work of George Spindler (1982) and George and Louise Spindler (1987) in the United States were also pioneering efforts in making the workings of schools in many different cultural contexts the focus of anthropologists' interests.

Madan Sarup (1978), in a review of anthropological studies in education from a neo-Marxist perspective, notes that these educational ethnographers could not ground their accounts of education in an objectively available social world because that world itself would be a feature of their method. Sarup (1978) asks, "What, then, is the justification of their own theorizing and how do they ground their accounts? What are the 'auspices' of their theorizing and on what grounds is their own enquiry better or more adequate?" (p. 33). He suggests that their orientation to political egalitarianism is the particular interest in which their accounts are grounded (Sarup, 1978). These are questions that deserve further consideration.

In my earlier work on the utility of anthropological approaches to the study of comparative education, I outlined various ways ethnographic studies could be useful. First, the cross-cultural study of socialization can provide information on the kinds of values and cognitive categories that children in various cultures learn before they even attend school (Masemann, 1976). It can illuminate the study of learning in natural settings from a natural history participant-observer approach and can provide detailed accounts of the cross-cultural study of cognition (Cole et al., 1971).

Second, the comparative study of schooling, as well as the interface between socialization and the formal demands of the school system, is enhanced by the holistic ethnographic study of schools within their communities. Third, the ethnographic study of the workings of schools themselves as formal institutions can yield valuable comparative insights into current issues of concern to educators, such as underachievement (a socially constructed term), and can provide the grounded theoretical perspectives from which more large-scale, survey-type studies can be developed (Masemann, 1976).

In terms of the theme of my article, which was immanent functionalism, the suggestions above about the use of ethnography in comparative education seem to be tied to an implicitly functionalist paradigm. Subsequently, I examined constraints on the development of a neo-Marxist school ethnography (Masemann, 1981). I argue that "school ethnography today is limited . . . in the same way early colonial anthropology was limited. It is essentially microcosmic, and can be carried out by researchers who see education as an essentially autonomous and isolated phenomenon" (Masemann, 1981, p. 86). (Thus the dialectic of the global and the local comes back to haunt us again. If ethnography is based on the liberal distinction that education and work are separate, then there is no need to postulate that education is related to the outside world.)

I asked if the trend to ethnographic studies could be likened to a metaphoric shift from "hard" to "soft" educational research in which, from a Bernsteinian perspective, educational researchers themselves had been socialized into an "elaborated code" of research (Masemann, 1981), "with its shades of meaning, the ambiguities, the ambivalences, the unwillingness to judge, the interest in social relations, the emphasis on context" (Bernstein, 1977, p. 69). In other words, just as Bernstein (1977) postulates that the middle class is more likely to be socialized into a code of language production that includes elaborate distinctions and complex syntax and lexicon, the ethnographers have become socialized into a more complex form of educational research in which their findings cannot be easily synthesized into results. Similarly, Bernstein postulates that, whereas members of the middle class are thus less likely to make judgments based on ideology because they might be able to see both sides of an argument at once, members of the working class have a certainty about ideology that is made possible by the form of discourse they command, in which answers are somewhat more sharply defined as positive or negative choices. I concluded in earlier editions of this book that the success of education itself leads to the inability of middle-class persons to think in ideological terms because they are involved in a form of knowledge production in which issues of ideology become subverted by issues of technique or, in this case, methodology (Masemann, 1981). The results of elections in the past two decades have led me to conclude that members of any social class in any country are less likely to cling to ideology than in previous times.

Thus school ethnography has become a technique widely used in colleges of education, but it has become deracinated from its place in the history of anthropological theory. (This situation has become even more evident since this textbook was first published in 1996. I attribute the ahistoricism in part to the prevalence of computer-based literature searches, although it may also have an ideological basis.)

I conclude that school ethnography with a neo-Marxist perspective would be unlikely to proliferate because the power of statistical research itself will increase with the spread of formal education, which is associated with the concept of modernization (Masemann, 1981). However, I also conclude that the value of neo-Marxist approaches to ethnography lies in the researcher's eschewing the assumptions of neutrality and objectivity of functionalist positivistic approaches and assuming the autonomy and isolation of the school and classroom (Masemann, 1981). Neo-Marxist approaches, instead, call for researchers to seize the opportunity of doing a political analysis in which their role, as well as that of the teacher, the student, and educational equality itself, is defined in new ways (Masemann, 1981).

In a further examination of the role of critical ethnography (studies that use an anthropological methodology but rely on a body of theory deriving from critical sociology and philosophy) in the study of comparative education, I raise the following issues:

> Is it the task of social scientists to seek ever more diligently to define objective methods of researching the social world (or education), with possibilities for change simply seen as the result of "reading out the data" and making choices on the basis of some cost-efficient or technological rationale? Or is it their task to attempt to understand as accurately as possible the subjective understandings that actors have of their own version of "social reality"? Or, third, is there some way of seeing social science in Marx's terms that would forever blur the objective/subjective distinction and thus make necessary the redefinition of social research itself? (Masemann, 1982, p. 1)

After discussing sociological and interpretive approaches to educational research, I examined the value of critical approaches in their treatment of social conflict and structuralism: "Neo-Marxist interpretations of school life have questioned the established categories of education and have raised fundamental questions about the social control functions of schools and the social contradictions they create or participate in" (Masemann, 1982, p. 11). Douglas Foley's (1979; 1990) work has been particularly noteworthy in this respect, in his studies of student alienation in Texas. He notes that critical ethnology offers the only way to study the techniques that schools and teachers use to organize, model, practice, and reward the behaviors that socialize students into technological rationality (Foley, 1979; 1990).

I concluded by suggesting various uses to which critical ethnography could be put in comparative education: the study of socialization of students into preferred language dialects or national languages, national political cultures, or elite values; the study of the penetration of dominant ideology or imported "innovative" rationality; comparative studies of systems of student credentialing, and the penetration of computer technologies (Masemann, 1982). Finally, I suggest the study of rationality itself could be an interesting new focus of comparative education (Masemann, 1982).

Since these papers were written in the 1980s, a great deal of ethnographic research has been done in educational settings, most prolifically in the United States and Great Britain, as well as in Latin America and Japan. It is doubtful if the majority of these studies have been done from a critical perspective. While an ethnographic method has been adopted as a tool of educational research, in many cases its theoretical basis in anthropology has been absent. Bradley Levinson, Douglas Foley, and Dorothy Holland (1996) summarized the major work in critical educational research over the last two decades of the 20th century to 1996. In their introduction, they review the then-current developments in critical educational studies: social reproduction, cultural reproduction, the cultural difference approach, ethnography and cultural reproduction, and cultural studies and the cultural production of the educated person. They also examine the Western schooling paradigm in a global context and explore "how concepts of the 'educated person' are produced and negotiated between state discourses and local practice" (Levinson et al., 1996, p. 18). Their work provides a very comprehensive and forward-looking assessment of the state of the art of critical educational studies. Another book addressing studies of education in a globalized context is that edited by Kathryn Anderson-Levitt (2003). It consists of studies exploring the question of whether education or schooling is becoming an increasingly homogenous institution or whether cultural differences create a diverse set of educational experiences, depending upon their context.

Other books published since 2000 fill in some of the gaps in the growing field of ethnography in comparative education. Bob Teasdale and Zane Ma Rhea (2000) edited a volume focusing mainly on indigenous knowledge in the context of higher education, including papers that were presented at the World Congress of Comparative Education Societies in Sydney, Australia, in 1996. Studies of indigenous perspectives of education are a growing area in ethnographic studies of education. In Judith Liu, Heidi Ross, and Donald Kelly's (2000) book, which focuses the "ethnographic eye" on education in China, the contributing authors cover many topics related to conducting ethnographic research. These topics range from policy issues to education for minority populations, juvenile delinquency, rural education, education in a girls' school, and problems of ethnographic methodology. Lui et al. (2000) presage the central issue that Frances Vavrus and Lesley Bartlett (2009) address—the problem of comparison at the local, intermediate, and national levels (Bartlett & Vavrus, 2019).

In general, papers on ethnographic studies of education since 2000 have largely been published in English-language journals, most notably in the U.S.-based *Anthropology and Education Quarterly*. In the United Kingdom, the journal titled *Ethnography and Education*, founded in 2006, has published articles deriving from a more sociological foundation. There has been a lack of communication about anthropologies of education among various countries because of language barriers and the realities of information flow and publishing in the postcolonial period. Kathryn Anderson-Levitt's (2011) edited book, *Anthropologies of Education: A Global Guide to Ethnographic Studies of Learning and Schooling*, seeks to remedy this gap by including chapters about the development of anthropology of education as a field in German, French, Spanish, Portuguese, Italian, Slavic languages, Japanese, and English as a second language. As a result, English-speaking anthropologists of education will be able to acquaint themselves with the rich heritage of studies that have heretofore been unavailable to them. One regrets the lack of a chapter on the work in the United Kingdom and Ireland on the anthropology of education. Brad Levinson and Mica Pollock's (2011) *A Companion to Anthropology and Education*, written mainly by members of the Council on Anthropology and Education (part of the American Anthropological Association), incorporates material from many different countries and language backgrounds to expose an encyclopedic range of ethnographic theories and methods from a global perspective. Over the last decade, several publications have carried on the work of school ethnography and related topics. The studies have expanded the scope of traditional ethnography with its notions of a bounded field site, a homogeneous population, and a common language and culture. The methodology has also expanded to take advantage of innovations in electronic data-gathering and interviewing. The increased movement of people worldwide has also resulted in heterogeneous school populations. In general, ethnographic studies of education are being done on a variety of topics that were not always characterized as comparative education—among them, migration and transmigration, global citizenship, indigenous education, education reform and innovation, policy linkages, and the world of big data.

Issues of migration and transnationalism are prominent in recent publications. Hamann, Wortham, and Murillo's (2015) *Revisiting Education in the New Latino Diaspora* contains a wide range of studies by many authors about the experiences of Mexican and other Latino students in schools across the United States. Newcomer immigrant youth from various backgrounds in the United States and Europe are also the subject of studies (Abu El-Haj et al., 2017; Bartlett & Vavrus, 2017; Jaffe-Walter & Lee, 2018; Mangual Figuerosa, 2017). Global citizenship education is the focus in studies by Chee and Jakubiak (2020), Dyrness and Abu El-Haj (2019), and Sant et al. (2018). Indigenous education was the focus of a special issue of the *Canadian Journal of Education* (Styres & Zinga, 2013). Ethnographic studies of education in countries outside of North America and Europe have been published by Kendall et al. (2019) on Malawi, Hoffman (2017) on Haiti, Janigan (2020) on Tajikistan, Levinson (2019) on Mexico, Thomas and Rugambwa (2011) on Tanzania, Kano (2019) on South Sudan, and Vavrus (2018) on East Africa, among others. Finally, the linkages of anthropology and education with context and public policy have been explored by Bartlett and Vavrus (2019), Demerath (2019), and Levinson et al. (2020). The development of cultural class theory and critical race theory was addressed by Foley (2010) and Woodson (2018) while decolonializing methodologies were addressed by Tuhiwai Smith (2012). This is not an exhaustive list, as the focus on research by scholars in or connected with the United States has dominated the major journals in this area. Diligent research will reveal many other studies from non-English-speaking countries and the Global South. International students at North American and European universities have also contributed to a much more diverse body of ethnographic studies carried out in their home countries, or among immigrant students and teachers in primary, secondary and tertiary levels of education within their host country. In the last decade, interest has taken a "postfoundational" turn. For example, the Comparative and International Education Society (CIES) now has a Post-Foundational Special Interest Group that seeks to explore beyond the traditional "foundations" in Western ideas of modernity, society, and development. A postfoundational lens focuses well beyond the uses of ethnographic methodology, which is our interest here.

In recent years, the power imbalance between the Global North and the Global South has shifted somewhat, as a result of postcolonial approaches to studying education and new ways of gathering, coding, and synthesizing data. I attribute these changes also to the spread of the use of computers as a research tool. For example, the invention of computer-based modes of synthesizing qualitative data, such as ATLAS.ti or NVivo (formerly called NUD*IST) software, has enabled researchers alternative ways to analyze and compare data sets. Computer communication has also enabled researchers to gather interview or survey data without ever speaking personally to the research subjects who may be in widely dispersed locations. Data sets can then be read as "text" in much larger-scale studies, which Noah Sobe (2018) discussed when addressing new modes of "problematizing comparison in a post-exploration age" (p. 325).

The power balance has also changed over the last several decades with an increase in literacy worldwide and the use of new technology. Brissett (2020) expresses this recent turn and brings out its inherent contradiction: "Demanding greater representation of the experiences of people from the Global South is a recognition that, **historically,** their voices have been marginalized and excluded from the very discipline that **is constructed to** supposedly understand and address their plight" (p. 594, bold added).

There has also been an expansion in the way ethnographic research can be conducted as evidenced by the use of autoethnography and collective or collaborative ethnography. Autoethnography consists of reflecting on one's biography or experience and then using the text as data to analyze it through a theoretical lens. By doing so, the researcher may also come to a better understanding of their positionality with their approach to the researchable question (Brissett, 2020).

Collective or collaborative ethnography refers to conducting research with other researchers, or to participating in the research process on an equal footing with those who might previously have been called the "research subjects." These two methods are a far cry from the traditional orally based mode of data-gathering by the "expert" anthropologist gathering data from persons in preliterate societies.

CONCLUSION

In conclusion, I return to the major themes of this chapter, particularly the relationship between culture and comparative education. Gail Kelly (as cited in Kelly, 1996) raised the question in her 1986 paper: "Vandra Masemann and Douglas Foley urged the field to engage in qualitative research that seeks to understand educational processes. No debate followed, nor for that matter did much research of a qualitative nature on school processes. The field neither accepted nor rejected the challenge; it simply acted as if it were never made" (Kelly, 1996, p. 99). I am not as pessimistic as Kelly, who measured the acceptance of research by its appearance in the major comparative education journals.

Other questions arise about the context in which critical perspectives thrive. From a Marxist perspective, there is a curious absence of focus on the dialectical struggle in comparative education, as if somehow the only struggle had been between East and West, when the epistemological struggle is being waged at a deeper cultural level between the north and the south and between industrial forms of culture and the more local, rooted forms of culture. Since schools are inherently sites of local cultural formation, this phenomenon should come as no surprise (Apple, 1996). Moreover, the struggle of cultural groups who have not accepted the major epistemological assumptions of scientism has been widely ignored in the field of comparative education. For example, the first Commission on Indigenous Education was held at the Ninth World Congress of Comparative Education in Sydney, Australia, in 1996 (Masemann & Welch, 1997).

Although cultural differences in education in industrial countries are perceived to be diminishing and the forces of standardization are growing ever stronger, even if only in the interests of sharing data on education, the struggle is still being waged between those who do not share the scientistic epistemology of the world and those who assume their view has triumphed. (The growth of this plurality of voices is addressed in other chapters in this book.)

With their emphasis on studying other cultures as complete wholes as well as on cultural relativism, anthropologists attempted to ignore the impact of the colonial endeavor itself on cultural change. The colonial enterprise was so laden with racist assumptions about the "other" people in the world that it became part of a convenient fiction to philosophize about human progress and the perfectibility to implement cost-efficient forms of government. Recent attempts to equalize educational opportunity on a global scale have led to the ignoring of local cultural values and traditional forms of knowledge and ways of thinking, which are in danger of becoming extinct. Anthropological studies of education in every country and setting can help bear witness to the rich diversity of modes of cultural transmission and the great variety of experiences that can be called educational.

NOTE

I would like to express my sincere thanks to Kara Janigan for her assistance in revising and editing this chapter. I am grateful for her technical support as well as her help in weathering the 2020 global viral pandemic. I also thank my colleagues Lesley Bartlett and Fran Vavrus for their suggestions about recent research in this area. My thanks also go to Iveta Silova and the organizing committee who organized the first virtual CIES annual conference in March/April 2020, which helped to keep the CIES community together.

REFERENCES

Abu El-Haj, T. R., Ríos-Rojas, A., & Jaffe-Walter, R. (2017). Whose race problem? Tracking patterns of racial denial in US and European educational discourses on Muslim youth. *Curriculum Inquiry, 47*(3), 310–335.

Altbach, P. G., & Kelly, G. P. (1978). Education and colonialism. In P. G. Altbach & G. P. Kelly (Eds.), *Educational policy, planning, and theory*. Longman.

Anderson-Levitt, K. M. (Ed.). (2003). *Local meanings, global schooling: Anthropology and world culture theory*. Palgrave Macmillan.

Anderson-Levitt, K. M. (Ed.). (2011). *Anthropologies of education: A global guide to ethnographic studies of learning and schooling*. Berghahn Books.

Apple, M. W. (1996). *Cultural politics and education*. Teachers College Press.

Barrett, S. R. (1996). *Anthropology: A student's guide to theory and method*. University of Toronto Press.

Barrett, S. R. (2011). *Anthropology: A student's guide to theory and method* (2nd ed.). University of Toronto Press.

Bartlett, L., & Vavrus, F. (2019). Rethinking the concept of "context" in comparative research. In R. Gorur, S. Sellar, & G. Steiner-Khamsi (Eds.), *World yearbook of education 2019: Comparative methodology in the era of big data and global networks*. Routledge.

Bartlett, L., & Vavrus, F. K. (2017). *Rethinking case study research: A comparative approach*. Routledge.

Bernstein, B. (1977). *Class, codes, and control: Theoretical studies towards a sociology of language* (Vol. 3, 2nd rev. ed.). Routledge & Kegan Paul.

Brissett, N. O. M. (2020). Teaching like a subaltern: Postcoloniality, positionality, and pedagogy in international development and education. *Comparative Education Review*, 64(4), 577–597.

Chee, W., & Jakubiak, C. (2020). the national as global, the global as national: Citizenship education in the context of migration and globalization. *Anthropology & Education Quarterly*, 51(2), 119–122.

Cohen, Y. (1971). The shaping of men's minds: Adaptations to imperatives of culture. In M. L. Wax, S. Diamond, & F. O. Gearing (Eds.), *Anthropological perspectives on education* (pp. 19–50). Basic Books.

Cole, M., Gay, J., Glick, J., & Sharp, D. (1971). *The cultural context of learning and thinking*. Basic Books.

Darwin, C. (1859). *On the origins of species, or, The preservation of favored races in the struggle for life*. John Murray.

Demerath, P. (2019). Maximizing impact in anthropology and education: Capitulations, linkages, and publics. *Anthropology & Education Quarterly*, 50(4), 448–458.

Dyrness, A., & Abu El-Haj, T. R. (2019). Reflections on the field: The democratic citizenship formation of transnational youth. *Anthropology & Education Quarterly*, 51(2), 165–177.

Escobar, A. (1992). Reflections on "development": Grassroots approaches and alternative politics in the third world. *Futures*, 24(5), 411–436.

Foley, D. E. (1979). *Labor and legitimation in schools: Notes on doing ethnography*. Paper presented at the Comparative and International Education Society, Ann Arbor, MI.

Foley, D. E. (1990). *Learning capitalist culture: Deep in the heart of Tejas*. University of Pennsylvania Press.

Foley, D. (2010). The rise of class culture theory in educational anthropology. *Anthropology & Education Quarterly*, 41(3), 215–227.

Fox, C. (1997). Metaphors of educational development. In T. J. Scrase (Ed.), *Social justice and third world education* (pp. 47–66). Garland Publishing.

Freire, P. (1974). *Pedagogy of the oppressed*. Seabury.

Galtung, J. (1973). *The European community: A superpower in the making*. Universitetsforlaget.

Hamann, E., Wortham, S., & Murillo, E. G., Jr. (Eds.). (2015). *Revisiting education in the new Latino diaspora*. Information Age Publishing.

Hoffman, D. M. (2017). Against all odds: The ethnography of hope among Haitian youth in difficult circumstances. In R. Hopson, W. Rodick, & A. Kaul (Eds.), *New directions in educational ethnography: Shifts, problems, and reconstruction* (pp. 15–33). Emerald Group Publishing Limited.

Ilon, L. (1994). Structural adjustment and education: Adapting to a growing global market. *International Journal of Educational Development*, 14(2), 95–108.

Jaffe-Walter, R., & Lee, S. J. (2018). Engaging the transnational lives of immigrant youth in public schooling: Toward a culturally sustaining pedagogy for newcomer immigrant youth. *American Journal of Education*, *124*(3), 257–283.

Janigan, K. (2020). Efforts to overcome barriers to girls' secondary schooling in rural Tajikistan: The importance of experiential activities. In I. Silova & S. Niyozov (Eds.), *Globalization on the margins: Education and post-socialist transformations in Central Asia* (2nd ed., pp. 229–248). Information Age Publishing.

Kano, S. (2019). "One" but divided: Tribalism and grouping among secondary school students in Southern Sudan. *Anthropology & Education Quarterly*, *50*(2), 189–204.

Keesing, F. M. (1960). *Cultural anthropology: The science of custom*. Rinehart.

Kelly, G. P. (1996). Vietnam. In D. H. Kelly (Ed.), *International feminist perspectives on educational reform: The work of Gail Paradise Kelly* (pp. 137–162). Garland Publishing.

Kendall, N., Kaunda, Z., & Majee, U. (2019). Decolonial approaches to AIDS, children's wellbeing, and education in Malawi. In I. Eloff (Ed.), *Handbook of quality of life in African societies* (pp. 275–292). Springer.

Kluckhohn, F. R. (1961). Dominant and variant value orientations. In F. R. Kluckhohn & F. L. Strodtbeck (Eds.), *Variations in value orientations* (pp. 1–48). Greenwood.

Levinson, B. A. (2019). Radical pluralism and the challenges of educating for democratic-ecological civic identities: Reflections from the Mexican school context. *Education, Citizenship and Social Justice*, *15*(1), 10–21.

Levinson, B. A., Foley, D. E., & Holland, D. C. (1996). *The cultural production of the educated person: Critical ethnographies of schooling and local practice*. State University of New York Press.

Levinson, B. A., & Pollock, M. (Eds.). (2011). *A companion to the anthropology of education*. Blackwell Publishing.

Levinson, B. A., Winstead, T., & Sutton, M. (2020). An anthropological approach to education policy as a practice of power: Concepts and methods. In G. Fan & T. S. Popkewitz (Eds.), *Handbook of education policy studies: Values, governance, globalization, and methodology* (Vol. 1, pp. 363–379). Springer.

Liu, J., Ross, H. A., & Kelly, D. P. (Eds.). (2000). *The ethnographic eye: Interpretive studies of education in China*. Falmer Press.

Mafeje, A. (1976). The problem of anthropology in historical perspective: An inquiry into the growth of the social sciences. *Canadian Journal of African Studies*, *10*(2), 307–333.

Malinowski, B. (1944). *A scientific theory of culture*. University of North Carolina Press.

Mangual Figueroa, A. (2017). Speech or silence: Undocumented students' decisions to disclose or disguise their citizenship status in school. *American Educational Research Journal*, *54*(3), 485–523.

Masemann, V. (1974). The "hidden curriculum" of a West African girls' secondary school. *Canadian Journal of African Studies*, *8*(3), 479–494.

Masemann, V. (1976). Anthropological approaches to comparative education. *Comparative Education Review*, *20*(3), 368–380.

Masemann, V. (1981). School ethnography: Plus ça change? In A. Kater (Ed.), *Anthropologists approaching education* (pp. 85–99). Centre for the Study of Education in Developing Countries.

Masemann, V. (1982). Critical ethnography in the study of comparative education. *Comparative Education Review*, *26*(1), 1–15.

Masemann, V. L., & Welch, A. R. (Eds.). (1997). *Tradition, modernity, and postmodernity in comparative education*. Kluwer Academic Publishers.

Mead, M. (1970). Our educational emphases in primitive perspective. In M. L. Wax, S. Diamond, & F. O. Gearing (Eds.), *From child to adult: Studies in the anthropology of education*. Natural History Press.

Morgan, L. H. (1877). *Ancient society*. Holt.

Noah, H. J., & Eckstein, M. A. (1969). *Toward a science of comparative education*. Macmillan.

Pai, Y., & Adler, S. A. (1997). *Cultural foundations of education* (2nd ed.). Prentice-Hall.

Radcliffe-Brown, R. A. (1948). *A natural science of society*. Free Press.

Sant, E., Davies, I., Pashby, K., & Shultz, L. (2018). *Global citizenship education: A critical introduction to key concepts and debates*. Bloomsbury Academic.

Sarup, M. (1978). *Marxism and education*. Routledge & Kegan Paul.

Sobe, N. W. (2018). Problematizing comparison in a post-exploration age: Big data, educational knowledge, and the art of criss-crossing. *Comparative Education Review*, 62(3), 325–343.

Spencer, H. (1896). *Principles of sociology*. D. Appleton. (Original work published in 1876).

Spindler, G. D. (1982). *Doing the ethnography of schooling: Educational anthropology in action*. Holt, Rinehart, and Winston.

Spindler, G. D., & Spindler, L. S. (Eds.). (1987). *Interpretive ethnography of education: At home and abroad*. Lawrence Erlbaum Associates.

Steiner-Khamsi, G., Appleton, M., & Vellani, S. (2018). Understanding business interests in international large-scale student assessments: A media analysis of *The Economist*, *Financial Times*, and *Wall Street Journal*. *Oxford Review of Education*, 44(2), 190–203.

Styres, S., & Zinga, D. (2013). Opening the circle: Welcoming brother sun. *Canadian Journal of Education*, 36(2), 1–3.

Teasdale, G. R., & Ma Rhea, Z. (Eds.). (2000). *Local knowledge and wisdom in higher education*. Pergamon.

Thomas, M. A. M., & Rugambwa, A. (2011). Equity, power, and capabilities: Constructions of gender in a Tanzanian secondary school. *Feminist Formations*, 23(3), 153–175.

Tuhiwai Smith, L. (2012). *Decolonizing methodologies: Research and Indigenous peoples* (2nd ed.). Zed Books.

Tylor, E. B. (1871). *Primitive culture*. John Murray.

Ulich, R. (1965). *Education in Western culture*. Harcourt, Brace, and World.

Vavrus, F. (2018). Andreas goes to Africa: A comparative historical study of the teachers for East Africa programs. *European Education*, 50(2), 171–184.

Vavrus, F. K., & Bartlett, L. (Eds.). (2009). *Critical approaches to comparative education: Vertical case studies from Africa, Europe, the Middle East, and the Americas*. Palgrave Macmillan.

wa Thiong'o, N. (1986). *Decolonizing the mind: The politics of language in African literature*. James Currey.

Williams, T. R. (1972). *Introduction to socialization: Human culture transmitted*. Mosby.

Winthrop, R., Bulloch, G., Bhatt, P., & Wood, A. (2013). *Investment in global education: A strategic imperative for business*. Brookings Institution.

Woodson, A. N. (2018). Racial code words, re-memberings and black kids' civic imaginations: A critical race ethnography of a post-civil rights leader. *Anthropology & Education Quarterly*, 50(1), 26–47.

Yang, S. (1991). *Shih and Kairos: Time category in the study of educational reform*. Paper presented at the National Science Council, Part C: Humanities and Social Sciences Taipei, Taiwan.

Young, M. F. D. (1971). *Knowledge and control: New directions for the sociology of education*. Collier-Macmillan.

5

The Question of Identity from a Comparative Education Perspective

Christine Fox
University of Wollongong

ABSTRACT

In an era of globalization, of far-flung diaspora both transnational and intranational, most of our 21st-century societies have multiple ways of being and defining ourselves. Cultural identities, once considered straightforward, are shaken, disrupted, by external pressures of population rise, armed conflict that drives millions of people from their homes and countries, and climate change that threatens their livelihood. The global spread of technology and social media should draw people together, creating an international forum for intercultural interaction. Yet in the 2020s, an alarming rise in "post-truth" or "fake news" phenomena in social media challenges the very foundations for creating truthful and sincere intercultural understanding. Concepts such as social justice, security, freedom of speech, and human rights are tossed around and twisted by white supremacists, dictators, and others to "justify" racism, misogyny, violence, exclusion, and other ideological fundamentalist views.

■ ■ ■

From a comparative education perspective, the question of identity is contextual and exceedingly complex. This revised chapter for the fifth edition explores a critical postcolonial perspective of comparative education that focuses more directly on the intersectionality of identity (e.g., Black feminism; poverty, class, gender, diverse sexuality, and "ethnic" identity) and education. Some examples from different international contexts are provided to illustrate the theoretical propositions. Sociocultural identities in the 21st century have one thing in common: fluidity. Since 2019, communities globally are being irrevocably altered by the impact of the coronavirus pandemic together with the devastating impact of climate change on the planet. Comparativists in education today are charged with searching for new meanings, creating new knowledge, and seeking new ways to answer questions of identity in comparative education.

We are like travelers navigating an unknown terrain with the help of old maps, drawn at a different time and in response to different needs. While the terrain we are traveling on, the world society of states, has changed, our normative map has not (Benhabib, 1992, p. 15).

In an era of globalization and transnational and intranational migration and in societies with multiple ways of being and multiple ways of defining ourselves, there are no longer clear-cut definitions or distinctions among groups of people. Nevertheless, some travelers still try to steer their followers along the old highways—into the ravines of discrimination, racism, and other ideological fundamentalist views of the Other. Educators around the world, particularly comparativists, are searching for new solutions and are creating new knowledge that is more appropriate for societies of the 21st century.

This chapter explores a perspective on comparative education that focuses on the intersection of identity and education as it affects our understandings of different educational contexts. The comparative educator seeks new theories and methodological approaches to investigate concerns involving all sectors of education, moving from within their society out to the challenges raised through globalization. These concerns particularly affect that curious breed of educators—international educational consultants—who are confronted and immersed in contexts other than their own, but who ideally claim some kind of universal moral right to speak about educational change and development that improve health and well-being.

My standpoint, drawing on Jürgen Habermas (1984), is that theoretically it is possible, as well as desirable, to reach uncoerced understandings *interculturally* that are based on trust and sincerity rather than through power or the domination so clearly demonstrated by the colonizers over the colonized in the past (Pratt, 1992). The coming together of common ideas across diverse societal conditions signals a potential to construct meaning; where this occurs, there is a transformation in education (Fox, 1992). In my work I have described three levels of attempted communicative action: successful communication; miscommunication; and systemically distorted communication. To be successful, the interlocutors need to show sincerity, truthfulness, and a belief that what they say is appropriate and comprehensible. Miscommunication may infer that linguistic or identity differences are contributing to misunderstanding or that some other impediment to understanding is occurring, which, with patience and sincerity can be corrected. The last category, distorted communication, includes intended strategic action that is power-based manipulation (concealed or open), or psycho-systemically based strategic action (Fox, 1992, p. 68) that perhaps is similar to unconscious bias.

We are in the middle of a post-truth era in the public and political domain as well as the private domain that strikes at the very heart of attempted successful communicative action. The distortions created by post-truths, by definition, eliminate even the possibility of successful intercultural communication. How can educators even begin the research that is truthful and that can be trusted (Connell, 2019, p. 32)? How can the distortions of intercultural communication—so evident in the political domain, in social media, and in the pronouncements of dictators and others in power—be anything other than "fake"? The perennial question is "Was Hitler a good leader?" Perhaps he was a leader, but not "good" in the moral sense. Similarly, we can ask, "Is Trump a good leader and successful communicator?" If post-truth is acceptable, and distortions of the facts are evident, but the result is a significant number of followers, the question remains.

As Unterhalter (2012) notes, if a researcher does not take into account the intersectionality of identity in education, both research and implementation of change may have limited relevance, as there may be systemic distortions in the data gathered. A student, for example, may be identified in the classroom as a girl, but she may also be white, Hindu, local, immigrant, lesbian, or living under poor or wealthy, secure or endangered conditions. Ignorance of such factors in such contexts would impede the validity of the research conclusions. Context is all-important, particularly when undertaking comparative research, and particularly when undertaking international research.

The disruptions occurring globally in the 2020s are indeed challenging what can be meaningful in education. Overarching global concerns that are creating havoc include, first, the emergency of climate change, as Naomi Klein (2014) and many others have warned. Since Naomi Klein's publication, political, socioeconomic, and environmental awareness of the crisis has multiplied. One of the most outspoken and influential global movements involving young people has been led since 2018 by young Swedish activist Greta Thunberg, using social media to organize massive School Strikes for Climate. A recent public global movement to bring about awareness of the plight of our planet is the Extinction Rebellion. Climate change is recognized as a long-term pattern that adversely impacts the lives and livelihood of communities where some areas are now uninhabitable, causing widespread migration of so-called climate refugees—groups who may face more prejudice, racism, and gender discrimination in several countries that are receiving refugees.

The second major emergency—the COVID-19 pandemic—is causing illness and death, fear, and mental health problems, loss of jobs, loss of security. Restrictions on movement, the resulting isolation, the closing of public places such as schools, and the struggle to have adequate food, water, and sanitation unequally impacts a society's poorer populations. The COVID-19 pandemic thus starkly reveals and exacerbates already existing (perhaps hidden?) inequalities. Families living in poverty have fewer resources, possibly no electricity and no access to technology. Many countries do not release accurate data on the spread of the virus, perhaps for lack of relevant technology or for political reasons. Communities in the United States are deeply divided socially and politically about how the pandemic should be addressed.

Third, the Black Lives Matter movement protesting against injustice and police brutality toward Black lives has been embraced not only by people of color but by millions of activists for justice throughout the world. Similarly, Eddo-Lodge (2018) highlights the intersectionality of race, class, and gender when she tries to reason with, for example, people in power, or to women who "see no color" whom she describes as "whitewashed feminists." The impact of racism on most intercultural human activity around the world has been a weeping sore over the centuries, particularly over the years of colonization and slavery. The sores have not healed; racism evokes bitterness, hatred, violence, and police brutality. The vulnerability in resistance is very real (see Butler et al., 2016). The vocal Black Lives Matter movement is not new but has emerged with greater visibility in the 2020s (Clayton, 2018).

A fourth overarching concern that has strong repercussions for the 2020s is the all-important struggle of inclusion and exclusion of people who identify as LGBTQ+ (lesbian, gay, bisexual, transgender, queer, and others). In many countries, it is still illegal to identify as lesbian or gay; those apprehended may even be subject to the death penalty. Refugees who identify as gay and are seeking asylum in other countries may be not be recognized as refugees. Comparative education scholars have been promoting research into the experiences, contexts, and sociopolitical implications of LGBTQ+ students in schools, higher education, and nonformal education for over 30 years (Connell, 1992). The 2020s mark a new era within the comparative and international education community to include publications on sexual orientation, gender identity, and expression (SOGIE). Academic research and discourses on the intersectionality of LGBTQ+ issues require volumes in themselves. Many other intersections of identity and education could be added, such as religion, disability, health, mental health, intelligence tests, feminism and masculinities, occupation, age, and so on.

In this new edition of *Comparative Education*, this chapter focuses on the changes that need to be recognized in an era of technological transformation, post-truth politics, a climate change emergency, and the COVID-19 pandemic.

The next section explores the literature of early intercultural interaction, highlighting how inequality, domination, and the distorted communication between colonizer and colonized set a scene that in effect created the racism, misogyny, and power-based control evident in modern industrialized societies. The chapter then discusses the intersectionalization of identity. Following are four cases studies taken from different contexts over time. A conclusion summarizes main issues and future actions that may be taken.

COLONIZERS AND COLONIZED: A BRIEF FORAY INTO THE LITERATURE OF INTERCULTURAL INTERACTION

Comparative education has traditionally been a search for similarities and differences in educational systems or activities, ideas, and ideologies. Early attempts to compare are reminiscent of early narratives, or travelers' tales, which presented vivid descriptions of groups of peoples, recognizing that they, like us, had intriguing differences in lifestyles. However, the tales of distant places soon became a mechanism for legitimating conquest and the stories expunged the humanness of colonized people. In the 19th and early 20th centuries, anthropological research came into its own, epitomizing Eurocentric interpretations of the Other, making much of the contrasts between two supposed opposites. As Raewyn Connell (2014, p. 522) notes, the colonialists saw the world of tribes and cultures, each unique, with only the colonizing power having an integrating view. Metaphors of *primitive* or *savage* placed the Other firmly in another world from the *civilized*. A case in point is the colonization of Australia by the British, where the colonialists, according to Bruce Pascoe (2014) "had their minds wrought by ideas of race and destiny. They arrived with a European cultural assumption that their science, economy and religion gave them natural superiority and authority to 'civilize' the original inhabitants and capture the wealth of the land they dispossessed." Bruce Pascoe, an Aboriginal historian, used the writings of early British colonizers, explorers, and settlers to construct his case. For example, in 1839, one of the early surveyors, Major Thomas Mitchell, recorded instances of widespread, organized agricultural activity, and villages that indicated the well-constructed buildings had been there for a very long time. By 1839, most of these areas and the habitation had been destroyed by the incoming pastoralists. Again and again, Pascoe shatters the still common myths that the original inhabitants of Australia were merely nomadic savages. Evidence abounds of pre-European systematic fishing practices, the building of dam walls along major rivers, and the harvesting and storing of natural grains. Yet even Pascoe's proven "Aboriginal identity" (disputed by some) and his sources taken directly from the colonizers' journals are still dismissed today by those deniers of the violence and destruction wrought by the colonists.

Postindependence history of what became known as "developing world" settings still tended to be dictated by European perceptions of what was good for the Other. With increased migration to the so-called First World, or the West, the complex process of intercultural interaction was often analyzed by Western educators as a one-way adaptation and integration of the Other into the dominant educational norm, rather like Young Yun Kim's theory of adaptation of strangers into a host society, since updated but not radically changed by her (Kim, 2001).

With the challenges of postmodernism, poststructuralism, and then postcolonialism, the notion of fundamental norms and values, or generalizable interests, lost its appeal. It is now widely recognized that there are multiple voices and that diversity can be celebrated. The danger, of course, lies in a belief by some that diversity indicates there are no common agreements on values and ethics, that all is culturally relative. Others may not even admit there are any worthwhile identities, values, or groups other than those of the dominant group in any society. The upshot of that argument is to claim that no worthwhile communication is possible across cultures. Now if this is the case, it may be argued that comparative education and international education are worthless disciplines, particularly when educators come from diametrically different cultural backgrounds. This chapter posits the opposite argument: that the visibly embodied difference of the Other is not a boundary, other than in the minds of those who create barriers. Bordering and rebordering, nay *un*bordering, is the outcome of globalization. Such boundaries are artificial, founded for the most part on historical racism (Majhanovich et al., 2012).

From postmodernism and poststructuralism has emerged a set of theories that address many of the conundrums of the current status and influence of places that were former colonial states (postcolonial *places*), or of people who are products of that colonial era down the generations and the diaspora of migration across the world society of states, a postcolonial disruption (Hickling-Hudson et al., 2004). The pioneers of postcolonialism included Edward Said (1978), whose classic work on Orientalism alerted the world to the debate about *us* and *them* as a very significant theoretical and practical issue. He particularly critiqued how those from the so-called Western nations stereotyped and denigrated those from the so-called Eastern nations, including the Middle East. Other important scholars in this vein include Gayatri Spivak (1990), who has been a vocal critic of the silencing of the subaltern by the dominant majority, particularly in the West. Homi Bhabha published *The Location of Culture* in 1994, in which he noted that the publication of Said's work "unleashed the exclusionary imperialist ideologies of self and other" (Bhabha, 1994a, p. 66). Bhabha is a key postcolonial theorist who set out to interrogate such broad notions as colonial discourse, identity, postmodernity, and semiotics and culture. He sought to relocate cultural representation through a critical, postcolonial perspective. His work on *hybridity* contains a complex discussion of identity—the ambivalence of identity, the creation of a *third space*—that challenges the colonial notion of *fixity*, or the essentialist representation of the colonial subject (Bhabha, 1994b). Fixity, as the sign of cultural/historical/racial difference in the discourse of colonialism, is a paradoxical mode of representation: it connotes rigidity and an unchanging order as well as disorder, degeneracy, and daemonic repetition. Stereotyping is its major discursive strategy.

In addition to postcolonial theory, this chapter draws on some key issues arising from Jürgen Habermas's (1984) communicative action. Habermas posits a hypothetical "as if" ideal speech situation, coercion-free, in which interlocutors can develop a mutual understanding through a rational dialogic process. Laudable as it is, Habermas's theory assumed that there must be a common cultural background between communicators for this to happen. He thus seemed to ignore most forms of communication in a postcolonial, intercultural world. However, Habermas's communicative action theory was written before the impact of globalization and before the latest diaspora of refugees, skilled workers, and sojourners flowing without boundaries to every corner of the globe. Challenged by sociological and political theorists in the 1990s, as the impacts of globalization were increasingly felt in the social and political arenas, Habermas responded to his critics by theorizing further on the concepts of law and democracy, sovereignty, and communicative power, while still interweaving the rational and moral elements of communicative action theory into his new work. There is still a question as to the extent that Habermas would accept multiple modes of reasoning or multiple differences of identity. As Bashir (2012) argues, "the inclusive, transformative, and empowering potential of Habermas' theory of deliberative democracy falters when confronted with particular types of historical injustices."

Authenticity in cross-cultural professional communication about education is not only desirable but also possible, despite the alternative facts bandied about in the media in the current era. An authentic communicative situation is an honorable kind of conversation based on mutual trust and a respectful sharing of intended meanings. It requires a sense of resonance between those who seek to reach agreement and mutual understanding—intuitively, poetically, or experientially—by identifying shared moral values or through rational discourse, or elements of each. The idea that cultural incompatibility is more or less inevitable is a logocentric view that stereotypes the Other and marginalizes those who identify with nondominant cultures. The ideas explored in this chapter show how people from contrastive worldviews can indeed bridge deep chasms of discursive difference, but only if they work together to create authentic (sincere, truthful, appropriate) intercultural communicative situations—that is, if they create their own intercultural space (Fox, 2016). It is important to keep in mind that too often intercultural communication is distorted—by deliberative deception, power inequalities, and by strategic action. The action (the communication) is not oriented to reaching understanding but rather oriented to success, or by concealing the intention of the dialogue and manipulating the situation in some way. Hence the manipulations of the powerful over powerless: by employer/employee, slave owner/slave, dictators/populace. They may seem to excel in intercultural communication, but they are not engaged in sincere, truthful, *authentic communication*.

Nevertheless, it is a pessimistic and dangerous view to dismiss the very real possibility of creating situations where two people (or groups of people) from very different cultures, power bases, class differences, and differences in their identities can get together and achieve real understanding in any special context, such as in creating positive educational change and renewal. The disastrous consequences of failing to find ways of working around differing values and goals of groups of people have seen whole nations and ethnic groups oppose each other with violence and hatred. Atrocities committed in the name of a group or an ideology are a violation of any human value system, as has been experienced to terrible effect in the first decades of the 21st century.

Dominant groups, particularly from highly industrialized and technologically advanced economies, have been adept at marginalizing the Other. And yet, in today's globalized world with rapid communication via new forms of information technology, it is impossible to maintain such separation or to believe that it can still be a West versus the Rest dichotomy. For example, in the second decade of the 21st century, divisions and discord emerged from within the many sectors of Middle Eastern and North African societies, once again demonstrating the absurdity of fixity of outsiders' views of the identity of, say, Muslim groups. Like Seyla Benhabid's words at the beginning of this chapter, the world has changed but the maps are old.

Authentic communication implies, as Hans-Georg Gadamer (1989) states, the opening of oneself to the full power of what the Other is saying. He shows that such an opening does not entail agreement but rather the to-and-fro play of dialogue. It is this potential that comparative educators and international educational consultants must pursue in response to the increasingly polarized context of global politics and its impact on education and intercultural research and, by implication, on the threat to authentic communication. These issues were eloquently discussed by Bradley Levinson and by Pauline Lipman in a special 35th anniversary issue of *Anthropology and Education Quarterly* in 2005.

COMPARATIVE EDUCATION AND THE INTERSECTIONALIZATION OF IDENTITY

Over many years, I have been involved in several educational projects that have raised important issues about the influence that formal education has on the development of individual identity—compared with, say, developing a nation, human resources, and participation rates in schooling. These projects have included research into the development of education in Western Samoa (Fox, 1992), the degree to which students from language backgrounds other than English are expected to participate in society (Iredale & Fox, 1997; Iredale et al., 1994); the participation of girls and women in education in Papua New Guinea (Fox, 1999); the experiences of girls and minority groups in schools in Laos (Fox, 2004); the experiences of Spanish-speaking students in some Australian schools (Plaza-Coral, 1998); the issues of undergraduate students in Sri Lankan universities (Fox, 2003); a comparison of perceptions of identity among Muslim girls in Australia and Saudi Arabia (El Biza, 2011) and the reforms of governance in a decentralized education system in Indonesia (Allaburton & Fox, 2006). What this work has indicated, and what my daily teaching at the university also indicates, is that the interplay of culture, education, and the state economy tends to create or support structural inequalities that mediate against the transformation of societies into just and peaceful places. Yet within these structures, there are enormous possibilities for cultural change through the agency of those who refuse to be relegated to the margins.

In this section, I discuss some of the issues that arise for those unfairly marginalized individuals and/or those who belong to subordinated groups. At stake here is how education has influenced the ways people construct their sociocultural, racial, and sexual identity and how others construct that identity for them. I posit that schooling is not necessarily unchangeable and is not merely a site for social and cultural reproduction. Rather, schools, schooling and alternative learning places (e.g., homeschooling), can present possibilities for transformation, even if those possibilities are today being attacked more than ever before. If such a transformation does take place, then it takes place largely through a *reconceptualization* of the identity of those who see themselves as agents of their destiny, or as resisters in a struggle to redefine who they are. The process itself transforms individuals, yet it takes place in a context of cultural identification of Other. The process challenges the conventional "wisdom" of the perceived inevitability of reproduction of inequality.

The explanations of cultural reproduction have changed as researchers focus more on documenting the transformative experiences of the heretofore invisible or silenced minorities. Well-known writings by Paulo Freire and others on development and literacy point to ways in which education can be transformative—as a process of conscientization. In a similar vein, the case study by Anne Hickling-Hudson points to new theories of how such a transformation takes place. Other comparativists have been influenced by anthropological, ethnographic literature, such as the work of Clifford Geertz, and by the intersections between culture and education, illustrating how subordinated groups seek to use schools as sites for cultural politics and challenges (see Chapter 4 in this volume).[1] They argue that through the production of cultural forms created within the structural constraints of sites such as schools, subjectivities form and agency develops (see, e.g., Sullivan & Day, 2019).

Some of the illustrative examples that I discuss raise further issues about the intersectional formation of identity and identities, typically the intersections of gender, poverty, and race. Identity is not fixed, nor is identity a single definable condition. Yet the construction of identity can be the construction of inequalities, as well as a powerful force in transforming the structures that seek to reduce the identity of Otherness to a single, stereotyped dimension.

The case studies that follow highlight such intersectional perspectives.

The "Single Story"

The stereotype is still frequently used by children and adults to recite a "single story" about communities of people that seem quite different from themselves. Chimamanda Ngosi Adichie (2013), an internationally recognized Black feminist author from Nigeria, encountered many "single stories" when she first arrived in the United States on a postgraduate scholarship—of all of Africa as a catastrophe, a place of poverty and war, a place waiting for aid from without. Coming from her urban, university background in eastern Nigeria, Adichie warns of the danger of the single story that risks critical misunderstandings. As Adichie claims, the single story robs people of their identity. One single story may be true in itself, but it is incomplete. Identity is explored through a multilayered construction of lives and cultures.

Similar "single stories" have been created of the imagined Muslim, a word often equated in non-Islamic countries with terrorists, as men with beards, or as subservient women wearing the hijab. In an article on critical literacy, Stephen Phelps (2010) has elaborated on ways in which to counter such single stories by using nonfiction to learn about Islam. Phelps points out, for example, that a popular stereotype and misconception of Muslims in the United States is that they are all Arab and that all Arabs are Muslim. This often quoted stereotype is despite the fact that most Muslims in many countries outside the Middle East are not Arab. Phelps provides descriptions of several recently published books that he has recommended for schools and colleges.

Another illustrative case is discussed by Douglas Foley (1996), who discusses the "silent Indian" stereotype that emerged in earlier literature on the experiences of Native Americans in schools set up by, and usually taught by, the dominant white majority in the United States. Foley revisits the myths and stereotypes of Native American schoolchildren by providing a close and personal inside view of how, and why, some Native Americans might choose silence as a resistance discourse, "a political retreat into a separate cultural space and identity far from the white world." The case of the "silent Indian" is still quoted today as a single story, although time has passed, and earlier assumptions were simplistic explanations for a multifaceted intercultural dialogic discourse in the Bakhtinian sense (Bakhtin, 1981).

The "Ethnic Minority" Australian

Despite nearly 40 years of multicultural policy in the schools of most states of Australia, a notion persists of students from overseas, or students from language backgrounds other than English (LBOTE), somehow fail to match up to the standards and culture of the dominant culture. The "ethnic minority" Australian has been stereotyped as nonparticipative, possibly dull-witted, and unimaginative. LBOTE students, who have left school and reflect on their schooling a decade ago, say that their participation was limited. They occurred when English as a second language programs tended to peter out after a couple of years of tuition. At the same time, curricula continued to draw much of their knowledge base from a fairly narrow band of cultural understandings that were confusing at best for someone unfamiliar with them, as well as disempowering and isolating (Iredale & Fox, 1997).

In the study of the experiences of Spanish-speaking students from Uruguayan, Chilean, and Spanish families in three high schools in New South Wales, David Plaza-Coral (1998) shows how the students try to resist the image they present in their schools of lacking ability through an approach similar to that of the "silent Indian"—that is, projecting a concept of themselves as bored and withdrawn and probably stupid. Yet, when interviewed, students proffered some differing explanations. One girl in a year 10 class commented that she did not like to read aloud in her English class because she was never encouraged and was afraid she might make a mistake and be ridiculed. The teacher explained that the girl was not interested in the subject and seemed unmotivated to try to move up to a higher level.

On the other hand, many of the students celebrated their multiple identities, being Uruguayan, Chilean, or Spanish at home, "wog" at school, and "gringo" (white foreigner) when visiting their parents' country of origin. They lived in two worlds in Australia, isolated by their minority culture but participating in a variety of ways at school, particularly if they were born in Australia and were bilingual. Plaza found that many of the differentiating characteristics of their minority group depended not just on how dark their skin was but on the accent detected in their English by the dominant group and in the extent to which the family remained in what Plaza calls their "cultural bubble." The children could go beyond the bubble and could go on to fulfill at least some of their dreams through various forms of both resistance and compliance. A similar theoretical approach to cultural identity but from a Muslim perspective was provided by Najah El Biza in her exploration of self-esteem and identity among Australian elementary school Muslim girls. They too tended to experience a "cultural bubble" with their families, while feeling able to participate with the non-Muslim society in their school.

Stories of identity differentiation such as the Australian examples above can be found across our global society of states, not only related to groups with nondominant language backgrounds, as in the above example, but also to the socioeconomic distinctions of affluence, or to distinctions among people of color, among people of nondominant religions, among people of different locations (e.g., rural and urban), and among people identifying as indigenous. In the United States, for example, Yuli Tamir (2011) has published a provocative essay on the fear among those in power of losing control through educational change. He states that to make a successful transformative shift in educational provision might change the social order, and that could loosen the hegemonic grip of the dominant group over society.

Comparative education literature has shown that there are plenty of ways to transform curriculum and pedagogy. What stands in the way to taking that path is that the directions do not appear on those old maps that Seyla Benhabib describes at the beginning of this chapter.

The "Gendered" Papua New Guinea Woman

To be a woman in Papua New Guinea is often not easy, although of course, it is not a "single story" of hardship, discrimination, poverty, sexual preference, age, and frequently a victim of violence. There are multilayered stories of the strength of women's participation in the home and community, culture and family finance, of their key roles in business and development, and of their increasing participation in public life. Over the last 20 years, the participation of females has increased markedly, particularly in primary schools. Comparative studies of basic human development indicators including educational access show that Papua New Guinea ranks quite low on the global index of development indicators, and yet the country with a population estimated in 2020 to have reached nearly nine million has significant mineral reserves,[2] forests, and agricultural land. Most of the predominantly rural population own their own land and grow their own crops.

Notwithstanding, the public profile of women's participation in Papua New Guinea society, including in education, is difficult to recount, given that historical policy documents and statistical analyses often failed to provide information relating to girls and women in education. Many analyses still omit to disaggregate enrollment figures, retention figures, teacher gender, achievement scores, or completion figures. Although local officials and international agencies working on educational development in Papua New Guinea attempt to collect up-to-date data from rural areas, much of the information is based on estimates drawn from earlier data. In addition, qualitative research in education is still rare. For example, in one doctoral dissertation on key factors affecting school effectiveness in Papua New Guinea there was scant information on girls or women in the thesis, as though the Papua New Guinea woman was somehow invisible. The statistical information in the thesis was gender "neutral," providing scant qualitative information on, for example, *why* girls tended to drop out more than boys, or *why* boys had more postschool opportunities than girls (Fox, 1999).

In the course of the research, we interviewed several women to discuss their perceptions of how girls and women were able to participate in schools, in adult education programs, and at the university level. The structural inequalities were obvious—girls' participation was far lower than boys', their job opportunities were fewer, and their status in society, on the whole, was far lower than for boys and men. It appeared that the greatest negative influence on female participation was an overwhelming and systemic subordination of women in much of Papua New Guinea society.

Some of the men interviewed during this same visit claimed that the subordination of women is a time-honored cultural factor in Papua New Guinea society. These interviewees claimed that any transformation of the role and status of women in society was a Western imposition of their concept of equity and equality, which went against traditional culture. When pressed, even those in high-status positions (males) who were responsible for implementing gender equity in the education system, agreed in principle with the policy, but they maintained, falsely, that yes, cultural traditions were stronger than school-based ideas. Thus, the perpetuation or reification of the image of a gendered Other tended to institutionalize the unequal state of affairs "as if it were permanent, natural and outside of time" (Thompson, 2013, p. 65). The illusion was reinforced by images of women depicted by the local media, in the community, in schools and other educational institutions, and in the workplace.

This claim of so-called irreversible cultural tradition, however, was disputed by all the women who were interviewed, as well as by several men interviewed who supported equity. The women maintained that it was merely convenient for the men to lock women into a subordinated position to maintain their power and that it could hardly be culturally determined if only the male half of the population was in agreement. They saw the dangers of being determined by cultural or gendered stereotypes. Labeling and fixing the Other is a form of colonial discourse that perpetuates unequal relationships of power, and it is perhaps nowhere more overt than in Papua New Guinea between the male as powerful and the female as Other.

One way in which women were able to use the school site to transform female experiences was evident in a particular girls-only secondary school managed by a Catholic nun. In an interview, she explained that she deliberately taught the girls at the school to be independent thinkers and to be conscious of the need to combat discrimination and violence against them when they went on to further education.

This approach to the construction of a gendered identity can be compared to that described by Debra Skinner and Dorothy Holland (2001) in their study of Nepalese females who challenged the so-called traditional compliant identity of girls in society. In their account, the authors describe how the Nepalese school was a forum for the development of critical discourses on the legacies of caste and gender privileges. The students had their ways of constructing their new identities and self-understandings, in this case, by writing their end-of-year revue of skits and song, in which, they expressed their anger and resistance.

The "Educated" Sri Lankan

Sri Lanka is fortunate in having successive governments that placed a high priority on education, even though there are inequalities in the supply of resources and access to higher education. The participation of females and males in the formal sector is fairly even; participation between rural and urban is far less even, with fewer opportunities for employment in rural areas and fewer resources supplied to schools. The government applies a quota system for admission to higher education in the 13 public universities, whereby a certain percentage of students must come from each of the country's provinces;[3] nevertheless, of the over 19% of the total of school leavers eligible to enter postsecondary schooling at the university level, only about 3.5% is admitted to these public universities.[4] Despite these barriers, many rural students, who otherwise would not have been able to study at this level, have become well-known scholars within these universities. Most of the students enrolled in universities are studying for external degrees, or are enrolled in private universities, some of which are affiliated with an overseas institution.

At the start of the 21st century, the proportion of graduates from education systems was extremely high, and graduates from Sri Lankan universities are seen as *educated*. The *educated* person, however, is not necessarily employable. The perceived identity of an educated person remains fixed on the white-collar employee or boss. Paradoxically for Sri Lanka, levels of unemployment among graduates in 2009 were over twice as high as in nongraduate cohorts. It is difficult to generalize the levels of unemployment among graduates, as both unemployed graduates from years back and new graduates since 2020 continue to seek work in various provinces and in many both formal and nonformal sites. The unemployment rates also vary significantly among the various academic disciplines.

In my reporting on the 2002 review (see also Monro, 2020) of the curriculum and student participation in Sri Lanka's then 13 national universities, it became clear that there was often a discrepancy between the concept of the "educated person" as one who has formal knowledge in the humanities compared with the "educated person" as one who can deal with change, manage resources, and be part of the workforce. Such complex and seemingly contradictory positioning is multifaceted and is by no means an either/or situation, not only in Sri Lanka, but as a global phenomenon. It rests on the definition of an educated person, on what characteristics pertain to such a label, and on examinations, which are seen as the gateway through which the ascribed identity of the "educated person" must walk.

CONCLUSION: TACKLING THE ISSUE OF IDENTITY AS A SOCIAL JUSTICE ISSUE

This chapter has highlighted the notion of identity as both a self-reflexive and an interactional process, one that is never determined and fixed but is bound in time, culture, and location. Comparative education research is realized through critiquing and comparing various interpretations of education in different times and places or by analyzing differing theories, issues, and experiences in education.

When joined with the study of "identity" as intersectional and fluid an even more complete and complex picture emerges. While the case studies in this chapter explain in part how international comparative education studies are themselves microcosms of a wider, globalized study of identity and education, they have not focused on other intersectional issues within the complexity of gender. These case studies have not focused, for example, on the intersectional issues of those who identify as LGBTQ+ that I highlighted at the beginning of this chapter. A greater focus on LGBTQ+ issues in the 2020s and beyond requires further examination of current research internationally and comparatively. As Surya Monro (2020) emphasizes in a recent article, when researching with an international perspective, it is crucial to consider the social contexts especially needed to address the materialist, cultural, neocolonial, and other forces that affect the formation of nonheterosexual and gender-diverse identities.

The concept of the "educated person" today is even more complex, fraught with assumptions, expectations, and cultural biases that are hard to resolve merely by imagining a return to a postpandemic "normal." What does education mean? Must it be wrapped up neatly and tied with a ribbon in a box that only contains formal education? Must children sit in rows in a classroom that one day may well be seen as a museum of the past, overtaken by various forms of distance learning? The current crisis is laying bare the inadequacies of attempts to homogenize the experience of education by means of regulation, credentialing, international measuring statistics, and selection in the schools and higher education institutions. Based on expectations that one size fits all, the system marginalizes, and discriminates against whole sections of student bodies, leaving behind the disadvantaged and the so-called Other. The pandemic has left questions: what is the "norm" of education, and what are the norms for everyday interactions? Can existing inequalities remain unattended? Around the world, while schools and other educational institutions were closed, at least, temporarily, because of the COVID-19 pandemic, the children and older students cope at home with a host of pressing issues not confined to keeping up with school learning. There is no longer any norm, least of all for those who have been left behind, including those who have often been considered deficient in language acquisition, perceived as helpless, vulnerable, poor, or lacking in experience of employability.

In conclusion, while the forces of globalization over the past few decades have seen greater internationalization of education, the new emergencies of climate change and the outbreak of the COVID-19 pandemic present challenges that are yet to be encountered or dealt with. Even the advantages of transformational technological developments in social media have been increasingly bombarded with misinformation and other post-truth communication. These challenges in recent times indicate a picture of a postcolonial crisis of populations.

The gradual demise of democracy, the rise of dictatorships, the chaos of social media, all contribute to a sense of unbelievable uncertainly that challenges the mental health of many. Education has a pivotal place to play in finding ways of navigating the crisis. In such an atmosphere of change, so must educational endeavors at local, national, and international levels respond in significantly transformed ways.

NOTES

1. A significant collection of ethnographic examples of the interplay of culture, identity, and schooling was compiled and edited in 1996 by Bradley A. Levinson, Douglas E. Foley, and Dorothy C. Holland.

2. The status of women has changed little in the intervening decade, as reported by Australian doctoral researcher and former resident of Papua New Guinea Suzanne Lipu, who has presented a number of unpublished papers on women's empowerment in Papua New Guinea (Pers.com). See also, for more recent discussion, A. McCormick (2014), Who Are the Custodians of Pacific Post-2015 Education Futures? Policy Discources, Education for All and the Millennium Development Goals. *International Journal of Educational Development*, 39, 163–172; N. B. Pham et al. (2020), Millennium Development Goals in Papua New Guinea: Towards Universal Education. *Educational Research for Policy and Practice*, 19, 181–209. https://doi.org/10.1007/s10671-019-09255-4

3. Information provided by the Sri Lanka Minister for Tertiary Education and Training, September 12, 2002.

4. "Strengthening Undergraduate Education" (2002) was a project managed by Melbourne University Private in Sri Lanka to provide recommendations to the government of Sri Lanka for a future five-year internationally funded higher education quality improvement.

REFERENCES

Adichie, C. N. (2013). *Americanah*. HarperCollins.
Allaburton, R., & Fox, C. (2006). Mid-term review. Unpublished report on two Basic Education Projects for the Indonesian Government. Australian Agency for International Development.
Bakhtin, M. (1981). *The dialogic imagination*. University of Texas Press.
Bashir, B. (2012). Reconciling historical injustices: Deliberative democracy and the politics of reconciliation. *Res Publica, 18*(2), 127–143.
Benhabib, S. (1992). *Situating the self*. Polity.
Bhabha, H. (1994b). Frontlines/borderposts, displacements. In A. Bammer (Ed.), *Displacements: Cultural identities in question* (pp. 269–272). Indiana University Press.
Bhabha, H, (1994a). *The location of culture*. Routledge.
Butler, J., Gambetti, Z., & Sabsay, L. (Eds.). (2016). *Vulnerability in resistance*. Duke University Press.

Clayton, D. M. (2018). Black Lives Matter and the Civil Rights movement. In D. McAdam, *The Wiley-Blackwell encyclopedia of social and political movements*. Blackwell.

Connell, R. W., & Messerschmidt, J. (2005). Hegemonic masculinity: Rethinking the concept. *Gender and Society 19*(6), 829–859.

Connell, R. (2014). Rethinking gender from the South. *Feminist Studies*, *40*(3), 522.

Connell, R. (2019). *The good university: What universities actually do and why it's time for radical change*. Zed Books.

Eddo-Lodge, R. (2018). *Why I am no longer talking to white people about race*. Bloomsbury Publishing.

El Biza, N. (2011). "Becoming me": Perceptions of identity and self-efficacy among Australian and Saudi Arabian Muslim girls. PhD diss, University of Wollongong.

Gadamer, H-G. (1989 [1960]). *Truth and method*. Crossroad.

Foley, D. (1996). The silent Indian as a cultural production. In B. Levinson, D. Foley, & D. C. Holland, *The cultural production of the educated person: Critical ethnographies of schooling and local practices*. State University of New York Press.

Fox, C. (1992). *A critical analysis of intercultural communication: Towards a new theory* Unpublished PhD thesis, Sydney University.

Fox, C. (1999). Girls, education and development in Papua New Guinea. *Gender, education and development for girls in Less Industrialised Countries*. Zed.

Fox, C. (2003). Higher education competencies required for Sri Lankan undergraduates to promote social harmony. Paper presented at UNESCO Conference on Intercultural Communication, Jyväskylä Finland (UNESCO).

Fox, C. (2004). Tensions in the decolonisation process: Disrupting preconceptions of postcolonial education in the Lao people's democratic republic. In A. Hickling-Hudson, J. Matthews, & A. Woods (Eds.), *Disrupting preconceptions: Postcolonialism and education* (pp. 99–106). Post Pressed.

Fox, C. (2016). Who is my neighbour? Unleashing our postcolonial consciousness. *International Education Journal: Comparative Perspectives*, *15*(3), 57–76.

Habermas, J. (1984). *The theory of communicative action* (Vol. 2). Beacon Press.

Hickling-Hudson, A., Matthews, J., & Woods, A. (Eds.). (2004). *Disruption preconceptions: Postcolonialism and education*. Post Pressed.

Iredale, R., & Fox, C. (1997). The impact of immigration on school education in New South Wales, Australia. *International Migration Review*, *31*(3), 655–669.

Iredale, R. R., Fox, C., & Sherlaimoff, T. (1994). *Immigration, education and training in new South Wales*. AGPS.

Klein, N. (2014). *This changes everything: Capitalism vs. the climate*. Penguin Random House UK.

Levinson, B. A. (2005). Citizenship, identity, democracy: Engaging the political in the anthropology of education. *Anthropology & Education Quarterly*, 329–340.

Levinson, B., Foley, D., & Holland, D. C. (1996). *The cultural production of the educated person: Critical ethnographies of schooling and local practices*. State University of New York Press.

Majhanovich, S., Fox, C., & Gok, F. (Eds). (2012). *Bordering, Re-bordering and new possibilities in education and society*. Springer.

Monro, S. (2020). Sexual and gender diversities: Implications for LGBTQ studies, *Journal of Homosexuality*, *67*(3), 315–324.

Pascoe, B. (2014). *Dark Emu: Agriculture or accident?* Magabala Books.

Phelps, S. (2010). Critical literacy: Using nonfiction to learn about Islam. *Journal of Adolescent & Adult Literacy*, *54*(3), 190–198.

Plaza-Coral, David. (1998). Australian Spanish-speaking background secondary school students and the construction and reconstruction of their cultural identity: A "wog" experience. PhD diss., University of Wollongong.

Pratt, M. L. (1992). *Imperial eyes: Travel writing and transculturation*. Routledge.
Said, E. (1978). *Orientalism: Western conceptions of the Orient*. Penguin.
Skinner, D., & Holland, D. (2001). Public education in Nepal. *The cultural production of the educated person*. In B. Levinson, D. Foley, & D. C. Holland, *The cultural production of the educated person: Critical ethnographies of schooling and local practices*. State University of New York Press.
Spivak, G. (1990). *The post-colonial critic: Interviews, strategies, dialogues*. Chatto & Windus.
Sullivan, C., & Day, M. (2019). Queer(y)ing Indigenous Australian higher education student spaces. *Australian Journal of Indigenous Education*, 1–8.
Tamir, Y. (2011). Staying in control; Or, what do we really want public education to achieve? *Educational Theory*, 61(4), 395–411.
Thompson, J. B. (2013). *Ideology and modern culture: Critical social theory in the era of mass communication*. Wiley.
Unterhalter, E. (2012). Poverty, education, gender and the Millennium Development Goals: Reflections on boundaries and intersectionality. *Theory and Research in Education*, 10(3), 253–274.

6

Equality of Education

Six Decades of Comparative Evidence Seen from a New Millennium

Joseph P. Farrell

ABSTRACT

Debates about (and occasional action on) educational reforms, which are common currency in the early years of this century (e.g., decentralization, privatization, education for "global competitiveness," use of "new technologies" such as the Internet, standards, testing, and "accountability") have a considerable history. They are in many fundamental respects current manifestations of debates and reform efforts that have spanned, in one form or another, the past six decades, and in some cases longer. To think seriously about the possible import of currently fashionable reform movements for equality of education, particularly for the most marginalized members of various societies, requires that we review and try to make some sense of that history. That is the intent of this chapter. Comparative education, as a field of scholarly inquiry and as an applied discipline, has been central to what has been learned.

■ ■ ■

BACKGROUND: THE OPTIMISTIC REFORMS OF THE 1960S

The 25 years following the end of the Second World War was an epoch of great and widespread optimism regarding questions of educational and socioeconomic equality. It was assumed generally that the evident gaps in wealth and power among nations could be rather quickly eliminated; that those already industrialized and "developed" nations that had been devastated by the war could be quickly put "back on their feet"; and that those nonindustrialized or generally poor nations (whether newly independent from European colonialism or long independent) could rather quickly and easily be placed on the "road to development," and that obvious gaps in access to income and power among individuals and collectivities within nations could be equally quickly reduced. It was also assumed that more general acquisition of education (understood mainly as the provision of formal schooling) was essential to the lessening of inequalities among and within nations. Increasing provision of education was seen as a major (in some views the most important) engine that would drive the world to a more equal provision of access to wealth, power, and opportunity. Poverty and inequality (absolute or relative; individual, collective, national, or international) came to be seen widely as relatively easily solved policy problems rather than necessary, unavoidable, or unresolvable human conditions.

The advent of human capital theory in the late 1950s and early 1960s put education even more squarely in the center of this optimistic vision. Education was no longer seen as simply one among many competing consumer goods to be acquired individually (for personal gain) or collectively (through taxes for perceived collective gain) to the extent that it could be afforded. Rather, education was constructed as an investment opportunity. Public expenditures on increasing the availability of education would produce net social benefits, increasing the total amount of wealth in a society and improving its distribution. The confluence of these events and ways of understanding them led to enormously increased expenditures on education around the world, a major increase in access to education (in poor nations, access to primary education and adult basic education; in richer nations, which had already achieved nearly universal primary education, in access to secondary and tertiary education), and major educational reform efforts attempting to make it more accessible and effective for marginalized or disadvantaged individuals or groups.

In rich nations primary education was already effectively compulsory and universal, and secondary and tertiary education was relatively widely available. The educational reforms focused on increasing the proportion of age-eligible youth who completed secondary schooling and went on to some form of postsecondary education, and on improving the educational "chances" of specifically targeted "educationally disadvantaged" groups, whether the disadvantage was based on race, ethnicity, socioeconomic status, gender, geographical location, or some combination of these. In many such nations there was a massive expansion of secondary education facilities, with the policy target often being universal access and usually universal completion. Existing universities expanded rapidly, large numbers of wholly new universities were created, and in many nations entire new systems of nonuniversity, technically oriented postsecondary institutions were established. For example, during the decade of the 1960s the province of Ontario, Canada, implemented a secondary education reform (the Robarts Plan) that aimed at (among other things) allowing all young people to complete that level of schooling. It built enough new universities and expanded the capacity of existing universities to more than double the capacity at that level, and established an entirely new system of more than 20 postsecondary colleges of applied arts and technology.

In the United States massive resources and political energy were devoted to attempting to end racial segregation of schooling and to develop and implement changes that might increase the educational success of disadvantaged groups. In much of Western Europe, "academic" secondary schooling led to attending a university (e.g., the English grammar school, the French lycée, the

German gymnasium) and served a small proportion of the eligible age-group—predominantly the children of already privileged families. Major attempts at "comprehensivization" of secondary schooling took different forms in different nations, but the general goals were to increase the proportion of youngsters who had access to a form of secondary schooling that could lead to postsecondary education and to equalize the opportunities to access to such education across social groups (Jallade, 1972–1973; Levin, 1978; Neave, 1982).

In developing nations, many children had no access to primary schooling and most adults were illiterate (although this varied dramatically from nation to nation). The main educational-change focus was on simple quantitative expansion, and many nations mounted national literacy "campaigns." In the early 1960s UNESCO convened a series of regional meetings of ministers of education that set broad targets for quantitative growth designed as a framework for national educational planning. The general aim was to move as quickly as possible (and it was assumed that this would be quickly indeed) to "universal primary education" and universal literacy, both seen as necessary components of national development. During this epoch, scholars fiercely debated the precise nature of "national development," but a fairly general consensus developed that it entailed at least three main components: (1) the generation of more wealth within a nation (economic development), (2) the more equitable distribution of such wealth or at least more equitable distribution of opportunities for access to that wealth (social development), and (3) the organization of political decision-making structures and development of "values" supporting them, which would be close approximations of those prevalent in "developed" nations (political development). More widespread and equitable provision of formal schooling was seen as essential to all three. Massive enrollment increases resulted from the application of this general view to educational policy in developing nations. Between 1960 and 1975, the number of children in school in developing countries increased by 122%; the proportion of age-eligible children in primary schooling increased from 57 to 75% during the same 15-year period, with corresponding increases at the secondary level (14% to 26%) and postsecondary level (1.5% to 4.4%) (World Bank, 1980).

RESULTS: MUCH LESS THAN ANTICIPATED

However, by the early 1970s, it was already apparent to many observers that this massive worldwide effort at educational reform in the name of growth and equality was not producing the expected results. As early as 1968, Coombs wrote the aptly titled book *The World Educational Crisis: A Systems Analysis*. The structural reforms in Western Europe were seldom fully implemented, if at all, and were not, in most cases, significantly changing the social composition of academic secondary schooling. In the United States, desegregation programs and other attempted reforms were not significantly improving the educational success of African Americans and other marginalized groups. In both instances, some individuals benefited, but the overall pattern of structural inequality remained intact. In developing nations, because population was growing rapidly relative to the rate of educational expansion, the absolute numbers of primary-age children out of school grew from 109.2 million in 1960 to 120.5 million in 1975 (World Bank, 1980). The same pattern held for adult literacy. Overall literacy rates were increasing (in some cases quite rapidly), but the absolute number of illiterate adults was increasing as well. Moreover, it was becoming clear that the rates of educational expenditure increase that had occurred during the 1960s and drove the expansion of school places could not be sustained over a longer period. Beyond this, although many developing nations had been experiencing economic growth, the already wealthy nations were for the most part growing even faster, creating an ever-widening gap between rich and poor countries. Furthermore, the gap between richer and poorer groups within many nations was also increasing, although this was a very mixed pattern (Seligson & Passe-Smith, 1993).

Within schooling systems themselves, in nations rich and poor, distributional inequalities were generally persisting, in some cases getting better and in some, worse. In many societies urban children benefited more than rural children from increased educational provision. In other societies, particular ethnic, tribal, or religious groups benefited more. In many societies boys received more of the newly available schooling than did girls. In most societies newly available school places, whether at the primary, secondary, or tertiary level, were occupied mainly, or almost exclusively, by children of the already well-to-do.

This led to a significant modification—for many a complete rejection—of the earlier optimistic view that had guided the actions of policymakers and advisers in rich and poor nations. Claims about the power of schooling to equalize the life chances of children who are born into very different social and economic circumstances generally became much more cautious. Don Adams (1977) once characterized this mood shift as the change from the "optimistic sixties" to the "cynical seventies."

As the comparative evidence continued to accumulate through the 1980s and into the 1990s, it strengthened and reinforced the "cynical" view established in the 1970s. It became increasingly clear that educational reforms aimed at increasing equality were very difficult to enact and implement successfully, and even when implemented reasonably well seldom had the intended effects on comparative life chances of the children of various social groups within and among nations. There were some success stories but far more examples of partial or complete failure. In many developing nations the situation was made even more difficult by the fiscal crises produced by the oil shock of the 1970s and the debt crisis of the 1980s. In most rich nations the difficulty was aggravated by economic restructuring, which produced significant reductions in public educational expenditures and severe reductions in the numbers of middle-class jobs that had been the traditional target occupations for youngsters from marginalized groups who had managed to use education as a vehicle for social mobility (it is hard to be mobile if there are few jobs into which to be mobile!). In 1997 I summarized the experience of the past three decades as follows:

One general lesson is that planning educational change is a far more difficult and risk-prone venture than had been imagined in the 1950s or 1960s. There are far more examples of failure, or of minimal success, than of relatively complete success. Far more is known about what doesn't work, or doesn't usually work, than about what does work. Moreover, when planned educational reform attempts have been successful, the process has usually taken a very long time, frequently far longer than originally anticipated. There are in the experience of the past decades a few examples where an unusual combination of favorable conditions and politically skilled planners has permitted a great deal of educational change to occur in a relatively brief period, but these have been rare and idiosyncratic (Farrell, 1997).

THEORETICAL ACCOUNTS OF REFORM FAILURE

Partly as a result of this experience, a very complex and confusing theoretical debate has developed. Although the details of the debate are discussed elsewhere in this book, some of the main features that pertain directly to the theme of this chapter are discussed next. Core aspects of the debate for present purposes can be framed by the title of George Counts's famous book from the 1930s, *Dare the School Build a New Social Order?* To pose the question at all assumes a positive answer to a previous question: Can the school build a new social order? The optimism of the 1960s was founded on a positive answer to that question. The schools could do it and we collectively should dare to do it, by marshaling nationally and internationally the appropriate mixture of knowledge, resources, and political will. One major set of theoretical explanations of and proposed remedies for the subsequent widespread failure continue to assume a positive answer. Schools can build a new social order. The problem is that we haven't yet "gotten it right." First, we have been operating from an incomplete or imperfect or badly interpreted knowledge base and, second, a wrong or incomplete set of political actors and stakeholder groups have been involved in the policy development and implementation process. The "problem" is a matter of technique and knowledge base. The "solution" is to continually improve the knowledge base (through basic and applied research and the dissemination of the results) and refine our interpretations of it, as well as to improve our micro- and macropolitical techniques. This understanding, in one variant or another, continues to be the dominant view. The literature here is vast (see, for example, Lockheed & Verspoor, 1990; Ross & Mahlick, 1990; 1993).

A wholly opposed view of the nature of the problem began to emerge strongly in the mid-1970s, arguing that schools could not build a new social order. The causal process works the other way round. Changing the socioeconomic order is a necessary precondition or co-condition for changing education in an egalitarian direction. Many scholars, particularly those arguing from a Marxist, neo-Marxist, or dependency theory approach, claim that formal schooling could necessarily do little more than reproduce structural inequalities in existing societies, at least capitalist ones; this is its basic sociopolitical and economic function; this is inevitably part of the normal development of capitalist societies and of developing countries linked to such nations through dependent economic, political, and social connections (see Bowles & Gintis, 1976; Carnoy, 1974). This view gained considerable popularity among some sectors of the scholarly community and among some policymakers in developing countries and international aid agencies. However, it never became the predominant view. By the mid-1980s some of the academic proponents of this view began to significantly modify their earlier position, arguing that formal schooling could function both to reproduce existing structural inequalities and to produce structural change, at least in democratic societies (see, for example, Carnoy & Levin, 1985; Liston, 1988). Following the collapse of the former Soviet Union and its associated state socialist nations, new evidence has become available suggesting that structural inequalities in those societies have been very nearly as resistant to the meliorating influence of education as in capitalist nations (Birzea, 1996). This may suggest that the problem of resistant structural inequality is endemic across political-economic regime types and is created by some deeper pattern that we have not yet identified—it simply takes different forms and manifestations in different societies.

An intermediate view has also developed. It suggests that educational change can affect the social order but only under particular circumstances and only if the educational change program is carefully tailored to the those circumstances. This can be seen as a profoundly pessimistic position in that the conditions for success are rare and idiosyncratic, and thus cannot be widely duplicated. A more optimistic take on this view has recently developed, arguing that the widespread failure has been due to a common tendency to try to design and implement (from whatever theoretical/ideological point of view) universalistic "one size fits all" educational reform approaches and strategies.

Thus, success in using educational change to promote social equality is widely possible but is contingent on carefully tailoring the reform to the specific local conditions. Some scholars have begun trying to work out possible relationships between particular sets of conditions and potentially successful educational reform approaches. I have argued elsewhere that taking this point of view seriously fundamentally challenges almost the entire corpus of modernist theory that has informed comparative education over the past several decades (see Farrell, 1997; Rondinelli et al., 1990).

CHANGING MEANINGS OF EDUCATIONAL EQUALITY

Running through this broad theoretical debate has been a constant modification, amplification, and nuancing of what is meant by the term "educational equality." Next, I shall briefly review these changes in meaning and introduce a model meant to bring together many of these changes in meaning in a way useful for thinking about the mass of accumulated evidence.

CATEGORIES OF DIFFERENTIATION

Thirty to 40 years ago discussions of social equality tended to focus on a limited set of categories of differentiation then considered to be most important in determining or influencing (depending on how deterministic or contingent and loosely coupled a view of large-scale social interactions one held) how large numbers of people were able to live their lives in rich, industrialized nations (especially social class and race/ethnicity) and to apply these Western categories to developing nations. The understanding of such potential categories of differentiation is now much more complex. All extant societies have some form of internal social differentiation, with some members being valued or rewarded more than others. However, the degree of such differentiation and its significance for the way individuals and social groups lead their lives varies dramatically across societies. Moreover, there are many different bases or criteria for such differentiation. Among the most common are race, occupation, ethnicity, gender, regional origin, lineage, income, political power, and religion. Both across and within societies there is considerable variation in which one of these, or which set of them, is most powerful as a determinant of how different people can and do live their lives. Those of us who are creatures of the historical experience and intellectual traditions of the industrial nations of the West, whether we embrace some form of structural, functional, or Marxist social theory, tend to collapse a common set of these—particularly occupation, income, and political power—into the notion of social class or social status. It is not at all clear now that these theoretical constructs are the most salient for understanding social differentiation in rich nations (feminist scholars, for example, would generally argue that gender is at least as important, if not more important, a category of differentiation) nor that they are directly applicable to all, or even most, less developed societies, either as accurate descriptors or as meaningful categories of social thought and behavior among individuals in those societies.

As the list of potential categories of social differentiation has expanded, some categories have come to be seen as more mutable or "disguisable" than others, which has an effect on the degree to which they may constrain children's life chances and what education can "do" about them. An instantly identifiable basis of social categorization is, in general, much harder to overcome by educational (or, more generally, social) policy. Race and gender, for example, have tended to be generally considered immediately identifiable characteristics. In contrast, the social class of origin of someone who has used education (or some other means) to become upwardly mobile is frequently nonidentifiable unless individuals choose to "advertise" it. Social class is a characteristic that is mutable and often easily disguisable. It is thus more easily altered by education than characteristics that seem to be immutable and nondisguisable. It has recently become apparent that consideration of the full implications of this set of issues is complexly related to the question of identity—the identity that people assign to themselves and the one that others assign to them. There is not enough space here to work out the full implications. However, it can be noted that some scholars, particularly those working from a postmodern feminist stance, are arguing that we must move from an idea of identity (as personally understood or socially assigned) as something essential and fundamentally unchangeable to a conception of identity, in both its senses, as something that is multiple and malleable. That is, we must move from thinking of identity to thinking of identities (Farrell, 1996). These new ways of thinking about educational equality represent a challenge to traditional modernist and grand theory approaches to comparative education, which are about as fundamental as the challenge represented by the contingency approach noted above. The implications of these ways of thinking for our understanding of educational equality are only beginning to be worked out, but it is becoming quite obvious that the meaning of the phrase is far more slippery and difficult to understand than we thought even a few years ago.

FROM OPPORTUNITY TO RESULTS

The notion of educational equality, which grew originally with the development of systems of tax-supported public schooling, focused on opportunity. The general assumption was that the job of the state was to ensure that all children (with the exception in some areas of groups that were consciously excluded, on the basis for example of race or gender) had access to schools that were free of direct cost, with generally similar facilities and curricula, at least through the stage of compulsory attendance. It was assumed that it was the child's responsibility to use the opportunity thus provided. Responsibility for a child who did not do well in school, through lack of intelligence, diligence, motivation, and so on, rested with the individuals involved, not the state. Over the past several decades it has become increasingly apparent that large numbers of children are unable to use the educational opportunity provided because of their social origins. The concept of educational equality has gradually been extended to include some notion of equal educational results. The task of the state has been extended to include ensuring that all children, whatever their social origin, have an equal ability to benefit from the educational opportunity provided, in terms of what they learn and how they can use that learning in later life, particularly in the labor market.

EQUALITY AS SIMILARITY OR EQUALITY AS VALUATION OF DIFFERENCE

Embedded within the standard discussions of equality of results is an even more complex set of questions: Do we really expect (indeed, do we want) the results to be similar, if not identical, for everyone? What do we actually mean by "results"? What do we mean by "an equal opportunity to benefit from" educational provision? Many discussions and arguments in both the scholarly and the popular literature imply quite directly that "equal results" means, for example, equal achievement test scores across social groups, schools, or nations (the "league table" approach), or equal access to highly valued occupational categories or salary levels. But it is increasingly argued that this view is too narrow and restrictive and that it is legitimate, indeed desirable, for different individuals and groups to want/need to learn different sorts of things and to use them for different life purposes. This alternative claim is expressed very strongly, for example, in many arguments for "relevant" education for particular subgroups within larger social/national groups (say, rural children in poor areas of developing nations) (Baker, 1989). This "valuation of difference rather than similarity" approach asserts that different types of learning, and ways of learning, as well as different uses of it throughout life, are equally (but differently) valuable socially and individually. If one accepts this concept of educational equality, it is not clear what "equality of results" might mean, let alone how we might assess it within or across societies.

EQUITY OR EQUALITY?

A useful distinction in sorting out debates on matters of equality is between equity and equality. Equity refers to social justice or fairness. It involves a subjective moral or ethical judgment. Equality deals with the actual patterns in which something (e.g., income or years of schooling) is distributed among members of a particular group. The equality of an income distribution can, for example, be assessed statistically by measuring deviations from some hypothetically completely equal situation. But individual or group judgments regarding the equity or fairness of any given observed degree of inequality can and do differ; equity involves value judgments and differing understandings of what is normal or inevitable. Since societies, groups within societies, and individuals within those groups differ in their value systems, a given statistically measured degree of inequality may be regarded as quite fair and reasonable, or equitable, by some as individuals or groups, and as very inequitable by others within the same society. Many of the most complex public political debates about education equality, and what might be done about it in terms of public policy, revolve around differing equity-based interpretations of differing equality-driven statistical indices. Differing interpretations of rates of female participation in education and the labor force is a striking case in point.

A REVIEW

The past several decades have been characterized by increasing conceptual confusion. This conceptual confusion has to a considerable degree resulted from the circulation of a bewildering quantity of comparative information regarding how different individuals and widely differing social groups utilize education and the effect it exerts on their destinies. Untangling some of that data and deriving meaning from it with respect to equality as a goal for education is the task of the remainder of this chapter. In the following pages, I present a model for thinking about educational equality that summarizes much of what we now understand by that concept, and I use that model to organize and summarize what much of the now available comparative data tells us about education's role in equalizing the life chances of children born into very different social circumstances as they grow into adults.

A "MODEL" OF EDUCATIONAL INEQUALITY

When considering problems of educational inequality in recent years, we have come increasingly to view schooling as a long-term process in which children may be sorted at many different points and in several different ways. We recognize that schooling, whatever else it may do, operates as a selective social screening mechanism. It enhances the status of some children, providing them with an opportunity for upward social or economic mobility. It ratifies the status of others, reinforcing the propensity for children born poor to remain poor as adults, and for children born into well-off families to become well-off adults. Recognizing this, we need to address the following questions: At what points in the process, to what degree, and how are children of which social groups screened out or kept in? From this point of view, several facets of equality can be usefully distinguished:

1. Equality of access—the probabilities of children from different social groupings getting into the school system, or some particular level or portion of it.
2. Equality of survival—the probabilities of children from various social groupings staying in the school system to some defined level, usually the end of a complete cycle (primary, secondary, higher).
3. Equality of output—the probabilities that children from various social groupings will learn the same things to the same levels at a defined point in the schooling system.

4. Equality of outcome—the probabilities that children from various social groupings will live relatively similar lives subsequent to and as a result of schooling (have equal incomes, have jobs of roughly the same status, have equal access to sites of political power, etc.).

The first three types of inequality refer to the workings of the school system itself. Equality of outcome refers to the junction between the school system and adult life, especially (but not exclusively) the labor market. With reference to the first three, each represents a mechanism by which children are sorted and screened by the school, and all three occur at each level or cycle of the system (i.e., a child may or may not enter primary schooling, may or may not survive to the end of the primary cycle, may or may not learn as much, or the same things, as other students by the end of the primary cycle; having completed primary, a child may or may not enter secondary schooling, may or may not survive to the end of secondary). Thus, in a three-level system (e.g., primary, secondary, higher) there are at least nine sorting points of children; in a four-level system (e.g., primary, junior secondary, higher secondary, higher) there are at least 12 sorting points. It should be noted that this classification of types of inequality is itself an oversimplification. For example, in systems that have different types of schools or "streams" at the same level (e.g., university-preparatory versus technical secondary schools or streams, or universities versus two-year technical colleges at the third level) the access question is not simply whether a student enters the cycle but the type of institution or stream to which the student is given access. We should also bear in mind that the same factors will not necessarily affect the destiny of children at all of the sorting points. Since children confronting a later sorting point are themselves "survivors" of earlier sortings, we can assume that factors which are critical at the earliest points may lose their significance at later points (having already had their effect), with new factors coming into play as the lengthy process moves along (see Farrell & Schiefelbein, 1982). It should also be noted that although the focus here is on formal schooling for young people, the four questions or issues can be addressed to any organized learning program, formal or nonformal, for learners of whatever age. For example, one can ask these questions of an adult literacy or vocational training program. Which people from which social categories have access to it? Which learners from which social categories "stay the course" to the end of the program? Which do not? Which learners from which social categories learn more or less of what is made available to them? Which learners from which social categories are more or less able thereafter to use their newly acquired knowledge/skills to improve their lives, and to what degree?

WHAT DO WE KNOW?

Our task here is to try to make some sense of the welter of comparative data regarding educational inequality that has been developed during the past several decades. With respect to some aspects of the model just presented, the evidence is sufficient to permit a reasonably coherent summary; with respect to other aspects, the evidence is spotty or inconsistent.

EQUALITY OF ACCESS

For the vast majority of children in developing nations, access is a problem at the primary level. As I noted earlier, a major objective of educational policy at the start of the 1960s was to provide school places sufficient to permit every child to have access to at least a few years of primary schooling. Although primary enrollment ratios have increased in all regions of the developing world, these general figures mask what is in some nations, often very populous ones, a much grimmer reality. Consider, for example, the three nations of the Indian subcontinent, whose combined population is approximately equal to that of China. Their net primary enrollment ratios in 2008 were 88% in India; 89% in Bangladesh; 60% in Pakistan (UNICEF, 2011). Moreover, during the decade of the 1980s primary enrollment ratios actually declined in 45 countries, leading many observers to refer to that period as a "disastrous decade for education" (UNESCO, 1993, p. 17). A UNESCO publication from the 1990s noted the not-surprising principal causes for lack of access to primary education: "Where are the 'missing children'? Most live in remote rural areas or in urban slums. Most are girls. Most belong to population groups outside the mainstream of society: they pass their days in overcrowded refugee camps, displaced by man-made or natural disasters, or wander with their herds. Often [they are] marginalized by language, life-style and culture" (UNESCO, 1993, p. 10). Faced with estimates that if the pattern of the 1980s continued there would be 162 million children without access to primary education, the World Conference on Education for All, held in Thailand in 1990, set a goal of universal access to basic education by the year 2000, and set in place elaborate international mechanisms to encourage and monitor progress. It seemed to many an unlikely quest. Resources would have had to be found, from shrinking national and international agency budgets, to create within a decade about as many new school places as were created in the 20 years between 1965 and 1985 (Lockheed & Vespoor, 1990, p. 31). Nonetheless, some progress was made, as noted at a follow-up meeting held in Dakar, Senegal, in 2000. Between 1990 and 1998 the number of children with no access to primary schooling dropped from 128 million to 113 million. By the end of the century the number of nations still experiencing post-1980 net primary enrollment ratio declines had dropped to 11; in the same period 21 nations had increased those enrollment ratios by 15% or more; and 32 developing nations had achieved near-universal access (net primary enrollment ratios above 90%), including such very populous nations as China, Indonesia, and Brazil. The Dakar meeting referred to these as "tangible but modest gains" and set a new target date of 2015 for universal primary access, while noting that the challenge was greatest in Sub-Saharan Africa and South Asia. By 2011 some agencies were suggesting that the target date should be set back yet again to 2025.

In the developing nations that have achieved nearly universal primary education and in rich nations generally, the main access problem occurs at a later point in the schooling process. In the former nations it is generally at the entrance to secondary schooling (among those 32 developing nations the secondary enrollment ratios at the beginning of this millennium ranged from 36% [Honduras] to 95% [South Africa], but generally ran between 50% and 70%) (UNESCO, 2000b; World Bank, 2000/2001). In the latter, the key access question is the type or stream of secondary schooling into which youngsters are admitted. In very rich nations that have achieved nearly universal secondary education, the access question arises most seriously at the entrance to postsecondary education. Not even the richest nations have seriously contemplated the universal provision of that level of education. In all nations, rich or poor, there is some point (or points) in the educational system at which schooling (or some favored types of it) is a scarce good that not all can acquire. The ideal equality model then becomes one of random access, with the paradigm case being a fair lottery. The available comparative data (as outlined earlier) indicate that the ideal random access situation is rarely even approximated. The same general set of factors that discriminate at the door of the primary school in poor nations simply operate in richer nations at a later point in children's lives.

It is commonly assumed that, particularly at the primary level, the problem of inequality of access is almost entirely a question of inadequate supply of schools and teachers; that an effective demand for primary schooling exists almost everywhere, and that if the resources and political will can be found to provide an adequate number of primary schools, all children will attend. As I have shown, the obstacles on the supply side are indeed formidable. However, there are obstacles on the demand side as well. In most middle-income nations (and in some favored regions of low-income nations), there are more than enough school places, in the appropriate locations, for all age-eligible children. In such circumstances, when children do not attend school, and they often do not, it is because their parents will not send them. Parents may regard the education provided there as inappropriate (e.g., on religious or cultural grounds), irrelevant or of little use, or not worth the opportunity cost of the child's labor (Bowman, 1984). This is a particularly serious obstacle to the enrollment of girls in many nations.

EQUALITY OF SURVIVAL

Among middle-income developing nations, between 80 and 100% of an entering grade-one cohort will complete the primary cycle. In low-income nations the completion proportions are lower, generally ranging between 50 and 80% (World Bank, 2011). These high rates of nonsurvival are a result of the combined effect of (1) high repetition rates and (2) high proportions of children dropping out of school—frequently after having repeated an early grade one or more times (UNESCO, 2000b; World Bank, 2011). Although the time-series data are spotty, there was a general trend for repetition rates to decrease and survival rates to increase between 1980 and 2010 (compare, for example, Lockheed & Verspoor, 1990; UNESCO, 2000b; UNICEF, 2011). In many developing nations, the survival rates at the secondary or postsecondary levels, for the very small proportion of the population who reach those levels, are also very low. However, the patterns at this level are highly variable. In some nations access to secondary schooling is very restricted and is based on scores on primary leaving examinations or socioeconomic privilege. The few who gain access to secondary or higher levels of schooling tend in large proportions to complete the cycle (Farrell, 1998).

In richer nations, survival becomes a serious policy issue at the point in the schooling cycle at which effective compulsory education ends, usually at some midpoint in the secondary cycle. Survival rates and patterns at this level vary greatly across such nations, in ways that are not easily accounted for. Policy expectations clearly have some effect. For example, in some nations, all students are expected to complete secondary schooling. High "dropout" rates are considered a major problem, and various policies are put in place to "keep kids in school." These are sometimes quite successful. For example, in Canada the official dropout rate in secondary schooling is around 30%, and a variety of avenues have been developed to allow such young people to "drop back in" in ways that fit with their life needs. Following these various alternative tracks, roughly 85% of an age cohort have attained a secondary diploma or equivalent by age 25. That is, about half of the officially identified "dropouts" eventually completed the cycle (Farrell, 1992; Levin, 1992; Paquette, 1995). A roughly similar situation exists in the United States (Bailey, 1991). On the other hand, in societies that do not expect all secondary-level students to complete the full cycle, dropping out is not seen as a policy problem but as a natural and normal circumstance. Here again, we see the importance of the distinction between equality and equity.

A survey of all available comparative evidence shows, generally, that in any given level of the educational system, poor children are less likely to survive educationally than are well-to-do children; that children born in rural areas are less likely to survive educationally than urban children; that repetition and dropout rates are higher among girls than among boys. However, the evidence regarding the relationship between any particular aspect of a child's personal or family circumstances and the probability of completing a given level of education is so scanty and contradictory that general conclusions cannot be drawn easily. The patterns vary dramatically from country to country in ways that cannot be explained simply. Variations in the influence of gender on survival potential are particularly striking. Among middle-income nations, primary-level survival rates for boys and girls are essentially identical. In the few cases where there is a noticeable gender difference, all three favor girls by 6%. Among low-income nations, there is much variation, which is difficult to interpret. The gender differences are somewhat larger (most in the 5% to 10% range) but they favor boys or girls in almost equal measure. Among the few cases of more extreme differences (greater than 10%), all are in Sub-Saharan Africa, five favor boys and two favor girls, but in the region overall there are about as many cases favoring girls as favoring boys. Secondary-level survival patterns are roughly similar. As the statistical assessment for the Dakar conference notes, "gender disparities at the national or regional level are minimal with regard to the internal efficiency of [i.e., survival within] the education system, and slightly favor girls in the majority of cases" (UNESCO, 2000b; World Bank, 2000/2001). Overall, there has been considerable progress toward gender equality on this dimension, and the remaining pockets of severe female disadvantage do not appear related in any obvious way to national income, geocultural area, religious tradition, or colonial heritage. It is a puzzle!

It is important to bear in mind that survival rates, for entire populations or for subgroups thereof, can only be understood correctly concerning educational policy by referring as well to access figures for the same societies. For example, at the turn of the present century, in both Syria and Mali, approximately 90 to 95% of children entering grade one would reach the end of primary schooling. In Syria almost all eligible children entered grade one, whereas in Mali only about 40% did so. In contrast, Ethiopia had about the same grade one access rate as did Mali, but only about 50% of its entrants completed primary schooling (World Bank, 2000/2001). Despite their similarity on either equality of access or equality of survival, the interaction between the two types of inequality produced three very different educational situations by the end of primary schooling. It is especially important to note the interaction between access and survival for particular subgroups of a nation's population in trying to assess the overall educational equality situation. For example, if a particular group is heavily discriminated against in terms of access to schooling, those few of its members who do get into schooling (any particular level or type thereof), being themselves the winners in a very rigorous previous screening process, may (and often do) have a very high subsequent survival potential.

EQUALITY OF OUTPUT

A system's output is whatever the system produces directly—in the case of an educational system, learning. Children with the same number of years of schooling (thus with equal access and equal survival) may have learned quite different things or the same subjects to quite different levels. There is a substantial amount of cross-national evidence which indicates that differences in levels of achievement are systematically associated with different social origins of children in a particular society. Generally, among those who have reached a given level of a nation's school system, children who are poor, rural, female, or from any other socially marginalized group, learn less. However, here too the differences among nations and cultures in the effect of such social characteristics on learning are impressive.

Given this comparative evidence, the following question has bedeviled educators: Considering the powerful influence of home background on relative levels of school learning, is there much if any room at all for changes in schooling policy and practice to improve the learning levels of socially marginalized children which will allow them, particularly as groups, to live better lives thereafter? Based on an increasingly large array of nation-specific studies, using many different methodological approaches and a smaller set of cross-national studies (many of which have turned out to be methodologically flawed), scholars identified what appeared to be a quite clear pattern emerging in the 1970s and 1980s (Riddell, 1997). The less developed the society, the less the effect of social origin on learning achievement, and the greater the effect of school-related (and thus social policy directed) variables (Heyneman & Loxley, 1983). However, the methodological critiques (particularly of those studies based on an "educational production function" approach) suggest that the overall pattern is not as clear as it once seemed (Riddell, 1997). Nonetheless, assessing all of the evidence, from several distinct methodological traditions, shows that the general pattern still seems to hold. Why should this be so?

Several different, and still quite tentative, explanations have been advanced. Quite early on, as the pattern was just beginning to become evident, Foster (1977) advanced the following:

> In broadest terms, as less-developed nations "modernize" the pattern of "objective" differentiation of populations becomes more complex with the growth of a

monetized economy and a greater division of labor. Not only this, possession of a "modern type" occupation becomes an increasingly important factor in determining the generalized social status of an individual. In other words, social strata defined in objective terms of occupations and income begin to emerge. Initially, however, this pattern of objective differentiation may not be accompanied by an equivalent degree of cultural differentiation as represented by increasing divergence of values, attitudes, and life-styles among various subgroups. In time, however, this may occur and we move, in effect, toward a pattern of stratification that more closely resembles that obtaining in developed societies. (pp. 224–225)

For example, child-rearing patterns, attitudes toward schooling, aspirations, and other family traits that may affect a child's school success in a newly rich African family may differ little from those of families not yet participating in the cash economy, or participating at a much more marginal level, at least during the early stages of the social change process. What we may be observing here is the educational effect of the process of class formation (in the Western sense), as poor nations become more like Western societies. This explanation fits rather well within Marxist, neo-Marxist and traditional structural-functional understandings of social change (which may be rather annoying to singular-minded and ideologically driven adherents of any of those theoretical stances). Of course, it is also observably the case that in societies in which standard Western indexes of social status are not (or are not yet) relevant to a child's educational destiny, other traditional stratification patterns may be very important, for example, caste, tribe, or lineage.

A different but related explanation is that there is much greater variation in the availability of school resources in developing nations than in developed nations. For example, in rich nations, almost all students have complete sets of textbooks, and the differences in the formal educational levels of teachers are relatively small. In developing nations, however, there are great variations in such indicators. In a poor nation, even modest increments in the provision of textbooks can thus have a major effect on student learning. In rich nations, students are already abundantly supplied with books, and increases in learning require difficult and costly improvements in the quality of books—assuming knowledge of the aspects of book quality that influence student learning. In a poor nation, many primary teachers have low levels of formal schooling and little if any pedagogical training. Thus, a very modest change in preservice or in-service training could significantly improve teacher performance and hence student learning. In a rich nation, almost all teachers have university degrees, high-level pedagogical training, and many opportunities for in-service education, and thus even small improvements in teacher performance are difficult to achieve and hard to identify

I have combined both of these explanations in a previous publication. In rich nations, which are close to the limits of the perfectibility of the "standard model of schooling" as we know it, "even modest additional gains in achievement require very difficult and costly educational effort." In developing nations "even the very modest improvements in school quality which a poor nation can realistically contemplate have the potential for providing important increases in student learning," particularly among the most marginalized students. The possibility of improving equality of output in developing nations, within the very modest resources available to them, is particularly important because the evidence indicates that levels of learning among students in developing nations are systematically lower than among students in rich nations. Cross-national comparisons of student achievement levels that have been carried out over these past decades, principally under the auspices of the International Association for the Evaluation of Educational Achievement (IEA), UNESCO, and the Organization for Economic Cooperation and Development (OECD) have consistently demonstrated that the achievement test scores of children from low- and middle- income nations are lower than those of children of comparable age or grade levels in industrialized nations. The differences are large in some subject areas and small in others, but they are consistent. Until quite recently these cross-national studies have compared young people at the secondary level, or in some cases the senior primary level. In most developing nations, as I noted earlier, children who are neither socioeconomically advantaged nor academically gifted do not typically survive to this level of schooling. Thus, the differences in learning output could be expected to be even greater at the early primary level, which is as far as most youngsters in developing nations progress in their formal education (Farrell & Heyneman, 1989). Evidence from an IEA study of reading levels among nine-year-olds in 29 nations, reported in 1992, plus a 1997 UNESCO study of grade four reading and mathematics achievement in 11 Latin American nations, and an analysis of Latin American performance on OECD tests of reading, mathematics, and science at grade three level reported in 2011, suggest that this may be the case. Unfortunately, the number of developing nations in these samples is too small to firmly ground the conclusion (Elley, 1992; Gaminian & Rocha, 2011; UNESCO, 2000a; Wolff et al., 2002).

Much recently published evidence indicates that the fiscal crisis in most developing nations, combined with expanding enrollments, is dramatically decreasing the instructional resources available per student, which is, in turn, increasing the learning gap between students in rich and poor nations (Farrell, 1989; Farrell & Heyneman, 1989). Regional assessments near the turn of the century indicate that the problem remains. Even where additional resources for education have been found they have typically increased access and/or survival without improving learning levels (UNESCO, 2000b; Wolff et al., 2002). A question that arises is whether individuals or societies benefit from increasingly equal access to and survival through a schooling system if student learning remains low, or even declines.

There is a problem with all of these analyses and studies, however. Many doubts have been expressed regarding the validity and utility of broad-scale international testing programs for close-grained cross-national comparisons (Farrell, 2004). It is not always clear what the results "mean" in any real policy or practice sense. For example, if one notes that the mean score on a mathematics test among, say, grade six students in country A is 10% higher than in country B, what real differences might that make in how the youngsters in the two nations develop as individuals or contribute to their nations' "development"? We don't really know. However, there is one basic learning goal assigned to schools all over the world. Whatever else they do, we expect that by the end of a full course of primary schooling young people will have become *literate*, at least to a basic functional level. Here the evidence is clear that schools in poorer nations are seriously failing. In 2006, Abadzi reported the following levels of minimum mastery of literacy among last-year primary students based on international or national tests: Malawi 7%; Mauritius 52%; Namibia 19%; Tanzania 18%; Colombia 27%:

Morocco 59%; Burkina Faso 21%; Cameroon 33%; Cote d'Ivoire 38%; Papua New Guinea 21%; Madagascar 20%; Senegal 25%; Togo 40%; Uruguay 66%; and Yemen 10% (Abadzi, 2006). Even in Latin America, generally considered to be a region with relatively high educational development in the "developing world," (primary enrollment ratios generally range above 90%), Schiefelbein (2006) reports that among the 63% of each cohort of entering students who actually complete the primary cycle, "no more than half of those who completed their primary education understand a short text published on the front page of a [popular] newspaper." I summarized the situation as follows: "Thus in the developing world there are more than one hundred million children who never enter primary school. Of those who do enter, hundreds of millions more do not complete the full cycle. Of those who do complete the full cycle, hundreds of millions more do not attain even a minimal level of literacy" (Farrell, 2009). All in all a rather dreary picture! Again, what really is the point of getting more and more bodies in seats in schools, if the learning results at even the level of basic functional literacy are so dismal? (This question was debated vigorously in *Comparative Education Review* 33, no. 1 [1989]).

EQUALITY OF OUTCOME

Relatively equal distributions of access to, survival through, or learning within the formal schooling system is considered socially beneficial by many only if it pays off for the recipients in relatively equal access to life chances (particularly but not exclusively jobs) as adults. To what extent can, or does, education have an intervening effect on the intergenerational status transmission? To what extent, and under what conditions, can it produce upward social mobility rather than simply ratify or reproduce existing patterns of structural inequality? Consideration of this question brings us back to the basic questions noted earlier in this chapter. Can, or under what conditions, the school build a new social order? Can it at least provide opportunities for individual social mobility for at least some children of marginalized groups within a society? A huge amount of evidence has been generated over the past decades regarding these questions, mostly within nations but occasionally comparatively across nations. The results are, at least in a comparative sense, systematic, but theoretically they are confusing. In 1975, Lin and Yauger reported data from a quite limited data set, from Haiti, from three Costa Rican communities at three levels of development, from Britain, and from the United States, and concluded that "the direct influence of educational attainment on occupational status is curvilinearly (concave) related to degree of industrialization" (Lin & Yauger, 1975). Schiefelbein and Farrell (1978) noted that data from Uganda at three points in time and from four Brazilian communities fitted the same pattern. More recent results from Chile have reinforced the same pattern (Farrell & Schiefelbein, 1985). The general pattern seems to be as follows. In very poor societies, almost everyone is engaged in subsistence agriculture, except for a few (typically young) occupants of newly created civil service posts and some commercial entrepreneurs. Education can have very little effect on occupational mobility because there are very few occupational destinations into which one could be mobile (partially explaining the lack of effective demand for education among such populations, as noted previously). As the local economy grows and becomes more differentiated, it creates a variety of new job openings. In the absence of a traditionally dominant class or group that can exploit all of the new opportunities, formal education becomes a predominant influence on the level of job acquired. Significant numbers of even very disadvantaged children can use education to obtain positions in the "modern" economy. (In many developing societies, the growth of the educational system has much surpassed the growth of the economy, producing a problem of "educated unemployment." Even in such societies, youngsters often continue in school as long as possible because the potential payoff is high if, or when, they can obtain any job at all.) As societies become very developed, their economies become so complex and rapidly changing, and the possible avenues to economic success are so varied, that the independent effect of formal education begins to diminish (see, e.g., Boudon, 1973; Jencks, 1972).

Evidence from the advanced state-socialist societies of Eastern Europe, which collapsed in the early 1990s, suggests that there too this general pattern has been evident (Birzea, 1996; Price-Rom, 2002; Zajda, 1980). Some economists have argued that in very advanced postindustrial economies the phenomenon of the "declining middle"—the elimination of well-paying industrial and middle-class jobs in favor of lower-paying service sector jobs—is reducing even further the mobility-generating potential of formal schooling. Pushing this argument a step further, Farrell and Schiefelbein (1985) have claimed that all the major studies that have provided data regarding the effect of education on intergenerational status transmission—which form the empirical foundation for the theoretical arguments on this question—are flawed and fundamentally uninterpretable because they fail to take into account long-term structural changes in the economy and how these necessarily constrain what education can do. However, despite this growing empirical and theoretical confusion, it is still clear that even in societies in which education has the weakest effect upon intergenerational status transmission, and the weakest effect upon social structural change, some individuals and social groups benefit from both its more widespread provision as well as increases in its quality. Rarely if ever does the provision of more formal education, or the improvement of its quality, have no mobility-generating or life-enhancing consequences for at least a few children of marginalized groups. Analyses by Paquette (1995) and by Levin (1992) in the 1990s, however, can be interpreted as suggesting that even that minimal effect of formal schooling on individual and collective life chances may be disappearing (or has already disappeared) in North American societies, and perhaps, by extension, in other societies as well.

CONCLUSION

In this final section, I wish to apply the massive amount of comparative data analyzed earlier to the central theme of this book: the effect of recent educational reform movements, proposals, and occasionally enacted policies (e.g., privatization, decentralization, educational change for "global competitiveness," the "testing" driven "standards" movement) on equality of educational opportunity and outcome among the most marginalized members of the many societies of our world. This is necessarily a highly speculative enterprise. As we have seen, major educational change is generally a failure-prone, slow, and long-term process. It takes even longer to begin to see and understand its eventual effects upon how today's students actually can and do live their lives. It has taken almost five decades for us to begin to understand the results of the massive educational change efforts of the "optimistic 60s," and even now we are still arguing about the quality and completeness of the available comparative information and about how to interpret and understand it. We could hardly expect less concerning the most recent waves of educational reforms. Moreover, local, regional, or worldwide events can significantly change the context of long-term reform efforts such that "results" can move in totally unpredictable directions. For example, if we had been creating this book in the late 1980s, none of the authors could have predicted the sudden demise of the former Soviet Union and its associated states, nor the consequences for our understanding of educational change and educational equality, which are still very unclear and will likely remain so for a long time. An ancient (probably apocryphal) proverb has it, "Prediction is always difficult, especially with respect to the future." A central lesson for the theme of this book from the comparative data assembled over the past several decades is this: Don't take seriously anyone who speaks with certainty about the probable effects of the current wave of educational reform proposals. We have, however, learned a few things since the end of the Second World War. These lessons can provide us with some guidance regarding how to think about outcomes, if not how to predict them. A central lesson learned is the necessity of a high degree of intellectual and moral humility, as well as tolerance for a high degree of ambiguity.

Another lesson learned is that the common tendency over the past decades to centrally directed and command-driven forms of educational change, most commonly following national and international "faddism" and a "one size fits all" view of educational change, have poorly served the interests of those who might benefit from increases in educational equality. This applies equally as well to the current wave of educational reform "fads." The possible or probable effects of the current reform fashions on educational inequality depend on specific local conditions and history. For example, university education in many nations of Latin America has long been highly "privatized." The effects on educational inequality vary dramatically from nation to nation, depending on specific national conditions. The effects of further privatization in any of these nations, however, would be almost certainly very different from the privatization of higher education in the completely state-controlled higher education systems of many other nations. Similarly, as Mark Bray notes in Chapter 8 of this volume, "decentralization" has different meanings and different possible long-term consequences, depending on where a particular nation starts on some sort of centralized-decentralized continuum. Moreover, serious critiques of some of these reform fads have begun to arise in their nations of origin. For example, Diane Ravitch (2011), one of the strongest proponents of the "testing, standards and accountability" reform movement in the United States for many years, has in 2010 "recanted," noting that testing "had become a preoccupation in the schools, and was not just a means but an end in itself." Just as there are no universally applicable solutions to educational inequality, there are no universally applicable predictions of reform consequences. There is, however, one general claim that can be made. If the experience of the past 60 years is any guide (the experience base in the United States goes back more than a century, but the "lesson" is the same) (Farrell, 2000), it seems that the broad reform proposals now being widely discussed will often not be enacted; if enacted, they will seldom be well or fully implemented; if implemented well, they generally will not have a significant effect on equality of access, survival, or output (as discussed in the "model" presented earlier), at least for large numbers of youngsters; and if they do manage to improve these "within-school" aspects of equality, they are highly unlikely to have a significant impact on equality of outcome by altering the life chances of large proportions of poor or marginalized children.

Overall, then, the picture appears rather bleak. There have been significant gains in educational equality over the past 60 years, but they have been for the most part not the result of broad-scale, centrally driven reform programs supported by international agencies. Rather, they have been the result of economic growth or social structural change outside the realm of the school, or of an option that is now generally unavailable or that political leaders are unwilling to choose: massive increases in educational expenditure. There are of course exceptions, nations that have found the political will to significantly increase educational expenditures and effectively implement reforms that appear to be having a positive impact on educational equality. Egypt is one such case (Farrell & Connelly, 1994; Spaulding et al., 1996). Chile is another such case. During the decade of the 1990s, a succession of democratically elected governments doubled spending on education, producing a significant improvement in all three within-school aspects of equality discussed here (see McGinn, 2000).

However, I end this chapter on a hopeful note. Throughout the world, particularly the developing world, there are small and large attempts to fundamentally alter the traditional teacher-directed model of schooling. They typically use some or all of the following modalities: combinations of fully trained teachers, partially trained teachers, para-teachers, and community resource people; radio, correspondence lessons, television, and in a few cases computers; peer tutoring; self-guided learning materials; student and teacher constructed learning materials; multigrade classrooms; child-centered rather than teacher-driven pedagogy; free flows of children and adults between the school and the community; locally adapted changes in the cycle of the school day or school year. They typically spread not by a centrally planned and commanded reform plan but through an innovation diffusion process. They depend for their success not on the ability and willingness of teachers to "follow orders" from on high, but rather on stimulating and unleashing the creative energy, enthusiasm, and personal practical knowledge of teachers. Such change programs do not simply alter one feature of the standard school (e.g., change one part of the curriculum), strengthen one or several parts of the standard schooling model (e.g., add more textbooks or improve teacher training), or add one or two new features. Rather, they represent a thorough reorganization and a fundamental revision of the standard schooling model such that the learning program, although often occurring in or based in a building called a school, is far different from what we have come to expect to be happening in a school. They tend to break down the boundaries between formal and nonformal education and to focus less on teaching and more on learning. Where they have been evaluated, the results have generally been very positive. New groups of learners are reached successfully, and the learning results are generally far better than those obtained in standard schools. More than 90% of children who start these primary programs complete them, and their assessed learning levels go far beyond the minimum level of literacy that the standard schools so often do not manage to provide. And the costs are typically no more than, if not less than, those of the standard model. Moreover, because they serve the most marginalized, hardest to reach and teach (in the standard model) students, the learning results from a value-added perspective are quite spectacular (Farrell, 2006; 2011).

Some major examples of these model-breaking educational change programs include the Escuela Nueva program in Colombia, which has now reached close to 30,000 rural schools and has been adapted on a large- or small-scale basis in at least 10 other Latin American nations; the multigrade program in Guinea, now operating in over 1,300 schools; the MECE Rural Program (Programa de Mejoramiento de la Calidad de la Educación para las Escuelas Multigrados Rurales) in Chile, which is now present in over 3,000 schools; the Nonformal Primary Education program of the Bangladesh Rural Advancement Committee, which operates in 35,000 villages in that nation and is spreading into urban areas and other nations, a wide network of community schools supported by the Aga Khan Foundation in Pakistan and other developing nations; the Schools for Life program in Central Ghana which has spread to several thousand schools, and the Community Schools Program in rural Egypt, which is now operating in thousands of schools. What is important about such programs is that they focus on learning rather than teaching and provide a pedagogically superior experience for highly marginalized young people. In addition, they generally operate either outside of or on the margins of the national school system (indeed, one of the major design issues with such systems, particularly at the early stages, is protecting or insulating them from the heavy bureaucratic hand of the state schooling system). They thus provide us with examples of successfully delivering opportunities for high-quality learning to the most disadvantaged children that do not depend on the eroding fiscal and managerial capacity of increasingly "fragile" states (Fuller, 1991). They present us with an operationally successful vision of a more hopeful future.

Even in these cases, however, it is far too early to tell whether these major increases in the availability and quality of schooling for poor and marginalized children will ultimately have any major effect on the socioeconomic and political structures that have created and maintained that poverty and marginalization in the first place. Indeed, ultimately we cannot know and predict that in advance. As I have argued elsewhere recently, human learning is, by its very nature, not subject to coercion and control nor to the prediction of its consequences. In the final analysis all we can do is enable it and hope for the best (Farrell, 1997). In that context, whatever the ultimate effects of these new schooling programs on the broad social-structural level, significantly improving the availability and quality of opportunities to learn through schooling is in and of itself a notable achievement and a very worthy social goal.

NOTE

We include this fourth edition chapter by Joseph Farrell (1939–2013) as a widely respected classic in our field that colleagues respect and have not wished to change. The chapter frames in very useful ways how to conceptualize the distinguishing features of educational equality and equity.

REFERENCES

Abadzi, H. (2006). *Efficient learning for the poor: Insights from the frontier of cognitive neuroscience.* World Bank Publications.

Adams, D. (1977). Development education. *Comparative Education Review, 21*(2/3), 296–310.

Bailey, T. (1991). Jobs of the future and the education they will require: Evidence from occupational forecasts. *Educational Researcher, 20*(2), 11–20.

Baker, V. J. (1989). Education for its own sake: The relevance dimension in rural areas. *Comparative Education Review, 33*(4), 507–518.

Birzea, C. (1996). Education in a world in transition: Between post-communism and post-modernism. *Prospects, 26*(4), 673–681.

Boudon, R. (1973). *Education, opportunity, and social inequality.* Wiley.

Bowles, S., & Gintis, H. (1976). *Schooling in capitalist America.* Basic Books.

Bowman, M. J. (1984). An integrated framework for analysis of the spread of schooling in less developed countries.

Carnoy, M. (1974). *Education as cultural imperialism.* McKay.

Carnoy, M., & Levin, H. (1985). *Schooling and work in the democratic state.* Stanford University Press.

Coombs, P. H. (1968). *The world educational crisis: A systems analysis.* Oxford University Press.

Counts, G. S. (1932). *Dare the school build a new social order?* John Day.

Elley, W. B. (1992). *How in the world do students read?* International Association for the Evaluation of Educational Achievement.

Farrell, J. (1992). Educational problems and learning solutions. *Curriculum Inquiry, 22*(3), 231–234.

Farrell, J. (1996). Narratives of identity: The voices of youth. *Curriculum Inquiry, 26*(3), 1–12.

Farrell, J. (1997). A retrospective on educational planning in comparative education. *Comparative Education Review, 41*(3), 277–313.

Farrell, J. (1998, December). Improving learning: Perspectives for primary education in rural Africa. In *A World Bank-and UNESCO-sponsored Regional Workshop with the Support of the Norwegian Trust, Lusaka, Zambia* (pp. 6–11).

Farrell, J. (2000). Why is educational reform so difficult? Similar descriptions, different prescriptions, failed explanations. *Curriculum Inquiry, 30*(1), 83–103.

Farrell, J. (2004). The use and abuse of comparative studies of educational achievement. *Curriculum Inquiry, 34*(3), 255–265.

Farrell, J. P. (2006). Community education in developing countries: The quest revolution in schooling. In *Sage international handbook of curriculum and instruction.* Sage.

Farrell, J. (2009). Literacy and international development: Education and literacy as basic human rights. In D. R. Olson & N. Torrance (Eds.), *The Cambridge handbook of literacy.* Cambridge University Press.

Farrell, J. (2011). Educational planning: Blind alleys and signposts of hope. In M. Bray & N. K. Varghese (Eds.), *Directions in educational planning: International experiences and perspectives* (pp. 63–87). International Institute for Educational Planning/ UNESCO.

Farrell, J., & Connell, M. (1994). *From a massive reform model to an innovation diffusion model of change, report for UNICEF-Egypt.* UNICEF.

Farrell, J., & Heyneman, S. P. (Eds.). (1989). *Textbooks in the developing world: Economic and educational choices.* World Bank.

Farrell, J., & Schiefelbein, E. (1982). *Eight years of their lives: Through schooling to the labour market in Chile.* International Development Research Centre.

Farrell, J. P., & Schiefelbein, E. (1985). Education and status attainment in Chile: A comparative challenge to the Wisconsin model of status attainment. *Comparative Education Review*, 29(4), 490–506.

Foster, P. (1977). Education and social differentiation in less developed countries. *Comparative Education Review*, 22(2–3), 224–225.

Fuller, B. (1991). *Growing-up modern: The western state builds third-world schools.* Routledge.

Gaminian, A., & Rocha, A. S. (2011). *Measuring up? How did Latin America and the Caribbean perform on the 2009 Programme for International Student Assessment?* Partnership for Educational Revitalization in the Americas.

Heyneman, S., & Loxley, W. (1983). The effects of primary school quality on academic achievement across twenty-nine high and low-income countries. *American Journal of Sociology*, 88(3), 1162–1194.

Jallade, J-P. (1972–1973). The evolution of educational systems in industrialized countries: A summary. *Western European Education*, 4(4), 330–336.

Jencks, C., et al. (1972). *Inequality.* Basic Books.

Levin, B. (1992). Dealing with dropouts in Canadian education. *Curriculum Inquiry*, 22(3), 257–270.

Levin, H. (1978). The dilemma of comprehensive secondary school reforms in Western Europe. *Comparative Education Review*, 22(3), 434–451.

Lin, N., & Yauger, D. (1975). The process of occupational status achievement: A preliminary cross-national comparison. *American Journal of Sociology*, 81(6), 543–562.

Liston, D. P. (1988). *Capitalist schools: Explanation and ethics in radical studies of schooling.* Routledge.

Lockheed, M., & Verspoor, A. (1990). *Improving primary education in developing countries: A review of policy options.* World Bank.

McGinn, N. D. (2000). Commentary. In F. Reimers (Ed.), *Unequal schools, unequal chances: The challenges to equal opportunity in the Americas.* Harvard University Press.

Neave, G. (1982). New influences on educational policies in Western Europe during the seventies. In P. Broadfoot et al., *Politics and educational change* (pp. 71–85). Croom Helm.

Paquette, J. (1995). Universal education: Meanings, challenges and options into the third millennium. *Curriculum Inquiry*, 25(1), 23–56.

Price-Rom, A. (2002). *The pedagogy of democracy in seven post-Soviet states.* Paper presented at the Annual Meeting of the Comparative and International Education Society, Orlando, Florida.

Ravitch, D. (2011). *The death and life of the great American school system: How testing and choice are undermining education.* Basic Books.

Riddell, A. R. (1997). Assessing designs for school effectiveness research and school improvement in developing countries. *Comparative Education Review*, 41(2), 178–204.

Rondinelli, D., Middleton, J., & Verspoor, A. (1990). *Planning educational reforms in developing countries: The contingency approach.* Duke University Press.

Ross, K. N., & Mahlick, L. (1990). *Planning the quality of education.* International Institute for Educational Planning.

Ross, K. N., & Mahlick, L. (1993). *Education and knowledge: Basic pillars of changing production patterns with social equity.* UNESCO-CEPAL.

Schiefelbein, E. (2006). *School performance problems in Latin America: The potential role of the Escuela Nueva system.* Paper prepared for the Second International New Schools Congress. Medellín, Colombia.

Schiefelbein, E., & Farrell, J. (1978). Selectivity and survival in the schools of Chile. *Comparative Education Review*, 22(2), 326–341.

Seligson, M. A., & Passe-Smith, J. T. (1993). *Development and underdevelopment: The political economy of inequality*. Lynne Rienner.

Spaulding, S., Klaus, B., Binayagum, C., & Nader, F. (1996). *Review and assessment of reform of basic education in Egypt*. UNESCO.

UNESCO. (1993). *Education for the twenty-first century: Learning to learn*. UNESCO.

UNESCO. (2000a). *Informe sub-regional de America Latina de EFA*. UNESCO Regional Office for Education in Latin America and the Caribbean.

UNESCO. (2000b). The Dakar framework for action. *Education for all: Meeting our collective commitments*. UNESCO.

UNICEF. (2011). *The state of the world's children: Special edition*. UNICEF.

Wolff, L., Schiefelbein, E., & Schiefelbein, P. (2002). *Primary education in Latin America*; Association for the Development of Education in Africa (ADEA), 14(2).

World Bank. (1980). *Education sector policy paper* (3rd ed.). World Bank.

World Bank. (2000/2001). *World development report. Attacking poverty*. World Bank.

World Bank. (2011). Elizabeth King. *The World Bank Group education strategy 2020*. World Bank.

Zajda, J. (1980). Education and social stratification in the Soviet Union. *Comparative Education Review*, 16(1), 3–11.

7

Women's Education in the 21st Century

Nelly P. Stromquist
University of Maryland

ABSTRACT

Given the simultaneous existence of the knowledge economy and oppressive gender relations, schooling is central to women's advancement. This chapter begins by revisiting gender theory and the condition of women's education at all levels across geographical regions. It then moves to examine from a critical feminist perspective the national and international actors influencing education policy. This review argues for the need to consider three key questions: (1) how do we change a patriarchal education system that has been in existence for so long and thus developed deep roots? (2) how can we further promote gender transformation through women-led nongovernmental organization (NGO) educational programs? and (3) how do we create spaces for change today amid social and economic situations that promote competition and access to the labor market rather than engagement with solidaristic and socially reflective practices? Crucial to the consideration of these three questions is the necessary action to modify the parallel worlds in which key actors in education and gender currently operate.

■ ■ ■

Given the simultaneous existence of the knowledge economy and oppressive gender relations, schooling is central to women's advancement. This chapter begins by revisiting gender theory and the condition of women's education at all levels across geographical regions. It then moves to examine from a critical feminist perspective the national and international actors influencing education policy. The interaction between global norms and national responses shows a tendency toward goal convergence; this agreement occurs in such areas as inclusion and quality while gender equality tends to receive symbolic attention and little transformative knowledge is conveyed. Nation-states as well as international agencies that support education, as consensually manifested in the United Nations Sustainable Development Goals, refrain from recognizing the substantial role that schools play in the continuous reconstitution of gender inequalities, preferring to promote instead education as a means to prepare women to enter the labor market under more competitive conditions. To secure a more complete approach to education, women's organizations emerge as indispensable agents in the provision of counterhegemonic knowledge. The potential of a multidimensional women's empowerment to heighten gender awareness and impel transformative action is highlighted here as a major political resource despite significant challenges created by neoliberal principles.

About 50 years have elapsed since the international women's movement first called attention to the social and economic inequalities confronting women, at the First World Conference on Women in 1975, held in Mexico. During this time, substantial progress has occurred in problem definition and theorization of gender, including the role of education and schooling in the advancement of women. Less progress has taken place in the type and degree of change within formal school systems. Industrialized countries, with greater resources, more organized women's groups, and institutions more sensitive to public pressure have attained greater changes than the developing countries, but even in the former much work remains to be accomplished.

When discussing the connection between gender and education, it is necessary to make a distinction between education and schooling. Education is used herein to refer to the transmission of broad and specific knowledge that includes but also goes beyond that imparted by national school systems. Education may occur in formal situations, nonformal situations (e.g., programs and classes provided for adults by community groups), and informal situations (notably the knowledge conveyed within the home and through the mass media). Schooling relates specifically to the structured and institutionalized type of knowledge transmitted through formal educational institutions, mainly schools and universities. This distinction is essential because, given the conservative nature of most schooling, it is within nonformal education settings that most gender-transforming processes have occurred and will likely occur. This chapter discusses schooling and education in developing countries, focusing on their implications for and linkage to gender issues. It emphasizes developments in recent decades and seeks to present an overview of the most recent developments along the lines of theory, policy, and practice.

Discussions of conceptual and practical changes must identify certain key groups involved in education—their positions regarding gender are not the same. Among governments and international development agencies (both bilateral and multilateral), the question of women's education has moved from invisibility to explicit recognition of the need to consider it a priority. However, official recognition tends to be more rhetorical than real and so far is based mostly on an acknowledgment of women as important mediators in the modernization process—not yet on an understanding of women as autonomous citizens. International development agencies have continued their policy of dealing exclusively with governments and thus their actions tend to side with governmental perspectives. Their education efforts to promote women have generally focused on access to schooling and skills for economic production. Among groups within or closely associated with the women's movement, education is considered an important avenue toward empowerment, and valuable knowledge has been gained from experiences in this direction. Gail Kelly (1978), one of the pioneer thinkers on the question of gender and education in the context of developing countries, admonished us to understand not only how the education of women can improve society but also how education can improve the lives of women themselves. This point has still not been fully recognized by either governments or international agencies.

Educational studies on gender in the 1970s concentrated on documenting sex inequalities in educational opportunity (primarily access to schooling). In the 1980s, the studies expanded this focus to examine such issues as the determinants of these opportunities, the relationship between education and work/remuneration, and the benefits of women's education for society (e.g., Smock, 1981). Later studies in the 1990s under the support of the World Bank continued the line of exploration of barriers to girls' education and, particularly, the personal and social benefits derived from their education (e.g., King & Hill, 1993). Such studies have been useful in highlighting the importance of education as a resource for women and the fact that it is neutral neither in its offerings nor in its consequences. A consistent finding has been that schooling increases women's earnings but does not remove their economic dependence on men. Women's years of schooling affect decisions on marriage, but there is no linear relationship between the two. These two critical shapers of women's lives indicate that although schooling is important for economic and social advancement, it is not sufficient to alter women's subordinate position. Even after higher levels of schooling, women have retained marginal positions in the political arena. Studies focusing on Latin America, a region in which gender parity is very close at all levels of education, have looked at issues beyond access and quality, such as the effects of coeducational settings on social outcomes, the participation and power of women in teachers' unions, women students in politics at the university level, and experiences in popular education for adult women (Stromquist, 1992; 1996).

The third generation of studies on gender and education, typical of the 2000 decade, has probed educational phenomena not often seen from a gender perspective, such as the role of women teachers in the process of educational change, the treatment of gender and ethnicity in history textbooks, and tensions between the professional and personal identities of women teachers. Such research has also given more attention to the contested experience of incorporating controversial subjects into the curriculum such as sex education and to the recognition of schools as unfriendly and even threatening environments for girls through such practices as sexual harassment and even rape, not infrequent events in African and Latin American countries. Studies in the 2010s have been more sensitive to the issues of sexual orientation and gender identity, both issues that have been much more felt in industrialized than developing countries (GCE & RESULTS, 2011).

THE CONTRIBUTION OF FEMINIST THEORY TO THE UNDERSTANDING OF EDUCATIONAL INSTITUTIONS

Most societies depend on hierarchies and divisions of labor to institute order and stability. Several markers (e.g., gender, social class, ethnicity, race, national origin) are used to create these hierarchies. Gender is not the only one but it is the most pervasive as the main type of differentiation and inequality in all societies. The intersection between gender and social class (poverty in this case) is particularly insidious, as evinced in the persistently high proportion of women among the global illiterate population, comprising about 63% (UNESCO, 2020).

Feminist theory seeks to place women and their lives in a central place to understand social relations as a whole. Feminism is best conceptualized as a form of critical theory and as a social movement that enables its adherents to see behind obvious manifestations and to understand the structures underlying it and giving meaning, albeit distorted, to their lives (Wilson, 1993). Feminist theory is crucial as it enables us to distinguish central from peripheral factors, cause from effect, solution from problem, and diagnosis from prognosis. Otherwise, we produce a long list of groups (women, immigrants, children, LGBTQ+, persons with disabilities, senior citizens, African Americans, Hispanics, etc.) and erroneously put them together, forgetting that they face different disadvantages and that there are women and men in all disadvantaged groups. Through a gender lens, we can understand mechanisms of subordination and oppression and identify forces that shape the apparent "free choices" that women and men make through various phases of their lives.

Feminist theory frequently invokes patriarchy as a coherent, cohesive, and permanent (albeit constantly adjusting) system of organizing society. Through the recognition of patriarchy as a crucial operating principle, feminist theory has highlighted the need to link analytically the symbolic and the material as well as the micro and the macro: the personal/intimate and the institutional, the family and the community, the individual and her society, the school and the state. These settings are interconnected in real life, and their mutual reinforcement must be taken into account when examining institutions such as schools and universities.

Schooling presents a paradoxical situation in the process of gender transformation. Schooling is undoubtedly a major source of cultural capital, employment, and social mobility. Its importance is so acknowledged that most countries have moved into mandating compulsory basic education for all. At the same time, however, educational institutions are conservative settings that reflect the values and rules of a patriarchal society (Kelly & Nihlen, 1982; Longwe, 1997) and, when change is proposed, parents usually emerge to protect the status quo. Nevertheless, there is also the possibility that when radical political change occurs in certain societies, both formal and nonformal education is used to transform gender relations and the subordinate status of women in their societies.

Among gender scholars today, there is an increased understanding of the necessity to undertake a comprehensive analysis of educational institutions so that the various aspects that constitute the totality of the schooling experience—curriculum, instructional methodologies, peer relations, extracurricular activities—are investigated. Schooling is organized in gendered ways and has differential impacts on girls and boys, often creating polarized forms of masculinity and femininity. Studies in industrialized countries—which tend to have more open social systems than those in developing countries—reveal that school authority structures, teacher expectations and classroom practices, and peer exchanges are organized along gender lines.

Knowledge about the gendered nature of schooling has certainly developed since the 1980s, but in recent years more evidence has been accumulated to demonstrate the pervasive nature of these conditions and their existence beyond variations in social class. The tools of qualitative research have been instrumental in documenting the everyday experience of students in educational institutions, noting the sometimes mild but cumulative nature of many events that gradually yet inexorably shape individuals' perception of self and their roles in society; an insightful example is Eisenhart and Holland (1990). Also in recent years greater conceptual attention has been given to the intersection between gender, social class, race, and ethnicity. These concerns, however, have not always materialized in studies of multiple intersections because this type of research requires substantial financial resources, due either to more complex research designs or to the need to enter into socially diverse school settings, which are not easy to access (especially those serving the elite). The conceptually important question of the intersection of social markers nevertheless runs the risk of introducing innumerable differences that, although correcting the conception of the "grand narrative" so criticized by postmodernism, also threaten to depoliticize social issues through the introduction of great variability of situations and elusive complexity. While there are diverse experiences through which women live, they are collectively lived because of their sex (Soper, 1991) and most women's existence is characterized by subordination and oppression on account of their sex. Gender analysis not only focuses on women but also on the permanent transactions between women and men.

Gender theories today are more sensitive to power and the role of the state in shaping society. The extension of this understanding to schooling has highlighted the role that schools play in the perpetuation of the stark categories of femininity and masculinity and how the state, through its quasi-monopoly on schooling, is implicated in this process. Thinkers such as Connell (1987; 1994) have been instrumental in explicating the centrality of organized state power and highlighting the function of schools in the development of gendered subjectivities. According to the analytic framework proposed by Althusser (1971), schooling functions as an ideological apparatus of state. Yet it is also a space into which students bring their own preconceptions and make them a reality through the power of peer pressure. Schooling does not act by itself. Students and teachers bring into the classroom an array of values, attitudes, and beliefs they have learned in their homes and community. These become reenacted in the school, through the treatment of women and men in textbooks, teacher-student interactions, peer-group transactions, and the school culture and organization in general.

A key feature of feminist theory is its emphasis on linking knowledge and action. Schools must be seen not only as they are now but also visualized as potentially transformative social spaces in which useful knowledge can be inculcated, reflection on existing knowledge and culture can take place, and alternative ways of being and living can be imagined and sought. The dominant global public debate regarding education and women has accepted the importance of women's participation in schooling, at least in terms of access to basic education. This defense of women's right to education is certainly crucial. At the same time, its emphasis on access has left unquestioned other aspects of schooling—curriculum content, teacher-student interactions, peer culture, and overall internal climate of the school—that tend to reproduce a patriarchal social order. This definition of the situation creates a significant challenge for the women's movement. Without access, the question of the knowledge to be acquired is a moot point; without questioning existing educational institutions, the knowledge gained might tend to affirm the unequal and inequitable status quo.

As part of critical theory, feminist approaches are sensitive to the notion of individual and collective agency—the possibility of resistance by those oppressed, a phenomenon derived from the Foucauldian principle that power exists not only in official institutions and hierarchies but also through the multiple and lower-level interactions in our everyday lives (Foucault, 1980). There is an increased emphasis on analyzing schooling as a contested terrain in which teachers and students try to create new definitions and personal identities, and students do not passively accept dominant gender representations but argue about values and meanings. The potential of teacher subjectivities and negotiations of the everyday life of schools is increasingly visualized as an avenue to attain the transformation of schooling.

In recent years, therefore, feminist work in schools and universities has moved toward more proactive strategies. At lower education levels, these include bringing patriarchy, sexism, and racism into the discussion of girls' and boys' lives, creating spaces within schools and classrooms in which young girls can explore their experiences and create situations of equal exchange. It also includes recognition and protection of the students' sexual orientation and gender identity, as increasing respect is being given to students who are gay, lesbian, bisexual, transsexual, queer, and other forms of sexual orientation and gender identity—a group collectively known as LGBTQ+. At the university level, proactive practices include participation in the various women's studies courses and in the creation of mentoring mechanisms by which younger scholars (doctoral students and junior faculty) are helped by senior academic professors in ways that range from fostering research production to "learning the ropes" for promotion to tenured status (Aaron & Walby, 1991).

Models of the impact of the expansion of schooling on life chances are becoming more complete than they have been in the past. If before they included variables such as forgone earnings, current and future benefits, direct costs, supply of school facilities, and the extent of mass communication (Bowman, 1986), today they are more open to questions of patriarchal ideology reflected in such variables as early marriage, early motherhood, and son preference. These variables do not directly address a society's belief in drastically distinct roles for women and men, but their incorporation into analyses of impact acknowledges that there are differential logics at work, rationales that are not necessarily economically based but reflect long-standing patriarchal norms. Researchers are also becoming more precise in their economic arguments. One example is Colclough (1996), who remarks that rates-of-return analyses compare the cost to parents of schooling with the economic returns to the child, but in practice what determines schooling is the cost and benefits to parents of sending a child to school. This observation illuminates why certain parents harm the educational opportunities for their children by depriving them of schooling in early years. Given the centrality of domestic work and, more specifically, the time invested in fuel and water fetching in rural households, it is becoming increasingly clear that opportunities for greater access of poor and low-income girls to school will have to pass through greater investment in infrastructure in electricity, water, and sewage by the government.

Ilon's (1998) study of macroeconomic and social variables reinforces this point. She finds that countries that become export intensive and improve their per capita GNP tend to increase the rate of females attending secondary school. This finding is compatible with the feminist argument and the empirical fact (observed in both the United States and Latin America) that women need more education to be as competitive as men in the labor force (reflected in women's need for about four more years of education than men to qualify for similar salaries). Also, as household incomes improve there is a diminished need for girls' domestic work.

In short, contributions from feminist perspectives to education underscore the need for holistic probing of the educational system, for a multidisciplinary analysis that considers influences at various forms and levels of social organization, and for policies or advocacy positions that exploit the opportunities for transformation within the narrow and somewhat temporary fractures that are possible.

THE CONDITIONS OF WOMEN'S SCHOOLING

Access to schooling has increased over time; comparisons of groups aged 20 to 24 with older cohorts invariably show higher levels of education among the younger generations. Ramirez and Boli-Bennett (1982) and others note that the expansion of educational systems occurs independently of economic, political, and social factors within national borders, thereby suggesting that influential "transnational forces" or a "world culture" are at work. Additional reasons for the expansion of schooling include international economic dynamics (countries becoming more export-intensive through value-added production of goods and services, or improving their per capita income), social imitation of promising innovations, and, in the case of women's schooling, the increasing pressure of the women's movement upon state policy for educational expansion. Supporting the latter assertion is the observation that over the past 25 years, according to UNESCO data, the participation of women in education has been generally increasing faster than that of men, even though gender gaps remain.

Official data regarding educational statistics are often inaccurate, especially in countries with underfunded ministries of education; in addition, the frequent reclassification of regions by the UNESCO Institute for Statistics (UIS) and the World Bank makes it difficult to analyze trends over time. Nonetheless, these data are the only figures to which we have access for regional and cross-national comparisons. Recent statistics indicate that women have closed the gender gap at all levels of schooling in industrialized countries, representing 49% of the total enrollment in primary education, 49% of the enrollment in secondary education, and 56% of the enrollment in tertiary education. In the developing countries, the situation shows marked disparities as women represent 46% of the enrollment in primary education, but only 43% and 40% of the enrollment in secondary and tertiary education, respectively (UNESCO, 2010). Disaggregation by country shows that the enrollment of girls is very low when the country is poor, heavily indebted, or affected by conflict (UNESCO, 2020). In part because of ongoing global education policies, primary school completion rates have increased in low-income countries from 44% in 1990 to 63% in 2018 (UIS, 2020). Yes, in Sub-Saharan Africa, the figures are dramatic: boys and girls have a 40% lower secondary completion and a 28% upper secondary completion (UNESCO, 2020). Many rural and ethnic minority populations still do not have access to formal education. Groups greatly excluded are the indigenous and Afro-Latino populations in Latin America, hill tribes in East Asia, scheduled castes and tribes in India, and rural and ethnic minorities in China. Data broken down by sex most likely indicate even lower proportions for girls' completion. Since girls have an average primary graduation rate of less than 50% in a large number of Sub-Saharan African countries, it may be predicted that the illiteracy rates of women in the region will continue to exceed those of men. It should be noted that statistics showing access to school should be juxtaposed to statistics showing the number of out-of-school children and youth, estimated to be 253 million in 2020. This population was in decrease during the 2000s but it has stagnated in recent years; more than half of those out-of-school are youth in upper secondary school age (UIS, 2019). In an era where knowledge is at a premium, out-of-school children will encounter a precarious existence as adults.

Table 7.1 presents enrollment data by specific developing regions. It uses the gender parity index (GPI) to show the enrollment of women compared to that of men; under ideal circumstances the index, representing the number of women for every hundred men, should be 1.0, indicating total equality. In most cases, women are still at a disadvantage compared to men. However, major shifts have emerged in the past three decades. Steady improvement has occurred in all developing regions in primary and secondary education; and significant increases have occurred in the representation of women in higher education. Within the Arab states, rather dramatic changes have developed at all levels of education. In Latin America and the Caribbean, women, on the aggregate, are slightly better represented than men at the secondary education level and now surpass men in tertiary education (see Chapter 12 in this volume).

Household survey data for 47 developing countries, which, unlike common educational statistics, include the collection of family income information, show that in all regions and across social class and age-groups, girls attend schools less than boys. As youths reach adolescence, the relative disadvantage of poor girls increases substantially, reflecting the interaction between gender and social class (Lloyd, 2005).

In several countries (e.g., Mauritius, Lesotho, Botswana, and Namibia in Africa; Mongolia and Korea in Asia; Jordan in the Middle East; and Honduras, Jamaica, Colombia, and Argentina in Latin America) there are more girls than boys attending primary school. This greater participation does not reflect a simple absence of gender differences but rather the particular gender dynamics in those societies. For instance, in the case of Lesotho and Namibia, where men have more physical mobility than women, male labor is exported to South Africa, leaving more women behind for schooling. Some small islands such as Jamaica suffered the destruction of the family under slavery, with the consequence that women assumed more economic responsibilities and thus had a greater need for schooling. Mongolia is a cattle-herding country in which boys, because of the sexual division of labor and sexual norms, are considered more suitable for unsupervised work. Colombia and Argentina reflect a higher propensity for young men to be incorporated early into the urban labor force despite lower levels of education than women. These explanations are not based on detailed studies exploring those phenomena—such investigations have yet to be conducted.

Statistics on lower secondary and upper secondary schooling completion show a clear move toward gender parity in all world regions. Progress still must

Table 7.1. Gender Parity Index for Gross Enrollment Ratios by Developing Region and Level of Education, Longitudinal Data

	Year	Primary	Secondary	Tertiary
Sub-Saharan Africa	1970	0.69	0.49	0.25
	1980	0.79	0.58	0.29
	1990	0.83	0.74	0.46
	2010	0.91	0.80	0.66
	2018	0.96	0.88	0.75
Latin America and the Caribbean	1970	0.95	0.93	0.55
	1980	0.95	0.99	0.77
	1990	0.95	1.07	0.87
	1992	0.91	1.07	0.92
	2010	0.97	1.04	1.25
	2018	0.98	1.04	1.30
East Asia and the Pacific	1970*			
	1980	0.83	0.70	0.56
	1990	0.89	0.78	0.66
	1992	0.92	0.83	0.68
	2010	1.01	1.03	1.01
	2018	1.00	1.02	1.18
Southern Asia	1970*			
	1980	0.61	0.47	0.34
	1990	0.71	0.52	0.66
	1992	0.73	0.62	0.68
	2010**	0.96	0.91	1.01
	2018	1.08	1.00	1.01
Arab States	1970	0.57	0.43	0.31
	1980	0.70	0.69	0.45
	1990	0.77	0.73	0.57
	2010	0.92	0.89	0.97
	2008	0.95	0.93	1.11

Source: UNESCO 1982, 1995, 2002, 2010, 2019.
*UNESCO statistics for 1970 provide only a single "Asian" category.
**UNESCO statistics for 2010 used the category South and West Asia to refer to the Southern Asia region.

be made in Sub-Saharan Africa and Southern Asia. An important statistic that must be juxtaposed to school completion concerns the number of adolescents (both girls and boys) out of school. It is estimated that 62 million adolescents are not attending lower-secondary school and 141 million adolescents are not attending upper secondary school. The majority of the out-of-school girls reside in Sub-Saharan Africa and South and West Asia, which reflects their limited access to facilities such as water and fuel, and the concomitant burdens for those assigned to domestic work. And of some 800 million illiterate youths and adults today about two-thirds are women, a proportion that has shown stubborn persistence (UIS, 2010).

It can be categorically affirmed that women's greater access to the various levels of schooling does not automatically reflect the disappearance of gender as a discriminating marker in their respective societies. If such were the case, there would be a much more even distribution in the salaries, professions, and political positions of men and women. One of the most accepted measures of equality between women and men in society, the Gender Empowerment Measure (GEM) developed by the Human Development Report (UNDP, 1995), reveals that the country closest to such parity is Sweden, with an index of 0.76 (showing that Swedish women have three-quarters the access to economic and political power that men have). The highest GEM score among developing countries is 0.54, held by Barbados. In 2011, GEM was replaced by an equivalent measure, the Gender Inequality Index (GII). It measures three dimensions (reproductive health, empowerment, and labor market participation). The GII is less easy to interpret; in the absence of inequality, the GII should be 0. The GII continues to register a serious gender inequality both within countries and between developed and developing countries. Nations with a very high level of human development have an average inequality of 0.224; in contrast, countries with low human development register a triple level of inequality, with a GII of 0.606 (UNDP, 2011).

Specific data for Brazil and India echo the global pattern. In general, 15% of the boys who enter first grade in India finish secondary school in India, but only 10% of the girls are similarly successful; further, most of those excluded from school belong to scheduled caste and scheduled tribe populations (NCERT, 1995). Brazil is a country in which some research on the intersection of race and gender has taken place. Rosemberg (1992) found that the average years of schooling of a Black woman from the northeast (the most rural area of Brazil, where African slave labor predominated until the late 19th century) is 2.1 years in contrast with 5.7 for a woman in the southeast (the most industrial and Europeanized area of the country) and 5.9 for a man of the southeast. In a subsequent study focusing on preschool education in seven Brazilian states, Rosemberg (1997) detected that Black children represented by far the largest group of preschool children over seven years of age. In her view, many Black children are placed for several years in preschool with little possibility of access to primary school. All the preschool teachers were women, but she found that 85% of them had not received training as preschool teachers and that 79% had not finished primary school. In other words, preschool black children in those seven Brazilian states, the slight majority of whom are boys, seem to be trapped in dead-end schooling, being taught mostly by unprepared teachers. If one were to look merely at aggregate access indicators, without disaggregating by geographic region, age, and ethnicity, the complex manifestations of multiple forms of discrimination would not be visible.

Aggregate enrollment statistics may miss important additional aspects. Indian scholars report that a preappraisal mission by the World Bank (a prerequisite to granting loans) found that the state of Kerala was quite close to attaining universal primary enrollment. Based on this finding, the World Bank declared that no gender interventions were required. Contrary to this declaration, fieldwork found a prevalence of dowry and women suffering the double burden of paid and unpaid work with no share in family or political decision-making (Nayar, 1995).

While there are problems in obtaining current data on enrollment patterns, research based on qualitative methodologies, such as the case studies discussed earlier and other ethnographic and inductive approaches reported in this chapter, provide useful insights and reveal the nuances, complexity, and social landscape that is needed to discern the conditions shaping who attends schooling and what experiences and outcomes these students face.

PRIMARY AND SECONDARY EDUCATION

As Table 7.1 shows, access to education is improving at both primary and secondary levels. Equally important indicators of access to schooling are cycle completion, academic achievement, and transition to a higher level of education (e.g., from primary to secondary school). These statistics are very scarce and, when available, seldom disaggregated by sex, although this is improving given the existence of several global policies promoting universal access (see the section in this chapter, Donor Agencies and Their Support of Education).

Few countries have engaged in policies and activities specifically designed to enable girls and women to overcome social obstacles. A few exceptions do exist. The most notable example is Prospera (originally called PROGRESA, then Oportunidades) in Mexico, a nationwide integrated approach that comprises education, nutrition, and health and provides education subsidies to poor families, with stipends slightly larger for girls than for boys in secondary school. In Guatemala, scholarships for primary school girls are being offered in the poorest regions of the country. In Bangladesh and Malawi, stipends (to compensate in part for forgone family income) for secondary school girls are being provided. Evaluations of these programs indicate that girls' enrollment increases when stipends are provided, which suggests that parental support for girls' education can be stimulated. On the other hand, some of the evaluation findings also indicate that rarely is the gender division of labor at home modified. The idea of providing monetary support to families to offset foregone costs is attaining popularity in the form of conditional cash transfers, which follow some elements of the Mexican model and can be found in approximately 130 countries throughout the world. These interventions today are designed to serve poor students in general and, except for a few countries, do not consider differential amounts to help girls' attendance to school.

Another important policy focused on girls is being implemented in India, where the government initiated the District Primary Education Program (DPEP) in 1994, which continues at present with the name Samagra Shiksa Abhiyan. DPEP pursued two objectives: access to quality education for all children and equality and empowerment for women. An early study of DPEP found that in only eight states were the textbooks relatively free of gender bias (Nayar, 1995). Through structured interviews of a variety of school actors in more than 400 villages and urban slums, researchers found that girls' domestic work, sibling care, and helping parents in remunerative employment were the main reason for dropping out among girls. The same study found that the girls perceived their illnesses as an important reason for dropping out in four of the eight surveyed states. Household poverty was strongly linked to girls' lower participation in schooling, but poverty in itself did not create cultural practices in favor of sons and boys. It simply made more acute the necessity of using girls and women in the biased division of labor; the study found that parents wanted girls to be educated, the most common reasons given being that parents recognized that education prepares girls for economic contribution and that it develops a positive self-image and confidence among girls. This finding corroborates another study in Baluchistan, one of the least advanced provinces of Pakistan. Contrary to popular belief, including that of the ministry of education officials, a large proportion of parents—especially mothers—recognized the importance of educating their daughters and were even willing to participate in the provision of school facilities (Stromquist & Murphy, 1995). By 2020, Samagra Shiksa Abhiyan covered preschool to grade 12. The program emphasizes issues of access rather than educational content; it includes the provision of residential girls' schools for marginalized castes and tribes in the country.

Yet another important insight regarding access to schooling comes from a study by Warwick and Jatoi (1994), based on a large survey of schools and teachers in Pakistan. The authors set out to trace the causes of low performance by girls in math. Using hierarchical linear modeling, they were able to decompose effects and locate as the main cause the training of girls in multigrade schools in rural areas staffed preponderantly by poorly trained women teachers. This finding verifies the complex relations among gender, patriarchal ideologies, and educational policies. Given patriarchal cultural norms, trained women teachers tend to avoid the rural areas for reasons of distance from their families and safety. Although more women are being trained as teachers, educational administrators' failure to recognize women's responsibilities as professionals, mothers, and care providers encourages a pattern of female teachers' avoidance of rural areas. Increasing research on female teachers in the African context indicates that there is a positive correlation between female teachers and female student enrollment and completion, which might reflect the female teachers' fostering of safe environments as well as their modeling of professional roles. Unfortunately, the majority of Sub-Saharan African countries have a small proportion of female teachers (Stromquist et al., 2017; UIS, 2010).

THE CONTENT OF KNOWLEDGE AND THE EXPERIENCE OF SCHOOLING

The discursive representations, as well as the material conditions of women and men, contribute to the definition of self and others. The role of schooling in differential gender socialization can be captured through content analysis of textbooks and through observations and in-depth interviews with teachers, administrators, and students. Studies of classroom dynamics and school climate are, unfortunately, very scarce in developing countries, although steps have been taken to expand this probe. Most of the educational investigations of this type have been conducted through MA theses and PhD dissertations. Since these products are not normally readily available in libraries, their contributions cannot be fully utilized by educators and researchers.

Studies conducted in the 1980s found that textbooks presented negative representations of women. As Smock (1981) observed then, textbooks did not make explicit statements on women's inferiority, but they presented them in limited roles and as reduced personalities. In many countries today, efforts are underway to "eliminate sexual stereotypes" from the textbooks and curricula (e.g., Pakistan, Malawi, Bangladesh, Mexico, and Sri Lanka). The most recent global review of textbooks in terms of gender representation took place in 2007. An extensive review of the academic and gray literature on gender-related teaching found few teacher training programs include gender-sensitive approaches in the content and ways of teaching of such programs (Miske, 2013).

Three levels of textbook modification can be conceptualized. First, the gender-neutral approach, the mildest effort, centers on the removal of biased language—excessive use of masculine pronouns and examples depicting mostly men. Second, the nonsexist approach eliminates stereotypical references to women and men in the work they do, the roles they play in society, and the traits that supposedly characterize them. Third, the antisexist approach presents alternative images of women and men, and it discusses ways to reach a different social organization (Streitmatter, 1995). As can be surmised, the antisexist approach is the most transformative. Typically, the role of governments in revising textbooks is limited to the first level of content change, making the textbooks gender-neutral. Increasingly, the efforts involve the nonsexist mode. Antisexist materials are proactive and aim at the construction of gender-egalitarian societies. Introducing alternative gender views is not an easy matter, since it calls for modifying how we think and requires a deep understanding of how language and images shape our thinking.

To assure the success of girls in schooling, careful monitoring of their everyday experience and their interactions with boy peers is needed. This type of research would not only produce rich insights into the creation of gender differences but would also enable us to understand what is required to achieve transformative action. Some research along these lines is being funded, albeit on a modest scale, by the Forum of African Women Educationalists (FAWE) in Sub-Saharan Africa (discussed later in this chapter).

In developed countries, research on girls' education has moved from documenting inequalities—which still exist—to (1) researching how these inequalities develop by looking at classroom situations, specifically the relations between students and teachers and among students, and (2) experimenting with how these inequitable situations can be transformed. In several school settings in the United States, new spaces are being created within schools so that lopsided patterns may be questioned and avoided and replaced with more equal relations. Many feminist pedagogical efforts are seeking to incorporate the experiences and voices of students, promoting self and social empowerment, and making the classrooms less teacher-centered. Recent efforts in U.S. schools have tried, for instance, to explore problems such as patriarchy, sexism, and racism in the context of girls' contemporary lives. In contrast, in developing countries, engagement in this type of effort has been minuscule. There is increased understanding, however, that a curriculum content that acknowledges the body and sexuality and addresses citizenship in its widest meaning should receive early attention.

Some qualitative work is unveiling gender practices in schools in developing countries. An ethnographic study of a Mexican lower secondary school focusing on how femininities and masculinities are created (Levinson, 2001) presented evidence that forceful groups of girls were called marimachas (tomboys) and that girls who excelled academically and sought leadership roles risked censure from both male and female classmates, even though these girls tended to defend their leadership on the grounds of greater discipline and moral superiority. Levinson found a prevailing belief that girls were unfit to serve as student body president, to carry the flag during parades, or to fulfill leadership roles, areas for which masculine force was seen as essential. But he also discovered that the climate in the school was open to change. Levinson notes that the new school leadership was causing innovative practices such as including girls in the flag escort and increasing participation of girls in classes and activities traditionally associated with boys, leading him to be optimistic about the possibility of changing gender beliefs in schools. In more recent times, research paying attention to the voices of girls and teachers has led organizations such as UNICEF to advocate for the provision of menstrual hygiene products, as lack of access to these products cause about one-third of poor and rural girls to miss classes every month.

Substantial efforts to develop more progressive curricular design regarding sex education have taken place in a few countries, notably Brazil. Often, efforts to modify the existing curriculum to include sex education or a discussion of the social relations of gender have encountered strong opposition from religious leaders. Two pieces of evidence come from Latin America, a region relatively open to modernizing forces. In Argentina, the National Program for the Promotion of Women's Equal Opportunities in Education (PRIOM), operating within the Ministry of Education, was able to deliver some nonsexist and antisexist teacher training workshops on the question of gender and education for several years (Bonder, 1994). PRIOM also worked during an extended period on the production of a comprehensive women's studies curriculum that was to be incorporated into the overall curriculum at the primary school level. PRIOM's curriculum also addressed linguistic sensibility and the unwarranted use of the masculine gender in words such as "citizen" (*ciudadano*), recommending instead collective nouns such as the "reading public" (*el público lector*) as opposed to "readers" (*lectores*—a noun in the masculine form) to make it easier to avoid the use of the masculine gender. Because of its efforts to introduce sex education, conservative parents and members of the Catholic Church accused PRIOM's staff of being antifamily and trying to introduce homosexuality in the schools, a complaint promptly heeded by the government. The document was reviewed to such an extent that PRIOM's technical team resigned. Persons closely involved in the development of the gender curriculum noted that the new document was not even concerned with nonsexist language.

In Mexico, in a twist that divided parents and government officials, parents denounced and succeeded in removing a textbook coedited by a state branch of the Ministry of Education that would have addressed adolescent sexuality with a discussion of the positive and negative consequences of engaging in sexual behavior during adolescence (Bayardo, 1996). Conservative parents and high officials of the Catholic Church invoked instead the principle of abstinence and insisted that sexuality should be practiced "at the right time" and "within marriage," a discourse amply indifferent to the reality of the country. Twenty-five years later, some parents—with clear Vatican endorsement—continue to attack the provision of sex education, charging that it oversexualizes children and promotes homosexuality (Garduño, 2018).

A significant backlash against the treatment of gender issues and the provision of sex education has become visible, widespread, and strong in several Latin American countries as well as in some Eastern and Western European countries. Through public demonstrations, parents who endorse fundamental Catholic and, on occasion, Evangelical beliefs have rejected textbooks that are perceived as challenging traditional norms of masculinity and femininity. This opposition also considers that the struggle by LGBTQ+ groups to characterize the discussion of "women" and "men" as a binary and useless way of seeing the world represents a significant challenge to the formation of "normal" families, defined as heterosexual and based on "natural differences" between women and men. In several countries, especially in Eastern Europe today, governments have taken an explicit position against feminist ideas that hold not only gender but also sex as a social construction. Consequently, the content of the curriculum has become an ongoing and highly debated issue (for coverage of developments in Europe, see Kuhar and Paternotte, 2007).

NONFORMAL EDUCATION PROGRAMS FOR PRIMARY SCHOOLCHILDREN

A development of considerable importance in recent decades is the use of non-formal education (NFE) settings to expand the education of girls. This approach is being tried primarily in populous Asian countries that have very low rates of school participation and sizable gender gaps in enrollment, notably Bangladesh, Pakistan, and India. The main NFE education program for girls in Bangladesh has been run by the Bangladesh Rural Advancement Committee (BRAC) since 1985. By 2019, this program enrolled 483,230 students at the pre-primary level and 186,406 at the primary level through NFE "centers" (BRAC, 2019). Each center serves a group of 30 to 33 students who become a cohort that moves together from first to fourth grade. The BRAC program was designed so that at least 70% of the students served in each center are girls, but by 2019 girls were only slightly more than half of the enrollment. The curriculum is highly innovative and includes many activities aimed to promote the development of confidence and assertiveness in girls. The fact that, unlike the formal schools, most teachers are women provides the students with positive role models. The BRAC centers have been highly successful in cycle completion, but problems have emerged in transferring the students to regular schools to complete their primary education (fourth and fifth grades). According to a 1996 study, about 30% of BRAC girls did not advance to the next educational cycle, possibly due to early marriage or the distance of the regular public school (Verma & Christie, 1996). In addition, when enrolled in the regular school, BRAC girls dropped out at higher rates than BRAC boys (it is unclear whether this occurs because the students find the new environment hostile or because school distance or domestic work prevents them from further attendance).

In Baluchistan, Pakistan, a program similar to BRAC's is conducted by an NGO, also working in cooperation with the provincial government. By design, this program serves a large number of girls and uses locally hired women teachers. It offers a gender-sensitive curriculum and has succeeded in attracting the cooperation of parents in the running of the school. According to program statistics, girls have not only enrolled in large numbers but also have shown good attendance rates. The participation of women as teachers and mothers in the running of Village Education Committees, which enable parents to make decisions about the schools in the Baluchistan program, has provided new and alternative roles for women in their traditional communities (Stromquist & Murphy, 1995). The

NFE programs in India and Pakistan operate primarily with external support. Although governmental funds have been increasingly assigned to cover part of the costs, it remains to be seen whether these programs will continue without donor funds.

The NFE programs in India—Shiksha Karmi and Lok Jumbish—present some of the features of the BRAC program, except that many of their rural teachers are men. On the other hand, the Indian programs cover the entire primary school cycle, and the work is not done separately by NGOs but in conjunction with government officials. This joint participation assures a coordinated and mutually supportive plan of action.

HIGHER EDUCATION

It might serve as a good point of contrast to remember that in May 1897, 125 years ago, Cambridge University roundly defeated a resolution that would have given women the right to the bachelor of arts degree. Such a position would seem unacceptable in many countries today. Should people, therefore, conclude that the educational situation of women in higher education has dramatically improved?

Between 2000 and 2014, the number of students in tertiary education more than doubled, from 100 million in 2000 to 207 million in 2014 (UNESCO & IIEP, 2017). Women have not only participated in this expansion but have attained parity and, as noted in Table 7.1, in most regions of the world there is a greater representation of women in universities. In only one region, Sub-Saharan Africa, women represent a minority. It is to be noted that the drastic increase in women's enrollment has occurred not only in terms of access to university but also to technical and commercial training institutions. Further, much of this expansion has taken place not necessarily through the expansion of public institutions but rather through the women's and their families' self-financing of education through access to private providers (UNESCO & IIEP, 2017). This development constitutes a very strong indication that it has been women's own agency behind their participation in higher education institutions, not the result of state objectives. What remains difficult to change is the concentration of women in typically feminine fields of study (particularly teaching and nursing) and, conversely, the overrepresentation of men in fields perceived as masculine, such as those dealing with science and technology. Globally, there is also a substantial underrepresentation of women as faculty in senior positions and as university administrators.

Despite the potential contribution of women's perspectives to such fields as agriculture and engineering, their representation in them remains insignificant. U.S. data for the past four decades (England et al., 2020) indicates that, while women have moved into previously male-dominated fields of study, men have not gone into fields of study that are seen as feminine. England et al. (2020) explain that, according to the index of dissimilarity (D), in which 0 represents no segregation and 1 total segregation, the D measure stood at 0.33 for bachelor's degrees and 0.20 for doctoral degrees in 2015. This rather surprising finding suggests that either there is less discrimination in doctoral programs or that men and women students at that level feel more confident about their academic choices; this issue remains to be further explored. These researchers also observe that in the past 20 years desegregation had stalled in some fields. Women's choice of fields considered socially appropriate for their gender reflects the confluence of multiple societal and cultural forces, but it also suggests that the academic experience of women and the knowledge acquired in higher education institutions, at least at the bachelor's level, does not challenge these forces.

Levy and Merry (1986) distinguish two levels of organizational change: First-order change seeks improvement in a few dimensions comprising supportive—though not central—aspects of organizational functioning; second-order change in contrast is multidimensional and interactive. Applied to universities, second-order change would mean engaging in synchronous ways faculty, administrators, and students, with efforts centered on enacting transformative institutional policies and practices. A few efforts are under way in higher education to increase the presence of women as students and in senior positions in teaching, research, and administration. The most complete set of measures dealing with students seems to be taken by the government of India to increase women's enrollment via the provision of scholarships, the establishment of women-only universities, the provision of hostels for working women, and the granting of maternity and leave care once during women's master's or doctoral programs (Hassan et al., 2020).

In several industrialized countries, including the United States and the United Kingdom, the national government offers grants for institutions to embark on multiple initiatives to facilitate the retention and advancement of women professors. ADVANCE, in the United States, has funded more than 100 universities to initiate a set of activities that include organizing several annual workshops to gain knowledge about university policies and practices, providing research funds for selected women professors, and promoting the development of women leaders. Athena SWAN, in the United Kingdom, has funded over 160 universities, and its objectives resemble those of ADVANCE. Evaluations of these programs reveal strong benefits for the women who participate in them but have found limited indications of institutional change. In the case of the United Kingdom, O'Connor et al. (2020) found that these benefits did not extend to nonparticipating women faculty, who were found less likely to be familiar with the criteria and process for promotion. Given this and related evidence, the authors concluded that "Athena SWAN is not an effective tool for transforming the structure and culture of higher education" (O'Connor et al., 2020, p. 135). Most interventions in higher education to advance the conditions of women and to reflect upon gender have been at the institutional level, since there are no national policies on this matter, except for the three instances mentioned a few lines earlier.

The most positive development in recent years within higher education in developing countries is the rapid expansion of women's studies programs and units. These can be quite extensive, as they are in India and Brazil, countries in which ties between feminist scholars and women in popular women's movements are strong. Women students in these universities are encouraged to produce master's theses and doctoral dissertations on gender issues, and they find intellectual spaces to discuss ways to analyze and combat gender discrimination and power asymmetries. Several graduates of women's studies programs have gone to work in gender units within national ministries and progressive NGOs, thus contributing to the dissemination of gender-sensitive values and perspectives through their positions in important venues of social action. With time, women in the feminist movement, for instance, are realizing that for change in gender ideologies and practices to take place, women need to develop a deeper understanding of economics and finances.

Unfortunately, under present neoliberal policies, university leaders are not paying much attention to the social sciences and the humanities—disciplines not known for securing large research contracts or producing patents. Neoliberal policies play a substantial role in decision-making, affecting the enactment of public policies and often determining a meager allocation of state funds to social programs, of which education is one of the most affected. In part because of neoliberal economic ideologies, universities have entered into a frenetic competition for financial resources, leaving little time and space for concerns of social justice. This in turn has affected women's and gender studies programs, which attract a rather small number of students compared to other programs with more marketable outcomes.

THE EDUCATION OF ADULT WOMEN

Since most formal education settings present endemic institutional barriers to gender-sensitive changes, it is essential to consider the transformative role of adult education, which lies outside schooling. The increased gender awareness of such education not only affects the students but—as they become adults—is also transmitted to their children. Women, as key organizers of the household environment, can influence what their children do and learn at home.

Transformative work in women's education—in the form of both oppositional discourse and practical actions against inequities—has been undertaken mostly by women-based or feminist NGOs. The areas they have addressed have included such issues as empowerment, legal literacy, domestic violence, and income generation. Many of these women-led NGOs also provide maternal health and childhood clinics, which serve as informal vehicles for the education of women even though their content is not transformative. A current theme within women-based NGOs in Latin America concerns citizenship training, lobbying and advocacy skills, health education practice, and the training of trainers. NGOs in Latin America are also moving from the denunciation of women's unequal and exploitative situations to making proposals based on statistics and information, creating spaces for training, and making concrete demands on government.

It is not easy to provide adult women with educational opportunities. Various studies focusing on the participation of low-income women in adult education programs have determined that women's domestic work, frequency of domestic violence, and the need for serving children and families leaves them with very little time and inclination for education, even though NFE programs often offer schedules and locations that make them accessible to the women (Stromquist, 1997).

Important lessons have been derived from these experiences. After many years of effort with literacy classes and condensed programs for which there were few takers, Indian scholars and practitioners have learned that skills and education cannot be forced on women (Jain & Krishnamurty, 1996). With the involvement of the Indian government and substantial funds coming from external sources, the Mahila Samakhya program has been implemented in India for 28 years and operated in 11 of the country's 29 states. Women in this program were not offered literacy training but were allowed to discuss in a social space their experiences and desires. Village-level forums were created exclusively for women, the assumption being that these women "in due time could emerge as strong pressure groups for raising genuine demands, fighting injustice and creating an environment for 'equal' treatment of women," and that these forums would enable them to "discover and re-discover their identities and problems as women, and mobilize around issues that were of priority to them." By most accounts, the women in the Mahila Samakhya have succeeded in changing their self-concept and have made successful demands on their local government. These women have acquired the skills and insights to analyze their situation of subordination and, as one observer summarized it, they have been able to turn fear into understanding. Despite Mahila Samakhya's being considered by many as the "most successful empowerment" program in India, the central government stopped funding it in 2016 and, thus, it became dependent on the discretion of individual states, provoking a considerable scaling down of the program.

Adult education offers much potential for gender transformation. It tends to unite women from different social classes, with low-income women as beneficiaries and middle-income (but increasingly low-income) women as leaders and staff members of the NGOs. These groups are usually confronted with two demands: to address immediate problems, mostly linked with basic needs (what have been called women's practical needs) and to address macro-level issues such as gender-fair legislation affecting the family, wages, access to credit, and so on (what are usually termed women's strategic needs) (Fink & Arnove, 1991; Molyneux, 1985; Stromquist, 2007). The resolution of these tensions is challenging, yet there are encouraging examples of women shifting toward more encompassing and long-term objectives that will call for transforming institutions and enacting new policies. It is becoming increasingly clear to these women-based NGOs that formulate large-scale change within society will require influencing the state, which will first require these NGOs to acquire mobilization and organization skills and engage in social action. Conversely, it is also becoming increasingly evident that major transformative educational efforts cannot bypass the engagement of women-led NGOs and, consequently, these groups will warrant much more funding than in the past, both from the state and from international sources. In Latin America, the unprecedented political mobilization of women in the 1980s due to the economic crisis and the existence of dictatorial regimes provided unexpected skills for many of the low-income women, skills and practices they have retained—speaking to express an opinion, making demands, and representing others. They have also been able to produce more accurate evaluations of the social functions of interpersonal relations and of their personal development (Guzmán, 1990; Stromquist, 2007).

At present, NGOs in general and women-based NGOs in particular are making efforts to redefine such taken-for-granted concepts as citizenship and social life, and introducing new ones such as empowerment (with its economic, political, psychological, and knowledge dimensions; see Stromquist, 2015). The mutual recognition of women's great burdens and logistical problems in becoming NFE students and simultaneously their preference to learn through imitation and informal apprenticeships has prompted feminist adult educators to recognize the importance of mediators in the process of social learning. These mediators can play an effective role in the provision of training. Walters (1997) explains: "This approach refocuses the problem away from the masses of poorly schooled people to the mediators. It is up to the mediators to learn to serve people across class, language, culture, etc., so that learning can occur more effectively through everyday experiences" (p. 33). One nonformal education program based on innovative and simplified curricula is centered on the concept of empowerment and concomitant teacher training. Developed in Honduras by an NGO devoted to transformative learning, the program addressed young women at the secondary school level. An unusual study employing a treatment-control research design showed that this program enabled women to engage in new behaviors such as seeking support from other women, speaking in public, and altering domestic relationships with their spouses (Murphy-Graham, 2012).

There are two instances in which NGOs are engaged in major efforts to improve schooling. The Forum of African Women Educationalists (FAWE) is a regional organization of some 44 countries that are represented by women who hold key official educational roles in their countries, such as ministers of education, vice chancellors, and other senior policymakers. FAWE is actively engaged in projects that include, among others, examining girls' and boys' performance in math and science, providing gender sensitization to educational personnel, organizing extracurricular activities such as clubs for girls as well as girls and boys together, exploring the occurrence of sexual harassment in secondary schools, and addressing women's issues in teaching and education management. Because of its prominent members, FAWE's work is expected to find a direct and relatively unblocked application in the school system. In Latin America, the Popular Education Network of Women (REPEM) is affiliated with the Adult Education Council of Latin America and the Caribbean. Composed of 150 women-based NGOs in 18 countries and committed to strengthening popular education with a gender perspective, REPEM has been working intensively on the development of nonsexist and antisexist educational materials. (See also Arnove et al. in Chapter 12 of this volume.)

THE STATE AND WOMEN'S EDUCATION

The state shapes social conditions and possibilities for changing them, including education, through public policies. In general, even democratic states have responded to gender issues in slow motion. In postsocialist countries, for instance, that used to have a more explicit welfare policy for both women and men, this is the case. Referring to the performance of Russian state policies, Ashwin and Supova (2018) remark that overall, current policies have not challenged the reproduction of gender ideologies.

Public education policies address such areas as curricular content, teacher preparation, and cost-related measures such as tuition fees, books, transportation, and other expenses that families could not otherwise afford. Education policies also address school access and retention by providing incentives such as scholarships or stipends for economically disadvantaged students to counterbalance the opportunity cost to parents. But, as noted earlier, despite the frequent reference to women and gender in global education policies, few national policies address this matter through comprehensive plans, much less seek to deconstruct gender through strategies deploying multiple venues and actions. Areas frequently covered by governments aim at the construction of more schools, more classrooms, and more bathrooms—the infrastructure of schooling. In terms of gender interventions per se, most often governments implement education "projects" only at the school level, and these efforts usually begin and end as pilot projects supported by donor agencies and are rarely incorporated into nationwide interventions. Efforts to help girls' education may include scholarships, stipends, boarding facilities, community sensitization, school feeding, mentoring, and tutoring (Miske, 2013), extracurricular activities (such as the creation of spaces where girls and boys reflect on gender norms), and providing teacher training to modify teachers' attitudes toward gender. Again, these efforts are typically limited in the number of schools and teachers they reach and are not offered regularly, thus reducing their effectiveness.

Three global policies have concentrated on education or mentioned it as a crucial goal: Education for All, the Millennium Development Goals, and today's Sustainable Development Goals (SDGs), in effect 2015–2030. All the documents approved at various conferences identify the education of girls as a top national priority. Some agreements also call for affirmative action as a method of reducing the access disparity that exists between boys and girls and women and men. Nonetheless, there continues to be a wide disjunction between rhetoric and actual action; it is to be hoped that as many of these documents are known and circulated, women and men who seek equality and equity in education will use these official promises to force governments into compliance.

DONOR AGENCIES AND THEIR SUPPORT FOR EDUCATION

Regarding education in developing countries, two international financial institutions play a significant role in shaping policies; the World Bank and the International Monetary Fund (IMF) are the most salient. Coburn (2019) remarks that while the 2008–2009 economic crisis brought attention to gender equity concerns, the IMF adopted a narrow argument around "women as smart economics." It framed gender issues as the underutilization of women in the paid economy, thus minimizing the fact that work not always increases social emancipation for women (often poorly paid, not being able to protect their income from demanding spouses, and, most of all, still subjected to relentless domestic work) and avoiding broader issues regarding their citizenship that transcend work. The World Bank, for its part, also endorses the notion of women as economic actors and downplays the role that gender ideologies play in the functioning of institutions that circumscribe women to the private sphere and create widely diffused notions of what men and women can be.

It must be noted that there is a stark divide between discourses of equality, enunciated in many global agreements and even conventions (which carry the force of international law), and the position by international financial institutions in favor of government austerity implemented through economic structural adjustment programs (SAPs, now replaced by Poverty Reduction Strategy Papers) and new loans approved by the World Bank and sanctioned by the IMF. Following such major world women's conferences as those in Nairobi and Beijing, and agreements crystallized in the global policies cited previously, gender has become a more serious policy objective of state, bilateral, and international development agencies. The advocacy in favor of girls' education and the financial support of donor agencies, albeit limited to basic education, have been instrumental in promoting attention to this issue since, as noted earlier, national governments are reluctant to invest their own funds on issues concerning gender. The strong leadership in favor of girls' schooling from institutions such as UNICEF, UNESCO, the UNDP, and the Scandinavian and Dutch agencies, has made gender an unavoidable issue in national development agendas. The influential Human Development Report for 1995 coined the slogan "If human development is not engendered, it is endangered," a phrase that seems to have lodged itself in the subconscious of many governments (UNDP, 1995).

Yet, the actual performance of development agencies is contradictory. Some staff members within these agencies believe (erroneously, given the high number of national and international declarations of commitment to the education of girls and women) that to press for attention to gender issues constitutes a form of cultural imperialism. Several agencies are now working with new principles of international assistance, such as "recipient responsibility" and "program support," which might end up discriminating against women. These two principles call for much greater dialogue with governments and for greater discretionary powers by the recipient state. For many issues regarding national development, government autonomy is a desirable situation. But in the case of gender, this autonomy could easily result in the avoidance of gender issues. A very strong indicator that governments are not interested in the pursuit of gender issues is that the large majority of projects focusing on girls' education continue to be funded through grants from international agencies, not by loans or by regular public budgets. A further weakness in dealing exclusively with governments in the area of gender and education is that they tend to operate mostly on questions of educational access and, if curricula and textbook revisions are involved, any changes operate at the gender-neutral level of change, now recognized as a first-level effort (see Streitmatter, 1995).

The SDGs, unlike the two previous global policies that preceded them, are paying constant attention to policy implementation. In this regard, they have established targets for each of the goals and have selected specific indicators to trace the implementation of each of the goals. While the targets are sensitive to the wording of the goals, the same cannot be said of the actual indicators selected. The indicators finally chosen tend to be very few, to focus on easily measurable outcomes, and to disregard important outcomes arguing that such data would be difficult to obtain (Wulff, 2020). Goal 4 of the SDGs focuses on education. The SDG indicators that refer to the curriculum (SDG 4.7.1) identify two academic subjects: global citizenship and education for sustainable development. Gender equality, along with human rights, will be treated within these two subjects. Indicator 4.7.1 will measure "the extent to which (i) global citizenship education and (ii) education for sustainable development, including gender equality and human rights, are mainstreamed at all levels in (a) national education policies; (b) curricula; (c) teacher education; and (d) student assessment." The current document on the implementation of indicator 4.7.1. goes on to say: "We are currently not aware of data for this indicator. You can notify us of available data for this indicator via our feedback form" (SDG Tracker, 2020). So, likely, this indicator will not be put in use. On the question of trained teachers, SDG Indicator 4.c.1 will measure "the proportion of teachers in (a) pre-primary; (b) primary; (c) lower secondary; and (d) upper secondary education who have received at least the minimum organized teacher training (e.g. pedagogical training) pre-service or in-service required for teaching at the relevant level in a given country" (SDG Tracker, 2020). There is no reference in the document to whether this includes training in gender issues. By the same token, no indicator has been selected on qualified and trained teacher educators. We know from research and experience that indicators play a major role in shaping policy implementation at local levels. By being weak or not spelled out, these indicators, and thus the policies linking curriculum and gender, will in the best of cases become aspirational—desirable rather than real.

Often development agencies present limited definitions of a situation even though their new principle appears to be quite appropriate. For instance, in recent years the World Bank has become very interested in the question of "good governance," a code phrase for countries eager to compete in the global economy. A 1995 World Bank publication on policies for gender equality identified four areas affecting the welfare of women to be addressed through legal action: land and property rights, labor market policies and employment law, family law, and financial laws and regulations. But since the prescriptions to make reforms in these areas are not based on a profound and complete understanding of the causes of women's inequality, the recipient state is assigned—quite unproblematically—the implementation of these reforms. Even though NGOs are acknowledged as important "players from civil society," there is no specific recognition of the role that women-based NGOs, and other elements in civil society identified with the women's movement, can play in these socioeconomic transformations.

Today, however, women are much more aware of the institutions that conduct key work in social and economic policies. The World Bank has been the object of strong feminist pressure. This emphasis started in 1995 at the Fourth World Women's Conference in Beijing when a letter signed by 900 women's organizations from around the globe was given to James Wolfensohn, the first president of the World Bank to attend a world women's conference. The letter requested that the World Bank act toward increasing participation of grassroots women in the design of macroeconomic policies, institutionalizing the perspective of gender as a standard practice in its policies and programs, and increasing the bank's investments in the sectors of education, health, agriculture, land ownership, employment, and financial services for women (Frade, 1997). After Beijing, the women organized an umbrella group called Women's Eyes on the World Bank, with chapters in different parts of the world. In 1997, this group wrote a second letter—widely circulated on the internet—to President Wolfensohn stating that it had reviewed the World Bank's initiatives during 1996 and found that "the admirable commitment from the top has yet to be translated into concrete action in the majority of Bank programs and operations, where there remains a lack of understanding among many Bank staff of gender inequities and their implications for development." To his credit, Wolfensohn initiated a series of institutional changes that gave more prominence to gender equity. In recent years, the World Bank has produced several studies dealing with women and education. Its attempts to theorize gender, however, remain anchored in economic rationales, disregard the impact of patriarchal ideologies in setting social institutions and norms that constrain women's life chances and minimize the importance of dealing with NGOs that advocate for transformation in the social relations of gender (O'Brien et al., 2000). Several observers of the World Bank's position in education criticize its instrumental conception of gender, in which women are useful because the more educated the women, the fewer children they will have and the more they will participate in the labor force, infant mortality will be lower, and possibilities for work and thus income will increase. Instead, these observers call for more social and political conceptualizing so that women are seen not as mere economic agents but as citizens with equal full rights and responsibilities (Stromquist, 2012).

A review of actual resources indicated that the assistance to basic education from bilateral donors in the mid-1990s in real terms was lower than it had been before the Jomtien 1990 conference. This study, based on a survey of 20 bilateral aid agencies, found that such assistance had increased in six of these agencies but remained static or fell in the other 14. The World Bank, which had been a major contributor in 1994 (US$2.16 billion), decreased considerably by 1996 (US$1.7 billion). It was not until 2012 that these loans reached US$5 billion. Both governments and donor agencies have endorsed helping women, but, persistently, they see education primarily as a vehicle for skills training so that women may increase their economic productivity and enter the labor force. The overwhelming emphasis on an economic rationale is rejected by feminist scholars. As Longwe (1997) remarks, "On the contrary, gender training must be largely concerned with providing the analytical tools for participants to become dissatisfied with the current unequal gender division of society, which they (may have) previously accepted and taken for granted." This means that the content of schooling and the experience of students within schools must be the object of educational policy as much as access to and completion of schooling are. Training, from a gender-transformative perspective, should also enable women to generate mobilization around the analysis of gender issues and subsequent public action to address these issues. So far, most agencies in the international education development field have evinced to be risk-averse and thus stay clear from working on gender-related curricular areas, whether they regard students or teachers.

A quantitative study based on 157 country behaviors between 1975 and 1998 (True & Mintrom, 2001) found that the strongest predictors of state adoption of "national machineries" for women (i.e., government units such as women's and gender ministries or offices) included (in addition to contact with transnational networks) the proportion of women in ministerial positions, the degree of democracy in the country, and the extent to which women had similar access to men's secondary education. (Interestingly, the study did not show an impact linked to the proportion of women enrolled, but rather to the degree of parity between women's and men's enrollment in secondary education, suggesting that equality is key.) These findings capture in telling ways what has become increasingly understood in the women's movement: that political mobilization at transnational levels is effective, that women in political positions do bring political agendas that men might not, and that access to higher levels of education (beyond primary) in equal numbers to those of men fosters strong empowering conditions among women. In other words, an educational agenda must be accompanied by a political agenda.

THE JUNCTURE OF ACTORS
BEHIND EDUCATION POLICY FORMATION

Multiple actors are activated in the educational arena. Multiple actors do not mean they have equal influence because states and their various agencies hold the decisive card. Governments, international development agencies, and international financial institutions have been working for several decades with the notion of gender inequality. The existence of global policies in favor of expanding and improving education, involving multiple governments and bilateral agencies, particularly the SDGs, can be considered a powerful signal in favor of the education of women. Despite this victory for the women's movement, the state and the agencies that represent it nationally and internationally still see women as economic agents and care providers rather than as human beings with rights to autonomy, equal treatment under the law, and not just advancement and protection within the unequal world in which they find themselves. The policies, projects, and related interventions that states and their agencies put in place are thus narrowly defined and do not challenge the prevailing social order. In part, this occurs because states and their agencies operate in a self-contained world, in which states talk only to states or international agencies, not to representatives of the feminist or women's movement, which could be done by recognizing women-led NGOs as interlocutors. Furthermore, global policies continue to be unfunded or funded to a degree that does not match their ostensible aims. Thus, as the SDG targets were operationalized, they were found to "give minimal attention to equity and inclusion, and place [them] in competition for scarce resources" (Benavot & Smith, 2020, p. 253). Specifically, a financial target is absent in SDG 4—the goal that deals with education (Sayed & Moriarty, 2020).

Women in the academic world, the main producers of feminist and gender theory, have limited contact with the women's movement, except in countries such as India and South Africa. Activists in the women's movement are not known for consuming the theoretical and research literature produced by feminist academics. They do not confront each other. Rather they live in parallel worlds. The international development agencies, for their part, seldom rely on feminist academics; they prefer instead to deal occasionally, on a consulting basis, with academic women who address economic and social issues affecting women, but who do not define themselves as feminists. The distance between the state or international development agencies and academics results in the underutilization of gender theory and research, with the consequent failure to register greater progress in the advancement of gender equality. Without reliance on conceptualization, theory, and empirical evidence, we might find, as in the case of interventions addressing domestic violence, that our prognosis (the programs we propose) is more developed than our diagnosis (an accurate understanding of the problem) (Verloo, 2006).

Feminism is an inclusive political movement striving for social justice (Acker, 1990; Pateman, 1986; Rottenberg, 2018). This means all voices must be heard and respected. Within the feminist movement, some dissent has emerged in recent years. One group considers it crucial to represent and express the voices of women who still experience great disadvantages in many areas of social life. This group can be found in industrialized countries and, particularly, in developing countries.

Another group, small in size and present almost exclusively in Anglo-Saxon countries, questions the use of women as a category, arguing that the term is part of an undesirable "binary" and thus detrimental to any effort toward social change in the relations of gender. They would prefer priority attention to the issues of gender identity and sexual orientation. The tension between working with broad categories such as women versus acknowledging complex and fluid gender identities has not been satisfactorily resolved (see Chapter 1 in this volume). While social issues of gender identity and sexual orientation are of great importance, it can be argued that for purposes of strategic action and political mobilization, it is essential to work with collective definitions and self-definition such as women and men. It is difficult to think we can operate politically based on multiple gender identities, some of which are not visible. We could not collect data about inequality if we eliminate the reference to women and men; there would be no clear basis for organizing; the subject for whom we seek social justice would disappear into myriad forms.

To reiterate, the feminist struggle is at heart a struggle for greater human rights, such as being recognized, having a political voice, and sharing more equally the riches that society can offer to its citizens. In this sense, minorities, including sexual minorities, have substantial rights in a democratic process and deserve full inclusion in any modern polity. These minorities, however, cannot impose a position that disqualifies the majority of women across the world by asserting that their identity as women and the identity of men as men should be abolished if progress is to take place. In a democratic process, we must be able to distinguish common interests beyond particular interests. Heterosexuality does not need to be construed as the main obstacle to a more just society and one in which values, practices, and attitudes are widely shared by women and men. Equality for women, from physical safety to income, access to wealth and leadership, and generalized well-being is far from being a reality in most countries of the world. Until that equality is achieved, the categories of women and men should remain fully operational and cannot be conceived as obstacles to social progress. On the contrary, it could be argued that the disappearance of women as a category would render invisible the agents whose interest must be recognized and respected and who have been struggling for social change for many decades now. Not surprisingly, the categories of women and men are not commonly questioned in developing countries, where injustices and inequalities are strongly felt in everyday life.

Parents—unquestionably a critical actor in education—tend to become organized mainly to defend what they see as appropriate or to challenge what they considered inappropriate in the curriculum or in teaching practices. In Western countries, a strong backlash against gender, drawn primarily from religious groups representing fundamental Catholic and Evangelical ideas, increasingly mobilize against educational public policies and textbooks they deem inappropriate. They often oppose sex education programs that portray gender identity, sexuality, and sexual orientation as entirely social constructions. Likewise, parents in several Muslim countries have presented strong obstacles to educational textbooks and curricula that defend the expansion of women's rights to economic, social, and political arenas. In the view of the protesting parents, feminist ideas are harmful to society as they threaten one of the most cherished institutions of society—the family—as well as promote sexual experimentation and homosexuality.

CHALLENGES IN DEVELOPING COUNTRIES

In the past decades, women have been gaining increased access to education. In several parts of the world, there is a clear tendency toward gender parity, at least at the basic level (commonly understood to cover between six and nine years of schooling). The positive content, experience, and outcomes of schooling are not so much taken for granted now, and efforts are taking place, albeit very modestly vis-à-vis the nature of the problem, to frame the issue of gender in education in a more complete and accurate manner. Against this background, five major challenges remain.

The first is the combined impact of globalization and neoliberalism, a process that is gearing up all countries—and their school systems in particular—for economic competition, not for critical social understanding. Globalization forces are promoting an increase in scientific and technological careers, yet it is not certain what efforts will be made to include women in this expansion (beyond some very narrow and sporadic concern with women's participation in STEM fields). Competitiveness has created a demand for quality of education, an issue several observers see as involving three dimensions: efficacy, process, and relevance. The positive side of efficacy resides in its focus on learning as opposed to merely attending school. The process dimension highlights the quality of inputs, such as good physical facilities, trained teachers, good textbooks, and adequate instructional methodologies—all necessary for a successful learning process. Relevance, however, can introduce some conservative thinking in that it tends to emphasize the economic usefulness of education rather than the social and affective development of individuals. For instance, efforts to renovate the educational system in Latin America recognize the poor quality of the educational system in such areas as reading, math, and science; the neglect of the teaching profession; and the existence of increasing inequality. Yet this last recognition tends to focus almost exclusively on social class, downplaying both gender and ethnic differences (Puryear & Brunner, 1997).

The second challenge derives from the serious economic crisis that many developing countries still face and the persisting effects of retrenchment imposed on the state by neoliberal policies enforced by the World Bank and the IMF. There is widespread consensus that these programs have generated more poverty than in the past as increases in the price of basic goods and cuts in social services such as health care, family planning, child care, and education have affected not only the poor but also middle-class households. Women and girls have absorbed the heaviest burden of SAPs (as noted earlier) through their increased household work and participation in formal and informal labor markets (Beneria & Bisnath, 1996). Sub-Saharan African countries are particularly affected as they have entered a cycle of unpayable external debt characterized by more funds going abroad to pay the debt than financial resources moving into the region. The initial loans continue to generate high interest. A case in point is that from 1987 to 1997, the IMF received $4 billion more from Sub-Saharan Africa than it provided this region in new finance (Development Cooperation, 1997). The retrenchment of the state, under today's neoliberal economic policies, has negative consequences for women because the state is a major institution capable of both applying pressure and creating large-scale change. In the case of women, a progressive tax structure would reduce the burden of social class, but the dynamics of privatization may be much less supportive of gender equality, especially among low-income parents, who continue to see girls' education as an expenditure rather than an investment. Obviously, less public money for education investments also means a reduced ability and willingness to consider disadvantaged populations. Since the countries with the heaviest per capita burden linked to economic indebtedness are also those with the largest disparities between men and women, this forecasts a period of disregard for girls' and women's education. A crucial consequence of the retrenchment of the state in social fields, such as education, is the increasing privatization at all levels of education, particularly in Africa. Initial expectations about the private sector were that it would be involved in education as a contributor to financial resources. Instead, the private sector has become a service provider and is thus involved in generating income directly from education (Archer & Muntasim, 2020). Private institutions now comprise about 33% of the world's enrollment in basic education and a similar proportion in higher education. Because the education of girls and women tends to be seen as consumption (not an investment) by many families, particularly low-income families, the growing privatization of schooling might end up having harmful effects on their participation, particularly their access to high-quality higher education. The massive and global economic crisis caused by COVID-19 will most likely worsen dramatically the availability of government funds to be assigned to public education and, with this, initiatives addressing gender issues in education might face disproportionate austerity.

Ironically, neoliberalism, as it relates to women, seems based on an assumption similar to that first introduced by Marxist thought. The "woman question" in Marxism argued that women's oppression was rooted in their exclusion from productive participation in economic activity so that their incorporation in the labor force would make their subordination disappear. Likewise, neoliberalism assumes that if women were to join the labor market, multiple benefits would accrue to them and to society. In both cases, it is the market that creates transformation for women. It must be noted that the unpaid work of women in reproduction, the gender division of labor and resources within the household and in society, and the pervasive influence of patriarchal ideology are ignored in both perspectives.

The third challenge emerges from the paucity of educational research in developing countries. Very limited national funds are available for research and development; most of the existing gender research has been conducted under the auspices of international assistance. Frequent calls by the World Bank and other institutions for developing nations to remove subsidies at the tertiary level of education and offer student loans instead suggests that funds thereby released may be used by educational systems to invest in other areas, research presumably being one of them. But several scholars doubt this. Colclough (1996), for example, contends that loans and scholarships involve higher administrative costs and are more expensive than the typical structure of subsidies. In his view, a better alternative measure would be to create better and more progressive tax structures. Research, especially of a qualitative kind, is urgently needed to identify spaces of rupture of dominant gender norms and representations, and to document the instances in which agency by women and their organizations is beginning to take place. A step in this direction can be found in Unterhalter et al. (2014). Research on innovative programs run by women-led NGOs serving adult women should receive much more attention.

The fourth challenge is perhaps the most significantly urgent and promising of the set. It concerns teachers. In the critical theory literature, teachers are perceived as major change agents, with tremendous potential for "border crossing"—their ability to bring themselves and their students to appreciate the position of other social and ethnic groups (Apple, 1983; Giroux, 1992). At the same time, since teachers, like everyone else, are products of their time and environment, many of them subscribe to traditional gender views. In several developing regions, Latin America especially, women constitute the larger proportion of primary schoolteachers and comprise a substantial number of secondary schoolteachers. Women teachers could be encouraged to play a role in promoting reflection on society and gender roles; they could also be assisted to work on the transformation of gender representations and norms. To be successful, the teachers themselves would need to transform; this would entail providing them with appropriate in-service and preservice teacher training and gender-sensitive curricula. Work on teachers' professional development is occurring in industrialized countries, but in developing countries this area has been considered only in exceptional circumstances (the Argentine case discussed above being one of them).

A fifth, but by no means less formidable, challenge regards the mainstream media. The media have always played a fundamental role in the production of images and representations of women and men. In earlier centuries, specifically Victorian times, it was the print media through novels, short stories, poetics, memoires of important people, which that affected us (Young, 2019). At present, with the pervasive presence of radio, TV, and the internet images and representations of women and men have acquired an even stronger influence upon us. This means that the study of "educational" impacts can no longer be limited to schooling and even adult education, but must involve an understanding of how the visual and oral mass media and constantly advanced information and communication technologies can be used to advance and alter women's conditions and change social arrangements. A much more solid and permanent form of collaboration between the commercial media and the education system is imperative and yet receives little attention from the state and the academy.

From this review of women's education, women and men alike should consider three key questions: (1) how do we change a patriarchal education system that has been in existence for so long and thus developed deep roots? (2) how can we further promote gender transformation through women-led NGO educational programs? and (3) how do we create spaces for change today amid social and economic situations that promote competition and access to the labor market rather than engagement with solidaristic and socially reflective practices? Crucial to the consideration of these three questions is the necessary action to modify the parallel worlds in which key actors in education and gender currently operate.

Although current students and scholars have limited regard for history, it might be suitable to end this chapter with a quote from the late Bella Abzug (1996), a former member of the U.S. Congress and a highly respected feminist:

In answer to those who think that women just want power for power's sake, it's not about that at all. It's not about simply main-streaming women. It's not about women joining the polluted stream. It's about cleaning the stream, changing stagnant pools into fresh, flowing waters. Our struggle is about resisting the slide into a morass of anarchy, violence, intolerance, inequality, and injustice. Our struggle is about reversing the trends of social, economic, and ecological crisis.

REFERENCES

Aaron, J., & Walby, S. (Eds.) (1991). *Out of the margins: Women's studies in the nineties*. Falmer.

Abzug, B. (1996). Women will change the nature of power. In B. Abzug & D. Jain. (Eds.), *Women's leadership and the ethics of development*. Gender in Development Monograph Series, No. 4. UNDP.

Acker, J. (1990). Hierarchies, jobs, bodies: A theory of gendered organizations. *Gender & Society, 4*(2), 139–158.

Althusser, L. (1971). *Lenin and philosophy and other essays*. Monthly Review Press.

Apple, M. (1983). Work, gender, and teaching. *Teachers College Record, 84*(3), 611–628.

Archer, D., & Muntasim, T. (2020). Financing SDG 4: Context, challenges, and solutions. In A. Wulff (Ed.), *Grading goal four: Tensions, threats, and opportunities in the sustainable development goal on quality education* (pp. 170–194). Brill Sense.

Ashwin, S., & Supova, O. (2018). Processes of reproduction and change in Russian women's gender ideology. *Gender & Society, 32*(4), 441–468.

Bayardo, B. (1996). Sex and the curriculum in Mexico and the United States. In N. P. Stromquist (Ed.), *Gender dimensions in education in Latin America*. Organization of American States.

Benavot, A., & Smith, W. (2020). Reshaping quality and equity: Global learning metrics as a ready-made solution to a manufactured crisis. In A. Wulff (Ed.), *Grading goal four: Tensions, threats, and opportunities in the sustainable development goal on quality education* (pp. 238–261). Brill Sense.

Beneria, L., & Bisnath, S. (1996). *Poverty and gender: An analysis for action*. UNDP.

Bonder, G. (1994, October). From theory to action: Reflections on a women's equal opportunities educational policy. Paper prepared for the expert group meeting on Gender, education, and training, Division for the Advancement of Women, United Nations.

Bowman, M. J. (1986). An integrated framework for analysis of the spread of schooling in less developed countries. In P. Altbach & G. Kelly (Eds.), *New approaches to comparative education*. University of Chicago Press.

BRAC. (2019). BRAC Education Program. www.brac.net/program/wp-content/uploads/2019/12/Factsheet-BRAC-Education-Programme-June-2019.pdf

Coburn, E. (2019). Trickle down gender at the International Monetary Fund: The contradictions of "femina economica" in global capitalist governance. *International Feminist Journal of Politics, 5*(21).

Colclough, C. (1996). Education and the market: Which parts of the neoliberal solution are correct? *World Development, 24*(4), 589–610.

Connell, R. W. (1987). *Gender and power: Society, the person, and sexual politics*. Stanford University Press.

Connell, R. W. (1994). Poverty and education. *Harvard Educational Review, 64*(2), 125–149.

Development and Cooperation. (1997). Borrowed burden. Development and Cooperation 2.

Eisenhart, M., & Holland, D. (1990). *Educated in romance*. University of Chicago Press.

England, P., Levine, A., Mishel, E. (2020). *Proceedings of the National Academy of Sciences. Progress toward gender equality in the United States has slowed or stalled.* National Academy of Sciences.

Fink, M. & Arnove, R. (1991). Issues and tensions in nonformal and popular education. *International Journal of Educational Development, 11*(3), 221–230.

Foucault, M. (1980). *Power/knowledge: Selected interviews and other essays.* Pantheon Books.

Frade, L. (1997). Women's eyes on the World Bank. *Social Watch, 1,* 67–68.

Garduño, V. (2018). Educación sexual: una polémica persistente. *Red, 2*(11), 24–32.

GCE & RESULTS. (2011). *Making it right. Ending the crisis in girls' education. A Report by the Global Campaign for Education and RESULTS.* Global Campaign for Education and RESULTS.

Giroux, H. (1992). *Border crossings: Cultural workers and the politics of education.* Routledge.

Guzmán, G. (1990). *Las organizaciones de mujeres populares: Tres perspectivas de análisis.* Centro de la Mujer Peruana Flora Tristan.

Hassan, M., Mirza, T., Hussain, M. (2020). The gender gap of teachers in the education sector of India. *Tathapi, 19*(45), 12–19.

Ilon, L. (1998). The effects of international economic dynamics on gender equity of schooling. *International Review of Education, 44*(4), 335–356.

Jain, S. & Krishnamurty, L. (1996). *Empowerment through Mahila Sanghas: The Mahila Samakhya Experience.* Sandhan Shodh Kendra.

Kelly, G. (1978). Research on the education of women in the third world: Problems and perspectives. *Women's Studies International Quarterly, 1*(4), 365–373.

Kelly, G. & Nihlen, A. (1982). Schooling and the reproduction of patriarchy: Unequal workloads, unequal rewards. In M. Apple (Ed.), *Cultural and economic reproduction in education.* Routledge.

King, E., & Hill, A. (Eds.) (1993). *Women's education in developing countries: Barriers, benefits, and policies.* Johns Hopkins University Press.

Kuhar, R., & Paternotte, D. (Eds.). (2007). *Anti-gender campaigns in Europe: Mobilizing against equality.* Rowman & Littlefield.

Levinson, B. (2001). *We are all equal: Student culture and identity at a Mexican secondary school, 1988–1998.* Duke University Press.

Levy, A., & Merry, U. (1986). *Organizational transformation: Approaches, strategies, theories.* Praeger.

Lloyd, C. (Ed.) (2005). *Growing up global. The changing transitions to adulthood in developing countries.* National Academies Press.

Longwe, S. (1997, February). Education for women's empowerment—or schooling for women's subordination? Paper presented at the international seminar-workshop on Promoting the Empowerment of Women through Adult Learning, Chiang Mai, Thailand.

Miske, S. (2013, June). Exploring the gendered dimensions of teaching and learning. background paper for the Education for All global monitoring report. UNGEI.

Molyneux, M. (1985). Mobilization without emancipation? Women's interests, state, and revolution in Nicaragua. *Feminist Studies, 11*(2), 227–254.

Murphy-Graham, E. (2012). *Opening minds, improving lives: Education and women's empowerment and Honduras.* Vanderbilt University Press.

Nayar, U. (1995). Planning for UPE of girls' and women's empowerment: Gender studies in DPEP. In National Council of Educational Research and Training (Ed.), *School effectiveness and learning achievement at primary stage.* National Council of Education Research and Training.

NCERT. (1995). *Education of the girl child in India: A fact sheet*. National Council of Educational Research and Training.

O'Brien, R., Goetz, A. M., Scholte, J., & Williams, M. (2000). *Global governance: Multilateral economic institutions and global social movements*. Cambridge University Press.

O'Connor, P., Harford, J., & Fitzgerald, T. (2020). Mapping an agenda for gender equality in the academy. *Irish Educational Studies*, 39(2), 1131–1171.

Pateman, C. (1986). Introduction: The theoretical subversiveness of feminism. In C. Pateman & E. Gross (Eds.), *Feminist challenges*. Allen & Unwin.

Puryear, J., & Brunner, J. J. (1997). An agenda for educational reform in Latin America and the Caribbean. In J. Puryear (Ed.), *Partners for progress: Education and the private sector in Latin America and the Caribbean* (pp. 9–13). Inter-American Dialogue.

Ramirez, F., & Boli-Bennett, J. (1982). Global patterns of educational institutionalization. In P. Altbach, R. Arnove, & G. Kelly (Eds.), *Comparative education* (p. 15–38). Macmillan.

Rosemberg, F. (1992). Education, democratization, and inequality in Brazil. In N. P. Stromquist (Ed.), *Women and education in Latin America* (pp. 33–46). Rienner.

Rosemberg, F. (1997, April). Educación, Género y Raza. Paper presented at the 20th Congress of the Latin American Studies Association, Guadalajara.

Rottenberg, C. (2018). *The rise of neoliberal feminism*. Oxford University Press.

Sayed, Y., & Moriarty, K. (2020). SDG 4 and the "education quality turn": Prospects, possibilities, and problems. In A. Wulff (Ed.), *Grading goal four: Tensions, threats, and opportunities in the sustainable development goal on quality education* (pp. 194–213). Brill Sense.

SDG Tracker. (2020). SDG Tracker. Measuring progress towards the sustainable goals. Ourworlddata.org.

Smock, A. (1981). *Women's education in developing countries: Opportunities and outcomes*. Praeger.

Soper, K. (1991). Postmodernism and its discontents. *Feminist Review*, 39, 97–108.

Streitmatter, J. (1995). *Toward gender equity in the classroom*. State University of New York Press.

Stromquist, N. P. (Ed.) (1992). *Women and education in Latin America: Knowledge, power, and change*. Rienner.

Stromquist, N. P. (Ed.). (1996). *Gender dimensions in education in Latin America*. Organization of American States.

Stromquist, N. P. (1997). *Literacy for citizenship: Gender and grassroots dynamics in Brazil*. State University of New York Press.

Stromquist, N. P. (2007). *Feminist organizations and social transformation in Latin America*. Paradigm Publishers.

Stromquist, N. P. (2012). The gender dimension in the World Bank's Education Strategy: Assertions in need of theory. In S. Klees, J. Samoff, & N. P. Stromquist (Eds.), *The World Bank and Education: Critiques and Alternatives* (pp. 159–172). Sense Publishers.

Stromquist, N. P. (2015). Women's empowerment and education: Linking knowledge to transformative action. *European Journal of Education*, 50(3), 307–324.

Stromquist, N. P., Klees, S., & Jing Lin, J. (Eds.). (2017). *Women teachers in Africa: Challenges and possibilities*. Routledge.

Stromquist, N. P. & Murphy, P. (1995). *Leveling the playing field: Giving girls an equal chance for basic education—three countries' efforts*. World Bank.

True, J., & Mintrom, M. (2001). Transnational networks and policy diffusion: The case of gender mainstreaming. *International Studies Quarterly*, 45(1).

UIS. (2010). *Global Education Digest 2010*. UNESCO Institute for Statistics.

UIS. (2019, September). *New methodology shows that 253 million children, adolescents and youth are out of school. Fact Sheet, No. 50*. UNESCO Institute for Statistics.

UIS. (2020). *Net enrollment rate by level of education*. UNESCO Institute for Statistics.

UNDP. (1995). *1995 Human Development Report*. UNDP.

UNDP. (2011). *Human Development Report 2011. Sustainability and equity: A better future for all*. UNDP.

UNESCO. (2010). *Global Education Digest 2010*. UNESCO.

UNESCO. (2020). *Global Education Monitoring Report 2020. Inclusion and education: All means all*. UNESCO.

UNESCO & IIEP. (2017). *Six ways to ensure higher education leaves no one behind*. UNESCO & IIEP.

Unterhalter, E., North, A., Arnot, M., Lloyd C., Moletsane, L., Murphy-Graham, E., Parkes, J., & Saito, M., et al. (2014). *Interventions to enhance girls' education and gender equality*. Department for International Development.

Verloo, M. (2006). Mainstreaming gender equality in Europe: A critical frame analysis approach. *The Greek Review of Social Research*, 117(B'), 11–34.

Verma, G. & Christie, T. (1996, December). *The main-streaming of BRAC/NFPE students*. Paper prepared for the Manchester Faculty of Education, University of Manchester.

Walters, S. (1997, February). *Democracy, development and adult education in South Africa*. Paper presented at the international seminar-workshop on Promoting the Empowerment of Women through Adult Learning, Chiang Mai, Thailand.

Warwick, D., & Jatoi, H. (1994). Teacher gender and student achievement in Pakistan. *Comparative Education Review*, 38(3), 377–399.

Wilson, J. (1993). The subject woman. In P. England (Ed.), *Theory on gender/feminism on theory* (pp. 343–356). Aldine de Gruyter.

World Bank. (1995). *Toward gender equality: The role of public policy*. World Bank.

Wulff, A. (Ed.) (2020). *Grading goal four: Tensions, threats, and opportunities in the sustainable development goal on quality education*. Brill Sense.

Young, A. (2019). *From spinster to career woman: Middle-class women and work in Victorian England*. McGill-Queen's University Press.

8

Control of Education

Issues and Tensions in Centralization and Decentralization

Mark Bray
East China Normal University (Shanghai) and University of Hong Kong

---

ABSTRACT

This chapter, focusing on the functional and territorial governance of education systems, begins by noting definitions and understandings of centralization and decentralization. The chapter then considers a range of motives for choosing various models and highlights the complexities of measurement of centralization and decentralization. Addressing themes and variations, the chapter considers control of school-leaving qualifications, textbooks, and universities. Subsequent sections consider implications for efficiency, social inequalities, and environments for administrative reform. The chapter remarks on patterns across a wide range of countries, cultures, and political environments.

Debates about the appropriate locus of control in education systems are often heated and are usually difficult to resolve. The reasons for this are political as well as technical, for the nature and degree of centralization or decentralization influence not only the scale and shape of education systems but also the access to education by different groups.

Much can be learned from a comparative study concerning the advantages and disadvantages of different arrangements. Comparative analysis can also enhance understanding of the reasons why some societies and systems have particular shapes and are moving in certain directions; and for politicians or administrators embarking on reforms, comparative study can demonstrate the need for certain preconditions and support systems.

This chapter commences by presenting some definitions, noting some of the motives for centralization and decentralization, identifying some models of governance, and outlining a discussion on ways to measure centralization and decentralization. The chapter then turns to some specific domains to show variations in administrative systems in different places. The three domains chosen as examples are school-leaving qualifications, textbooks, and universities. The next two sections comment on the implications of different types of arrangements for efficiency and for social inequalities. The penultimate section notes some specific factors that must be taken into account during the design of administrative reforms, and the last section concludes the discussion.

MEANINGS, MOTIVES, MODELS, AND MEASUREMENTS

Meanings

The words *centralization* and *decentralization* can mean different things to different people. This chapter must therefore begin by noting some possible meanings of the terms.

A starting point is to note that centralization and decentralization are processes—they are "-izations"—rather than static situations. This chapter is therefore concerned with a variety of starting points. It discusses centralization in systems that were previously decentralized; but it also discusses further centralization in systems that were already centralized. Similar points apply to systems in which control was centralized but is then made less centralized, and to systems that were already decentralized but become even more decentralized.

A second observation is that the terms centralization and decentralization usually refer to deliberate processes initiated at the apex of hierarchies. However, sometimes patterns change by default rather than by deliberate action. Also, power may be removed from the center either with the acquiescence of or in the face of resistance by the center.

Next it is necessary to distinguish between various types of centralization and decentralization. The literature on this topic is not entirely consistent, but there is general agreement on some major points (see, e.g., Daun & Siminou, 2009; OECD, 2019; Varghese, 2011). Among them is the distinction between functional and territorial dimensions. *Functional* centralization and decentralization refers to a shift in the distribution of powers between various authorities that operate in parallel. For example:

- In some countries, a single ministry of education is responsible for all aspects of the public system of education. A move to split such a body into a ministry of basic education and a separate ministry of higher education could be called functional decentralization.
- In some systems all public examinations are operated by the ministry of education. Creation of a separate examinations authority to take over this role could be called functional decentralization, even if that examinations authority remained directly controlled by the government.
- In many countries, schools are operated by voluntary agencies as well as by governments. A loosening of government control on voluntary-agency schools could be called functional decentralization. Conversely, a tightening of control could be a form of functional centralization. Nationalization of voluntary agency schools, to place them under direct government control, would be an even more obvious form of functional centralization.

Territorial centralization and decentralization, by contrast, refers to a redistribution of control among the different geographic tiers of government, such as nation, states or provinces, districts, and schools. A transfer of power from higher to lower levels would be called territorial decentralization. This is a spatial conception of the term. The category of territorial decentralization includes three major subcategories.

- *Deconcentration* is the process through which a central authority establishes field units or branch offices, staffing them with its own officers. Thus, personnel of the ministry of education may all work in the same central building, or some of them may be posted out to provinces and districts.
- *Delegation* implies a stronger degree of decision-making power at the local level. Nevertheless, powers in a delegated system still basically rest with the central authority, which has chosen to "lend" them to the local one. The powers can be withdrawn without resort to legislation.
- *Devolution* is the most extreme of these three forms of territorial decentralization. Powers are formally held at subnational levels, the officers of which do not need to seek higher-level approval for their actions. The subnational officers may choose to inform the center of their decisions, but the role of the center is chiefly confined to the collection and exchange of information.

Some writers describe privatization as another form of decentralization (e.g., Zajda, 2006). Certainly privatization may be a form of decentralization in which state authority over schools is reduced. However, it is not necessarily decentralizing. Some forms of privatization concentrate power in the hands of churches or large private corporations. In these cases, privatization may centralize control, albeit in nongovernmental bodies.

Motives

The motives for centralization and decentralization of the control of education are commonly political but may also be administrative, or a combination of both. Politically motivated reforms aim to strengthen the power of the dominant group (in the case of centralization) or to spread power to other groups (in the case of decentralization). Administratively motivated reforms aim to facilitate the operation of bureaucracies. Often the origin of education reforms lies in wider political or administrative changes rather than in the specifics of the education sector.

Among the most dramatic examples of politically motivated reforms have been territorial decentralization schemes in Ethiopia, the Philippines, and Spain. Regionally based separatist movements in these countries were sufficiently powerful to threaten secession if not granted stronger autonomy. The central authorities conceded power to persuade the secessionist groups to remain within the national framework.

However, secessionist threats can lead to different reactions. For example, in 1961 the Ghanaian government reacted to separatist stirrings in the Ashanti confederacy by creating a strongly centralized unitary state. The Indonesian government reacted similarly during the 1960s to secessionist tendencies in the province of Irian Jaya. Alternatively, central governments may respond to secessionist threats with a strategy of "divide and rule." For example, when Nigeria's federal government was threatened by Biafran secession in 1967, it decided to split the country's four regions into 12 states. To respond to further political demands, the number of states in Nigeria was increased to 19 in 1976, 21 in 1987, 30 in 1991, and 36 in 1996.

Other examples of political motivations include the desire through reforms to include or exclude certain groups from decision-making. A 1989 Colombian initiative sought to promote unity by involving dissident groups and by incorporating all major segments of the population (Hanson, 1999). In contrast, decentralization in Mexico reduced the power of the teachers' union by transferring salary negotiations from the central to the state government level (Ornelas, 2006).

On a more bureaucratic plane, both centralization and decentralization may be advocated to improve efficiency. The main centralizing argument is that operations can be directed more efficiently by a small group of central planners without cumbersome duplication of functions in parallel or subnational bodies. The main decentralizing argument is that specialist parallel bodies are better able to focus on the needs of clients and that territorially decentralized subnational units are closer to the clients and are better able to cater for local diversity. Efficiency arguments for territorial decentralization typically focus on the high unit costs of primary and secondary education provided by the central government. The internet has much reduced communication costs, but personnel in the capital city may not be aware of local labor market conditions, price differentials for construction, and so on.

Allied to this set of justifications are others based on cultural differences. Weiler (1993) pointed out that decentralization may be advocated to provide greater sensitivity to local variations in educational needs:

> Except in very small or culturally very homogeneous societies, most countries vary considerably across regions, communities, and language groups in terms of cultural and social frameworks of learning. The frames of reference for the study of history, botany, social studies, and other fields vary obviously and significantly between southern and northern Italy, Alabama and California, or Bavaria and Berlin. Differences such as these, in countries such as the Federal Republic of Germany and the United States, historically have sustained the argument for a federal or local structure of educational governance and for varying degrees of cross-regional differentiation, as far as the content of education is concerned. (p. 65)

In contrast, centralization may be advocated because intranational diversity in the cultures of learning is excessive and there is a need for standardization of at least the core elements in curriculum and instruction. This was among the justifications for partial centralization in the United States during the 1930s (Tyack, 1993, p. 3), and more recently has been a motive in England, the government of which introduced a centralizing national curriculum in 1988 (Daun & Siminou, 2009; Roberts, 2019). In the same vein, in many African countries the curriculum has remained centralized since their governments have considered the curriculum to be an important tool for nation-building.

Finally, one negative motive for decentralization is a desire by the center to reduce its responsibilities for education because of financial stringency. Central governments that realize that they do not have sufficient resources for adequate provision of services may choose to evade the problem by decentralizing responsibility to lower tiers or to nongovernmental bodies. This has been an underlying consideration of reforms giving subnational bodies greater responsibility for education in Nigeria and several other West African countries (Geo-Jaja, 2006; Lugaz & De Grauwe, 2010; UNESCO, 2005). It has also been a major motive in various privatization initiatives (Ball & Youdell, 2008; Belfield & Levin, 2002).

Models

As already implied, the range of models for the governance of education is very wide. Decisions on the choice of models must be made in the context of political ideologies, historical legacies, and such factors as linguistic plurality, geographic size, and ease of communications.

An obvious starting point is with the overall structure of government. Australia, Canada, India, Nigeria, and the United States all have federal systems in which substantial powers are vested in state or provincial governments. The degree of provincial decision-making in Canada, for example, is so great that the structure and content of education are substantially different in such provinces as Alberta and Quebec. Most obviously, in the former, the education system is mainly conducted in English, whereas in the latter, it is mainly conducted in French. Differences are not quite so marked between the individual states of the United States, but they are still substantial in that country. These systems therefore appear to be highly decentralized.

Many unitary systems also appear to have high degrees of decentralization. For example, in 1976 Papua New Guinea adopted a quasi-federal system with 19 provincial governments, each of which had considerable autonomy including in matters of education (Bray, 1984; Hawksley, 2006). The United Kingdom, although not a federal system, has a strong degree of decentralization to its constituent parts—England, Northern Ireland, Wales, and Scotland. The education systems of England and Wales are closely linked, but those of Scotland and Northern Ireland operate separately (Bray & Jiang, 2014; Brock, 2015).

Some confederal systems have even greater degrees of decentralization. Switzerland, for example, has 26 cantons, each of which has its own school laws and education system (Barakay & Lockwood, 2007; Behren, 2015). Cantonal authorities are empowered to decide on the structure of the system, the curriculum, the language of instruction, and the time spent on each subject in each grade. The national government plays hardly any role in the decision-making process.

Linguistic pluralism plays a major role in several of the countries already mentioned, particularly Nigeria, Canada, and Switzerland. Belgium has parallel education systems serving French speakers and Flemish speakers, and linguistic pluralism was among the factors behind the territorial decentralization initiatives in Papua New Guinea. In Vanuatu, by contrast, efforts have been made to coordinate the separate English-medium and French-medium systems under a single ministry—an initiative that is a form of functional centralization.

Concerning geographic size, one might be tempted to look at countries with large areas, such as Canada, India, Russia, and the United States, all of which have federal systems, and assume that all large countries have decentralized administrations. However, the fact that this is not the case is demonstrated by consideration of Indonesia and China, which until recently have had highly centralized administrations. Conversely, it cannot be assumed that small states necessarily have centralized systems. This is certainly true in some small states, such as Malta and Brunei Darussalam; but it is not true of St. Lucia and The Gambia. The latter two countries have district administrations and also permit some decision-making at the school level.

The importance of the school as a level of consideration deserves emphasis. Since the mid-1980s, school-based management has received considerable emphasis in a wide range of countries (Bruns et al., 2011; Caldwell, 2009). In New Zealand, for example, a far-reaching initiative abolished the government's Department of Education and formed school-level boards of trustees (New Zealand, 1988). The boards were required to enter contractual agreements with their communities and were empowered to manage school budgets and hire and fire teachers. Similar initiatives were launched at about the same time in Australia, Canada, the United States, and the United Kingdom (Caldwell, 2003). A reform in Spain took democratization to the extent of requiring School Councils to elect the principals of schools (Luengo et al., 2005).

Finally, models of administration are influenced by the ease or otherwise of communication. In the Democratic Republic of the Congo, for example, the administration is decentralized by default simply because communications are poor. The center does not know what the periphery is doing, and the periphery would be unable to secure regular and detailed instructions from the center even if it wanted to. In other parts of the world, the advent of the internet has greatly reduced remoteness and has permitted stronger central supervision.

Measurements

The complexities of centralization or decentralization become even more apparent when efforts are made at measurement (Kostas, 2020). Many people suppose that countries can be ranked on a scale, with some having strongly centralized systems at the top and others having strongly decentralized systems at the bottom. However, attempts to create such rankings usually produce findings that are questionable and potentially misleading.

An initial problem arises from the custom of taking the nation-state as the unit for analysis. National boundaries are in most cases arbitrary, and they form countries of greatly differing sizes. Thus, to describe Japan (population 122,600,000) as having a centralized administration would mean something very different from describing Tonga (population 97,000) as having a centralized administration. Likewise, although at one time the government of India devoted much publicity to its decentralized District Primary Education Project (Mukundan & Bray, 2006; Varghese, 1996), the fact that some of these districts had populations above five million, which is considerably greater than the total populations of many countries, might make some observers feel that the unit of government is still very large.

Enlarging on this point, when the Soviet Union was a single country, the autonomy held by individual republics such as Azerbaijan, Georgia, and Latvia made the administrative system appear decentralized. Now that those republics are independent countries, the administration of their education systems, from the perspective of the nation-state, is commonly described as centralized. Conversely, when Hong Kong was a self-governing colony, its administration was widely described as centralized (Morris, 1996, pp. 91–95). However, after the 1997 reincorporation of Hong Kong into the People's Republic of China, Hong Kong remained a Special Administrative Region with considerable autonomy that, at least from the perspective of Beijing, seemed a highly decentralized arrangement (Bray & Koo, 2005; Tse & Lee, 2017).

A different difficulty in measurement arises from value judgments on the importance or otherwise of different powers. Thus the power to determine the structure of school systems, or the language of instruction, might be considered very important. In contrast, the power to hire school cleaners might be considered rather less important. This would require weighting within any model for measurement.

Further complexity is that reforms might move systems simultaneously in opposite directions. During the 1980s, the government in England greatly changed the nature of educational decision-making (Turner, 2006). As already noted, one component of reforms was the introduction of a national curriculum, which centralized power in the hands of the national government. Another component was the requirement for all schools to have boards of governors that had considerable powers at the school level over such matters as budgets, recruitment of teachers, and facilities. The coexistence of trends that are both centralizing and decentralizing creates major difficulties for classification (Hautala et al., 2018).

Also creating major difficulties is the fact that some systems might seem to be centralized and decentralized at the same time. Thus Malaysia, for example, has been described as having "centralized decentralization" (Lee, 2006); and China has been described as simultaneously undergoing centralization, decentralization, and recentralization (Hawkins, 2006; see also Guo & Guo, 2016). Related to this point is that the extent to which a system of government is centralized or decentralized cannot be prejudged from the existence or absence of subnational institutions. Many constitutions give federal governments powers of veto that act as a considerable constraint on state or provincial governments, which means that the systems are not as decentralized as they appear at first sight. Also, the power of federal and quasi-federal governments is commonly strengthened by the control of major sources of finance. By contrast, even in countries with no state or provincial governments, national authorities may be willing to decentralize substantial powers to the school level (Chapman, 2004; Chikoko, 2009).

Finally, while deconcentration is usually described as a form of decentralization, it can be a mechanism for tightening central control of the periphery instead of allowing for greater local decision-making. When central government staff posted to the periphery are permitted to take local decisions to reflect local needs and priorities, then deconcentration may reasonably be described as a form of decentralization. But when staff in the periphery are responsible for tightening implementation of policies determined by the central government, deconcentration is more reasonably described as a form of centralization.

Yet despite all these complexities and the questions they raise, some analysts have persisted with efforts at measurement. One such attempt is presented in Table 8.1. The table seems to describe Luxembourg as the most centralized of the 16 countries covered, followed by Italy and Mexico. At the other end, the Czech Republic seems to be the most decentralized, followed by England.

Table 8.1. Balance Between Levels of Decision-Making for Public Lower Secondary Education (%)

	Central	State/Province	Local	School	Multiple	Total
Australia	0	48	0	52	0	100
Austria	32	22	0	46	0	100
Czech Republic	2	4	26	68	0	100
Denmark	21	0	22	29	28	100
England	0	0	6	65	29	100
Estonia	0	0	13	58	29	100
Iceland	8	0	31	60	0	100
Ireland	42	0	0	46	13	100
Italy	52	11	0	36	0	100
Japan	13	33	21	21	13	100
Korea	29	15	8	15	33	100
Luxembourg	83	0	0	17	0	100
Mexico	49	34	0	17	0	100
Scotland	0	0	44	48	8	100
Spain	8	69	0	10	13	100
Sweden	21	0	35	35	8	100

Source: OECD (2018, p. 418).

Although these figures shed some light on the topic, they should be viewed with extreme caution. First, Luxembourg is a very small country, with a population and area much smaller than most Australian states, for example. Second, to establish the distributions, the authors counted functions, assigned each of them a score, and calculated percentage distributions at each level. The publication showed different tables for specific functions, including organization of instruction, personnel management, planning, and resourcing. These were all assigned equal weight, even though arguably some functions are more important than others. And finally, although the table refers specifically to lower secondary education in public systems rather than to all levels of education, including in private systems, the definitions of lower secondary and of public may not have been consistent. As such, the example shows the dangers as well as the benefits of efforts to place countries on a single continuum for comparison.

THEMES AND VARIATIONS

The factors behind different models, and the implications of different arrangements, may be further illustrated with a few examples. Three specific foci of decision-making are presented here. They are school-leaving qualifications, school textbooks, and the operation of universities.

Control of School-Leaving Qualifications

Considerable diversity may be found in the control of qualifications awarded at the end of secondary schooling. In some jurisdictions control is tightly held by Ministries of Education, while in others examination boards operated by government agencies or by private bodies play major roles. As with other aspects of administration, the factors underlying different arrangements reflect a combination of historical legacies and deliberate policies. The United Kingdom has a long tradition of independent examination boards, some associated with tertiary institutions such as the Universities of London, Oxford, and Cambridge. In a break with tradition, in 2003 a company called London Qualifications Ltd. was established. In 2004 it changed its name to Edexcel, and in 2005 became the only large examination board in private hands when Pearson plc took complete control. Other countries, such as Poland, Romania, and Russia, have more centralized traditions with examination units under the direct control of the Ministry of Education.

Yet other countries, such as Spain and Sweden, have no formal final examinations (Kellaghan & Greaney, 2019, pp. 3, 31). Students in these countries are instead subject to school-based assessment throughout their secondary school careers, with forms of external review for consistency of standards. Institutions of higher education may set entrance examinations of various kinds, but that process can be a separate activity from certification of completion of secondary education. In the Republic of Korea, higher education selection is based on school records, involvement in extramural activities, and scores in nationwide university entrance examinations (Boyle, 2008). Sweden also has a university entrance examination, but in the Republic of Korea students don't have to sit for this type of examination to gain admission.

Table 8.2 elaborates on the balance between external and internal assessment in 16 jurisdictions. Although the first column is headed "mainly using external assessment," Ireland occupied an extreme in which no school-based assessment contributes to qualifications and all assessment is external. At the other end, Japan had no formal national systems of assessment for students in compulsory education, and the grade for the Certificate of Graduation from Upper Secondary Education was based largely on teacher assessment without external moderation. However, arrangements for the majority of jurisdictions, in the words of the author, "could be conceived of either as moderately favouring internal or external assessment, or of having mixed systems" (Boyle, 2008, p. 30). This remark again underlines the difficulty of classifying systems.

Table 8.2. Categorization of Jurisdictions Using Mainly Internal or Mainly External Assessment for Secondary School-Leaving Qualifications

Mainly using external assessment	*Mainly using internal assessment*
Denmark	Japan
Estonia	Republic of Korea
Greece	Queensland, Australia
Ireland	Spain
Latvia	Sweden
Netherlands	Switzerland
Poland	Turkey
Slovenia	
England	

Source: Boyle (2008), p. 30.

Focus on examinations also helps to show that the locus of real control over educational processes may be hidden. Although one might expect a public examination system to be related to the degree to which an education system is centralized, the relationship is not straightforward (Kellaghan & Greaney, 2019, p. 6). It is true that the United States, which can be an example of a decentralized system, does not have national examinations; but centralized examinations may be considered necessary to monitor standards in a system, such as that in Norway, in which control is predominantly local. Further, examinations are a major determinant of actual (as opposed to officially intended) school curricula; and where there is a divergence between what is taught and what is tested, students generally pay greater heed to the latter.

Control of Textbooks

Commonality and diversity of textbook policies may be illustrated by comparing patterns in four parts of East Asia which themselves have much in common but also display major differences. The following account focuses on mainland China, Taiwan, Hong Kong, and Macao. All four are mainly inhabited by people of Chinese ethnicity, and their dominant cultures have Confucian roots. One has had a communist government since 1949, whereas the other three have always had capitalist governments. Hong Kong and Macao share histories of colonization by European powers, but despite this commonality they have significant differences in the nature of educational provision.

The government of China, chiefly to spread the official ideology of communism, at one time held tight control over curricula and textbooks. Shortly after the foundation of the People's Republic in 1949, the government decided that only one basic set of textbooks, published in Beijing by the People's Education Press, would be permitted for use in schools. After 1985, however, the central government permitted increasing diversification in the production and contents of textbooks. The change reflected the introduction of a market economy and increased tolerance of pluralism in both economic and social sectors. The relaxation of control began with Shanghai, which was followed by other economically advanced coastal areas and then by other regions (Qi, 2011; Zhang, 2004). Showing political swings, however, regulations were tightened again in the following decade (China, 2020).

Taiwan contrasts with mainland China in many aspects of political ideology. Most obviously, whereas China became a communist society after the 1949 revolution, Taiwan remained a capitalist society that was strongly antagonistic to the political changes on the mainland. Yet despite this ideological difference, the Taiwanese authorities were for a long time just as keen as their counterparts in mainland China to control the content of the curriculum. A 2001 reform, taken further in 2007, gave schools autonomy to design their own curricula (Lo, 2010). Before that change, textbooks were standardized and published by the National Institute for Compilation and Translation. Official goals for primary education included inculcation of patriotism and anticommunism, and textbooks were seen as a major vehicle for achieving these goals (Young, 1995).

Hong Kong, another society with long capitalist traditions, was a British colony between 1842 and 1997. As one might expect, the colonial authorities were also concerned about the content of textbooks, and particularly about the extent to which such books could disseminate ideas that conflicted with those promoted by the government. However, the policies of the Hong Kong colonial government were not as rigid as those in China or Taiwan. The authorities only permitted schools to use books that had been placed on an official list, but the schools could choose books produced by independent publishers and sold on the open market (Lo, 2005). Subsequently, the government moved only to a recommended list (Hong Kong, Education Bureau, 2020).

Macao provides yet another model. Like Hong Kong, Macao was a colony of a European power but the administration of Macao was much more laissez-faire than that of Hong Kong. Macao became a Portuguese colony in 1557 and remained under Portuguese administration for over four centuries. In 1987, the governments of Portugal and China agreed that sovereignty over Macao would revert to China in 1999, two years after the transition in Hong Kong. That political initiative did cause some changes in the education system, but the schools remained completely free to decide which textbooks on the market they wished to use. The government of Macao did not itself produce any textbooks for schools, and the lack of controls resulted in the considerable diversity in what was taught in different institutions (Bray & Tang, 2006). This picture evolved in the decades following the reintegration of Macao with the rest of China, with the government particularly paying attention to history textbooks but still permitting schools to choose according to preferences (Zhu, 2019).

This set of examples shows on the one hand that similar administrative systems may be found in different political environments, and on the other hand that different administrative systems may be found in similar political environments. The governments of both mainland China and Taiwan exerted tight control over textbooks, even though one was communist and the other was capitalist. Mainland China's move to a market economy was accompanied by relaxation of control, and at that point contrasted with Taiwan which had always had a market economy but in which schools had never been permitted freedom of choice in textbooks. Hong Kong and Macao were both colonies of European powers, but the colonial government in Hong Kong only permitted schools to use books that had been vetted, whereas the colonial government in Macao adopted a completely laissez-faire policy. The difference in this case partly reflected the colonies' importance to the metropolitan authorities. Hong Kong was a sizeable colony in which the British government was anxious to maintain stability; Macao was a very small colony that had been important to the Portuguese empire up to the 19th century but subsequently declined in significance. The resulting neglect was evident in all sectors, including education. However, the decades following reintegration with the rest of China at the end of the 20th century brought some convergence of patterns in both Hong Kong and Macau.

Control of Universities

Concerning relationships between governments and universities, two main models may be identified (Fielden, 2008; Varghese, 2009). The first is the state-control model, which historically can be exemplified by higher education systems in continental Europe and particularly by that of France. These systems were created by the state and have been almost completely financed by it. At least formally, the state has controlled nearly all aspects of the dynamics of these higher education systems. The national ministries of education have regulated the access conditions, curriculum, degree requirements, examinations, and appointment and remuneration of academic staff. One objective of this detailed government regulation is the standardization of national degrees, which in several countries are awarded by the state rather than by the universities themselves.

In this model, the power of the state is combined with strong authority at the level of senior professors. The latter holds considerable collegial power within the faculties and the institutions. This model is therefore characterized by a strong top (the state), a weak middle (the institutional administration), and a strong bottom (the senior professors).

In contrast is the state-supervising model, which was employed for public universities in the United States and the United Kingdom up to recent times, as well as many former British colonies. In this model, senior professors have strong powers, while the institutional administrators have modest powers and the state also accepts a modest role. Each institution recruits its own students, hires its own staff, and determines its own curricula. Many systems influenced by the U.K. model have buffer bodies modeled on the University Grants Committee, which operated in the United Kingdom from 1919 to 1988. Table 8.3 summarizes information on buffer bodies in nine countries. Although the table shows variation in their roles, the bodies typically liaise between the institutions and the government, seeking on the one hand to respect institutional autonomy but on the other hand to secure accountability in the use of public resources. Also in the state-supervised model are systems such as that in the Philippines, which have large numbers of private institutions that are to some extent regulated by the state.

During the 2000s, an increasing number of governments shifted from the control model to the supervisory model (Fielden, 2008, p. 2). Many felt that the supervisory model would more easily permit and stimulate the types of innovation within institutions that were considered necessary to cope with rapidly changing circumstances. Reforms in Chile, Argentina, and China were oriented toward this model. However the state-controlled model may also have advantages, and other higher education systems, for example at various points in history those in Kenya, Uganda, and Ghana, have moved in that direction. The reasons for this countermovement include a government desire to control high-level human resources output, to restrict political threats from universities, and to contain pressure on resources through a relatively elitist system. In connection with the last of these, movements in the United Kingdom are instructive. In that country the University Grants Committee was replaced in 1988 by a University Funding Council through which the government could take much more direct control (Walford, 1991). This was a form of functional centralization that permitted the government to require institutions to demand measures of research output and the quality of teaching.

At the same time, governments must recognize that higher education has increasingly been provided across borders. Online education is increasingly common, as are foreign campuses of universities. Governments therefore have to consider foreign providers as well as domestic providers, and regulation of such providers is much more challenging (Chapman et al., 2010; Knight, 2010).

Table 8.3. Functions of University Buffer Funding Bodies in Nine Countries

	Canada (Manitoba)	Hong Kong	India	Kenya	Nigeria	South Africa	Sri Lanka	England	Zimbabwe
Strategic planning	✓	✓		✓	✓		✓		✓
Policy analysis/problem resolution	✓	✓	✓	✓	✓		✓	✓	
Mission definition of higher education institutions	✓			✓	✓				
Academic program review	✓			✓	✓	✓			✓
Budget development/funding advice/allocation	✓	✓	✓	✓	✓	✓	✓	✓	✓
Program administration	✓			✓	✓	✓			
Monitoring/accountability		✓		✓	✓	✓	✓	✓	
Quality assurance/standards review		✓	✓		✓	✓	✓		✓
Deciding the total number of student admissions	✓		✓			✓	✓		✓

Source: Fielden (2008, p. 10).

Implications for Efficiency

As noted previously, in various circumstances arguments for efficiency may be used to support both centralization and decentralization. These points deserve elaboration to identify the types of factors involved.

Experiences in Papua New Guinea provide a good starting point for discussion (Bray, 1984, pp. 99–114). In 1977, the government of Papua New Guinea launched a major scheme for territorial devolution to 19 newly created provincial governments. The reform was not without critics. For example, in 1978 the Leader of the Opposition (Okuk, 1978, p. 21) highlighted the costs of an increase in the number of provincial-level politicians:

> Papua New Guinea is to have more than 600 paid politicians. We have three million people. Australia has about 600 paid politicians, and it has 14 million people. It took Australia almost 100 years to develop to the stage where it now has 600 politicians. It has taken us three years. Britain, which has a population of 40 million, has about as many politicians as Papua New Guinea. Does anyone seriously believe that a developing country like Papua New Guinea can afford that much government?

Nevertheless, the reform went ahead. Provincial governments were formed with substantial responsibilities in most sectors including education—and including for each a provincial minister of education.

One result of the reform was a massive expansion of the bureaucracy. This was especially visible at the provincial level but was also evident at the national level, since more staff were required for coordination and training. In one province between 1977 and 1983 primary school enrollments expanded by 15% and secondary school enrollments expanded by 7%, but the number of senior administrative officers expanded by 208%. The smallest province had just 25,000 people (which elsewhere would have been equivalent in size to a small town) but nevertheless acquired a bureaucracy with the same major components as all other provinces. Moreover, at that stage in its development, Papua New Guinea was severely short of skilled personnel. Adjustments to the distribution of roles of national, provincial, and local governments were made in 1995, but review a decade later still lamented that "the interface between national and sub-national levels of education is weak with the [National] Department of Education having no oversight or quality assurance function over responsibilities decentralised to provinces, districts and local-level governments" (Papua New Guinea, 2004, p. 26). In addition, the government recognized, the national authorities themselves lacked organizational capacity to administer and monitor the education system.

However, other types of decentralization can increase efficiency. Among them are school-based management projects of the types launched in Australia, England, and New Zealand. Typical features of these projects include competition between institutions for pupils and teachers, and allocation of block grants to the school level so that principals and other administrators can switch between budget categories according to needs and priorities. Most schemes also allow some funds to be retained from one year to the next, which gives an incentive to school-level administrators to save money rather than simply disburse all surpluses toward the end of the financial year. Evaluations have shown increased personal stress at the school level, and critics have asserted that some of the pedagogic goals of school principals have been subsumed by the demands of managerialism (Zajda & Gamage, 2009). Nevertheless, it generally appears that the reforms have led to a much greater consciousness of costs and of ways to improve efficiency.

Also related to issues of efficiency is the need for coordination in decentralized systems. This may consume considerable time as well as labor. The Swiss model has been described as permitting efficiencies because of close links between the people and their education system (Barakay & Lockwood, 2007). The response from advocates of decentralization might be that the changes, although slow, are more likely to be solid because they should be grounded in general acceptance. This viewpoint implies that speed of change is only one indicator of efficiency and that effectiveness of change must be included as another. The example once again indicates the complexity of the subject and of the implications of administrative reform.

Implications for Social Inequalities

In general, decentralization is likely to permit and perhaps encourage social inequalities. Conversely, centralization provides a mechanism for reducing inequalities; but whether that mechanism is used depends on goals and willpower at the apex of the system.

Concerning geographic disparities, discussion can usefully begin with territorial devolution to the provincial or state level. Such devolution permits subnational bodies to determine the nature and direction of development. Some bodies are likely to be more active than others, in which case regional disparities in the quantity or quality of education will increase. Further down the spatial hierarchy, the same point would apply to districts and to individual schools. Devolution is not usually just a matter of decision-making; it is also a matter of resource allocation. Highly decentralized systems commonly permit subnational bodies to retain most or all of the resources that they generate. Since prosperous communities can afford better quality or greater quantities of education, disparities remain or even widen.

To expand on the earlier example, one major part of the devolution package in Papua New Guinea was the provision for provincial governments to retain much larger proportions of locally generated revenue than had previously been permitted. The national government controlled external aid and various other revenues, and it was able through this mechanism to ameliorate some disparities. However, the national government was not able to make full compensation for the structural imbalances created by the devolution framework (Bray, 1984; Walton & Davda, 2019).

Administrative structures have also created major imbalances in the United States, both within and between states. The U.S. Constitution does not give a direct educational role to the federal government, though increasing federal funds have in fact been allocated to the education of disadvantaged groups. Within states, the problem is that some school districts are able much more easily than others to mobilize resources for education from property taxes and other sources. Taking a historical perspective, Table 8.4 shows the changing balance between federal, state, and local financing for elementary and secondary schooling. Whereas in 1919–1920 the bulk of revenue was raised at the local level, by 2016–2017 both federal and state government revenues were more prominent. This showed the existence of a mechanism to reduce some imbalances, though disparities remained.

Table 8.4. Sources of Revenue for Public Elementary and Secondary Schools, United States (Percentage)

School Year	Federal	State	Local
1919–1920	0.3	16.5	83.2
1929–1930	0.4	16.9	82.7
1939–1940	1.8	30.3	68.0
1949–1950	2.9	39.8	57.3
1959–1960	4.4	39.1	56.5
1969–1970	8.0	39.9	52.1
1979–1980	9.8	46.8	43.4
1989–1990	6.1	47.1	46.8
1999–2000	7.3	49.5	43.2
2009–2010	12.7	43.4	43.9
2016–2017	8.1	47.0	44.9

Sources: *Digest of Education Statistics* (National Center for Education Statistics, 2019). Retrieved September 30, 2020, from https://nces.ed.gov/programs/digest/d19/tables/dt19_235.10.asp?current.asp

Inequalities may also be exacerbated within socioeconomic groups. For example, the literature on community financing of education points out that richer communities are more likely and better able to embark on self-help projects than are poor communities (Bray, 2003; Mekolle, 2019; Nishimura, 2017).

Preconditions and Support Systems for Administrative Reform

The literature on administrative reform pays much greater attention to ways to achieve effective decentralization than to ways to achieve effective centralization (Farrell, 2011, p. 75). This probably reflects the value judgments of the individuals and organizations producing that literature, though it may also reflect a perception that decentralization is more difficult to achieve than centralization. As the examples in this chapter have pointed out, in some cases centralization is more desirable than decentralization, and it should not be assumed that centralization can be achieved simply by issuing decrees.

Prawda (1993, p. 262) focused on lessons learned from decentralization efforts in the education sector in Latin America. He presented seven lessons, some of which would presumably also apply to attempts at centralization. Successful decentralization, he suggests, requires the following:

1. full political commitment from national, regional, provincial, municipal, and local leaders;
2. a model addressing the issue of which educational functions and responsibilities could be more efficiently and effectively delivered at the central level, smaller decentralized government units, and/or the private sector, and explicitly defining the degree of accountability of the different participants;
3. an implementation strategy and timetable;
4. clear operational manuals and procedures;

5. continuous training for the skill levels to be performed at the central and decentralized units of government;
6. relevant performance indicators to be continuously monitored through a management information system by policymakers and senior government officials; and
7. adequate financial, human, and physical resources to sustain the process.

Turning to reforms of the opposite type, most analysts would consider the most important requirements for centralization to be full commitment from the central leadership and acquiescence at lower levels. Questions about capacity may be just as relevant to centralization as to decentralization initiatives, since both may collapse if they fail to deliver promised benefits.

Missing from Prawda's list is a public relations campaign to explain the need for reform, which would be equally valuable for centralization and for decentralization reforms. Allied to such a campaign would be the need to secure cooperation from teachers' unions and similar groups.

Also important in all reforms is the time element. The exigencies of political forces sometimes require results before reforms have had time to become fully effective. This is one reason for the swings evident in some countries from centralization to decentralization and back again. Prawda (1993, p. 262) pointed out that the first accomplishments from decentralization in Mexico and Chile surfaced only five years after the reforms had been launched. However, such a period may be too long for many political regimes. Between 1991 and 2000 the average duration of service of Ministers of Education in Latin America was 2.81 years (Poggi, 2011, p. 245).

CONCLUSION

The political context of reforms is among the points most deserving emphasis. Although centralization and decentralization are often officially justified by technical criteria, political factors are usually the most important (Berkhout, 2005; Romanowski & Du, 2020). Centralization and decentralization are about matters of control, about the distribution of resources, and, in the education sector, about access to opportunities that can fundamentally influence the quality of life for both individuals and social groups.

For scholars who are more concerned with dispassionate analysis than with manipulation of variables, the first task in any review of centralization or decentralization is to identify precisely what is meant by the terms as used in each case. This chapter has shown that the words "centralization" and "decentralization" can have many different meanings. Not only are the terms vague, they may even have contradictory meanings depending on the circumstances and perspectives of the persons making the judgments. Deconcentration, for example, may seem like a form of decentralization when viewed from the central ministry but may be a mechanism to exert tighter control on the periphery and may thus be seen as a form of centralization by those in the periphery. Likewise, splitting a single ministry into two parts may seem like decentralization from the perspective of those who are closely involved but may appear to make little difference to those who are more distant. Although attempts to empower local communities may appear to be laudable attempts at decentralization, the fact that such communities may be dominated by factional elites may leave other groups feeling at least as marginalized as before.

Also important to note are rather sober assessments about the impact of structural reforms on teaching and learning in classrooms. In the United States, for example, Elmore (1993) remarked that:

> Whatever the politics of centralization and decentralization is "about" in American education ... it is not fundamentally or directly about teaching and learning. This disconnection between structural reform and the core technology of schooling means that major reforms can wash over the educational system, consuming large amounts of scarce resources—money; time; the energy of parents, teachers, and administrators; the political capital of elected officials—without having any discernible effect on what students actually learn in school. (p. 35)

More recently and on the other side of the world, Saguin and Ramesh (2020, p. 172) were similarly disappointed with the "lackluster performance" of education in the Philippines despite administrative reforms over the decades.

Yet although analysts around the world recognize the thrust of these points, it would be an overstatement to suggest that shifts in the locus of control do not impact life in classrooms. Certainly, the reforms may not be tied fundamentally or directly to teaching and learning, but many reforms have had marked implications for school curricula and for the access to education by different groups. Indeed it is mainly for this reason that the battles over control of education are so intense.

As was noted at the beginning of this chapter, comparative analysis can highlight the advantages and disadvantages of different models of governance. It can also enhance understanding of the reasons why some societies and systems have particular shapes and are moving in certain directions; and for politicians and administrators embarking on reforms, comparative study can show the need for certain preconditions and support systems. However, it is impossible to reach a single recipe that will be appropriate for all countries. Societies with strongly entrenched democratic values and well-educated populations are more likely than others to demand decentralized systems and to make them work. But even this is a broad generalization that does not hold in all cases. The future, like the past, is likely to bring continued shifts in forms of governance in all parts of the world. Some of these shifts will be centralizing, others will be decentralizing, and yet others will be both centralizing and decentralizing at the same time. This need not be cause for bemusement or despair. Rather, it can be taken as part of the ever-present dynamic of human endeavor.

REFERENCES

Ball, S. J., & Youdell, D. (2008). *Hidden privatisation in public education*. Education International.

Barakay, I., & Lockwood, B. (2007). Decentralization and the productive efficiency of government: Evidence from Swiss cantons. *Journal of Public Economics, 91*(5–6), 1197–1218.

Behren, M. (2015). Switzerland: Between the federal structure and global challenges. In T. Sprague (Ed.), *Education in non-EU countries in Western and Southern Europe* (pp. 75–97). Bloomsbury.

Belfield, C. R., & Levin, H. M. (2002). *Educational privatization: Causes, consequences and planning implications*. UNESCO International Institute for Educational Planning (IIEP).

Berkhout, S. J. (2005). The decentralisation debate: Thinking about power. *International Review of Education*, 51(4), 313–327.

Boyle, A. (2008). *The regulation of examinations and qualifications: An international study*. Office of the Qualifications and Examinations Regulator.

Bray, M. (1984). *Educational planning in a decentralised system: The Papua New Guinean experience*. University of Papua New Guinea Press; Sydney University Press.

Bray, M. (2003). Community initiatives in education: Goals, dimensions and linkages with governments. *Compare: A Journal of Comparative Education*, 33(1), 31–45.

Bray, M., & Koo, R. (Eds.) (2005). *Education and society in Hong Kong and Macao: Comparative perspectives on continuity and change*. Comparative Education Research Centre, University of Hong Kong; Springer.

Bray, M., & Jiang, K. (2014). Comparing systems. In M. Bray, B. Adamson, & M. Mason (Eds.), *Comparative education research: Approaches and methods* (2nd ed., pp. 139–166). Comparative Education Research Centre, University of Hong Kong; Springer.

Bray, M., & Tang, K. C. (2006). Building and diversifying education systems: Evolving patterns and contrasting trends in Hong Kong and Macau. In C. Bjork (Ed.), *Educational decentralization: Asian experiences and conceptual contributions* (pp. 71–95). Springer.

Brock, C. (Ed.) (2015). *Education in the United Kingdom*. Bloomsbury.

Bruns, B., Filmer, D. & Patrinos, H. A. (2011). *Making schools work: New evidence on accountability reforms*. World Bank.

Caldwell, B. (2003). Decentralisation and the self-managing school. In J. P. Keeves & R. Watanabe (Eds.), *International handbook of educational research in the Asia-Pacific region* (pp. 931–944). Kluwer.

Caldwell, B. (2009). Centralisation and decentralisation in education: A new dimension to policy. In J. Zajda & D. T. Gamage (Eds.), *Decentralisation, school-based management, and policy* (pp. 53–66). Springer.

Chapman, D. (2004). *Management and efficiency in education: Goals and strategies*. Comparative Education Research Centre, University of Hong Kong; Asian Development Bank.

Chapman, D., Cummings, W. K., & Postiglione, G. A. (Eds.) (2010). *Crossing borders in East Asian higher education*. Comparative Education Research Centre, University of Hong Kong; Springer.

Chikoko, V. (2009). Educational decentralisation in Zimbabwe and Malawi: A study of decisional location and process. *International Journal of Educational Development*, 29(3), 201–211.

China, Ministry of Education (2020). *Notice of the Ministry of Education on the issuance of the measures for the administration of teaching materials in primary and secondary schools and the measures for the administration of teaching materials in general higher education institutions*. Ministry of Education. [in Chinese] http://www.moe.gov.cn/srcsite/A26/moe_714/202001/t20200107_414578.html

Daun, H., & Siminou, P. (2009). Decentralisation and market mechanisms in education: Examples from six European countries. In J. Zajda & D. T. Gamage (Eds.), *Decentralisation, school-based management, and policy* (pp. 77–101). Springer.

Elmore, R. F. (1993). School decentralization: Who gains? Who loses? In J. Hannaway & M. Carnoy (Eds.), *Decentralization and school improvement: Can we fulfill the promise?* (pp. 33–54). Jossey-Bass.

Farrell, J. P. (2011). Blind alleys and signposts of hope. In M. Bray & N. V. Varghese (Eds.), *Directions in educational planning: International experiences and perspectives* (pp. 63–87). UNESCO International Institute for Educational Planning (IIEP).

Fielden, J. (2008). *Global trends in university governance.* World Bank.

Geo-Jaja, M. (2006). Educational decentralization, public spending, and social justice in Nigeria. In J. Zajda, S. Majhanovich, & E. M. Sabina (Eds.), *Education and social justice* (pp. 125–148). Springer.

Guo, S., & Guo, Y. (Eds.) (2016). *Spotlight on China: Changes in education under China's market economy.* Sense.

Hanson, E. M. (1999). Democratization and decentralization in Colombian education. In N. F. McGinn & E. H. Epstein (Eds.), *Comparative perspectives on the role of education in democratization. Part I: Transitional states and states of transition* (pp. 143–203). Peter Lang.

Hautala, T., Helander, J. & Korhonen, V. (2018). Loose and tight coupling in educational organizations: An integrative literature review. *Journal of Educational Administration*, 56(2): 236–258.

Hawkins, J. N. (2006). Walking on three legs: Centralization, decentralization, and recentralization in Chinese education. In C. Bjork (Ed.), *Educational decentralization: Asian experiences and conceptual contributions* (pp. 27–41). Springer.

Hawksley, C. (2006). Papua New Guinea at thirty: Late decolonisation and the political economy of nation-building. *Third World Quarterly*, 27(1), 161–173.

Hong Kong, Education Bureau. (2020). *Selection of quality textbooks and learning and teaching resources for use in schools: Circular memorandum No. 26/2020.* Education Bureau. https://applications.edb.gov.hk/circular/upload/EDBCM/EDBCM20026E.pdf

Kellaghan, T., & Greaney, V. (2019). *Public examinations examined.* World Bank.

Knight, J. (2010). Cross-border higher education: Issues and implications for quality assurance and accreditation. In C. Findlay & W. Tierney (Eds.), *Globalisation and tertiary education in the Asia-Pacific: The changing nature of a dynamic market* (pp. 73–92). World Scientific.

Kostas, T. (2020). Centralized and decentralized educational systems: A comparative quantitative approach. *International Journal of Educational Innovation*, 2(6), 112–123.

Lee, M. N. N. (2006). Centralized decentralization in Malaysia. In C. Bjork (Ed.), *Educational decentralization: Asian experiences and conceptual contributions* (pp. 149–158). Springer.

Lo, J. Y. C. (2005). Curriculum Reform. In M. Bray & R. Koo (Eds.), *Education and society in Hong Kong and Macao: Comparative perspectives on continuity and change* (pp. 161–174). Comparative Education Research Centre, University of Hong Kong; Springer.

Lo, W. Y. W. (2010). Educational decentralization and its implications for governance: Explaining the differences in the four Asian newly industrialized economies. *Compare: A Journal of Comparative and International Education*, 40(1), 63–78.

Luengo, J., Sevilla, D., & Torres, M. (2005). From centralism to decentralization: The recent transformation of the Spanish education system. *European Education*, 37(1), 46–61.

Lugaz, C., & De Grauwe, A. (2010). *Schooling and decentralization: Patterns and policy implications in Francophone West Africa.* UNESCO International Institute for Educational Planning (IIEP).

Mekolle, P. M. (2019). Decentralization and the financing of access to secondary education in Cameroon: Community contributions counts? *European Journal of Education Studies, 5*(2), 82–98.

Morris, P. (1996). *The Hong Kong school curriculum: Development, issues, and policies.* Hong Kong University Press.

Mukundan, M. V., & Bray, M. (2006). The decentralisation of education in Kerala State, India: Rhetoric and reality. In J. Zajda (Ed.), *Decentralisation and privatisation in education: The role of the state* (pp. 111–131). Springer.

New Zealand, Government of (1988). *Tomorrow's schools: The reform of education administration in New Zealand.* Government Printer.

Nishimura, M. (2017). Community participation in school management in developing countries. *Oxford Research Encyclopedia of Education.* doi:10.1093/acrefore/9780190264093.013.64

OECD. (2019). *Making decentralisation work: A handbook for policy-makers.* Organisation for Economic Co-operation and Development.

Okuk, I. (1978). Decentralisation: A critique and an alternative. In R. Premdas & S. Pokawin (Eds.), *Decentralisation: The Papua New Guinean experience* (pp. 21–25). University of Papua New Guinea.

Ornelas, C. (2006). The politics of privatisation, decentralisation and education reform in Mexico. In J. Zajda (Ed.), *Decentralisation and privatisation in education: The role of the state* (pp. 207–228). Springer.

Papua New Guinea, Department of Education. (2004). *Achieving a better future: A national plan for education 2005–2014.* Department of Education.

Poggi, M. (2011). Key issues in educational agendas: New perspectives for educational planning in Latin America. In M. Bray & N. V. Varghese (Eds.), *Directions in educational planning: International experiences and perspectives* (pp. 241–251), UNESCO International Institute for Educational Planning (IIEP).

Prawda, J. (1993). Educational decentralization in Latin America: Lessons learned. *International Journal of Educational Development, 13*(3), 253–264.

Qi, T. (2011). Moving toward decentralization? Changing education governance in China after 1985. In A.W. Wiseman & T. Huang (Eds.), *The impact and transformation of education policy in China* (pp. 19–41). Emerald Group Publishing.

Roberts, N. (2019). *The school curriculum in England.* House of Commons. https://dera.ioe.ac.uk/34766/1/SN06798.pdf

Romanowski, M. H., & Du, X. (2020). Education transferring and decentralized reforms: The case of Qatar. *Prospects,* https://doi.org/10.1007/s11125-020-09478-x

Saguin, K. I., & Ramesh, M. (2020). Bringing governance back into education reforms: The case of the Philippines. *International Review of Public Policy, 2*(2), 159–177.

Tse, T. K. C., & Lee, M. H. (Eds.). (2017). *Making sense of education in post-handover Hong Kong: Achievements and challenges.* Routledge.

Turner, D. (2006). Privatisation, decentralisation and education in the United Kingdom: The role of the state. In J. Zajda (Ed.), *Decentralisation and privatisation in education: The role of the state* (pp. 97–107). Springer.

Tyack, D. (1993). School governance in the United States: Historical puzzles and anomalies. In J. Hannaway & M. Carnoy (Eds.), *Decentralization and school improvement: Can we fulfill the promise?* (pp. 1–32). Jossey-Bass.

UNESCO. (2005). *Decentralization in education: National policies and practices* (pp. 17–20). UNESCO.

Varghese, N. V. (1996). Decentralisation of educational planning in India. *International Journal of Educational Development, 16*(4), 355–365.

Varghese, N. V. (2009). *Higher education reforms: Institutional restructuring in Asia.* UNESCO International Institute for Educational Planning (IIEP).

Varghese, N. V. (2011). State is the problem and state is the solution: Changing orientations in educational planning. In M. Bray & N. V. Varghese (Eds.), *Directions in educational planning: International experiences and perspectives* (pp. 89–108). UNESCO International Institute for Educational Planning (IIEP).

Walford, G. (1991). The changing relationship between government and higher education in Britain. In G. Neave & F. van Vught (Eds.), *Prometheus bound: The changing relationship between government and higher education in Western Europe* (pp. 165–183). Pergamon Press.

Walton, G. W., & Davda, T. (2019). School-community relations and fee-free education policy in Papua New Guinea. *Pacific Affairs, 92*(1), 71–94.

Weiler, H. N. (1993). Control versus legitimation: The politics of ambivalence. In J. Hannaway & M. Carnoy (Eds.), *Decentralization and school improvement: Can we fulfill the promise?* (pp. 55–83). Jossey-Bass.

Young, Y. R. (1995). Taiwan. In P. Morris & A. Sweeting (Eds.), *Education and development in East Asia* (pp. 105–124). Garland.

Zajda, J. (Ed.). (2006). *Decentralisation and privatisation in education: The role of the state*. Springer.

Zajda, J., & Gamage, D. T. (Eds.). (2009). *Decentralisation, school-based management, and quality*. Springer.

Zhang, X. (2004). New curriculum reform and basic education experiment. In D. Yang (Ed.), *China's education bluebook* (pp. 226–251). Higher Education Press.

Zhu, J. (2019, September 24). Education: Standardized history textbook adopted by more grades. *Macao Daily Times*, https://macaudailytimes.com.mo/education-standardized-history-textbook-adopted-by-more-grades.html

9

Transforming Adult and Community Education

A Theory of Literacies for Analyzing Change in Grenada's Revolution and After

Anne Hickling-Hudson
Queensland University of Technology

ABSTRACT

In this chapter I propose a theory of socio-educational analysis blending various scholarly conceptualizations of "literacies" to evaluate the role of adult education in national development. Using this social theory of literacies, I explore, as a case study, how adult education was designed and implemented during the Grenada Revolution of 1981–1983, and then after its collapse as a new polity was put in place. I discuss the role of adult education in maintaining a hierarchical status quo, and its potential to contribute to decolonizing, transformational sociopolitical change. Literacy strategies used in the Grenada revolution show the extent to which a radical model of adult education can help participants develop and master sets of "literacies" in the spheres of epistemology, identity, technical skills, and public/political capabilities that enable them to challenge structures of injustice and dysfunctionality. Flaws limit the effectiveness of both the revolutionary and the traditional approaches to adult education. Comparing these approaches, and discussing experiments in other countries, I consider clues about how we might "rewrite literacy" to transform the old model that consigned adult education to being a subordinated educational channel at the bottom of the education sector.

POSTCOLONIALISM, LITERACIES AND COMPARISONS

This chapter explores the concept of "literacies" as a tool for considering the role of adult education in national development. The context refers particularly to postcolonial societies that were until recently part of the former European empires, attaining their independence only with the ending of World War II. The analysis of "literacies" in a social context is arguably relevant to any society stratified by socioeconomic inequities. Using a case study, I discuss lessons that inequitable societies can learn from comparing the Caribbean experience of two approaches to adult basic and popular education which are intended to develop the "literacies" of adults affected by socioeconomic disadvantage.

The case of Grenada, a Caribbean microstate of about 90,000 people, helps to explore this because of the comparative analysis made possible by its socialist-oriented revolution (1979–1983), the overthrow of this process of change, and the return to a traditional path of market-led development between 1984 and the present. The discussion in this chapter compares two models of adult education utilized in Grenada: one designed within the context of postcolonial socialist orientation, and the other tending to characterize the neocolonial capitalism that continues, notwithstanding the postcolonial space (Hickling-Hudson, 1995; Jules, 1992).[1] Drawing on criteria developed from a blended theory of literacies that I propose, I consider strengths and flaws in both models, arguing that we need to go beyond them to meet today's imperatives.

It is the question of the role of adult education as a system-maintenance structure versus its potential as a transformational structure that makes it pertinent to discuss educational experiments in this tiny country several decades ago. In the unspeakable trauma of October 1983, the much-loved leader of the revolutionary government, Prime Minister Maurice Bishop, and seven other political leaders were killed by soldiers said to have been directed by another faction of political leaders, who have consistently denied this, drawing on international legal support (see Mandle & Mandle, 2020). Since then, there has been an outpouring of social science studies that explore not only this tragic event, and the U.S. invasion of Grenada that followed, but also the positive legacies of the Grenada Revolution, using political, social, economic, and cultural frameworks (Ambursley & Dunkerley, 1984; Coard, 2017; 2018; Cushion & Bartholomew 2018; Heine, 1991; Grenade, 2015b; Lewis et al., 2015; Meeks, 2015; Scott, 2014). My emphasis in this chapter is that this revolution, lasting only four and a half years, still has extraordinary significance, especially for countries of the Global South, in the achievements of its strategies for building adult literacies in new ways, as well as in the flaws in these experiments that perhaps contributed to the inability of the adult education sector to survive the revolution's collapse.

Locating my discussion of adult education in the Grenada Revolution involves describing my background of personal participation as an educator in the process. I spent two years in Grenada, 1981–1983, one of many Caribbean professionals working at the invitation of the Grenadian government in the new projects of the revolution. Having obtained unpaid leave from my position as a senior lecturer in teacher education in my home country, Jamaica, I taught in Grenada's National In-Service Teacher Education Programme (NISTEP), as well as being part of the planning team working in the Ministry of Education to research and plan future change in each sector of education. I was therefore in a position of deep engagement in the transformational educational plans and practices of the Grenada revolution and made this the subject of two of my postgraduate dissertations (Hickling-Hudson, 1986; 1995). Nearly 40 years later, I still argue that it is important to reflect on the policies and achievements of the Grenada Revolution and their significance in starting to reshape education, given the dominance of the postrevolutionary continuation of a traditionally elitist model. Studying this dimension of Grenada puts me in the role of blending an insider/outsider position (participant as well as regional colleague, narrator as well as policy analyst) in my comparison of two episodes of policy and practice (see Bray et al., 2007).

In comparing the two models of adult education in the revolution and after its collapse, I put forward in this chapter a theoretical framework for analysis. First, I use a postcolonial perspective to explain the context of the case. Next, I combine three concepts of "literacies" into a theory of literacies that is powerful for analyzing education in class-stratified societies. I apply this theoretical frame to understanding the case study, an approach that has significance for comparative analysis of selected dimensions of education in any society. I then draw attention to the need for studying global approaches to transforming the adult education sector in ways that have the potential for bringing about meaningful change for the people who seek to challenge their imposed disadvantage.

COLONIALITY, THE POSTCOLONIAL SPACE AND GRENADA'S REVOLUTION

A perspective drawn from postcolonial theory starts by analyzing context since this influences the cases being investigated. It pays particular attention to understanding the ideological power of the colonial historical context, how this power continues to influence material conditions across the globe, and how it is challenged. It explores the extent to which the colonial is embedded in the postcolonial, in economies, societies, institutions and ideologies, and analyzes contradictions and ambiguities in the process of change (Coloma, 2009; Enslin, 2017; Hickling-Hudson et al., 2004; Rizvi, 2007).

Grenada's revolution is an example of a postcolonial event. Some scholars argue that the term "postcolonial" is misleading because of the current and enduring strength of colonial structures even after the colonizer has left. While they prefer terms such as "anticolonial" and "decolonial," I argue that both these terms are aspects of postcolonialism. With the demise of the political structures of colonialism, there is a new space, one in which we can put terms such as "anticolonial," and "decolonizing" into the service of challenging neocolonialism and coloniality in the struggle to bring about transformative change. The postcolonial space after independence gives rise to new opportunities for change. In each sector of education, from preschool to grade school to tertiary and adult education, new approaches become possible (Hickling-Hudson, 2010).

Yet, change is always difficult because of the entrenched power of coloniality. This makes it almost inevitable that conflicts will accompany the hard task of changing from a mindset typical of coloniality. As Christie (2021) argues, reforms in education can be seen as a palimpsest in which the changes do not erase the previous structures of colonialism but are shaped on top of them. Grenada in the 1980s, a developing society caught in the contradictions of the postcolonial condition, was shaped by contesting currents. On the one hand, the society was impoverished, underdeveloped, economically dependent on the Global North, class-stratified with a large agricultural peasantry and a small, highly educated and well-off elite, all features inherited from the centuries of British colonialism that had only ended in 1974. On the other, internal social movements were struggling to challenge these malformations and move to more equitable and viable ways of living.

Grenada's revolution, although brought to an end by the fratricidal conflict between factions that paved the way for invasion and overthrow by the United States in October 1983, left a social legacy of deep significance. The path of "socialist transition" tried there was an example of an alternative development model characterized by private sector dominance coexisting with state sector growth—certainly not "socialism," but oriented toward it. The revolution's mixed economy succeeded in taking initial steps on the path of transformation. In its short four years, it made a start, and achieved remarkable success in:

- restructuring and revitalizing the stagnant economy, seen in figures such as a rise in the gross domestic product (GDP) from 2.1% in 1979 to 5.5% in 1983, and a decrease of unemployment from 49% in 1978 to 14% in 1983,
- establishing better and new social services in health and housing,
- implementing legislation that provided new rights for disadvantaged groups, especially women and workers' unions,
- redesigning and massively expanding education for adults,
- establishing a new program and approach in teacher education that offered at least two in-service years of certificate level training (NISTEP) to the 70% of unqualified (pre-trained) teachers in Grenada,
- making initial improvements in primary and secondary schools including designing new textbooks, launching student councils, providing free school meals and uniforms, repairing decaying schools, expanding secondary school places to accommodate 40% of the age-group, building a new high school, providing teacher professional development seminars, and encouraging high schools to adopt a Caribbean curriculum and examination system instead of a British one,
- expanding and redesigning vocational education for young people as well as in the adult education program
- forging communities and groups into alliances for improving community life and articulating a more culturally confident national vision. (Cushion & Bartholomew, 2018; Hickling-Hudson, 1986; 2012, pp. 228–230)

So striking were these advances that the process was described locally and regionally as a revolution—a popular movement led and organized by Grenada's PRG (People's Revolutionary Government), which drew most of its members from the NJM (New Jewel Movement), a coalition political party. The PRG regarded itself as a rigorous and responsible "vanguard" of leaders, and indeed followed an exacting standard of assiduous hard work, study, and political engagement. But this vanguard turned out to have weaknesses including those of highly restricted membership and inadequate structures of conflict-resolution and public accountability. This proved an inadequate foundation for supporting deep social change and ultimately contributed to the collapse of the revolution (Meeks, 2015; Thomas, 1988; Thorndike, 1991; Whitehead, 1991).

After the U.S. invasion, the society returned to the regional model of a neoliberal version of capitalism which is aggressively advocated and endorsed by the United States and other governments of the North for developing countries (e.g., see Chomsky, 1999). This model, while expanding some global business opportunities for impoverished economies, at the same time opens these economies even further to "free" trade and foreign capital seeking cheap and minimally protected labor. The model maintains traditional export agriculture based on undervalued tropical crops and traditional tourism, both of which, despite bringing jobs and income, also have significant drawbacks for new nations seeking developmental change. Further, there are cutbacks in public sector employment and state services, including education. In this model, indicators such as GDP or GNI can sometimes show economic improvement ("growth"—see World Factbook, Grenada (2022) while there is little or no reduction of the gap between already impoverished majorities and wealthy minorities (Ferguson, 2000; Thomas, 2001). In the current situation some 38% of the population live below the poverty line, with unemployment of about 24% (World Factbook, Grenada, 2022). It is estimated that in 2016 in Grenada there were about 4,000 unemployed young adults. "While youth represent 30% of the total number of unemployed, 70% of the unemployed are not youth. This suggests that Grenada suffers a more systemic employment problem than a youth specific one" (United Nations, 2021).

Like most Caribbean people at the current juncture, Grenadians vote for the various parties that sustain the neoliberal model in a context in which there appears to be no other viable option but globalizing capitalism. This swing back to tradition is inevitable, given the disastrous circumstances in which the revolution collapsed as well as the general failure of socialist revolutionary leadership globally to have established a consistently viable change process or economic model.[2] But in Grenada, despite the overthrow of the revolution, the reversal of most of its programs, and the swing back to conservative, dependent capitalism, the memory of the revolution's social and economic achievements has not been erased. Shalin Puri's landmark cultural study of memory in Grenada's present explores how people remember both the joyous creativity of the revolution and the traumatic destruction of a process that was loved (Puri, 2014). Adult basic and popular education is an important element of this social memory, since it was seen as a particularly creative achievement of the revolution. This kind of sociocultural memory may also be important in informing future political development in other impoverished countries. As observed by Wendy Grenade (2015, p. 258), "the struggle for control of the state by the political class can promote electoral democracy at the expense of genuine substantive democracy. The case suggests the need for a democratic ethos that finds creative mechanisms for ordinary people to be involved in their governance."

The next sections discuss a theory of literacies, the revolution's experiments in adult basic and popular education, and the strengths and limitations of these experiments compared to those in the neoliberal model.

A THEORY OF LITERACIES FOR ANALYZING EDUCATIONAL CHANGE

A theory of literacy and literacies embedded in a sociopolitical framework is necessary for analyzing issues in the practice and improvement of adult education. This section briefly suggests a literacy theory that facilitates comparison of the conservative, system-maintenance role of adult education with the role that it would play were it to make a significant difference in contributing to change in society. The term *adult education* is used in this chapter as a comprehensive reference to compensatory or second-chance schooling and vocational training (basic education), and community education organized in popular or voluntary structures accessible to all citizens. I refer to the latter as popular community education, while acknowledging that it is sometimes known as nonformal education. In my usage, adult education consists of the dual components of formal basic education and nonformal popular education.

A politically aware theory of literacies enables the analyst to explore questions that are often neglected in reports and analyses of adult education that have a technicist focus on narrowly interpreted notions of efficiency and effectiveness. Do adult basic and popular education structures reflect and reinforce the deep-seated inequities in decolonizing societies? Or do they challenge inequity to establish greater democracy? Or perhaps some combination of these? Why is it so difficult to achieve democratic change in and through adult education? How might such change be pushed forward?

Scholars of literacy see it not as a unitary skill of reading and writing but as a set of discourses and competencies applied to tasks in a given culture. Drawing from varied theorizations of the nature of literacy discourses, I contend that, for analysts of the social role of education:

- It is inadequate to understand "literacy" in a unitary way as the skills of reading, writing, and numeracy. It is also inadequate to understand it only as the popular concept of "multiliteracies" relating to areas of skills and content knowledge such as media, politics, mathematics, the sciences, or the arts.
- More sociologically useful for educators is to weave together theories that would help us to assess how literacies, including skills, content, and epistemologies, perform in society.
- People are initiated into the discourses and competencies of varied literacies in different ways according to their socioeconomic and cultural status.
- Different groupings of people practice literacies along a continuum that ranges from basic to critical and powerful.
- The outcomes of acquiring literacy and literacies are not necessarily empowering—people can acquire disempowering or subordinate literacies rather than powerful or dominant ones. (Gee, 1991; Lankshear et al., 1997)

The model put forward by Rob McCormack (1991) is useful in conceptualizing literacy as comprising at least four domains, each of which embodies a type of knowledge and a set of competencies. The domain of *epistemic literacy* refers to the uses of written text associated with formal knowledge conceptualized along the lines of academic disciplines. *Technical literacy* is interpreted as procedural knowledge in areas of practical action. A high degree of technical literacy in the modern workplace would demand competence in technology-based forms of creating, storing, and conveying information, although in developing societies, technical and mechanical skills are still as economically important as the skills of information technology. *Humanist literacy* refers to the ability to construct narratives that conceptualize, explain, and draw personal strength from cultural, social, and gender identities. *Public literacy* is seen as the competencies underlying meaningful participation in the public sphere, understanding and being able to contribute to opinion, debate, political judgment, and the shaping of collective identity.

The approach that I propose is to combine these concepts and apply them to social analysis. Utilizing this blended approach to analyzing education (Hickling-Hudson 1995), I argue for evaluating education policies, systems and structures along the following lines:

- Identify how the education structure incorporates the four "literacies" (the domains proposed by McCormack, 1991).
- Evaluate the nature and quality of each literacy domain as to: (i) how far along the continuum it can be assessed, from basic to powerful (Gee, 1991), and (ii) how far it inculcates the dominant or the subordinate literacies (Lankshear et al., 1997, pp. 63–79) offered by the society.
- Evaluate the structure according to this analysis (how basic or powerful, how dominant or subordinate, are the "literacies" provided by the society?).

This allows us to apply the construct of "literacies" sociologically, exploring the acquisition of literacy domains along lines of social class. The underlying theory—the set of explanatory ideas—is that such an approach is a foundation for understanding the role of socially divided literacies in maintaining the status quo. It would show how socially stratified education systems such as those in the Caribbean and other postcolonial societies across the globe, inculcate literacy domains into citizens according to their socioeconomic class or status. This has far-reaching effects on individuals and society.

Through schooling, people are placed on a certain track or channel in the educational hierarchy. Some are initiated by their education and upbringing into the content and techniques of dominant literacy in each domain, which is then used to justify their continuance in the elite educational channel (lined by the best schools and colleges) and their socioeconomic dominance and political power. In the Caribbean, this is illustrated by the elite educational channels of those who go to the traditionally privileged and influential schools modeled on the British grammar style school, fee-paying, grant-aided, and nearly always single-sex. Such schools in Grenada include the Grenada Boys' Secondary School, Presentation Boys' College, and the Anglican High School for girls, in which many of the leaders of the Grenada Revolution were schooled before acquiring professional degrees and qualifications and high-status jobs. The majority of the population is denied this initiation into dominant literacies, and are made to follow a very different pathway. They are shunted into the less adequate, often grossly under-resourced and neglected government-funded schools (always coeducational), sometimes followed by vocational training. These low-status educational channels provide subordinate literacies, which are then penalized as being of inferior worth in society. Needless to say, the outcome of the subordinate path is access to the society's low-status and low-income jobs, or unemployment. The "literacies" of these economically poorer people may be functional for survival in the disadvantaged layers of society, but do not gain them any systematic access to the corridors of power or the levers of political change. This is the case in every Caribbean society that has so far inadequately reshaped the coloniality of its European heritage.

This stratified model of literacies exists in any class-divided society, but the divisions are deepest, and the barriers to mobility highest, in postcolonial societies whose recent colonial history left them with maldeveloped and distorted economies subordinated in the world capitalist system. Across the Caribbean region, although functional literacy is widespread, it is at a minimal and subordinate level for the majority (with the possible exception of Cuba). Adult education, with its catch-up schooling to a primary level and its vocational training for subsistence jobs, is too underdeveloped to provide adequate opportunity for adults either to gain the epistemic literacies necessary for well-paid employment and social mobility or to gain the political literacies necessary to put consistent pressure for democratic change on the system. Instead, it entrenches them in their position in the lowest levels of the socioeconomic pyramid. Yet, it enables the state to claim that it is looking after the needs of disadvantaged adults. Thus the social role of traditional adult education is, arguably, largely one that maintains unjust hierarchical systems and at the same time legitimizes them (Arnove & Graff, 1992; LaBelle & Verhine, 1975; Torres, 1990).

When a political process is serious about putting in place change with equity, it has to learn how to change the stratified nature of hierarchical education channels and hierarchized literacies. In postcolonial experience, it tends to have been socialist-oriented regimes that have taken this task seriously, since it has been in their interest to provide conditions, including more and better education, that will encourage people to support and defend revolutionary change (Torres, 1990). The option of socialism in its 20th-century form may have been largely superseded, but seeking radical change remains vital for people marginalized by social injustice. Change that challenges inequity must include forging a system in which the entire population acquires literacies that are powerful enough to enable an informed critique of negative social patterns and democratic participation in changing them. From the perspective of striving for social justice, education should be contributing toward improving the entire society's material conditions by helping people to establish viable self and group employment in economic projects and to demand from the state a commitment to develop policies that are fair, sustainable, and accountable. It should be changing the contextual pattern of stratified channels of education and occupation to help reduce the barriers that sustain an obscene level of inequality between social classes, strata, and gender groups. Politically, education should prepare people to assess the quality and performance of their political systems, to analyze international patterns of injustice and trends for change, to hold politicians accountable, to discuss and experiment with problem-solving, both nationally and in alliance with international movements, to run for local and national political office based on informed and creative platforms.

To consider the potential of adult and community education for playing such roles, experiments need to be examined for their strengths and limitations, and new ones designed on this basis. The focus of such an analysis is not primarily on the scale or efficiency of adult education—for example, on how many adult education programs there are or how many adult students pass the tests they offer. It is on the *social role* of these programs, and therefore needs the tools of literacy theory within the postcolonial political economy framework suggested earlier.

ADULT BASIC EDUCATION: CHALLENGES IN DEVELOPING EPISTEMIC AND TECHNICAL LITERACIES

Studying adult education in the Grenadian revolution and after its collapse is useful to a comparative education approach in that it allows the analysis of a unique, socially significant case that can be compared with other cases. Comparisons of this sort throw light on the working of the education system as a whole.

Educators in Grenada's revolutionary process designed a new structure to provide adult basic education for impoverished people, mostly subsistence farmers, and seasonal agricultural laborers. The new structure became known as the Center for Popular Education (CPE) and initially attracted four thousand learners to enroll—about 24% of the approximately 17,000 adults assessed as ranging from nonliterate to minimally literate. The Revolution's emphasis on and drive for adult education also included the provision of popular education in existing and new community groups and other informal groups. These community groups (such as groups of women, youth, and people in citizens' councils) were not organized by the CPE, but by political leadership in the revolutionary state. I will consider the potential for changing adult education first by reflecting on its formal dimension (the CPE structure), then by considering nonformal, popular education elements of the community and political associations. It is useful to separate them to understand the kind of adult learning possible in each area.[3]

Many postcolonial societies, including several Caribbean ones, have designed and implemented structures and programs of compensatory and vocational adult education. Cuba through its 1959 revolution and Jamaica in its social-democratic period of the 1970s paid special attention to designing and implementing adult literacy and further education programs that sought to transform traditional approaches. Revolutionary Grenada's CPE drew on these ideas and crafted its way of creatively tackling the problems of articulation of levels, access, and program design, set out in detail in Hickling-Hudson (1995, pp. 164–184). These features are important in providing sites of comparison between programs in different geographical or temporal spaces. Each feature may be evaluated for the extent to which it promoted epistemic, technical, humanist, and public literacies, and for the extent to which empowerment was envisaged in the design.

1. In creating CPE, the PRG designed a new and completely government-funded program which was incorporated in the annual national budget. The CPE did not depend on private funds.
2. The CPE's administration was democratically structured along lines in which program designers and teachers regularly consulted with and reported to learners' councils and area committees.

3. The CPE's learning program was sequential, with one educational level leading to another (literacy, primary, secondary, postsecondary, and tertiary).
4. The program's content was intended to be equivalent to but not the same as the content taught in schools. After the initial literacy phase, which was assisted by many community volunteers, adults would access a specially designed curriculum geared to workplace needs and adult interests and maturity.
5. Each level from primary onward included compulsory vocational education and certification that prepared adults for jobs. CPE educators also taught in the vocational education offered in work-based programs: the Farm Schools, the Hotel School, the new Fisheries School, and Grencraft, the new Craft School, as well as in new workplace training for producer cooperatives and for workers constructing the new airport.
6. Successful completion of the secondary level of the program could lead to scholarships for vocational or university education either at home, where the tertiary education level was being expanded, or abroad, most likely in Cuba, which was assisting the Grenadian government through tertiary education scholarships.
7. The political ethos of the program, illustrated in its newly designed textbooks, reflected the government's desire to contribute to the confident and creative reconceptualization of cultural and national identity.
8. The impetus of the revolution led to a high degree of community participation by adult education students in organizing their own CPE programs as well as extracurricular activities in their neighborhoods, including events such as panel discussions, sporting and domino competitions, audiovisual presentations, and so on. (Jules, 1993)

Apart from my research in the 1990s, since then there seems to have been no scholarship that has studied the reinterpretation of adult education in its formal and nonformal dimensions in the 40 years after the revolution. What has been studied, by Laura Perez Gonzalez (2020), is the postschool educational opportunities that now exist for young Grenadian adults seeking vocational training after problematic school experiences, including failure, dropout, or expulsion. Gonzalez examines how these postschool programs are designed and operated by educators, and how young adults experience and respond to them.

The wider historical view that I want to take here observes how the new adult education model forged in the Grenada Revolution disappeared after its collapse, the U.S. invasion, and the resumption of a British style 'Westminster model' of political governance. The CPE was brought to an end, and its sequential pathways, programs, and textbooks were discarded by the postrevolutionary local governments. Formal adult education was taken over by a department within the newly amalgamated Grenada National College, later renamed the T.A. Marryshow Community College. It was redesigned along the lines of the old model common to the rest of the anglophone Caribbean. The focus shifted to the preparation of adults for actual school programs. They were now charged fees for retaking the annual secondary school-leaving exams set by the Caribbean Examinations Council or the British General Certificate of Education. In 1992–1993, there were about 800 students in these programs, mostly people who had attended high school but failed or dropped out of their final exams. Since then, the numbers in these examination streams have continued to increase. Vocational work-preparation programs are also provided, separate from school. The study by Perez Gonzalez (2020) shows that many young adults have benefited from Grenada's sharing in Caribbean-designed programs such as the Caribbean Vocational Qualification, which guides countries in content, assessment, and qualifications for vocational occupations.

In this traditional policy approach, relatively minor attention is given to the most disadvantaged adults, those who seek literacy and the primary level of education—the people who had received the most attention during the revolution. Adult literacy postrevolution was still government-funded, but became a minimal beginners' program involving fewer than a hundred learners, with no provision of specially designed literacy materials. Adult primary education was no longer conceptualized as a program specially designed for maturity and workplace needs, as it was in the revolution. Instead, adults were expected to access the senior primary program of the under-resourced "all-age" schools, designed in colonial times for less privileged adolescents who had been denied entry to secondary schools. The senior primary exam in the 1990s was being taken by up to a hundred adults each year, which was far less than the number needing that level of education.

The features of this model of adult education include a drastic reduction of government funding, a promotion of "user pays" funding in both government and nongovernment programs, the slotting in of adults to the grade school curriculum and its selective examinations as soon as they became sufficiently literate, and a reduction of vocational training attached to workplaces. The strength of the model, from the vantage point of efficiency, is that with minimal cost to the state it provides some level of schooled epistemic literacy for adults who already have basic schooling, so adults can "catch up" with the schooling they missed. But offering adults schooling designed for children and adolescents, especially in societies that suppress political study in schools, is not likely to provide them with opportunities for developing literacies at the level of maturity they deserve—particularly not public literacies. The approach does not provide a free, specifically designed, sequential education process for nonliterate adults—those who are least able to pay. With the ongoing high rate of poverty and unemployment, custom-designed adult education is needed for many groups of adults in Grenada, including groups of women, prisoners, school dropouts, and adults who are functionally nonliterate.

The revolution's establishment of the CPE as a new institution to design, organize, and implement a novel education process was an immense achievement in a region in which most of the newly independent countries, weighed down by coloniality, had not yet tackled the colonial tradition of educational discrimination against the majority. The CPE can be celebrated for its culturally innovative structure and programs (see Jules, 1993), its attention to developing some level of political literacy in these programs, its enrollment of more than four thousand adult learners, and its success in helping over a thousand adults achieve basic literacy as well as postliteracy competencies. Yet, it had weaknesses that should be examined if an effort is to be made to understand the lessons of the model to develop a more appropriate one in the future.

The CPE was able, in the three or so years of its existence, to organize, prepare, and offer two of the three phases of adult education that it designed. Four thousand adults enrolled in Phase 1, the basic literacy program, and about 1,000 adults enrolled in Phase 2, called Adult Primary. Phase 3, Adult Secondary, was planned for 1984. With 1,500 adults out of the 4,000 that enrolled completing the first phase (basic literacy), there was an increase in functional literacy in the population, despite the dropout rate of about two-thirds, a common feature of adult education programs throughout the world (Arnove & Graff, 1992, p. 287). This occurred partly because the CPE structure was more complex and more ambitious than available government resources in the short-lived revolution could handle efficiently. The scale and ambitions of the project compared to limited resources strained both volunteer teachers and economically impoverished learners. It may be that the revolutionary government should have considered making the CPE a statutory body with the independence to invite philanthropic assistance from nongovernmental organizations (NGOs) and other bodies, and to seek funding from more countries than Cuba (which had helped with the production of materials). This would have improved the breadth and depth of the program. The complete dependence of the CPE on the revolutionary state made it vulnerable to being erased with a change of government.

The research has not been done, but it may be that those who dropped out of the CPE, did not, in their local circumstances, have the material opportunity to fulfill the learning goals of a formal "schooled equivalence" program. Jules [1993] points out that some learners demanded that the new program provide them with accredited certification, but the high dropout number suggests that many may have been discouraged by the perceived difficulty of the formal content and assessment aspects of the program. This leads to the reflection that education traditions bound up with stratification are so entrenched that often even the most radical educators (and participants) have little idea of how to change the old hierarchical assumptions and practices inculcated under European colonialism, which had only recently ended. Among these are traditions of prescriptive rather than critical texts, didactic pedagogy based mainly on written text, written examinations, and the necessity of providing learning in sequential, lock-stepped stages similar to those of the formal education system. This "schooled" model of adult education may suit adult learners who are motivated or in relatively favorable circumstances, and the CPE did well in successfully preparing over a thousand adults in the first two phases of the program. But the high dropout rates in Grenada, as in many countries, suggest that the model does not adequately meet the educational needs and conditions of disadvantaged majorities.

Some features of the CPE's "schooled equivalence" program were, perhaps, like pouring new wine into old bottles. New and promising were the elements of radical content, which provided opportunities to discuss revolutionary goals for the society as well as introducing extracts from novels and poetry that celebrated agricultural and other manual workers in different Caribbean countries. Full of potential, also, were the participatory elements in the structure (such as the volunteer teachers), and the strategies designed to provide systematic paths for adult learners to link to vocational or professional education. Old and constraining were the continuation of the didactic, prescriptive educational philosophy particularly unjust for the majorities brought up in a folk tradition rather than a middle-class one. It may be that this explains the low attractiveness, relative to need, and high dropout rates common in adult education programs. Even if adults gain some epistemic and technical/vocational literacy through them, these literacies will likely remain subordinate. They are not the dominant literacies that would enable disadvantaged people to surmount the barriers to social, political, and economic mobility, much less the powerful literacy that can empower them to make structural changes that would remove these barriers. The politically radicalizing and humanist potential of new content and structures is constrained by inadequate building on vernacular literacies and insufficient development of pedagogies combining learner-centeredness and expert facilitation.

It is for this reason that I argue that adult basic education providing individual catch-up school equivalence and job training has inadequate potential for carrying out some of the radicalizing aims of change that challenges inequity as outlined earlier. Popular education based on the development of political and cultural capacities in local communities has greater potential for carrying out such aims. This is not to say that adult basic education is not necessary; it is to say that it needs to be redesigned within the nourishing context of a popular education structure. In the next section I lay the basis for discussing this by considering the strength and limits of popular education as it was experienced in Grenada.

COMMUNITY EDUCATION: CHALLENGES IN DEVELOPING HUMANIST AND PUBLIC LITERACIES

To what extent can the experiences of popular education contribute to transforming the power relations within civil society? Can participants take the opportunities for growth offered to them by leaders who are usually middle class and "run with them" in creative ways that are not necessarily directed? If they could learn this role, and help others to learn it, it would indeed have the potential to become part of a cultural revolution or the kind of "cultural action for freedom" described by Paulo Freire (1972; 2000). Light is thrown on these questions by the attempt during the Grenadian revolution to mobilize a level of popular involvement in community education and social reform that had never been experienced in Grenada, indeed, in the Caribbean, before. This popular education movement was led by the New Jewel Movement (NJM), Grenada's revolutionary political party from which most of the political leaders and members of the government were drawn. In the years of challenging the dictatorial regime that had ruled Grenada in the 1970s, the NJM had established a tradition of educated activism in community-based and workplace-based groups. The People's Revolutionary Government continued and expanded this community education work of the NJM, keeping it outside of educational structures that promoted formal and vocational knowledge—that is, separate from the CPE's literacy and vocational training programs of a quasi-school nature. Since the community education groups involved a broad cross section of the population and combined political and educational aims, I shall refer to them as community associations and to their educational aspect as the popular education process.

There were two categories of community association representing two types of activity. First, communities of citizens gathered to discuss and contribute ideas to local and national goals and policies of transformation. In this category were nationwide peoples' councils (comprising associations called Workers' Parish Councils and Zonal Councils) and the people's budget process in which local communities all over the country met politicians and technocrats to help plan the national budget. Second, interest groups worked for improvements in their particular group, on a national rather than a local scale. These were called mass organizations and were grouped around women, youth, farmers, and trade union members (Coard, 2018; Jules, 1993; Thorndike, 1991). These mass organizations were similar to those in the Cuban and Nicaraguan revolutions (see Samoff, 1991; Torres, 1990).

The political role of the community associations was inextricably linked to their role in developing public and humanist literacy. They were the chief means of giving Grenadians a new voice in national affairs traditionally handled by the government. Through the associations, the broad population got increasingly pulled into an ongoing cultural revolution in an experiential way that involved affect as well as intellect, identity as well as politics.

"Humanist" Literacy and Cultural Identity

The role of the community associations in developing humanist literacy was to contribute to challenging traditional images related to social class roles, gender, and national identity and reshaping them in new ways. For example, the preconceptions about stratified economic roles started to be reshaped. Through the activities of the community associations, all became "workers." Middle-class professionals were seen as intellectual workers, and they frequently met and interacted with manual workers in the same discussion groups. Political and social roles started to be reshaped in that people from different social class groupings had to learn how to interact—cooperating in identifying, prioritizing, and carrying out tasks, listening to and communicating with each other. Most of the members of the community associations would not have attended elite schools and would therefore have been deprived of the chance to acquire skills in the public and humanist literacy domains that are provided for in the curriculum and extracurricular activities in elite schools. The community associations helped give them "public" and humanist knowledge, supplementing the education provided through the school equivalence programs of the CPE, which had their main focus on the epistemic and technical domains of literacy.

The community associations were the main locations in which people could engage with what it meant to develop a self-confident national identity in a global context. Through them, people experienced visits and speeches from famous international figures associated with political transformation, such as Jamaica's Michael Manley, Mozambique's Samora Machel, African American activists Harry Belafonte and Angela Davis, and those associated with cultural transformation such as Barbadian novelist George Lamming and Guyanese poets and writers Martin Carter, Robin Dobreau and Jan Carew. They listened also to their leaders' explanations of international events, and they became associated with campaigns such as fund-raising to assist countries that had experienced natural disasters. In the collectives, Grenadians worked closely with and became friendly with many internationalist workers from other countries in the Caribbean and beyond, who had also joined these groups. Ideas of national identity were increasingly expressed through the cultural activities of the community associations, especially the mass organizations, which were the chief vehicles in the communities for organizing cultural events that publicized the unprecedented outpouring of artistic expression in vernacular Creole poetry, drama, and music that was taking place (see Searle, 1984).

In the sphere of gender identity, it proved necessary to persuade some women as well as many men that women were entitled to equal rights with men. New images of women's social and political roles took shape through the community associations, especially the National Women's Organization (NWO), which at one time had some 8,000 members. There was a long way to go before some men yielded to this challenge, but it started. The NWO played a key part in mobilizing women, regardless of traditional political divisions, to articulate and represent to the government the legal and social changes for women that they wanted (Coard, 2018, pp. 194–198; Franklin, 1988; NJM Women, 1983; Philip-Dowe, 2015). The uneven process of development showed in the fact that the institutional/political advances won by women did not stop sexism. On the one hand, the government passed laws such as those institutionalizing paid maternity leave without loss of job, a minimum wage, and equal pay for women, and those that imposed sanctions on the sexual exploitation of women workers in an attempt to bring this to an end. On the other hand, sexism continued to exist, even in the NJM itself. Male double standards in sexual behavior were rife, and NJM men refused on several occasions to make any concessions to the women in consideration of their extra burden of domestic responsibilities. Further problems of sexism that had to be overcome were male reluctance to take on equivalent responsibilities for the financial support of all their children, and their overwhelming predominance in employment and leadership positions (see Hickling-Hudson, 1999).

The women's confrontation of many spheres of gender inequality was initial and tentative. Little attention was given to reconceptualizing masculinities and femininities. Yet these flaws, together with the problem of a sometimes didactic conception of leadership education, could not blunt the real achievements and the powerful potential of the national women's organization. The NWO showed how a systematic women's movement could substantially increase the strategic power of Grenada's women to make changes benefiting them and the whole society. The foundation for this was laid in the revolution.

"Public" Literacy and Political Participation

Community associations played an enormous role in developing public literacy. Reflection on their work might facilitate adult educators both to appreciate and to move beyond the conceptualization of this dimension of literacy put forward by McCormack, who defines it broadly as "the nature and structure of opinion, political judgement and political argument, the dynamics of political action, the forms of political consciousness, and the way a political community appropriates its past, projects its future, and conceptualises its historical continuity." My involvement in the Grenada process led me to see that public literacy has at least three major aspects. One aspect relates to people's understanding of what governments, institutions, and political parties do in their own and different societies, and how they operate. Another is the development of people's participation, responsibility, and leadership. Another has to do with power relationships, including gender and ethnic relationships, between and among social classes and strata. The development of critical knowledge and competencies in all these aspects is what would lead to a high level of public literacy. Thus, people would develop public literacy by combining a theoretical with a practical understanding of public or political participation in policy-making and implementation.

In the anglophone Caribbean, the traditional political parties, shaped by the British model of parties as electoral vehicles, tend to be hostile to each other—in Jamaica, sometimes to the point of hundreds of murders being committed in the tense run-up to elections. This is a tragic outcome of a neocolonial tradition of political socialization within competing and hostile party organizations. I had witnessed this tragedy in my society, Jamaica, and was struck by the Grenada contrast in which the mass organizations, citizens' councils, and worker education classes sought to involve and unite broad cross-sections of Grenadians in educational, social, and political activity, regardless of their past or current political allegiance. Some mass organizations, such as the National Women's Organization, were more successful than others in achieving this goal of uniting a political cross-section. The National Youth Organization and the Productive Farmers Union, for example, had a reputation of consisting mainly of members and supporters of the NJM.

The community associations in the Grenada Revolution help us to understand the three dimensions I propose for public literacy. Involvement in them drew people into seeing how government institutions operate (at least in their own country), into participating in this work, and in starting to change the power relationships of class and gender. The associations were the vehicles that engaged people in shaping structures that could facilitate change: speaking at meetings, pressing demands, becoming leaders. This affected both privileged and less privileged social groups. For working-class and agricultural workers, the associations provided an opportunity for participation open to everyone, not just those who had registered as adult learners in the CPE. As far as middle-class people were concerned, the community associations pulled more of them into political activity than is usual in Caribbean multiparty systems. Workers' parish councils consisted of regular meetings between NJM politicians, government officers, and local communities to discuss their needs, as well as to shape policy ideas in the context of social and economic developments in the nation. At one meeting at which I was present in the local audience, for example, the manager of Grenlec, the newly established state electric company, explained the problems of the old electric equipment and the policies of repair and development. At another, the government town planner explained some of the present regulations and future national plans for land use (see Hudson, 1991). These representatives would then have to answer the people's questions, write down their concerns, and respond to any challenges. At each meeting, the NJM leader who was present would have to explain to the people what progress had been made on attending to matters brought up at a previous meeting. A workers' parish council meeting had the right to request in advance the presence of any government official it wished to question.

Within a year, attendance at these parish meetings had grown so large that there was no hall big enough to hold the hundreds who wanted to get in. The workers' parish councils were then subdivided into zonal councils, the zone being a cluster of villages in a parish. At the high point of development, there were about 36 zonal councils. Although the government was willing to listen to and assist with local suggestions for change, funds were scarce, and it became clear that little could be achieved without a national volunteer effort. The importance of volunteer donations of time and effort was highlighted. Taken together, the CPE, the parish and zonal councils, and the mass organizations involved thousands of Grenadians in voluntary work and activities that not only started to raise their levels of education but also mobilized their hope and power to confront poverty and begin the long and complex process of working to eradicate it.

The political activity that took place in the parish and zonal councils and the mass organizations ensured the success of the revolutionary government's "People's Budget," unique and unprecedented in the Caribbean. This transformed the annual, traditionally secretive, and technocratic exercise of making a national budget, controlled by the Ministry of Finance, into a planning operation that directly involved the participation of the masses of the people. Launched in 1982 and repeated in 1983, the People's Budget exercise was an extended procedure lasting about three months, during which the national economic plan was presented to communities all over the country for their study, criticisms, and recommendations. Then it was modified in the light of this interaction between politicians, technical advisers, and people:

> First, expenditure requests from all government departments were studied by the Ministry of Finance, headed by Bernard Coard. A preliminary draft was then submitted to the PRG Cabinet for discussion. This was followed by a period during which officials from the ministry went before the trade unions, mass organizations, zonal and parish councils to discuss the draft with them. The high point . . . was the national conference on the economy, which was attended by delegates from all the mass organizations. Breaking up into workshops devoted to specific areas of the economy, the delegates made detailed comments and criticisms on the draft proposals. The budget then went back to the Ministry of Finance for final revisions and then to the cabinet for approval. Finally, a detailed report was made to the people by the ministry and an explanation was given as to which recommendations had been rejected and why. (Ambursley & Dunkerley, 1984, p. 38; Coard, 2018, pp. 283–287)

Personal involvement in these activities is at the basis of my understanding of them as being a deeply educative process. Like most of my colleagues implementing the new teacher education program (NISTEP), I attended all of the large meetings of the workers' parish council in the parish of St. George's. We also went to many of the smaller zonal council meetings in our neighborhood to discuss local community matters and the draft of the national budget. It was possible to merge anonymously with the crowded audience at the Workers' Parish Council meetings and simply listen with interest to the proceedings in which government officials explained national programs, answered questions, responded to criticism, and noted suggestions from members of the crowd. But mere listening was not possible at the smaller zonal council meetings. These involved our neighbors and the people in our local district, and everyone engaged in a lively discussion.

In our small groups studying the budget proposals, we had to help each other come to terms with economic concepts like the GDP, inflation rate, real growth, balance of trade, the social wage, and many others. We sent our suggestions to the government and attended the final budget conference. The climax was the realization that what was eventually adopted as the national budget was the product of a unique three-month process of consultation involving a broad spectrum of social interests and strata. Public technocrats had been required to describe the economic situation in accessible language; and the people, in turn, were challenged to grapple with national development issues (Jules, 1992, pp. 183, 327).

The third major aspect of public literacy relates to power relationships between privileged and less privileged social strata. Community associations went beyond the CPE's circumscribed sphere of teaching and learning, in which middle-class teachers had, compared to the learners, demonstrably more power derived from their high-status cultural capital and their dominant role in shaping the CPE materials and controlling the pedagogy. A contribution of the community associations to public literacy, then, was their role in gradually reshaping this traditional, stratified relationship. The associations were a forum in which people who had been marginalized learned to recognize and value their contribution to shaping change, and middle-class people started learning how to share power. The mutual interaction involved in the community and political work was a process in which teachers and other educated volunteers learned immensely from the people they were teaching. A teacher involved in the process of community consultations on the preparation of the national budget remarked that it was "an eye-opener" to realize that "these people who did not go to a secondary school and did not have a degree had such good ideas" (Jules, 1992, p. 327). Angus Smith, a young Grenadian who at the age of 23 was appointed accountant general in the Ministry of Finance, described how his development was enhanced by the process of interacting with community groups in discussing the People's Budget:

> Like many others, I was surprised at the high level of consciousness of the people throughout the budget process, at their knowledge of general affairs and their eagerness for involvement. Numerous practical and useful ideas were constantly coming out, things that technicians like ourselves would never have thought about, things which gave us a much wider perspective of the issues and ideas in the minds of the people around the country. . . . The experience brought home to us the need for our technicians to have a much wider view of things, to look at the country from the widest possible angle, and not just from behind a desk. Everybody in our society has a viewpoint and we must pool all these together. For us it was genuinely exciting to be able to translate these budget figures that pass across our desks every day into the living reality of people's lives, and doing so learn more and more about how our people live. (Smith in Searle & Rojas, 1982, pp. 56–58)

The community associations showed the importance of the language question. A wider range of middle-class people other than literacy teachers were involved in them and had to start to grope for an appropriate form of communication—perhaps not in the vernacular Creole, as some critics felt should be the case (Devonish, 2007), but at least in the sense of struggling to get away from jargon and elitist language. This was particularly evident in the People's Budget process. Ministry of Finance technocrats were given the responsibility of compiling a book that set out information about the economy and the budget issues for the community meetings at which they were to discuss the issues. They sought help from educators at the Teachers College in doing this, and the budget books were compiled only after these educators had helped them make the language more direct and clear. Using the books assisted the discussion groups, and the discussion groups forced Ministry of Finance facilitators to clarify concepts even further.

The community associations had immense democratic potential, but they also had problems associated with being at the beginning of a change process. They were to a large extent led by members of the NJM, although local, nonparty leaders were starting to emerge. Some leaders of local or workplace groups tended to expect members to listen to sessions based on prepared texts that sought to promote the messages of the revolution. A didactic communication process could characterize occasions when the leaders sought to implement classes of "political education" based on their often inflexible images of socialist vision. This sometimes occurred although these same group leaders had gained a lot of knowledge from listening to the people with whom they were interacting in community work. That is, some had not yet learned to combine theory with daily life.

In a paper analyzing some of the weaknesses of the NJM leaders, Charles Mills (2010) argues that many of them seemed to regard their political analysis of the Grenadian situation as the only correct interpretation, based as it was on the "scientific thought" of Marxism. This argument holds that NJM philosophy, despite some strengths, did not take enough into account the contribution of local Caribbean thought and popular traditions. If Mills is right that some NJM leaders tended to push a single, prescriptive voice rather than strive for the powerful synergies of blending several visions of change, this may throw light on areas of weakness in many revolutions, including the one in Grenada. The Grenadian revolutionary party's internal conflicts over strategy, leadership structure, and pace of reform were not resolved because each faction, convinced it had the correct view, took this to the point of armed struggle against each other. Too late, Bernard Coard, the PRG's Minister of Finance and one of the imprisoned survivors of the struggle, reflected on how the potential power of the community associations could have been further tapped:

> I have thought, often, over the past five years what would have happened if either the minority or the majority faction had taken the matter in a principled manner to the masses. And what better fora for doing it than the Zonal Parish and Workers, Women, Youth . . . Assemblies [and] meetings? With copies of all relevant minutes printed and distributed to the people; with representatives of both trends in the leadership putting their view forward to the people in the Assemblies . . . and being questioned and grilled by the people in return and hearing their views . . . what better way could there have been for resolving our differences? (Coard, 1989, pp. 10–11)

Comparing the revolution's popular community education process with the traditional approach resumed after the revolution throws light on the significant issues that need to be considered in striving for the improvement of popular education. The new community structures in the revolution sought what should be the basic thrust of popular education—to produce a reorganization of the social basis of power in the communities, and on this foundation, in the overall society. Marginalized people were educated into adopting more powerful ways of behaving politically—articulating demands, building organizations to carry out specified purposes, exchanging views with educated government officials and party politicians, holding these people accountable for the carrying out of their promises, uniting across the partisan divisions of the past. The associations reflected the strengths of genuinely participatory learning and leadership. The next step would have been for educators to find a way of encouraging adult learners to blend their political participation and their formal study. However, the potential for this kind of change was weakened by flaws in the wider social context that contradicted the rhetoric and promise of people's power, for example, by the tendency of some leaders to resort to didactic ways of interacting with grassroots people, by a lack of electoral processes, and by the secrecy of a Marxist-Leninist style of centralist political organization that limited the public accountability of national leaders (Meeks, 1993, pp. 153, 160–165).

In the traditional British style, the old political model was resumed after the revolution and the electoral processes reverted to a competitive government-versus-opposition structure. This allows for a multitude of rival political parties (in Grenada at least nine political parties were jostling for power in the decade after the 1983 U.S. invasion) but provides little potential for cooperation or consensus (Ferguson, 1990; Grenade, 2015). Popular education is on a minimal local scale rather than a national scale interacting with social change. Instead of being multiclass, it is directed by the educated classes toward the economically disadvantaged. It takes the form of raising awareness about specific, narrowly defined social problems, and carries out some pressure-group advocacy through religious groups, drama groups, and fragmented women's groups. Limited political information-giving, such as talks about current events, occurs in some groups, for example, in Grenadian groups funded by the Agency for Rural Transformation, an NGO that was one of the few institutions established during the revolution that survived. In general, there is minimal development of education that fosters political and humanist literacy, encourages public and community voice, or facilitates collective political activism for change. The challenge for the future is to find a way of balancing an open electoral process with the kind of popular community education that promotes participatory democracy—collective activism for meaningful community development on a national scale—and through this, the production of powerful, transformational knowledge.

WAYS FORWARD FOR ADULT EDUCATION: GLOBAL EXPERIMENTS

A comparative view of Caribbean experiments in adult basic and popular education in the Grenada revolution and in traditional polities provides postcolonial societies with clues about how adult education can seek ways forward out of the model that consigns it to being the minimalist educational channel at the bottom of the social hierarchy. UNESCO's Institute for Lifelong Learning also engages with this question, urging and assisting countries across the world to commit to meaningful equity goals in adult learning and education as well as to global citizenship education. This broadens the context of my discussion in this chapter of the importance of analyzing sociopolitical dimensions of adult education to enable evaluation and planning for its improvement. UNESCO identifies three key domains of learning and skills of central importance for adult education: literacy and basic skills; continuing education and vocational skills; and liberal, popular and community education and citizenship skills. It also highlights the great potential of information and communication technologies to promote inclusion and equity for adult learners, including people with disabilities and other marginalized groups. It supports regular reports providing a comprehensive picture of the global state of adult education, showing how far it is being implemented in over 150 countries to support health and well-being, employment and the labor market, and social, civic, and community life (see UNESCO, 2016; 2021).

For the researcher, such reports make more sense when they are put into analytical context. Understanding the context is the foundation for evaluating and developing adult education. What pushed forward educational change in the Grenada revolution was a combination of the political goals of a socialist-influenced vision and the achievement of successful economic changes that increasingly required skilled and educated workers. Such workers are even more urgently required in today's context (Hickling-Hudson, 2004), as postindustrial changes and new trade blocs are making the neocolonial, dependent economic model redundant. A socialist-oriented path based on the classical model of revolution may not be viable in most of the postcolonial world, but new models are needed since the answer does not lie in neoliberal capitalist structures such as the ones that continue in the Caribbean (see Chomsky & Waterstone, 2021; Farrell, 1993; Sivanandan, 1989; Sutton, 2006; Thomas, 1993; 2001). In these, only a minority elite is highly developed for the new opportunities in the high-tech and global markets. The majority remains in an exploited or marginalized position. Furthermore, the kind of dependent capitalism experienced in many postcolonial countries makes tackling the existential crisis of ecological destruction politically problematic, with inadequate pushback against the "massive commercial assaults on our life support systems" (Monbiot, 2021; Shiva, 1999; 2001). Countries of the Global South are in a weak position, also, concerning the burgeoning deployment of social media, which can spread both factual and life-saving information, and dangerous disinformation based on cynical lies which are used by political partisans to "divide, dominate, disorient, and ultimately demoralize the people on the other side" (see Graham, 2021; Helsper, 2021; Wehner, 2021). Changemakers need to put continuing and united pressure on the international economic system for altering structures and processes that maintain injustice for impoverished countries.

Against this background of immense local and global challenges, comprehensive rethinking is needed about the structure, goals, and practices of adult education. Several edited books on adult education explore these dimensions with analyses of philosophies, models, and programs in various countries (e.g., English & Mayo, 2012; Jarvis, 2009; Mayo, 2013; Milana & Nesbit, 2015). Educational change to meet equity goals has to be an integral part of any vision of interrelated political, economic, and cultural activism: no section of the population can be omitted from this. Current developments in online learning can facilitate this process. Some governments can be pushed into supporting the kinds of changes needed if articulate social groups among the population are informed and motivated enough to push them. Social alliances in civil society could more effectively engage in local action for change if they joined forces with global transformative movements such as those for ecologically sustainable development, feminism, literacy, and media reform. Local action could become more effective if based on the kind of community action research dubbed "Thirdworldist Participatory

Action Research" by Masalam and Kapoor (2021), documenting this process in Indonesia, and described by Arnove (1989) in his evaluation of the effective use of aid funding in Costa Rica, Honduras, and Guatemala. The essence is to work within the progressive tradition of popular education which, although not necessarily involving formal skills of reading and writing, nevertheless creates a participatory education approach that enables community organizations in impoverished and marginalized communities to define their problems systematically, and design and implement action strategies for tackling them.

This approach reflects the philosophy popularized by Paulo Freire of the learner as subject rather than as the object into which predetermined content is "banked." In 1980, the second year of the Grenada Revolution, Freire led a two-week workshop for teachers, in which he and his team modeled how education could become "communication praxis," combining the voices of learners and teachers into a cycle of social analysis, social activism, and reflection (Hickling-Hudson, 1988). This must become part of the philosophical base of teachers and learners engaged in transformative educational change. Another essential for reconceptualizing literacy is the incorporation of a feminist and "green" perspectives that challenge the older concept of integrating women in development. Critiquing the socially and ecologically disastrous impact of the present development model of international capitalism, such perspectives search for gender-sensitive and sustainable development (Antrobus, 1993).

Brazil provides an important example of grassroots adult education change through the Landless Workers Movement (MST), one of the largest social movements in Latin America, globally famous for its success over the last 35 years in occupying land, winning land rights, and developing alternative economic enterprises for over a million landless workers. The MST has linked education reform to its vision for agrarian reform. It has carried out life-changing initiatives such as "itinerant schools, multi-level learning settings in tents, popular education initiatives with adults and younger ones learning together in intergenerational spaces and much lauded landmarks in social movement education as the Escola Nacional Florestan Fernandez" (Mayo, 2021). It also strives to exert influence on publicly funded schools and universities by helping some of them develop pedagogical practices that foster activism, direct democracy, and collective forms of work. The schools and the movement support each other in the recruitment of new activists and the increase of technical knowledge (Tarlau, 2019). This struggle for an alternative approach has an impact on political power. Another Brazilian example is that of the Cajamar Institute, founded by workers to promote opportunities for social analysis in a region of northeastern Brazil dominated by plantation agriculture. Paulo Freire was elected president of the council of this institute in 1986. He describes how workers managed to acquire a 120-room building that used to be a motel and created there the Cajamar Institute as an organization for the "training of the working class, peasants and the urban workers under their responsibility." Seminars and courses were offered to workers, some on a weekend basis. Worker institutes such as Cajamar could play the role of allowing men and women to achieve the distance from their daily work that facilitates studying society theoretically, "in order to understand the reason for the struggle and to make better methods for this struggle, and how to choose" (Horton & Freire, 1990).

Adult education organizers, to achieve equity goals, usually cannot rely on the cash-strapped, timid, neoliberal, conservative governments in the current political context of the Global South. Sometimes, the best hopes of development lie outside of government control or interference, and beyond the limited horizons of narrow, instrumentalist adult education institutions. One of the most famous independent NGOs with an adult education component is BRAC (the Bangladesh Rural Advancement Committee), developed by the people of Bangladesh since the 1970s. Starting as a national NGO dedicated to empowering millions of impoverished people to bring about change in their own lives through microfinance and nonformal education, BRAC is now an international organization helping other communities in at least nine countries of Africa and Asia to do the same. The important role of international NGOs such as Greenpeace, Oxfam, and World Learning for International Development has expanded in response to the challenges of globalization, as discussed by Hoff and Hickling-Hudson (2011) and Milana and Nesbit, (2015). In the Caribbean, examples of small NGOs include the Social Action Centre in Jamaica and SERVOL in Trinidad (Ellis & Ramsay, 2000). They could form the basis of a potentially strong alternative adult education movement.

Existing and new groups could be strengthened by interacting with each other regionally for systematic knowledge exchange and development and by drawing on the support of international institutions and networks. This networking would be a source of empowerment and independence outside of the parameters of state control. Yet state-led initiatives can sometimes be a catalyst for development through dynamic structures for lifelong learning. The potential for this seems strong. For example, the adult education structure in St. Lucia, established at the turn of this century, was reengineered to prepare adults with educational, practical, civic, and cultural skills and with capacities for self-directed learning. Courses were systematically articulated in a new accreditation system that linked to school and tertiary education. Course materials were designed by individuals, groups, and agencies on the island, thus enhancing content responsiveness and content flexibility. Literacy in folk culture and Kweyol (Creole), as well as global culture and English, were promoted (Jules, 1999; Nwenmely, 1999). Trinidad and Tobago is another Caribbean nation with a state-run adult education division that appears to cater well for adult learners, both by collaborating with nongovernment agencies and by operating nationwide centers offering a range of classes from basic to workplace education, from civic affairs to leisure and family-life education (Ellis & Ramsay, 2000).

An urgent need in adult education is that of training in modern communications technology, especially the internet and social media, that can enhance local and international activist links. In a study of this kind of communication in Pacific societies, Harris (2007) points out that the process of message-making, rather than the finished product, is essential to empowerment, and emphasizes the capacity of radio, video, and the internet to bring the voices of the marginalized into the public sphere. Training adult learners in skills of radio production and community radio is particularly important for impoverished communities that depend largely on the radio for information and entertainment (O'Donnell, 1991, pp. 110–141).

Reconceptualized literacies and pedagogy need not depend on the kind of text-based, school-imitative adult education model taken for granted in many postcolonial countries. Adult education can be creatively located as one component of economic, cultural, artistic, or political projects, as discussed in examples that I have analyzed in Jamaica, Grenada, and Australia (Hickling-Hudson, 2014). It does not have to take the form of a unitary national system that is a subordinate shadow of the centrally designed curriculum levels, texts, and examinations of schooling. Each project could have an education team working collaboratively with participants to design learning experiences related to the project, to levels of education, to aspirations, and to other needs that may be expressed. Methods and ideas do need to be coordinated between projects, but in such a way that there is an enriching relationship between local and central concerns in a search for effective socioeconomic, political, and cultural development.

CONCLUSION : LITERACIES AND EDUCATIONAL CHANGE IN THE POSTCOLONIAL SPACE

In the postcolonial space provided by a process of change such as occurred in the Grenada Revolution, educators in some countries have forged new, experimental pathways for adult education. Evaluating such cases of adult education would benefit from utilizing the analytical tools proposed in this chapter, with the researcher asking: what spaces for change emerge from the sociopolitical and economic context? What kinds of literacies can be identified in structures, curricula, and activities? What is the position of each type of literacy along a continuum of subordinate to powerful? This goes beyond documenting the why, how, and what of change. It would explore the epistemologies underpinning the new adult education system, wrestling with questions of how far the change process has been able to supersede the constraining knowledge of coloniality and Eurocentric modernity. All this would be a foundation for comparative case studies that could inform policy and practice to move the sector forward. This kind of case study documentation and evaluative analysis of experimental pathways would comprise an important conceptual base for those seeking transformative adult education.

This chapter has discussed the significance of the new model of adult education forged in a few short years in the Grenada Revolution of 1979–1983. The Centre for Popular Education brought educational benefits seeking to meet in a novel way the needs of thousands of historically disadvantaged adult learners, notwithstanding the flaws of design inevitable in a new process. The community associations that complemented and interacted with the CPE had an immense impact on raising political and humanist literacies, seen in the popular outpourings of creole expressive culture, and the collaboration between people and government to articulate and meet new political demands. After the collapse of the revolution, adult education reverted to the traditional neocolonial model that continues to neglect the majority of disadvantaged adults, providing catch-up schooling only for that minority who can negotiate the cost and qualification gateposts to access the system.

At the stage of development that characterized the CPE educators during the Grenadian revolution, educational transformation tended to be seen as combining socialist ideals of celebrating worker or peasant roles and culture with middle-class interpretations of epistemic literacy. Were a transformative program to be developed now, it would have to expand equity goals to include educational respect for orality, folk discourse, and the border-crossing flexibility that empower learners to experiment with a range of perspectives and learning experiences. Popular education of the type experimented with in the Grenadian community associations has strong potential for building humanist literacy as the foundation of a self-confident cultural identity, without which few challenges to negative aspects of tradition can be mounted. This is the first step toward rewriting epistemic literacy for most postcolonial countries in which the literacy of the folk roots has been subordinated. Fashioning epistemic literacy anew requires blending a people's literacy with postcolonial epistemological advances such as those contained in the work of Caribbean scholars C. L. R. James, George Beckford, and Walter Rodney, and Brazilian scholar Paulo Freire, to name a few. It may well be, as Devonish (2007) argues, that validation of vernacular or Creole literacy for serious study rather than informal communication and entertainment is essential for this.

The "way forward" examples discussed in this chapter give insights into how adult and popular or community education, particularly in impoverished countries, can facilitate the development of literacies for tackling material and cultural problems simultaneously. A combination of the literacies proposed would be needed for adult learners to utilize cutting-edge media to promote the best of local culture, design small-scale enterprises that suit both local and global niche markets, seize work opportunities with international concerns while protecting worker rights and the environment, utilize governments and international agencies while not relying on them, and struggle against hegemonic regimes of the Global North for national control of the region's resources. Such goals require crossing boundaries of class, gender, and location in sharing and extending knowledge. They can be better sought by collective networks of like-minded people operating globally and locally. To utilize this range of approaches, it would be more necessary than ever to draw on and rework the best of the changes implemented by the Centre for Popular Education and the community associations of the Grenada Revolution to overcome the neocolonial tradition of dominant, exclusionary literacies for ruling minorities and subordinate literacies for working-class majorities.

NOTES

1. Both writers of these doctoral dissertations are Caribbean educators who worked in Grenada during the revolution and have had extensive experience in education in other countries of the Caribbean and elsewhere. The dissertations discuss education in the Grenada Revolution in the national and Caribbean context of the period.

2. Jamaica in the 1970s and Guyana from 1979 to 1990 were the other English-speaking Caribbean countries that experimented with variants of a socialist orientation. Economic and ideological weaknesses as well as "great power" hostility meant that the approaches could not be sustained. See "National Experiments: The Radical Options," in Clive Thomas, *The Poor and the Powerless: Economic Policy and Change in the Caribbean* (Monthly Review Press, 1988), 210–237, 251–264.

3. There is an area of confusion in accounts that assume that the CPE organized all aspects of popular adult learning under its umbrella. In fact, the CPE was responsible for organizing adult literacy, school equivalent programs, vocational education programs attached to workplaces, and some community events. It was the political leadership that was responsible for community associations such as the Parish and Zonal Councils, the National Women's Organization (now), and the National Youth Organization (NYO). However, elements of popular, informal education took place in both the CPE and in these community associations, and of course, many of the same people participated in both. So there was a crossover of cultural and civic learning in both.

REFERENCES

Ambursley, F., & Dunkerly, J. (1984) *Grenada: Whose freedom?* Latin American Bureau.

Antrobus, P. (1993). Gender issues in Caribbean development. In S. Lalta & M. Freckleton (Eds.), *Caribbean economic development: The first generation.* Ian Randle Publishers.

Arnove, R. (1989). *An evaluation of the Program of Education for Participation (PEP).* United States Development Agency, Bureau of Latin America and the Caribbean.

Arnove, R., & Graff, H. (1992). National literacy campaigns in historical and comparative perspective: Legacies, lessons, issues. In R. Arnove, P. Altbach, & G. Kelly (Eds.) *Emergent issues in education: Comparative perspectives.* State University of New York Press.

Bray, M., Adamson, B., & Mason, M. (Eds.). (2007). *Comparative education research: Approaches and methods.* Comparative Education Research Centre, University of Hong Kong.

Chomsky, N. (1999). *Profit over people: Neoliberalism and the global order.* Seven Stories Press.

Chomsky, N., & Waterstone, M. (2021). *Consequences of capitalism: Manufacturing discontent and resistance.* Hamish Hamilton Publishers.

Christie, P. (2021). Colonial palimpsests in schooling: Tracing continuity and change in South Africa. *Postcolonial Directions in Education, 10*(1), 51–79.

Coard, B. (2017). *The Grenada revolution: What really happened?* (Vol. 1). McDermott Publishing.

Coard, B. (2018). *Forward ever: Journey to a new Grenada.* (Vol. 2). McDermott Publishing.

Coard, B. (1989). *Village and workers, women, farmers and youth assemblies during the Grenada revolution: Their genesis, evolution, and significance.* Karia Press.

Coloma, R. S. (Ed.). (2009). *Postcolonial challenges in education.* Peter Lang.

Cushion, S., & Bartholomew, D. (2018). *By our own hands: A people's history of the Grenada revolution.* Caribbean Labour Solidarity. http://cls-uk.org.uk/wp-content/uploads/2018/10/Pamphlet-compressed.pdf

Devonish, H. (2007). *Language and liberation: Creole language politics in the Caribbean.* Arawak Publications.

Ellis, P., & Ramsay, A. (2000). *Adult education in the Caribbean at the turn of the century.* (pp. 136–154). Office of the UNESCO Representative in the Caribbean.

English, L., & Mayo, P. (2012). *Learning with adults: A critical pedagogical introduction.* Springer.

Enslin, P. (2017). Postcolonialism and education. *Oxford Research Encyclopaedia of Education.* Oxford University Press.

Farrell, T. (1993). Some notes towards a strategy for economic transformation. In S. Lalta & M. Freckleton (Eds.). *Caribbean economic development* (pp. 330–342). Ian Randle Publishers.

Ferguson, J. (1990). *Revolution in reverse.* Latin American Bureau.

Ferguson, T. (2000). Social disintegration in the context of adjustment and globalisation: The Caribbean experience. In K. Hall & D. Benn (Eds.), *Contending with destiny: The Caribbean in the 21st century* (pp. 185-195). Ian Randle Publishers.

Franklin, D. (1988). *The role of women in the struggle for social and political change in Grenada, 1979–1983*. B.A. dissertation, University of the West Indies.

Freire, P. (1972/2018). *Pedagogy of the oppressed*. Penguin.

Freire, P. (2000). *Cultural action for freedom*. Harvard Education Press.

Gee, J. (1991). What is literacy? And discourse systems and aspirin bottles: On literacy. In C. Mitchell & K. Weiler (Eds.), *Rewriting literacy: Culture and the discourse of the other* (pp. 3-12). Bergin and Garvey.

Gonsalves, R. (2015) The spirit and ideas of Maurice Bishop are alive in our Caribbean civilization. In W. Grenade (Ed.), *The Grenada revolution: Reflections and lessons* (pp. 264–274). University Press of Mississippi.

Graham, D. (2021, July 10). The rise of anti-history. *The Atlantic*.

Grenade, W. (2015). Exploring transitions in party politics in Grenada. In W. Grenade (Ed.), *The Grenada revolution: Reflections and Lessons* (pp. 241–263). University Press of Mississippi.

Grenade, W. (Ed.). (2015). *The Grenada Revolution: Reflections and lessons*. University Press of Mississippi.

Harris, U. S. (2007). Community informatics and the power of participation. *Pacific Journalism Review*, 13(2), 29–45.

Heine, J. (Ed.) (1991). *A revolution aborted: The lessons of Grenada*. University of Pittsburgh Press.

Helsper, E. (2021). *The digital disconnect: The social causes and consequences of digital inequalities*. Sage.

Hickling-Hudson, A. (1986). *In-service teacher education in Grenada 1981–1983: Case study of a problem-solving strategy*. Master of Arts dissertation, University of the West Indies.

Hickling-Hudson, A. (1988). Towards communication praxis: Reflections on the pedagogy of Paulo Freire and educational change in Grenada. *Journal of Education*, 170(2), 9–38.

Hickling-Hudson, A. (1995). *Literacy and literacies in Grenada: A study of adult education in the revolution and after*. PhD dissertation, University of Queensland.

Hickling-Hudson, A. (1999). Experiments in political literacy: Caribbean women and feminist education. *Journal of Education and Development in the Caribbean*, 3(1).

Hickling-Hudson, A. (2004). Caribbean "knowledge societies": Dismantling neo-colonial barriers in the age of globalisation. *Compare*, 34(3), 293–300.

Hickling-Hudson, A. (2010). Curriculum in postcolonial contexts. In B. McGraw, E. Baker, & P. Peterson (Eds.), *International encyclopedia of education* (3rd Ed.; pp. 299–305). Elsevier Science.

Hickling-Hudson, A. (2012). Grenada, education, revolution. In R. Lewis (Ed.), *Caribbean reasonings: Caribbean political activism, essays in honour of Richard Hart* (pp. 227–253). Ian Randle Publishers.

Hickling-Hudson, A. (2014). Striving for a better world: Lessons from Freire in Grenada, Jamaica and Australia. *International Review of Education*, 60(4), 523–543.

Hickling-Hudson, A., Matthews, J., & Woods, A. (2004). Education, Postcolonialism and Disruptions. In A. Hickling-Hudson, J. Matthews, & A. Woods (Eds.), *Disrupting preconceptions: Postcolonialism and education* (pp. 1–18). Post Pressed Publishers.

Hoff, L., & Hickling-Hudson, A. (2011). The role of international non-governmental organisations in promoting adult education for social change: A research agenda. *International Journal of Educational Development*, 31(2), 197–195.

Horton, M., & Freire, P. (1990). *We make the road by walking: Conversations on education and social change* (pp. 213–214). Temple University Press.

Hudson, B. (1991). Physical planning in the Grenada revolution: Achievement and legacy. *Third World Planning Review*, 13(2), 179–190.

Jarvis, P. (2009). (Ed.). *The Routledge international handbook of lifelong learning*. Routledge.

Jules, D. (1992). *Education and Social Transformation in Grenada*. PhD dissertation, University of Wisconsin.

Jules, D. (1993). The challenge of popular education in the Grenada revolution. In C. Lankshear & P. McLaren (Eds.), *Critical literacy: Policy, praxis and the postmodern*. State University of New York Press.

Jules, D. (1999). *Adult and continuing education in St. Lucia: Addressing global transformation and the new millennium*. Ministry of Education, Human Resource Development, Youth and Sports.

LaBelle, T., & Verhine, R. E. (1975). Nonformal education and occupational stratification: Implications for Latin America. *Harvard Educational Review*, 45(2), 161–190.

Lankshear, C., Gee, J., Knobel, M., & Searle, C. (1997). *Changing literacies*. Open University Press.

Lewis, P., Williams, G., & Clegg, P. (Eds.). (2015). *Grenada: Revolution and invasion*. University of the West Indies Press.

Mandle, J. R., & Mandle, J. D. (2020). The Coards and the Grenada revolution: Review article. *New West Indian Guide* [Nieuwe West-Indische Gids], 94(3–4), 293–299.

Masalam, H., & Kapoor, D. (2021). Third Worldist Participatory Action Research (PAR), Development Dispossession (DD) and learning in indigenous and peasant struggles in Indonesia. *Postcolonial Directions in Education*, 10(1), 103–138.

Mayo, P. (2013). *Learning with adults: A reader*. Springer.

Mayo, P. (2021). Review of Rebecca Tarlau's occupying schools, occupying land: how the landless workers movement transformed Brazilian education. *Postcolonial Directions in Education*, 10(1), 182–187.

Monbiot, G. (2021, April 7). Seaspiracy shows why we must treat fish not as seafood, but as wildlife. *The Guardian*.

McCormack, R. (1991). Framing the field: Adult literacies and the future. In F. Christie et al. (Eds.), *Teaching English literacy in the pre-service preparation of teachers*. Northern Territory University.

Meeks, B. (1993). *Caribbean revolutions and revolutionary theory*. Macmillan.

Meeks, B. (2015). Grenada once again: Revisiting the 1983 crisis and collapse of the Grenada revolution. In W. Grenade (Ed.), *The Grenada revolution: Reflections and lessons* (pp. 87–113). University Press of Mississippi.

Milana, M., & Nesbit, T. (Eds.). (2015). *Global perspectives on adult education and learning policy*. Palgrave Macmillan.

Mills, C. (2010). Getting out of the cave: Tension between democracy and elitism in Marx's theory of cognitive liberation. In C. Mills (Ed.), *Radical theory, Caribbean reality* (pp. 128–163). University of the West Indies Press. First published in *Social and Economic Studies*, 39(1) (March 1990), 1–50.

NJM Women. (1983). *Proposals for women with children within the NJM*. Report for the New Jewel Movement, Grenada.

Nwenmely, H. (1999). Language policy and planning in St. Lucia: Stagnation or change? *Language and Education*, 13(4), 269–279.

O'Donnell, P. (1991). *Death, dreams, and dancing in Nicaragua*. Australian Broadcasting Corporation.

Perez Gonzalez, L. (2020) "Second chance" education: redefining youth development in Grenada. *Postcolonial Directions in Education*, 9 (2), 226-271.

Philip-Dowe, N. (2015). Women in the Grenada revolution, 1979–1983. In P. Lewis, G. Williams, & P. Clegg (Eds.), *Grenada: Revolution and invasion* (pp. 45–80). University of the West Indies Press.

Puri, S. (2014). *The Grenada revolution in the Caribbean present. Operation urgent memory*. Palgrave Macmillan.

Rizvi, F. (2007). Postcolonialism and globalization in education. *Cultural Studies, Critical Methodologies*, 7(3), 256–263.

Samoff, J. (Ed.). (1991). Education and socialist (R)Evolution. Special issue, *Comparative Education Review*, 35(1).

Scott, D. (2014). *Omens of adversity: Tragedy, time, memory, justice*. Duke University Press.

Searle, C. (1984). *Words unchained: Language and revolution in Grenada*. Zed Books.

Shiva, V. (1999). *Biopiracy: The plunder of nature and knowledge*. South End Press.

Shiva, V. (2001). Globalization and poverty. In V. Bennholdt-Thomsen, N. Faraclas, & C. Von Werlhof (Eds.), *There is an alternative: Subsistence and worldwide resistance to corporate globalization* (pp. 57–66). Zed Books.

Searle, C., & Rojas, D. (1982). *To construct from morning: Making the people's budget in Grenada* (pp. 56–58). Fedon Press.

Sivanandan, A. (1989). New circuits of imperialism. *Race and Class*, 30(4).

Sutton, P. (2006). Caribbean development: An overview. *New West Indian Guide [Nieuwe West-Indische Gids]*, 80(1–2), 45–62.

Tarlau, R. (2019) *Occupying schools, occupying land. How the landless workers movement transformed Brazilian education*. Oxford University Press.

Thomas, C. (1988). *The poor and the powerless: Economic policy and change in the Caribbean* (pp. 210–237, 251–264). Monthly Review Press.

Thomas, C. (1993). Alternative development models for the Caribbean. In S. Lalta & M. Freckleton (Eds.), *Caribbean economic development: The first generation*. Ian Randle Publishers.

Thomas, C. (2001). On reconstructing a political economy of the Caribbean. In B. Meeks & F. Lindhal (Eds.), *New Caribbean thought: A reader*. University of the West Indies Press.

Thorndike, T. (1991). People's power in theory and practice. In J. Heine (Ed.), *A revolution aborted: The lessons of Grenada* (pp. 29–50). University of Pittsburgh Press.

Torres, C. A. (1990). *The politics of nonformal education in Latin America*. Praeger.

UNESCO. (2016, February). Recommendation on adult learning and education, 2015. https://uil.unesco.org/adult-education/unesco-recommendation/unesco-recommendation-adult-learning-and-education-2015

UNESCO. (2021, May). Caribbean consultation held on adult education challenges and opportunities in preparation of CONFINTEA VII. https://en.unesco.org/news/caribbean-consultation-held-adult-education-challenges-and-opportunities-preparation-confintea

United Nations. (2021). Transition from education to employment in Grenada. https://easterncaribbean.un.org/sites/default/files/2021-01/undp-bb-Transition-from-Education-to-Employment-in-Grenada-January-2021_0.pdf

Wehner, P. (2021, July 9). You're being manipulated. The Atlantic, https://www.theatlantic.com/ideas/archive/2021/07/jonathan-rauch-americas-competing-totalistic-ideologies/619386/

Whitehead, L. (1991). Democracy and socialism: Reflections on the Grenada experience. In J. Heine (Ed.,) *A revolution aborted: The lessons of Grenada* (pp. 309–319). University of Pittsburgh Press.

World Factbook—Grenada. (2022). Retrieved March 2022, from https://www.cia.gov/the-world-factbook/countries/grenada/

10

Between the State, Society, and Global Markets

Three Roles of Higher Education

Susan Wiksten
European Institute of Education and Social Policy

Daniel Schugurensky
Arizona State University

ABSTRACT

This chapter addresses three roles that universities have performed throughout history: (1) serve the interests of the state, (2) contribute to emancipation and social change, and (3) participate in the global education market. The status of global higher education development is outlined in terms of international policy efforts and as reported in comparative data on higher education collected by international organizations. Drawing on examples of the three roles of higher education, the discussion considers questions that pertain to the quality of higher education and its purposes in the context of professional integrity issues and ethical frameworks. The chapter concludes by arguing that growing diversity in higher education in terms of both providers and participants represents an opportunity for a better understanding of how higher education institutions can develop—specifically, to better fulfill their roles in societies that face demographic, environmental, economic, social, technological, and political change. Comparative education research plays an important role in contributing to the knowledge base on which universities stand to respond to the challenges of the 21st century.

■ ■ ■

In the 20th century, higher education systems around the world experienced significant changes in terms of growth and scope, and most countries transitioned from educating an elite to enrolling larger portions of relevant age-groups. Despite this impressive expansion, inequalities in access, completion, and quality are still pervasive. Debates on the most effective policies to diminish inequalities are still unresolved, as are debates on the financing of higher education, public-private provision, institutional autonomy, and issues related to the academic profession such as job security, academic freedom, positive work environments, and the hiring and retention of minority faculty. Other contemporary debates relate to the best ways to assess the impacts of universities in their traditional functions (research, teaching, and service), the strengths and weaknesses of rankings to compare university performance, and issues related to inclusion, equity, and diversity. In terms of instruction, in the last decades, higher education institutions have increased their offer of online courses, a trend that has accelerated during the COVID-19 pandemic. In response to an increasingly challenging and competitive context, many universities are designing new strategies for internationalization, exploring new curriculum development, establishing new international partnerships, and developing innovative approaches including hybrid online-offline offerings and micro-credentialing (Altbach, 2016; Chao, 2021).

Taking a longer perspective—specifically, a longue durée approach to understanding the incremental development of institutions over time (Braudel, 1958; Wallerstein, 2004)—we observe that the history of the modern state and the history of higher education have been intertwined. As the geopolitical landscape has evolved, so has the role of higher education. Due to the political realities in which universities function, they have played different roles, some of them complex and even contradictory. Historically, the university has served both the interests of imperial rule—in modernity referred to as a hegemonic role (Gramsci, 1971)—but it also has contributed to social change. In other words, higher education has served both the maintenance of forms of power and also its contestation. Universities have contributed to legitimizing and reproducing dominant knowledge, but also to creating and advancing new knowledge; universities have been tools of ideological control (legitimizing and reproducing dominant knowledge) but also engines of change (creating and advancing new knowledge).

This chapter starts with a contextualization of the status of global higher education development as articulated in international policy efforts and as reported in comparative data on higher education collected by the United Nations Organization for Education, Science and Culture (UNESCO) and the Organization for Economic Collaboration and Development (OECD). It then proceeds by discussing examples of three historical and contemporary roles played by universities: (1) their role in the construction and government of empires and states, (2) their role in promoting social change, and (3) their role in the global education market. The first of these roles is associated with the selection and formation of elites. The second role is associated with the role of higher education as a site for critical thinking, a site for the development of emancipatory social movements, and a site of personal development. The third is associated with labor market functions, as envisioned in, for example, human capital theory (Schultz, 1962). Elaborating on these roles, this chapter considers questions that pertain to the quality of higher education and the purposes of higher education development in terms of professional integrity and ethical frameworks; it also connects these questions to the responsibilities and roles of higher education in different societal contexts.

It is of course possible to categorize the roles of the university in several other ways depending on the theory that is in each case promoted by a given scholar for addressing the roles of the university. However, this perspective that draws on a long historical perspective (Braudel, 1958) with a simple and somewhat crude focus on three historically pervasive roles of the university serves in this chapter as a guide for a broad-strokes analysis to support a global comparison of the development of the university and higher education sector across the globe. Our focus on these three roles allows us to highlight some of the shared albeit distinct histories, concerns, and dynamics that contribute to molding the role of higher education in a global comparative perspective.

The chapter concludes by arguing that growing diversity in higher education in terms of both providers and participants represents an opportunity for better understanding how higher education institutions can develop to better fulfill their roles in societies that face important demographic, environmental, technological, economic, and political change. Comparative research in higher education plays a crucial role in contributing to the knowledge that is needed for the articulation of relevant responses to these challenges in the 21st century.

A note on the positioning and limitations of the chapter is warranted. While neither of the authors speaks English as their first language (our first languages are Swedish, Finnish, and Spanish), we write our analysis in English. Although this chapter does not specifically address language issues, we discuss some of the power relationships that have rendered moot the question of why we write in English. The question is moot as English is the dominant language in higher education—why this is so remains a critical question. The languages we are limited by (English, Spanish, French, Portuguese, Finnish, Swedish, Danish) and our professional experiences that for the most part are from higher education in the Americas and Europe, as well as our intersectional positionalities, have played a role in the choice of examples that we discuss and the examples of which we are familiar. Both of us benefit in our comparative analyses from collaborations that we concurrently work on with colleagues representing different intersectional perspectives and languages from the Global South and the Global North; for this we are grateful as feedback and interactions with peers helped us to admit our limitations and identify relevant historical and current examples that we are unable to address sufficiently, in part due to space constraints. Among them are the early development of higher education in China (predating the Common Era); the early development of universities in the Maghreb (northwest Africa) as exemplified by al-Qarawiyyin in Morocco; the historical relevance of the Córdoba Reform and the universidades populares in Latin America; the role of higher education in colonial and postcolonial Africa in forming elites and a sense of nationhood (see also Lee, 2017); the role of higher education in forming elites in colonial India; the reception of higher education students from the Global South in China today and historically in the former Soviet Union; racism in higher education (see e.g., Cantwell & Lee, 2010); indigenous higher education research (Durie, 2005), efforts to decolonize higher education (Bhambra et al., 2018), and transnational efforts to promote knowledge democracy (Tandon et al., 2016).

However, our theoretical analysis is of some relevance also to examples that are not specifically elaborated on. The power dynamics and relationships between higher education and societies we discuss have impacted and continue to be relevant for a broad range of contexts, albeit in variegated regional and localized forms.

INTERNATIONAL POLICY FRAMEWORK FOR HIGHER EDUCATION

The United Nations' declaration for human rights represents the first effort to articulate international policy for the development of education globally (United Nations, 1948). The signatories of that post–Second World War declaration agreed that providing free primary education to all social groups in society was a shared goal that each country wanted to work for. At that time, higher education was not defined as a right or need for the broader population, but instead equally accessible based on merit for a few individuals only. Policy thinking on the role of higher education has changed over the years. In line with human capital theory (Becker, 1962; Schultz, 1962) a consensus has formed that the development and economic competitiveness of countries are linked to the development of higher education and the research sector in 21st-century knowledge economies (Dale, 2005).

Higher education with its historically long-standing traditions of international student mobility has alongside international organizations played a leading role in the formation of what today is a global market of education (Shields, 2013; Torres, 2015; Verger et al., 2016). This development is currently characterized by league tables, rankings (Hazelkorn, 2018), and ever-accelerating competition in the face of which higher education systems of peripheral countries—even where long-standing traditions in higher education exist—struggle to survive (see, e.g., Brajdić Vuković et al., 2020). Market-based expansion has taken place since the 1990s, and the higher education field has been bustling with entrepreneurs and actors that provide access to higher education for a greater number of students. At the same time, this has raised concerns about the quality of higher education and the differentially valued categories of higher education providers (Horta & Feng, 2021; Wiksten, 2020). As higher education has become more accessible, the competition between higher education institutions has become more accentuated. The competition for status increases the pressure on students to not merely complete an advanced degree but to receive it from a renowned higher education institution.

In the context of a growing and diversifying global higher education industry, the international policy agenda is framed by the fourth goal of the United Nations Sustainable Development Agenda (specifically target 4.3), in which signatories have committed to ensuring by 2030 "equal access for all women and men to affordable quality technical, vocational and tertiary education, including university" (United Nations, 2015). A distinction between types of postsecondary learning in this policy recognizes that postsecondary education includes universities and also vocational and continued professional learning. The latter have not traditionally been understood at par with higher education in universities, albeit education system-specific practices show some variation. For instance, professionally oriented graduate schools at universities in the United States have historically contributed to the idea of a multiversity (Kerr, 1982). In France, the history of engineering schools, *écoles polytechniques*, is associated with the development of a branch of elite higher education, the *grandes écoles*, that has served the education of a professional elite (Belhoste, 2002). The 2021 closing of the École nationale d'administration—an institution that has served as the alma mater of several prominent public officials in France, including President Emmanuel Macron—represents an important change in the latter tradition and signals a political effort to reduce inequality in higher education in France (Le Monde, April 9, 2021).

These examples notwithstanding, many education systems have traditions that track, orient, and select students by cognitive skills to so-called general or academic tracks for university, whereas certain forms of vocational education have not been formally as recognized and in many societies have not been appreciated as education pathways but as educational dead ends. However, this is changing as education systems in the 21st century are developing qualifications frameworks that aim at supporting progression in education pathways in a flexible manner that formally recognizes also varieties of professional secondary and professional postsecondary learning (Singh, 2017; UNESCO, 2019; Wibrow & Waugh, 2020).

The policy stance of the UN represents an unprecedented international policy effort to support postsecondary education in all its various forms for all social groups and is a key reference for the development of higher education globally. There are many challenges to this undertaking due to the different circumstances in which higher education takes place across the globe. One of these challenges is associated with limitations of the information provided by population-wide data on higher education that traditionally have been used for gauging the progression of higher education development globally. Large-scale population data for individual countries and for global comparisons provide important indicators but will also often mask inequities within populations. This calls for efforts to develop disaggregated data for better understanding inequities in higher education participation and access (UNESCO, 2018; 2020).

Comparative education has studied variations in higher education systems and institutions across different societies. As is the case for a variety of societal institutions and practices, higher education is subject to societal changes that are brought on by social, economic, political, demographic, environmental, and technological changes. Critical scholarship has underscored the role of geopolitics and histories of unequal trade relations and colonization as factors that have contributed to relationships of power and domination that characterize different positions of peripheral and dominating higher education systems—power relationships that are reflected and reproduced in higher education practices to this day (de Sousa Santos, 2014). Although societal changes that impact higher education play out differently in different contexts, comparative data on the state of higher education in the world illustrate patterns that shed light on the development of higher education globally. We explore this in the next section.

COMPARATIVE DATA ON PARTICIPATION IN HIGHER EDUCATION

Comparative data shows that higher education participation rates are comparatively lower in low-income countries (4%) and higher in high-income countries (55%), although significant variations among countries grouped by income categories can be observed (UIS, 2021). Figure 10.1 shows higher education attainment rates among 25–34 years old in 43 high-income or upper-middle-income countries. The averages among those countries range from 6% to 70%. The range of attainment rates is reflected by higher education participation rates that range

Figure 10.1. Higher Education levels in OECD member and partner countries

Source: Data compiled and analyzed by Wiksten using data retrieved on January 10, 2021, from OECD at https://data.oecd.org/chart/6e7p. Data refers to % in age-group of people aged 25-34 years in 2019, or latest available data in the time period 2017-2019.

from 10 to 90% in high-income countries globally (UIS, 2021). This underscores the fact that even though participation in higher education is more frequent in high-income countries, country income categories alone do not sufficiently explain variation in the provision of higher education. This suggests the pertinence of considering differences associated with the political economy and social policy traditions in individual countries (Esping-Andersen, 1990).

Indeed, within many countries, there are important differences in the higher education participation of different social groups. To begin with, the disparity in higher education participation between populations in rural and urban areas is a global phenomenon, and the disparity is comparatively greater in high-income countries. That is, higher income country status is associated with higher differences between participation in higher education in urban and rural areas (Figure 10.2). For example, the difference between urban and rural participation in low-income countries is on average 9% whereas the difference between urban and rural participation in higher education in high-income countries is on average 17% (UIS, 2021).

Regarding gender, in low-income and lower-middle-income countries, women participate in higher education at lower rates than men. In high-income countries, women participate in higher education in greater numbers than men (UIS, 2021). However, disparities associated with the participation of historically disadvantaged groups are also present in high-income countries. Data show lower participation in higher education among men from social groups that have historically experienced exclusion from higher education based on race, ethnicity, and socio-economic status (Brey et al., 2019).

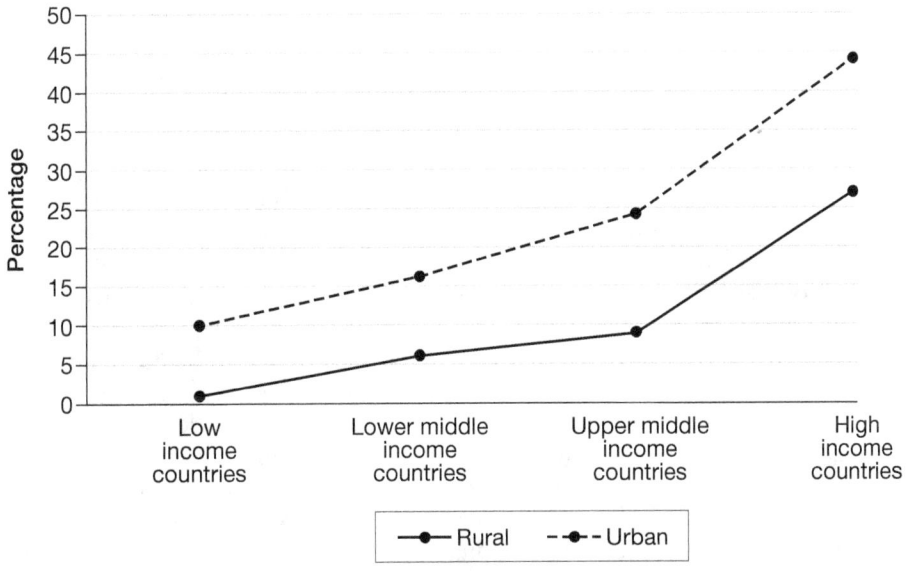

Figure 10.2. Higher education attendance in rural and urban areas by country income groups

Source: Figure constructed by Wiksten. Data obtained from the UIS World Inequality Database on Education (UIS, 2021) in January 2021, from https://www.education-inequalities.org/indicators/higher_1822#?sort=mean&dimension=community&group=all&age_group=attend_higher_1822&countries=all

Qualitative research on the reproduction of habitus and social capital (Hadjar et al., 2021; Lehmann, 2021; O'Shea, 2021; Reay, 2021) shows that in some countries with high participation in tertiary education such as Canada, Australia, United States, Switzerland, Luxembourg, and the United Kingdom, first-in-family students and students from working-class backgrounds—also referred to as first-generation students—continue to experience comparatively greater difficulties in higher education environments and in transitioning to the labor market. This is due not only to the reproduction of values from student home environments unfamiliar with higher education but also to inadvertent and explicit practices of exclusion in higher education (Reay, 2021). At the same time, there is an increasing realization that higher education institutions need to change to become more welcoming to diverse students; supporting students to develop a sense of belonging and especially helping first-generation students to navigate an unfamiliar and intimidating space (O'Shea 2021; Weiss, 2021).

Global statistics indicate that much remains to be done for achieving equitable participation in higher education, including the need for policies to support the participation of populations from rural areas, women in low-income countries, minority men in comparatively higher-income countries, and other historically disadvantaged social groups (UIS, 2021; UNESCO, 2018). The compounded effects of several intersectional social group markers do not show up in the current UNESCO data but should also be recognized, especially where individuals experience combined effects of two or multiple disadvantages associated with social group markers in specific contexts; for example, barriers to participation based on combinations of factors such as gender, race, age, health, and poverty. It is important that limitations in addressing intersectional factors in aggregate data are acknowledged by policymakers and that policy decisions are informed also by qualitative research.

Other factors to consider when comparing data on higher education are those that impact the lives of individuals before enrollment in higher education and the circumstances following degree completion. Some factors to consider before enrollment include the rates of primary and secondary school access and completion as well as health-related factors. Relevant factors during and after the pursuit of higher education pertain to the flexibility of the labor market, flexibility in degree completion, including policies that support completion of degrees at a later stage in life (Desjardins, 2017), as well as technical measures such as professional recognition mechanisms and supporting regulation such as qualifications frameworks or certification practices.

The combined effect of selected factors that contribute to the life opportunities of individuals, notably in terms of health and education, have been aggregated by the World Bank into an index titled the Human Capital Index. Although all aggregate data are limited in the ability to represent the diversity of populations, the index is an interesting composite indicator for a comparison of the life opportunities of individuals in different countries. In this index, 100% (or 1) represents an ideal situation in which all individuals in a given society have the opportunity to participate in education through higher education, where mortality rates are low and where health indicators are high. Comparing the averages of low-income, lower-middle-income, upper-middle-income, and high-income countries, this index illustrates a part of the combined effect of factors before and following higher education that contribute to a fuller understanding of the role of higher education in different countries. As illustrated in Figure 10.3, lower-income countries perform consistently lower in the Human Capital Index and higher-income countries perform higher. However, the performance among high- and low-income countries varies importantly—some lower-middle-income countries can provide better life opportunities than some upper-middle-income countries, whereas some upper-middle-income countries are performing better than some high-income countries in this comparison. As noted earlier, these data indicate that individual life opportunities are not directly explainable by the income category of individual countries but depend on the political economies of individual countries and other local circumstances. Indeed, prominent factors that impact the context of education and higher education include political conflicts and political instability.

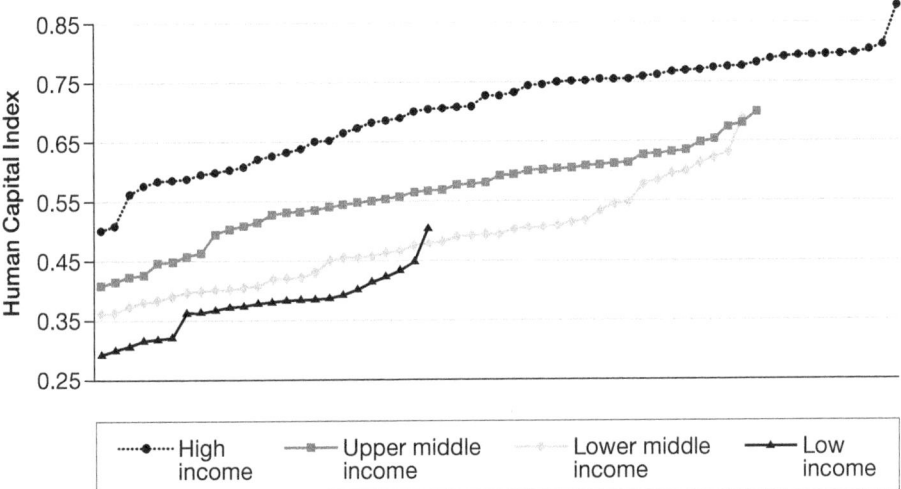

Figure 10.3. Human Capital Index 2020 by Country Income Groups

Source: Figure constructed by Wiksten (2021). Data retrieved from the World Bank, data retrieved January 2021 from https://www.worldbank.org/en/publication/human-capital#Index. The Human Capital Index combines data on health and education for 174 countries to provide an overall estimation of the life opportunities of individuals born and educated in these countries. The index combines health and education related indicators; specifically: the probability of survival to age five; expected years of school; harmonized test scores; learning-adjusted years of school; adult survival rate to age 60; healthy growth (not stunted rate).

THREE ROLES OF HIGHER EDUCATION

In a long historical perspective (Braudel, 1958), the history of the modern state and the history of higher education are intertwined. It is for this reason not surprising that the origin of universities in established narratives of the birth of the university is often located in northern Italy, a region that played a crucial role in early conceptualizations of the modern state (Skinner, 1978). Due to the geopolitical realities in which higher education institutions function, their roles in the production and reproduction of knowledge and in promoting social reforms are very complex and are contradictory. In a long historical perspective, universities have served both the maintenance as well as the contestation of forms of power;

they have served both the purposes and aims of elites and have served revolutions both great and small.

That universities from their earliest days have been products, servants, and tools of power is reflected in the conventional narrative of the birth of the university in 12th-century Europe in Bologna and Paris. The University of Bologna was founded by religious authorities, as reflected in the early curriculum in which the study of religious laws was a prominent focus. The university in Paris grew as an agglomeration of schools around the cathedral Notre Dame (Verger, 1986). The curriculum in Paris included the study of religious laws but notably also the study of the liberal arts as promoted by the Carolingian palatine school; a comparatively more liberal site of study that retained the official recognition of the Pope only later. A comparison of the early stages of these two contemporary early universities reflects two roles of the university that are confirmed by several historical examples, namely (1) the university as the servant of the political interests of the current political authority on knowledge and (2) the university as the site of construction of competing political authorities on knowledge—that is, the university that supports emancipation and contests the current political authority on knowledge. The tension between these two roles characterizes questions and concerns associated with the quality, equity, and interests served by higher education to this day, despite historical shifts in dominating doctrines of knowledge over the past thousand years.

The following section elaborates on three roles—reflecting the themes *control*, *emancipation*, and *market*—played by higher education institutions historically and today. We start by discussing the role of higher education in the construction and government of empires and states. Next, we address the role of higher education in driving societal change. Finally, the role of higher education in the global education market is described. Our focus highlights some of the shared albeit distinct histories, concerns, and dynamics that contribute to molding the role of higher education in a global comparative perspective in the 21st century.

The framework of concepts that we use for our analysis is distinct from Clark's (1986, p. 143) triangle of coordination in that we focus on the role of higher education institutions as arbiters of power and as actors contributing to societal change. However, Clark's analysis serves as a predecessor in that his analysis similarly to ours highlights the power relationships between state, academia, and the market.

The University of the Empire and the State
During the 1600s, the Swedish empire sought to establish itself over an area that today corresponds to northern Germany, Sweden, Finland, and Estonia by taking over older institutions and by establishing new universities. The network of universities of the Swedish empire in the 1600s included the University of Greifswald (1649) in current-day northern Germany, the University of Dorpat (1632) in what today is Tartu, Estonia, the Royal Academy of Åbo (1640) in what today is Turku, Finland, and the Universities of Lund (1666) and Uppsala (1477) in what today remain parts of Sweden. The Baltic Sea was at this time an interior sea of the Swedish empire and the universities served the practical purposes of training a literate elite loyal to the king that could be deployed for the administration

of the empire. This helped to assert Swedish rule symbolically, administratively, culturally, and intellectually; and thereby to consolidate the distant corners of the empire. The strategy of asserting power and presence through an administrative elite was something that Charles VI of Sweden did not need to invent himself. Charlemagne, already in the latter part of the first millennium of the common era (CE), had fostered what has been called the Carolingian renaissance. The latter promoted the study of the liberal arts for much the same purpose, the training of a literate elite to support a consolidation of the administration of a large multi-ethnic European empire (Sullivan, 2020).

Similarly in Asia, higher education practices established already in the latter half of the millennium before the common era, following the Confucian tradition, aimed at supporting existing power structures by molding obedient commoners and a nobility skilled in administration and warfare to consolidate and maintain the power of the Chinese empire (Palmer et al., 2001, p. 2). The tradition of imperial examinations continues in that one of the important functions of higher education in many countries to this day is to serve as a mechanism for selecting a privileged elite to administer and govern the state (Liu, 2007; see also Zhang, 2020, p. 390). In this vein also in Europe, universities following the Napoleonic reforms of the 19th century embodied the principle of central control and state monopoly over instruction (Green, 1990, p. 150).

Green notes how higher education in England, in contrast to continental Europe, reflected specifics of the prevalent liberal political economy of the country. It was characterized by a less centrally controlled development of the education system (Green, 1990, pp. 242–243). Indeed, specificities of regional variations have contributed to recognized historical models of higher education including the German model and the U.S. model. The German (or Humboldtian) model was influenced by reforms of the Prussian empire characterized by the privileged education of an administrative and military middle class (Green, 1990, pp. 128–130). The U.S. model in turn was in important ways influenced by the American Revolution (Geiger, 2014). A shared feature of each of these influential models is that they have contributed to the establishment and maintenance of various states and constellations of power—be it the British empire or other manifestations of power, such as individual nation-states, or what is understood as the modern state (Green, 1990; Skinner, 1978).

In the 21st century, neoliberal global policies exercise an influence in higher education that can be compared to the powerful influence of the empires of previous millennia (de Sousa Santos, 2014; Schugurensky, 2013; Torres, 2013). As a result of neoliberal policies promoted in higher education globally since the 1990s, the competition to be part of a controlling power elite legitimized by recognized higher education degrees has increased inequities in education. An unfair playing field has been exacerbated, for example, by the growth of an unregulated private supplementary education sector (Ghosh & Bray, 2020; Kim et al., 2020; Liu & Bray, 2020). Indeed, a host of scholars, who cannot all be listed here, have provided well-founded arguments and good reasoning for describing the various ways in which the global implementation of neoliberal policies in higher education has impacted higher education in negative ways. For example, by increasing inequity in higher education, by decreasing funding to basic research, and by adding pressure on scholars in arbitrary or market-directed ways that raise concerns regarding the quality and integrity of research (Brajdić Vuković et al., 2020; Giroux, 2011; Torres, 2015).

The Carolingian palace school model outlined the higher education curricula in early European universities; a comparable situation influencing higher education curricula today is the global power of the neoliberal agenda (Gyamera & Burke, 2018; Schugurensky, 2013; Torres, 2009).

The effects of neoliberal policies in higher education have been identified as challenging notably the common good or public good dimensions of higher education (Piketty, 2014). In the long history of the liberal movement such a development represents a paradox. It reflects a development in which the liberal movement has over a long period developed from an underdog position to a common-sense hegemony (Gramsci, 1971; Torres, 2013). The following section—on the role of higher education in revolutions and in contesting established power structures—will briefly outline the role of early European universities in the liberal revolution that has culminated in a global hegemony in the 21st century.

The Contestatory and Emancipatory University or the University of the Revolution

The early universities in Europe developed in the context of a tension between the interests of ruling sovereigns, religious institutions, and a growing class of artisans and merchant-traders.

The early universities of Bologna, Paris, and Oxford were born in centers of trade that by 1150 CE held a growing middle class of merchant-traders (see also, Creighton & Wright, 2016; Loveluck, 2013, p. 3; Verger, 1986). The Hanseatic League is an example of the power associated with the wealth of merchant traders, a notable nonstate, nonchurch organization that represented the self-directed collaborative interests of trade networks across the coastal regions of northwestern and northeastern Europe (Fink, 2010).

Religious authority provided education and privileges for the clergy to maintain its specific corporate administrative form with representations throughout much of Europe. The royal houses in turn provided privileges for the nobility to control and develop military power and an increasingly centralized legislative and administrative control of geographic territory. The merchant traders operated within the ideological and regulatory frameworks defined by the sovereign and religious doctrine in which they formally had little influence, despite increasing wealth and a vested interest in regulations.

With the establishment of the University of Paris, it became possible for independent students—that is, students not supported financially by a religious order or by the royal court—to obtain advanced skills necessary for establishing legally recognized contracts and thereby to contribute to a formally recognized administration of capital; not least, in forms such as the legal transfer of inheritances. The latter in particular was crucial for the autonomy of the class of merchants and trades professionals and thereby a fundamental cause for the early liberal movement. The 12th-century University of Paris was an agglomeration of schools, organized similarly as medieval guilds, in the vicinity of the cathedral of Notre Dame (Verger, 1986)—political sanctioning of the university by king and pope were obtained in the early 13th century.

The curriculum at the early universities in Europe comprised the seven liberal arts of the Carolingian palace school, the trivium (grammar, rhetoric, dialectic), and the quadrivium (geometry, arithmetic, astronomy, and music) (Deubel et al., 2007, p. 11), for statesmanship and warfare—and of the study of religious doctrine, for those who were to serve as clergy. The training of clergy remained a key function of higher education institutions in parts of Europe until the 19th century—despite the Enlightenment movement's insistence on separating the religious organization from the university (see, e.g., Geiger, 2014). This insistence of the Enlightenment movement led notably in countries of Catholic education traditions to a distinction articulated by the terms *laïcité* and *l'école laïque*; that is, the definition of education as a secular institution and the forms of knowledge advanced in higher education as secular forms of knowledge. As noted by Deubel et al. (2007, p. 19), this insistence and distinction led in some countries to the separation of church and state.

Numerous later examples of how the university has been associated in contesting the status quo or power constellations in countries across the globe include independence struggles and nationalist movements seeking autonomy from ruling European empires both in Europe and in former colonies in the 19th century and early 20th century. A notable example of this is the 1918 Córdoba Reform (Schugurensky & Davidson-Harden, 2003). More recent examples include the youth movements of the 1960s and 1970s in North America, Europe and in the early part of the 21st century in Northern Africa and Chile. Both the university revolutions of 1968 and the Arab spring of 2012, and developments following these historical contestations, were fueled by a university educated youth population calling for structural societal changes, developments that in part depended on the massification of access to higher education in previous decades.

In this vein, Xabier Gorostiaga suggested a new role for universities of the South. He called for using university resources such as extension programs and research and development institutes for experimentation, training, and popular education. This approach recognizes the role of rural and marginalized populations as knowledge producers. The knowledge generated by rural-based centers would contribute to a higher education better aligned for playing an empowering role in meeting the needs of local societies. It can provide a framework to establish closer and more dynamic connections between research, service and teaching. Moreover, this approach could also help to develop structures to facilitate South-North collaborations (Gorostiaga, 1993; see also Torres, 2011).

The University of the Global Market

The end of the 20th century saw an intensification of global contacts and a variety of forms of globalizations. Internationalization in higher education contributed as one variant of globalization to the acceleration in the frequency of global contacts. However, in the first part of the 21st century, as a result of reactions against societal changes brought on by forms of globalization, the higher education sector along with other sectors is experiencing the effects of different forms of localism, protectionism, nationalism, and calls for curbing international exchanges. A concrete example is Brexit, the withdrawal of the United Kingdom from the European Union (EU)—and thereby also from the European Union's effort to foster a European Higher Education Area (EHEA) and a European Research Area

(ERA) for the benefit of student mobility, cooperation in research (Vukasovic & Stensaker, 2018)—and not least for competing as a regional block with the higher education sector in the United States.

The EU defines education as a national interest area. The development of the EHEA and other shared references for education in the EU depend for this reason on the voluntary participation of EU member states. To some extent, Brexit disrupts established connections for institutional cooperation in higher education in Europe; however, countries with comparatively large economies like Germany may be able to use state funding to support bilateral agreements to offset prior EU frameworks (Jungblut & Seidenschnur, 2018, p. 56). Smaller EU countries who previously have charged comparatively lower tuition will likely experience a greater decrease in cooperation (van der Wende & Rienks, 2018, p. 96). Courtois notes that since the Brexit decision was announced there is a reluctance among academics in Europe to involve British partners in research bids and there is a concern that joint research initiatives no longer are economically tenable (Courtois, 2018, p. 21).

Brexit can be understood as a political reaction to some of the effects of various forms of globalization including growing migration to Europe. The political discourses supporting Brexit have promoted articulations of autonomy and sovereignty and other nationalist characterizations that seek to revalorize and underscore the role of the nation-state as a political entity. The EHEA has been a joint effort by European countries with traditions for state-funded higher education and a broad range of higher education institutions, including small and internationally little-known institutions. The EHEA has sought to foster greater opportunities for students also from peripheral contexts to participate in a diverse higher education sector across Europe. Although promoting new management practices, the EHEA has also promoted the utopic Enlightenment idea of education as a common good resource. The EHEA has also served as a strategy by which a conglomeration of larger and smaller countries joined forces to compete in a global higher education market dominated by the United States. For UK higher education, Brexit entails a distancing from the EHEA project and thereby by necessity an even greater commitment to a liberal, unregulated, global higher education market.

Both the separation of the United Kingdom from the EU and the EU's effort to form the EHEA represent efforts to hold on to traditional ideas of the nation-state. For the United Kingdom, Brexit is about underscoring autonomy and sovereignty. For the EU, the EHEA collaboration is an effort to support the survival of national higher education systems facing the domination of English language higher education systems in a global higher education market. Higher education in the United Kingdom in some sense already has, without the EHEA, a given set of English language higher education systems with which to collaborate globally, including higher education systems in the United States, Australia, Canada, and New Zealand.

Whereas the English language higher education systems dominate globally, a number of regional collaborations have, similarly to the European Union, sought to collaboratively strengthen their positions in a global higher education context. These include collaborations in the Association of Southeast Asian Nations, the Southern African Regional Universities Association, the Unión de Universidades de América Latina y el Caribe, and the Asociación de Universidades Grupo Montevideo in the southern cone.

Ethical Challenges of the Global Higher Education Market

A prominent development in an increasingly competitive higher education sector—with high stakes associated with admission to highly ranked universities—is the private supplementary education sector, sometimes referred to as *cram-schools*, *private tuition*, or *shadow education*. This private business sector that runs parallel to education systems has proliferated over the past three decades notably in Asia—a development that Baker expects to become a global phenomenon (Baker, 2020). Such an expectation—that students should participate in private supplementary education—exacerbates inequities in entry to higher education. Also, the expectation for private supplementary tutoring impacts curricula and education in concrete and systemic ways, as has been illustrated in case studies from Myanmar, South Korea, China, and India (Ghosh & Bray, 2020; Kim et al., 2020; Liu & Bray, 2020; Zhang, 2020). In this vein, competition and inequity in education are driven by systemic practices that encourage, for example, teachers to reserve parts of the curriculum for students who can afford to pay additional tuition. The latter allows notably teachers in low-income contexts to supplement low salaries and contributes to a private unregulated industry of tutoring jobs for university and high school graduates. Private supplementary education has mushroomed on all levels of education and is now a prominent feature also in higher education.

For example, higher education students in China compete for study-abroad opportunities by paying for services that assist the wealthiest students in editing personal statements and constructing extracurricular profiles to optimize admission opportunities to universities in the United States (Horta & Feng, 2021). Practices that allow students from wealthy families to pay teachers for better access to curricula and services that place students in an advantageous position in university admissions processes raise several questions about the impact of an unregulated private education service sector on the quality of education; the quality of curricula and the quality of the student body; notably, questions that pertain to merit-based selection; equity; professional integrity, the ethical frameworks that guide practices in higher education and the quality of higher education. A concern is that the supplementary education system encourages in some cases favoritism and cheating on examinations of students who might, at the same time, be private students as well as students in the university classes of the instructor.

DISCUSSION

Focusing on the role of universities and higher education as power arbiters in societies and in a global market of education is both necessary and problematic. The degree of specialization and technical focus required for advancing science in modern universities has alienated many researchers, lecturers, students, and research projects from the societal context of knowledge production. This has not happened by coincidence but was to some extent put forth as a necessity for objective research. Scholars in line with the Enlightenment movement proposed that the only way to advance science was to separate religious authority from the academy. In modernity, this willingness to establish distance to normative and ethical frameworks has in some cases been interpreted in extreme iterations. One example of this was the development of eugenics, a pseudoscience developed to promote a racist political agenda. Other examples of efforts within academia to promote theoretical frameworks that explicitly take distance from ethical considerations of equal human worth and humane societies are not uncommon. Rational choice theory can be considered another example of this.

Whereas it is easy to discern the political agendas that have promoted a pseudoscience such as eugenics (racism), it is important to recognize the ease with which technically specialized research can omit societal and ethical contextualization and a consideration of the ethical and societal impacts of research. Examples of failures of well-intended modern efforts have been detailed, for example, by Scott (2020). Recognizing ethical blind spots in research is particularly important for pervasive forms of societal inequities that may not be a focus or interest of a given study. Failing to recognize agendas served by research may inadvertently worsen conditions for vulnerable populations. The problem then lies in that modern stances that claim neutral nonnormative positions also downplay the need for researchers to invest time and resources in understanding both the particularities of specific research and in addition to understanding the bigger picture of the role that their research plays in academia and in society. That is, to understand not only the technical specialty of one's field but also how one's specialized research is meaningful to other research and society. The modern stance in higher education tends to deemphasize the role of the latter which is a problem as it is a necessity for the development of ethically relevant practices and professional integrity among researchers.

The global market of higher education and research generates further significant pressures for scholars and researchers to produce metrics and competition that are decontextualized. These activities, in some contexts, can be arbitrary and irrelevant; they also may misrepresent local concerns. The global market of higher education challenges individual institutions and programs to compete for students and resources. The challenges have been characterized by pressures to adapt to and adopt global power languages such as English and pressures to adopt neoliberal policies and associated so-called *new public management* practices that include, for example, *performance-based funding* practices. An important part of adapting to the global market of education has entailed efforts to internationalize higher education, to implement organizational changes, and adapt structures for catering to a global customer base of students (e.g., Fumasoli, 2021). Universities in English-speaking countries have in many cases used revenue from foreign students to compensate for budget cuts to higher education following neoliberal policies. In the second decade of the 21st century, however, the work of universities, scholars, and researchers has been disrupted in various ways by a global coronavirus disease pandemic and the proliferation of nationalist protectionist discourses. The latter is here understood as a political backlash to the globalization that resulted from the opening up of the global markets in the 1990s.

Another emerging trend is that some universities are creating organizational structures to promote lifelong learning after graduation. In the 21st century, the pioneering university extension programs of the 19th century that focused on agricultural techniques have evolved into a multifaceted approach that includes a wide range of topics (from professional development opportunities to multiple areas of general interest), and a variety of modalities (from short workshops and seminars to internships and full programs), locations (online, offline, and hybrid), entry points and certification arrangements (see, e.g., O'Connor, 2014).

Without seeing what the future brings, it is nevertheless possible to predict based on what we know from the history of universities as institutions that higher education will continue to serve interests of control, emancipation, and markets. Higher education continues to serve both hegemonic political interests and contestation of who determines the ends, means, and outcomes of education. Higher education continues to play a role in serving a global market of knowledge production. Important questions pertain to: *how in practice, in specific localities, the three roles of higher education come into play*, and how universities can best support the goals of quality and equity in their roles. Whereas a few broad strokes as presented in this chapter are not sufficient for addressing local particularities, we hope to have provided a framework for analysis with a few examples of comparative empirical evidence that may be useful for further comparative efforts to contextualize developments in higher education.

CONCLUSION

This chapter presented a comparative global analysis of higher education that proposes a theoretical lens that identifies three contradictory purposes of higher education. First, universities have historically been established as part of efforts to build empires and assert dominance. Second, universities have nurtured both great and small revolutions, including structural, technological, normative, and societal shifts. Third, universities serve a global knowledge economy and a global education market. The role of universities as power arbiters was introduced using the early development of the universities of Bologna, Paris, and Oxford as examples. The role of power arbitration was problematized in the discussion section. The need for research to connect to ethical considerations that pertain to humane societies and equitable practices was underscored. We reviewed empirical data on the development of higher education globally and the three themes of different roles of the university were highlighted in three thematic sections.

Although universities, scholars, and students face challenges of entrenched inequalities, competition, precarity, and many uncertainties, it is important to acknowledge that a growing number of young and older persons have gained access to higher education over the past five decades and the numbers continue to increase despite global difficulties. It is therefore pertinent to raise a concern regarding the quality of education in an increasingly diverse field of higher education providers. This is particularly relevant as parts of the higher education sector are currently driven by market interests by for-profit actors. The incorporation of a broader range of providers of higher education can at best be seen as a form of democratization of higher education, but it also contributes to the further entrenchment of already existing societal inequities. An uneven playing field may even push entire education systems toward standards established by families who can pay for additional private tuition (see, e.g., Ghosh & Bray, 2020).

Means for addressing the question of quality in systems with a diversity of higher education providers (private, public, denominational, and guided by other agendas) have historically been established in English-speaking countries such as the United Kingdom and the United States in the form of certification requirements governed by professional associations. The movements for standardization and modularization of education that have emerged across the globe for the past 20 years serve as complementary mechanisms to certification processes. Examples of these developments that seek to increase the transparency and standardization of study requirements and study loads include the establishment of qualifications frameworks (Cort, 2010; EHEA, 2005; Knight, 2013; Singh, 2017; UNESCO, 2019; Wibrow & Waugh, 2020).

Liberal universities have benefited from the guidance from professional associations for the quality control of degrees. However, negotiation and coordination beyond local and regional efforts are needed for promoting ethical and relevant practices in the global 21st century higher education market. To remain relevant in a context of global competition, universities need to continue reinventing their practices, their agendas, and the awareness of their roles as they face ongoing societal changes. This global competition is not fair, as it is dominated by power relations, hegemonic languages, and by geopolitical interests. Researchers of professional integrity need to be able to recognize the power vested in the role of a scholar and need to be able to, intelligibly and persuasively, articulate their own positions.

For articulating such positions, comparative researchers have in many cases focused on the characteristics of national higher education systems and how systems might be typologized by specific characteristics of higher education systems and global positions, such as the distinction made between universities and scholars from the Global South and the Global North (for a helpful overview of this distinction, see Demeter & Toth, 2020). A more nuanced approach for comparative research in higher education proposed by Marginson and Rhoades (2002), the glonacal heuristic, identifies three interacting levels on which higher education institutions and actors operate (global, national, and local), amid multiple and reciprocal flows.

As we have shown with the review of data and research literature on higher education in this chapter, specific challenges facing the development of higher education—and therefore important topical areas that call for the attention of comparative education researchers—pertain to the participation of women in higher education in low-income countries; the participation of minority men in high-income countries and the increasing disparity in access to prestigious higher education that is in part driven by a global higher education market. Higher education presents itself as an international playing field that is out of reach for the children of comparatively lower socioeconomic status families, as noted in a survey of approximately 4,600 Indian academics across the globe (Czaika & Toma, 2017), and as has been confirmed by qualitative comparative research (see, e.g., Ghosh & Bray, 2020; Liu & Bray, 2020).

Recent propositions for how comparative higher education research should advance have called for reconnecting to the emancipatory mission of higher education reflected in the development of students' critical thinking skills and common good values (Torres & Bosio, 2020, see also de Wit, 2020). There has been a call to advance the methodologies of research in comparative higher education research, suggesting that methodologies have suffered from incoherence and a lack of critical attention (Kosmützky & Nokkala, 2020). Lee and Stensaker (2021) note that the theoretical underpinnings of research in comparative research on higher education have not been articulated in a clear manner. One of the reasons for the latter is that there is not a single explanation that will suffice for advancing comparative higher education research; unless, perhaps, the explanation that several different perspectives and theoretical stances are needed to understand different and changing societal contexts. Efforts, such as this chapter, to provide a wider comparative reflection on comparative research in higher education are by necessity limited. We proposed a conceptual framework identifying three historical roles of higher education institutions (control, emancipation, market) and presented a discussion with examples of power relationships in different societies that influenced the form and prevalence of those roles. In this way, we have responded to the call for critical and theoretical reflections on which methodology in comparative higher education research can build. The perspective we have presented underscores the agentic and political role of higher education and scholars.

Continued comparative education research using historical, glonacal, and other perspectives can contribute to a better understanding of the challenges and opportunities in higher education in the 21st century. Growing diversity among higher education participants and providers represents both opportunities and urgent needs for understanding how universities can better fulfill their roles as power arbiters in societies that face important challenges due to demographic, environmental, social, economic, technological, and political changes.

REFERENCES

Altbach, P. (2016). *Global perspectives on higher education*. Johns Hopkins University Press.

Baker, D. P. (2020). An inevitable phenomenon: Reflections on the origins and future of worldwide shadow education. *European Journal of Education, 55*(3), 311–315. https://doi.org/10.1111/ejed.12410

Becker, G. S. (1962). Investment in human capital: A theoretical analysis. *Journal of Political Economy, 70*(5), 9–49.

Belhoste, B. (2002). Anatomie d'un concours: L'organisation de l'examen d'admission à l'École polytechnique de la Révolution à nos jours. *Histoire de l'éducation, 94*, 141–175. https://doi.org/10.4000/histoire-education.827

Bhambra, G. K., Nisancioglu, K., & Gebrial, D. (2018). *Decolonizing the university*. Pluto Press.

Brajdić Vuković, M., Vignjević Korotaj, B., & Ćulum Ilić, B. (2020). STEM colonization: Applying hard sciences' socio-organisational patterns and evaluation procedures to the soft sciences in Croatia. *European Journal of Education, 55*(4), 542–559. https://doi.org/10.1111/ejed.12421

Braudel, F. (1958). Histoire et Sciences sociales: La longue durée. Annales. *Histoire, Sciences Sociales, 13*(4), 725–753.

Brey, C., Musu, L., McFarland, J. (Eds.). (2019). *Status and trends in the education of racial and ethnic groups 2018*. U.S. Department of Education, National Center for Education Statistics. https://nces.ed.gov/pubsearch/

Cantwell, B., & Lee, J. J. (2010). Unseen workers in the academic factory: Perceptions of neo-racism among international postdocs in the US and UK. *Harvard Education Review, 80*(4), 490–517.

Chao, R. (2021, February). A time for innovation in international higher education post-COVID-19. *University World News*.

Clark, B. R. (1986). *The higher education system: Academic organization in cross-national perspective*. University of California Press.

Cort, P. (2010). Stating the obvious: The European Qualifications Framework is not a neutral evidence-based policy tool. *European Educational Research Journal, 9*(3), 304–316. https://doi.org/10.2304/eerj.2010.9.3.304

Courtois, A. (Ed.). (2018). *Higher Education and Brexit: current European perspectives*. Special report. Centre for Global Higher Education, UCL Institute of Education. https://www.researchcghe.org/perch/resources/publications/he-and-brexit.pdf

Creighton, O. H., & Wright, D. W. (2016). *The anarchy: War and status in 12th-century landscapes of conflict*. Liverpool University Press.

Czaika, M., & Toma, S. (2017). International academic mobility across space and time: The case of Indian academics. *Population, Space and Place, 23*(8), e2069. https://doi.org/10.1002/psp.2069

Dale, R. (2005). Globalisation, knowledge economy and comparative education. *Comparative Education, 41*(2), 117–149. https://doi.org/10.1080/03050060500150906

Demeter, M., & Toth, T. (2020). The world-systemic network of global elite sociology: The western male monoculture at faculties of the top one-hundred sociology departments of the world. *Scientometrics, 124*, 2469–2495. https://doi.org/10.1007/s11192-020-03563-w

de Wit, H. (2020). Internationalization of higher education: The need for a more ethical and qualitative approach. *Journal of International Students, 10*(1), i–iv. https://doi.org/10.32674/jis.v10i1.1893

Desjardins, R. (2017). *Political economy of adult learning systems*. Bloomsbury Academic. https://www.bloomsbury.com/us/political-economy-of-adult-learning-systems-9781474273664/

Deubel, P., Huart, J. M., Montoussé, M., & Vin-Datiche, D. (2007). *100 fiches pour comprendre le système éducatif*. Bréal.

Durie, M. (2005). Indigenous knowledge within a global knowledge system. *Higher Education Policy, 18*(3), 301–312.

EHEA. (2005). The framework of qualifications for the European Higher Education Area. http://www.ehea.info/Uploads/qualification/QF-EHEA-May2005.pdf

Esping-Andersen, G. (1990). *The three worlds of welfare capitalism*. Princeton University Press.

Fink, A. (2010). Under what conditions may social contracts arise? Evidence from the Hanseatic League. *Constitutional Political Economy, 22*(2), 173–190. https://doi.org/10.1007/s10602-010-9099-z

Fumasoli, T. (2021). Purposive design or ecology? A critique of teleological perspectives on internationalisation in higher education. *European Journal of Education, 56*(2).

Geiger, R. (2014). *The history of American higher education: Learning and culture from the founding to World War II*. Princeton University Press.

Ghosh, P., & Bray, M. (2020). School systems as breeding grounds for shadow education: Factors contributing to private supplementary tutoring in West Bengal, India. *European Journal of Education, 55*(3), 342–360. https://doi.org/10.1111/ejed.12412

Giroux, H. (2011). The disappearing intellectual in the age of economic Darwinism. *Policy Futures in Education, 9*(2), 163–171. http://dx.doi.org/10.2304/pfie.2011.9.2.163

Gorostiaga, X. (1993). New times, new role for universities of the South. *Envio: The Monthly Magazine of Analysis on Central America, 12*(144), 29–40.

Gramsci, A. (1971). *Selections from the Prison Notebooks*. International Publishers.

Green, A. (1990). *Education and state formation*. Macmillan.

Gyamera, G. O., & Burke, P. J. (2018). Neoliberalism and curriculum in higher education in Africa: A post-colonial analysis. *Teaching in Higher Education*, 23(4), 450–467. https://doi.org/10.1080/13562517.2017.1414782

Hadjar, A., Scharf, J., & Hascher, T. (2021). Who aspires to higher education? Axes of inequality, values of education and higher education aspirations in secondary schools in Luxembourg and the Swiss Canton of Bern. *European Journal of Education*, 56(1). https://doi.org/10.1111/ejed.12435

Hazelkorn, E. (2018). Reshaping the world order of higher education: The role and impact of rankings on national and global systems. *Policy Reviews in Higher Education*, 2(1), 4–31. https://doi.org/10.1080/23322969.2018.1424562

Horta, H., & Feng, S. (2021). Brokers of international student mobility: The roles and processes of education agents in China Siyuan Feng & Hugo Horta. *European Journal of Education*, 56(1).

Jungblut, J., & Seidenschnur, T. (2018). Germany: Much ado about nothing? Perceptions in German universities regarding the impact of Brexit. In A. Courtois (Ed.), *Higher Education and Brexit: Current European perspectives* (pp. 47–59). Centre for Global Higher Education, UCL IOE.

Kerr, C. (1982). *The uses of the university* (3rd ed.). Harvard University Press.

Kim, Y. C., Jo, J., & Jung, J.-H. (2020). The education of academically gifted students in South Korea: Innovative approaches in shadow education. *European Journal of Education*, 55(3), 376–387. https://doi.org/10.1111/ejed.12399

Knight, J. (2013). A model for the regionalization of higher education: The role and contribution of Tuning. *Tuning Journal for Higher Education*, 1(1), 105–125.

Kosmützky, A., & Nokkala, T. (Eds.) (2020). Towards a methodology discourse in comparative higher education. *Higher Education Quarterly*, 74(2), 115–217.

Lee, J. J. (2017). Neo-nationalism in higher education: Case of South Africa. *Studies in Higher Education*, 42(5), 869–886.

Lee, J. J., & Stensaker, B. (2021). Research on internationalisation and globalisation in higher education: Reflections on historical paths, current perspectives and future possibilities. *European Journal of Education*, 56(2).

Lehmann, W. (2021). Conflict and contentment: Case study of the social mobility of working–class students in Canada. *European Journal of Education*, 56(1). https://doi.org/10.1111/ejed.12431

Le Monde. (2021, April 9). La fin de l'ENA, une étape vers le renouveau de l'Etat. Retrieved from https://www.lemonde.fr/education/article/2021/04/09/la-fin-de-l-ena-une-etape-vers-le-renouveau-de-l-etat_6076136_1473685.html

Liu, H. (2007). Influence of China's imperial examinations on Japan, Korea and Vietnam. *Frontiers of History in China*, 2(4), 493–512. https://doi.org/10.1007/s11462-007-0025-5

Liu, J., & Bray, M. (2020). Accountability and (mis)trust in education systems: Private supplementary tutoring and the ineffectiveness of regulation in Myanmar. *European Journal of Education*, 55(3), 361–375. https://doi.org/10.1111/ejed.12409

Loveluck, C. (2013). *Northwest Europe in the Early Middle Ages, c.AD 600–1150: A comparative archaeology*. Cambridge University Press.

Marginson, S., & Rhoades, G. (2002). Beyond national states, markets, and systems of higher education: A glonacal agency heuristic. *Higher Education*, 43(3), 281–309. https://doi.org/10.1023/A:1014699605875

O'Connor, K. (2014). MOOCs, institutional policy and change dynamics in higher education. *Higher Education*, 68(5), 623–635. https://doi.org/10.1007/s10734-014-9735-z

O'Shea, S. (2021). "Kids from here don't go to uni": Considering first in family students' belonging and entitlement within the field of higher education in Australia. *European Journal of Education*, 56(1), https://doi.org/10.1111/ejed.12434

Palmer, J., Bresler, L., & Cooper, D. (Eds.). (2001). *Fifty major thinkers on education: From Confucius to Dewey*. Routledge.

Piketty, T. (2014). *Capital in the twenty-first century*. Harvard University Press.

Reay, D. (2021). The working classes and higher education: Meritocratic fallacies of upward mobility in the United Kingdom. *European Journal of Education*, 56(1). https://doi.org/10.1111/ejed.12438

de Sousa Santos, B. (2014). *Epistemologies of the South: Justice against epistemicide*. Paradigm Publishers.

Schugurensky, D. (2013). Higher education restructuring in the era of globalization: Toward a heteronomous model. In R. F. Arnove, C. A. Torres, & S. Franz (Eds.), *Comparative education: The dialectic of the global and the local* (pp. 283–304). Rowman & Littlefield.

Schugurensky, D., & Davidson-Harden, A. (2003). From Córdoba to Washington: WTO/GATS and Latin American education. *Globalisation, Societies and Education*, 1(3), 321–357.

Schultz, T. (1962). Reflections on investment in man. *Journal of Political Economy*, 70(5), 1–8.

Scott, J. C. (2020). *Seeing like a state: How certain schemes to improve the human condition have failed*. Yale University Press.

Shields, R. (2013). Globalization and international student mobility: A network analysis. *Comparative Education Review*, 57(4), 609–636. https://doi.org/10.1086/671752

Singh, M. (2017). National Qualifications Frameworks (NQF) and support for alternative transition routes for young people. In M. Pilz (Ed.), *Vocational Education and Training in times of economic crisis: Lessons from around the world* (Vol. 24, pp. 3–23). Springer. https://doi.org/10.1007/978-3-319-47856-2_1

Skinner, Q. (1978). *The foundations of modern political thought: The Renaissance* (Vol. 1). Cambridge University Press.

Sullivan, R. (2020). Charlemagne. *Encyclopaedia Britannica*. https://www.britannica.com/biography/Charlemagne

Tandon, R., Singh, W., Clover, D. E., & Hall, B. L. (2016). Knowledge democracy and excellence in engagement. Online article. *IDS Bulletin*, 47(6). https://bulletin.ids.ac.uk/index.php/idsbo/article/view/2828/ONLINE%20ARTICLE

Torres, C. A. (2013). Neoliberalism as a new historical bloc: A Gramscian analysis of neoliberalism's common sense in education. *International Studies in Sociology of Education*, 23(2), 80–106. https://doi.org/10.1080/09620214.2013.790658

Torres, C. A. (2015). Global citizenship and global universities: The age of global interdependence and cosmopolitanism. *European Journal of Education*, 50(3), 262–279. https://doi.org/10.1111/ejed.12129

Torres, C.A. (2009). *Globalizations and education: Collected essays on class, race, gender, and the state*. Teachers College.

Torres, C.A. (2011). Public universities and the neoliberal common sense: Seven iconoclastic theses. *International Studies in Sociology of Education*, 21(3), 177–19.

Torres, C. A., & Bosio, E. (2020). Global citizenship education at the crossroads: Globalization, global commons, common good, and critical consciousness. *Prospects: Comparative Journal of Curriculum, Learning, and Assessment*, 48, 99–113. https://doi.org/10.1007/s11125-019-09458-w

UIS. (2021). *World Inequality Database on Education (WIDE)*. Database. UNESCO Institute for Statistics. https://www.education-inequalities.org

UNESCO. (2018). *Handbook on measuring equity in education*. UNESCO Institute for Statistics. http://uis.unesco.org/sites/default/files/documents/handbook-measuring-equity-education-2018-en.pdf

UNESCO. (2019). *Global convention on the recognition of qualifications concerning higher education*. UNESCO. http://portal.unesco.org/en/ev.php-URL_ID=49557&URL_DO=DO_TOPIC&URL_SECTION=201.html

UNESCO. (2020). *Global education monitoring report: Inclusion and education*. UNESCO.

United Nations. (1948). *Universal Declaration of Human Rights*. United Nations. http://www.ohchr.org/EN/UDHR/Documents/UDHR_Translations/eng.pdf

United Nations. (2015). Transforming our world: The 2030 agenda for sustainable development. United Nations. https://sustainabledevelopment.un.org/post2015/transformingourworld/publication

van der Wende, M., & Rienks, J. (2018). Netherlands: Stages of uncertainty: Brexit and the unknown future of UK-Dutch higher education cooperation. In A. Courtois (Ed.), *Higher Education and Brexit: Current European perspectives* (pp. 84–97). Centre for Global Higher Education, UCL IOE.

Verger, A., Lubienski, C., Steiner-Khamsi, G. (Eds.). (2016). *The global education industry*. Routledge.

Verger, J. (1986). À propos de la naissance de l'université de Paris: Contexte social, enjeu politique, portée intellectuelle. *Vorträge Und Forschungen: Schulen Und Studium Im Sozialen Wandel Des Hohen Und Späten Mittelalters, 30*, 69–96. https://doi.org/DOI:10.11588/VUF.1986.0.15808

Vukasovic, M., & Stensaker, B. (2018). University alliances in the Europe of knowledge: Positions, agendas and practices in policy processes. *European Educational Research Journal, 17*(3), 349–364. https://doi.org/10.1177/1474904117724572

Wallerstein, I. (2004). *World-Systems analysis: An introduction*. Duke University Press.

Weiss, S. (2021). Fostering sense of belonging at universities. *European Journal of Education, 56*(1). https://doi.org/10.1111/ejed.12439

Wibrow, B., & Waugh, J. (2020). *Rationalising VET qualifications: Selected international approaches*. National Centre for Vocational Education Research. https://www.ncver.edu.au/__data/assets/pdf_file/0035/9662417/Rationalising_VET_qualifications_selected_international_approaches.pdf

Wiksten, S. (2020). A critically informed teacher education curriculum in Global Citizenship Education: Training teachers as field experts and contributors to assessment and monitoring of goals. *Journal of International Cooperation in Education, 23*(2), 107–130. https://cice.hiroshima-u.ac.jp/wp-content/uploads/2021/02/8.Susan_.pdf

Zhang, W. (2020). Shadow education in the service of tiger parenting: Strategies used by middle-class families in China. *European Journal of Education, 55*(3), 388–404. https://doi.org/10.1111/ejed.12414

11

Education for All in Africa— Not Remediation, but Transformation and Innovation

Joel Samoff
Stanford University and University of Johannesburg

Bidemi Carrol
RTI International

ABSTRACT

Education held extraordinary promise at Africa's independence. Nearly unbounded aspirations. Imaginative innovations. Yet the initial rapid progress was not sustained. By the late 20th century crisis was common. Schools in many countries had no teachers' guides, no textbooks, not even chairs. The new century has seen reflection and rejuvenation, often accompanied by significantly increased dependence on external resources. While some of its excitement has reappeared, education in Africa—widely understood as critical to national development and the focus of a major share of national budgets—combines high expectations and enthusiasm with distress and dependence. Ironically, many of the strategies intended to achieve education for all in practice render it a distant dream. The rhetoric of liberation and empowerment notwithstanding, the commonly held view is that education must enable Africa to run faster as it tries to catch up with those who are ahead rather than forge new paths or transform the international economy and Africa's role in it. As African countries struggle to provide quality education for all, their major challenge is to shift the focus from catching up to leaping ahead, specifying their direction. Needed is not remediation but transformation and innovation, indeed, developing learning strategies that others emulate.

■ ■ ■

Education held extraordinary promise at Africa's independence. Nearly unbounded aspirations. More schools. More teachers. More learners. Imaginative innovations. Yet the initial rapid progress was not sustained. By the late 20th century crisis was common. Schools in many countries had no teachers' guides, no textbooks, not even chairs. The new century has seen reflection and rejuvenation, often accompanied by significantly increased dependence on external resources. While some of its excitement has reappeared, education in Africa—widely understood as critical to national development and the focus of a major share of national budgets—combines high expectations and enthusiasm with distress and dependence. As African countries struggle to provide quality education for all, their major challenge is to shift the focus from catching up to leaping ahead, specifying their direction. Needed is not remediation but transformation and innovation, indeed, developing learning strategies that others emulate.

Where education systems are not functioning well and do not provide productive learning environments for many of their students, it is tempting to limit expectations and focus on basic mastery. Doing so, however, is self-limiting. Education systems that do not encourage learners to excel, to challenge and surpass their teachers, to experiment and innovate, cannot develop the education culture and institutional strengths necessary to enable all learners to achieve basic mastery. Unless they leap ahead—for Julius Nyerere, "We must run while they walk"—Africa's education systems will continue to copy the stunted models of the European schools they inherited at independence.[1] As Levin has shown, Africa's development requires acceleration, not remediation.[2]

Africa has been the site of imaginative experiments, innovations in the content and forms of education, and critical reflections on the role of education in society. Long before Europeans arrived, and to this day, Africa's intellectual contributions have had global influence. How, then, to make sense of this transition from expansive expectations to pervasive degeneration to renewed growth, from promise to progress to crisis to new hope? While we must not underestimate the achievements or lose hope, moving beyond crisis requires careful analysis of its origins and persistence. That analysis requires attention to both content and forms, and especially process. In the remainder of this brief overview, we explore major issues and themes in education in contemporary Africa,[3] considering both outcomes and analytic frameworks.

"Education in Africa," like "African education," is, of course, a simplification fraught with risk. For most purposes, neither exists. With care, it is possible to study education in Guinée and to explore the unique characteristics of, say, Ugandan education. But since the diversity within countries is vast, it is foolhardy to speak in general terms about a continent comprising more than 50 countries. Still, the craft of comparative education requires just that. Identifying and understanding similarities and commonalities sometimes requires deferring attention to individual variations. Our continuing challenge and responsibility are to use each sort of analysis—detailed examination of what is unique at the small scale and synthetic overview of what is common at the larger scale—to illuminate and strengthen the other. Hence, as we consider shared patterns across Africa, we must at the same time constantly recall and respect Africa's rich diversity.

EDUCATION IN AFRICA: FROM CRISIS TO RENEWED HOPE

The early 21st century has been a period of reflection and reevaluation for African development. The optimism that accompanied the decolonization of the late 1950s and early 1960s was displaced by deep dismay at persisting poverty and a profound pessimism about the viability of any strategy of social transformation. For many, the objective was no longer broad improvement in the standard of living or self-reliance but simply survival.

Education experienced a similar transition.[4] Earlier, education (formal and nonformal) was expected to be the principal vehicle for social change, both helping to define the new society and enabling its citizens to function effectively within it. Not only were the unschooled to learn reading and writing, but the newly educated were also to foster innovation, accelerate the generation and diffusion of ideas and technologies, and monitor and manage a responsive political system. Education was to be the vehicle for redressing discrimination and inequality, both in daily practice and in popular understanding.

There was progress and, in some countries, very substantial achievements. Still, as the 21st century dawned, in much of Africa many children received little or no schooling, illiteracy rates remained high, school libraries had few books, laboratories had outdated or malfunctioning equipment and insufficient supplies, and learners lacked chairs, exercise books, even pencils. The common term was crisis. Many, both inside and outside Africa, were pessimistic about the ability of national authorities to address the crisis effectively.

In this setting, recourse to foreign aid, always important for education in Africa, became a way of life. Almost without exception, education reform proposals were presumed to require external funding. Increasingly, even the day-to-day operation of the education system depended on overseas support.

External aid agencies proffered development advice as well as finance. Notwithstanding its critical role, historically their funding remained a very modest portion of total education expenditures. Consequently, their influence was far greater than the absolute value of their aid suggests. Indeed, some agencies, and especially the World Bank, insist that their development expertise is even more important than their funds. "[The World Bank's] main contribution must be advice, designed to help governments develop education policies suitable for the circumstances of their countries" (World Bank, 1995, p. 14).

Two approaches clash here. One insists that education is a right and a public good. The other addresses education primarily in terms of its contribution to national growth and well-being through the development of the knowledge and skills that societies are deemed to need. Notwithstanding the common rhetoric of the rights approach, however, most often education is regarded as distinctly instrumental, an investment in a country's future, a production system that (more or less successfully) turns out people with particular competencies and attitudes, and a delivery system that transfers wisdom, expectations, ways of thinking, and discipline to the next generation (see Samoff, Chapter 1, this volume). The voices that continue to insist that education is liberating, that learning is inherently developmental, and that therefore education is a public responsibility, struggle to be heard and rarely prevail in policy deliberations. As we shall see, within the instrumental orientation two powerful currents—on the one hand, the expanded role for foreign aid and its providers and with it the tendency to address education through the prism and with the tools of finance and, on the other, the understanding of education primarily as preparation for the world of work—reinforce each other with enduring consequences for education in Africa.

Promise, Decay, and Rejuvenation

Nearly all African countries became independent with an inherited education system that excluded most of the population. In Tanzania (then Tanganyika), for example, both Christian missionaries and the British government-operated schools. But at independence in 1961 those schools accommodated fewer than half the country's children. For most of them, the course of study was four (or fewer) years. As former Tanzanian president Julius Nyerere noted, at independence "85 percent of [Tanzania's] adults were illiterate in any language. The country had only two African Engineers, 12 Doctors, and perhaps 30 Arts graduates" (Nyerere, 1998, p. 8). Although the schooled population was larger in a few African countries, many faced the new era with as few educated citizens as Tanzania.

If education were to transform society, access had to be extended massively and rapidly. Indeed, expanded access had become both a popular demand of the anticolonial nationalist movement and a promise of the newly installed postcolonial leadership. The premise was personal as well as political. Access to education was the primary route by which nearly all of Africa's initial leaders escaped (or rather mitigated) the discrimination and domination of European rule. Wherever there was a clear effort to reject race and other ascriptive criteria for employment and promotion, education's selection role became even more important. Opening schools in urban neighborhoods and rural villages was the most readily achievable and visible manifestation of the new government's accomplishments. Progress in this regard was indeed remarkable.

Let us consider the record. Doing so requires recognizing that the apparent precision provided by numbers is often fundamentally misleading. Put sharply, the margin of error on reported African education data is often far larger than the observed variation. Hence, many apparent changes, sometimes invoked to support policy or programs, are simply reflections of inconsistencies in the data or the categories used to organize it. Unfortunately, while the quality of data collection and analysis has continued to improve, problems of accuracy and comparability, and thus inference, persist.

There are three sorts of problems here. First, as we have noted, commentators and analysts regularly use the term Africa to refer to Sub-Saharan Africa. More problematic, we may not be able to determine to which notion of Africa a particular report or recommendation refers, rendering comparisons over time difficult or impossible.

Second, even foundation data may reflect political decisions more than careful counting. Jerven (2013; 2015) provides compelling evidence that major increases in the reported gross domestic product (GDP), making a low-income country middle income overnight, have resulted from revised calculation and reporting rather than from what appears to be substantial and rapid expansion of the national economy. As Jerven (2013) concludes, "the most basic metric of development, GDP, should not be treated as an objective number but rather as a number that is a product of a process in which a range of arbitrary and controversial assumptions are made" (p. 121).

Third, available figures are often inaccurate, inconsistent, and not readily comparable. Schools, districts, and other sources provide incomplete and inaccurate information. Sources differ on periodization and on the specification of expenditure categories. Some reports confuse budget and actual expenditure data and compare budget figures in one year with expenditure reports in another. Recurrent and development (capital) expenditures are treated inconsistently. Often the available data do not include individual, family, local government, and direct foreign spending. Discussions of the cost of education generally refer to government expenditures on education and sometimes only to education ministry spending. Inflation, deflation, and exchange rates are treated inconsistently. Data series are frequently too short to be sure that observed variation reflects significant change, and longer series are usually not comparable.[5]

The implications seem clear. First, it is essential to take the margin of error seriously, that is, to treat most national education statistics as rough approximations. Second, even relatively large observed changes may reflect nothing more significant than random fluctuations, annual variations, and flawed statistics. Consequently, apparent changes may be a weak foundation for broad inferences and public policy. Third, both researchers and policymakers must reject statistics whose underlying assumptions require a level of precision, linearity, or continuity that the data do not reliably support. Finally, effective use of available data requires seeing through the facade of precision and demystifying the use of statistics. Although number-density is the order of the day in international education policy and planning, pages bristling with numbers may obscure far more than they reveal.

Duly cautious, let us consider the accomplishments. Primary school enrollments in Sub-Saharan Africa increased sixfold from 1970 to 2018 (Table 11.1). In the same period, secondary enrollments were 12 times larger and tertiary enrollments 23 times larger. Over the past few decades, post-primary enrollments have been growing at a remarkably fast rate. If current sources permitted us to extend the data series back to 1960, the expansion would be even more dramatic. In societies in which less than a 10th of the population was deemed literate at the end of colonial rule, literacy rates have been increasing steadily (Table 11.2). Even so the absolute number of illiterate adults has increased (UIS database).[6]

Clearly, access to education in Africa expanded dramatically and rapidly. Yet, the initial high growth rates were not uniformly sustained. For many countries the primary enrollment ratio stagnated or even declined in the 1980s, one indication of the deterioration of public services and of the inability of governments to meet their commitment to move toward schooling for all their citizens (Table 11.3).

Table 11.1. Enrollment Trends in Education in Sub-Saharan Africa, 1970–2018 (in thousands)

	1970	1980	1990	2000	2010	2018
Pre-Primary		4,968	6,668	7,578	13,987	26,360
Primary	27,149	49,940	63,056	90,722	139,860	173,562
Secondary	5,413	9,978	16,221	23,914	46,553	63,406
Tertiary	384	746	1,476	2,811	8,371	8,798

Source: World Bank, Education Statistics (EdStats), https://datatopics.worldbank.org/education/home, retrieved May 17, 2020.

Table 11.2. Estimated Adult Literacy Rates in Sub-Saharan Africa, 1990–2018 (Percentages)

	1990	2000	2010	2018
Adult literacy rate, population 15+ years, both sexes (%)	53	57	60	66

Source: World Bank, Education Statistics (EdStats), https://datatopics.worldbank.org/education/home, retrieved May 17, 2020.

Table 11.3. Gross Enrollment Ratio in Primary and Secondary (both sexes), Sub-Saharan Africa, 1970–2018 (Percentages)

	1970	1980	1990	2000	2010	2018
Primary	54	77	73	82	97	98
Secondary	13	19	23	26	40	44

Source: World Bank, Education Statistics (EdStats), https://datatopics.worldbank.org/education/home, retrieved May 17, 2020.

At the same time, the supporting infrastructure for expansion was sorely stretched. In many countries buildings were not maintained, crash teacher recruitment programs were not accompanied by in-service professional development, low salaries forced teachers to look outside their classrooms to supplement their incomes, curriculum revision and textbook preparation proceeded slowly if at all, and morale plummeted. By the late 1980s African education was in crisis:

> It is not uncommon to find a teacher standing in front of 80–100 pupils who are sitting on a dirt floor in a room without a roof, trying to convey orally the limited knowledge he has, and the pupils trying to take notes on a piece of wrinkled paper using as a writing board the back of the pupil in front of him. There is no teacher guide for the teacher and no textbooks for the children. (UNESCO, 1989)

Decay was also apparent in higher education, especially as the emphasis on basic education was accompanied by efforts to shift resources from post-primary to primary schooling. Indeed, the rhetoric became accusatory, insisting that universities had become unaffordable and therefore exploitive luxuries that benefited only a small elite.[7]

By the end of the century, education growth in most countries resumed and higher education received renewed recognition and additional funding. Several countries have had many years of relatively high-volume external funding, both targeted at specific programs and from some sources provided as sector or budget support. Notwithstanding a strong initiative to shift from project to budget support, currently, budget support is a very small percentage, perhaps less than 1%, of external assistance to education. Schooling in those countries, however, continues to confront very large classes, teachers with little preparation and limited instructional materials, and periodic promising reforms that rarely progress beyond the pilot stage or receive too little funding or political support to flourish. As well, the primary indicator of progress toward global goals, substantially increased enrollment in the first year of school, often has not been sustained. Throughout the region it is not uncommon to find that many of the new students do not return for their second year and that most do not reach the end of the primary school cycle. For example, in Sierra Leone, Mozambique, and Uganda, where enrollment growth has been rapid, the rates of surviving to the last grade of primary in 2016 were 47%, 39%, and 36%, respectively (UNESCO Institute of Statistics, 2021). The very rapid expansion that followed the abolition of primary school fees, and increasingly secondary school fees, in several countries has been followed not only by high attrition but also by very large classes for those who remain in school. Even where it was achieved, expanded access to school was not readily translated into learning for all.

In 1990 governments and international and nongovernmental organizations (NGOs) enthusiastically committed themselves to Education for All (Inter-Agency Commission, World Conference on Education for All, 1990). Small meetings, big conferences, national plans, and many reports followed. Meeting in Dakar a decade later, the world's education community considered a sobering assessment.[8] Notwithstanding the reaffirmation of the goals, education for all in Africa remained a long way off. As they renewed the commitment, educators and policymakers deferred the targets, strengthened the infrastructure, and maintained optimistic expectations (World Education Forum, 2000). Once again in 2015 the monitors reported a similar conclusion as the world gathered in Incheon, South Korea, to review progress. Despite important achievements, uneven across countries, socioeconomic strata, gender, and urban/rural residence, "Overall, not even the target of universal primary education was reached, let alone the more ambitious EFA goals, and the most disadvantaged continue to be the last to benefit" (UNESCO, 2015, p. xv).

Once again, the major targets, now somewhat expanded and included as Goal 4 in the UN's Sustainable Development Goals, were deferred for another 15 years, that is 40 years from the 1990 conference (*Education 2030*, 2015). At the current pace, the EFA monitors had projected, universal lower secondary education for poor rural girls in Sub-Saharan Africa will require nearly a century to achieve.

While an extended analysis of the education for all campaign and the Jomtien (1990), Dakar (2000), and Incheon (2015) meetings is not possible here, four observations are important.[9] First, since in some countries there has been little or very slow progress toward education for all over more than a half-century, it is reasonable to conclude that despite the rhetoric and formal pronouncements, education goals and priorities lie elsewhere. Second, it is far from clear that massive international conferences, an international secretariat, and insistence on national plans and reports are an effective or cost-efficient strategy for transforming and shaping education policy and practice in Africa: "The assumption that global and regional conferences are powerful enough to hold countries and the international community to account has not proved to be valid . . . it is less clear that new knowledge or tools have helped develop appropriate capacity for evidence-based national policymaking or that they have strengthened national EFA policy and practice" (UNESCO, 2015, p. xv).

Third, the progress noted here has been confronted by a persisting pessimism about achieving global education goals. Several of the countries with the lowest enrollments have witnessed remarkably expanded access in the few decades, but even at that pace still cannot make the international goals (Education Policy

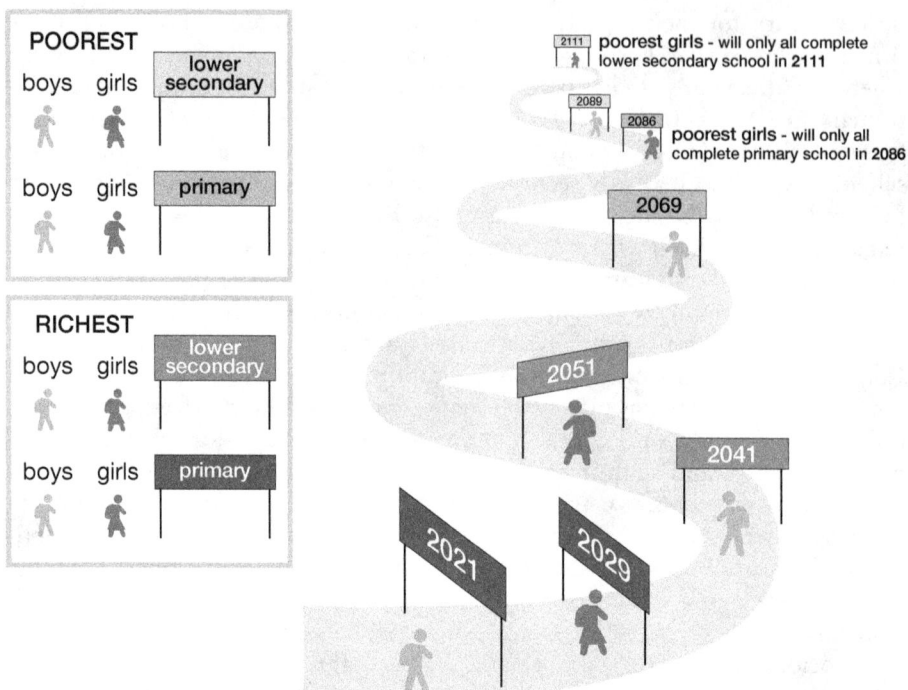

Figure 11.1. The Journey to Complete Education in Sub-Saharan Africa
Source: UNESCO. "Infographics from the GMR 2013/4: Teaching and Learning: Achieving Quality for All." Accessed February 22, 2021. https://en.unesco.org/gem-report/infographics/infographics-gmr-20134-teaching-and-learning-achieving-quality-all.

Data Center, 2005). Education for All was more a campaign than a plan and clearly has included targets that some countries could not reach. The monitors of progress toward those goals have issued 16 reports since 2002. All incorporated specially commissioned studies, careful data collection, and systematic analysis. Although their primary emphasis varies, and although they chronicle progress in several domains, their refrain for Africa is common: the Education for All targets have not been met (e.g., gender parity in 2005) and are unlikely to be met by the new deadlines. Other reports reached similar conclusions. Even those that remain upbeat highlighted the slow progress in Africa and the difficulty of reaching the final 5–10% of the school-age population: "Four years from the deadline for achieving the targets set in Dakar, the central message of this year's EFA Global Monitoring Report is that governments have failed to meet their collective commitments" (UNESCO, 2011, p. 24).

> Sub-Saharan Africa is home to 43% of the world's out-of-school children, levels of learning achievement are very low, gender disparities are still large, and the learning needs of young children, adolescents and adults continue to suffer from widespread neglect. After much progress in increasing government investment in education, the financial crisis has reduced education spending in some countries and jeopardized the growth in spending required to achieve EFA in others. External aid to basic education declined in 2008, resulting in a significant decrease in basic education aid per child. (UNESCO, 2011, p. 1)[10]

The most recent analysis reports that the number of children not in school in Africa is growing, not decreasing. Disadvantage stems not only from poverty, but also from location, gender, ethnicity, and language (UNESCO, 2020a, pp. 6–7).

Fourth, the periodic reports that highlight progress and accomplishment—Africa rising—are both encouraging and incomplete (Association for the Development of Education in Africa, 2001). The evidence certainly shows significant education accomplishment and innovation, but for some people in some parts of the continent. Much of Africa, however, has not participated in that progress. Most important, education systems that provide universal access and reasonable quality and that support the generation, integration, and effective use of new knowledge—that enable African learners and researchers to set the pace rather than scrambling to catch up—have yet to emerge. Below, we explore more fully the evolving relationship between education and the state.

Experimentation and Innovation

Like much of education, experimentation, and innovation are contested terrain. As we have noted, Africa has witnessed important experiments and innovations in education at larger and smaller scales. In the late 1960s Tanzania rejected manpower planning in favor of education for self-reliance. At independence, the priority was developing higher-level skills. Projected skills need guided allocations. As the 1960s proceeded, Tanzania's leaders became increasingly critical of that approach, primarily because it constrained the expansion of primary education, a benefit of independence and a requisite for democratic development. Major resources were focused on a small part of the population, creating an arrogant elite detached from its social roots. The priorities must be reversed, leaders insisted. Scarce resources must go to those with little or no education rather than to those with the most (and the most alienating) education. Reversing the earlier orientation, Nyerere's (1967; 1968) widely read and cited *Education for Self-Reliance* shifted the emphasis to primary and adult education. Schools were to become community institutions, intimately connected with the patterns and rhythms of the local setting. Schools were also to have farms and workshops, both to value directly productive activities and to generate supplementary income.

Africa has been the site of imaginative and exciting education innovation. In Botswana, production brigades sought to integrate learning and the local setting by creating community schools in which learners and teachers were also producers (Gustafsson, 1985a).[11] To expand access rapidly, several African countries experimented with preservice and in-service teacher education. Others explored how to draw effectively on the local setting to develop lessons and materials. For just one example, in the early 1980s Zimbabwe developed imaginative curriculum kits to enable primary school teachers to engage learners in basic science by exploring rain puddles, tree leaves, and seed germination where labs with microscopes and other equipment were unavailable. Several countries have explored the uses of radio, television, and computers to extend the reach of a limited pool of experienced educators and to extend learners' access to resources unavailable at local schools. Dispersed and locally managed resource centers for teachers have proved effective in providing continuing support to instructional staff. Imaginative and energetic literacy campaigns have brought rapid progress in several countries.

Innovative community-based nonschool education programs have emerged across Africa, often with the support of a local or international NGO.

Though materially poor, several of Africa's higher education institutions are intellectually rich, exploring ideas and constructs with contacts and influences around the world. Ghana, for example, from the 1960s nurtured the rejuvenation of studies and debates about pan-Africanism. Through seminars, research, and major student holiday research projects scholars at the University of Dar es Salaam in the 1960s and 1970s explored the claims and problems and refined the methods of oral history, thereby joining and advancing an international debate among professional historians. Africa's laboratories and research institutes have developed systematic analyses, assessed standard responses, and generated new approaches for dealing with outbreaks and epidemics—HIV and AIDS, Ebola, coronavirus—along with their work on endemic diseases.

Recognizing the importance of interchanges across Africa, especially since it has often been easier for African scholars to communicate with colleagues in Europe than with colleagues in a neighboring country, researchers have established several continent-wide organizations. A few examples must suffice. Especially active has been the Council for the Development of Economic and Social Research in Africa (CODESRIA, Dakar), founded in 1973. Through its annual conferences, journals and publication series, collaborative research projects, international links, and support to young scholars, CODESRIA has energized and sustained imaginative innovations and critical analysis. Some organizations and their activities have proved difficult to sustain. Founded in Dar es Salaam in 1973 but inactive in recent years, the African Association of Political Science periodically brought scholars together, published a journal, supported participation in international meetings, and generally challenged Africa's political scientists to be critical and to cooperate. Two parallel networks, sometimes very active, sometimes hardly noticed, link education researchers in West and Central Africa and in Eastern and Southern Africa, concerned especially with the role of research in making public policy. Several externally initiated cross-national initiatives, for example, the African Virtual University and the African Economic Research Consortium, seek to play similar roles, though their organization and management continue to reflect the constructs and orientations of their funders.

Thus, despite a parched and bleak landscape, education innovation and experimentation have periodically flourished in Africa. While some initiatives have won wide recognition and influence, most have struggled to survive after the founders departed or initial funding was exhausted (Samoff et al., 2011). Although foreign funds have periodically supported reforms and experiments, overall, aid dependence has generally discouraged experimentation, especially activities that are oriented toward broad national political and social goals rather than more narrowly defined instructional tasks.

Large Commitments, Little Wealth

What explains the spurts and reverses and the difficulty in sustaining progress? In Africa as elsewhere it is common to blame governments for education problems. Particularly striking, however, is the extent to which African governments have generally maintained their commitment to education even in periods of dire economic distress. Two indicators are of interest, allocations to education as part of total spending and of national wealth.

Expressed as a percentage of the national budget, spending on education in Sub-Saharan Africa has consistently averaged between 15% and 18% (Table 11.4).[12]

Table 11.4. Public Expenditure on Education as % of Total Government Expenditure, 2000–2013

Year	2000	2005	2010	2013
Sub-Saharan Africa	15.6	18.0	17.4	16.6

Source: World Bank, Education Statistics (EdStats), https://data topics.worldbank.org/education/home, retrived May 17, 2020.

In terms of the overall economy, the level of spending on education in Sub-Saharan Africa has increased, though it remains less than in the world's most affluent countries (Table 11.5).

Table 11.5. Public Expenditure on Education as a Percentage (%) of GDP, 2000–2010

	2000	2005	2010
East Asia and Pacific		3.6	3.6
Europe and Central Asia	4.2	4.9	5.3
Latin America and Caribbean	3.9		4.8
North America	5.4	4.8	5.4
South Asia	2.6	3.2	3.4
Sub-Saharan Africa	3.2	3.6	3.8
World	4.0	4.1	4.6

Source: World Bank, Education Statistics (EdStats), https://data topics.worldbank.org/education/home, retrieved May 17, 2020.

Even a large part of a small budget, however, is still small. Although most African governments maintained their commitment to education through difficult economic circumstances and pressures to constrain social spending, the actual amounts spent were very small. That most African countries came to independence with few educated people and very small education infrastructure and have a large school-aged population highlights the challenge. The major constraint has been total government revenue, although in many countries there has been limited political support for education and ineffective and inefficient education (and national) management.

Indeed, funding education is more complex than this suggests. While of course colonial rule has ended, African countries remain inserted in a global political economy that constrains autonomy. As well, African governments have proved reluctant to tap the national resources available.

Pressed by the international financial institutions, initially in the 1980s and broadly continuing, many African countries adopted structural adjustment programs, commonly termed "liberalization," that generally emphasized substantial devaluation, decreased direct government role in the economy (especially in productive activities), reductions in the size of the civil service, encouragement of foreign investment, and support for the privatization of many activities, including public services. Nearly everywhere the implementation of these policies meant increased prices for consumer goods and new or increased fees for social services, including education. Notwithstanding pressures to constrain or reduce education spending, for example by employing paraprofessional or other lower-paid instructional personnel, many African governments maintained their basic commitment to funding education. Increasing indebtedness, another consequence of efforts to expand public services with limited resources, consumes an increasing portion of the revenue that is available. Even with great sacrifices, in absolute terms, there was little money for education.

Still, the widespread notion that African countries cannot afford stronger education systems is at best a partial understanding. Systematic reviews show substantial private spending on education that could be tapped to support education expansion and innovation. As well, increasing tax revenue—both more effective collection of taxes that are due and progressive revision of tax laws—could finance more and better schools (Samoff & Irving, 2014; International Commission on Financing Global Education Opportunity, 2016). Ironically, African governments' recourse to the grants and loans of foreign aid reinforces their reluctance to modify taxes to increase revenue for public services.

Education was to be the developmental engine, the principal strategy for eliminating poverty and closing the gap between the most and least affluent countries. To play that role, however, education required resources that were not readily available. A consequence of this dilemma is that for poor countries (most of the world's poorest countries are in Africa), the development gap is likely to continue to expand.

In its current forms, foreign aid is unlikely to close that gap. The very public and regularly reiterated global commitment to education for all, and the explicit assertion that "no countries seriously committed to education for all will be thwarted in their achievement of this goal by a lack of resources" (World Education Forum, 2000, p. 9), have not been accompanied by a clear strategy for financing education for all (Samoff & Irving, 2014). A global education fund, similar to the Global Fund to Fight AIDS, Tuberculosis, and Malaria, has been proposed but has not materialized. A global education tax—progressive and redistributive as is common within affluent countries, where the most affluent segments of the population bear the largest share of supporting the education system, including educating the poorest children—seems even more distant.

The world education community clings to the hope that foreign aid can close the funding gap. For education, the 2015 EFA Global Monitoring Report calculated that even with optimistic assumptions about economic growth, efficient financial management, and increased foreign aid, achieving the 2030 goals would require annual supplemental funding of $39 billion, and that is assuming low-income countries increase their domestic funding of education as a share of GDP by 50% (UNESCO, 2015). Yet, external support to education, and particularly funding for basic education, has declined sharply over the past two decades (UNESCO, 2002, p. 23 and Chapter 5; UNESCO, 2010). As we have noted, historically foreign aid provided a very small percentage of Africa's total spending on education,[13] and whatever its magnitude, much of that support is spent on personnel, services, products, and scholarships in the aid-providing country. Hence, in at least some settings, far from redistribution toward Africa, foreign aid may in fact function to generate a net outflow from Africa of both capital and skills. Figure 11.2 shows trends in official development assistance to Africa, in terms of gross disbursements, from all providers (governments, multilaterals, and private donors) that report aid statistics to OECD's Development Assistance Committee (DAC). Notably missing from the providers list are several countries, including China, India, and Qatar, that have increased their development assistance to Africa, but do not report to the DAC (OECD, 2015). Of the nonreporting countries, China is the most influential. And while it is difficult to secure a reliable estimate of China's contribution to education in Africa, its education focus is less on basic education and more on skills development and higher education.

The Fast Track to Planned Dependence

As we have noted, modern education in Africa has both local and foreign roots. For most African countries, the continuing external role looms large. Governments pay teachers' salaries. They also build and maintain schools, purchase textbooks, and sometimes support students' accommodation and board. Very little public funding is available for chalk or wall maps or copying machines or other supplies and equipment. Hardly any is available for innovation, experimentation, and reform. There lies foreign aid's powerful roar. Its leverage has not been its total volume but rather that educators with exhausted budgets can use it to expand, to alter priorities, to modify practices, and more generally to respond to their own and others' sense of what needs to be done. Across Africa foreign aid has become the center of gravity for education and development initiatives.

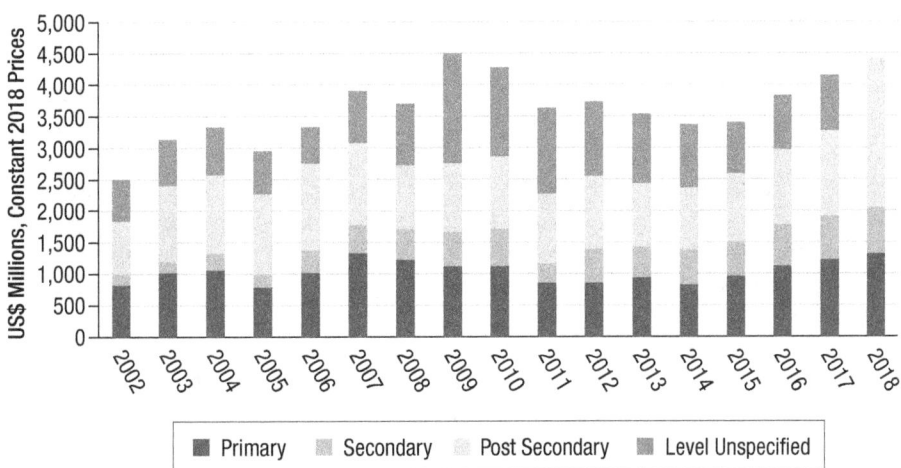

Figure 11.2. Official Development Assistance to Education to Africa, Gross Disbursements, 2002–2018.

Note: Includes all donors (bilateral, multilateral), all channels (budget support, NGO, education institutions, etc.), and all types of aid (budget support, scholarships, project funding, etc.).

Source: Organisation for Economic Co-operation and Development (OECD). "Creditor Reporting System (CRS)," April 16, 2020. https://stats.oecd.org/Index.aspx?DataSetCode=crs1#.

Beyond the need for additional resources, over time it has come to seem not only obvious but unexceptional that new initiatives and reform programs require external support, and therefore responsiveness to the agenda and preferences of the funding agencies: aid dependence.

Thus, aid dependence refers not to the volume of aid or to education systems whose principal funding comes from abroad. Rather, aid dependence is the internalization within those education systems of the notion that improvement and change require external support, advice, and often personnel. Aid dependence is as well the adoption and institutionalization of constructs, analytic frameworks, and assessment strategies developed elsewhere (Samoff, 2019). That internalization and institutionalization, supplemented by the elaborate reporting routines now required by funding agencies, make the policies and preferences of the foreign funders far more consequential than could be explained by the volume of their assistance.

That orientation is dramatic in several African countries. Not only education development efforts but also recurrent expenditures have become significantly dependent on external funding. Effectively, foreign aid pays the teachers. Net Official Development Assistance received in 2018 accounted for over 50% of total government expenditure in seven countries: Central African Republic (292%),[14] Malawi (86%), Mali (71%), Rwanda (62%), Mozambique (62%), Ethiopia (54%), and Madagascar (51%) (World Bank, Education Statistics, 2021). While that seems unsustainable, there is little discussion of how African countries will wean themselves from that support. Indeed, the effort to increase and accelerate aid has become a fast track to planned dependence. Even more important than the unsustainability of that reliance on foreign aid is the tension between intensified and entrenched dependence and a country's ability to orient and manage its education system. That reliance on foreign support carries both the promise of immediate benefits and the risk of undermining education's developmental role.

At the same time, the major international conferences have been accompanied by an ever-increasing collection of indicators, country reports, and reviews. As the education goals were incorporated into still broader poverty reduction goals, governments of the affluent countries launched major commissions to study poverty and foreign aid, generally with a strong focus on education and often followed by promises of substantially increased funding. In 2005 the major affluent countries agreed to double foreign aid to Africa and to forgive at least part of Africa's encumbering aid debt. Increased and more rapidly delivered support were founding premises for the Fast Track Initiative and the Global Partnership for Education.

While the international conferences and the parallel efforts to modify the aid process, especially to shift from supporting individual projects to subsidizing the national budget, are not specific to Africa, their consequences weigh heavily on Africa. First, the global conferences established international reporting machinery, generally in addition to the large number of project- and country-specific reports required of aid recipients. Effectively, that establishes external accountability well before accountability within the country has been developed and institutionalized. The advantage: greater clarity on what is (and is not) being done and by whom. The disadvantage: the external focus undermines efforts to create direct accountability of leaders to communities and organizations within the country.

The eligibility rules of debt relief (Heavily Indebted Poor Countries [HIPC]) and related accelerated aid (Fast Track Initiative [FTI], Global Partnership for Education [GPE]) programs become in practice an externally set policy agenda for African education, at least as powerful as explicit conditions set by aid providers. Third, the associated planning and reporting requirements further constrain national education policy even as they proclaim their commitment to nationally led development.[15] Fourth, although intended to reduce the duplications and distractions of reporting to multiple foreign agencies, the required reports remain a significant administrative burden and, more important, reinforce an imposed orthodoxy in the constructs and analytic frameworks used to review the education system, indicate and measure progress, analyze problems, and suggest remedies. Over several decades, periodic conferences and declarations have envisioned a code of conduct for funding and technical assistance agencies and have reiterated the importance of national goals and plans. There remains, however, far more external direction than genuine transnational partnerships. Thus, like the aid relationship, the international conferences and the global goals promote progress along specific paths (say, expanded schooling for girls) at the cost of further entrenching external direction and accountability. A critical perspective must not create a caricature of the role of foreign assistance. Aid is a relationship that depends on the active participation of both providers and recipients. Many African countries have proved imaginative in asserting a national agenda, even as in others, foreign aid protects leaders' security of tenure against local challenges.

This overview of education in Africa has provided a series of snapshots of evolution and change, highlighting both progress and problems. Understanding that evolution requires exploring policy and programmatic initiatives and regarding both policy and practice in education as sharply contested terrain.

Learning for All
The global commitment to education for all explicitly asserted the importance of *learning*, not schooling. Subtitled "Meeting Basic Learning Needs," the World Declaration on Education for All insisted that:

> Whether or not expanded educational opportunities will translate into meaningful development—for an individual or for society—depends ultimately on whether people actually learn as a result of those opportunities. . . . The focus of basic education must, therefore, be on actual learning acquisition and outcome, rather than exclusively upon enrollment, continued participation in organized programmes and completion of certification requirements. Active and participatory approaches are particularly valuable in assuring learning acquisition and allowing learners to reach their fullest potential. (World Declaration on Education for All, 1990 Article 4)

The importance of learning was reaffirmed at the subsequent global meetings in Dakar (2000) and Incheon (2015), where the education objectives, with basic education extended to include lower secondary, became Goal 4 of the Sustainable Development Goals (World Education Forum, 2000; *Education 2030*). Yet, in practice, most EFA activities have focused on access to primary school. Although some educators have reminded the world of its inattention to learning and to learners beyond school age or otherwise not in school, the major focus has been schooling, with progress toward EFA goals commonly reported as primary school enrollment. As more African countries have reached or are nearing universal primary education, however, attention has increasingly shifted to education quality. Most recently that transition is reflected in Sustainable Development Goal 4: Ensure inclusive and equitable quality education and promote lifelong learning opportunities for all.

Unfortunately, that apparent refocusing retains a narrow construction of education, concerned far more with inputs and outputs than with what happens in between, and is little attentive to the learning process. Particularly striking is the World Bank's 2020 education strategy, which notwithstanding its title, *Learning for All*, says very little about learning (World Bank, 2011; Samoff, 2012a). A similarly narrow approach troubles several other major global education analyses (World Bank, 2017; Bashir et al., 2018). The concern is acquiring information (used synonymously with knowledge) and then repeating it in class and in examinations, presented uncritically as the measure of education quality. The major recent analyses we have noted all refer to learning, all take learning to mean acquisition of information, and all assess that through tests of reading skill, which are presented as measures of cognitive achievement, itself a proxy for all learning. Unaddressed are nurturing curiosity, framing questions and intellectual puzzles, undertaking systematic comparisons, developing constructs, preparing evidence-based analysis, and most important for a continent that must escape its underdevelopment, creating knowledge. Schooling is to be a passive activity, delivered by teachers to largely passive students, very much the banking model of education criticized by Paulo Freire (1970). Equally frustrating in this approach is the inattention to and lack of support for the education research infrastructure necessary to enable Africa's educators to understand and promote learning for all (Samoff, 2012b).

While expanding access can accomplish schooling for all, achieving that falls far short of learning for all. There are two related issues here. First, enabling more children to enter schools that have maintained the curriculum and organization of institutions designed to educate elites cannot secure learning for all. Effective mass education requires a different schooling model. It is useful to compare a school whose primary concern is selection (as students proceed up the education ladder, their number decreases sharply—the common education pyramid) with a school organized around inclusion (all students who begin the basic education cycle are expected to complete it). Selective schools are very concerned with sifting and sorting (determining who will proceed), rely on ability grouping and tracking, use examinations to measure individual achievement, and understand failure in terms of individual student performance. The differences are sharp. Since they believe all students can learn and since they expect the students who begin basic education to complete it, inclusive schools focus on cooperation and collaboration rather than competition and selection, organize heterogeneous student groups, use examinations primarily to assess where the curriculum and pedagogy are effective and where they must be modified, and understand failure in school and systemic terms. Schooling intended to educate a small elite—the inherited pattern that has been maintained in most of Africa—cannot achieve mass education. Without a fundamental transformation of the schooling model, learning for all will remain an unattainable goal.

Second, the common narrow construction of education quality is itself an obstacle to learning for all. Of course, learners must master basic literacy and numeracy skills. Confusing that skills mastery with learning, however, fosters unimaginative teaching and teacher education, reinforces hierarchical and non-participatory classroom practice, and provides little incentive or reward, at any level, for the creativity, the willingness and ability to challenge standard models, and the innovation and knowledge production that are essential for Africa.

CHALLENGES, ISSUES, AND INITIATIVES

Equality and Equity

Another commitment of Africa's postcolonial leadership was to use the education system to address the inequalities and injustices of the larger society. Expanded access was an important but insufficient step in that direction.

Historically, schools had been primary agents in reproducing a sharply unequal social order. Limited recruitment and severely constrained academic pathways restricted most Africans to less-skilled and lower-paid jobs and to their social status. There were important exceptions. A few Africans did reach the highest levels of the education system, surpassing many of their European peers. A few poets, novelists, and playwrights found ways to publish their work. A few West Africans were elected to the French parliament and served in the cabinet. Especially in places that had a longer history of missionary education, a few families could point to several generations of university graduates. Still, most Africans simply never had a chance to go to school. Of those who did, few advanced far. Hence, converting schools from institutions that functioned to create and maintain inequality into vehicles for achieving equality requires a fundamental transformation. What has occurred in this regard? To address this question, we must first consider several issues of terminology and public policy.

First, common to much of the analysis of education is a confusion of equity and equality. This confusion is potentially quite problematic for public policy. Although over the long term equity generally requires equal treatment, in some circumstances achieving equity may require differentiation. Equality has to do with sameness, or, in public policy, with nondiscrimination. Equality has to do with making sure that some learners are not assigned to smaller classes, do not receive more or better textbooks, or are not preferentially promoted because of their race, gender, regional origin, or family wealth. Although there may be valid educational grounds for differentiating among students, equal access requires that status differences not function to limit or guide admission, promotion, and selection.

Equity, however, has to do with fairness and justice. And there is the conundrum. Sometimes the two do not go together, at least in the short term. A history of discrimination (at the core of the colonial experience) may mean that justice requires providing special encouragement and support for those who were disadvantaged. For example, given its history, what is equitable education in post–apartheid South Africa? Repealing discriminatory laws cannot in itself quickly achieve equality of access. Wherever it is deemed reasonable, affirmative action to redress injustice may involve pursuing policies that treat different groups of people in different ways. Achieving equity—justice—may thus require structured inequalities, at least temporarily. Assuring equal access, itself a very difficult challenge, is a first step toward achieving equity. But conflating equity and equality diverts attention from addressing the links between discrimination and injustice and sets nondiscrimination, rather than justice, as the major objective.[16]

Even when equity is specified as equality, what is generally envisioned is equality of opportunity. But how is it possible to know whether opportunities have been equal without considering outcomes? A careful study might, for example, find no visible gender discrimination in selection to secondary school or in the secondary school pedagogy. But if that study also finds that attrition and failure rates are much higher among girls, it seems likely that opportunities were not equal after all. That is, measures of access are insufficient for assessing equality of opportunity. Discovering and redressing inequalities of opportunity require considering outcomes as well as starting points. (See Chapter 6 in this volume.)

Second, discussions of equality and equity commonly assume a fundamental tension between those goals and economic growth. African governments must of course make development choices. Yet, it is far from clear that growth and equality are alternatives, especially in education. Reducing inequality by expanding access to education, for example, may fuel growth as increased consumer demand for goods and services stimulates the expansion of production and productive capacity. Similarly, broader diffusion of competencies and understandings may reduce the reliance on much more expensive imported labor and facilitate reorienting the workforce as forms and circumstances of production change. As well, persisting inequality is both a barrier to broad participation in democratic governance and a breeding ground for socially disruptive discontent. There are thus strong grounds for rejecting the assumption that there is a necessary tradeoff between growth and equality and for concluding instead that growth and equality are mutually dependent, each requiring and advancing the other.

Third, as access has expanded, while the base of the education pyramid has broadened, its top remains very narrow in most of Africa, in part because of the massive resources required to transform primary education for a selected elite into basic education for all. The exclusion point has moved farther along in the school cycle. As Table 11.6 shows, in Sub-Saharan Africa, 37% of those in primary school can expect to reach the secondary level and 5% to go beyond that. Mindful that these numbers represent different student cohorts, it seems clear that for most Africans, schooling is a process of ever-narrowing selection, with only a few learners proceeding to the advanced levels.

Table 11.6. Education Enrollment and Selection in Sub-Saharan Africa, 2018

	Enrollment (millions)	Enrollment as % of preceding level	Enrollment as % of primary
Primary	173.6		
Secondary	63.4	37%	37%
Tertiary	8.8	14%	5%

Source: World Bank, Education Statistics (EdStats), https://datatopics.worldbank.org/education/home, retrieved May 17, 2020.

Fourth, although earlier discussions of (in)equality and (in)equity in education were generally concerned with region (a surrogate for ethnicity and, more commonly, tribe), in recent years gender has received priority attention.

In a very short period, women's experiences in education have become a central focus of education analysis and, in at least some countries, of education policy and planning (Bloch et al., 1998; UNESCO, 2016; 2020b; see also Chapter 7 from Stromquist, this volume). A review of nearly 150 broad studies of African education undertaken during the late 1980s found little explicit attention to girls' education. A review of some 240 studies completed in the early 1990s found that essentially all addressed that topic (Samoff, 1996). Here we see the direct influence of foreign aid on African education policy and practice. Initially led by Swedish feminists whose parliamentarians insisted that Swedish aid include a priority for girls' education, the foreign aid community elevated the importance of this issue, with obligatory attention but uneven enthusiasm across Africa. That increased attention has been accompanied by the development of organizations, institutions, and networks concerned with girls' education at the continental, national, and local levels. Several external funding agencies provide significant support for efforts to increase girls' recruitment and school success.

Efforts to encourage and support girls to enter and succeed in school have been extensive but only partially successful. Although there has been clear progress toward equal gender access to primary school, in the countries of Sub-Saharan Africa as a group, females do not yet constitute half of the enrollment. From lower starting points (one-fourth of the secondary school population and one-tenth of tertiary enrollment in 1960), there has been remarkable progress at secondary and tertiary levels. Still, in 2018 females constituted only 43% of total tertiary enrollment (Table 11.7). The variation among African countries is substantial. At the secondary level, for example, the gender parity index (GPI) for secondary gross enrollment rate in 2017 varied from 0.67 (Central African Republic) to 1.35 (Lesotho).[17] For the tertiary gross enrollment rate, GPI varied from 0.42 (Mali) to 2.31 (Seychelles) (World Bank, Education Statistics, 2021). Note that in some countries, especially those where young boys are sent to mind the cows (e.g., Lesotho), the disparity moves in the other direction: males are under-enrolled.

Table 11.7. Female Enrollment as a Percentage (%) of Total Enrollments in Sub-Saharan Africa, 1990-2018

Year	Preprimary	Primary	Secondary	Tertiary
1990	49	45	43	34
2000	49	46	44	41
2010	50	48	45	41
2018	49	48	47	43

Source: World Bank, Education Statistics (EdStats), https://datatopics.worldbank.org/education/home, retrieved May 17, 2020.

Table 11.8 shows that the percentage of literate adult females in Sub-Saharan Africa has increased by about 16 percentage points over the past three decades, and the ratio of female literacy rate to male literacy rate has increased from 0.64 to 0.81. Nevertheless, slightly less than a third remain illiterate. As with all other data, the regional averages hide wide variations per country with the female adult literacy rate ranging from 26% in Mali to 96% in Seychelles.

Table 11.8. Estimated Adult (15+) Literacy Rates in Sub-Saharan Africa, 1985–2018

Year	1985	1990	2000	2010	2018
Population 15+ years, both sexes (%)	50	53	57	60	66
Population 15+ years, female (%)	39	42	50	51	59
Gender Parity Index	0.64	0.66	0.71	0.75	0.81

Source: World Bank, Education Statistics (EdStats), https://datatopics.worldbank.org/education/home, retrieved May 17, 2020.

The persistence of differentiation is striking. A 1995 research overview concluded that:

> although tremendous gains have been made since the 1960s in most places, participation levels of girls still remain lower than those of boys. Repetition, drop-out and failure is very high among girls, beginning at the primary level and continuing throughout the system. . . . The small number of girls who remain in the system tend to be directed away from science, mathematics and technical subjects. . . . Consequently, female participation in the [formal] labour market is limited. . . . Female illiteracy remains high. (Odaga & Heneveld, 1995, p. 14)

Nearly a decade later:

> Sub-Saharan Africa has low enrollments rates and strong gender disparities and inequalities. . . . Gender disparities concern not only access to school but also participation in the learning process. Sub-Saharan Africa is the region with the highest repetition rate . . . girls repeat more often than boys. . . . Survival rates to grade 5 in sub-Saharan Africa are lower than elsewhere, and it is the only region where they are higher for boys than girls . . . . Gender disparities in primary education increase with the level of education . . . . In tertiary education, girls are not only much less represented (fewer than five girls to 10 boys) but often confined to so-called "feminine" fields, such as social sciences, humanities, services and health-related courses, that do not boost their chances of equal job opportunities with men. Women account for nearly two-thirds of the illiterates, a figure not expected to change much by 2015. Most countries show substantial gender gaps, with female literacy no more than half that of males. (UNESCO, 2003, pp. 1–2)

Nearly another decade later the EFA Global Education Monitoring Report projected that poor rural girls in Africa will achieve universal primary education in 2086 and universal lower secondary education in 2111. The monitors' 2016 Gender Review reported: "Girls face the biggest barriers in sub-Saharan Africa. Of out-of-school girls, 50%, or 9 million, will never enter a classroom" (UNESCO 2003, p. 15).

The most recent data from the UNESCO Institute for Statistics estimates that 97.5 million children, adolescents, and youth were out of school in Sub-Saharan Africa, and of those 52 million (53%) were female.[18]

The increased attention to gender in education highlights important issues of approach and method in comparative education and in the links between research and policy. The prevailing research orientation in this arena clearly reflects both the dominance and the limitations of what has come to be the standard model for social science research. Generally, the starting point is a set of instrumental assumptions about the value and importance of educating females, especially expanding and strengthening workforce skills, increasing employability, improving family health, and reducing fertility. Yet, if educating females produces clear social and individual benefits, why do they not constitute half the school population? To address this question, researchers seek to identify factors that explain lower enrollment or higher attrition. The candidate causes are by now well-known: parental attitudes, gender-differentiated expectations for future income, the labor and household responsibilities of women, the absence of role models at home and in school, explicit and implicit discouragement for pursuing particular courses of study, parents' educational achievement, family religious and moral precepts, sexual harassment, child marriage, early pregnancy, and more.

Some analysts, however, insist that the fundamental problem is power and authority relations, not exclusion (Unterhalter, 2005; Heward, 1999). From this perspective, schools reflect the social order in which they function, and thus it is not surprising that societal gender distinctions infiltrate and orient the schools. That is, to confront gender inequality in education requires not so much identifying individual causative factors but modifying social, and therefore economic and political, relations. In this approach, rather than working to incorporate females into a nonegalitarian society, schools must become locations and agents of social transformation. This understanding of the problem, though forcefully presented in the general literature on African development, is with few exceptions little evident in studies of African education, which for the most part continue to list variables and attempt to test their relative importance. (For further discussion, see Chapter 7 in this volume.)

It is useful to consider briefly the persistence within education of other societal cleavages. Substantial and reliable evidence indicates that access to and success in school continues in many countries to be sharply differentiated by region, religion, race or national origin, and class. Available country data, for example, Nigeria and Ghana, indicate that Christian communities generally have more schools, more children in school, and more graduates than Muslim communities. Within Africa, Qur'anic and other Muslim schools have generally not been a serious academic alternative to secular (i.e., Western and at least unofficially Christian) education. When relevant data are collected, the systematic finding is that children from more affluent and higher-status families are more likely to find places in school and to proceed to higher levels. For example, in Rwanda inequalities due to region, ethnicity, and socioeconomic status are much larger than gender inequality (Figure 11.3; data from the 2015 Demographic and Health Survey). The data show the widest disparities in transition by household wealth and the smallest in terms of gender. This pattern is similar for many other countries. Yet, these inequalities are far less often the focus of discussion and systematic research than gender differentiation. Several countries have implemented gender affirmative action programs. But there seems to be no comparable initiatives to assist

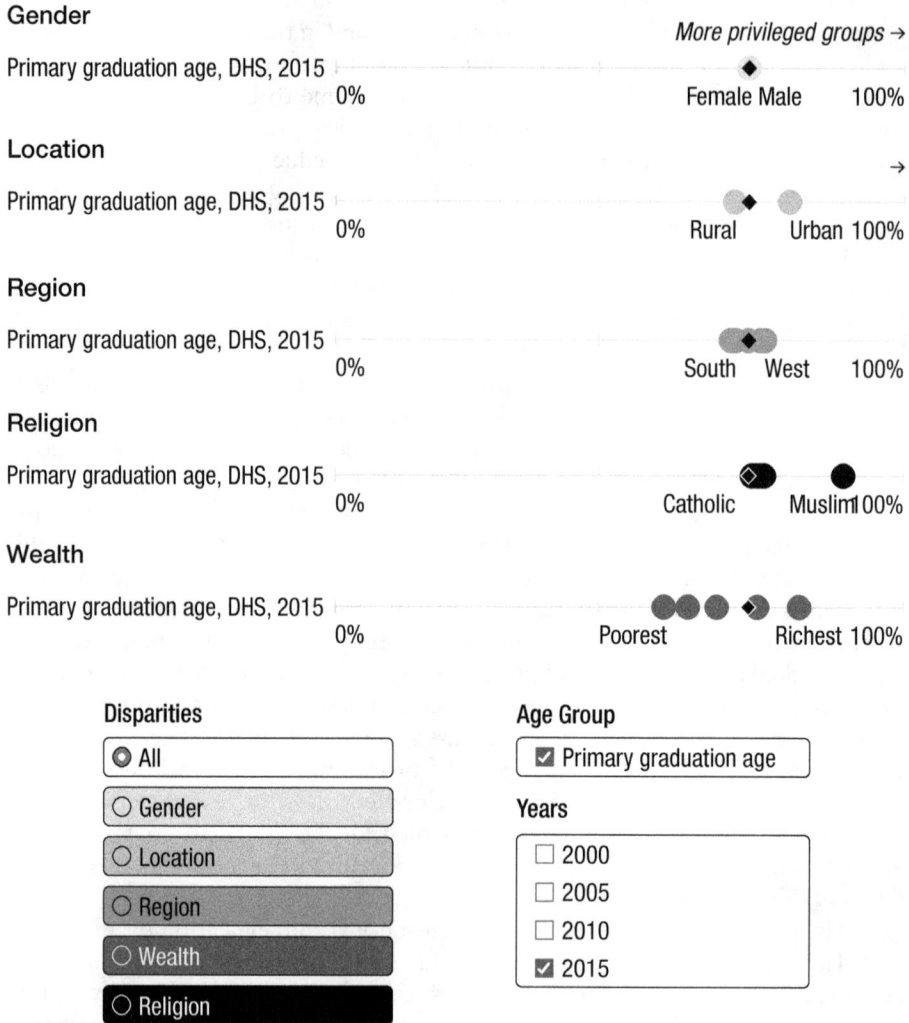

Figure 11.3. Inequalities in transition rate to lower secondary, Rwanda, 2015

Source: The World Inequality Database on Education. https://www.education-inequalities.org/countries/rwanda#?dimension=all&group=all&year=latest; Generated on July 26, 2020.

prospective learners who are discouraged or disadvantaged by region, ethnicity, race, national origin, religion, or socioeconomic status.

There are other areas of disadvantage, such as disability status, which until recently have received little attention and little systematic data collection. However, available data show that children with disabilities are less likely to be in school, and if they are in school they lag behind other students in measured learning outcomes (Global Education Monitoring Report Team, 2020).

Education, Conflict, and Emergencies

As we write (mid-2020), the world is experiencing a global health pandemic that has resulted in school closures and learning disruptions. UNESCO reports that more than one billion children were affected in over 100 countries. While this is undoubtedly the largest education emergency and the most school closures we have faced in modern times, there are millions of children at any time who are out of school or whose learning is disrupted due to other crises, emergencies, and conflicts. In addition to wars and other conflict-related crises, health emergencies (e.g., coronavirus pandemic, Ebola epidemic) and climate disasters (e.g., earthquakes, floods) have resulted in prolonged school closures. Often, countries and learners in Africa are the most vulnerable to these crises.

Half of the 35 countries identified in the UNESCO Global Monitoring Report as conflict-affected countries, where education performance is at its lowest, are in Africa. As well, 42% of the out-of-school children are in conflict-affected countries (UNESCO, 2011, p. 24). In addition to the negative consequences of conflict for education, the unequal distribution of education and other public services can themselves be a root cause of conflict (Sierra Leone Truth and Reconciliation Commission, 2004). In some countries, for example, Sierra Leone, young men, conscripted into fighting forces, deliberately targeted and destroyed education institutions that had failed them or from which they had been excluded (O'Malley, 2007; 2010).

Health and climate emergencies are especially consequential for African children in fragile states with poor infrastructure. The Ebola epidemic in West Africa in 2014–2015 led to school closures for over a year, and the education systems have still not recovered. The prolonged closures due to COVID-19 have powerful and long-lasting consequences for students in Africa, where despite government efforts to maintain learning through radio, television, and other mobile technologies, many children do not have access. Remote schooling becomes no schooling. Since creating remote learning opportunities is costly, many countries rely on external funding to accomplish that. The Global Partnership for Education has established a fund to help African governments finance their COVID-19 mitigation plans, but there can be long delays between seeking and receiving funds.

While all children suffer during these prolonged school crises, children are impacted differently based on several factors including gender and socioeconomic status. During wartime, young boys can be abducted and forced to become soldiers as occurred in Sierra Leone, Uganda, Democratic Republic of Congo, and other countries, while abducted girls are forced to become wives or sex slaves of soldiers. In Northern Nigeria, Boko Haram has specifically targeted girls and became infamous internationally for kidnapping over 200 girls from their school in Chibok (Maiangwa & Agbiboa, 2014). During long school closures due to the Ebola epidemic as well, girls in Sierra Leone and Liberia were more vulnerable to sexual abuse and exploitation in their communities, and both countries saw increased rates of teenage pregnancies, which led many girls not to return to school after the crisis (Onyango et al., 2019). Finally, children from low-income households are less likely to benefit from initiatives aimed at continuing learning, both because they lack access to needed technologies and because they need to support the livelihoods of their families. Many will not return to school.

These conflicts and crises have led to forced displacement worldwide. At the end of 2019, 79.5 million people had been displaced from their homes; 26 million refugees and 45.7 million internally displaced. Six Sub-Saharan African countries are among the world's 10 countries with the greatest displacement: South Sudan

(2.2 million), Somalia (0.9 million), Democratic Republic of Congo (0.8 million), Sudan (0.7 million), and Central African Republic (0.6 million) (UNHCR, 2019). Conflict and violence in these countries caused the refugee population in Sub-Saharan Africa to triple over the last decade. Most of the refugees from these countries are in camps in neighboring countries including Uganda, Sudan, Ethiopia, and Kenya, under the auspices of the UNHCR. The UNHCR's Global Education Strategy calls for the integration of refugees into the host country's national systems, but this usually means integration in schools with fewer resources and lower learning outcomes amongst refugee children (Dryden-Peterson et al., 2019).

Within the dark clouds of education and conflict, there has also been innovation in education. For example, in Namibia's liberation movement's bush schools, constantly under attack, instructors became skilled at developing teacher-made materials and fostered peer-assisted learning and learner-centered instruction. Sierra Leone refugee teachers started schools under mango trees in Guinea. Alternative primary education programs in Sierra Leone and Liberia provided a contracted primary school education to young people who had missed out on schooling during the war. Those two countries initiated radio instruction programs during their Ebola epidemic, as many other countries have done during the COVID-19 pandemic. Though the programs are still nascent and have limited reach, education ministries have developed partnerships with telecommunication companies to provide free access to educational materials and learning opportunities for parents and learners with cell phones.

As long as African countries continue to move in and out of conflict, education progress will be hindered and universal education will remain an elusive goal.

From Private to Public to Private

For most of Africa, colonial education was a significantly private affair, with churches in the central role, often with government funding. Decolonization shifted the center of activity. Education and health became the most visible of public goods, to be publicly funded and managed by the government. Not only was there widespread recognition of education's value to the community, but as well the postcolonial context carried the expectation that the new government, successor to the nationalist movement, would replace selective and discriminatory schooling with broad access and progress by merit. As we have seen, public schools and enrollments mushroomed, with progress toward universal primary school access in many countries. More recently, the very visible abolition of primary and secondary school fees and the EFA campaigns have reinforced the government's role.

At the same time, the pressures to [re-]privatize have gathered steam. Privatization advocacy comes from several directions. In some settings, the churches have remained active education providers, not infrequently with public funds. In Lesotho, for example, churches own and manage most schools. That prominent education role for religious institutions is not simply a legacy of the past. Several countries are considering integrating Koranic schools into the public education system and providing them at least partial funding. Second, high-fee private schools have retained a role, serving the children of the most affluent. Third, the visible failures of government schools fuel demand for nongovernmental alternatives. In several countries, private chains of low-fee schools have captured public attention, relying on centrally developed curriculum delivered electronically to teachers with limited professional education and rudimentary facilities to reduce their operating costs. Finding that it has not met government standards for certified teachers and accredited curriculum, the Uganda and Kenya governments have brought legal action to close one chain's schools (Reip & Machacek, 2016). The larger issue concerns government responsibility and accountability for basic education, especially for a country's poorest citizens. The right to education is replaced by an opportunity to purchase education. School fees for the poor deepen their poverty. Rather than strengthening public education, this pattern of privatization leaves government schools as the last resort for the most disadvantaged (Lewin, 2017).

A fourth current has been the foreign funders' pressure to privatize, especially prominent in the World Bank's periodic analyses and recommendations. A fifth impulse comes from external vendors who seek access to African education, protected by the rules of the international trade agreements and organizations. While most students attend public schools, enrollment in private schools across sub-Saharan Africa has increased significantly. Recent data record a 40% increase in the percentage of students in private primary schools (Table 11.9). The country variation is even more striking. In 2017, the share of enrollment in private pre-primary ranged from 100% in Uganda to 5% in Tanzania. The share of enrollment in private primary schools ranged from 48% in Liberia to 1% in Sao Tome, and in secondary from 57% in Mauritius to 4% in South Africa.

Table 11.9. Percentage of Enrollment in Private Education Institutions in Sub-Saharan Africa, 2000–2018

	2000	2005	2010	2015	2018
Pre-Primary	32	31	34	30	32
Primary	10	10	11	13	14
Secondary	17	17	20	21	21

Source: World Bank, Education Statistics (EdStats), https://datatopics.worldbank.org/education/home, retrieved May 17, 2020.

Education privatization in Africa—shifting responsibility for funding education from government to learners and their families—has several forms. School fees at any level transform at least part of the learning environment from a public good supported by the entire populace to a private user benefit.

While the abolition of primary school fees has somewhat reinforced the notion of publicly supported education, ostensibly free schools continue to find ways to demand payments from their students. As well, parents across the continent seek to improve their children's prospects through paid supplementary lessons, generally after-school tutoring, often by learners' regular teachers.

Thus, though initially banned or discouraged in some countries, private schools—some nongovernmental nonprofit and some for-profit institutions, some high quality and some learning environments in name only—have increased nearly everywhere. For some commentators, they provide a better alternative for the poor (see, e.g., Tooley & Dixon, 2005). While some have a long history (e.g.,

Harambee secondary schools in Kenya), community schools at multiple levels, funded entirely or in large part by communities' direct and in-kind contributions, have also expanded across Africa. Notwithstanding several national initiatives, textbook production has remained significantly private and foreign. In many countries, private higher education institutions now outnumber government colleges and universities. Numerous and prominent, foreign vendors have proved difficult to accredit and regulate. Increasingly, government-sponsored access to higher education, reflecting the notion that university students are both the implementers and the trustees of the public good and therefore reasonably publicly supported, has been replaced by significant student fees. Government universities are expected to generate more revenue through student fees, charges for products and services, and perhaps direct involvement in commercial enterprises.

As this privatization has proceeded, the gray area that overlaps public and private has also expanded. Schools of many sorts receive direct and indirect government funding and are sometimes responsive to government direction. Some use their private or quasi-private status to secure exemption from government regulations or to offer courses of study not entirely congruent with national education objectives, policies, or priorities.

The broad consequences of this increased private role are not yet fully clear or systematically assessed. What is clear is that for many people postprimary education, and for some even basic education, is increasingly viewed as a commodity whose price is set in a complex and difficult to understand market whose major drivers may lie outside Africa. Since information on value and pricing is at best incomplete and certainly not readily available to most parents, individual choices are regularly guided by the prominence and persistence of claims in discussions largely dominated by privatization advocates. Where significant elements of the education system lie outside public control and where even well-managed resources are insufficient, the right to education disappears. It is difficult to hold the government responsible and accountable for schooling and unlikely that the government will innovate and initiate. The understanding of education as a public good has eroded, with very limited discussion of how, why, and who benefits.

Nongovernmental Organizations

With few exceptions, the government has played the central role in postcolonial African education, both setting policy and creating and managing schools. That reflects the global pattern of education as a public good and the specifically African circumstances. Education was to enable a developmental leap, to reduce inherited inequalities, and to promote national integration. We have noted what was initially the persistence of a small private sector and what has become a set of powerful pressures to privatize.

At the same time, the United Nations and NGOs of various sorts—international, national, and local—have played an increasing education role in Africa. In addition to UNESCO, UN agencies have sought to address special circumstances (e.g., United Nations High Commission for Refugees support to schools for displaced people), underserved education domains (United Nations Children's Fund support for early childhood education), and high priorities (United Nations Girls' Education Initiative). Several international NGOs have had long-standing broad education initiatives (e.g., Save the Children), while others have a narrower focus (Room to Read, Friends of African Village Libraries). Other service NGOs have education programs (Oxfam, Catholic Relief Services, International Rescue Committee). While these NGOs are formally apolitical, regularly the momentum of their work requires advocacy and involves them in education policy issues.

A few NGOs are explicitly activist, committed to influencing education policy, for example eliminating school fees or promoting girls' education. Founded in 1999 by ActionAid, Oxfam, Education International (an association of teachers' unions), and the Global March Against Child Labour, the Global Campaign for Education has regional and national affiliates across Africa. Education activism has also emerged within Africa. Recognizing the challenges in achieving education for all, the Africa Network Campaign on Education for All provides an umbrella for education alliances and coalitions across Africa. Initially, with support from the Association for the Development of Education in Africa (ADEA) and the Rockefeller Foundation, the Forum for African Women Educationalists has developed continent-wide and country-specific programs to support girls' education initiatives. Focused on adult literacy among women in Senegal, Tostan ("breakthrough" in Wolof) has played an influential local and national role in addressing female genital cutting.

Activist education organizations in several countries have sought to navigate between supporting government initiatives and periodically using research, media access, and citizen mobilization to highlight the education system's inadequacies, for example, HakiElimu (Tanzania), Twaweza and Uwezo (East Africa), and Equal Education (South Africa). Challenging authority of course carries risks. HakiElimu's critical reports on EFA progress and teachers' conditions led in 2005 to sharp responses by senior political officials and efforts to restrict its activities and a formal ban on access to schools, subsequently lifted.

It seems likely that NGO activity will continue to expand, though to date Africa has not seen the emergence of NGOs committed to creating independent parallel schools,[19] and that activists will have uneasy relationships with governments. While education NGOs can be especially responsive to unique local needs and conditions—indeed, that is commonly their founding rationale—most continue to rely heavily on external funding and are periodically buffeted by its vagaries. As well, where NGOs provide education services, they may reduce government responsibility and accountability and thereby diminish citizens' ability to demand and secure education.

Setting Education Policy

Education policy and agenda-setting in Africa have taken many forms, from broadly inclusive to narrowly authoritarian (for case studies, see Evans, 1994; Association for the Development of African Education, 1996; Fredua-Kwarteng, 2016). The inherited model was distinctly bureaucratic, oriented more toward control and management than innovation and development, a pattern that has been widely retained and reinforced. In some countries, key individuals (often the education minister but occasionally the head of state) have played the central role in defining problems and charting directions. In other countries, select commissions have gathered evidence, sponsored studies, and recommended new policies. In still other settings, a major national conference (in francophone Africa, états-généraux) provided opportunities for the diverse interests of the education community to present their views and construct coalitions to support particular policies.

Tanzania's experience is again instructive (we draw here on Samoff, 1994a). Both the policies and the policy-making process reflected the changing times, influences, and balance of forces. With a very small pool of educated officials at its independence in 1961, Tanzania (Tanganyika), like many other African countries, sought external advice and assistance in setting priorities and developing concrete plans. Guided by consultants recruited by the World Bank, Tanzania decided initially to emphasize postprimary education and a manpower planning approach. With the 1967 publication of *Education for Self-Reliance* (Nyerere, 1967), the priority shifted to primary and adult education. Earlier, the principal education policy advisers had been external experts. By the end of the 1960s, the influential voices were those of the president and Tanzania's single political party (TANU).

As primary education expanded, public discontent and especially middle-class protest focused on limited access to secondary school. Appointed in the early 1980s by President Nyerere to review education policy, a national commission toured the country, heard testimony, commissioned studies, and offered analyses, projections, and recommendations. Publicly released and then abruptly withdrawn, its report initiated a national debate, including contentious exchanges on the introduction of secondary school fees. Thus the education policy-making process had again been modified. Whereas in the preceding decade the president and the party had initiated the new policies, by the 1980s the circle of participants in policymaking had widened.

By the early 1990s, the situation had again changed. A new national review of education policy was launched. This time the initiative lay with the Ministry of Education and Culture, and the principal participants were not politicians but rather academics, who relied heavily on external funding.[20] Here, then, is another approach to formulating education policy, directed by the education bureaucracy with education experts in the central roles. This orientation was quite consistent with the general 1990s trend of seeking to depoliticize the public policy process. That orientation in turn coincided with the vastly increased role of the World Bank in Third World education research and policymaking, a role that was particularly evident in Tanzania in the early 1990s. By the turn of the century, education policymaking in Tanzania had come full cycle, with a prominent role for the World Bank and its experts as the Poverty Reduction Strategy Paper became the umbrella process for policymaking in education and other sectors.

In short, over the years Tanzania experimented with several different policy-making models: reliance on externally recruited experts, initiative by the president and the party, consultation managed by an inclusive and distinctly political national commission, renewed recourse to education experts, though heavily dependent on external funding.

Note that often studies of education policy are frustratingly narrowly gauged. Most of the writing on public policy focuses on formal pronouncements by authoritative institutions. Since making policy is assumed to be the prerogative of those in power, policy researchers study elites and formal documents. Most often, this perspective understands policymaking as a sequence of activities and feedback loops, moving from vision to formulation to negotiation to policy specification and from announcement to implementation to evaluation. This understanding of policy is widespread and regularly asserted in Africa.

Yet policy is made as much (or often a good deal more) in practice as by pronouncement. Indeed, effective policy analysis requires moving beyond the equation of policy with official statements that may have little or no influence on what occurs. Consider, for example, policy on language of instruction. An education ministry may have formal rules, officially recorded and publicly announced, specifying that instructors are to use a particular language to teach certain subjects. Suppose, however, that an onsite study shows that nearly all of the instructors use other languages to teach those subjects. When asked, a school principal might say, "Our policy in this school is to use the language that our students understand. To do otherwise will make their examination marks even worse." What, then, is the policy? From one perspective, the policy is what the ministry has promulgated, and what the teachers do is a deviation from official policy. From the other perspective, the actual policy (i.e., the working rules that guide behavior) is what the teachers are doing. In this view, the ministry documents are just that: official statements that may or may not be implemented and certainly not guides to what people actually do.

Recognizing that policy results from practice as well as from official pronouncements helps identify other major influences on education policy in Africa. Regularly, education policy in Africa results from the intersection of national initiatives and external expectations. Increased reliance on foreign funding has expanded the direct role of both the finance ministry, which generally manages all external aid, and the funding and technical assistance agencies, whose agendas have come to guide and constrain education initiatives and reforms in Africa. Explicit conditions attached to foreign aid may require particular policies or priorities. Even if there are no explicit conditions of that sort and foreign aid is a very small portion of total national spending on education, external influence can still be decisive. Consciously or unconsciously, African policy and decision-makers shape their programs and projects, and thus policies and priorities, to fit what seems most likely to secure foreign funding. As the director of planning in Tanzania's education ministry explained, planning had become marketing (Samoff, 1994b). His task was less a process of exploring needs and developing strategies to address them than an effort to study the market set by prospective funders. He then identified its priorities and value points, using that market knowledge to craft, advertise, and sell projects and programs. That strategy was perhaps effective for coping in difficult circumstances. Nevertheless, it entrenched the role of the funding agencies in setting national education policies and priorities. It also reinforced the status and influence of a particular set of actors within the country, not those with the clearest or most dynamic education vision or those with the most solid national political base but rather those who proved to be most effective in securing foreign funding. In these ways, too, aid dependence becomes a vehicle for internalizing within African education establishments externally set policies, priorities, and understandings.

THE BROADER CONTEXT

Education and Development

A widely used term, *development* has many meanings (Decker & McMahon, 2020). In all, education is central. Understandings of the role of education in African development (broadly, improved standard of living and the economic changes required to achieve that) diverge sharply, with important educational and political consequences. Efforts to expand access, desegregate schools and curriculum, and promote equity reflect the premise and promise of decolonization. Viewed from that perspective, education has a broad and transformative mission. Parallel to that orientation and often in tension with it is a narrower view of the relationship between education and development. Often mechanically economic, this view assigns primary importance to the instrumental role of education in expanding production and productive capacity and generally considers other education objectives to be societal luxuries that must be deferred as currently unaffordable. In this view, however desirable, the humanist aspirations of liberal education, the moral obligation to redress inequalities, the expected social benefits of promoting equity, and the potential power of political mobilization and expanded democratic participation all must wait or, alternatively, must be achieved as by-products of insisting that schools focus on preparing the next generation for its expected role in the national and global economies. These are indeed difficult choices, its advocates insist, but unavoidable for poor countries.

That instrumental orientation is reinforced by widespread concern with what is generally termed "educated unemployment." This terminology is itself revealing. What is the problem here? What distinguishes the unemployment of the more educated from the joblessness of those with little or no schooling? Surely neither the society at large nor the young people who cannot find jobs would be better off if they were illiterate as well as unemployed.

That young people who finish school are frustrated in not finding jobs (or the jobs they think they should have) is primarily a function of job creation, not schooling. That those in power feel threatened by rising levels of education among the unemployed is primarily a problem of politics, not education.

Modifying the content and practice of education is expected to increase employability, alter expectations, or both. But even with better trained and better paid teachers, less crowded classrooms, and sufficient instructional materials, the education system cannot single-handedly overcome the consequences of a stagnant economy. If job seekers outnumber job openings, modifying school curriculum and pedagogy may affect which students find employment but not how many. Life experiences, far more than school lessons, shape expectations. In the absence of economic growth, neither the subject content taught in schools nor the political education they provide will do much to reduce frustration or relieve the anxiety of the political elite.

Together, the instrumental view of education's role in development and the concern with educated unemployment have generated efforts to link education closely with perceived skills needs. Over time, strategies for forging that link have evolved. An earlier notion was "manpower planning," which relied on projected labor needs to guide education programs and allocations. Widely criticized, that approach is still used. Yet, projecting needed skills far into the future is difficult, perhaps impossible, especially in economies experiencing rapid industrial and technical change. Just a few years ago, human resources planners in Africa had no entries in their job lists for computer programmer, microelectronics technician, or education technology instructor. Yet today every African economy needs those skills. This approach commonly underestimates the extent and rapidity of career changes. As well, it tends to disregard intellectual growth, the development of critical and problem-solving ability, the encouragement of creativity and expression, and many other dimensions of education that have no immediate or direct vocational outcome (see Klees, Chapter 2).

Several alternative approaches have emerged. One emphasizes society's broad interest in access to education and uses social demands to shape education programs. Focusing on demand enables education institutions to be sensitive to changing perspectives and preferences. But this approach is also subject to misunderstandings, fashions, and special circumstances that make it difficult to develop a coherent and integrated national education agenda. A different response to human-power planning is to locate principal programmatic decision-making within education and training institutions. If institutions are especially sensitive to their economic, political, and social context, that institutional autonomy may be very desirable. Yet, this approach is not readily compatible with efforts to set national policies and priorities. Nor does it facilitate coordinating the activities of different institutions. And when institutions are primarily responsive to their own internal pressures for new and enlarged programs, the risk of a mismatch between labor market demand and graduates' specializations is very high.

The effort to link curriculum and the education system more generally to the labor market has also led to the regularly reiterated complaint that schooling is too academic and too humanist. Education must be, the constant refrain goes, relevant to national needs. In this view, national needs, relevance, and their curriculum implications tend to be construed very narrowly. Beyond a rate and pattern of economic growth that enable people to improve their standard of living and develop spiritually as well as materially, what exactly are national needs?[21] Steel mills and a microelectronics industry? More village boreholes and grain mills? Do national needs include reliable, high-quality public services or the demand—often termed "need"—for more video players and other consumer goods? Should moral and ethical behavior, nonviolent conflict resolution, and the equitable treatment of all citizens also be considered national needs? Where to rank cultural, aesthetic, and literary needs? Everywhere, needs and priorities are regularly debated and redefined. In all societies, some groups assert that their particular demands are national needs. Education surely has a role in both shaping and addressing national needs, but equally surely has no linear paths to be followed.

Relevance makes sense only in terms of context and process. Often, for example, the observation that most people in Africa are rural agriculturalists leads to the assertion that education should focus on the tools and skills of farming. Unemployment is attributed to miseducation—that is, to studying history and language rather than soil chemistry and accounting. From that perspective, schools that teach languages to introduce young people to other cultures or assign books intended to expose learners to new ideas and different ways of thinking or insist that students use microscopes to understand and master systematic observation and comparison are wasting time with irrelevant programs. If so, how will Africa ever escape its dependence on the ideas and technologies of others? How will Africa move beyond exploiting nonrenewable resources to creating and developing new resources? If no Africans experiment with subnuclear particles, write new computer programs, or devise new approaches to dysentery, malaria, and AIDS, how can Africans assume responsibility for their own direction? If education is to expand rather than limit horizons, determining what is relevant requires not a simple statement of the obvious but an ongoing engagement with values, expectations, and constraints. Relevant programs emerge not from an authoritative decision but from collaboration and negotiation.

In summary, two sharply divergent perspectives on education and development have emerged in Africa. In one, education's role is transformative, liberating, and synthetic. Education must enable people to understand their society in order to change it. Education must be as much concerned with human relations as with skills, and equally concerned with eliminating inequality and practicing democracy. Education must focus on learning how to learn and on examining critically accepted knowledge and ways of doing things. Favoring innovation and experimentation, that sort of education is potentially liberating, empowering, and, as such, threatening to established power structures, both within and outside the schools. This orientation has remained the minority view.

Occasional initiatives to redefine the core and practice of education notwithstanding (e.g., education for self-reliance in Tanzania and production brigades in Botswana), the dominant perspective understands education primarily as skills development and preparation for the world of work. The emphasis on relevance assigns low priority to educating historians, philosophers, poets, and social critics, and thereby to cultivating the historian, philosopher, poet, and critic in all learners. Fearing unemployed graduates, leaders expect schools to limit learners' aspirations. Shaped by national examinations, curriculum revolves much more around information to be acquired than around developing strategies and tools for acquiring that information, generating ideas, or crafting critiques.

Global Goals and Assessments

Throughout this discussion, we have highlighted the intersection of external and internal dynamics in education policy and practice in Africa. Two global education currents warrant additional attention.

The first concerns the international education conferences and the elaborate management, monitoring, and reporting structure associated with them. The world—hundreds of governments, international organizations, funding and technical assistance agencies, NGOs, and more—met in 1990, 2000, and again in 2015 to review progress and reaffirm its commitment to education for all. Those large events were preceded and followed by many smaller-scale meetings, studies, and reviews. Assuring that education, including its funding, the world asserted, is now a global responsibility. Perhaps.

The annual EFA Global Monitoring Reports have been clear that education, and certainly education of "good quality," was not universal by the twice-revised target, 2015, that for many learners the universal access goal is still well in the future, and that notwithstanding the funding agencies' promise of adequate resources, the aid that has been provided is far less than the aid needed to meet calculated costs. How, then, to assess the extensive EFA campaign?[22]

The campaign has focused attention on education and its value and perhaps accelerated progress toward universal primary education in some countries. The general EFA campaign has likely assisted targeted initiatives, for example, to promote girls' education. It may be that the campaign has generated additional resources for education in poor countries. It may be that the spending on the conferences, international and national secretariats, national reporting, global monitoring, and related activities are reasonable costs for the additional education resources.

At the same time, the EFA campaign has clearly reinforced and solidified external intervention and continuing roles in education in Africa. It has established and strengthened external lines of accountability, perhaps weakening those within countries. We can see here how the widely articulated rights approach to education remains rhetorical. Rights are societal constructs that require guarantors. The assertion of rights without corresponding attention to who is responsible for assuring those rights, makes them at best aspirational, not foundations for policy, and at worst a cover for entrenching inequalities. As Tomasevski pointed out, when providing education is the responsibility of everyone, no one is directly responsible or legally accountable for failure.[23] When citizens press their governments for more and better education, leaders can disclaim responsibility, pointing to the failure to deliver promised foreign aid. For many African countries, the EFA campaign has also increased indebtedness and reinforced and entrenched aid dependence. With occasional exceptions, the EFA campaign reinforces the outsiders' assertion that they are the most effective protectors of Africa's poor and disadvantaged and that African governments are more often the problem than the solution.

Even more problematic for the longer term is the shift of focus from national responsibility to external support. The EFA campaign has obscured, deferred, and likely obstructed the discussion of the disadvantages of leaving so much control over education, widely understood to be central to Africa's development, to outsiders and the political debate about how revenue might be generated within the country to design and manage the education system. Put sharply, the world has set an education agenda and strategy that have immediate benefits and potentially significant costs for Africa. As we shall explain, that education agenda converges with the preferences of national elites who prioritize accumulation and security of tenure over democratic participation and mass education.

Here, too, we must not understand the aid relationship to have initiative and influence in only one direction or to ignore the agency of African leaders. As we have noted, countries have used EFA resources to expand and strengthen their education systems. Extending school access and especially eliminating school fees have periodically featured prominently in political campaigns, for example in Uganda, Sierra Leone, Ghana, and Kenya. Our observation is simply that when education expansion and reform, and leaders' own security in the office, are dependent on external resources, the aid providers become active participants in African education, regularly influencing policy and imposing constraints on practice.

The second global education current is the product of the increasing prominence of the cross-national achievement education assessments. Parallel and intersecting international initiatives, most subject-specific, are intended to establish and validate universal standards that permit comparing the measured accomplishment of, say, grade 4 pupils in mathematics in Country A with the accomplishments of grade 4 students in Countries B, C, D, and E.[24] Especially since they are comparative, reported results become a widely discussed progress marker. Embarrassed that their SACMEQ assessment results are weaker than those in neighboring, much smaller and much poorer countries, for example, South Africans decry the inadequacies of their education system and shout their recommended remedies.

Assessing education programs is of course important, and the cross-national testing may both reinforce the general importance of monitoring and assessment and point to specific problems. At the same time, they embed a notion of learning that privileges what is deemed to be the universal content of knowledge and skills and that devalues the understanding of knowledge as fundamentally local, context- and culture-grounded, and contingent. Often, a narrow assessment of reading ability becomes the measure of the broad development of cognitive skills and the proxy for the quality of a national education system. In the absence of a single global education system with agreed objectives, standards, and measures, effective cross-national comparison is likely unattainable, since meaning and learning are always contextual. Even were that not so, their validity for Africa will remain of limited utility until there is much deeper African involvement in the conception, development, and management of the assessments.

The cross-national testing is better understood as another strategy for urging, rewarding, and localizing within Africa externally specified notions of knowledge and skills, of the knowledge that matters, and of how that knowledge should be acquired, and for urging and rewarding education systems for adopting and implementing particular learning objectives and pedagogical approaches: "Measuring educational quality and using those measurements to fault 'bad' education for a host of ills in society is highly functional to maintaining the highly preferred position of the very elites who spread this ideology" (Carnoy, 2016, p. 32).

When African students fare poorly in the international comparisons, the common response is to adopt the curriculum and pedagogy of the countries where students score higher. When, occasionally, African students are the high scorers, the common response is not to learn from Africa's educators but rather to wonder how that exception occurred.

Their allure is blinding. Both the EFA campaign and the cross-national testing are powerful and generally unremarked vehicles through which African countries willingly embrace globalizing trends that undermine African initiative and autonomy.

Education and the State

In Africa as elsewhere, education and the state are intimately interconnected. Developing our analysis of education in Africa requires exploring that link. The state in Africa plays a major role in the processes of accumulation and legitimacy.[25] Sometimes on behalf of an emerging indigenous bourgeoisie and often in a context where foreign capital dominates in the absence of local capitalists capable of controlling the national political economy, the state in Africa assumes responsibility for fostering and managing the accumulation and reinvestment of capital that are essential both for economic growth and development and for the security of the tenure of the national leadership. In practice, that often requires the African state to manage conditions for accumulation that are largely specified externally (structural adjustment programs are one example). As it does so, the African state must at the same time maintain its own legitimacy. As students of industrialized capitalist states have stressed, there is a necessary tension between legitimacy and accumulation. (For further discussion, see Chapter 3 in this volume.)

Within a peripheral capitalist economy with fragile political authority, accumulation requires a relatively weak, poorly integrated, and politically disorganized labor force. A liberal democratic capitalist system requires even more: a state that can successfully present itself as a representative of the popular will and not an agent of the dominant class(es). The policies the state pursues to maintain its universalist image, however, threaten its ability to manage, or even assist, accumulation. Each arena in which citizen participation is encouraged and democratic choice is permitted becomes a point of potential vulnerability for the state itself, and for the capitalist order. Promoting legitimacy through controlled democratic practice—which surely has been occurring in Africa—risks threatening the accumulation process. Empowered peasants may organize and demand greater control over both the organization of production and the distribution of wealth. At the same time, facilitating accumulation by constraining participation—which has also occurred in Africa—undermines legitimacy. The tension between these two is also reflected in the demands of external actors. To maximize extraction from the periphery, the earlier preference was for strong leaders who could control labor and dissent. But as authoritarian rule was challenged within Africa, leaders required popular legitimacy to implement harsh structural adjustment measures. Increasingly, aid providers insisted on democratization.

Accumulation is particularly problematic for the leadership of peripheral conditioned capitalist states (Carnoy, 1990). As Fanon (1963) foresaw, the structural interests of Africa's postcolonial leadership maintained and reinforced their dependence. The rhetoric of decolonization notwithstanding, the agenda of most who assumed office after the European rulers left was neither radical transformation of the peripheral economy nor the risk-taking required for capitalist innovation. Fragile states with insecure elites were unable or disinclined to take a long-term view of what national development would require and reluctant to make a continuing investment in a skilled, disciplined, and accountable public service.[26] One consequence has been a constellation of interests and power that found it difficult to create conditions conducive to accumulation and sustained investment in the development of new production and productive capacity. Another consequence has been a generally inefficient and not infrequently corrupt administration. For education, this situation has been manifested in the ineffective use of limited resources. Funds are poorly managed, both nationally and locally, with little accountability and reliable oversight. Inefficiency becomes normal, both expected and tolerated.

This tension between accumulation and legitimacy is regularly reflected in education policy, perhaps the most contested of public policies. Establishing and managing the conditions for accumulation favor regarding education instrumentally, primarily as a set of institutional arrangements concerned with preparing the future labor force, which includes developing both skills and work discipline. That orientation reinforces the inclination to link schooling with projected labor needs, to emphasize acquiring information, to regard teachers as transmitters and students as receivers of knowledge, and to rely heavily on examinations and other selection and exclusion mechanisms. The commonly asserted view that young Africans must be prepared for their role in the global economy (i.e., that their jobs and the skills those jobs require are likely to be defined not within the country but at distant centers of economic and political power) bolsters the external orientation of this instrumental view of education.

Legitimacy, however, is rooted in popular participation and consent. Beyond opening new schools,[27] maintaining the legitimacy not only of particular officeholders but of governing arrangements more generally requires the active involvement of an informed public that is aware of the power that it wields and is willing to use it. From this perspective, education must be concerned with, and must be seen to be concerned with, encouraging participation, redressing inequality, promoting social mobility, and fostering cooperation and nonviolent conflict resolution. This orientation reinforces the inclination to regard learners as active initiators, not passive recipients.

In short, as it struggles with its own fragility, the state adopts two different and at times incompatible postures toward the education system. Most often its orientation is functional and technical. Periodically, however, its expectations for schools are more liberal and transformative. The appropriate institutional configurations, even spatial arrangements, for these two orientations also differ. The school-as-factory architecture so common throughout the world—classrooms with the teacher-authority at the front, separated by a buffering space from students in orderly rows, and hierarchical administrations within schools and school systems—reflects the instrumental role of schooling. Open classrooms, activity-group seating patterns, and shared leadership responsibilities generally reflect a preference for the liberal and transformative perspective.

At work here are two related but distinct tensions. One is confronted in the political system as the state works to promote both accumulation and economic growth and at the same time to establish and reinforce its legitimacy. The second is confronted in the education system, which is charged both with preparing students for the world of work and at the same time with nurturing the development of individual potential, critical imagination, risk-taking innovation, and societal well-being. These two tensions, each with its own characteristics, participants, institutional configurations, and consequences, are interdependent but not identical. Although they intersect frequently and are often mutually reinforcing. Neither fully determines the other.

Understood somewhat more broadly, education in Africa has a dual charter. Its major task is to reproduce the economic, political, and social order.[28] Schools become the mechanism by which society selects young people who will proceed far in their education, sorts, tracks, and trains them, and certifies their accomplishments. The internalization of the reasonableness of that certification is crucial. For schools to serve their reproductive role, students who fail must attribute their problems to their own lack of skill or application, to circumstances beyond their control, or perhaps to bad luck. What the schools must avoid is the understanding that tracking, achievement, and certification, and their consequences for subsequent life chances, are planned and controllable outcomes of schools and schooling. (Consider for a moment teachers whose students all achieve specified goals and receive high marks. Rather than congratulating the students and teacher on their achievement, the immediate assumption is that the teacher must be doing something wrong since the classes of teachers who behave appropriately have both successes and failures.) Schools must legitimize as well as track, select, and certify. Their assessments must be accepted as just and appropriate and internalized. When students do not secure the jobs they seek, the emphasis on schooling as job preparation functions to direct their frustrations toward the apparent deficiencies of their education rather than toward the economic and political system that has not created sufficient jobs.

Reproducing the social order, however, also requires critique and innovation. To survive in capitalism's fiercely competitive environment, national economies must have some people who reject the old ways of doing things, insist on looking for better alternatives, and are willing to run the risks associated with criticism and innovation. Hence, schools have a radical as well as a conservative role. They must enable and encourage at least some students to ask difficult questions, to be impatient with the answers they receive, to trust their own judgment at least as much as their teachers' opinions.

The education system is thus charged with contradictory tasks in reproducing society: preserving and protecting the major features of the social order and at the same time challenging and changing them. Carnoy and Levin (1985) characterize this tension as between education as a democratizing force (social mobility, public education as an equalizing experience, instruction on the democratic ideal) and education as a mechanism for reproducing capitalist inequalities (class, race, or gender division of labor, unequal access to knowledge). Commonly, education systems try to manage that combination by separation—emphasizing the conservative role in most schools for most students and encouraging critique in a few schools, generally for elite students. In practice, that separation is difficult to establish and maintain. Each orientation is corrosive of the other. Critique and innovation have a momentum of their own. Schools become sites for rebellion, indirect (withdrawal, rejection) and direct (militant organization).

During the nationalist and liberation struggles, education emphasized its critical role. After minority rule was dismantled and the new order emerged, education in Africa turned back to its conservative charter, more concerned with preserving order than with challenging common understandings and forging new paths. In the circumstances of the peripheral conditioned state and dependent legitimation, accumulation is deemed more important than redistribution. The preference persists: an elitist, not mass, education system.

FROM EDUCATION AS SOCIAL TRANSFORMATION TO EDUCATION AS (AND FOR) PRODUCTION

Let us pull the threads together. Our concern is to understand education in contemporary Africa. We have found both exciting experimentation, innovation, and rapid expansion and also little change in inherited models, large numbers of out-of-school children and illiterate adults, and a very small higher education sector that strains to prepare sufficient teachers and struggles to reach the frontiers of knowledge generation and application. Major progress. Even more major problems.

After decades of an Education for All campaign, universal access to quality education is still many decades in the future. The message of that experience is powerful: more of the same is not sufficient (Samoff, 2012a). Like poverty, or more accurately, impoverishment, the spasmodic education progress and troubling education outcomes we observe are not accidental. They cannot be explained by notions of African backwardness or any of the other stereotypes of primitive and undeveloped Africa. Nor, more than a half-century after the end of colonial rule can they be explained by lethargy, slow steps, or time lags. Rather, we see here the powerful convergence of external and internal dynamics that reflect an active process of structured and institutionalized underdevelopment.

Postcolonial education in Africa has confronted two major hurdles, one conceptual and political, the other financial (Mbembe, 2001).[29]

Colonial education was used to structure economic, political, and social roles, to segregate and subordinate. Central to maintaining colonial (in South Africa, minority) rule and to organizing and managing a sharply differentiated society, education was at the same time an escape valve for a selected elite.[30] Few Africans reached school, and those who did found programs focused on the basic literacy, numeracy, and other skills deemed necessary to manage the colony. Among those a small group had access to more advanced education, to provide the administrative staff, the teachers, the nurses, even a few doctors and lawyers that the system required. Across the continent, from that elite came both the lower-level officials and administrators of colonial/minority rule and the activist leaders who militantly opposed it. Periodically education became a mobilization strategy, focused on raising political consciousness and enabling disadvantaged groups to seize the initiative. Education was thus both a powerful control system and a sharply contested terrain, in many countries both a motivator and an organizing ground for anticolonial nationalism.

That tension—education for liberation and social transformation versus education whose primary roles are differentiation, elite formation, and social control—has persisted into the postcolonial era. Where education is primarily concerned with structuring roles, it is the experience of schooling that matters, not learning. Where schooling eclipses learning, education is more concerned with preservation and reproduction than with innovation and transformation. Schools are the markers of modernity, the entry gates to desired futures, the fruits of the defeat of the old order. With a long history of attention to examinations and certification, generally the education system and its officials are more comfortable dealing with schooling than with learning. The moment of education as politics yields to education as administration.

Education had been at the center of the liberation struggle. Its task, it seemed clear, was social transformation. Very quickly, however, the commitment to rapidly expanded access, the inclination, supported by external funders, to regard education as a technical task revolving around policy statements, detailed plans, and implementation strategies, and insecure leaders' confrontations with students' and teachers' discontent combined to shift the focus from learning and liberation to schooling and examinations, and more generally to education as preparation for the world of work. With surprising speed, education's conservative charter once again became paramount.

At the same time, resources were everywhere inadequate. In many countries, the rate of education expansion could not be sustained. Facilities deteriorated, out-of-date textbooks were not replaced, libraries and laboratories were empty, gross enrollment ratios stagnated or declined, and universities could support neither library nor laboratory research. Measures of education quality, school efficiency, and teacher and learner satisfaction showed similar distress. Far from being an engine for social transformation, Africa's education systems found it increasingly difficult to provide even basic schooling. Some imaginative experiments continued, but in general promising innovations were localized and rarely sustained.

As they confronted this education crisis, whose roots lay in poverty, the international division of labor, fragile dependent states, deteriorating public service, and leadership more concerned with schooling for skills than with learning for development, African countries turned increasingly to foreign funding. Innovation and reform, and in some countries even textbooks and desks, were assumed to require external support. With the foreign funding came ideas and values, advice and directives on how education systems ought to be managed and targeted. Foreign aid's relatively small volume has large leverage and impact. A wide range of approaches to setting education policy notwithstanding, its imprint on education agendas and priorities is clearly visible across the continent. More recently, education in some countries has become even more directly dependent on external resources, increasing that influence. As external agencies undertake research as well as providing funding and development advice, their perspectives on scholarship and science shape approaches, methodologies, and the definition of universities' missions and more generally the scientific enterprise. Throughout Africa, unable to find local support, education researchers became contracted consultants. As they did so, those imported understandings of research, from framing questions to gathering data to interpretive strategies, were internalized and institutionalized, no longer foreign imports but now the unexceptional everyday routines of universities, research institutes, and indeed informed discourse.

We see here international convergence at several levels. Increasingly, the specification of education quality is presumed to be universal rather than nationally, culturally, or situationally specific. Similarly, notions of effective schools, good school management, and community participation are also treated as universals.

Far from the globalization of the knowledge era that is expected to be developmental and democratizing, this globalization is one form of the integration of African political economies into a world system on terms largely set outside Africa. Clearly the international integration of African goods, technology, labor, and capital has a long and energetic history. Colonial rule was, among other things, a general strategy for exploiting African resources, institutionalized in the dependent re-integration of Africa into the global political economy. Colonial rule's end changed the managers, centering the international financial institutions, World Bank and IMF. As capital and production move more easily around the world, the movement of labor remains sharply controlled and restricted by nationally set rules. For aid-dependent Africa, trade treaties, structural adjustment, and the poverty reduction strategy process set participation rules and constrain initiative. Strategies for reducing debt have become the fast track to planned dependence.

In a context of persisting poverty, aid dependence, increasing debt, and powerful pressures from within and without to adopt a particular understanding of development, African governments have been inclined to emphasize accumulation over legitimacy. Similarly, though pockets of innovation and radical reform persist, the trajectory of education policy and practice in Africa has generally been to discard or devalue education's role in economic and social transformation in favor of education's role in maintaining particular patterns of economic, social, and political organization. In practice, the productivist and conservative charter for education contributes to entrenching still further the conditioned state and Africa's dependence. Within Africa the consequence is to acquiesce in (even see as necessary) fundamental societal inequalities and the politics they breed.

Consistent with that conservative role for education, attention has increasingly focused on efficiency, quality, and school improvement, often modeled on approaches and experiences elsewhere. Ironically, many of the strategies intended to achieve education for all in practice render it a distant dream. The rhetoric of liberation and empowerment notwithstanding, the commonly held view is that education must enable Africa to run faster as it tries to catch up with those who are ahead rather than forge new paths or transform the international economy and Africa's role in it. Scrambling to catch up always leaves those presumed to be in front to determine where they, and thus everyone else, are going.

NOTES

1. Quoted in Smith, 1972, p. 284. While Smith links Nyerere's comment to catching up with the "modern world," a fuller reading of Nyerere's intent, including many other quotations in this book, make clear that for Nyerere, closing the gap required setting the pace. See Mkandawire, 2011.

2. Levin, 2004, 2001. The institutional manifestation of this approach is the Accelerated Schools Project.

3. As we shall see, beyond the mystification and exoticism associated with the "dark continent," the terminology commonly employed regularly structures the discussion in ways that are not immediately apparent, even to careful readers and active participants in policy debates. The specification of what is "Africa" is an instructive case in point. Nearly all World Bank documents on Africa, as well as many others, include a note that indicates, "Most of the discussion and all of the statistics about Africa in this study refer to just thirty-nine countries south of the Sahara, for which the terms Africa and Sub-Saharan Africa are used interchangeably" (this example is from World Bank, 1988, p. viii). The World Bank's recent education analysis carries the subtitle "Schooling for Learning in Africa" but begins by explaining that it "meticulously documents the access and learning levels of many *Sub-Saharan African* countries" (Bashir et al., 2018, p. xxv; emphasis added). That is, "Africa" is not the Africa specified either by geography—countries on the African continent and its adjacent islands—or by African states themselves—membership in the African Union—but rather a subset of those states grouped to reflect the foreign policy interests and categories of the World Bank, the United States, and other countries of the North Atlantic. Unfortunately, there is currently no straightforward resolution to this dilemma. Much of the most readily available data on education in Africa come from publications of those organizations, and to date no one has systematically revised those data to include North Africa or reorganized other data that do include North Africa to make them directly comparable. In this discussion, other than explicitly noted exceptions, our comments generally refer to the entire continent.

4. We are concerned here primarily with formal education through secondary school. While as appropriate we will address postsecondary, distance, and vocational education, they are not our major focus here. After a period of severely reduced support, higher education is receiving renewed attention and funding. In some countries, privatization is progressing rapidly at that level.

5. Historical comparisons are especially problematic. The major data sources, for example, the UIS and the World Bank, regularly revise data for particular years. While that may improve accuracy, it also renders their own annual reports not readily comparable. Those authoritative sources also note that since categories and classifications were revised in 2000, pre-1999 and post-1999 cannot easily be compared. We rely here primarily on the UIS database, http://data.uis.unesco.org, aware that the most recently reported numbers may not be more accurate than numbers reported earlier and subsequently revised.

6. Except where otherwise noted, data presented here are from the UIS database.

7. Among the funding agencies, the World Bank was often sharply critical of allocations to higher education. For an exploration of the World Bank's role in this arena, see Samoff & Carrol, 2004. Unless otherwise noted, URLs cited in this chapter were accessible 2020.07.14.

8. As coordinating agency, UNESCO published the major preparatory and follow-up documents. Since 2002 Education for All global monitoring reports have highlighted progress and problems. The annual EFA Global Monitoring Reports are at: https://en.unesco.org/gem-report/allreports [2020.07.04].

9. Rosa Maria Torres provides an insightful and critical perspective on the 1990 and 2000 conferences (2000a, 2000b). For an early analysis of SDG 4, Klees, 2017.

10. With 14.1% of the world's population in 2019, Africa's out-of-school children were 37.8% of the global total.

11. For a parallel effort in Zimbabwe, see Gustafsson, 1985b.

12. As we have noted, changes in categorizations in the major data sources preclude longer-term comparisons. Our reading of the available evidence suggests that with a dip in the late 1980s and early 1990s, the percentage allocation across sub-Saharan Africa has been generally consistent over four decades.

13. Unfortunately, beyond the EFA Global Monitoring Reports, there have been few systematic studies of the volume of education aid to Africa and its impact on the direction of capital flows. As we note, in some countries the situation has changed dramatically, with foreign aid supporting a major portion of education expenditures, especially as the funding agencies have provided direct budget subsidies.

14. Though seemingly impossible, official accounting of when aid is recorded shows more aid received than the government spent for this year.

15. Overview, guidelines, papers, and progress reports are at www.imf.org/external/np/prsp/prsp.asp [2020.07.10].

16. Note that treating equality and equity as synonyms muddles the issues in many of the major World Bank education reviews and policy statements as well as other documents that take the World Bank presentation as the starting point. Among the examples of this persisting confusion are World Bank, *Priorities and Strategies for Education* and World Bank, *Learning for All, The Learning Generation*, and Bashir et al., *Facing Forward*.

17. The gender parity index is the ratio of girls' enrollment in primary, secondary or tertiary education. World Bank, Education Statistics (EdStats) Online Database, http://databank.worldbank.org. See also the UNESCO eAtlas of Gender Inequality in Education: https://tellmaps.com/uis/gender/#!/tellmap/-1195952519

18. As noted above, with 14.1% of the world's population in 2019, Africa's out-of-school children were 37.8% of the global total. UNESCO Institute for Statistics, "New Methodology Shows That 258 Million Children, Adolescents and Youth Are Out of School."

19. The international models are BRAC in Bangladesh, Lok Jumbish in India, and Escuela Nueva in Colombia. Notwithstanding their national successes and international recognition, their models have not yet stimulated or encouraged similar education initiatives in Africa, through BRAC supports programs in several African countries.

20. Note that *politicians* here is not a pejorative term but simply refers to individuals who hold political office or whose concerns and activities revolve around the expression, confrontation, integration, and mediation of political interests. Nor do we assume that education policy ought to be set by professional educators or that decisions guided primarily by the findings of education researchers will necessarily produce better policy.

21. We draw here on critical discussions of education and relevance in two major Namibian policy statements: Namibia, 1993; 1998.

22. We use "EFA campaign" to refer the general process of goals and conferences, including the specific EFA goals and conferences, the associated funding mechanisms (Fast Track Initiative/Global Partnership for Education), and the related United Nations Millennium Development Goals and Sustainable Development Goals.

23. From 1999–2004 Katarina Tomasevski was the United Nations, Economic and Social Council, Commission on Human Rights, Special Rapporteur on the Right to Education. The Rights to Education Project provides links to her reports, http://www.right-to-education.org/node/417.

24. Among the most prominent of the cross-national assessment programs are: International Association for the Evaluation of Educational Achievement (IEA), Monitoring Learning Achievement (MLA [UNESCO]); Programme d'Analyse des Systèmes Éducatifs de la CONFEMEN (PASEC); Progress in International Reading Literacy Skills (PIRLS); Programme for International Student Assessment (PISA); and Trends in International Mathematics and Science Study (TIMSS). An African regional initiative is the Southern and Eastern Africa Consortium for Monitoring Educational Quality (SACMEQ).

25. Since an extended discussion of the state in Africa is far beyond the scope of this chapter, we limit our attention here to the tension between accumulation and legitimation and its implications for education. For a fuller development of these and related themes, see Carnoy & Samoff, 1990, especially part 1; Carnoy, 1992; Carnoy, 2016. For a synthetic and critical review of analyses of the state, see Jessop, 2015.

26. The World Bank and other external agencies have increasingly focused major attention on problems of governance and administration, though generally without addressing the structural roots of managerial inefficiency and the lack of transparency and accountability. "The principal purpose of the World Bank Group's engagement on governance and anticorruption is to support poverty reduction." (World Bank, Strengthening World Bank Group Engagement on Governance and Anticorruption. [World Bank Governance and Anticorruption Strategy, March 2007], i. [http://siteresources.worldbank.org/EXTGOVANTICORR/Resources/3035863-1281627136986/GACStrategyPaper.pdf])

27. Hans Weiler explores what he terms compensatory legitimation: Weiler, 1989.

28. Samuel Bowles and Herbert Gintis have developed and refined the notion of the correspondence between school and society: Bowles & Gintis, 1981.

29. Mbembe's seminal work on the post-colony has informed our thinking and is reflected in our analysis. Fuller attention to the richness of Mbembe's and others' work on the post-colony is beyond our scope here.

30. For South Africa the 1994 transition, three decades after most African countries, was from minority to majority rule. For the evolution of education in South Africa, see Cross & Chisholm, 1990; Jansen, 1991; Vally, 2007; Badat & Sayed, 2014.

REFERENCES

Association for the Development of African Education. (1996). *Formulating education policy: Lessons and experiences from Sub-Saharan Africa*. Association for the Development of African Education.

Association for the Development of Education in Africa. (2001). *What Works and What's New in Education: Africa Speaks! Report from a Prospective, Stocktaking Review of Education in Africa.* Association for the Development of Education in Africa.

Badat, S., & Sayed, Y. (2014). Post-1994 South African education: The challenge of social justice. *Annals of the American Academy of Political and Social Science, 652*(1), 127–148.

Bashir, S., Lockheed, M., Ninan, E., & Tang, J. P. (2018). *Facing forward: Schooling for learning in Africa.* World Bank.

Bloch, M., Beoku-Betts, J. A., & Tabachnick, B. R. (1998). *Women and education in Sub-Saharan Africa: Power, opportunities, and constraints.* Lynne Rienner.

Bowles, S., & Gintis, H. (1981). Education as a Site of contradictions in the reproduction of the capital-labor relationship: Second thoughts on the "correspondence principle." *Economic and Industrial Democracy, 2,* 223–242.

Carnoy, M. (1990). Education and the transition state. In M. Carnoy & J. Samoff (Eds.), *Education and social transition.* Princeton University Press.

Carnoy, M. (1992). Education and the state: From Adam Smith to perestroika. In R. F. Arnove, P. G. Altbach, & G. P. Kelly (Eds.), *Emergent issues in education: Comparative perspectives* (pp. 143–159). State University of New York Press.

Carnoy. M. (2016). Educational policies in the face of globalization: Whither the nation state? In K. E. Mundy, A. Green, B. Lingard, & A. Verger (Eds.), *The handbook of global education policy.* Wiley.

Carnoy, M., & Levin, H. M. (1985). *Schooling and work in the democratic state.* Stanford University Press.

Carnoy, M., & Samoff, J. (1990). *Education and social transition in the Third World.* Princeton University Press.

Cross, M., & Chisholm, L. (1990). The roots of segregated schooling in twentieth-century South Africa. In M. Nkomo (Ed.), *Pedagogy of domination: Toward a democratic education in South Africa* (pp. 43–74). Africa World Press.

Decker, C., & McMahon, E. (2020). *The idea of development in Africa: A history.* Cambridge University Press.

Dryden-Peterson, S., Adelman, E., Bellino, M. J., & Chopra, V. (2019). The purposes of refugee education: Policy and practice of including refugees in national education systems. *Sociology of Education, 92*(4), 346–66

Education 2030: Incheon Declaration and Framework for Action for the implementation of Sustainable Development Goal 4. (2015). UNESCO.

Education Policy and Data Center. (2005). *Educating the world's children: Patterns of growth and inequality.* Education Policy and Data Center.

Evans, D. R. (Ed.). (1994). *Education policy formation in Africa: A comparative study of five countries.* USAID.

Fanon, F. (1963). *The wretched of the earth.* Grove.

Fredua-Kwarteng, Eric. (2016). Democratization and participation: National education policy-making in Africa. *International Education Journal: Comparative Perspectives, 15*(4), 1–19.

Freire, P. (1970). *Pedagogy of the oppressed.* Herder and Herder.

Global Education Monitoring Report Team. (2020). *Inclusion and education: All means all.* Global Education Monitoring Report.

Gustafsson, I. (1985a). *Integration between education and work at primary and post-primary level—the case of Botswana.* University of Stockholm, Institute of International Education.

Gustafsson, I. (1985b). *Zimbabwe Foundation for Education with Production, ZIMFEP: A follow-up study.* Swedish International Development Authority.

Heward, C. (1999). Introduction: The new discourses of gender, education and development. In C. Heward & S. S. Bunwaree (Eds.), *Gender, education, and development: Beyond access to empowerment.* Zed Books; St. Martin's Press.

Inter-Agency Commission, World Conference on Education for All (UNDP, UNESCO, UNICEF, World Bank) (1990). *Final Report, World Conference on Education for All: Meeting basic learning needs.* UNICEF.

International Commission on Financing Global Education Opportunity. (2016). *The learning generation: Investing in education for a changing world.* International Commission on Financing Global Education Opportunity.

Jansen, J. (1991). Knowledge and power in the world system: The South African case. In J. Jansen (Ed.), *Knowledge and power in South Africa: Critical perspectives across the disciplines.* Skotaville Publishers.

Jerven, M. (2013). *Poor numbers: How we are misled by African development statistics and what to do about it.* Cornell University Press.

Jerven, M. (2015). *Africa: Why economists get it wrong.* Zed Books.

Jessop, B. (2015). *The state: past, present, future.* Polity.

Klees, S. J. (2017). Will We Achieve Education for All and the Education Sustainable Development Goal? *Comparative Education Review, 61*(2), 425–440.

The learning generation: Investing in education for a changing World. (2016). International Commission on Financing Global Education Opportunity.

Levin, H. M. (2001). Pedagogical challenges for educational futures in industrializing countries. *Comparative Education Review, 45*(4), 537–560.

Levin, H. M. (2004). Learning from school reform. In J. Chi-Kin Lee, L. Nai-kwai Lo, & A. Walker (Eds.), *Partnership and change: Toward school development* (pp. 31–51). Chinese University Press.

Lewin, K. M. (2017). Making rights realities: Does privatizing educational services for the poor make sense? In B. S. Ndimande & C. Lubienski (Eds.), *Privatization and the education of marginalized children: Policies, impacts, and global lessons.* Taylor and Francis.

Maiangwa, B., & Agbiboa, D. (2014). Why Boko Haram kidnaps women and young girls in north-eastern Nigeria. *Conflict Trends, 3,* 51–56.

Mbembe, A. (2001). *On the postcolony.* University of California Press.

Mkandawire, T. (2011). Running while others walk: Knowledge and the challenge of Africa's development. *Africa Development, 36*(2), 1–36.

Namibia. (1993). *Toward education for all.* Ministry of Education and Culture.

Namibia. (1998). *Investing in people, developing a country: Higher education for development in Namibia.* Ministry of Higher Education, Vocational Training, Science, and Technology.

Nyerere, J. K. (1967). *Education for self-reliance.* TANU.

Nyerere, J. K. (1968). *Freedom and Socialism/Uhuru na Ujamaa.* Oxford University Press.

Nyerere, J. K. (1998). Africa: The current situation. *African Philosophy, 11*(1).

Odaga, A., & Heneveld, W. (1995). *Girls and schools in Sub-Saharan Africa: From analysis to action.* World Bank.

OECD. (2015). *Development Co-operation by countries beyond the DAC: Towards a more complete picture of international development finance.* OECD.

O'Malley, B. (2007). *Education under attack 2007.* UNESCO.

O'Malley, B. (2010). *Education under attack 2010.* UNESCO.

Onyango, M. A., et al. (2019). Gender-based violence among adolescent girls and young women: A neglected consequence of the West African Ebola outbreak. In D. A. Schwartz, J. N. Anoko, & S. A. Abramowitz (Eds.), *Pregnant in the time of Ebola: Women and their children in the 2013–2015 West African epidemic* (pp. 121–132). Springer.

Riep, C., & Machacek, M. (2016). *Schooling the poor profitably: The innovations and deprivations of Bridge International Academies in Uganda.* Education International.

Samoff, J. (1994a). Education policy formation in Tanzania: Self-reliance and dependence. In D. R. Evans (Ed.), *Education policy formation in Africa: A comparative study of five countries* (pp. 85–126). USAID.

Samoff, J. (2012a). More of the same will not do: Learning without learning in the World Bank's 2020 Education Strategy. In S. J. Klees, J. Samoff, & N. P. Stromquist (Eds.), *The World Bank and education: Critiques and alternatives* (pp. 109–121). Sense Publishers.

Samoff, J. (2012b). "Research shows that . . . ": Creating the knowledge environment for learning for all. In *The World Bank and education* (pp. 143–157). Sense Publishers.

Samoff, J. (2019). *Higher education for self-reliance: Tanzania and Africa*. HakiElimu.

Samoff, J., with Assié-Lumumba, N. T. (1996). *Analyses, agendas, and priorities in African education: A review of externally initiated, commissioned, and supported studies of education in Africa, 1990–1994*. UNESCO.

Samoff, J., & Carrol, B. (2004). *From manpower planning to the knowledge era: World Bank policies on higher education in Africa*. UNESCO Forum on Higher Education, Research and Knowledge.

Samoff, J., Dembélé, M., & Sebatane, E. M. (2011). *'Going to scale': Nurturing the local roots of education innovation in Africa*. EdQual: Research Programme Consortium on Implementing Education Quality in Low Income Countries, EdQual Working Paper, No. 8.

Samoff, J., & Irving, M. (2014). *Education for all: A global commitment without global funding*. Open Society Foundations.

Samoff, J., with Sumra, S. (1994b). From planning to marketing: Making education and training policy in Tanzania. In J. Samoff (Ed.), *Coping with crisis: Austerity, adjustment, and human resources*. Cassell.

Sierra Leone Truth and Reconciliation Commission. (2004). *Witness to the truth: Report of the Sierra Leone Truth and Reconciliation Commission*. Graphics Packaging.

Smith, W. E. (1972). *We must run while they walk: A portrait of Africa's Julius Nyerere*. Random House.

Tooley, J., & Dixon, P. (2005). *Private education is good for the poor: A study of private schools serving the poor in low-income countries*. Cato Institute.

Torres, R. M. (2000a). *One decade of education for all: The challenge ahead*. UNESCO, International Institute of Education Planning (Buenos Aires).

Torres, R. M. (2000b). What happened at the World Education Forum? (n.p.)

UNESCO. (1989). *United Republic of Tanzania: Education in Tanzania, vol. 1, : Overview*. UNESCO.

UNESCO. (2002). *Education for all: Is the world on track?* UNESCO.

UNESCO. (2003). *Gender and education for all: The leap to equality*. EFA Global Monitoring Report 2003/4. Regional Overview: Sub-Saharan Africa. UNESCO.

UNESCO. (2011). *The hidden crisis: Armed conflict and education*. Education for All Global Monitoring Report 2011. UNESCO.

UNESCO. (2015). Pricing the right to education: The cost of reaching new targets. *Education for All Global Monitoring Report: Policy Paper, 18*.

UNESCO. (2016). *Gender review: Creating sustainable futures for All*. Global Education Monitoring Report 2016. UNESCO.

UNESCO. (2020a). *Inclusion and education: All means all*. Global Education Monitoring Report 2020. UNESCO.

UNESCO. (2020b). Global education monitoring report. *Gender Report, A New Generation: 25 years of efforts for gender equality in education*. UNESCO.

United Nations High Commissioner for Refugees (UNHCR). (2019). *Global trends: Forced displacement in 2019*. UNHCR.

Unterhalter, E. (2005). Fragmented frameworks? Researching women, gender, education, and development. In S. Aikman & E. Unterhalter (Eds.), *Beyond access: Transforming Policy and practice for gender equality in education* (pp. 14–35). Oxfam.

Vally, S. (2007). From people's education to neo-liberalism in South Africa. *Review of African Political Economy, 34*(111), 39–56.

Weiler, H. (1989). Education and power: The politics of educational decentralization in comparative perspective. *Educational Policy, 3*(1), 31–43.

World Declaration on Education for All. (1990). UNESCO.

World Education Forum. (2000). *The Dakar framework for action.* WEF/UNESCO.

World Bank. (1988). *Education in sub-saharan Africa.* World Bank.

World Bank. (1995). *Priorities and strategies for education.* World Bank.

World Bank (2011). *Learning for all: Investing in people's knowledge and skills to promote development. World Bank education strategy 2020.* World Bank.

World Bank. (2017). *Learning to realize education's promise.* World Bank.

12

Education in Latin America

From Dependency and Neoliberalism to Alternative Paths to Development

Robert F. Arnove
Indiana University

Stephen Franz
Indiana University

Carlos Ornelas
Metropolitan Autonomous University

Carlos Alberto Torres
UCLA

ABSTRACT

This chapter starts with the premise that to understand education in Latin America in the third decade of the 21st century, it is necessary to view the nature of the state and how the interaction of global and local forces influence the governance, financing, workings, and outcomes of school systems. Those forces significantly changed the landscape for education over the past 10 years. Among them was a dramatic shift to autocratic, nationalist/populist governments. The following sections then examine who attends and completes different levels of education with what outcomes by race/ethnicity, economic class, gender, and geography (all of which intersect with and reinforce one another to determine advantage or disadvantage). In doing so, we identify promising trends in comparative research, that highlight the sets of factors that advance or hinder the achievement of more equitable, high-quality education for the vast majority. Other sections critique the negative consequences of neoliberal decentralization and privatization initiatives, as well as the emancipatory possibilities of regional counterhegemonic and popular education movements. The concluding section examines the potential of progressive social movements to contribute to Latin American countries achieving more democratic and just societies in the face of daunting challenges posed during a global pandemic.

To understand education in Latin America in the third decade of the 21st century, it is necessary to view the nature of the state and how the interaction of global and local forces influence the governance, financing, workings, and outcomes of school systems. In the 2013 edition of *Comparative Education*, we identified several progressive, leftist political regimes that initiated bold distributive policies to counteract the dominant neoliberal economic and social policies followed by most states during the last two decades of the 20th century to gain access to international capital and markets. The neoliberal policies led to a growing gap between the rich and poor within countries, cutbacks in state funding for public education, and consequently highly inequitable education systems.

The sustained success of egalitarian distributive initiatives in the region, however, is problematic. Since 2013, there have been notable reversals of political trajectories in several countries. In 2019, in Brazil, a reactionary government came to power that immediately set out to dismantle policies that benefited the working class, the landless, African descendants, and indigenous peoples. A less dramatic shift to austerity, neoliberal policies occurred two years earlier in Ecuador. In Venezuela and Nicaragua, grassroots mass mobilizations around education and health have given way to one-party dictatorial rule. In Venezuela, in recent years, an ongoing economic crisis of historic proportions has made it extremely difficult for even essential staples and basic health care to be made available to the most vulnerable.

In other cases, neoliberal-oriented governments (e.g., Argentina in 2019) were replaced by more nationalist, populist-oriented ones. Nontraditional parties also emerged. In Mexico, in 2018, a third party occupied the highest office of the land for the first time. In Central America politicians with unusual backgrounds won presidencies: in Guatemala, a popular TV comedian held power between 2016 and 2020, to be replaced by the former head of the country's penitentiary system; and in El Salvador, in 2020, a former member of the revolutionary Farabundo Marti National Liberation Front was elected heading the ticket for a conservative, business-oriented party. In 2022, progressive governments were elected in Chile and Honduras, which now has its first female head of state.

As of 2022, there is no discernible dominant trend across the region concerning the nature of political regimes or initiatives to remake highly inequitable socioeconomic and education systems. Previous reforms—such as deregulation, decentralization, and privatization—are undergoing modifications in countries that once touted them as panaceas for dysfunctional governance structures and schooling. About privatization, the most notable case is that of Chile. Significant efforts also have been made to reassert centralized control over unwieldy systems—in Mexico, that involved efforts to curb the power of the national teachers' union; in Peru, attempts to regain national authority over highly autonomous regions.

What remains clear is that Latin America continues to have persistent levels of widespread poverty and deeply entrenched inequalities in society and education. Latin America, furthermore, continues to be the world's most inequitable region regarding wealth and income. According to Mahoney (2015) and Webber (2017), although Latin America is not the poorest region in the world, it has a long history of inequalities "flowing in the first instance out of the colonial legacies of highly concentrated landholdings, means of production, credit, and political power."

Since 2020, attempts to overcome past injustices are challenged by the COVID-19 pandemic that has exacerbated enduring problems. In several countries, negative growth in gross domestic product (GDP) has accelerated. For the second half of 2020, the International Monetary Fund (IMF; 2020) estimated substantial declines in GDP in the already wracked economies of Venezuela (-15%), Nicaragua (-11%), Argentina (-11%), and Nicaragua (-6%). Other economies with sluggish growth at the beginning of 2020—Mexico (estimated 1%)—and others with estimated growth rates over 3% before the pandemic—for example, Peru and El Salvador—were expected to decline between 4 and 11% by 2021.

The sharp reversals in growth patterns reveal the fact that in many countries in the region, a majority of the populations work in what has been variously called informal or shadow economies—in short, the "economies of the poor." As a case in point, street vendors, many of them children, are particularly vulnerable to contagions, as are the hundreds of millions living in crowded barrios without access to potable water and functioning sewage systems. Health care is beyond the reach of the majority in many countries. All these factors impact the well-being of the majority, and, of course, who can attend and complete types and levels of education.

In the following pages, we will examine who attends and completes different levels of education with what outcomes by race or ethnicity, economic class, gender, and geography (all of which intersect with and reinforce one another to determine advantage or disadvantage). In doing so, we point out interesting advances in comparative research that highlight the sets of factors that advance or hinder the achievement of more equitable, high-quality education for the vast majority of students.

We then discuss various reform initiatives according to where they originate—the top, the bottom, and the middle. Among these reforms are targeted cash transfer programs to channel resources to low-income families to send their children to school as well as have access to adequate nutrition and health services; curriculum innovations that involve, for example, bilingual-intercultural education in countries with large indigenous populations; efforts to extend the outreach of higher education to serve disadvantaged populations; and adult education programs based on the pedagogical principles of Brazilian educator Paulo Freire. We argue that the achievement of more equitable and democratic education systems, critical to achieving more participatory and just societies, depends not only on state initiatives but on the existence of strong grassroots movements and a strong civil society that serve as a counterforce to elite interests and the dictates of authoritarian governments, no matter how well-intentioned they may be.

DEFINING THE STATE AND ITS RELATIONSHIP TO EDUCATION

Generally, the state may be conceptualized as a pact of domination, as an arena of conflict, and as a purposeful actor that must select among competing political projects. According to Cardoso (1979), the state should be considered to be the "basic pact of domination that exists among social classes or factions of dominant classes and the norms, which guarantee their dominance over subordinate strata." As an arena of confrontation, the state displays the tensions and contradictions of competing political projects as well as the political agreements of civil society. Moreover, social class, racial, ethnic, gender, geographical, ethical-moral, and religious factors influence the actions of the state in legislating and executing social policies.

Although the state in a capitalist society, by its very nature, favors policies that are directed toward the constitution and reproduction of the capitalist system (Offe, 1984; Offe & Ronge, 1975), it also is the representative of the nation as a whole, and, in liberal democratic societies, the state is a proponent of the extension of personal rights and greater mass participation in the determination of public policy (Bowles & Gintis, 1986; Carnoy & Levin, 1985). Hence, as noted earlier, the state has a dual character: it is both a pact of domination and a contested terrain. Various groups intervene to shape public policy to serve their interests. Although education can be used to legitimate a political system, it also can serve to interrogate it; although an education system may function to perpetuate the social division of labor, it also can equip individuals with the skills and knowledge to humanize the workplace and change the class structure of a society.

THE "CONDITIONED" STATE

Historically, education policies and programs have been significantly limited in their ability to bring about fundamental social change or improvements in the lives of the majority by the fact that Latin American countries, until the advent of the Cuban Revolution of 1959, could be considered dependent or "conditioned" capitalist states (Gott, 2000; Lutjens, 1996). According to Cardoso and Magnani (1974) and Cardoso (1981), an "associate-dependent development" long characterized Latin America. As Cardoso (1981) notes, the economic systems of Latin America were built upon an alliance among the state bureaucracy and state managers, the multinational corporations, and the highest strata of the national bourgeoisie. Not only multinational corporations but also U.S. hegemony exercised in the region for more than 100 years—exemplified by various forms of colonialism that, until recently, has involved frequent military interventions, particularly in the Caribbean region and Central America. This hegemony thwarted alternative and more independent models of economic development (Chomsky, 2002; LaFeber, 1993). The typical political economy of Latin America strengthened a more concentrated economic system that was inherently less redistributive and excluded the subordinate classes.

According to Martin Carnoy (as cited in Torres, 1990), the educational implications of dependent capitalism in Latin America were that "(1) the state was often unwilling or unable to mobilize enough resources to make public education (state-defined knowledge) generally available; and (2) even if education was made generally available, the private production sector and the state were often unable to provide sufficient wage employment to absorb those with average education" (p. x).

Income Inequality and Educational Equity

Not only the "conditioned state" and "dependent development" but also the attendant disparities in wealth greatly determined who would complete the highest levels and most prestigious types of education and thereby have access to the most lucrative and desirable jobs in the modern sector of the economy. Latin America is characterized by greater income inequality than other developing regions. According to *Social Panorama of Latin America 2019*, Latin America's Gini index registered at 0.47—higher than other world regions (0.45 for Sub-Saharan Africa; 0.40 for East Asia and the Pacific; 0.37 for the Middle East and North Africa; 0.34 for South Asia; 0.33 for Eastern Europe and Central Asia; and 0.30 for OECD countries) (CEPAL, 2019). And, as Psacharopoulos et al. (1997) have noted: "Education is the variable with the strongest impact on income inequality" (p. 196).

According to the Inter-American Development Bank (1998) report "Education: The Gordian Knot": if you want to find a root cause for Latin America's income inequality, you don't have to look much further than its skewed educational system. This report, issued on the eve of the April 1998 Summit of the Americas in Santiago, Chile, found that the region's public schools were mired in crisis. Rather than contributing to progress, the report stated, schooling was "reinforcing poverty, perpetuating inequality and holding back economic growth." The problem was not access but completion rates. By the fifth year, nearly 40% of the poor dropped out, while 93% of the richest students were still in the system. By the ninth year, only 15% of poor students remained in school, compared to 58% of the richest (Inter-American Development Bank, 1998).

We would argue, however, that the root cause of economic stagnation resides not in the education system, but in the social and economic inequality generated by the economic policies that have been implemented by many governments in the region since the mid-1980s. According to a report in the January–March 2005 Newsletter of UNESCO's International Institute for Educational Planning on "Education and Equity in Latin America," 10 years after undertaking various economic growth and social recovery policies, "the social situation in the region has not improved and the impact of educational reform in terms of equity is minimal" (IIEP & UNESCO, 2005). The report continues:

> On the one hand, poverty no longer stems from an economic scenario of crisis and inflation, but is the result of new growth strategies adopted by most countries in the region.... The divide between rich and poor in the region has considerably widened and wealth distribution has become central to an analysis of the social situation. (IIEP & UNESCO, 2005, p. 1)

The report describes "wealth distribution patterns which benefit the better off, allowing some to enjoy one of the highest standards of living in the world"—very similar, we would add, to the privileged position enjoyed by whites in apartheid South Africa—a situation of internal colonialism which also may serve as an apt description of the condition of rural indigenous populations in Bolivia, Ecuador, Peru, and Guatemala, and African Americans, especially, in the northeast region of Brazil. Not only these countries, but also Nicaragua, El Salvador, Honduras, and Haiti (all of which have suffered civil war and natural disasters as well as a history of foreign interventions and neocolonialism), not surprisingly, had the highest illiteracy and dropout rates in the region. In the cases listed, the majority of their populations live in poverty and, according to the *Social*

Panorama of Latin America 2019, the average poverty rate through the region in that year was 30.8 percent (CEPAL, 2019).

Education and Enrollment Patterns

Although Latin America, historically, has had a greater percentage of children and youth enrolled in schools in other developing areas of the world, enrollment patterns reflected the particular history of the region. In several countries, there was a bimodal distribution of enrollment. Large numbers of students from the least privileged sectors of society (ethnic minorities, rural populations, and women) did not attend or complete primary schooling while a substantial number of students attending universities, often at rates, in the past, exceeding those of European countries. At the same time, Latin American workers had fewer years of schooling than their counterparts in Eastern and South-Eastern Asia (UNESCO Institute of Statistics: http://data.uis.unesco.org/).

In 2013, the average amount of schooling of the adult population (15 to 64 years of age) was less than six years. Despite the disadvantage in school access and attainments experienced by older generations, younger generations have had greater opportunity to attend and complete primary and lower-secondary levels of education: according to the UIS (http://data.uis.unesco.org/), data show a lower secondary net enrollment rate of 93%; and completion rate of 76%. The Organization for Economic Cooperation and Development (OECD; 2020) found that post-1990s students, for example, are likely to attain two more years of second schooling than their parents' generation.

Despite increases in primary school enrollment following the "Lost Decade" of the 1980s, as of 2013, six countries still had less than 90% enrollment for ages 6 to 18. In Colombia, Ecuador, El Salvador, Guatemala, Honduras, and Nicaragua, 25% to over 40% of children between 6 and 18 years of age were not in school (UNESCO Institute for Statistics, 2020). In the Dominican Republic, Ecuador, El Salvador, and Nicaragua, one-fourth of the students did not reach the sixth grade (CEPAL, 2019).

At the same time, despite the slower expansion of higher education since 1990 relative to that of Europe, 2018–2019 enrollment rates for Latin America and the Caribbean were higher than the world average of 39%. The regional rate varied between 52 and 53% (depending on whether or not high-income countries were excluded). According to the World Bank (2020), in 2018–2019, regions with lower rates included the Arab World (33%), East Asia and the Pacific (between 46 and 49% percent depending on the inclusion of high countries or not), South Asia (25%), and Sub-Saharan Africa (9%).

World Bank (2020) data further show that 2017–2018 gross enrollment rates. Argentina (90%), Chile (91%), Uruguay (63%) compared favorably with those of Italy (64%), Portugal (60%), Hungary (50%), and Romania (51%). Earlier data on the Bolivarian Republic of Venezuela show that in 2009, before the current economic crisis, 79% percent of students were enrolled in some form of higher education.

In the following sections, we analyze enrollment and completion patterns by geography, gender, ethnicity, and their intersections with economic class.

Urban-Rural and Income Level Differences

Differences in urban-rural enrollment patterns are significantly shaped by levels of poverty as well as access to land ownership. Between 2012 and 2018, for example, poverty rose from 28.7% (166 million) to 30.8% (191 million), and extreme poverty from 8.2% (47 million) to 11.5% (72 million). In 2018, rural poverty registered at 45.2%, and extreme poverty, 20.0%; for urban areas, the rates were 26.3% for poverty, and 8.4% for extreme poverty (CEPAL, 2019).

Furthermore, according to the Food and Agriculture Organization of the United Nations (n.d.), it is the "region with the greatest inequality in the distribution of land." Without adequate land on which to live and prosper, malnutrition and insecure shelter face hundreds of million rural families and their children, necessarily curtailing the ability to attend and succeed in formal schooling.

Secondary attendance and completion rates by urban and rural differences reveal how national contexts have a significant impact. By 2013, the countries that have taken the most significant strides to decrease the urban-rural gap in attendance rates were Brazil, Chile, Peru, and Venezuela. Rural attendance rates are climbing and are now 90% of those found in urban areas for these countries.

By contrast, five countries—El Salvador, Guatemala, Honduras, Nicaragua, and, surprisingly, Uruguay—had rural attendance rates about 20% less than urban rates (UNICEF, 2019). Startling were the completion rate disparities by geography. In the four Central American countries, rural student completion rates were over 65% lower than their urban counterparts. These countries reveal the geographical disparities in poverty and household stability found throughout the region but were exacerbated by civil wars, revolutionary upheavals, and growing violence from drug-related gangs that disrupted rural life.

In addition to generally inadequate facilities and the distance of schools from communities, as well as the need for child labor at home or in the field, another variable affecting school completion rates and academic achievement is the quality of teachers. Luschei's (2012) research in two Mexican states (Aguascalientes and Sonora) found that teachers with those positive qualities most strongly correlated with student scores on national examinations were more likely to be located in urban schools and especially those with lower poverty rates. However, Luschei's (2012) data lead him to hypothesize that strong positive incentives were likely to lead more experienced and high-equality teachers to serve in rural areas.

These incentives, in most cases, are not likely to be present. Teacher stability is a major issue for rural schools as turnover is high, given harsh living conditions and schools often lacking running water and electricity as well as current textbooks. Research on the negative impact of temporary teacher status on student achievement, especially for low-income students who do not receive needed personal support and feedback from their teachers, pertains also to urban school contexts (Lusechi, 2012; Marotta, 2019).

Gender

There are gender differences in literacy levels and educational attainments. Females in Latin America fare well compared with women in poorer regions of the world. For example, in 1994, estimated illiteracy figures for developing countries were 32.8% overall and 42.0% for females, whereas the corresponding figures for Latin America were 15.7% overall and 17.2% for females (Marotta, 2019;

Urquiola & Calderón, 2006). By 2018, however, that rate had not improved. Worldwide comparisons of the estimated illiterate 800 million males and females over the age of 15 worldwide, show that 35 million reside in Latin America—an average of 10 percentage points higher than the rest of the world average of 60% (Adult Education and International Literacy Benchmarks) (UNESCO Institute for Statistics, 2002).

By contrast, female enrollment rates were on a par with those of "developed" countries: 45% at the primary level, 52% and the secondary level, and 59% at the tertiary level. (For further discussion, see Chapter 7 in this volume.) As of 2008, females surpassed males in enrollment rates not only at the secondary education level but also in higher education by at least seven percentage points. In Argentina, Brazil, Colombia, Cuba, El Salvador, Nicaragua, Panama, Uruguay, and Venezuela, women comprise the majority of higher education students (CEPAL, 2010).

In Latin America, despite increasing access to education, approximately 21% of females over the age of 15 are illiterate. When the combined effects of social class, region, and gender are taken into account, the highest illiteracy rates are found among poor women living in rural areas (UNESCO, 2010). Gender differences in literacy attainment become even sharper when ethnicity is taken into account. It is not uncommon to find illiteracy rates greater than two-thirds to three-quarters of indigenous women living in rural areas.

Nelly Stromquist (see Chapter 7 of this volume) has pointed out that while gender parity in education remains on the agenda for Latin American females, more pressing policy and research questions involve the following:

> [T]he effects of coeducational settings on social outcomes, the participation and power of women in teachers' unions, women students in politics at the university third generation of studies on gender and seen from a gender perspective, such as the role of women teachers in the process of educational change, the treatment of gender and women teachers. Such research has also given more attention to the contested experience recognition of schools as unfriendly and even threatening environments for girls through such practices as sexual harassment and even rape, not infrequent events in African and Latin American countries.

Stromquist further notes that "A significant backlash against the treatment of gender issues and the provision of sex education has become visible, widespread, and strong in several Latin American countries as well as in some Eastern and Western European countries."

The Catholic Church in Mexico, for example, has strongly objected to sexuality education in school curricula and textbooks, since its introduction in the 1930s. Currently, comprehensive sexuality education (CSE), in various forms, reaches students 10 to 17 years of age. Analysis trends over four historical periods by Chandra-Mouli et al. (2018) indicate that in recent years there have been more organized and large-scale mobilizations by both opponents and proponents of CSE. The conclusion of their study suggests "Mexico's experience with sexuality education can inform other countries' efforts to consider the drivers, responses, support, and resistance that may be present in their own contexts" (Chandra-Mouli et al., 2018, p. 138) (For discussion of the positive results for sexual and reproductive health of Mexico high school students results associated CSE, see De Castro et al., 2018.)

Civil society nongovernmental organizations (NGOs), discussed later in this chapter, have played a major role in advancing women's rights in education as well as in all domains of civil and political rights. In a penultimate section of the chapter, we also mention the promising research on the interplay between gender, education, and social mobility within and across countries.

Ethnicity

Indigenous populations or "first peoples" and ethnic minorities (especially Afro-Brazilians) are the most discriminated against populations concerning access to educational services for two reasons. First, they are commonly located in the most impoverished and underdeveloped regions of their countries, and second, the language of instruction, until recent reform initiatives were invariably Spanish (Portuguese in Brazil). Even when efforts are made to begin instruction in maternal languages during the first year or two of schooling, Spanish (or Portuguese) becomes the language of instruction as one progresses through the education system. The countries with the largest indigenous populations—Bolivia, Peru, and Guatemala—tend to have the highest illiteracy rates and lowest school attendance and completion rates. This is also true of Brazil, with a large number of descendants of former African slaves who inhabit the destitute northeast region. In Brazil, in the mid-2010s, completion rates for Afro-Latin children were 84% of those for their peers at the upper-secondary level. Although this was not ideal, the initiatives of the Workers' Party of President Luiz Inácio Lula Da Silva (2003–2011) and Dilma Rousseff (2011–2016) helped increase the college-going rates of Afro-Latinos. Subsequent governments, especially that of reactionary populist Jair Bolsonaro (2019–), do not bode well for systematic efforts to overcome past racialized policies disadvantaging Afro-Brazilians. A qualitative case-based study by Scott et al. (2019, p. 377) in Central Brazil found that policies promoting ethnocultural diversity and intercultural understanding, as viewed by K–12 teachers, "were unsupported by institutions and thus almost completely reliant on teachers' personal efforts."

Research by Canales and Webb (2018), where indigenous groups constitute approximately 10% of the population, indicates that ethnicity and social class interact to shape student achievement. They found that "In schools where the ethnic composition is higher than the national average, the test score disadvantage of indigenous students is larger, especially those students whose parents both identify as indigenous" (Canales & Webb, 2018, p. 231). While family background is important also significant are school curricular and pedagogical factors. Marks (2005, as cited in Canales & Webb, 2018, p. 256) refer to research in Guatemala, Mexico, and Peru that suggests "language and reading tests are more closely affiliated with sociocultural and family attributes while mathematics learning depends more on school contexts."

In countries with a large indigenous-nonindigenous achievement gap (such as Guatemala, Mexico, and Peru, as well as Bolivia and Ecuador) intercultural and bilingual education programs endeavor to provide more inclusive curricula and teaching contexts. Unfortunately, according to Canales and Webb (2018, p. 257) "limited learning opportunities and low capacity to hire quality teachers in high ethnic composition schools show up in low student achievement."

Peru offers an example of difficulties confronting efforts to implement bilingual-interethnic education reform initiatives in countries with large indigenous populations. In Peru, 51 indigenous peoples represent approximately 45% of the total population. In 2003, bilingual-intercultural education legislation was passed to promote a more egalitarian and democratic society. But such well-intentioned initiatives have faced historical and contextual realities of still deeply entrenched racism that leads to an emphasis on indigenous populations learning Spanish, but not Spanish speakers learning indigenous languages. Efforts at intercultural language tend to take place in rural schools, but not urban ones. When indigenous populations are valorized in textbooks and school extracurricular activities, the picture is a romanticized version of quaint villages and "Indians in their place," as opposed to upward mobile migrants to the cities. Discrimination previously expressed in racial-ethnic terms is now masked as basic differences in culture with Indians transiting to Mestizo status viewed as lacking the appropriate cultural and social capital.

Guatemala represents another interesting case study of a country where racial discrimination played an important role in a civil war in the country between 1960 and 1996. Constituting, at a minimum, 45% of the population, Mayan indigenous groups aligned with rural poor Ladinos and leftist groups to contest a brutal military government. During that period, it is estimated that the army murdered approximately 200,000 indigenous individuals, at least 40,000 of whom were classified as "disappeared"; whole villages were burned to the ground and hundreds of thousands were displaced. According to Bellino (2016):

> The Peace Accords [UN Peacemaker, 1996], negotiated among state and guerrilla sectors, acknowledged the role of the educational sector in perpetuating racism via unequal access to schools, poor treatment of indigenous students, and discriminatory representations of culture in curricula. The accords outlined a number of steps toward making education a more equitable system, including access, bilingual instruction, community involvement, and institutional decentralization, in addition to curricular reform. (p. 58)

According to a 2019 report by the Committee on the Elimination of Racial Discrimination that reviewed progress toward implementing the Accord on Indigenous Peoples' Identity and Rights, special attention was given to the right of self-identification in the 2018 national census, and, for the first time, acknowledged the option for individuals to identify as a "person of African descent/Creole/Afro-mixed race." Priority was also given to the accuracy of gender representation. The report further acknowledged a Constitutional Court ruling that "upheld the right of indigenous peoples to participate in the elaboration, implementation and evaluation of development plans—whether they were economic, social, or cultural—that could affect them directly" (OHCHR, n.d.).

The very outset of the report by Committee Experts noted that problems remained and that Guatemala had experienced setbacks, unfortunately, despite the progress achieved. Questions remained concerning government efforts "to strengthen its institutions to better serve the vulnerable segments of the population and address their concerns." Also questioned was whether "law enforcement officers [were] trained to ensure that indigenous groups allowed to demonstrate without being silenced" (OHCHR, n.d.).

In the third edition of *Comparative Education*, Arnove et al. (2013, p. 23), noted that K'ekchi'May people in Guatemala had an average of 1.8 years of schooling, compared with 6.7 years for Spanish speakers. More recent data indicate that in rural communities, the literacy rate is 81%, with Ladino (nonindigenous) students reaching a rate of 86% and indigenous students at a lower rate of 76%. According to the Guatemala Literacy Project (n.d.), although the **current** (bold in text) levels of literacy of **indigenous** (ditto) youth are lower than those of their Ladino peers, despite this discrepancy, the author notes that literacy in **Guatemala** (ditto) has increased significantly in the last decade.

Even so, Guatemala, like El Salvador and Honduras, is a country wracked by gang violence and the inability of corrupt governments to defend the most vulnerable populations. Consequently, tens of thousands of families, as well as great numbers of unaccompanied children and young adults, have attempted to seek refuge first in Mexico and then the United States, which has shut its doors to those fleeing violence and seeking a better life in the north (Mayers & Freedman, 2019; Sami, 2012).

Education, the Debt Crisis, and the Neoliberal Agenda

The distorted economic policies being pursued by countries throughout the region reflect the hangover from the debt crisis of the 1980s, often referred to as the "lost decade" of development. Economic expansion, experienced at high rates from the 1950s through the 1970s, slowed considerably in the 1980s and 1990s. In the 1960s, the average annual gross national product (GNP) growth rate for Latin American economies was 5.7%. In the 1970s, the growth rate was 5.6%, despite difficulties caused by the oil crisis. By the 1980s, the average annual GNP growth rate for Latin American countries dropped to 1.3% (CEPAL, 2002). The falling GNP translated into decreasing per capita income for the majority of Latin Americans. On average, Latin American per capita incomes fell 9%.

In response to the ever-deepening economic crisis, most Latin American governments adopted the neoliberal fiscal stabilization and economic adjustment policies promoted by international donor agencies like the IMF and the World Bank. The term *neoliberal* derives from the neoclassical economic theories expounded by these agencies and their consultants. The theories are based on the work of the classical economists Adam Smith and David Ricardo, who believed that the role of the state consisted in establishing the conditions by which the free play of the marketplace, the laws of supply and demand, and free trade based on competitive advantage would inevitably redound to the benefit of all. Government policies based on these notions have led to a drastic reduction in the state's role in social spending, deregulation of the economy, and liberalization of import policies. The educational counterparts of these policies have included moves to decentralize and privatize public school systems.

Consequently, education ministries were, to an extent, obligated to subscribe to donor agency policy. As a result, "[donor agencies] advocated a decrease in the amount of government involvement in the education process, an increase in the private sector's role, and greater application of market principles to the organization of Third World educational systems."

It should be noted that since the late 1990s, educational expenditures once again have been on the rise. The overall funding picture for Latin America, however, is more complicated because increasing expenditures on education as a percent of GNP are not adequate to meet the increased demands on education due to the age distribution of Latin American populations. Given the disproportionately large number of school-age children, the countries of the region would need to invest a greater percentage of GNP to achieve adequate levels of education expenditures per child. Furthermore, achieving a workforce with a level of education appropriate for countries with comparable incomes would require an additional investment of 0.5% per year over 25 years (CEPAL, 2002). Accomplishing these goals is very problematic in light of economic policies, in several countries—but not all, as will be seen later—that have cut social spending and have unevenly distributed the benefits of economic growth to the wealthiest segments of Latin American societies.

A key question here is who is benefiting from neoliberal and education policies promoted, if not imposed, by international financial and technical assistance agencies. In briefly reviewing major initiatives to privatize and decentralize education systems in Latin America, as well as elsewhere, we argue that these reforms have benefited primarily the rich and powerful.

PRIVATIZATION

Privatization has taken a variety of forms, including charging user fees in public schools that were previously free of charge. As the educational sector turned toward private interests to fund educational endeavors, policy planning changed to accommodate private investors. Parallel to education ministries' desire to conform to private interests was their need to create self-supporting school systems. This does not mean that education ministries abandoned the finance and support of public education. Rather, education ministries allowed for accelerated development and accreditation of private institutions (primary, secondary, and higher education). Some states, notably Chile, also subsidized private schools or provided tax credits to parents who opt out of the public school system. Selective, high-quality private institutions are attractive to middle- and upper-class students because they offer smaller classes, improved facilities, and an overall atmosphere that is more conducive to learning. At the university level, private institutions are seen as less politicized and therefore not prone to student demonstrations that disrupt classes or cancel an academic semester/year.

Many private schools, especially for-profit ones, are just the opposite. Crowded classrooms, inadequate facilities, poorly paid and overworked teachers, and low-quality instruction characterize them. As low-income students are likely to attend these schools, at great cost to their families, they are offered a second-rate education that is unlikely to open opportunities for them at the postsecondary level.

The Chilean case is noteworthy for illustrating how "the most market-oriented education system in the world has functioned to segregate students by social class" (Verger et al., 2016, p. 223). Based on vouchers established during the dictatorship of Augusto Pinochet (1974–1989), private school enrollment by 2012 represented 61% of all students. This high percentage of enrollment reflected a 1994 government Law of Shared Financing that provided additional funding for private subsidized schools by allowing them to charge fees beyond what they received from public vouchers. According to Verger et al. (2016) a "creaming" occurs when families choose schools primarily on characteristics such as discipline, size, religious affiliation, values extolled, proximity, social class, and fees—overriding features such as academic achievement (measured by national examinations) or innovative curricula and pedagogy (pp. 226, 235). These outcomes, according to Verger et al. (2016) "derive less from the initiatives of private schools than from "bureaucratic or public policy interventions, not market forces" (p. 249).

Public policy, during the center-left government of Michelle Bachelet (2014–2018), however, did take a bold turn toward greater equity. According to Ávalos and Bellei (2019, p. 44), education reforms were launched "to diminish the relevance of market dynamics in Chilean education, including ending public subsidies to profit schools." A 2014 Inclusion Law, for example, "modified the relationship of the state to private education, establishing free education in all schools, ending discrimination in student selection, as well as terminating profits (*lucro*) from schools receiving public resources" (Stuardo & Cayuela, 2019, p. 72).

Changing public perceptions of urban public schools as being inferior, however, is not that easily accomplished. Stuardo and Cayuela (2019, p. 94) underscore, "the political and cultural difficulty of reforming private education services, especially when media groups participate massively in a culture permeated by neo-liberal values in which selection, the educational market, and the 'right to choose' based on economic resources, are the norm." For now, the Chilean education system serves as the most useful mechanism for perpetuating social differentiation and managing class relations (Stuardo & Cayuela, 2019).

At the tertiary level of education, public universities in many countries are faced with an expanded demand from the growing number of secondary school graduates and insufficient state funds. Public universities, therefore, have resorted to charging tuition and other fees that often are the same as those charged in elite private universities.

In Argentina, which has the fewest private university students (20%) of any large state in the region, tuition is charged at the graduate level and for specialized courses. At the undergraduate level, access is both open and free (Rabossi, 2012). The same holds for other left-leaning countries, such as Nicaragua, that have attempted to eliminate barriers to higher education for previously marginalized populations.

In 2011, considerable press coverage was given to student and faculty protests in Colombia that stopped the passage of legislation that would have favored the privatization of higher education. In 2010, in Chile, high school student protests paralyzed the education system over what they considered to be a dehumanizing education, major student demonstrations erupted; their concerns were followed-up in 2011 by widespread demonstration and building occupations by university students and faculty, joined by teachers, labor unions, and other dissatisfied groups over the neoliberal economic model that remained entrenched even after the downfall of the Augusto Pinochet dictatorship in 1989 (Sami, 2012).

Students were protesting the high cost of tuition, the lack of public funding for education, and the very economic model and its values that had led to the most privatized education system in Latin America. Tens of thousands joined in public demonstrations. The newly installed conservative government of Sebastian Piñera (2010) offered substantial concessions. They included a US$4 billion increase in the education budget over the following four to six years, increased access to preschool, reforms in teacher education and certification, and local public-school governance. At the university level, Piñera offered to increase "funding for public universities, [to] ease payment conditions for outstanding debtors, [to] lower the interest rate on educational loans and give full-tuition scholarships to the poorest 40 percent of students" (Sami, 2012). The students, however, found these offers unacceptable, as they were based in a paradigm that depended on students paying high tuition fees, instead of the state offering a free public higher education accessible to all. For the students, increased state revenues should fund the costs of public education; this would require a reformed tax system.[1] According to Bernasconi (2012, p. 28), "Mere adjustments to the educational system would not suffice. They want[ed] to transform what they see as Chile's 'free market,' 'neoliberal education'—as a means of changing the Chilean free market, neoliberal model of development." The government then withdrew its offers and left the resolution of the issues raised to the Chilean Congress, where action on the student demands has stalled, if not died.

In 2018, conservative politician Sebastian Piñera replaced President Michelle Bachelet once again in October 2019, according to Alarcón (2020, p. 20). What had begun as civil disobedience against a metro-ticket price hike had escalated to encompass decades' worth of political, economic, and social grievances, and the impact was everywhere. Known as "*el estallido*" (the explosion), Alarcon noted, "what had begun as a relatively small protest by a couple of hundred high-school students ["institutinos" from the prestigious National Institute in Santiago] had become an existential crisis for the country's political order." Piñera mobilized both police and army security forces, who responded brutally to large-scale demonstrations involving thousands—in ways reminiscent of the Pinochet dictatorship.

Higher education in Latin America will contain to be contested terrain over the extent to which access remains available at low- or no cost to the most disadvantaged populations. Arresting the movement of established and emerging middle-class students to private higher education institutions, furthermore, will not be easy, as they represent a closer gateway to the most prestigious fields and positions in the marketplace and polity, and they are generally considered safer, less politically volatile environments in which to study with a higher quality of instruction in elite institutions.

As a generalization: at whatever level of education, when middle-class parents leave the public school system, the most vocal advocates for quality in the schools disappear. The lower classes, although constituting the majority of the population, lack the political and economic clout necessary to promote quality in the public school system. Without middle-class support, and facing decreased funding, many public school systems fall into decline. Both educational quality and facilities deteriorate significantly

Problems stemming from the privatization of education are exacerbated by the decentralization of national education systems.

DECENTRALIZATION

Decentralization is another option pursued by educational ministries in response to the financial crises of recent years. It also accords with efforts to strengthen civil society in countries undergoing a transition to democracy following the collapse of authoritarian regimes. Unlike the highly decentralized U.S. school system, in most Latin American countries a strong central education ministry controlled all budgetary and curricular decisions.

The decision to decentralize, while popular in certain countries, has been controversial. Many nations have taken steps to decentralize their educational systems, shifting many financial and curricular planning responsibilities as well as personnel decisions to the provincial, departmental, municipal, and even local (as in Nicaragua, between 1993 and 2006) school levels. Prominent examples of countries that have implemented a national decentralization policy are Colombia (1968 and 1986), Argentina (1976), Mexico (1992), and Chile (1981)[2] (De Carvalho & Verhine, 1999; Hanson, 1997). Lower territorial/political units have been given significant funding responsibilities for local schools. The idea is that schools considered superior in quality and services would attract more students and thereby increase their funding capacity. The state partially subsidizes education, but the local territorial/political units are responsible for paying the balance. For example, the Chilean government subsidized, until the Bachelet government reforms, approximately 50% of education costs at the preprimary and primary levels (grades one and two); and at the general secondary education and the upper levels of technical secondary education, roughly 60% (Matte & Sancho, 1993).

Decentralized systems may be successful in resource-rich urban and suburban areas, but present serious problems for lower-class municipalities and rural areas. These areas do not have the resources necessary to make up for educational costs not covered by government subsidies. Nor do they have the same resources to make informed decisions regarding market mechanisms and cost-containment incentives introduced by the government as new educational practices (Prawda, 1993). Both privatization and decentralization exacerbate preexisting socioeconomic inequalities in the education system. Although the elite continues to benefit from quality education, the marginalized sectors of the population have been disproportionately the victims of the growing educational crisis, as well as the 2020/2022 COVID-19 pandemic. Results of national standardized tests in countries like Chile are considered by knowledgeable observers to be a direct proxy for social class with students in urban private schools tending to score highest and students in rural public schools lowest.

Decentralization also refers to government initiatives to establish school councils involving, in some cases, substantial parent and community input to decisions affecting teaching and staff hiring and firing, school budgets, curricula, and extracurricular activities. The effectiveness of decentralization at the school level depends on the knowledge and skills possessed by parent and community members (often a reflection of social class); a clear delineation of responsibilities that involves (a) willingness of teachers and principals to accord significant tasks to nonschool members, while (b) protecting the professional authority and autonomy of teachers within their areas of competence.

At the system level, decentralization to be truly effective must involve a successful balancing of fiscal and curricular initiatives. Past policies, to our way of thinking, had the wrong set of policy thrusts: they emphasized financial deregulation with a tightening of curricular regulations involving high-stakes national examinations that determined what was to be taught Instead, we have found that what Latin American teachers generally prefer is centralized public funding that guarantees equitable financing of education for all areas of a country with a more decentralized curricular policy to reflect local realities.

Locally responsive educational policies are more likely to be achieved to the extent that grassroots movements and civil society pressure central authorities to adopt policies that run counter to strong international, as well as national, currents emphasizing standardized testing. Such testing is viewed as the single most important indicator of how well an education system is performing—a prevalent assumption with which we disagree as well as several countries forming a bloc of resistance to economic and social reforms emanating from abroad (for further discussion, see chapter by David and Leslie Rutkowski [2023], chapter 1 by Joel Samoff in this volume, and Samoff [2013]).

COUNTERHEGEMONIC STATE INITIATIVES

In the first decade of the 20th century, with a "pink tide" of leftist-oriented governments coming to power, efforts were undertaken to form a counterhegemonic bloc to the United States and European influence in the region. These countries undertook bold measures to address not only poverty but also the inequitable education system. The bloc was known as ALBA (Bolivarian Alliance for the Peoples of Our America). Initiated by Venezuela in 2003 (with the support of Cuba, and subsequently incorporating Bolivia, Ecuador, Nicaragua, and the Caribbean island countries of Antigua, Barbuda, Saint Vincent and the Grenadines, and the Commonwealth of Dominica). ALBA views itself as a counter-hegemonic bloc to U.S. influence in the area. It promotes values opposed to the reigning neoliberal economic agenda emphasizing marketization and privatization of all areas of society, a reduced role of the state in the provision of basic social services, competitive relations between countries, and individualism. Instead, ALBA advocates an expanded role for the state in redirecting resources to the neediest regions and populations within a country; regional integration and cooperative relations among countries; and assertion of national sovereignty against external interference in the region not only from the United States and Europe and their aid agencies, but also from intergovernmental agencies such as the World Bank and the IMF. The countries forming ALBA took initial steps to form alternative financial and technical assistance agencies (e.g., *Banco del Sur*, the Bank of the South) and mutual security arrangements. Cooperation in education, for example, involved Cuba sending teachers to Venezuela and Nicaragua to advise on literacy campaigns as well as sending doctors to staff health clinics in poor urban neighborhoods. In turn, Venezuela provided low-cost, subsidized petroleum to Cuba and gave substantial financial assistance to Argentina to help it recover from its economic collapse in 2001–2002.

Since 2013, ALBA's consequential influence has diminished significantly. By 2020, as described earlier, key countries like Brazil and Ecuador now follow conservative, neoliberal economic and social policies. The economy of Venezuela, a major source of funds for regional development efforts, is now bankrupt.

Social movements that protest these external and top-down pressures—informed by the neoliberal and neoconservative economic and education agendas—in many instances are inspired by the philosophy and pedagogy of Brazilian educator Paulo Freire, arguably one of the most important public intellectuals of the second half of the twentieth century.

POPULAR EDUCATION AND OTHER INNOVATIONS

In contrast to state-sponsored education programs, some grassroots education programs in Latin America form part of a "popular education" movement. For a more detailed description of the history and extent of grassroots education efforts as part of social mobilization efforts to change the world, see Rebecca Tarlau's (2023) chapter on Latin America. Although generally limited in resources and small in scope, these programs nonetheless are significant in that they offer an alternative model of education that empowers individuals and communities to place demands on national governments for social services and resources that should be the right of all citizens of a country.

Since the 1960s, nonformal and popular education programs, inspired by the critical consciousness-raising philosophy and pedagogy of the late Brazilian educator Paulo Freire have been important alternatives to the formal education sector. *Nonformal education* implies an educational experience that occurs outside the standard education sphere. *Popular education*, a subset of nonformal education, is distinguished by its pedagogical and political characteristics (Fink & Arnove, 1991).

Pedagogically, popular education programs emphasize nonhierarchical learning situations in which teachers and students engage in dialogue, and learners' knowledge is incorporated into the content of instruction. According to Torres (1994), "education appears as the act of knowing rather than a simple transmission of knowledge or the cultural baggage of society" (p. 198). Politically, popular education programs tend to be directed at meeting the special needs of marginalized sectors of society (women, the unemployed, peasants, and indigenous groups). They have played a significant role in facilitating the development of collective survival strategies to confront the economic crises of the past two decades in the region. Furthermore, the ultimate aim of many popular education programs is not just adaptation or survival for hard-pressed populations but sweeping social change that leads to more just societies (Gadotti, 1992; Torres, 1995; Torres & Puiggrós, 1995).

The most far-sweeping social movement that involves multiple levels and types of education is the Landless Workers Movement (MWT) in Brazil. As described by Tarlau (2023) MST is a *socio-territorial movement* (Fernandes, 2005) that not only makes demands on the state but attempts to control and transform entire territories. As she notes, "over the past thirty years, the MST has helped to develop programs for adult literacy, primary and secondary schooling, high school, and bachelor's and graduate degrees in partnership with over 80 different higher education institutions, involving hundreds of thousands of students. . . . These formal educational programs have transformed the MST from a movement of farmers with at most an elementary or middle school education, to a movement of farmers who are college graduates, in a diversity of disciplines and professions" (Fernandes, 2005, p. 325).

A number of these programs have involved cooperation with municipal and local school systems where the movement has introduced progressive pedagogies that involve greater student and parent involvement and community-oriented action. Whether not these incursions into Brazilian education will be able to transform the federal education system is problematic. Arnove and Bull (2015, as noted by Tarlau, question the appropriateness of the MST movement having such an impact). Arnove and Bull did so, because of what they consider to be restrictive features of the movement's education programs that frame individual collective identities and the very nature of the world from a totalizing perspective—namely, the ideological perspective of the MST (for further discussion, see Tarlau chapter in volume two of *Comparative Education*).

An example of a large-scale education program based on gender is REPEM (*Red de Educación Popular Entre Mujeres de América Latina y el Caribe*), located in Montevideo. The NGO links over 100 organizations at the global, regional, and national levels. It serves as a focal point for research, information dissemination, and advocacy on behalf of low-income women with little formal education. A major goal of both *Peru Mujer* and REPEM is to meet women's demands for greater equality and opportunity and the chance to participate actively in the formulation of alternative social change strategies.

Although popular education programs are generally effective on the community level, they often fail to bring about change at the level of governmental policy. Governments implementing neoliberal policies, for example, frequently view popular education programs as substitutes for national efforts. Of concern to those working in literacy, adult basic education, and various forms of popular education is that state funding for such programs has begun to dry up in recent years. National school systems are increasingly focusing their literacy efforts on school-aged children or adults under 35 years of age. One reason for this trend is that the World Bank, the largest source of external funding for education change initiatives, allocates less than 2% of its budget to literacy programs; and, in past years, encouraged recipients of its loans to focus on younger populations (Arnove, 2012).

State-Civil Society Collaboration

There are, nonetheless, cases of ambitious state-sponsored educational innovations that do benefit traditionally underserved populations. One significant example of a state-sponsored innovation is *La Escuela Nueva* (the New School) in Colombia, which was designed to meet the special needs of rural schools and communities by creating a curriculum that emphasizes communal needs and values. The New School model actively encourages a strong relationship between schools and communities, and a flexible school calendar and promotion policy that is adapted to local agricultural production cycles. One of the goals of the New School is to teach civic values by encouraging student and parent participation in important decisions concerning local educational policy. The emphasis the New School places on participation and decision-making accords with the overarching child-centered, constructivist philosophy framing the program.

The effectiveness of this education reform may explain why Colombia was the only country in the 1997 UNESCO study of academic achievement in which rural third-grade schoolchildren outperformed their urban counterparts on standardized language tests and, except for students in Colombian megacities, their urban counterparts on standardized mathematics tests. New School students also demonstrate strong democratic values on various measures related to civic knowledge, skills, and attitudinal dispositions.

As Gómez (2000) notes, "the New School was consolidated as a framework for resolving . . . [the problems of rural schooling] in an economically sustainable and pedagogically skilled manner" (p. 233). Between its creation in 1989 and the mid-1990s, the program expanded from 8,000 to over 20,000 schools reaching approximately 40% of rural schoolchildren.

A key to the success of this reform, and others, is the preparation of teachers and, as Levin (1992) has pointed out, constant monitoring, problem-solving, and adjustment. Vicky Colbert, one of the founders of the New School Movement and a past vice minister of education, became somewhat disenchanted with how (over time) it had become overly bureaucratized under centralized Ministry control. She left the government to form, in 1987, her private foundation (*La Fundación Escuela Nueva Volvamos a la Gente*) to disseminate the guiding principles of the reform to grassroots groups who would be the initiators of improvements in their schools.[3]

Although widely admired and emulated, attempts to replicate the New School, without significant adaptation to local circumstances, have proven problematic, even within Colombia itself. In Brazil, Tarlau (2017) points out how the New School was viewed as a nonradical foreign transplant competing for valued resources with the education projects of the more politically inspired MWT.

Whatever the limitations of the New School Program may be, its positive features resonate with those of an ideal model of what Latin American countries need to do to achieve more equitable education for all. A review of relevant research from Latin America and other regions suggests that several general policy initiatives would contribute to greater equality of educational opportunities and more equitable outcomes for the most marginalized and disadvantaged populations.

The recommended reforms include quality preschool, early childhood programs with supplementary nutrition and health care services; more adequate school infrastructure so that poor, rural, and indigenous children have the same amenities (schools, desks and chairs, electricity, running water, and toilets) enjoyed by their more advantaged peers in urban and private schools; a flexible academic calendar responsive to the socioeconomic context of schools in different regions of a country; sufficient supplies of textbooks and culturally sensitive as well as socially relevant curricular materials in the appropriate languages; teaching guides matched to transformed curricula; student-centered, more active pedagogies that involve collaborative work as well as personalized attention to each child; significantly improved preservice and in-service teacher education and professional development programs and opportunities; incentive pay for teachers working under difficult conditions (as noted earlier in the Luschei study) and, generally, more adequate remuneration and social recognition of the importance of teaching; and, importantly, greater participation of teachers, parents, and communities in the design of education programs to meet their self-defined needs. A final set of policy initiatives pertain to family income support, payments for school attendance, and completion.

The last initiative is particularly important in the light of the extensive poverty in the region, where there is often a trade-off between the income derived from child labor and school attendance with a problematic promise of future greater earnings for a family. In 2020, the largest programs involving cash transfer to poverty-stricken families—*La Bolsa* in Brazil—benefited 3.8 million families (more than 40 million individuals) with incentive funds for their children to complete basic education as well as attend to basic health needs with vaccinations. In Mexico, a similar program (*Prospera*), by 2020, reached 6.5 million families and 34 million individuals with conditional cash funds to improve students' health and educational attainment (Food and Nutrition Security Platform, 2018). A rigorous evaluation of an earlier version of the program (*Progresa*) found that children in schools receiving transfer funds that include money for staples (such as rice and beans) and school supplies were healthier and stayed in school longer than children in a control group (Duggan, 2004). According to Wolff and De Moura Castro (2003), the *Progresa Programa* in Mexico increased entry rates into lower secondary schools in rural areas by almost 20%.

Targeting funds for disadvantaged populations, known as *focalización* in Spanish, is not without controversy. Several eminent scholars of Latin American education have indicated that such policies often fail to discriminate among different levels of poverty and therefore do not provide enough support to help the most desperate families. They have criticized these fund transfers as largely ameliorative and not attacking the root causes of poverty; and they argue for more comprehensive policies that meet the needs of the vast majority of students in a country (Bonal & Tarabini-Castellani, 2006).

A less progressive reason, according to Kidd et al. (2017), is that a majority of a country's population is paying taxes to finance targeted-cash transfer programs without the ability to access them. As a case in point, *Prospera*, in Mexico, was scheduled to be terminated in 2021. Once touted by the World Bank as a "model for the world" (Villa & Niño-Zarazúa, 2019), according to Kidd et al. (2017), the fate of *Prospera* was "a tragedy foretold."

We argue, however, that these programs are essential, especially in countries, such as Brazil, which has one of the most inequitable distributions of income in the world and, in 2021, ranked second in the world in the number of people dying from COVID-19, as well as in Mexico, among the top 10 countries affected by cases of COVID-19. The pandemic is especially mortal and crippling for countries characterized by high levels of poverty, urban or rural differences in access to health care, and substantial ethnic minorities who have suffered institutionalized discrimination and disadvantage.

The Role of Universities

One of us has written recently on the contributions of Latin American universities to international affairs (Torres, 2020), and the commentary deserves to be quoted at length in this section:

Central trends in the political economy of universities are concerned with economic development and growth, as well as environmental protection, democracy, and the role of education in a contemporary capitalist system. To a great extent, the conversation about development has been substituted for theories of globalization and, not surprisingly, an important topic in this century has been the internationalization of higher education within Latin America itself (De Wit et al., 2005; see Torres, 2021, p. 41).

Another recent significant trend in the region has been the loss of faith in neoliberal policies, which reflects the growing clamor of discontent by sectors of the population, scholars, social movements, and a few governments (Burdick et al., 2009; Stiglitz, 2002). Neoliberal governments have steadily promoted deregulation, free trade, and reduced state intervention. Historically, these policies have been associated with structural adjustment programs and a broad range of policies recommended by the World Bank, IMF, the OECD, and financial institutions. Neoliberalism has taken a stronghold on university life in many industrially advanced societies. However, given the tradition of autonomy of public universities in Latin America, both academics and students have criticized neoliberalism, rejecting the importance of university rankings and the notion of world-class universities.

Multiculturalism and integration have posed another concern for higher education. In many parts of the world, immigrants have been demonized by nativist neopopulists and neofascists. In Latin America, however, immigrants have often been received in the spirit of the Kantian right of hospitality as described by Theologian Boff (2015). Both domestic migration and international immigration occur frequently in the region, and Latin American universities, with their principles of autonomy and free education, receive students from all over the world and accommodate them at a very low cost. However, a central polemic in the region, which spans many other parts of the world given the growing presence and affirmation of indigenous forces, is the question of indigenous rights and multiculturalism (Eisenstadt et al., 2013; Lehmann, 2016; Sieder, 2002). This debate on the recognition of rights aligns with the fourth generation Frankfurt Critical Theory, particularly on the work of Axel Honneth (Sauerwald, 2008; Schiermer & Pettenkofer, 2017).

Experiences of Latin American integration that began in the 20th century survive today with varying degrees of success. Successes include the Mercosur promoting free trade and the fluid movement of goods, people, and currency, as well as the Federal University for Latin American Integration, a bilingual university created in the tripartite frontier of Brazil, Paraguay, and Argentina. Another model of integration is the University for International Integration of the Afro-Brazilian Lusophony (UNILAB), founded in 2010 as a federal university in Brazil with campuses in the northeastern states of Ceará and Bahía. UNILAB (n.d.) offers fellowships for foreign students and seeks to aid the process of integration.

In the 1960s and 1970s, public universities were further impacted by the critical theories developed by international organizations and university scholars, alongside several social movements (Bielschowsky, 2016; Bondy, 1969; Cardoso & Faletto, 1979; Dussel, 2011; Freire, 1972; Leopoldo, 1969; O'Donnell, 1982; Rodolfo, 1977; Roig, 1981). Not surprisingly, the postcolonial tradition continues to be nourished in recent decades. Postcolonialism is an academic field that studies the cultural legacy of colonialism and imperialism, and postcoloniality in academia provides an important commentary on identity construction. Beyond politics, postcolonialism is intimately connected with method, ontology, and epistemology. Hence new epistemological perspectives from the Global South have emerged through a variety of projects in scholarship and universities (Acosta, 2015).

One such project with significant global reach is the ALICE project. This project is a legacy of the Reinventing Social Emancipation project (EMANCIPA), coordinated by Portuguese sociologist Boaventura de Sousa Santos between 1999 and 2001 (de Sousa Santos, 2018). EMANCIPA stemmed from the growing awareness that the social sciences had exhausted their ability to renew and innovate. In pursuit of the reinvention of social emancipation, the project explored what is now termed the "Epistemologies of the South," fostering an understanding of knowledge and practices made invisible by mainstream social sciences. The work was carried out by a team of 69 researchers and resulted in a series of publications in various languages focused, for instance, on "counter-hegemonic globalization," participatory democracy, emancipatory multiculturalism, and new labor internationalism (ALICE, n.d.).

Since the creation of the Bologna project in Europe, the relationships among European universities and Latin American universities have increased considerably. The RIAIPE (2021) project, a collaboration among many European and Latin American universities, exemplifies these increasingly positive relationships. The project executed between 2010 and 2015 engaged a consortium of 31 research teams from Latin American universities and seven teams from European universities, along with teams from the Organization of the Iberoamerican States (Centre for Social Studies, University of Coimbra, n.d.; Teodoro & Guilherme, 2014).

From a different perspective, the UNESCO Chairs and UnitWin Networks have their global reach. These UNESCO Chairs promote the Sustainable Development Goals (2015–2030) of the United Nations, and with more than 700 such chairs all over the world and sizable influence in Latin America, these chairs have conceived of a new orientation for education. This orientation is expected to reach the same heights as that of previous emblematic and seminal publications of UNESCO like the Faure (1972) report titled *Learning to Be* and the Delors (1996) report titled *Learning: The Treasure Within*. The latest report indicates these newest developments in higher education is titled *Humanistic Futures of Learning: Perspectives from UNESCO Chairs and UNITWIN Networks* (UNESCO, 2020).

This selective reading of the generative themes that animate the research and teaching agendas in the public universities is not complete, nor should it be considered a guide for a systematic introduction to the field. There are hundreds if not thousands of books, research papers, reports, videos, and articles in multiple languages that have not been covered in this analysis. Latin American national and international politics remain in tension with the U.S. policies in the region and the perception that the United States is no longer the dominant power of the Cold War. Hence, not surprisingly, China has become an increasingly vital presence in Latin American development in the 21st century.

Finally, it is necessary to point out the important role that universities can play, through their research, development, and dissemination activities, in contributing to income and job generation to overcome the devastating effects of the debt crisis and the current neoliberal agenda. Higher education leaders like the late Xabier Gorostiaga of the Central American University (UCA) of Nicaragua have proposed a vision of a new role for "universities of the South." His vision calls for utilizing existing university departmental extension programs and research and development institutes affiliated with the UCA as nuclei for experimentation, training, and popular education. Building a university education around the knowledge generated by rural-based centers would contribute to the formation of professionals who, because they had a more realistic understanding of their society, would be better prepared to address its most pressing problems. Moreover, the work of such centers would contribute to empowering the "producing majority" to become major historical actors involved in the transformation of an unsatisfactory status quo that has marginalized and exploited them. These engagements are critical to the development and dissemination of appropriate and self-sustainable technologies; and, according to Gorostiaga (1993), they offer prospects of collaboration between universities of the north and the south (Torres, 2011).

PROMISING COMPARATIVE RESEARCH

In updating and revising this chapter, the authors encountered several interesting approaches to the study of education in the region of Latin America. Briefly, we discuss four studies.

Carnoy et al. (2017, p. 726) provide insights on the significance of examining subnational differences in student academic achievement in large federal states such as Brazil. Their research focuses on the "'effectiveness' of state education administration in delivering education." Their study further disaggregates data on mathematics test scores on national examinations over an extended period (1990–2013) to identify "differences in state[s] with similar demographic characteristics." Among contributions to political theory is the following finding: "Even controlling for individual socioeconomic background and the average socioeconomic background of students in school, students in states with higher proportions of families in poverty (family income less that one minimum wage) may average lower scores than students attending state and municipal schools in states with lower levels of poverty. . . . [S]tudents of all social classes may be affected academically in living in states with higher levels of poverty" (Carnoy et al., 2017, p. 752).

While where a student lives may have a determinative impact on students' academic performance, the researchers note that national and subnational education policy and practices can lessen the negative impact of poverty. According to Carnoy et al. (2017, p. 748), "Studies show that providing a coherent approach to curriculum, teaching practices, professional development, and the implementation of change in these educational inputs in administrative units such as schools and districts increase student achievement."

Other promising research draws attention to the importance of ideographic personality traits shaping how students negotiate their schooling experiences. In their Chilean case study, Gómez Vera et al. (2015) note "there are students who, despite living in impoverished conditions, achieve solid academic performance" (p. 693). Their research employs "resilience" as a key factor in explaining this outcome on PISA (Programme for International Student Achievement) language test scores. As defined by Masten and Obradovic (2008, as cited in Gómez Vera et al., 2015, p. 698), resilience is "the ability to maintain normal performance despite adversity." Of particular value is how this individual personality trait plays out in a school system that is considered to be "one of the most socially segregated school systems in the world" (OECD, 2019). Introducing different levels of analysis, from the individual to the institutional, the researchers select PISA language scores as their dependent variable. Focusing on the lowest socioeconomic quartile. Gómez Vera et al. (2015, p. 704) find "resilient students tend to have more educated parents and have a higher index of cultural possessions than nonresilient students but less than the average group. Family environment is an important determinant of resilience." School and classroom variables, not surprisingly, turn out to be very significant concerning both resilient and average students. Among the most significant findings are these: they attend more selective schools that use academic criteria in their admissions process; they attend schools with lower rates of violence; the average level education of classmates' families is higher among resilient and average students than among nonresilient students—all three of these differentiating factors turn out to more important than parents' education. Finally, what distinguishes resilient students from both average and nonresilient students turns out to be the "classroom environment, which is reported to be better in the classes attended by resilient students" (Gómez Vera et al., 2015, p. 710). One individual variable that stood in the study was gender: more girls than boys tended to be located in the resilient category.

Gender is an important variable in Valentine et al.'s (2017) study of migration patterns and the pursuit of education in Oaxaca and Chiapas, Mexico. Adolescent mobility in search of opportunities to complete secondary education in more urban areas in the country and beyond has a major impact on rural communities in various ways, one being remittances that are sent home; if not, large-scale exodus diminishes even more local resources for schooling. The researchers find "An increasing emphasis on the value of education is emerging particularly for girls" (Valentine et al., 2017, p. 167). They note, "Young women were pursuing post high-school training and university to secure higher payment employment at higher rates than previous generational cohorts of women in their families." It is hoped that antipoverty programs will narrow and transpose "the gap between male and female schooling outcomes" (Valentine et al., 2017, p. 169). Among the contributions of Valentine et al.'s (2017) study is placing migration and education patterns not only within a national, but within regional, and international contexts.

A fourth study, one of many others, that provides a remarkable theoretical framework is that by Verger et al. (2016) on the heavily market-based Chilean education systems (discussed earlier in the chapter). Briefly, the researchers employ "A realist evaluation perspective" to study "Public-private partnership (PPPS) in education . . . as a cost-effect policy solution to the access and quality problems that many education systems, especially in developing countries face" (p. 223). According to Verger et al. (2016), the advantages of this perspective over more conventional evaluation methods is this: "[It] is especially appropriate for analyzing education policies whose implementation depends so decisively on the strategic behavior, 'logics of action,' and preferences of the intended beneficiaries of the intervention—clearly the case for PPPs in education" (p. 225).

Recent studies cited in this chapter were selected for precisely the types of sophisticated analysis illustrated in the country studies of Brazil, Mexico, and Chile. The researchers employ multilevel analysis (that can range from the individual to the international), situate individuals and their groups within specific contexts and a variety of intervening factors shaping actions and outcomes, and examine not only the limitations but the potential of education policies and practices to bring about more equitable school systems and just societies.

A fifth study commissioned by UNESCO on people in conditions of mobility and written by Carlos Alberto Torres offers a systematic analysis of the main trends that impact the region in the last decade, and particularly how education plays a major role in receiving and promoting the insertion of immigrants in Latin American societies. The document titled "Educación para la Ciudadanía Global y Personas en Situación de Movilidad Propuestas para América Latina y El Caribe" (in press) seeks to promote at the regional level a contextualized discussion of the concept of global citizenship education. The theoretical context of this discussion identifies eight larger global trends and how they impact Latin America and the Caribbean region. The analysis of global citizenship education focuses on the role of human rights, democracy, and government institutions in a context affected by inequality and the search for alternatives to promote sustainability goals for development.

REFLECTIONS ON THE REGION IN THE TIME OF COVID-19

As we write this update, we would be remiss if we did not discuss the significant negative impact of the coronavirus pandemic in the region. The years 2020/2022 was very hard on the health, well-being, and economies of Latin America. As well as its education systems. Several economists early on predicted that it was a year in which domestic growth would decline, amounting to losses equivalent to the decade of the 1980s, considered the "lost decade" of development worldwide (Ridley, 1989). One important factor is the complete loss of faith in the neoliberal policies that have inspired conservative governments in the region, and the possibility that after the way some of them have mismanaged the pandemic, most prominently President Jair Bolsonaro in Brazil, that the next electoral cycle will punish elected governments.

Some analysts have spoken about the need for a large-scale mobilization of resources that would be akin to a Marshall Plan for Latin America. But in the context of the confusing policies of the United States in recent years, the slow process of growth of the global economy, and the growing unrest in the region, it is difficult to predict that a recovery is around the corner. However, vignettes and personal observations of the authors indicate that the hope for education, its role in social mobility, values of decency, dignity, and solidarity, which are quintessential values in the construction of democratic citizenship, and the possibility of a new global pact for sustainable growth cannot be discounted.

CONCLUSION

The implementation of structural adjustment policies in the 1980s to liberalize the economies of Latin America and integrate them more tightly into the world capitalist system provoked several crises throughout the region. In diminishing the role of the state in the provision of basic social services—part of the cost-cutting policies recommended by the World Bank and the IMF—the social safety net provided the most marginalized populations was significantly dismantled over the ensuing two decades. The disparity between the wealthy and the poor increased. This situation limited educational access and opportunities for the most vulnerable populations to gain access to quality education and equitable life chances. Moreover, moves to decentralize and privatize economies were paralleled by initiatives to reduce the role of the state in the financing of education. Another intended outcome of such initiatives was the erosion of the bargaining power of national teacher unions, in many cases the single most important voice for a universal, free education system that prepares individuals not only for productive economic roles but the exercise of democratic citizenship rights.

These fiscal austerities and structural adjustment policies resulted in growing social unrest and mass demonstrations that both threatened and toppled governments, Bolivia and Ecuador being two notable examples. In the education field, the introduction of these neoliberal economic policies and a conservative ideological agenda into the education system led to numerous protests—teacher strikes and student and parent occupations of schools and Ministry of Education offices in countries ranging from Argentina to Mexico. As was documented in Arnove's (1994) case study of Nicaragua, these initiatives polarized education, despite the ostensible goals of governments to use education as a means of achieving social consensus.

As we have argued in previous editions of *Comparative Education*, it is possible, but unlikely, that consensus concerning education can be achieved without a national agreement being reached around a model of economic development. This model must be based on protecting the autonomy and sovereignty of individual countries to devise economic and social policies that are reflective of their individual histories and social and cultural dynamics, rather than economic agendas determined in the major metropolitan centers of the north. It would be a model that recognizes and supports autonomous, sustainable development at the grassroots level and in the informal sectors of the economy, the so-called industries of the poor, providing employment for as much as one-half of the workforce of many Latin American countries (Gorostiaga, 1993). One model, for example, draws upon features of a free-market economy to generate goods and services but also upon those of social democracies that provide a social safety net—the basic conditions for all to live decently. Other models may involve more radical distributive policies.

A struggle is now taking place in Latin America, as elsewhere, as to who will determine the goals, processes, and outcomes of national economic and social policies. The achievement of more equitable development is integrally related to the ability of countries to affirm their national sovereignty as well as their collective interests. To do so requires the joining of like-minded countries to challenge the external constraints imposed upon them by the dominant hegemonic power in the region—the United States—but also by transnational actors ranging from the international financial, technical assistance, and trade agencies—most recently the World Trade Organization. The growing number of more progressive governments that came to power in the first years of the 21st century was a sign that populations were fed up with the existing status quo. Leaders from these countries attempted to form alternative economic blocs to the Free Trade Area of the Americas (FTAA) and the Central American Free Trade Area (CAFTA) while reaching out to counterparts in Africa and the Middle East to shift the terms of trade and unequal relationships between north and south. From the more rapid economic growth of Argentina, which rejected IMF conditionalities and renegotiated its external debt on more favorable terms (Rohter, 2004), to the leading role played by progressive Latin American governments and other third world countries in challenging harmful free trade agreements of the World Trade Organization, in Cancun in September 2003, there was evidence that things were beginning to change.

Unfortunately, these promising trends evident in the 2013 edition of *Comparative Education* have encountered strong resistance and dramatic reversals. Instead, populist governments of both the left and right have come to power. Whether fascist or socialist in orientation, they are authoritarian in nature. They do not bode well for democratic governance or the achievement of more equitable societies and education systems. If enduring progressive change is to occur it necessarily will have to come from sociopolitical mobilizations and mass protests from below.

The technologies that are now in place to facilitate the international flow of capital and the global assembly line also can be used to connect progressive social movements across national borders. Such has been the case with labor unions, peasant federations, and indigenist, feminist, environmental, and other movements that now mobilize transnationally to protect their habitats, affirm and preserve their cultural identities and communities, receive a living wage in safe places, and achieve more equitable societies.[4] Such social movements have been the driving force for the election of more populist and nationalist governments as well as the overthrow of corrupt governments that have sold out national rights. In the field of education, networks exist to connect scholars, policymakers, and practitioners concerned with issues of globalization and "Education for All."[5] In the spring of 2005, Mary Compton, the president of the National Union of Teachers in England, called for "solidarity among teachers around the world to combat forces of globalization and privatization" (Compton & Weiner, 2008). She notes, "We Are the World" (Compton, 2005).

If a more satisfactory consensus is to be achieved between the various protagonists and antagonists over how economic and social development is to occur and the nature and role of education systems in contributing to a more desirable future for the countries of Latin America and the Caribbean, it will not be the result of the beneficence of the multinational corporations and international organizations, nor even of popularly elected governments. It will be the outcome of the sustained, collective efforts of these grassroots movements inspired by alternative visions of the future. As researchers, educators, and activists concerned with issues of social justice around the world, we can contribute to those struggles through our multiple engagements with the production and dissemination of knowledge. The role of education, in the continent that gave us so many philosophers of liberation, and so many experiences of popular culture and popular education, may indicate that the future will be brighter than the actual present.

NOTES

The authors wish to acknowledge the invaluable assistance of Li Yan in formatting and verifying the references, as well as the substantive contributions of Lauren Misiaszek to the chapter.

1. If there were an equitable tax system with effective enforcement, using public taxes to finance an essentially free higher education system for all might be possible. But getting the rich and powerful to pay their fair share of taxes is extraordinarily difficult in Latin America.

2. Furthermore, Cuba, as part of its 1986 "rectification" overhaul of centralized government, also initiated a process of decentralization in education. Unlike municipalization plans in other Latin American countries, it tended to shift more power to local school councils and various forms of "popular power" (see Lutjens, 1996).

3. Conversation with Vicky Colbert, president of the Fundación Volvamos a la Gente and co-founder of La Escuela Nueva, August 19, 2002, Bogotá, Colombia; summary information available in the pamphlet Improving the Quality of Basic Primary Education: The Case of Escuela Nueva from Colombia (Bogotá, Colombia: Ministry of Education, Back to the People Foundation, and National Federation of Coffee Growers Association, n.d.).

4. Typical of these efforts was a coming together of indigenous, labor, environmental, feminist, and antiglobalization movements in Cochabamba, Bolivia, December 8–9, 2006, to discuss an alternative to the neoliberal agenda, at the same time that the heads of state of twelve South American countries met to discuss regional integration. The meeting represented a joining of transnational forces initiated by the Comunidad Sudamericana de Naciones (CSN) with the interstate initiatives of President Evo Morales of Bolivia. See "Evo Morales Propone CSN para 'Vivir Bien.'" Contact information is available at info@alainet.org.

5. See, for example, the initiatives of Rosa María Torres (fronesis.org/prolat.htm) as a follow-up to the Jomtien 1990 and Dakar 2000 international conferences.

REFERENCES

Acosta, W. S. (2015). Ciencias sociales y relaciones internacionales: Nuevas perspectivas desde América Latina [Social sciences and international relations: New perspectives from Latin America]. Escuela de Relaciones Internacionales de la Univesidad Nacional.

Alarcón, D. (2020, October 5). Chile at the Barricades. *The New Yorker*. Retrieved from https://www.newyorker.com/magazine/2020/10/12/chile-at-the-barricades

ALICE. (n.d.). *ALICE background—"Reinventing social emancipation."* Retrieved from http://alice.ces.uc.pt/en/index.php/about/where-does-alice-come-from/

Arnove, R. F. (1994). *Education as contested terrain: Nicaragua, 1979–1993*. Westview Press.

Arnove, R. F. (2012). The World Bank's "education strategy 2020": A personal account. In C. S. Collins & A. W. Wiseman (Eds.), *Education strategy in the developing world: Revising the World Bank's education policy* (pp. 63–80). Emerald Group Publishing.

Arnove, R., Franz, S., & Kubow, P. K. (2013). *Comparative education*. Rowman & Littlefield.

Ávalos, B., & Bellei, C. (2019). Recent education reforms in Chile: How much of a departure from market and new public management systems? In C. Ornelas (Ed.), *Politics of education in Latin America* (pp. 43–71). Sense-Brill Publishers.

Bellino, M. J. (2016). So that we do not fall again: History education and citizenship in "postwar" Guatemala. *Comparative Education Review*, 60(1), 58–79. doi:10.1086/684361

Bernasconi, A. (2012). Chile: The rise and decline of a student movement. *International Higher Education, 66*, 27–29. doi:10.6017/ihe.2012.66.8596

Bielschowsky, R. (2016). *ECLAC thinking: Selected texts (1948–1998)*. United Nations.

Boff, L. (2015). *Hospitality: Everyone's right and everyone's duty*. Retrieved from https://www.alainet.org/en/articulo/173624

Bonal, X., & Tarabini-Castellani, A. (2006). Focalización educativa y lucha contra la pobreza:un debate acerca de los límites y posibilidades del Programa Bolsa Escola [Educational targeting and the fight against poverty: A debate about the limits and possibilities of the Bolsa Escola Program]. In X. Bonal (Ed.), *Globalización, educación, y pobreza en América Latina* [Globalization, education, and poverty in Latin America] (pp. 355–380). Editorial Bellaterra.

Bondy, A. S. (1969). *Existe una filosofía de nuestra América?* [Is there a philosophy of our America?]. Siglo XXI.

Bowles, S., & Gintis, H. (1986). *Democracy and capitalism: Property, community, and the contradictions of modern social thought*. Basic Books.

Burdick, J., Oxhorn, P., & Roberts, K. (Eds.). (2009). *Beyond neoliberalism in Latin America? Societies and politics at the crossroads*. Palgrave Macmillan.

Canales, A., & Webb, A. (2018). Educational achievement of indigenous students in Chile: School composition and peer effects. *Comparative Education Review, 62*(2), 231–273. doi:10.1086/696957

Cardoso, F. H. (1979). On the characterisation of authoritarian regimes in Latin America. In D. Collier (Ed.), *The new authoritarianism in Latin America* (pp. 33–57). Princeton University Press.

Cardoso, F. H. (1981). Political regime and social change: Some reflections concerning the Brazilian case. *Boletín de Estudios Latinoamericanos y del Caribe, 30*, 3–20.

Cardoso, F. H., & Faletto, E. (1979). *Dependency and development in Latin America*. University of California Press.

Cardoso, F. H., & Magnani, J. G. C. (1974). Las contradicciones del desarrollo asociado [The contradictions of associated development]. *Desarrollo Económico, 14*(53), 3–32. doi:10.2307/3466046

Carnoy, M., & Levin, H. (1985). *Schooling and work in the democratic state*. Stanford University Press.

Carnoy, M., Marotta, L., Louzano, P., Khavenson, T., Guimarães, F. R. F., & Carnauba, F. (2017). Intranational comparative education: What state differences in student achievement can teach us about improving education—The case of Brazil. *Comparative Education Review, 61*(4), 726–759. doi:10.1086/693981

Centre for Social Studies, University of Coimbra. (n.d.). *RIAIPE 3: Inter-university framework program for equity and social cohesion policies in higher education*. Retrieved from https://ces.uc.pt/en/investigacao/projetos-de-investigacao/projetos-financiados/riaipe-3

CEPAL. (2002). *Panorama Social de América Latina* [Social panorama of Latin America]. CEPAL.

CEPAL. (2010). *Panorama Social de América Latina* [Social panorama of Latin America]. CEPAL.

CEPAL. (2019). *Panorama Social de América Latina* [Social panorama of Latin America]. CEPAL.

Chandra-Mouli, V., Garbero, L. G., Plesons, M., Lang, I., & Vargas, E. C. (2018). Evolution and resistance to sexuality education in Mexico. *Global Health: Science and Practice, 6*(1), 137–149. doi:10.9745/GHSP-D-17-00284

Chomsky, N. (2002). *Hegemony or survival: America's quest for global dominance*. Metropolitan Books.

Colbert, V. (n.d.). Improving the Quality of Basic Primary Education: The Case of Escuela Nueva from Colombia. Ministry of Education (Bogotá, Colombia), Back to the People Foundation, and National Federation of Coffee Growers Association (pamphlet).

Compton, M. (2005). *We are the world: A call for solidarity among teachers around the world to combat forces of globalization and privatization.* Retrieved from https://rethinkingschools.org/articles/essay-we-are-the-world/

Compton, M., & Weiner, L. (2008). The global assault on teachers, teaching, and teacher unions. In M. Compton & L. Weiner (Eds.), *The global assault on teaching, teachers, and their unions stories for resistance* (pp. 3–9). Palgrave Macmillan.

De Carvalho, I. M. M., & Verhine, R. E. (1999). A descentralizaçao da educaçao [The decentralization of education]. *Revista Sociedade e Estado, 16*(2), 299–321.

De Castro, F., Rojas-Martínez, R., Villalobos-Hernández, A., Allen-Leigh, B., Breverman-Bronstein, A., Billings, D. L., & Uribe-Zúñiga, P. (2018). Sexual and reproductive health outcomes are positively associated with comprehensive sexual education exposure in Mexican high-school students. *PLoS One, 13*(3), e0193780. doi:10.1371/journal.pone.0193780

De Sousa Santos, B. (2018). *The end of the cognitive empire: The coming of age of epistemologies of the South.* Duke University Press.

De Wit, H., Jaramillo, I. C., Gacel-Avila, J., & Knight, J. (Eds.). (2005). *Higher education in Latin America: The international dimension.* World Bank Publications.

Delors, J. (1996). *Learning: The treasure within.* UNESCO Publishing.

Duggan, C. W. (2004, January 3). To help poor be pupils, not wage earners, Brazil pays parents. *New York Times.* Retrieved from https://www.nytimes.com/2004/01/03/world/to-help-poor-be-pupils-not-wage-earners-brazil-pays-parents.html

Dussel, E. (2011). *Filosofía de la liberación* [Philosophy of liberation]. Fondo de Cultura Económica.

Eisenstadt, T. A., Danielson, M. S., Corres, M. J. B., & Polo, C. S. (Eds.). (2013). *Latin America's multicultural movements: The struggle between communitarianism, autonomy, and human rights.* Oxford University Press.

Faure, E. (1972). *Learning to be: The world of education today and tomorrow.* UNESCO Publishing.

Fernandes, B. M. (2005). The occupation as a form of access to land in Brazil: A theoretical and methodological contribution. In S. Moyo & P. Yeros (Eds.), *Reclaiming the land: The resurgence of rural movements in Africa, Asia and Latin America* (pp. 317–340). Zed Books.

Fink, M., & Arnove, R. F. (1991). Issues and tensions in popular education in Latin America. *International Journal of Educational Development, 11*(3), 221–230. doi:10.1016/0738-0593(91)90022-Z

Food and Agriculture Organization of the United Nations. (n.d.). *Food and nutrition security in Latin America and the Caribbean.* Retrieved from http://www.fao.org/americas/prioridades/seguridad-alimentaria/en/

Food and Nutrition Security Platform. (2018). *Mexico: Social inclusion program "PROSPERA."* Retrieved from https://plataformacelac.org/en/programa/264

Freire, P. (1972). *Pedagogía del oprimido* [Pedagogy of the oppressed]. Tierra Nueva.

Gadotti, M. (1992). Latin America: Popular education and the state. In C. Poster & J. Zimmer (Eds.), *Community education in the third world* (pp. 125–141). Routledge.

Gómez, A. S. (2000). Equity and education in Colombia. In F. Reimers (Ed.), *Unequal schools, unequal chances: The challenges to equal opportunity in the Americas* (pp. 203–244). Harvard University Press.

Gómez Vera, G. G., Valenzuela, J. P., & Sotomayor, C. (2015). Against all odds: Outstanding reading performance among Chilean youth in vulnerable conditions. *Comparative Education Review, 59*(4), 693–716. doi:10.1086/683108

Gorostiaga, X. (1993). New times, new role for universities of the South. *Envio: The Monthly Magazine of Analysis on Central America, 12*(144), 29–40.
Gott, R. (2000). *Hugo Chávez and the Bolivarian revolution.* Verso Books.
Guatemala Literacy Project. (n.d.). *Why Guatemala?* Retrieved from https://guatemala literacy.org/why-guatemala
Hanson, M. (1997). *Educational decentralization: Issues and challenges.* Retrieved from https://gsdrc.org/document-library/educational-decentralization-issues-and-challenges/
IIEP & UNESCO. (2005). Education and equity in Latin America. *Newsletter, 23*(1), 1–16.
Inter-American Development Bank. (1998). *Education: The Gordian knot.* Inter-American Development Bank.
International Monetary Fund. (2020). *World economic outlook database.* Retrieved from https://www.imf.org/en/Publications/WEO/weo-database/2020/April/select-countries?grp=205&sg=All-countries/Emerging-market-and-developing-economies/Latin-America-and-the-Caribbean
Kidd, S., Gelders, B., & Bailey-Athias, D. (2017). *Exclusion by design: An assessment of the effectiveness of the proxy means test poverty targeting mechanism.* International Labour Organization.
LaFeber, W. (1993). *Inevitable revolutions: The United States in Central America.* W. W. Norton.
Lehmann, D. (Ed.). (2016). *The crisis of multiculturalism in Latin America.* Palgrave Macmillan.
Leopoldo, Z. (1969). *La filosofía americana como filosofía sin más* [American philosophy as philosophy no more]. Siglo XXI.
Levin, H. (1992). Effective schools in comparative focus. In R. F. Arnove, P. G. Altbach, & G. P. Kelly (Eds.), *Emergent issues in education: Comparative perspectives* (pp. 229–245). State University of New York Press.
Luschei, T. F. (2012). In search of good teachers: Patterns of teacher quality in two Mexican states. *Comparative Education Review, 56*(1), 69–97. doi:10.1086/661508
Lutjens, S. L. (1996). *The state, bureaucracy, and the Cuban schools: Power and participation.* Westview.
Mahoney, J. (2015). Explaining the great continuity: Ethnic institutions, colonialism, and social development in Spanish America. In M. M. Charrad & J. P. Adams (Eds.), *Patrimonial capitalism and empire* (pp. 43–62). Emerald Group Publishing.
Marotta, L. (2019). Teachers' contractual ties and student achievement: The effect of temporary and multiple-school teachers in Brazil. *Comparative Education Review, 63*(3), 356–376. doi:10.1086/703981
Matte, P., & Sancho, A. (1993). Primary and secondary education. In C. Larroulet (Ed.), *The Chilean experience: Private solutions to public problems* (pp. 106–118). Editorial Universitaria.
Mayers, S., & Freedman, J. (Eds.). (2019). *Solito, Solita: Crossing borders with youth refugees from Central America.* Haymarket Books.
O'Donnell, G. (1982). *1966–1973 El estado burocrático autoritario: Triunfos, derrotas y crisis* [1966–1973 The authoritarian bureaucratic state: Triumphs, defeats, and crises]. University of California Press.
OECD. (2019). *Balancing school choice and equity: An international perspective based on PISA.* Retrieved from http://www.oecd.org/education/balancing-school-choice-and-equity-2592c974-en.htm
OECD. (2020). *OECD education statistics.* Retrieved from https://www.oecd-ilibrary.org/education/data/oecd-education-statistics_edu-data-en
Offe, C. (1984). *Contradictions of the welfare state.* MIT Press.
Offe, C., & Ronge, V. (1975). Theses on the theory of the state. *New German Critique, 6,* 137–147. doi:10.2307/487658

OHCHR. (n.d.). *Committee on the Elimination of Racial Discrimination*. Retrieved from https://www.ohchr.org/en/hrbodies/cerd/pages/cerdindex.aspx

Prawda, J. (1993). Educational decentralization in Latin America: Lessons learned. *International Journal of Educational Development, 13*(3), 253–264. doi: 10.1016/0738-0593(93)90033-V

Psacharopoulos, G., Morley, S., Fiszbein, A., Lee, H., & Wood, B. (1997). *Poverty and income distribution in Latin America: The story of the 1980s*. World Bank.

Rabossi, M. (2012). Why Argentine private universities continue to lag. *International Higher Education, 66*, 29–30. doi:10.6017/ihe.2012.66.8597

RIAIPE. (2021). *Introduction to Riaipe*. Retrieved from http://riaipe.org/index.php/riaipe/

Ridley, C. (1989). *The 1980s was a "lost decade" for development in . . .* Retrieved from https://www.upi.com/Archives/1989/12/20/The-1980s-was-a-lost-decade-for-development-in/6776630133200/

Rodolfo, K. (1977). *El pensamiento indígena y popular en América* [The indigenous and popular thought in America]. Hachette.

Rohter, L. (2004, December 26). Economic rally for Argentines defies forecasts. *New York Times*. Retrieved from https://www.nytimes.com/2004/12/26/world/americas/argentinas-economic-rally-defies-forecasts.html

Roig, A. A. (1981). *Teoría y crítica del pensamiento latinoamericano* [Theory and Criticism of Latin American thought]. Fondo de Cultura Económica.

Rutkowski, D., & Rutkowski, L. (2023). The promise and methodological limits of international. In L. I. Misiaszek et al. (Eds.), *Emergent trends in comparative education: The dialectic of the global and the local*. Rowman & Littlefield.

Sami, F. (2012). *Higher education in Latin America 2011: The burden of the youth*. Retrieved from https://www.coha.org/higher-education-in-latin-america-2011the-burden-of-the-youth/

Samoff, J. (2013). Institutionalizing international influence. In R. F. Arnove et al. (Eds.), *Comparative education: The dialectic of the global and the local* (pp. 55–87). Rowman & Littlefield.

Sauerwald, G. (2008). *Reconocimiento y liberación: Axel Honneth y el pensamiento latinoamericano: por un diálogo entre el Sur y el Norte* [Recognition and liberation: Axel Honneth and Latin American thought: For a dialogue between the South and the North]. Lit Berlag.

Schiermer, B., & Pettenkofer, A. (2017). *E-special: Four generations of critical theory in Acta Sociologica*. https://journals.sagepub.com/pb-assets/cmscontent/ASJ/Intro_Four_Generations.pdf

Scott, D., Kawalilak, C., Dressler, R, & Alves de Paiva, W. (2019). Investigating educational responses to diversity in Brazil during a time of curriculum change. *Comparative Education Review, 63*(3), 377–397. doi.org/10.1086/703982

Sieder, R. (Ed.). (2002). *Multiculturalism in Latin America: Indigenous rights, diversity and democracy*. Palgrave Macmillan.

Stiglitz, J. E. (2002). *Globalization and its discontents*. W. W. Norton.

Stuardo, G. M., & Cayuela, J. W. (2019). The difficult process in Chile: Redefining the rules of the game for subsidized private education. In C. Ornelas (Ed.), *Politics of education in Latin America* (pp. 72–100). Sense-Brill Publishers.

Tarlau, R. (2017). State theory, grassroots agency, and global policy transfer: The life and death of Colombia's Escuela Nueva in Brazil (1997–2012). *Comparative Education Review, 61*(4), 675–700. doi:10.1086/693923

Tarlau, R. (2023). Social movements, popular education, and counterhegemonic schooling in Latin America. In L. I. Misiaszek et al. (Eds.), *Emergent trends in comparative education: The dialectic of the global and the local*. Rowman & Littlefield.

Teodoro, A., & Guilherme, M. (Eds.). (2014). *European and Latin American higher education between mirrors*. Sense Publishers.

Torres, C. A. (1990). *The politics of nonformal education in Latin America*. Praeger Publishers.

Torres, C. A. (1994). Paulo Freire as secretary of education in the municipality of São Paulo. *Comparative Education Review, 38*(2), 181–214. doi:10.1086/447241

Torres, C. A. (2011). Public universities and the neoliberal common sense: Seven iconoclastic theses. *International Studies in Sociology of Education, 21*(3), 177–197. doi:10.1080/09620214.2011.616340

Torres, C. A. (2020). The owl of Minerva: The political contributions of Latin American public universities. *Georgetown Journal of International Affairs, 21*, 142–149. doi:10.1353/gia.2020.0034

Torres, C. A. (2021). La universidad pública en América Latina. Ensayo en celebración del treinta aniversario de la Revista Educación Superior y Sociedad (UNESCO-IESALC). *Educación Superior y Sociedad, 33*(1), 21–56], iSSN: 07981228/ iSSNe: 26107759instituto internacional de la uNESCo para la Educación Superior en América latina y el Caribe

Torres, C. A. (in press). Educación para la Ciudadanía Global y Personas en Situación de Movilidad Propuestas para América Latina y El Caribe.

Torres, C. A., & Puiggrós, A. (1995). The state and public education in Latin America. *Comparative Education Review, 39*(1), 1–27. doi:10.1086/447287

Torres, R. M. (1995). *Para revencer la educación de adultos* [To reveal adult education]. UNICEF.

UNESCO Institute for Statistics. (2002). *Table on literacy and nonformal education sector, regional adult illiteracy rate and population by gender*. Retrieved from www.uis.unesco.org/en/stats/statistics/UIS_Literacy_Regional2002.xls

UNESCO Institute for Statistics. (2020). *Table 12: Measures of progression and completion in primary education*. Retrieved from http://data.uis.unesco.org/?ReportId%20167

UNESCO. (2010). *Education for all global monitoring report 2010*. UNESCO.

UNESCO. (2020). *Humanistic futures of learning: Perspectives from UNESCO chairs and UNITWIN networks*. UNESCO Publishing.

UNICEF. (2019). *Education overview*. Retrieved from https://data.unicef.org/topic/education/overview/

UNILAB. (n.d.). *Unilab—Institucional*. Retrieved from http://www.unilab.edu.br/institucional-2/

Urquiola, M., & Calderón, V. (2006). Apples and oranges: Educational enrollment and attainment across countries in Latin America and the Caribbean. *International Journal of Educational Development, 26*(6), 572–590. doi:10.1016/j.ijedudev.2006.02.001

Valentine, J. L., Barham, B., Gitter, S., & Nobles, J. (2017). Migration and the pursuit of education in Southern Mexico. *Comparative Education Review, 61*(1), 141–175. doi:10.1086/689615

Verger, A., Bonal, X., & Zancajo, A. (2016). What are the role and impact of public-private partnerships in education? A realist evaluation of the Chilean education quasi-market. *Comparative Education Review, 60*(2), 223–248. doi:10.1086/685557

Verger, A., Fontdevila, C., & Zancajo, A. (2016). *The privatization of education: A political economy of global education reform*. Teachers College Press.

Villa, J. M., & Niño-Zarazúa, M. (2019). Poverty dynamics and graduation from conditional cash transfers: A transition model for Mexico's Progresa-Oportunidades-Prospera program. *Journal of Economic Inequality, 17*(2), 219–251. doi:10.1007/s10888-018-9399-5

Webber, J. R. (2017). Contemporary Latin American inequality. *Latin American Research Review*, 52(2), 281–299. doi:10.25222/larr.34

Wolff, L., & De Moura Castro, C. (2003). *Education and training: The task ahead.* Institute for International Economics.

World Bank. (2020). *School enrollment, tertiary (% gross)*. Retrieved from https://data.worldbank.org/indicator/SE.TER.ENRR?end=2020&start=2020&view=bar

13

The Education of Youngsters in Conflict-Ridden Regions of the Middle East

Challenges and Opportunities

Muzna Awayed-Bishara
Tel Aviv University

ABSTRACT

This chapter examines the dialectic between the local and the global in the education of youngsters in conflict-ridden regions of the Middle East. The complexity of evaluating educational challenges/opportunities in this context is examined through intersecting global categories and local structures that take on particular dimensions in educational contexts that are ubiquitously challenged by: globalization in the form of international war against terrorism; the ongoing internal conflict and foreign involvement in Syria; the Arab Spring; the antigovernment protests in Lebanon; the expansion of settler colonialism in Israel/Palestine; and the global crisis of refugees. The chapter investigates how access to and quality of education are challenged/enabled to Middle Eastern learners, be they in their home country (e.g., Syria, Lebanon, Egypt, Israel/Palestine) or those who fled and found refuge in host countries (e.g., Germany, Sweden). It tackles how impeding factors impact their education both locally (e.g., lack of accessibility, destruction of schools, unsafe environments) and globally (e.g., assimilation policies, linguistic and sociocultural barriers, xenophobia). What opportunities could emerge in these highly problematic contexts is also examined by focusing on the way those who are socially harmed exercise their agency for the sake of contesting the local-global forces that work to their disadvantage.

■ ■ ■

Education in many regions of the Middle East has been drastically affected in light of the devastating circumstances of the last decade. Most noticeable among these are the civil war in Syria and the humanitarian crisis of refugees, the long aftereffects of the Arab Spring in Egypt, the antigovernment protests in Lebanon, and the expansion of settler-colonialism in Israel/Palestine. Granted that multiple forces of globalization shape educational policies and practices at various local levels, I argue in this chapter that conflict and war-zone contexts offer a particular vantage point from which to understand power relations and epistemological tensions between the global and the local concerning educational policies, practices, and systems. My focus on these specific contexts in the Arab world aims to offer a nuanced insight into the complexity of the educational experiences of youngsters in conflict or war zones. While including the experiences of those in other Middle Eastern locations, whether inside or outside the Arab world (e.g., Jordan, Yemen, Iran) is equally important, it is beyond the scope of this chapter.

The premise of this study is that the voice of those who are most affected by the tensions between the local and the global forces that shape their country's troubled reality is often stifled. To methodologically enable an examination of how global forces are dialectically related to educational processes in conflict-ridden regions of the Middle East (hereafter CRME), this chapter sets out to emphasize the voices of those who suffer the most from regional tensions while undertaking a Southern perspective. "North" and "South" are understood as two epistemological sites involved in hegemonic relations of power both locally and globally. It is safe to argue that the direction of influence and the flow of power and knowledge are still from the European center to the southern periphery (Santos, 2014). For example, ranking educational systems in various regions of the world, including the Middle East, is largely conducted through the lenses of neoliberal and market-related standards and terms that dominate the field of comparative and international education (Torres, 2016). Through the global dissemination of Western ideas, thinking about education has itself become an almost "universal" practice (Samoff, 1999). This so-called universal practice is dominated by a set of neo-imperial assumptions concerning economic progress and notions of human capital and development that constitute a broader discourse of capitalist triumphalism often overlooking the sociocultural needs and orientation of the "nontriumphant" other in the story.

The fact that access and quality are two central principles that guide the evaluation of whether the right to education is granted falls within this "universal" educational discourse that aims to increase enrollment rates worldwide. Putting every child in school and improving the quality of education constitute two of the main three pillars of the 2012 UN Global Education First Initiative (GEFI) offered by former secretary Ban Ki-Moon, to whom education is about more than only literacy and numeracy, and must "fully assume its essential role in helping people to forge more just, peaceful and tolerant societies" (cited in Torres, 2017, p. 4). The GEFI also marked Global Citizenship Education (GCE) as a third central educational goal aimed at increasing the attention to the global community and the well-being of humanity as a whole. As a form of intervention searching for a theory, GCE supports global peace and "encourages interventions regarding economic, social, and cultural inequality" (Torres & Bosio, 2020, p. 2). Yet, the priority is given to access to and quality of education in the GEFI does not only reinforce their centrality as universal educational goals but also, sadly, that they are still far from being accomplished. To understand the complexity entangled in meeting the GEFI's first two principles in conflict-ridden zones, we first need to consider the tensions between multiple forms of globalization and local educational realities and "their implications for reshaping the limits or potential for civil society" (Torres, 2017, p. 20). The point of departure is that access to and quality of education, their benefits and usages, are highly political.

Specifically, to understand how aspects of globalization interrupt education in countries suffering from continuous violence, displacement, destruction, and violation of the most basic human rights, this chapter deviates from both the neoliberal and the traditional aid methods (i.e., those held by humanitarian aid organizations) that are frequently used to assess and implement educational initiatives. Namely, instead of focusing on the victimization of those whose right to education is mostly infringed in the Middle East, this chapter focuses on their agency as an engaged community struggling to access equal educational opportunities. In her study of the education of Syrian refugees in neighboring countries (e.g., Lebanon and Turkey), Cain (2020) invites us to reevaluate the role traditional aid methods play in places with no access to education. Despite their well-intended inclinations, the fact that providing food, shelter, and health care to people in war zones is still the main priority means that "long-term needs, like education, are often overlooked in favor of short-term goals" (p. 7). Considering how pivotal education is for the future building of troubled countries and that of its younger generations as both local and global citizens, Cain (2020) invites us to reexamine education questions *with* and not for the people to whom these questions matter. Paulo Freire (2005/1970) would have also urged us not to "expect positive results from an educational or political action program which fails to respect the particular view of the world held by the people" (p. 95).

The chapter is empirically based on an extensive review of academic literature that provides a variety of interdisciplinary perspectives on the education of Middle Eastern youngsters, be they in their home country (e.g., Syria, Lebanon, Egypt, Israel/Palestine) or those who fled and found refuge in a host country (e.g., Germany, Sweden). Two goals guide the way questions of (access to and quality of) education in the Middle East are tackled in this chapter. Against the background of a long history of colonialism in the region and the deficit thinking that still dominates discourses about the Middle East; the first goal is to draw a picture of the educational challenges and opportunities without reproducing harmful stereotypes of Middle Easterner youngsters who are reluctantly forced to face—whether from the inside or from the outside—the devastating outcomes in their turbulent home country. Hence, the focus on agency and voice is meant to safeguard against the risk a study on conflictual regions of the Middle East might run in perpetuating stereotypes about the region. The second goal is to offer a nuanced understanding of what "the right to education" in conflict and troubled zones means. Despite the international legal and official acknowledgment of education as a basic human right (e.g., Article 26 of the Universal Declaration of Human Rights), and its central role in peace-building and social justice, there is still a scarcity of research on what adequate investments in education within conflict and war zones are needed (Shalhoub-Kevorkian, 2008).

The chapter consists of four parts. The first section examines the intersection between the "troubled" local and the "influential" global in various CRME education contexts. The second section examines the challenges that deny many children equitable educational opportunities, as well as jeopardize their future employment and development possibilities. Additionally, it examines the challenges refugee children face in the educational systems of Europe. The third part considers what opportunities might still arise and shows that hope emerges from the agency subaltern groups (such as women and youth) exercise in the way they contest the precarious realities into which they are driven. To empower marginalized populations in conflict-ridden zones, the chapter concludes that global educational programs (e.g., GCE) must aim for transformative remedies that work toward restructuring the underlying frameworks that generate inequitable outcomes (Fraser, 1995).

THE INTERSECTION BETWEEN GLOBAL CATEGORIES AND LOCAL STRUCTURES IN THE MIDDLE EAST

The Troubled Local

December 2010 marked a point in the history of the Arab World that has turned since then into a contested site for ongoing protests and uprisings. The tragic incident of the now-iconic Tunisian Mohamed Bouazizi setting light to himself in a protest against the confiscation of his unlicensed cart led to the revolts in Tunisia in 2011. Egypt followed suit when civil society organized a protest around Tahrir Square in Cairo bringing President Mubarak to resign on February 11, 2011 (Kiwan, 2015). Notwithstanding the country's first democratic experiment with an elected government, a military coup has brought an end to this government "pushing the democratically elected Mohammed Morsi and the Muslim Brotherhood out of power" (Öniş, 2014, p. 204). What was metaphorically conceived at the onset as an Arab Spring promising a Summer of Liberation from authoritarian regimes turned into a devastating human tragedy.

The Syrian civil war and the crisis of Syrian refugees are perhaps the most tangible manifestations of this tragedy described by the World Health Organization as the worst humanitarian crisis yet in the 21st century. In Syria, things began to deteriorate when the security forces killed several demonstrators who were protesting against the arrest of some teenagers for painting revolutionary slogans on a school wall (Yassin-Kassab & Al-Shami, 2016). These protests soon transformed into a civil war between those loyal to Bashar Al-Assad's government and those who oppose it and were thus targeted by the government. The civil war started on March 15, 2011, and was responsible for over 191,369 certified violent deaths out of Syria's formerly 22 million inhabitants in five years, including at least 16,970 children (Elsafti et al., 2016, p. 874). By the end of 2019, there were 5.6 million registered refugees, 6.2 million people displaced internally, and 700,000 children out of school in the region (El-Gamal, 2019). El-Gamal (2019) further reports massive waves of displacement in addition to the arbitrary barrel bombs, torture, rape, mass execution, and chemical attacks that stole the lives of children as they slept.

Besides being a product of colonialism with a long history of sectarianism, Lebanon has also been destabilized while trying to welcome the highest rate of refugees (mainly Syrian and Syrian-Palestinian) currently constituting over 25% of Lebanon's population (Cain, 2020). Human Rights Watch (2016) reports that 1.1 million refugees are registered in Lebanon and another estimated 400,000 are unregistered. Recently, the long-ruling sectarianism that reached violent turns in Lebanese history during the 15-year Lebanese Civil War (1975–1990) has been challenged by the way "many of the sects have come together to protest corruption and inefficiencies in their government" (Cain, 2020, p. 10).

Finally, the ongoing Israeli-Palestinian conflict plays a fundamental role in architecting the routes for stability in the Middle East. While Palestinians in the West Bank live under strict military occupation, Palestinians inside Israel, who constitute almost 20% of Israel's population, are discriminated against by over 65 laws (Bishara, 2020). In July 2018, Israel passed a Nation State Law that defines Israel as the homeland of the Jewish people alone, reinforcing the second-class status of its Palestinian citizens. On the linguistic level, the Nation State Law transformed the status of Arabic from one of Israel's official languages, and the mother tongue of its Palestinian minority, into a language with a *special* status (Awayed-Bishara, 2020).

Such politico-historical events significantly shape the structuring of education realities in the region and determine the future roles the young generations might play in the rebuilding of their countries. To further understand how access and quality to education are challenged or enabled in CRME, it is essential to situate the local factors surveyed above within a larger global context.

The Influential Global

Although the waves of the Arab revolutions have been to a large extent internally driven—that is, movements from below (Hollis, 2012)—the militaristic and political engagement of the United States and its European and Arab states allies cannot be underestimated (Kiwan, 2015). While foreign involvement in the region is often framed as a commitment Western countries have in leading *an international war against terrorism*, Western interest in the Middle East has a long history of colonialism justified as the West's "moral" obligation to educate or civilize the East—that is, *Orientalism* in Edward Said's (1978) terms. Yet, Torres (2017) identifies the international war against terrorism as a form of globalization *from above* that gained prominence following the events of September 11, 2001. While such value-based militaristic initiatives of Western countries would ostensibly appear to script geopolitics of hope (Sparke, 2007), this so-called commitment to protect human rights is often used as a cover for other hidden agendas (e.g., see Spivak (2004) on how narratives of Western humanism conceal the exploitation of the non-Western "Other").

Initiatives to protect human rights generate emerging norms of human rights and democracy at the international level that often enshrine new rules, roles, and obligations for sovereign states and "script states' rulers as guardians of extraterritorial human rights and democratic freedoms" (Perkins & Neumayer, 2009, p. 249). The growing ideology of human rights in this sense is often referred to as the *globalization of human rights* (Torres, 2017). Torres (2017) problematizes some of the global concerns with human rights and explains that "in the international system and in international law, many traditional practices endemic to the fabric of particular societies or cultures (from religious to esoteric practices) are now being called into question, challenged, forbidden or even outlawed" (pp. 27–28). Against this backdrop, a critique of the shortcomings of rights discourses as a basis for transformative processes emanating from the Western Hemisphere presents itself particularly since articulations of human rights are predominantly produced in the Global North.

In her study of the ethical and political dilemmas posed by the construction and international circulation of discourses on women's rights in the Middle East, Lila Abu-Lughod (2009) postulates that priorities and possibilities for Arab women are defined by "the liberal language of human development and the neoliberal discourses of structural adjustment and global markets" (p. 91). Notwithstanding how commendable some reports on human development in the Arab world (e.g., the Arab Human Development Report (ADHR) of 2005, as cited in Abu-Lughod, 2009) are in terms of the multiplicity of voices and perspectives they present, *what* is reported, and the way it is framed is often taken up as evidence of the pathology of Arab culture in general and its gender one in particular (p. 86). Abu-Lughod (2009) provides an insightful critical reading of the ADHR report and concludes that "there is no hint of a marginalized but reemerging international language whose vocabulary includes exploitation, underdevelopment, injustice, or revolution and no questioning of priorities such as military spending, Western investment, export economies, profligate consumerism, or international debt" (p. 92).

Along different yet relevant lines, the notion of "the right to education" in CRME needs also to be critically examined against the background of global attempts to universalize the thinking about education. The problem is, according to Arnove (see the introduction to this volume) that "education policy makers cannot simply uproot elements of one society and expect them to flourish in the soil of another society." Namely, the question of whether a one-size-fits-all global approach to compare who has access to education and what quality of education they get is contentious. The overarching principle guiding this claim is that when children grow up in precarious situations, they do not have the same opportunities as other children in the world, educational or otherwise. Considering the devastating outcomes children in conflict and war zones like the Middle East have to endure, the notion of "the right to education" as a fundamental human right must be revisited. This is because tension exists between the ostensible commitment of the Global North (e.g., European member states) to protect human rights, and the way local communities in the Global South suffer from harmful actions performed under the auspices of this commitment. Harm is caused not only by the tangible outcomes of militaristic actions but also by the long history of Western civilizational discourses that reproduce and maintain an Orientalist representation of the Arab world. What seems to be missing in human rights reports on the Arab world, according to Abu-Lughod, is a systematically critical and comparative perspective. The following section demonstrates the tension between the right to education as a basic universal human right and the challenges people in CRME face while exercising this right.

CHALLENGES AT LOCAL AND GLOBAL LEVELS

The Conundrum of the Right to Access Education: The Case of Syria

In Syria, destruction of infrastructure, internal displacement, lack of health care, loss of one (or both) parent(s), and destruction of schools are factors that impact whether children have access to education. The question is: How could a comparative approach be utilized to evaluate access to and quality of education in a country where almost half of its inhabitants have been either killed, severely injured, internally displaced, traumatized, or forced to flee their houses and find refuge across the borders? Before delving into the details of such challenges, it is important to start with how things were in prewar Syria.

Article 37 of the Syrian 1973 Constitution defines the objectives of education as "to bring up a national Arab generation, which is socialist and scientific in its manner of thinking, attached to its history and land, proud of its patrimony, and satiates [sic] with the struggling spirit" (Syria National Republic Report, 2000, cited in Hos & Cinarbas, 2017). From Syria's independence from the French Mandate in 1946, it is reported that education in Syria developed consistently and gradually and that the government of Syria was among the best in the Arab world providing basic education to its citizens (Huitfeldth & Kabbani, 2005). Regardless of the challenges, Syrian education system underscored the right to education by providing many opportunities to its citizens to receive education (Hos & Cinarbas, 2017). Sadly, the current situation in Syria removed education aside, leaving many Syrian children without access to education (Elsafti et al., 2016).

In their study of the humanitarian crisis in Syria with a special emphasis on its devastating impacts on children, Elsafti et al. (2016) report that "the real death toll is estimated at 300,000 people, including over 100,000 civilians, of whom 23% are children [whereas] an estimated 300,000 Syrians have been injured, of whom 17% were children" (p. 874). They conclude that more than half of school-aged children have no access to education. Politics and war become central in such chaotic environments rendering military and parliament as the most important and functional institutions while incapacitating other units of government particularly the ministry of education (Hos & Cinarbas, 2017). In terms of quality of education, the authors caution "as there is no or very little control over educational units in Syria, the educational institutions that manage to stand are used to convene supporter for either loyals or rebels" (Hos & Cinarbas, 2017, p. 226).

Along different lines, voices from the inside provide some critical insights about what "education" and "schools" mean in conflict-ridden contexts. According to the testimony of one school administrator, many of the schools "have been burned down and people have burned the desks and chairs in the schools to warm up from the cold" (cited in Hos & Cinarbas, 2017, p. 226). Voices of 12 children from Syria (ages 5–16) are amplified by Thabit and Rusmusson (2019) as they appear in three documentaries: *Children of Aleppo*, *Children of Syria*, and *Generation in Crisis*. Speaking of his right for childhood, Jalal (age 11) states: "I have lived a great childhood, but with the crisis, I honestly feel that I'm not living one second of the childhood I once had" (Jalal in Thabit & Rusmusson, 2019, p. 2).

The interplay between the way Jalal describes how his foundational right as a child to live a life without violence is stolen from him and the administrator's description of burning schools as a means for warming up from the cold problematizes the universal concern with putting every child in school. This becomes even more evident in Baraha (age 8) who despite expressing her most basic desire to practice her right to education spelled out as "I'd like to go to school," realizes that her current educational reality is nothing but a contradictory practice wherein: "Instead of learning to read and write, I learn about weapons" (Thabit & Rusmusson, 2019). Despite breaking down in tears, Kifah, a 13-year-old boy, also courageously advocates: "The children shouldn't be left like this. They should be getting an education for their future" (Kifah in Thabit & Rusmusson, 2019).

Along even more affirmative lines, Daad (age 11) appropriates the language of universal human rights and offers an alternative, more holistic, conception of the right to education as she perceives it from her troubled perspective: "A child has the right to learn and play, families have a right to a home, to learn, eat and drink. There is no love left in Syria. Syria has been wrecked, it's now completely unlivable" (Daad, Thabit & Rusmusson, 2019, p. 3).

In Daad's understanding, the right to education cannot be compartmentalized and must entail the whole package of what a child needs to lead a normal childhood beyond asking whether or not a child has access to education. The package includes having a home, love, food, and above all, a livable life.

To conclude, these critical voices indicate the achievement of an in-depth understanding of the world which allows these children to perceive and expose social and political contradictions, an achievement that we can understand in Freirean terms as *conscientization* (2005/1970). Such understanding transforms our perception of people in war zones from mere victims to critical agents who provide insights into what "education" and "schools" mean in these contexts. Aside from their educational values, schools should constitute a space where children feel protected, sheltered, and socially valued. Yet, if such a space is lost, there is a risk of turning our global concern with putting every child in school into no more than an ambitious goal. When children miss education, their future and that of their country are undermined. Suffice it to say here that the voices we hear from Syria evoke a philosophical conundrum: *Does the right to education even matter when people lose the roof over their heads and when children lose their childhood?*

When Quality of Education Is at Stake
The Case of Egypt

Placed at the core of the Egyptian Constitution is the right to free education as a fundamental right of every Egyptian citizen. As in many countries, Egypt has been concerned with increasing enrollment rates. A report from UNESCO in 2015 shows that net enrollment rates in primary education have increased from 64% in 1978 to 96% in 2009. Similarly, the average school years attained went from 2.7 to 7.1 putting Egypt among the top 20 countries globally vis-à-vis the increases in school attainment over that same period (Campante & Chor, 2012). Notwithstanding the promising numbers, neglect of other important dimensions of education is often manifested in low school quality and low levels of learning (Assaad, 2014). Assaad and Krafft (2015) question although education in Egypt is free, does it exempt families from additional spending to ensure that their children learn and succeed within the education system? Basing themselves on other scholars, the authors caution that "the need for additional [family] spending contributes to young people's unequal opportunities to attain education or achieve learning" (Assaad & Krafft, 2015, p. 16). El-Baradei (2013; cited in Assaad & Krafft, 2015) attributes the low-quality school to the inadequate public funding of basic education, which, from an economic perspective, means that in the long run "investments in education may generate low returns in the labor market" (Assaad & Krafft, 2015, p. 16). When compared to other countries, returns to all levels of education are significantly low while basic education has lower returns than secondary or higher education (Said, 2015).

The poor quality of education in public schools compels families who can afford it to rely on other resources to ensure their children succeed in school. Assaad and Krafft (2015) describe how the poor quality of public basic education in Egypt "has generated substantial demand for educational supplements or substitutes, such as private schooling, parental help, help groups, and especially private tutoring" (p. 17), which constitutes an increasingly substantial share of the budgets of Egyptian households with school-age children (El-Baradei, 2013, cited in Assaad & Krafft, 2015). Sadly, private spending has become central in determining the educational outcomes of both the haves and the have nots. The lack of equal educational opportunities and the low returns to education constitute some of the major causes of the youth frustrations that drove the Arab Spring uprisings (Assaad & Krafft, 2015). While questioning whether free education is a reality or a myth, the authors postulate that: "Education in Egypt had traditionally meant access to formal (mostly public) jobs that paved the way to a middle class existence, but it has failed to live up to these expectations for recent cohorts of youth. The devaluation of education in recent decades has not only led to a great deal of anger and frustration on the part of educated youth, but also to persistent demands for social justice and more equal opportunities" (p. 17).

Such sociopolitical realities of poor educational opportunities and high levels of unemployment might lead to states of youth alienation as we will also see, though along different lines, in the case of Lebanon.

The Case of Lebanon

The commonly accepted mission of education as a means for facilitating social unity and preparing generations of responsible citizens for the social, political, and economic development of a nation (Heyneman & Todoric-Bebic, 2000) takes on a different direction in a destabilized place like Lebanon—a country with many minority groups and heterogeneous religious communities all living in delicate balance (Cain, 2020). Following a long history of sectarian conflicts, the end of Lebanon's 15-year civil war (1975–1990) was marked with a peace settlement known as the Taif Accord, which instigated a power-sharing system with equal representations of Muslims and Christians. Education plays a central role in perpetuating the hegemony of sectarian ideology in Lebanon, specifically due to poor educational policies that "have de-emphasized national identity and permitted the establishment of religiously segregated schools leading to the growth of sectarian divisions among Lebanese communities" (Baytiyeh, 2017, p. 546). The most tangible form of this hegemony is the dominance of private, nongovernmental schools and the marginalization of public schools.

A study presented during the World Economic Forum in Dakar in 2000 identifies how weakness in educational structure and content contribute to civil conflicts, and how an education system that reinforces segregation is itself a dangerous source of conflict (Frayha, 2009). In the case of Lebanon, Baytiyeh (2017) postulates that the sectarian structure of the political system "has penetrated the educational system, leading to the reduction of social resilience and greater risk of sectarian violence in the country" and "has contributed tremendously to the current sectarian division in Lebanese society" (p. 547). This division is reinforced in the quality of education that greatly differs between private and public schools, between the different regions, and among the different communities (Youssef, 2020). In terms of education inequality in the Middle East and North Africa region, Lebanon is ranked as the third-worst country (following Morocco and Egypt) in terms of inequality in opportunity for education. These inequalities are manifested in large differences in school achievement among children and youth (Dibeh et al., 2017, cited in Youssef, 2020) and are mainly related to the fragmented nature of Lebanese society and to the high level of privatization of education. Despite the high rates in the quality of its education, low efficiency rates contribute to increasing the gap between the country's economically advantaged youth (who can afford private education) and their poorer peers (who can afford only public education) (Cain, 2020).

In addition to an educational atmosphere of escalating intolerance and sectarian hostility, the political impasses in the country, corrupt, maladministration of the ruling political class, and an economic collapse, have altogether resulted in nationwide antigovernment protests that started in October 2019 (Parreira, 2019). However, whether these uprisings against the refusal of inept politicians to respond to essential demands that concern the future of the young generations in Lebanon point at an emerging form of youth agency and activism is a question for future research. Up until the uprisings, the voices of young Lebanese students—"the hope of the future"—rather indicate that they are withdrawing from their active citizenship, less willing to take on their roles as social changemakers, and "rejecting all forms of public discourse and civic engagement" (Khalaf, 2014, p. 114). Analyzing the voices of university students from different social strata in Lebanon, Khalaf (2014) cautions that students perceive the obstacles to change as insurmountable and not worth fighting for and that "with enthusiasm dissipating, even ongoing regional uprisings seem only to strengthen youth apathy and post-ideological stances" (p. 114). It is precisely for the sake of mitigating such tragic outcomes whereby the young generations lose hope in building a future in their own country that Baytiyeh (2017) calls for reforming the Lebanese educational system "in terms of its content and pedagogical approaches to achieve sustainable peace in the country" (p. 556). Notwithstanding these sincere voices and calls, the recent devastating destruction of Beirut due to the massive explosion in the port area might constitute an additional impediment to setting in motion the long-awaited educational reform.

The Right to Education in Israel and Palestine

Despite their different living conditions in terms of *inter alia* freedom of movement, exposure to military forces, and citizenry status, when it comes to education both the Palestinians outside and inside the Green Line deal with Israel's settler-colonial policies and practices.[1] While education in the Occupied Palestinian Territories (OPT) is systematically disrupted and often obstructed by the Israeli military occupation (Shalhoub-Kevorkian, 2008; 2019; Traxler et al., 2019), education in Israel is controlled by the state and its ethnonational ideology that "legitimizes ethnic hierarchy, purification, superiority and differentiation" (Agbaria, 2018, p. 219), although Article 26 of the Universal Declaration of Human Rights—ratified by Israel in 1991—states that "The right to education is a fundamental human right and basic to human freedom."

The decades following the war of 1967 have determined the current shape of what is often referred to as the West Bank or the occupied Palestinian territories (Efrat, 2006) that the Israeli administration divides now into three areas, often called zones (Traxler et al., 2019). Only what is known as "Area A," and in particular the even smaller enclave around *Ramallah*, tends to have the appearance of normalcy. While "Area B" is administered by both the Palestinian Authority and Israel, "Area C"—which forms 18.1% of the total land space in the OPT—is fully under Israeli military and civilian control (Handel, 2009, p. 180). In such a complex geopolitical order, school life is massively disrupted by ongoing "Israeli armed and police forces and by periodic security 'spikes,' shootings, riots, lockdowns, unrest, and disturbances" (Traxler et al., 2019, p. 1). Exercising their right to education becomes contingent on the geographically diverse nature of the schools Palestinian children and teachers must arrive to daily. Where refugee camp schools endure the most violent confrontations, arriving at schools in villages entails inter-city travel and requires crossing Israeli checkpoints. In the case of city schools, some are located on the line of contact with the occupation forces while others are in areas under Israeli control often compelling teachers (and students) to travel to schools in other areas (Traxler et al., 2019, p. 9).

Voices of Palestinian teachers speaking of their experiences and those of their students under these precarious conditions point to how the Israeli occupation constitutes a threat to the educational process by violating the right to freedom of movement (Traxler et al., 2019). Not only is the educational process interrupted but also teachers' performance is affected as a result of what one teacher describes as "The daily checkpoints between the school and the house, involuntary returning from the checkpoint to the house, the late arrival to the school, the separation wall and standing in front of the gates for hours" (Traxler et al., 2019, p. 9). Others describe the continuous denial of access to the school as exhausting and fearful as one teacher states: "Arriving late to school affects my emotions, it causes exhaustion and it affects my performance as a teacher" (Traxler et al., 2019, p. 10). But mainly, teachers' accounts of the obstructed access to schools as a result of crossing nearby checkpoints or locations in "Area C," and the military acts of destroying schools should altogether call the world's attention to how the right to education in conflict zones must be addressed. Perhaps the voice of Nora, a 15-year-old girl from Rafah, provides an insight:

> When they demolished my school, I felt that I lost my own home. Maybe the world can't understand, but for Palestinian girls like me, the school is all we have. Girls in the world can go places, visit each other, find the books they want to read, organize field trips with their school and teachers, but Palestinian children have nothing. We the Palestinian girls feel that our schools are the only place we can meet friends, share books, meet, talk, play, sing, write, love . . . and now they demolished my school. (Nora in Shalhoub-Kevorkian, 2008, p. 189)

Inside Israel, the education of the Palestinian minority offers a complex educational experience where curricula, textbook design, policy, and schooling practices are intertwined with sociopolitical and ideological agendas. While Palestinians constitute the largest indigenous minority, they used to constitute the majority in Palestine before 1948 (Al-Haj, 2002, p. 72) after which Israeli citizenship was imposed on them. Many Palestinians see themselves as "the legitimate owners of the land, and the pursuers of a historical legacy of Palestinian struggle against Israel's military, land-confiscating, oppressive, and Zionist neocolonialist incursions inside and outside of the green line" (Awayed-Bishara, 2020, p. 4). As Israeli citizens, they are discriminated against at the social, educational, economic, and political levels. Dwairy (2004) summarizes how Israel has treated its Palestinian citizens since its inception, as "foster citizens" whose national identity and cultural heritage are rejected by the Jewish majority. The Nation State Law that Israel legislated in 2018 lawfully reinforced the second-class citizenship of its Palestinian minority.

Since its establishment, Israel has maintained two separate school systems: one for the Jewish majority, and another for the Arab minority. Considering Israel's ethnic diversity, the subdivisions in the educational system might falsely appear to accommodate cultural differences and educational pluralism. However, they mainly serve the interests of the dominant ethnic group, while maintaining the marginalization of the indigenous Palestinian-Arab community (Al-Haj, 2002; Awayed-Bishara, 2020). The educational institutions and working conditions of the Arab educational system have long been seen as deteriorating and vulnerable and in genuine need of an intervention (Jabareen & Agbaria, 2010) particularly regarding equal budgetary allocations; participation of the Arab community in policy-making and design of curricula; and acceptance of Palestinian Arab students' cultural and linguistic needs. However, the provision of equal educational rights is contingent on appeals to the ruling regime, which aims at maintaining Jewish-Israeli supremacy, and Palestinian-Arab subalternity (Awayed-Bishara, 2020). Official data from the Ministry of Education consistently reveal a substantial gap in achievement between Jewish and Arab students. Jabareen and Agbaria (2010) report that the proportion of students eligible for the matriculation certificate required to access tertiary education in 2009 was highly unequal: for Jewish students it was 59.74% but for Arab students it was 31.94%, just over half. Comparison with figures published in the following years suggests a gap that is, if not widening, not closing either.

Challenges in European Educational Contexts
The right to access compulsory education is often granted in European Union (EU) countries (Crul, 2017, p. 5). Yet, the absence of a coordinated central policy approach results in limited or even no access to education for refugees in some EU member states (Koehler, 2017). In Sweden and Germany, for instance, some groups of refugee children whose asylum procedures are still ongoing or who do not yet have a residence permit are under no obligation to attend school. Accommodating refugees in distant and rural locations and moving them frequently also limit their choice of school and hinder their attendance (Koehler & Schneider, 2019). As a result, segregation not only becomes customary but also "remains a relevant obstacle to the integration into mainstream education for refugees in general" as it "inhibits equal opportunities and has negative effects on the school performances of native and immigrant students and can lead to increased negative personal and social effects such as xenophobia, social exclusion, radicalization

and violence" (Koehler & Schneider, 2019, p. 11). Another challenge that hinders the education of refugees is the contesting views in the way EU member states conceptualize diversity, often through the lenses of a deficit model (Fejes & Dahlstedt, 2017; Koehler, 2017; Panagiotopoulou & Rosen, 2018). In contrast to the potential view that sees diversity as an asset and an educational opportunity, the deficit model sees diversity as a challenge to be dealt with (Ahmadi et al., 2017). The Public Policy Management Institute (2017) found that despite the increasing recognition of the benefits of cultural, linguistic, religious, and social diversity, many EU member states are mainly informed by deficit views (p. 102) constituting migrants as in deficit, ignorant, and unhealthy and therefore need to be (re)cultivated (Fejes & Dahlstedt, 2017; Panagiotopoulou & Rosen, 2018).

Denied inclusion of migration-related multilingualism constitutes another challenge since language policies determine, at both the macro and micro levels, what opportunities for education are open to refugee children. In their ethnographic observations of the way refugee children are integrated into mainstream classrooms in Germany, Panagiotopoulou and Rosen (2018) show how teachers' appropriation of the government policy "not only reinforces a monolingual 'German only' assimilation policy, it also denies children the right to use their home and other languages in learning the German language" (p. 394). In one of the classrooms for Arabic-speaking migrants, for example, the observer reports how students are aware that using Arabic, even during recess, is not permitted by their teacher who threatens that "Rana and Saida [two Arab female students] 'will be in trouble' if they do not stop using their Arabic" (p. 402). When asked about her practice, the teacher implies that the use of ethnic minority languages will risk the children's acquisition of German and, hence, to ensure their learning progress, she leaves the Arabic-speaking newcomers with two options: to speak German or not to speak at all. Against the background of monolingual policies, the use of students' linguistic repertoires—often conceptualized as "translanguaging" (García, 2009)—has been gaining recognition in bilingual and multilingual education. Translanguaging, as defined by García and Kano (2014), is: "A process by which students and teachers engage in complex discursive practices that include ALL the language practices of ALL students in a class in order to develop new language practices and sustain old ones, communicate and appropriate knowledge, and give voice to new sociopolitical realities by interrogating linguistic inequality" (p. 261).

In contrast to previous theories and conceptualizations, translanguaging regards these shifts as normal practices (García, 2009). Translanguaging is perceived as a highly creative practice that opens up possibilities for teachers and learners to solve situations of misunderstanding, bridge language and knowledge gaps, and promote learning (García, 2018). That being said, the requirement to speak only German, as we have seen in the earlier example, has the systematic potential to silence the students (Panagiotopoulou & Rosen, 2018).

Suffice it to say that pending resident permit applications, regulating the description of immigrants through a deficit model, and denying opportunities for a multilingual education are among the most prominent challenges the literature on refugees education in Europe underpins. A critical evaluation of the level of compatibility between stated policies and implemented practices is required so refugees are not trapped between the proverbial hammer and the anvil: at the crossroads between a desperate attempt to build a new life after escaping war back home, and educational assimilation policies that curtail their agency and stifle their voice.

OPPORTUNITIES EMERGE FROM YOUTH AND WOMEN AGENCY

The most prominent perception of women, children, and youth borne out of (armed) conflicts is that of "victims of war/conflict." What often goes unreported or even unrecognized is the ability of the "victims" to agentively act against the challenges and harms from which they suffer to rebuild hope and peace for themselves and others in their community. To challenge the dominance of victimization discourses, I argue that opportunities in conflict-ridden zones arise at the grassroots level; namely when those who are socially harmed exercise their agency for the sake of contesting the local-global forces that work to their disadvantage (Awayed-Bishara, 2020). Focusing on agency is not meant to undermine the hardships people in conflict zones confront, nor does it exempt local and global stakeholders from their responsibility for eliminating inequalities and social injustices. Rather, the focus on how women and youth in various CRME contexts are constructing new educational, sociocultural, and economic opportunities aims to offer a counter-model for empowerment.

Whereas accessing education remains a great challenge for many Syrian refugees specifically those living in camps (UNHCR, 2016), Asaf (2017) points at an increased emphasis and realization of the important role women and girls can play within the refugee community. For refugee women of Syria education has become so important to an extent that "when they were to make a choice between sending either their sons or their daughters to school, they preferred educating their daughters" (Asaf, 2017, p. 10). The reasons these women provide for this preference are that girls have better chances to provide for their families if they have education, and that boys can find work in places girls cannot. The case of Bekaa Valley at the Syrian-Lebanon border offers a distinctive case where refugee women and girls are undergoing an educational revolution (Human Rights Watch Report, 2016). International organizations, local universities, and volunteers, among other organizations, are lending a hand in "empowering a new generation of Syrian women, with tools and knowledge they will need to build their future" (Asaf, 2017, p. 10). Through "taking care of all the responsibilities of the public and domestic spheres of their lives; from sending their children to school for education to taking care of the residency papers" (Asaf, 2017, p. 10), women in the valley have become the leaders of their community (Gatten, 2015, cited in Asaf, 2017). Asaf further reports that currently there are five schools for one million, plus registered Syrian refugees in the valley including an all-girls high school where more than 200 Syrian girls are enrolled for a better future. The importance of education in this place goes beyond the mere experience of learning since the focus is on preparing women for long-term development goals for themselves and their community. Going back to Syria and rebuilding it has become the dream of these women (Collins, 2016, cited in Asaf, 2017).

Lastly, acts of youth in CRME play a significant role in challenging discourses of victimization and discourses that tend to construct them as "risky" or "dangerous." Whether through street protests, social media, or other forms of cultural expression, Arab youth are increasingly constructing themselves politically in new ways (Kiwan, 2015). For example, studying Palestinian youth media practices at the Lajee Center in Aida Refugee Camp (in the West Bank) shows how *participatory media* open up new avenues for youth expression at both local and global levels. In contrast to how prevalent media representations of Palestinian youth depict them as victims who invite pity rather than compassion, participatory media focus on the active role alternative voices of young Palestinians play in meaning-making constructions. Participatory media create a new space for offering alternative narratives of the Palestinian-Israeli conflict to those dominant in mainstream media while also inspiring new spaces for exploring culture, education, community, and conflict (Norman, 2009).

CONCLUSION

Focusing on the interplay between global forces and local responses, this chapter has examined the challenges and opportunities for the education of youngsters in conflict-ridden zones of the Middle East. Set out to emphasize the voices of the people in this region, this chapter concludes that the troubled voices that we hear from the Middle East urgently call for the need to reevaluate how the right to education is both conceptualized and assessed. Global educational initiatives that aim to empower marginalized groups and grant them greater and more equal shares in society must build on the capacity of local communities to take an active part in the struggle for social transformation and educational justice. Transformative educational programs aim at restructuring the underlying frameworks that generate unequal educational opportunities (Fraser, 1995), and focus on the agency of local communities and their ability to actively design and critically consider their future possibilities. This requires a view of the people in conflict and war zones (or otherwise marginalized communities) as *partners* whose epistemological knowledge contributes to better conceptualizations of contentious universal notions such as the "right to education." If we continue to fail in considering the imbalances of current global and local processes, we may end up as Andreotti (2006) warns us promoting a new "civilizing mission." Contrariwise, a global-local partnership approach is a key for transforming social and educational inequities and injustices.

NOTE

1. The Green Line refers to the areas that the 1949 armistice lines established between Israel and its Arab neighbors in the aftermath of the 1948 War of Independence.

REFERENCES

Abu-Lughod, L. (2009). Dialects of women's empowerment: The international circuitry of the Arab human development report 2005. *International Journal of Middle East Studies*, 41(1), 83–103.
Agbaria, A. K. (2018). The "right" education in Israel: Segregation, religious ethnonationalism, and depoliticized professionalism. *Critical Studies in Education*, 59(1), 18–34.
Al-Haj, M. (2002). Multiculturalism in deeply divided societies: The Israeli case. *International Journal of Intercultural Relations*, 26, 169–183.

Andreotti, V. (2006). Soft versus critical global citizenship education. *Policy and Practice: A Development Education Review*, 3, 40–45. https://www.developmenteducation review.com/issue/issue-3/soft-versus-critical-global-citizenship-education.

Asaf, Y. (2017). Syrian women and the refugee crisis: Surviving the conflict, building peace, and taking new gender roles. *Social Sciences*, 6(110), 1–18; doi:10.3390/socsci6030110

Assaad, R., (2014). Making sense of Arab labor markets: The enduring legacy of dualism. *IZA Journal of Labor and Development*, 3(1), 1–25.

Assaad, R., & Krafft, C. (2015). Is free basic education in Egypt a reality or a myth? *International Journal of Educational Development*, 45, 16–30.

Awayed-Bishara, M. (2020). *EFL pedagogy as cultural practice: Textbooks, practice, and policy for Arabs and Jews in Israel*. Routledge.

Baytiyeh, H. (2017). Has the educational system in Lebanon contributed to the growing sectarian divisions? *Education and Urban Society*, 49(5), 546–559.

Bishara, A. (2020, Spring). Looking beyond the struggle for Palestinian statehood. *Middle East Report*, 294.

Cain, K. (2020). Refugees, identity, and the fight for education: A study of the cultural and political context of education policy for Syrian refugees in neighboring host countries. *Senior Theses*, 44. https://research.library.fordham.edu/international_senior/44/

Campante, F. R., & Chor, D. (2012). Why was the Arab world poised for revolution? Schooling, economic opportunities, and the Arab Spring. *Journal of Economic Perspective*, 26(2), 167–188.

Chaaban, J., & el Khoury, A. (2016). *Spotlight on youth in Lebanon*. UNDP.

Crul, M. (2017, February). Refugee children in education in Europe. How to prevent a lost generation? *SIRIUS Network Policy Brief Series*, 7.

Dwairy, M. (2004). Culturally sensitive education: Adapting self-oriented assertiveness training to collective minorities. *Journal of Social Issues*, 60(2), 423–436.

Efrat, E. (2006). *The West Bank and Gaza Strip: A geography of occupation and disengagement*. Routledge.

El-Gamal, J. M. (2019, July 2). Innocent victims of a brutal war, Syria's "lost generation" can still be saved. *Atlantic Council*. https://www.atlanticcouncil.org/blogs/syriasource/innocent-victims-of-a-brutal-war-syria-s-lost-generation-can-still-be-saved/

Elsafti A. M., van Berlaer G., Al Safadi, M., et al. (2016). Children in the Syrian civil war: The familial, educational, and public health impact of ongoing violence. *Disaster Medicine and Public Health Preparedness*, 10, 874–882.

Fejes, A., & Dahlstedt, M. (2017). Popular education, migration and a discourse of inclusion. *Studies in the Education of Adults*, 49(2), 214–227.

Fraser, N. (1995, July/August). From redistribution to recognition? Dilemmas of justice in a "post-socialist" age. *New Left Review*, 212, 68–91.

Frayha, N. (2009). *The negative face of the Lebanese education system*. Lebanon Renaissance. Retrieved from http://www.lebanonrenaissance.org/assets/Uploads/0-The-negative-face-of-the-Lebanese-education-system-by-Nmer-Frayha-2009.pdf

Freire, P. (2005[1970]). *Pedagogy of the oppressed*. (M. B. Ramos, Trans.) (30th Anniversary). Continuum.

García, O. (2009). *Bilingual education in the 21st century: A global perspective*. Wiley-Blackwell.

García, O. (2018). Translanguaging, pedagogy and creativity. In J. Erfurt, E. Carporal, & A. Weirich (Eds.), Éducation *plurilingue et pratiques langagières: Hommage à Christine Hélot* (pp. 39–56). Peter Lang.

García, O., & Kano, N. (2014). Translanguaging as process and pedagogy: Developing the English writing of Japanese students in the US. In J. Conteh & G. Meier (Eds.), *The multilingual turn in languages education: Opportunities and challenges* (pp. 258–277). Multilingual Matters.

Handel, A. (2009). Where, where to, and when in the occupied territories: An introduction to geography of disaster. In A. Ophir, M. Givoni, & S. Hanafi (Eds.), *The power of inclusive exclusion: Anatomy of Israeli rule in the occupied Palestinian territories* (pp. 179–222). Zone Books.

Heyneman, S. P., & Todoric-Bebic, S. (2000). A renewed sense for the purposes of schooling: The challenges of education and social cohesion in Asia, Africa, Latin America, Europe and Central Asia. *Prospects*, 30, 145–166.

Hollis, R. (2012). No friend of democratization: Europe's role in the genesis of the "Arab Spring." *International Affairs*, 88(1), 81–94.

Hos, R., & Cinarbas, H. I. (2017). Education interrupted: English education policy from the rubble in Syria. In R. Kirkpatrick (Eds.), *English language education policy in the Middle East and North Africa*. Language Policy (Vol. 13). Springer.

Huitfeldt, H., & Kabbani, N. (2005). Labor force participation, employment, and returns to education in Syria. *Twelfth annual conference of the Economic Research Forum (ERF)*.

Human Rights Watch. (2016). "Growing up without an Education": Barriers to education for Syrian refugee children in Lebanon. https://www.hrw.org/report/2016/07/19/growing-without-education/barriers-education-syrian-refugee-children-lebanon#

Jabareen, Y. T., & Agbaria, A. (2010). *Education on hold: Israeli government policy and civil society initiatives to improve Arab education in Israel (Executive Summary)* (p. 23). DIRASAT: The Arab Center for Law and Policy and The Arab Minority Rights Clinic at the Faculty of Law, University of Haifa.

Khalaf, R., (2014). Lebanese youth narratives: A bleak post-war landscape. *Compare: A Journal of Comparative and International Education*, 44(1), 97–116.

Kiwan, D. (2015). Contesting citizenship in the Arab Revolutions: Youth, women, and refugees. *Democracy and Security*, 11(2), 129–144.

Koehler, C. (2017). Continuity of learning for newly arrived refugee children in Europe. Network of Experts working on the Social Dimension of Education and Training (NESET II Working Paper No. 1). Retrieved from http://nesetweb.eu/en/library/continuity-of-learning-for-newly-arrived-refugee-children-in-europe/

Koehler, C., & Schneider, J. (2019). Multi-country partnership to enhance the education of refugee and asylum-seeking youth in Europe—National Report Germany. *European forum for migration studies, verikom and SIRIUS*—Policy Network on Migrant Education.

Norman, J. (2009). Creative activism: Youth media in Palestine. *Middle East Journal of Culture and Communication*, 2, 251–274.

Öniş, Z. (2014). Turkey and the Arab revolutions: Boundaries of regional power influence in a turbulent Middle East. *Mediterranean Politics*, 19(2), 203–219.

Panagiotopoulou, J. A., & Rosen, L. (2018). Denied inclusion of migration-related multilingualism: an ethnographic approach to a preparatory class for newly arrived children in Germany. *Language and Education*, 32(5), 394–409.

Parreira, C. (2019). *The art of not governing: How Lebanon's rulers got away with doing so little for so long*. Synaps. https://www.synaps.network/post/lebanon-protests-uprising-poor-governance

Perkins, R., & Neumayer, E. (2009). The organized hypocrisy of ethical foreign policy: Human rights, democracy and Western arms sales. *Geoforum*, 41(2), 247–256.

Public Policy and Management Institute (2017). *Preparing teachers for diversity: The role of initial teacher education*. European Commission. Retrieved from https://publications.europa.eu/en/publication-detail/-/publication/b347bf7d-1db1-11e7-aeb3-01aa75ed71a1/language-en.

Said, M. (2015). Wages and inequality in the Egyptian labor market in an era of financial crisis and revolution. In R. Assaad & C. Krafft (Eds.), *The Egyptian labor market in an era of revolution* (pp. 52–69). Oxford University Press.

Samoff, J. (1999). No teacher guide, no textbooks, no chairs: Contending with crisis in African education. Paper presented at the Annual Meeting of the African Studies Association, 43rd, Philadelphia, PA, November 11–14, 1999.

Santos, B. (2014). *The epistemologies of the south*. Paradigm.

Shalhoub-Kevorkian, N. (2008). The gendered nature of education under siege: A Palestinian feminist perspective. *International Journal of Lifelong Education, 27*(2), 179–200.

Shalhoub-Kevorkian, N. (2019). *Incarcerated childhood and the politics of unchilding*. Cambridge University Press.

Sparke, M. (2007). Geopolitical fear, geoeconomic hope and the responsibilities of geography. *Annals of the Association of American Geographers, 97*, 338–349.

Spivak, G. (2004, Spring/Summer). Righting wrongs. *Southern Atlantic Quarterly, 103*(2/3), 523–581.

Thabit, N., & Rasmusson, X. (2019). Understanding the health and mental health impact of the Syrian civil war through children's voices. *Journal of Community Medicine and Health Research, 1*(2), 1–6.

Torres, C. A. (2016). Teaching comparative education: The dialectics of the global and the local. In P. Kubow & A. Blosser (Eds.), *Teaching comparative education: Trends and issues informing practice* (pp. 163–181). Symposium Books.

Torres, C. A. (2017). *Theoretical and empirical foundations of critical global citizenship education*. Routledge.

Torres, C. A., & Bosio, E. (2020). Global citizenship education at the crossroads: Globalization, global commons, common good, and critical consciousness. *Prospects, 48*, 99–113.

Traxler, J., Khaif, Z., Nevill, A., Affouneh, S., Salha, S., Zuhd, A., & Trayek, F. (2019). Living under occupation: Palestinian teachers' experiences and their digital responses. *Research in Learning Technology, 27*, 1–18.

UNHCR. (2016). *5 Challenges to accessing education for Syrian Refugee Children*. UNHCR.

Yassin-Kassab, R., & Al-Shami, L. (2016). *Burning country: Syrians in revolution and War*. Pluto Press.

Youssef, S. (2020). *Adolescent boys and youth in Lebanon. A review of the evidence*. Gender and Adolescence: Global Evidence.

14

Education in the Asia-Pacific Region

Achievements and Challenges

John Hawkins
Anthony Welch
University of Sydney

ABSTRACT

The first challenge faced by any analyst of Asia-Pacific education is that of diversity. The Pacific island nations are themselves very culturally and linguistically diverse, presenting a substantial test for national education systems. For Asia, which includes some 50 countries of East, and South East Asia, Central Asia, South Asia, as well as parts of the Middle East, and the Caucasus, diversity is at least as large a feature, with associated opportunities and challenges in education. So, the following chapter is necessarily selective, with most examples taken from the highly dynamic and diverse East and South East Asian regions. Key themes addressed often relate to the dramatic rise of Asia in recent decades: quality assurance and the quest for world-class universities; the changing demands of the knowledge society; the push for and limits of equality; the limited impact of regionalism; changing modes of governance amid rising neoliberalism; the influence of COVID-19; the influence of rising U.S.-China tensions on higher education; the effects of corruption; and the ongoing quest for an East-West synthesis in higher education. The portrait that emerges is of great dynamism and diversity, a substantial set of ongoing achievements, as well as ongoing issues.

■ ■ ■

Any account of education in the Asia-Pacific region presents an immediate difficulty, not least since Asia itself is highly diverse, while the countries of the Pacific are different again. The latter, including Micronesia, Polynesia, and Melanesia, embraces countries such as Fiji, Vanuatu, Solomon Islands, and Papua New Guinea, which are in some cases very diverse internally, and have little in common with the countries of Asia (Crossley et al., 2011). Significant educational aid partnerships with regional neighbors such as Australia and New Zealand are now under threat, as the former, if not the latter, cut its aid budget significantly in recent years (Tolley & Coxon, 2014; Wood, 2020). Measures taken in response to COVID-19 led to large increases in debt levels in both donor and recipient nations in 2020. These will very likely constrain educational efforts in Pacific nations in succeeding years.

Yet much remains to be done. Across the small states of the Pacific, while early childhood education is growing, around 14% of children are still not in school, amid a wide range of teacher-pupil ratios. The Pacific Education Development Framework, adopted in 2009, expressed common goals among the four million or so inhabitants of island nations. Quality concerns, including of teachers, some of whom are untrained, are prominent, as are curriculum issues, access and equity, language of instruction, physical infrastructure, and preservation of Pacific cultures (Thaman, 2014). High population growth is common, urbanization a growing phenomenon, and ethnic differences significant (the latter, as in Fiji, a legacy of a deliberate policy of British colonialism) (Sharma et al., 2014). Each has consequences for educational provision, as also for access and equity. By many measures, educational quality remains generally low and effectiveness limited. Some attribute these outcomes to the persistence of Western values and orientations, including the legacy of colonialism and earlier missionary endeavors, rather than Pacific worldviews, and epistemologies (see, e.g., the brief reference to Talanoa epistemologies and research approach in Chapter 18 in this volume; Johannson-Fua, 2014; Bakalevu et al., 2014; Underwood et al., 2014). This point, at least, is held in common with many of the countries of Asia, regarding the purposes of education, and the importance of reflecting local cultures and epistemologies (Reagan, 2018).

It is the rise of Asia, however, which is undoubtedly one of the major global phenomena of the last century and a half. Beginning with Meiji, Japan's reaching out to acquire the best knowledge from around the world, in 1868, to the much later rise of Korea and Taiwan, and the most recent rise of recent mainland China and India, Asia's ascent is changing the world. Its spectacular economic growth is the dimension most often pointed to, with China's annual growth rate having only moderated in recent years from an average of around 10% (since the late 1980s). South East Asian nations such as Việt Nam have also shown strong economic growth in recent times. The political dimension, including alternative governance models, is less often a focus, although the so-called developmental state model, in which the state plays an active role in fostering economic and social development, has often been seen as productive of the strong development of East Asia in particular (Carroll & Jarvis, 2017). The pivotal role played by an interventionist, *dirigiste* state in fostering an industrial, and perhaps now a postindustrial, economy, presents a clear counterpoint to the more *laissez-faire*, neoliberal Western model of the state, and socioeconomic development (Welch, 2021a). Asian cultural and philosophical models, too, differ significantly from dominant Western frameworks, often rejecting, for example, the taken-for-granted dualisms and antinomies of the West in favor of more relational forms of thought, and preferring the more mutually beneficial orientation that is more characteristic of East Asia, to the individualism of the West (Mou, 2009; Yang & Gao, 2020). This, too, plays out in different governance traditions in higher education within the Asia Pacific, for example (Yang, 2020; Zhou, 2011).

The second arena of difference to the West is the demographic profile of Asia-Pacific nations. While Japan, Korea, and, increasingly, China face challenges that flow from aging populations, including significant implications for education, India, and ASEAN member states reveal a much younger population profile, with 25 to 35% of their populations under the age of 15 (Welch, 2011; UNESCO, 2014). Thus, while in East Asia, for example, numerous private higher education institutions (HEIs) faced closure due to insufficient enrollments, in South East Asia systems are largely still expanding, to cater both to demographic demand and rising aspiration levels. In India, enrollments increased fourfold from 2001 to 2018 (Ravi et al., 2019).

The fact that in East Asia in particular, and also in India, learning and teachers have traditionally been held in high esteem is another feature of the context. It plays out in the schools of countries of migration, such as the United States, Canada, and Australia, where students from Confucian-heritage countries of China, Việt Nam, and Singapore, as well as from India, generally perform well above the national average and gain entry into leading schools and universities (Dandy, 2018; Mohanty, 2012; Volante et al., 2018; Welch, 2017). In international tests of student achievement such as the OECD's Programme for International Student Achievement (PISA), too, the leading nations are mostly from East and South East Asia: China and Singapore, for example (see OECD, 2019). But the rise of Asian education and the development of a more multipolar world of knowledge is also reflected in the recent rise of Asian universities in the proliferating range of global university rankings. Once again, China offers the most spectacular example: a decade or more ago, barely a handful of its universities were listed among the top 500 higher education HEIs in the well-regarded *Academic Ranking of World Universities* (ARWU), popularly known as the Shanghai Jiaotong index. By 2019, some 58 Chinese universities were listed among the top 500, with four among the top 100. Both Singapore's major universities are among the top 100, as is one from Malaysia. India, however, lags on this measure: despite the size of its higher education cohort, only one HEI is listed among the top 500 (Academic Ranking of World Universities [ARWU], 2019; Institute for International Education, 2015; Welch, 2019, 2020a). A further index of rising prestige was evident in changing international student flows, with China exceeding its target of 500,000 by 2020, to become (pre-COVID) the second-largest destination for international higher education students, and Japan setting a target of 300,000 students.

But, just as economic history underlines that the dominance of Western economies is a relatively recent phenomenon, so too, a longer perspective reveals it should be no surprise to see Asian HEIs assuming a more prominent profile in the ranks of the world's leading universities (Chaudhuri, 1983; Holodny, 2017; Jacques, 2012).[1] The rich history of higher learning in the region shows that there were major centers of higher learning and influential models of education more than a millennium ago. Major scholarly centers in other parts of Asia, such as Cairo's Al Azhar and Baghdad, were paralleled in India by Nalandar (now being reestablished in Bihar), and Takshashila, in current Punjab. Angkor Wat, the cultural and political heart of the mighty Khmer empire, contained temples and libraries that attracted scholars from across the region. But the most influential model of higher learning was Confucian, which matured in the Tang and Song dynasties, and was based on a core curriculum of the Four Books and Five

Classics. Beyond China, it proved of enduring influence in Korea and Việt Nam and somewhat more briefly in Japan. Given this illustrious, if uneven, history, it is probably more accurate to characterize Asia's recent rise to prominence in education as a renaissance, rather than a rise (Welch, 2019).

There is both a history of educational achievement, as well as growing contemporary prominence. At the same time, several significant challenges remain, in which education is implicated. While Asia remains the fastest-growing region in the world, with the World Economic Forum predicting that, in 2020, Asia's economic output would surpass the rest of the world's gross domestic product (GDP), the extraordinary diversity evident across Asia situates some nations much more highly than others. Even within member nations of the Association of Southeast Asian Nations (ASEAN), for example, highly developed economies such as Singapore are paired with very poor nations such as Laos and Timor l'Este.

Such differences are mirrored across the Asia-Pacific, notably in education. Within nations, too, inequality remains a major issue, along lines of class/caste, gender, and ethnicity, and there is evidence that globalization has widened such internal differentiation. A 2020 UN Report castigated the failure to do more to reduce real poverty, in part due to the reliance on an arbitrary, dated World Bank measure that radically understates its extent (UN Human Rights Council, 2020). In China, as an example, while income levels have risen strongly overall in recent decades, and hundreds of millions have been lifted out of poverty, differentials between rich and poor, and rural and urban, have risen. Its GINI coefficient (a measure of income inequality) increased from 0.30 to 0.55 between 1980 and 2002, and in 2019 was 0.465 (CIEC, 2020; Xie & Zhou, 2014). This translates into highly differential outcomes in education, with students from wealthier families, in major urban centers, faring far better than those from poorer rural families. To a greater or lesser degree, similar patterns are evident in many parts of Asia. But the striking rise of the middle class in Asia is also of clear relevance to education. Projections are that almost 90% of the next billion entrants into the global middle class will be from Asia: 380 million from India, 350 million from China, and 210 million from other Asia (OECD, 2014). A combination of rising aspiration and greater capacity to pay has major implications for educational expansion in Asia, especially at upper secondary and higher education levels.

The destabilization of the world also has substantial implications for education. Consequent in part upon the increasingly rivalrous and rancorous relations between China and the United States (especially after the U.S. presidential elections of 2016), which were initially presented as a trade war, but quickly came to be recognized as a technology and even Culture War, significant geostrategic implications became apparent. Especially in the Asia Pacific region, the world's most dynamic, it became a major cause of concern, that threatened the so-called Asian Century (see Lee, 2020; Medcalf, 2020; Mozur and Myers 2020) The rapid global bifurcation, that by mid-2020 was being characterized as a new cold war, had direct implications for both scholarly mobility and international research collaboration, with the United States, for example, restricting both the number and duration of visas to Chinese researchers and students in STEM subjects in 2019 and 2020, and threatening to send home international students (mostly from Asia) who, through no fault of their own, were only able to enroll in online programs, in the aftermath of the COVID-19 pandemic (Kennedy, 2020; Marginson

& Yang, 2020). Notwithstanding rising political pressures and some internal tensions, however, a common ASEAN view was that they did not wish to be forced to choose between the two superpowers (Schuman, 2019; SCMP, 2020). Indeed, regional research collaboration with China remained healthy, with China forming a major knowledge partner to several ASEAN systems, and Australia (Chubb, 2013; Laurenceson & Zhou, 2020; Welch, 2014).

But the effects of the COVID-19 pandemic threatened more than scholarly mobility and international research collaboration, within and without Asia, particularly between the United States and China (Connected World, 2020; Kennedy, 2020; Lee & Haupt, 202;). The economic devastation wrought on the region was itself destabilizing, with International Institute of Finance data showing global debt rising by US$15 billion in 2020, and reaching a possible US$360 billion by 2030 (International Institute for Finance, 2020; IMF, 2020). The effects on children were dramatic: UNICEF data projected that a further 86 million children were likely to be pushed into poverty, while UNESCO charted school closures in 160 countries, including numbers in the Asia Pacific (UNESCO, 2020). The worst effects were on the poor. Together with the rising geostrategic contest between the United States and China in the Asia Pacific region, as well as various competing claims to areas of the South China sea, the net effect was seen as producing an Asia-Pacific that was "poorer, more dangerous and more disorderly" after COVID-19. In a major speech in mid-2020, the Australian prime minister warned that "the Indo-Pacific is the 'epicentre' of rising strategic competition and 'the risk of miscalculation—and even conflict—is heightening'" (Grattan, 2020; Macmillan & Greene, 2020).

The long-term consequences of the COVID-19 pandemic and rising global polarization and tensions for academic mobility and international research collaboration were not entirely clear at the time of writing. But the precedent of the late 1990s' regional currency crisis that tipped tens of millions of families in the region into poverty, with many children forced to withdraw from school, and many Asian research candidates compelled to return from abroad, due to cuts to national scholarship programs in countries such as Malaysia, was worrying. The fact that students from Asia represented such a high proportion of overall international enrolments, not merely within major Western destinations such as Australia, the United States, United Kingdom, and Canada, but also within Asia, meant that the potential implications were likely to be profound. The outcomes for universities in the Asia-Pacific region were nowhere more evident than in Australia, whose universities were the most highly dependent on income derived from fee-paying international students, nearly all of whom were from the region. When tens of thousands of Chinese students, for example, were trapped abroad by travel bans in 2020, and unable to return to resume their studies, the bleak financial implications for all Australian universities were starkly revealed (Babones, 2020; Welch, 2020a; 2022).

Countries in the region risked becoming collateral damage in the great power dispute between China and America, although most preferred not to have to take sides. As Parag Khanna, author of *The Future Is Asian*, responded in a 2019 interview, "No one wants to choose sides. We live in a multipolar system. No smart country sides with only one power. Instead, they play all the powers off each other to derive maximum benefit for themselves" (Schuman, 2019).

A further challenge that flows from the massification of both secondary education, as well as the dramatic growth of higher education in the region, is employment. Continuing effort is needed to raise employment prospects, an area linked to education and essential for social stability. In many parts of Asia, credentialism induces many to enroll in higher education without corresponding job prospects, leading to what has been called a Diploma Disease, that can be not merely wasteful in economic terms but also crushes the hopes of generations of young students (Dore, 1997; Jonbekova, 2020). As more and more young people gain degrees, the benefits of having the qualification decline. Faced with numerous well-qualified applicants, employers raise the bar when selecting for jobs. Increasing domestic demand for goods and services will also likely be a priority in the years ahead, for many Asian systems, with important effects in the technical and vocational training sector.

An earlier Asian Pacific Economic Cooperation (APEC) meeting revealed several enduring issues that most members of the region agreed were critical to higher education transformation for the 21st century. At the top of the list were access and equity. Although some national educational systems, such as Japan, Korea, and Taiwan, have come close to universal access (K–12 and higher education), many nations in the region continue to struggle with rural-urban differences, peri-urban lack of access, discrimination against minorities, women, and other excluded groups. Even among those with more open access and capacity, equity continues to be a challenge, as social stratification dominates educational systems. In most systems, high socioeconomic status groups still command a disproportionate number of spaces in the best secondary and HEIs, at times through the use of supplementary "shadow" education (Bray & Lykins, 2012).

A second area directly related to access and equity is quality assurance (QA). As regional educational systems have grown and more capacity becomes available, the question of "how good is it?" is raised by various stakeholders. QA has become a hot topic, especially in higher education as nations in the region have bought into the rankings race and the quest for "world class" status. While numerous Asian universities have, as a result, achieved much higher profiles, the impact on local scholarship, particularly in the social science and humanities, is a widespread source of concern (Chou, 2014; Chou & Chan 2016, Li, 2020).

As capacity and quality have been linked in Asian educational development, so has the notion that an increase in both will bring about a new kind of society, that is, a knowledge society transforming the region from the previous "developing" paradigm to the world of technology, knowledge creation, discovery, and a changing labor force. All this of course requires a new kind of educational system. Asia has been at the forefront of the digital revolution, especially as it relates to education at all levels. Some societies such as Singapore and South Korea are leaders in this domain, while others such as Bangladesh and Afghanistan are far behind. Nevertheless, among educational policymakers, the notion of the emergent knowledge society looms large in the region and fuels a variety of debates, especially in the access, equity, and QA sectors.

Although student and scholar mobility and migration has long been an important dimension of the educational landscape in Asia, it has assumed new importance as it has shifted from being largely outward-oriented (targeted to the West) to being a mix of inward and cross-border regional exchanges. This represents a third enduring trend as students and scholars, programs and ideas move into and through the region in increasing numbers, only to be confronted by a variety of questions as to the appropriateness, and the degree of impact that this movement represents.

A fourth area to be explored, inspired largely by efforts to "harmonize" education in the European Union, is the issue of regionalism. This has assumed renewed importance in Asia, as nations seek ways to expand their historical economic cooperation to one including education and human resource development. Based on a varied mix of a desire for status and soft power, as well as a need to supplement state funding, this has proved more difficult than expected but opens up many new challenges for education and national development in the Asian region (Hawkins et al., 2012; Welch, 2018a).

ACCESS AND EQUITY

The concepts of access, equity, and capacity and the varying practices that flow from them have commonly been the "stuff" of basic and secondary education policy. Since the early 1990s, however, especially in Asia-Pacific, the powerful combination of national development and demographic shifts has propelled each—in different ways—to the center of higher education policy discourse.

It has become commonplace to see the Asia-Pacific region as characterized by three different development trajectories. The more historically developed systems in the region—Japan, South Korea, and Taiwan—are rapidly aging. As they continue to pursue familiar patterns of economic development, they find themselves with labor shortages, especially at the lower end of the employment structure, as well as overdeveloped higher education capacity. Built to accommodate the rapidly escalated demand for higher education in the late 1970s through to the most recent period, these structures are now proving excessive in some regards concerning their domestic populations. Some private HEIs in both Japan and Taiwan have been forced to close (see Green, 2020; Huang & Welch, 2021). By contrast, the massive economies of India and China are rapidly expanding, creating ever-new labor force needs both to meet their own requirements as well as those of highly segmented global labor markets. (It should be noted, however, that, unlike India, China faces an imminent demographic decline—a result of its One Child policy, and the subsequent failure of more liberal policies.) In both countries, a succession of government policies has been introduced to enhance perceived higher educational capacity. In the middle of this continuum are other countries in the region—most particularly Indonesia, Malaysia, Thailand, the Philippines, and Vietnam—whose patterns of economic development are less uni-dimensional, and whose continued high birth rates result in a much younger demographic profile, that exerts pressure for continued higher education expansion through enlarged capacity and enhanced access.

Educational policymakers became aware of the more complex nature of the relationship between educational expansion, access, and equity and the ultimate goal of providing more equality for those who would attend higher education (Neubauer & Tanaka, 2011). There was, of course, the issue of equity of access; that is, who gets into the expanded higher education system. It is difficult to find a case in Asia where there is not a diversified population, divided by social class, geography, gender, ethnicity, language, religion, or caste. Decisions, or lack of decisions, must be made to account for these differences, and actions taken or not taken to facilitate access to higher education.

But even if "affirmative" action is taken to ease admittance to the tertiary sector, it is not always effective, as the complex Indian example shows concerning caste and other distinctions. But, beyond making the grade, once in, how does one survive? Is this important at all to educational policymakers? As in India, are programs in place to assist "underrepresented" populations to compete with those who more traditionally attend higher education (Agarwal, 2009)? Once in, how do you stay in? This may or may not be of concern to educational policymakers, but is related to the issue of output. Will those populations now admitted learn the same things at the same level as the more traditional populations? And once they graduate, do they have the same life and work experiences as the dominant groups? These are all difficult questions and often ignored in the typical "access to higher education" discussion.

The issue gets further complicated when we examine the relationship between access and equity more closely. Family income is the most obvious variable when looking at these relationships. Income distribution among those admitted to higher education is strongly related to such measures as "capability poverty," where such basics as nourishment, health, and education factor into the capacity of certain populations to compete equitably with others on the road to higher education admissions. Decentralization can become a disincentive for equity and access and a case can be made for state intervention to level the playing field.

Great regional diversity across the Asia-Pacific region, as well as within countries, factors into the access and equity equation. Regional disparities of certain groups may hinge on structural, political, religious, or ethnic issues as certain groups occupy "marginal lands" and find their opportunities for entrance to higher education are also marginalized. The Muslim Rohingya minority in Myanmar is a stark example; but there are many others (Jonaid, 2019). Numerous policy issues exist and many approaches have been tried: enhancing the relevance and improving quality of rural schools, utilizing vocational and technical education to address the alignment question (although often an inferior type of education), and improving efficiencies so that there is more equitable distribution of resources between and across regions. Whatever the approach, the regional disparity issue often looms large and, in cases such as China, has influenced national policy at the highest levels.

Beyond regional diversity lies the wider issue of sociocultural diversity. Here the familiar categories of differentiation such as ethnic, linguistic, religious, caste, gender, and other distinguishing characteristics become central to policymaking and influence higher education access and equity strategies. A wide range of responses to this diversity can be found; from outright discrimination to various forms of affirmative action. Often, the relationship between regional marginality and sociocultural marginality is strong.

Finally, structural responses and mechanisms round out the policy-making dilemma. A principal one in the case of most of Asia is the issue of high-stakes national testing regimes, in what are often highly competitive education systems. The primary screening, gate-keeping mechanism for higher education in much of Asia is some form of national entrance examination, known in China as the *gaokao*. Usually occurring at the end of secondary education, these examinations determine who is granted admission to the various levels of higher education but, more importantly, who is granted admission to the most prestigious HEIs—those that will determine the occupational and income future of graduates. There is a large literature critiquing these systems, particularly the national examinations of East Asia, Singapore, and India (Ash, 2016; Kim & Cho, 2014). These critiques focus on the contradiction between the supposed "merit-based" nature of the examinations, and the net results that are usually stratified by race, ethnicity, income, gender, region, and the other variables discussed previously—or, as pointed out earlier, the reproduction of ruling elites. Reforms of these systems have been attempted over the years (the most dramatic in Japan when the U.S. occupation forces recommended eliminating them, and in China during the Cultural Revolution when Red [Ideology] was favored over Expert [academic attainment]). In all cases, they have proved to be resilient and continue to this day to play the role of gatekeeper for higher education admission, and often drive the curriculum at all lower levels, as primary and secondary teachers "teach" to the national entrance exam (Yeom, 2013).

Streaming mechanisms often guide selected secondary school leavers toward the world of work and others to HEIs. Wealth and the public-private debate are significant, given that versions of neoliberalism are increasingly adopted as policy in the region. This gives further support to responses such as preparatory or "cram" schools (*juku* in Japan; *buxiban* in Taiwan, China, Hong Kong, and Singapore; *hakwon* in Korea) that provide a shadow educational system, available to all—at a price.

To gain traction on these long-standing questions, several basic questions seem important. One model seeks out countries, regions, or cities that purposefully address questions of access, equity, and capacity. Joseph Farrell examined "novel" educational responses to the various crises and predicaments that have developed in elementary education as it has sought to address the same issues. Farrell's work provided many surprises, not the least being that often it is people in situations that are not particularly well disposed in terms of conventional resources (in conventional terms they lack capacity) that develop some of the most innovative solutions to addressing issues of access and equity (for further discussion, see Chapter 6 in this volume; see also Prasad, 2009).

Another potential question might be whether higher education is "all that it is cracked up to be." As various societies have pushed to address access and capacity, the dominant tendency has been to add capacity, along existing lines, rather than reform institutions and curricula. In turn, this can lead institutions to "water down" curriculum and standards or face the prospect of finding large numbers of students unable to meet established standards. Seeking to solve access issues in this manner also has often resulted in the "simple" reproduction of existing systems put in place simply to achieve more "seats" for more students. This is certainly the case in much of Asia. Evidence in some countries, for example, India, suggests that this propensity is a powerful driver of the alignment disparities that so bedevil the national administration.

One suggestion is that the dominant discourses that constitute these three values, especially those that purport to link capacity with access, may need to be reconceptualized, perhaps with a new equity base. A key question here would be "who benefits most from existing financial resources," which leads to the further question: higher education graduates for what purpose? Very disparate answers to such an inquiry might well result, not all of which necessarily link higher education outcomes solely in terms of occupational outcomes. It may indeed be the case that in the shifting climate of increased global interaction and dependence, as well as in societies increasingly based on ever-shorter innovation and adoption cycles, we need to give renewed attention to how the kinds of inputs that are being mobilized within nations are being employed (Hawkins, 2011; Welch, 2008). Should questions of access, equity, and capacity be framed more explicitly in terms of mixes of formal and nonformal higher education or tertiary education? Such a move would lead us toward a more differentiated education model that looks less at world-class, elite HEIs, and looks more at other forms: community colleges, rural cooperatives, and open universities that cater to diverse national and local needs. Such a shift of focus would allow us to identify discourses and outcomes that have wider value in society. The rising demand for higher education in Asia, especially since World War II, has resulted in the massification we see today but it has also spawned a "diploma disease" and the rise of credentialism, often disconnected from the world of work (Dore, 1997; Neubauer & Tanaka, 2013). The differentiation in higher education that has occurred in the changing social structures of the late 20th century extends across a long continuum of quality leading in turn to a resurgence of the quality assurance movement.

All this has occurred in the context of rising neoliberalism and its many and differentiated manifestations in the Asia-Pacific region: privatization, deregulation, marketization, decentralization, and corporatization (Welch, 2021a). While different systems respond to this agenda according to their circumstances, East and South East Asia, for example, faced both a regional currency crisis in the late 1990s, and a decade later, a major global financial crisis. Both had implications for education, including the mix of public and private higher education. Another decade on, the global COVID-19 pandemic was predicted to push as many as half a billion people, worldwide, back into poverty, many in the Asia Pacific (Oxfam, 2020). The implications for education were ominous, for both schools and HEIs. The regional currency crisis of the late 1990s, for example, pushed tens of millions of families into poverty, with the result that many children dropped out of school, and many studying at universities overseas, on government scholarships, were forced to return home and enroll in local universities, due to the sudden shortage of funds. Early evidence showed the COVID-19 pandemic having the same effect.

Much more could be said about the complexity of access and equity in the Asian region. The factors discussed briefly, however, underline how a variety of barriers exist to those seeking admission to various levels of education, and help frame the discussion for the issues that flow from this fundamental, ongoing challenge.

QUALITY ASSURANCE

No less than elsewhere, HEIs in the Asia-Pacific are caught up in the push for quality assurance. Organizations such as the Asian Pacific Quality Network, founded in 2003 and based in Shanghai, offer members the opportunity to stay abreast of new developments in this rapidly changing field (Neidermeier & Pohlenz, 2019). A further related regional initiative was the enactment of the Tokyo Convention on mutual recognition of degrees in higher education, in October 2018 (UNESCO, 2018).

The issue of accreditation for the many new HEIs launched in the region, however, is a shifting one, as the growth and massification of higher education across the region have often been poorly regulated. In several systems, the growth of private sector HEIs has outpaced public sector growth, leading to the rise of many HEIs of questionable quality (such as some semiprivate *minban* institutions in China, affiliated colleges in India, and private HEIs in Afghanistan). In some instances, staff qualifications are weak, or fraudulent, and facilities and overall quality poor. Public HEI faculty moonlighting in private HEIs is common, and corruption surrounding accreditation is not unknown (Welch, 2011; Welch & Wahidyar, 2012; 2019).

The context in which the heightened interest in QA occurs in Asia is worth noting. Universities in Asia are experiencing a changing relationship between themselves and their host societies. While higher education decentralization is occurring on the one hand, a contradictory "centralizing" (i.e., the Ministry of Education [MOE] or other state body) obsession with QA is occurring on the other; resulting in what some scholars are referring to as "centralized decentralization" (Lee & Gopinathan, 2013). This ambiguity has prompted both enthusiasm and cynicism regarding QA. The rise of QA in Asia coincided with several forces and factors including the philosophies of neoliberalism managerialism, corporatization, among others, all of which have contributed to the establishment of national QA or accreditation agencies, societies, associations, and other schemes that purport to measure higher education quality. Higher education stakeholders are understandably concerned with how their HEIs are performing. Massification plus diversity in higher education in Asia has resulted in an increased demand for more information regarding the myriad universities and colleges that represent the higher education landscape in the region. For their part, colleges and universities can use QA for branding purposes, and to find their niche in the tangle of institutions that represent the region. At the state level, governments find QA useful to increase their control and leverage over higher education, and increasingly, continued state funding (albeit often diminished as a result of decentralization) is often conditional, based on the results of various reviews. While the introduction of QA procedures is justified by appeals to accountability, demands for greater performativity often make accountability feel more like accountancy to harried faculty and administrators. This includes research performance audits, leading to common critiques across Asia of what has been dubbed the Social Science Citation Index (SSCI) syndrome, which fail to adequately acknowledge valuable locally based research (Chou, 2014, Chou & Chan 2016; Li, 2020).

What is observable is that there has been a shift from a "bottom up" higher education change process, to an increase in "top down" external influences, and a shift to more control. Often, QA occurred during the process whereby the HEI was established, and apart from periodic demands by the MOE for quantitative data, and for approval of changes in the institutional structure, there was little by way of formal, regular evaluation. One consequence of this movement is that "quality management" has replaced a more loosely coupled, and more academic, management style to ensure that the ideas spawned from QA permeate the organization, that the data that are collected and the internal assessments that occur comply with external demands. For better or worse, an evaluative culture has emerged in the region, as the two following cases illustrate (Chou, 2014, Chou & Chan 2016; Welch, 2016).

China

Of the two largest higher education systems in the region, China and India, approaches to QA in higher education are quite distinct. In China, except for examples such as the National Defence University that is administered by its relevant ministry, the MOE plays a central role in the overall regulatory responsibility system. This centralization has allowed for a more unified system of qualification standards to be applied in the areas of learning, accreditation, and degree-granting. This has become particularly challenging and important because of the rise of the nongovernmental sector (*minban* HEIs such as Huang He University in Zhengzhou, Xi'an Fanyi University, and Xian Eurasia University, both in Xi'an, and Sanda College in Shanghai), which has developed some impressive educational capacities and challenges prevailing notions of academic excellence (Welch, 2021b). Provincial accreditation committees are responsible for auditing *minban*. This includes some impressive examples of Sino-foreign collaboration, such as the well-regarded Xian Jiaotong Liverpool University, in Suzhou, although recent research shows that, in general, "The autonomy granted to Sino-foreign cooperation universities has surrendered to the re-centralized regulation by the Beijing elites" (Mok & Han, 2017).

The financial self-responsibility movement has also had an impact on QA development. Whereas in the past HEIs received 80% or more of their budgets from the state, HEIs now must generate the majority of funds needed to cover recurrent costs and research. A question here is the degree to which this has helped or hindered QA. The OECD notes that the movement toward the market has had mixed results and has not necessarily improved learning outcomes. It was reported that the MOE was aware of this and was taking action to "initiate further quality monitoring and assurance reforms, including providing more information to consumers" (Li, 2010). This resulted, *inter alia*, in the cancellation of 234 Sino-foreign programs in mid-2018 (Sharma, 2019). The general QA system that has evolved since 2002 consists of a variety of levels of review. While central, bureaucratic authorities have major responsibility for QA and accreditation in general, the movement since 1994 has been toward independent assessment bodies such as the NGO National Evaluation Institute for Degree Granting Education. However, this approach did not yield expected results and the MOE more recently became interested both in external models such as the U.S. model of accreditation, and agencies such as the European Foundation for Quality Management. By the early 2000s, three basic types of institutional assessment had emerged: qualification assessment, excellence assessment (*xuan yu ping gu*), and random assessment (Liu & Liu, 2017). The first mechanism is focused on HEIs with recognized weak institutional capacities. Excellence assessment is reserved for HEIs with generally recognized strong institutional capacities, and random assessment, for those that fall in between these two categories.

The establishment of the Higher Education Evaluation Centre (HEEC, 2007), responsible for undergraduate education, enabled a first round of reviews of 589 HEIs to be conducted by 2008; by 2013, a further 121 HEIs with new humanities programs had been completed. The China Academic Degrees and Graduate Education Development Center, responsible for postgraduate education, including the quality of various disciplines, conducted reviews of 4,235 disciplines from 391 HEIs in the 2011–2012 round (CDGDC, 2015). In addition, provincial-level bodies such as the Jiangsu Agency for Education Evaluation conduct quality assessments of higher vocational education institutions and random inspections of postgraduate students' research theses (Liu & Liu, 2017). Internal QA processes have also been introduced into HEIs.

Standardized assessment procedures consist of the three elements common to many procedures in the region: (1) self-assessment report; (2) onsite visits by specialists; and (3) reform and improvement of practices. There are both first-level indicators (such as those associated with the educational philosophy, faculty, learning resources, teaching, and learning), and second-level indicators (such as basic learning facilities, quantity and structure of the teaching force, majors, morals, and values) that are considered in the overall assessment process. The system appears to be moving more toward qualitative measures than quantitative measures (e.g., written tests that were previously required for the campus site visits are no longer part of the process) and assessment indicators are more focused on "soft" themes such as institutional philosophy, faculty issues, course development, and so on. At the same time, a rising culture of performativity is evident concerning research. Within the overall QA process, there is also some evidence of a greater emphasis on ideology and a reassertion of the leading role of the party, in recent years, with particular implications for the social sciences and humanities (China Copyright and Media, 2015; Phillips 2016, 2016; Sharma, 2018).

Finally, the time-tried Chinese approach to change of using exemplars upon which others model, has been used via two major higher education initiatives: Project 211 and Project 985. Both of these projects (211, strengthening 100 universities for the 21st century; 985 referring to a speech by Jiang Zemin in May 1985) sought to create models of excellence in higher education that could demonstrate what is meant by "high quality" and thus influence the overall QA system. The most recent *Shuang Yi Liu* (Double First Class) initiative is a further initiative to emphasize quality. One outcome has been recognition that evaluation and monitoring of higher education should involve independent external agencies as well as NGOs. Another has been a call for better internal QA efforts on behalf of China's key universities. Such measures are not disconnected from China's ongoing drive to boost its universities' profiles in the various global rankings.

China's QA system is a work in progress currently consisting of a mix of levels (central government, MOE, local provincial and institutional, and continued interest in the involvement of external, international agencies). Like many other Asian higher education systems, it faces several challenges and questions: Should QA be formative or terminal? How much to emphasize rankings? What should the relationship be between governmental QA and other "buffer" agencies? Does the emphasis on QA exacerbate the highly stratified nature of the Chinese system? Is there too much emphasis on competition? How should the QA assessment be used? Is there too much emphasis on natural science and technology? What seems clear is a strong policy interest in using QA to build a core of first-class HEIs (Wang, 2014).

India

While India is the other large higher education system in Asia, with a population comparable to China, a higher education student enrollment of 37.4 million, and a gross enrollment ratio of more than 26% in 2018–2019, its education profile is distinct. Recently, the government has been harshly critical of the system, and of higher education in particular. Indian higher education has a long history of British regulatory mechanisms. This included the University Grants Commission (UGC) established in 1994, and the National Assessment and Accreditation Council, which employed a familiar QA mechanism of self-evaluations, peer review (based on predetermined criteria for assessment), and the application of a voluntary, graded five-point scale. The primary problem India has faced has been the tradition of affiliation whereby one college takes the lead in undergraduate education and is loosely connected to other colleges and universities. As Stella (2002) notes: "Most Indian universities are of the affiliating type where the affiliation university legislates . . . courses of study, holds examinations centrally on common syllabi for its affiliates, and awards degrees of successful candidates." As in several other Asian higher education systems, capacity is also a problem: some universities have over 400 affiliated colleges, rendering QA highly problematic. Many of the affiliates are known to be substandard. Again, the poorly regulated expansion of the private sector is a problem, with much of the growth in recent years occurring in the private sector. About 70% of all HEIs are run by private trusts (even though many receive substantial levels of state funding through "grant-in-aid college funds"). Private deemed universities, mostly run by powerful families, have mushroomed since the mid-1990s, with many transformed from private colleges. Agarwal (2009; 2015) is only one scholar to point to the somewhat arbitrary and opaque nature of this process, which raised concerns of political influence and patronage. Attempts to regulate the process in the early 2000s, and make it more transparent, largely failed. While private deemed universities are often entrepreneurial, they are often focused narrowly on certain disciplines, are short on infrastructure, and lax on fees and admissions to boost profits (Agarwal, 2009; 2015).

The scale of the "quality" problem of Indian higher education was divulged by the leaking of a confidential report by the National Assessment and Accreditation Council, a division of the UGC. The report indicated that 123 universities and 2,956 affiliated colleges across India had been evaluated and that 68% of the universities and 90% of the colleges were found to be of "poor quality" (Neelakantan, 2007b, p. 2). Additional QA issues included that enrollments were down, faculty positions were unfilled, teachers lacked credentials, preferential admissions were granted, and technology was lacking. Moonlighting is a fact of life, for many faculty, lowering the quality of higher education (Jain, 2014). Former Prime Minister M. Singh lamented that,

> The country's university system is in a state of disrepair, we need better facilities, more and better teachers, a flexible approach to curriculum development

to make it more relevant, more effective pedagogical and learning methods and more meaningful evaluation systems. . . . (We have) a dysfunctional education system, which can only produce dysfunctional future citizens. There are complaints of favouritism and corruption . . . we should free university appointments from unnecessary interventions on the part of governments and must promote autonomy and accountability. (Neelakantan, 2007b)

The challenges for QA in India are thus substantial. To address the issue of "affiliated nondegree-granting institutions" that make up the bulk of the colleges in India, Singh proposed that new degree-granting central universities be established in each of the 16 states that lacked one. Each new institution should symbolize academic excellence, run to the highest academic standards, and be a model of efficiency. The Prime Minister directed India's higher educational regulatory bodies and Planning Commission to prepare a strategy for the establishment of these new institutions (Neelakantan, 2007a). Thus a major higher education development effort seemed to begin a more rigorous QA effort in India. In 2017, the government planned to link future funding of the 43 Central Universities to performance to boost accountability and address the gap between the actual cost of providing programs and the low fees. The current QA mechanisms are also being questioned but the focus is on redefining higher education in India through the establishment of new institutions that meet world standards. But a recent proposal to deem certain key universities "Institutes of Excellence," with enhanced autonomy and additional funding, has been labeled a farce, with one of the listed institutions not even established at the time (Bothwell, 2019; Niazi, 2018).

Although India has many advantages that facilitate progress toward quality higher education, there are substantial disadvantages that the current QA system highlights but seems unable to address. High-quality HEIs, such as the Indian Institutes of Technology, the All India Institute of Medical Sciences, and the Tata Institute of Fundamental Research, enroll well under 1% of the student population (Altbach, 2005). India's proposed action to create a new set of globally competitive institutions thereby raising the QA level for all Indian higher education is both bold and risky (and expensive). But as Altbach (2005) notes, "Without these universities, India is destined to remain a scientific backwater." A related problem is that too many of India's leading graduates leave for better prospects abroad. In part a response to high levels of graduate unemployment, there is now evidence of a pattern of reverse brain drain, where limited opportunities abroad since the global financial crisis (GFC) of 2008–2009 is paralleled by growing opportunities at home (Kumar, 2013; PTI, 2014).

Japan

While China and India struggle to push their massive higher education systems forward and at the same time raise quality standards, Japan, as the traditionally undisputed higher education leader in the East Asia region, struggles to redefine what it means by QA and to maintain the quality that it has already earned. Japan has a long history of formal accreditation, modeled on the U.S. system inherited as a result of the U.S. post–World War II Occupation. The Japan University Accreditation Association (JUAA) was formed in 1947, founded by 47 universities but currently embracing many private universities, as well as around half of the National HEIs, and some public universities. By 2018, HEIs totaled 780, of which 603 were private, 93 public, and 86 national. Until 2004, the JUAA was the sole organization for accreditation and evaluation in Japan (the MOE of course had the sole authority to approve the creation of all HEIs but provided minimum standards). All HEIs were required by the MOE to undergo a self-review periodically and the results were publicly released, but there was no explicit requirement that the institutions be reviewed by an external agency. JUAA accreditation was a voluntary and autonomous system of QA that many HEIs joined largely to help improve their pedagogical mission.

The QA process began to change in 2000 when the MOE launched its system of evaluation conducted by its agency: the National Institute for Academic Degrees and University Evaluation (NIAD-EU). Modeled on the British QA system, the NIAD-EU was not accreditation in the strict sense. Stimulated by the World Trade Organization (WTO) and the European accreditation movement, the NIAD-EU approach "referred to trends in European countries regarding accreditation and explained the need for QA in the context of international competitive and cross border provision of education, rather than in terms of domestic requirements for quality improvement" (Yonezawa, 2015). In 2016, the NIAD-QE was launched, with the QE denoting quality enhancement. It operates three evaluation and accreditation schemes: Certified Evaluation and Accreditation (CEA), Institutional Thematic Assessment, and National University Corporation Evaluation. The MOE never made much use of the JUAA, but universities liked it as being symbolic of participation in the international QA movement.

The School Education Act was amended in 2002, and a new accreditation scheme was enacted in 2004: the CEA system. There are now 13 certified evaluation and accreditation organizations (Yonezawa, 2015). The Japan Institute for Higher Education Evaluation was founded in 2004, and the Japan Accreditation Board for Engineering Education, founded in 1999, is involved in the accreditation of programs to train technicians in engineering, science, and agriculture departments within HEIs.

While Japan seemed to be following the global trend of establishing national bodies of accreditation, the results are somewhat confusing, as Yonezawa (2015) points out:

> The strong insistence by the government on its ownership of accreditation in Japan has unarguably contributed to confusion regarding the concept. Currently, the only reliable model of accreditation for Japan is the American, nongovernmental one, while the Japanese approach itself corresponds somewhat to newly developing European (and some other Asian) initiatives. A sense of ownership of the accreditation system is hardly shared by the Japanese universities ... Japanese higher education institutions have never consolidated to protect their ownership of accreditation after (it) being introduced by the American forces in the mid-20th century. (pp. 21–22)

The plethora of organizations involved, and lack of perceived ownership hamstring any serious efforts by the MOE or any other accreditation agencies to gain overall credibility in the QA process. Mori noted that the CEA has little to do with excellence. More likely is that international and local market pressures, especially the push to boost Japan's profile in the range of international league tables, such as Academic Ranking of World Universities, Times, and QS, will have a much greater QA impact, especially in the natural and applied science areas (Ishikawa & Sun, 2016; 2021). JUAA has been diminished and must now report (as do all other QA agencies) to the MOE. Once again, tensions exist between a push for centralization (more from the Ministry), and decentralization (preferred by the university sector). The numerous private institutions in Japan, for example, decided at one stage to launch their accreditation agency, although the current demographic decline weakened the sector, and undermined the attempt to establish yet another agency. For-profit and even international agencies could be certified as accreditation agencies under the new legislation. One feature of the system is competition. If a university or college does not like the results of one QA evaluation, it can switch agencies for the next seven-year round. Again, it is argued that an improvement in QA methods in Japan would be to strengthen internal QA and empower HEIs to be individually accountable. The complex and confusing situation inevitably raises questions about the seriousness of QA in Japanese higher education.

Taiwan

A parallel search for QA alternatives has evolved in Taiwan (Hsu, 2019). Since 1966, Taiwan's higher education system expanded; from 21 HEIs to 159 in 2014. The expansion, combined with the international competitive forces of globalization, have put QA on the front burner for educational leaders and analysts. The MOE has put pressure on Taiwan's HEIs to compete internationally and be able to enter the "rankings" along with high-quality institutions in other Asian settings. Three basic mechanisms have been utilized to spur the QA movement: (1) offering HEIs more basic autonomy; (2) offering increased funding as an incentive for change; (3) at the same time, developing a new and better QA system to perform periodic evaluations of both institutions and programs. The institutional accreditation methods familiar in the United States influenced Taiwan early in its QA development beginning in 1975 up to the 1990s. The process was always centralized, with the MOE playing a central role. In 2005, the MOE commissioned a new organization called the Taiwan Assessment and Evaluation Association (TWAEA) and authorized it to conduct both programmatic and institutional evaluations.

The Higher Education Evaluation and Accreditation Council (HEEACT), established in the same year and funded by the MOE, conducted a nationwide university program evaluation and laid the groundwork for the ranking of research performance. Its primary mission consists of developing performance indicators, implementing higher education evaluations, and providing evaluation reports to the MOE. Institutional accreditations, conducted every five years, have the goal of self-improvement. The process is based on a system of rewards and punishment that is largely mirrored at the institutional level, with successful departments and individuals rewarded with extra funds and poor departments merged with others. Under the Programme for Developing First-Class University and Top Research Centre, additional funding could be awarded by the ministry, while a poor rating might trigger the Exit Mechanism, designed to close weak HEIs. In 2014, three private HEIs were closed, and in 2020 the MOE announced plans to close at least 10 more (Green, 2020). The University Evaluation Act of 2007 mandated regular self-evaluation of teaching, research, administration, and services by HEIs that required them to introduce internal QA processes that were subsequently refined. Further reforms, introduced in 2012 to respond to criticisms from the sector of the burden of QA processes, instituted "self-conducted external evaluations," reports that were submitted directly to the MOE rather than to HEEACT. Further reforms instituted in 2017, mandated that HEIs conduct program accreditation themselves. But the overall emphasis on publication in Science Citation Index (SCI) and SSCI journals as a key metric was strongly criticized by many academics, as distorting academic production and restricting freedom (Hsu, 2019). The cancellation of research-oriented performance indicators in 2006 did little to dent the pressure to publish in key English-language international journals, at the cost of teaching.

TWAEA is a nonprofit organization founded by academics and individuals from the business sector. HEEACT is a MOE body, although reduced in the latest reforms to an accreditation role, rather than conducting evaluations. This is an ongoing process viewed by some scholars as focused more on international rankings and league tables than on improving teaching, research, and learning. Hsu (2019) pointed to unintended consequences and set the analysis against a backdrop of rising managerialism and a compliance culture among HEIs.

The methods used are also a mix of the U.S. accreditation approach and the experiences derived from the Bologna Process in Europe. This means more fully involving the HEIs themselves, involving students in the evaluation process, focusing on the quality and employability of graduates, and becoming competitive internationally. Like Japan and China, the QA process remains highly centralized with the MOE and its agencies playing lead roles and external agencies increasingly being involved in specific aspects of QA review. At least one scholar of QA in Taiwan has suggested a preferred future where the MOE would retreat to a position of assuring the integrity of the process while relying on external, more independent agencies to conduct the actual audits and evaluations.

Singapore and Hong Kong
Singapore and Hong Kong offer further, albeit different, examples of a QA process whereby general decentralization and increased autonomy of HEIs are coupled with a continued strong presence of the state concerning QA. Mok refers to a "re" regulation of HE in the context of QA, at the same time as the state loosened its controls of HE in general, although the passage of the Hong Kong National Security Law in 2020 was seen by many as a tightening of control (Tsoi & Wai, 2020). Hong Kong may have been the first higher education system in the region to systematize QA when, in 1997, the Executive Council empowered the University Grants Committee (UGC) to institute a QA process for all HEIs:

> The UGC in its mission statement pledges to uphold the academic freedom and institutional autonomy of institutions while at the same time seeking to assure the quality and cost-effectiveness of their education provision, and being publicly accountable for the sums of public money devoted to higher education. . . . [T]he term quality assurance (the UGC means) the maintenance of the highest standards both in teaching and learning and in research and services commensurate with an institutions' agreed role and mission . . . [S]uch terms as "fitness for purpose,"

"doing the right thing right the first time," "value added," "performance indicators," and so on, proliferate. (Mok, 2000, p. 158)

The focus at the central level in Hong Kong, then, is determining that HEIs in Hong Kong have the appropriate mechanisms for QA in place, rather than assessing quality itself. The passage of the National Security Law in mid-2020 by the central government in Beijing, however, raised concerns about the potential politicization of education, including higher education (Altbach & Postiglione, 2020, Tsoi and Wai 2020).

Quality assurance committees and performance, planning, appraisal, and development offices were established within universities to focus on four meta-areas of evaluation: the quality program framework (mission statements, vision, goals, etc.), formal quality program activities, quality program support, values and incentives (what is the reward structure for carrying out QA?). Hong Kong initiated (and Japan and Taiwan followed) a "center of excellence" scheme to encourage strong programs to develop and conversely identify weak programs. Mok (2005) concludes, "All these changes illustrate how the ideas and practices of managerialism have affected the university sector in Hong Kong. Without a doubt, university governance in Hong Kong has shifted from the traditional collegial approach to management-oriented and market models" (p. 538). Hong Kong has more recently moved toward the "total quality control" model utilizing the audit method and a variety of outcome measurement tools. A form of decentralization has emerged (steering at a distance) which maintains a muted but effective government presence.

Singapore in some ways offers a contrasting approach to QA. Whereas in Hong Kong the emphasis has been on cost-cutting and efficiency, in Singapore the focus is on maintaining global competitiveness, which includes significant investment in higher education and research and development (R&D). About the same time QA began in earnest in Hong Kong (1997), Singapore's then Prime Minister Goh stated, "We have to prepare ourselves for a bracing future—a future of intense (global) competition and shifting competitive advantages, a future where technologies and concepts are replaced at an increasing pace, and a future of changing values. Education and training are central to how nations will fare in this future" (Mok, 2000). To prepare for this competition, Singapore's two primary universities (National University of Singapore [NUS] and Nanyang Technical University [NTU]) put in place internal QA mechanisms intending to transform both institutions into "world class" universities. As seen earlier, both are ranked within the world's top 100 HEIs. The MOE adopted a novel approach by forming an international QA team of 11 prominent academics from highly ranked American, European, and Asian universities to conduct an external QA analysis of the two universities. The goal was to provide recommendations that would transform them into the Boston of the East, with NUS representing Harvard and NTU representing MIT. The reviews were conducted at the institutional level and the MOE buttressed these efforts by introducing policies that tightened up tenure rules, provided financial incentives for good teaching and research, promoted a more favorable faculty-student ratio, and so on (Tan, 2011). In both the Hong Kong and Singapore cases, QA is very much a presence, and while occurring during a period of the hollowing out of the state, the state, through the respective MOEs is very much involved: another two cases of the government-directed centralization of decentralization.

Other Settings

QA policy change is not limited to East Asia but is occurring throughout the region. Efforts in Indonesia, Afghanistan, Pakistan, Cambodia, Vietnam, and Thailand, to name just a few, are occurring apace and as was suggested in the introduction to this section, attract both enthusiasm and cynicism (Welch and Wahidyar 2019; Faiz et al 2020). ASEAN regional initiatives include those listed previously. In Indonesia, accreditation is still viewed by some with some suspicion as a "foreign" concept, at odds with Indonesian higher education traditions. In Pakistan, the goal and challenge for educational policymakers are to find a way to legitimate QA and find accreditation mechanisms that fit national and cultural circumstances, while aligning HEIs with international standards. Vietnam, Thailand, and Cambodia have all opted for a more centralized approach to accreditation and it appears unlikely as of this writing that there will be any movement toward a more independent process. The process is bedeviled by corruption in several systems (Welch, 2011; 2020b; Welch & Wahidyar, 2012; 2019).

MOBILITY AND MIGRATION

A growing feature of contemporary globalization has been the extraordinary degree of migration and mobility, including of the highly skilled, over the past three to four decades. During this period, the world has witnessed unprecedented movements of people between countries, within and between major regions of the world, and within countries. Framed by the enormous movement of capital and manufacturing between the developed and the developing areas of the world—arguably the harbinger of this period of globalization—millions of people have moved to systems that offer more focused economic development and the jobs it has created. Fueled by continuing global population growth, these economic relocations have resulted in a fundamentally urban world: by 2000, more people lived in cities than in the countryside, a trend that will continue throughout the 21st century. In ways that almost stagger the imagination, remittance economies have sprung up around the world, many of them in Asia, creating a circuit of labor exchange and economic return that comes to fuel many economies to the point of dependency. Within Asia, the Philippines forms a dramatic example, with remittances totaling US$33.5 billion in 2019, or around 10% of GDP. In sum, the worlds of location, work, economic return, and sustainability have been significantly transformed during this period, and the structure and dynamics that have been responsible for it in turn frame and determine a whole range of other social institutions, including education.

Higher education is among those institutions that have been transformed. Massification in the Asia Pacific resulted in the vast expansion of capacity for both existing institutions and spawned significant numbers of new ones, in both public and private sectors. Higher education systems and institutions were transformed, touching on fundamentally important issues, as we have seen, of quality and quality assurance, curricula and pedagogy, and intense national debates on what is taught in higher education and how these subjects align with the needs of evolving labor markets, and long-standing national values and cultures. Indeed, foremost among challenges facing higher education is how it seeks to remain relevant in the face of the significant social, economic, and cultural changes posed by the steadily emergent knowledge society, that is often seen in Asia as Western-centric. A related quest is to find a balance between preserving national culture and tradition, on one hand; and drawing on international innovation on the other. In Japan this attempted synthesis is called *Wakon Yosai*; in China, *Zhongti xiyong*: "Chinese Learning as Substance; Western Learning as Application." The quest is ongoing.

Higher education migration and mobility are central to these other broad currents of social change, especially the movement of talent within the region, and also between the region and beyond. As seen earlier, such movements have a long history but have reached extraordinary proportions with major implications for higher education and national development. While many aspects of globalization have received significant attention (mobility of goods, services, technology, capital, unskilled workers) talent mobility is only now receiving much attention. Mobility patterns of both students and higher education faculty—phenomena that were traditionally referred to as brain drain, but more recently as brain circulation, involves consideration of what are termed knowledge diasporas, of which the Chinese and Indian are major examples, as previously discussed. Several countries have established national strategies to recruit their overseas academic talent, either to return and contribute to national development, or, if not, to liaise and collaborate with colleagues back home (Welch, 2018b; Welch & Cai, 2011; Hao & Welch, 2012; Welch & Hao, 2016; Welch & Yang, 2010; Welch & Zhang, 2008). East Asian systems have been among the more successful.

Such patterns of migration and mobility are increasingly important in the Asia Pacific region, especially as some countries have developed excess higher education capacity. In some cases, this is deliberate, for example in the Philippines, which overproduces nurses and doctors, who then work overseas and remit part of their salaries to families back home. Other regional systems, such as Australia, and New Zealand aggressively pursued a higher education funding model based on the recruitment of international students (which, among other things left them highly vulnerable, as student mobility dried up as a result of travel restrictions imposed in response to the COVID-19 crisis). But other forms of mobility are also involved. This embraces the movement of ideas within the region, including ideas about how universities might (should) be organized, financed, supervised, or governed; ideas about what it means to be "globally competitive" and what this implies for what should be taught and researched within higher education settings; ideas about nationalism versus regional approaches in higher education (such as ongoing efforts to develop an ASEAN "consciousness" in higher education); or the development of "scholarly" exchanges within the region, for example, journals, jointly funded research projects or consortia, scholarly meetings. Related to this is the transfer and transformation of higher educational "forms." This process has gone beyond the previous one-way "borrowing" that took place in the early 20th century and post–WWII period and now is poised to take place within and without the Asia Pacific region. Some have argued that, while ASEAN for example is now generally recognized as a region, China-ASEAN relations, including in education, are now well-developed enough, to begin to conceive of China-ASEAN as a region (Welch, 2014; Wen, 2016).

The demographics of migration within the Asia Pacific region reveal exceptional change. Over half of the world's population lives in the Asia Pacific region—specifically, given the most recent data, of a global population of about 7.75 billion, around 60% live in Asia. Just as important, some of the larger countries in the region, such as India, Indonesia, Malaysia, and the Philippines, have some of the highest birth rates. As Table 14.1 indicates, even as birth rates fall over the coming decades, as they are throughout much of the world (sending some of the rapidly aging countries such as Japan, Korea, and China into a decline), overall regional birth rates will remain relatively high.

At the heart of the matter is the fact that in 2025, the planet will have roughly an additional 1.3 billion residents, most of whom will live in Asia and most of whom will also live in cities, including their burgeoning slums (Davis, 2006). The challenges for education are profound.

Within-country migration in Asia has—due to the huge population bases of countries such as China, India, and Indonesia—dwarfed that of other countries in the world. As an example, internal migration in China during the decade of the 1990s constitutes perhaps the largest single migration in the history of the world, as over 150,000,000 people moved from the countryside to cities. There are enormous implications for education at all levels but especially for heavily impacted higher education (Iredale & Guo, 2015).

The degree of urbanization during the past few decades is stunning. Fifty years ago, 30% of the world lived in urban settings; 20 years ago, that figure was 45%; today, it is 55% plus. In the year 2000, 2.8 billion people lived in cities, some 411 of which had populations over one million. Up to the latter part of the 20th century, the majority of the world's urban population lived in Europe and North America. In this century, the largest share will accrue to cities in other continents, mainly Asia. By 2020, the urban population total had reached 4.8 billion—an increase of two billion over 2000. Again, the majority of this urban concentration is in Asia.

One can cite particular patterns of migration to underscore the relative volatility of the region. For example, the period from the early 1970s through the 1980s witnessed significant international migration from Asia principally to

Table 14.1. Population Growth 1990–2050, Selected Asia (Millions)

Country	1990	2019	2050 (projected)
China	1,177	1,434	1,402
India	873	1,366	1,639
Indonesia	181	271	331
Japan	125	127	106
Pakistan	108	217	338
Bangladesh	103	163	193

Source: UN World Population Prospects 2019: Highlights, 14; Population Pyramid: Japan 2050.
Note: Japan's population decline is projected to be large enough to fall out of the world's Top 10 by 2050.

North America. Migration to Australia and the oil states in Middle East grew dramatically from the 1990s on, and, within the region, migration grew dramatically from less developed Asia Pacific nations to new emerging nations.

Within Asia, we can distinguish between those that have been primarily destination countries (Brunei, Hong Kong, Japan, Singapore, South Korea, Taiwan); those that show evidence of both significant emigration and immigration (Malaysia, Thailand); and those that have been primarily source countries (Afghanistan, Bangladesh, Burma/Myanmar, Cambodia, China, India, Indonesia, Laos, Nepal, Pakistan, Philippines, Sri Lanka, Việt Nam). Some of these, China and India foremost, have witnessed some newer patterns of return migration, especially in the high-skill categories of electrical engineering and medicine as these countries have launched focused campaigns to encourage such returns. China notably introduced an array of "foreign talent schemes," that have drawn many high-skilled Chinese academics back from abroad, while the declining job market in Western countries after the GFC also induced more Chinese to return to greener pastures back home (Welch & Cai, 2011).

While these trends represent gross movements of people, largely for occupational reasons, of more interest here are the academic exchanges that have come to characterize the Asia Pacific region. While it remains true that a handful of Western countries (the United States, the United Kingdom, France, Germany, Australia) continue to host over 60% of international higher education students, China now hosts over 500,000, and Japan has set a target of 300,000 (by 2018, the total was 208,900). Newer competitors such as Malaysia and Singapore have been very successful in attracting international students from the region to their universities; the former also attracts significant numbers of Muslim students from beyond the region. Of the 5.2 million international higher education students in 2020, the largest group (at around 30%) is from the Asia Pacific region, with China in the lead followed by India, South Korea, and Japan. Thus the movement of students and scholars within Asia and between Asia and the rest of the world represents a significant portion of what some have dubbed the "great brain race" (Wildavsky, 2010).

As these aspects of global knowledge capital and circuits within the Asia Pacific region are mapped, a research agenda for the future would be to pay particular attention to specific impacts on higher education institutions. One impact is the migration/diffusion/circulation of governance ideas, patterns, and practices. An example from the 1990s was the rise of managerialism, efforts to organize and operate universities more as freestanding business organizations. In one way or another, the policy reform spread rather quickly throughout the Asia Pacific region and changed the nature of higher education.

REGIONALISM AND HIGHER EDUCATION

Harmonizing disparate national higher educational systems is easier said than done, even in the European Union, where rising nationalist sentiments in some states are currently undermining regional engagement. In Asia, too, nationalism is rising among some systems, tensions between nations and subregions are evident, as well as a reluctance on the part of national ministries to cede (much) control to regional entities and organizations. All these mean that regionalism is at a more embryonic stage of development (Jayasuriya, 2003). Economic regionalization may well continue in some form, given that most countries within the Asia Pacific, including almost all of the ASEAN member states, have China as a major trading partner. The signing of the 11-country Trans-Pacific Partnership in 2018 (that did not include China), and the subsequent 15-country Regional Comprehensive Economic Partnership in 2020 (that included China) both promised to boost regional trade. But would this herald educational regionalization, thus uniting economic internationalization and education?

Regionalism in Asian higher education is thus caught between what may be called centrifugal forces—those that pull away from regionalization and harmonization of higher education—and centripetal—those that pull toward this vision. These of course are not necessarily new arguments. Clark Kerr (1990), former president of the University of California system, posited years ago that two laws of motion in higher education pull in opposite directions—internationalization of learning and knowledge, and the nationalization of the purposes of higher education (Chou & Chan, 2016; Ishkawa & Sun, 2016). It has been noted elsewhere that quality assurance within the higher education movement is increasingly driven by economic agendas, with its prevalent emphasis on metrics and learning outcomes that align with the world of business (Neubauer & Bilgalke, 2009; Welch, 2016; 2021a). The rising influence of neoliberalism has driven HEIs toward justifying their existence and funding on how well they serve national if not local interests; a far cry from cross-national regional concerns. The expansive and convergent discourses of globalization so prevalent in framing higher education policy discussion in Asia-Pacific are often belied by the national sense of what it takes to gain "global recognition," which is to be recognized as having "globally competitive" (and ranked) universities (see Chou, 2014; Ishikawa & Sun, 2016). Within more narrow economic frames of reference, the seemingly robust and boundless energies that produced the WTO extended to regional counterparts have within the past 10 years been supplemented by bilateral agreements (*University World News*, 2013). So where do regional organizations (ROs) and higher education fit in? The answer is complicated by the often highly stratified nature of many Asian higher education systems, particularly in East Asia, where local HEIs tend to be more focused on domestic concerns, whereas the top-tiers of HEIs are more internationally focused.

An interesting hypothesis might be that forms of regional higher education organization and governance are more likely to occur in a narrow rather than broad sense. Furthermore, the nation-state is also a centrifugal force when it comes to regionalization, a force pulling away from this concept, largely due to neoliberalism, economic competition, accountability, QA, and alignment issues. In other words, as neoliberal economics becomes more globalized, higher education gets caught up in the centrifugal local forces mentioned previously. It needs to be recognized that both centrifugal and centripetal forces are happening simultaneously and will continue to occur, which makes it important to forge a sensible conceptual language that permits us to understand that both forces are in continual and constant dynamic tension. As Steger (2009) and others have argued, this attribute seemingly typifies globalization as a phenomenon, or as a set of aggregate phenomena.

The late Ezra Vogel (2010) pointed to centrifugal forces that militate against further expansion of ROs, especially in Asia, and therefore regional HEIs. Reminding us that we need to consider the historical context in which regionalization must take root and be nurtured, he pointed to two difficult issues that remain unresolved. The two posed a major barrier to the establishment of a successful regional organization that would involve the participation of the three largest social and economic powerhouses in the region (Japan, Korea, and China): historical disputes, and military balance of power. Japan-China tensions, as well as China-Korea and Korea-Japan tensions, complicate harmonizing their HEIs. Much further progress on regionalism cannot be assumed, notwithstanding regional initiatives like Campus Asia, and the Asian University Alliance (Chao, 2018; Jung & Kim 2018; Kuroda et al., 2018). Vogel concludes that the small-scale structures that already exist and the one large-scale structure (ASEAN) are probably sufficient for now, and policy energy and funding should not be wasted on efforts to create any new ROs designed to somehow "harmonize" higher education in the region.

Regionalism may focus on political structures, security, and international relations, economics, geography, literature, art and architecture, popular culture and sport, or education. Generally speaking, two main phases of regionalism can be identified in the Asian region: old and new. From 1950–1980, efforts consisted of country groupings of peer economies, intraregional interactions, trade and security, and education. ASEAN is the prime example of this exclusive form. From 1980, we see reflections of neoliberalism (to differing degrees) and market deregulation in the rise of broader-based interregional organizations such as APEC, the Asia/Europe Meeting, the Asia Cooperation Dialogue, ASEAN +3, and so on. Educational regionalism has been built on organizations such as these, in particular the Southeast Asian Ministers of Education Organizations (SEAMEO), Regional Centre for Higher Education and Development (RIHED), the Association of Southeast Asian Institutions of Higher Learning (ASAIHL), among others. These groupings focus on a diverse set of higher education issues such as QA, collaborative R&D, teaching and learning, student mobility, and do not exclude interacting with national settings outside of the immediate Asian orbit (such as Australia, the United States, and the EU) (Robertson, 2008; Shameel, 2003). So we see here, in these two phases, a wide range of ROs from exclusive to inclusive, from intraregional to interregional, and covering an equally wide range of social issues, one of which is education and especially higher education.

All of this warrants ongoing research and observation as ROs continue to grow and develop, including in higher education. Yepes (2006) points out that the relationship between regionalism and higher education in Asia is developing in the context of interaction between the ROs and those regional efforts in other global settings. The exemplar and paradigm that is most often mentioned is Europe, the EU, and the Bologna Process, which puts the Asian efforts into a more comparative perspective.

Efforts have been made to include higher education in existing regional organizations since ASEAN began to explore collaboration with East Asia by establishing the ASAIHL in 1956. In the 1960s, UNESCO's Asia and Pacific Regional Bureau for Education began to work with SEAMEO to better integrate higher education in the region. Expanded to include Japan and other non-ASEAN nations, the RIHED was established to "respond to needs related to policy and planning, administration and management of higher education" (Yepes, 2006). For its part, ASEAN instituted the Asian University Network (AUN) in 1995 at Chulalongkorn University in Thailand to manage collaborative exchanges of students and faculty and grant scholarships, provide information networking, joint research, and an ASEAN-wide course syllabus. It now includes ASEAN+3 and ASEAN+6 and is now seeking to extend links with the EU, India, and Russia.

UMAP (University Mobility in the Asia-Pacific) was established in the 1990s, the ASEAN-EU University Network Programme in 2000, and the Asia Link Program around that same time, all designed to create regional opportunities, promote Asia knowledge and links with other world regions, a strong regional identity, and "East Asian Consciousness" (Azmawati & Quayle, 2017; Yepes, 2006). The goals and objectives of these various regional higher education efforts are summarized as follows:

- Regional lifelong learning collaboration
- Regional credit transfer systems and mutual recognition of degrees (such as the Tokyo Convention and the Malaysia-China agreement) (*University World News*, 2013)
- Mobility and scholarships for students and faculty (from, e.g., the China Scholarships Council)
- Cooperative R&D
- Promotion of centers of excellence for e-learning
- Curriculum development
- Regional-wide QA cooperation (e.g., AUN-QA and AQAN)

These goals are similar to those proposed by the Bologna Process. But progress in the Asian region reveals little in the way of coordination of these various efforts, and indeed many of the initiatives mentioned above have either stalled or are no longer very active. Yepes suggested that an organization such as UNESCO could provide the umbrella coordinating organization, the WTO could assist with reviewing regional conventions on diplomas and degrees, and the World Bank, or the Asian Development Bank, could provide funding for such an effort. None appear likely.

Other scholars have concluded that true regionalization in Asia will not occur as long as the previous exclusive organizations (ASEAN, SEAMEO, etc.) are not able to effectively draw in at least the "big three" East Asian nations (China, Japan, and Korea). The argument is that Japan and China's unresolved historical tensions and animosities presented a major obstacle to moving forward with a form of regionalism that would include harmonization of higher education: "The problematic state of relations between Beijing and Tokyo has increasingly emerged as the foremost hurdle for East Asian regionalism" (Armstrong, 2020; Rozman, 2005), although Japan succeeded in mending relations significantly in the years to 2020. Student mobility in the region is still dominated by China, Australia, and Japan, although Korea, Singapore, and Malaysia also now each host large numbers of international students.

ASEAN's progress, as also the other regional associations, are highly dependent on the big three East Asian countries and further integration between East and Southeast Asia. Further regionalism is not necessarily the wave of the future in Asia, and probably not in the EU either, both due to rising nationalism and the growth of separatist "illiberal democracies." The increasing economic and cultural interdependency of the region may lead to a slow, tortuous regional community, but is balanced against rising nationalism in China and growing authoritarianism in selected ASEAN member states, such as the Philippines. History and cultural memory cast a huge shadow over trust in such areas as higher education harmonization, shared curriculum, and other educational policies.

This rather bleak projection of bringing together East Asia and Southeast Asia (ignoring for the moment South Asia) into some form of educational harmonized relationship was echoed by such scholars as Robert Scalapino who argued that "the diversities within Asia far exceed the commonalities. . . . Asia has nowhere near the cultural affinities of West Europe" (cited Dent, 2016; Lee & Scalapino, n.d.; Rozman, 2005). Seen from the inside, however, Asian nations have much more in common with each other than they do with the West and therefore, there is a basis for forging substantive regional affiliations (a centripetal force). Hence, while a full-fledged Asia regional organization capable of harmonizing. East and Southeast Asian higher education, with member countries participating on an equal basis, remains elusive, some have argued that the outline of a potential East and Southeast Asian regionalism in higher education are becoming visible. Ultimately, however, HE regionalization in the Asia Pacific remains in a more embryonic form, compared to Europe; much more needs to be done.

Several scholars including Kuroda et al. (2018) and Nguyen (2009) agree that at the very least, some questions need to be addressed:

- How much and what kind of regional higher education cooperation already exists?
- What governing principles and policies exist that encourage or discourage higher education harmonization?
- What does analysis of existing frameworks and organizations (ASEAN+3, APRU, etc.), reveal?
- What would a study of the actors involved, not only countries but also HEIs, tell us?
- What can be learned from a comparative study of other examples such as Europe?

Nguyen (2009) concluded that comparisons with other world regions show that the efforts at developing a harmonized higher education regime in Asia remain for more embryonic (Jayasuriya, 2003; 2010; Nguyen, 2009; Welch, 2018b). Of particular interest to Asians, she argued, are the following features of the Bologna Process:

1. Readable, comparable degrees
2. Three-cycle degree system
3. System of credits based on European Credit Transfer and Accumulation system (ECTS)[2]
4. Student and staff mobility
5. QA cooperation

6. Promotion of a European Dimension in higher education, curriculum development, programs of study, etc.
7. Promotion of lifelong learning
8. Marketing the idea of a European Higher Education Area

Given, however, that recent assessments of the progress of the EU toward higher education harmonization and the list of capacities are less than enthusiastic, questions regarding the scale, scope, progress, and indeed feasibility of Asian higher education harmonization are naturally raised (Nguyen, 2009; McDermott, 2017).

While much has been said about the common interests of the Asian region, and the rational reasons behind promoting some sort of harmonization process, several centrifugal forces, some of which were already discussed, present formidable obstacles to the realization of such a policy. Echoing the Scalapino (n.d.), and Rozman (2005) arguments, several writers point to the vast and diverse nature of the region, its ethnicities, cultures, languages, religious traditions and beliefs, political-economies, and diverse higher education histories, as being factors that work against such ROs and higher education cooperative arrangements (Musselin, 2009). Although student and faculty mobility in the region is one area of progress, overall, this has remained limited when one considers percentages of these cohorts represented in any given national HEI. When compared with other world regions, Nguyen (2009) notes: "Asia is lagging far behind other regions of the world in promoting even the most basic level of policy harmonization to achieve common objectives and interests in the area of higher education" (p. 76; Jayasuriya, 2003; 2010; Welch, 2011).

Somewhat more successful in terms of usage is the AUN designed in 1995 to support student mobility in the region. While open to all HEIs in the region, in fact, it has become primarily an elite program, as "elites prefer to cooperate with elites" (Nguyen, 2009, p. 80). Therefore, it is somewhat self-limiting and as of 2020 had 30 members. If the "plus three" nations of China, Japan, and Korea are added, membership expands to 51. More interesting was the subregional networking on QA practices, which seeks to establish some common standards for the region. AUN-QA reaches out to all institutions in the region that wish to get the AUN-QA label.

Finally, SEAMEO's RIHED is another program designed to promote regional cooperation in higher education in the region, established in 1959, and more directly interested in governance as a key component to regional higher education harmonization. This organization focuses on areas such as higher education management and administration.

A RIHED workshop on the topic of harmonization, regional organizations, and higher education in Asia concluded that the future of this movement would consist primarily of a series of small steps rather than the establishment of a Bologna-type overarching mechanism that "invites doubts and suspicions among Asian countries" (Nguyen, 2009, p. 80). Furthermore, this study and others have concluded that a major goal of the current crop of ROs in the region is to raise awareness in the region of the value of regionalization. UCTS and other such efforts are small steps in the right direction. This "small step" approach likely is the most appropriate for Asia.

In summary, the centrifugal forces seem to far outweigh the centripetal forces and include the following:

- Diversity and disparity of countries and HEIs in the region
- Historical and cultural tensions among the top three East Asian nations (China, Japan, and Korea)
- Variety of languages and ethnicities
- Differences in credit systems, curricula, and grading systems
- Lack of uniform QA standards
- Lack of financial resources and capacity for ROs to promote and market cooperation
- Lack of commitment at both national and institutional levels
- Risky "step by step" approach, no guarantee that there will be any spillover to the other levels
- Weak approach by AUN in building a cohesive community
- The ongoing debt mountain faced by countries around the world, as a result of the global COVID-19 pandemic in 2020. This will inhibit further progress toward regional higher education harmonization. The International Institute of Finance estimated that global debt reached US$277 trillion in 2020, and by 2030 could reach US$360 trillion. Once again, the effects will be unequal, with developing economies caught in a debt trap, at just the point when past debts, accruing from the GFC of 2008, were coming under control. Making matters worse, developed countries, seeking to reduce their expenditure, began cutting back on aid programs, including in education.

CONCLUSION

The immense complexity of the region called "Asia Pacific" reveals a potent mix of achievements and challenges. Several enduring challenges face education in general and higher education in particular, including the common aspiration in both Pacific nations as well as in many parts of Asia, to balance preserving and honoring local cultures and epistemologies, on one hand, and drawing on ideas from outside, largely from the West, on the other. These have been briefly discussed. This is not to say that there are not others, and other ways to dissect and analyze education in the Asia-Pacific. Certainly, there is a large and interesting literature on the notion of "the knowledge society" and what it means for such a dynamic region. The issue of diversity, equity, and intergroup relations remains substantial. One could discuss at length the complexities of education and occupational alignment. Religion is becoming a more significant feature of education in parts of Asia, with some concerns about rising extremism, in countries such as Afghanistan, Indonesia, Malaysia, Sri Lanka, and Myanmar (Alam, 2020; De Alwis, 2019; Van Bruineissen, 2013; Welch, 2015; Welch & Wahidyar, 2012).

However, it should be remembered that the challenges treated here are not bounded by impermeable borders but are conceptually porous. Capacity, access, and equity of course include issues of diversity; and regionalism has implications for mobility and migration. Furthermore, quality assurance is of importance for each of these challenges.

Quantitative and qualitative growth is evident in the Asia Pacific, albeit very differentially. Asia's leading universities now compete on the world stage, attracting staff and students from around the world, and collaborating with leading HEIs worldwide. At the same time, a further element threatens further progress. The "cancer of corruption," as a former president of the World Bank termed it, afflicts much of Asia, including in education (Welch, 2020b; World Bank, 2020). While the phenomenon is worldwide, the following table reveals a troubling pattern of substantial corruption afflicting many Asian systems.

The effects in education are pervasive. Defined as the abuse of entrusted power for private gain, corruption takes many forms, including fake degrees; paying others to write assignments or research; sexual abuse of students; financial misappropriation of research, teaching or other funds; accepting bribes to allow entry to underqualified applicants, award higher grades to students, or to institutional QA results; cronyism in institutional leadership appointments; sale of positions and promotions; plagiarism; misrepresentation of student research as being by the professor; payment for publication; misuse of research funds; falsification of research results; and ensuring that students cannot pass exams within the regular curriculum, and must thus enroll in private after-school classes, for fees. While such practices occur in both public and private HEIs (as well as in ministries and QA agencies), the poorly regulated expansion of private HEIs in several Asian systems in recent decades has made such invidious practices more pervasive (Transparency International, 2005; Welch, 2021b).

A chapter covering such a complex and large topic as "Asia-Pacific education" cannot detail all of the issues involved. The approach taken was to raise questions that provoke discussion and invite others to explore at more length and in greater depth the variety and excitement of how education is done in the world's most dynamic and diverse, rapidly changing world region.

Table 14.2. Corruption Perceptions Index (CPI) 2018, Selected Asia.

Country	CPI score	World Ranking
Singapore	85	3
Australia	77	13
Japan	73	18
South Korea	57	45
Malaysia	47	61
India	41	78
China	39	87
Indonesia	38	89
Philippines	36	99
Thailand	36	99
Việt Nam	33	117
Myanmar	29	132
Cambodia	20	161
Afghanistan	16	172

Source: Transparency International. Corruption Perceptions Index 2019.

NOTES

The current version draws on, and significantly amends, an earlier chapter by the late John Hawkins.

1. Until around the 18th century, the economies of China and India accounted for close to 50% of the world's economy.

2. This has been boosted through the EU's SHARE program, a component of which focuses on extending credit transfer both within the region, and with the EU, via the AECTS scheme.

REFERENCES

Academic Ranking of World Universities. (ARWU). (2019). http://www.shanghairanking.com/

Agarwal, P. (2009). *Indian higher education: Envisioning the future*. Sage.

Agarwal, P. (2015). Private Deemed Universities in India. *International Higher Education*, 49, 15–17.

Alam, S. (2020). The Rohingya and their fight for education. *Anadolu Agency*. https://www.aa.com.tr/en/asia-pacific/the-rohingya-and-their-fight-for-education/1743113

Altbach, P. (2005). India: World class universities? *International Higher Education*, 40, 18–20.

Altbach, P., & Postiglione, G. (2020). Will new security law prove a turning point for HE? University World News. https://www.universityworldnews.com/post.php?story=20200724110105165

Armstrong, S. (2020, November 17). Japan visit cements strategic ties for Prime Minister Morrison. *East Asia Forum*. https://www.eastasiaforum.org/2020/11/17/japan-visit-cements-strategic-ties-for-prime-minister-morrison/

Ash, A. (2016). Is China's Gaokao the world's toughest school exam? *The Guardian*. https://www.theguardian.com/world/2016/oct/12/gaokao-china-toughest-school-exam-in-world

Azmawati, D., & Quayle, L. (2017). Promoting ASEAN awareness at the higher education chalkface. *Contemporary Southeast Asia*, 39(1), 127–148.

Babones, S. (2020). Is there a future for Chinese students in Australia? In M. Natzler (Ed.). *UK Universities and China*. Higher Education Policy Institute. HEPI Report No. 132.

Bakalevu, S., Dorovolomo, J., & Liligeto, A. (2014). Melanesia: An overview. In M. Crossley, G. Hancock, & T. Sprague (Eds.), *Education in Australia, New Zealand and the Pacific* (pp. 267–268). Bloomsbury.

Bothwell, E. (2019, August 26). India's "institutes of eminence" scheme a "huge farce." *Times Higher Education*. https://www.timeshighereducation.com/news/indias-institutes-eminence-scheme-huge-farce#:~:text=Indi"s%20scheme%20to%20promote%20a,20%20campuses%20with%20the%20award

Bray, M., & Lykins, C. (2012). *Shadow education. Private supplementary tutoring and its implications for policy makers in Asia*. ADB and Comparative Education Research Centre (CERC) University of Hong Kong.

Carroll, T., & Jarvis, D. S. (Eds.). (2017). *Asia after the developmental state: Disembedding autonomy*. Cambridge University Press.

Chao, R. (2018). Regionalism, regionalisation of higher education, and higher education research: Mapping the development in regionalisation of higher education research. In J. Jung et al. (Eds.), *Researching higher education in Asia Quality excellence and governance* (pp. 73–109). Springer.

Chaudhuri, K. (1983). Foreign trade and balance of payments, 1757–1947. In D. Kumar (Ed.), *The Cambridge economic history of India: c1757–c1970* (Vol. 2). Cambridge University Press.

China Academic Degrees & Graduate Education Development Centre (CDGDC). (2015). *Introduction to the China Academic Degrees & Graduate Education Development Center in China*. http://www.cdgdc.edu.cn/ (in Chinese).

China Copyright and Media. (2015). Opinions concerning Further strengthening and improving propaganda and ideology work in higher education under new circumstances. Retrieved from https://chinacopyrightandmedia.wordpress.com/2015/01/19/opinions-concerning-further-strengthening-and-improving-propaganda-and-ideology-work-in-higher-education-under-new-circumstances/

Chou, C. P. (Ed.). (2014). *The SSCI syndrome in higher education: A local or global phenomenon*. Springer Science & Business Media.

Chou, C., & Chan, C-f. (2016). Trends in publication in the race for world-class university: The case of Taiwan. *Higher Education Policy, 29*(4), 431–449.

Chubb, I. (2013). *Partners in influence: How Australia and China related through Science*. Speech, Australian Centre on China and the World.

Connected world: Patterns of international collaboration captured by the nature index. (2020). Nature Index. https://www.natureindex.com/country-outputs/collaboration-graph/

Crossley, M., Bray, M., & Packer, S. (2011). *Education in small states: Policies and priorities*. Commonwealth Secretariat.

Dandy, J. (2018). Why some migrant school students do better than their local peers (they're not "just smarter"). *The Conversation*. https://theconversation.com/why-some-migrant-school-students-do-better-than-their-local-peers-theyre-not-just-smarter-93741

Davis, M. (2006). *Planet of slums*. Verso.

De Alwis, Dinesh. (2019, May 31). Fear of campus islamophobia after Easter bombings. *University World News*. https://www.universityworldnews.com/post.php?story=20190531074954315

Dent, C. (2016). *East Asian regionalism* (2nd ed.). Routledge.

Dore, R. (1997). *The diploma disease. Education, qualification and development*. Allen & Unwin.

Faiz, A., Karimi, A., & Teter, W. (2020). Universities are the key to pandemic recovery. *University World News*. https://www.universityworldnews.com/post.php?story=20200707083611676

Grattan, M. (2020). Scott Morrison pivots Australian Defence Force to meet more threatening regional outlook. *The Conversation*. https://theconversation.com/scott-morrison-pivots-australian-defence-force-to-meet-more-threatening-regional-outlook-141727

Green, B. (2020, January 30). Taiwan's universities are fighting for their lives, as birth rates plummet. *Ketagalan Media*. https://ketagalanmedia.com/2020/01/30/taiwans-universities-are-fighting-for-their-lives-as-birth-rates-plummet/#:~:text=According%20to%20the%20Ministry%20of,in%20which%20these%20universities%20operate.

Hao, J., & Welch, A. (2012). A tale of sea turtles: Job-seeking experiences of Hai Gui (high-skilled returnees) in China. *Higher Education Policy, 25*(2), 243–260.

Hawkins, J. (2011). The rhetoric and reality of mobility and migration in higher education. In D. Neubauer & K. Kuroda (Eds.) *Mobility, migration, and higher education transformation: The view from the Asia/Pacific region*. (pp. 105–123). Palgrave Macmillan.

Hawkins, J., Mok, K-h., & Neubauer, D. (Eds). (2012). *Higher education regionalism in Asia Pacific: Implications for governance, citizenship and university transformation*. Palgrave.

Higher Education Evaluation Centre (HEEC). (2007). *The handbook of quality assessment of undergraduate education: Questions and answers*. Higher Education Evaluation Centre. (in Chinese)

Holodny, E. (2017). The rise, fall, and comeback of the Chinese economy over the last 800 years. *Business Insider*. https://www.businessinsider.com.au/history-of-chinese-economy-1200-2017-2017-1?r=US&IR=T

Hsu, Y-p. (2019). The evolution of quality assurance in higher education in Taiwan: The changes and the effects at different levels. *Higher Education Policy*, *32*(3), 339–357.

Huang, F., & Welch, A. (2021). Asia Pacific: Introduction. In J. Thondhlana et al. (Eds.), *The Bloomsbury handbook of internationalization in the Global South* (pp. 41–46). Bloomsbury.

Institute for International Education. (2015). *Asia: The next higher education superpower*. Washington, IIE. https://www.iie.org/Research-and-Insights/Publications/Asia-The-Next-Higher-Education-Superpower

International Institute for Finance. (2020, November 18). *Global debt monitor: Attack of the debt tsunami*. https://www.iif.com/Research/Capital-Flows-and-Debt/Global-Debt-Monitor

International Monetary Fund. (IMF). (2020). *Regional economic outlook. Asia and the Pacific. navigating the pandemic: A multispeed recovery in Asia*. https://www.imf.org/en/Publications/REO/APAC/Issues/2020/10/21/regional-economic-outlook-apd#top

Iredale, R., & Guo, F. (Eds.). (2015). *Handbook of Chinese migration. Identity and well-being*. Cheltenham, Edward Elgar.

Ishikawa, M., & Sun, C. (2016). The paradox of autonomy: Japan's vernacular scholarship and the policy pursuit of "super global." *Higher Education Policy*, *29*(4), 451–472.

Ishikawa, M., & Sun, C. (2021). The paradox of autonomy: Japan's vernacular scholarship and the policy pursuit of "super global." In A. Welch & J. Li (Eds.), *Measuring up in higher education*. (pp. 249–274). Palgrave Macmillan.

Jacques, M. (2012). *When China rules the world: The end of the Western world and the birth of a new global order*. Penguin.

Jain, M. (2014, January 8). Teaching plays second fiddle as teachers with 'other jobs' reach disturbing proportions. *India Today*. https://www.indiatoday.in/magazine/education/story/19870531-teaching-plays-second-fiddle-as-teachers-with-other-jobs-reach-disturbing-proportions-798906-1987-05-31

Jayasuriya, K. (2003). Introduction: Governing the Asia Pacific, beyond the "new regionalism." *Third World Quarterly*, *24*(2), 199–215.

Jayasuriya, K. (2010). Learning by the market: Regulatory regionalism, Bologna, and accountability communities. *Globalisation, Societies and Education*, *8*(1), 7–22.

Johannson-Fua, S. (2014). Polynesia: In search of quality education. In M. Crossley, G. Hancock, & T. Sprague (Eds.), *Education in Australia, New Zealand and the Pacific* (pp. 287–314). Bloomsbury.

Jonaid, J. N. (2019). We, the Rohingya youth, demand our right to an education. *Al Jezeera*. https://www.aljazeera.com/opinions/2019/12/31/we-the-rohingya-youth-demand-our-right-to-an-education/

Jonbekova, D. (2020). The diploma disease in Central Asia: Student views about purpose of university education in Kazakhstan and Tajikistan. *Studies in Higher Education*, *45*(6), 1183–1196.

Jung, J. & Kim Y. (2018) Exploring regional and institutional factors of international students' dropout: The South Korea Case. *Higher Education Quarterly*, *72*(2), 141–159.

Kennedy, A. (2020, November 24). What's at stake in decoupling innovation? *East Asia Forum*. https://www.eastasiaforum.org/2020/11/24/whats-at-stake-in-decoupling-innovation/

Kerr, C. (1990). The internationalization of learning and the nationalization of the purposes of higher education: two laws of motion in conflict. *European Journal of Education*, 25(1), 5–22.

Kim, M., & Cho, J. (2014). An exam so stressful even planes are banned to avoid noise. ABC News. https://abcnews.go.com/International/exam-stressful-planes-banned-avoid-noise/story?id=26885757

Kumar, R. (2013, November 16). The reverse brain drain: why NRIs are returning to India. *NDTV*. https://www.ndtv.com/business/the-reverse-brain-drain-why-nris-are-returning-to-india-372361

Kuroda, K., Sugimura, M., Kitamura, Y., & Asada, S. (2018). Internationalisation of higher education and student mobility in Japan and Asia. Paper for the GEMR 2019 Report, *Migration, displacement and education. Building bridges not walls*. UNESCO. https://en.unesco.org/gem-report/report/2019/migration

Laurenceson, J., & Zhou, M. (2020). *The Australia China science boom*. Australia-China Relations Institute. https://www.australiachinarelations.org/sites/default/files/20200722%20Australia-China%20Relations%20Institute%20report_The%20Australia-China%20science%20boom_James%20Laurenceson%20Michael%20Zhou.pdf

Lee, H. L. (2020). The endangered Asian century: America, China, and the perils of confrontation. *Foreign Affairs*, 99(4), 52–64.

Lee, J., & Haupt, J. (2020). Winners and losers in US-China scientific research collaborations. *Higher Education*, 80, 57–74.

Lee, K-y, & Scalapino, R. (n.d.). Will East Asia's economic miracle return? http://www.nikkei-events.jp/future-of-asia/2000/000609_01.html

Lee, M., & Gopinathan, S. (2013). Centralized decentralization of higher education in Singapore. In H-H. Mok (Ed.), *Centralization and decentralization* (pp. 117–136). Comparative Education Research Centre, The University of Hong Kong. CERC Studies in Comparative Education.

Li, M. (2020). *Coping with Global asymmetries: A Study of China's English-language academic journals in the humanities and social sciences*. Unpublished PhD, University of Hong Kong.

Li, Y. (2010). Quality assurance in Chinese higher education. *Research in Comparative and International Education*, 5(1), 58–76.

Liu, S., & Liu, J. (2017). Quality assurance in Chinese higher education. In M. Sha & Q. Do (Eds.), *The rise of quality assurance in Asian higher education*. Chandos

Macmillan, J., & Greene, A. (2020) Australia to spend $270 building larger military to prepare for poorer, more dangerous; World and rise of China. Retrieved from https://www.abc.net.au/news/2020-06-30/australia-unveils-10-year-defence-strategy/12408232

Marginson, S., & Yang, L. (2020). *Higher education and public good in East and West*. Centre for Global Higher Education. https://www.researchcghe.org/perch/resources/publications/research-findings-no-5june-2020.pdf

McDermott, D. (2017). Towards a Southeast Asian higher education area. UWN. https://www.universityworldnews.com/post.php?story=20170704111700957

Medcalf, R. (2020). *Contest for the Indo Pacific: Why China won't map the future*. LaTrobe University Press.

Mohanty, S. (2012). India: Culture and learning. In P. Jarvis & M. Watts (Eds.), *Routledge International Handbook of Learning* (pp. 530–531). Routledge.

Mok, K-h. (2000). Impact of globalization: A study of quality assurance systems of higher education in Hong Kong and Singapore. *Comparative Education Review*, 44(2), 148–174.

Mok, K-h. (2005). Fostering entrepreneurship: Changing role of government and higher Education Governance in Hong Kong. *Research Policy*, 34, 537–554.

Mok, K-h., & Han, X. (2017). Higher education governance and policy in China: Managing decentralization and transnationalism. *Policy and Society*, 36(1)44.

Mou, B. (2009). On some methodological issues concerning Chinese philosophy: An introduction. *History of Chinese philosophy*. Routledge.

Mozur, P., & Myers, S. L. (2020). U.S. and China, caught in "ideological spiral," drift toward Cold War. *New York Times*. https://www.nytimes.com/2020/07/14/world/asia/cold-war-china-us.html

Musselin, C. (2009). The side effects of the Bologna Process on national institutional settings: The case of France. In A. Amaral, G. Neave, C. Musselin, & P. Maassen (Eds.), *European integration and the governance of higher education and research* (pp. 181–205). Springer.

Niazi, S. (2018, July 12). "Institutes of Eminence" named, but not all exist yet. *UWN*. https://www.universityworldnews.com/post.php?story=20180712000904958

Neelakantan, S. (2007a, June 4). Indian Prime Minister promises to establish many more universities and colleges. *Chronicle of Higher Education*.

Neelakantan, S. (2007b, June 25). India's Prime Minister assails universities as below average and "dysfunctional." *Chronicle of Higher Education*.

Neubauer, D., & Tanaka, Y. (Eds.). (2011). *Access, equity and capacity in Asia-Pacific higher education*. Palgrave MacMillan.

Niedermeier, F., & Pohlenz, P. (2019). *State of play and development needs. Higher education quality assurance in the ASEAN region* (2nd ed.). DAAD.

Neubauer, D., & Bilgalke, T. (2009). *Higher education in Asia/Pacific: Quality and the public good*. Palgrave MacMillan.

Nguyen, A. T. (2009). The role of regional organizations in East Asian regional cooperation and integration in the field of higher education. *Asian Regional Integration Review*, Waseda University, I, 69–82.

OECD. (2014). The unprecedented expansion of the global middle class: An update. *OECD Observer*, 12–13. https://oecdobserver.org/news/fullstory.php/aid/3681/An_emerging_middle_class.html

OECD. (2019). PISA 2018 Results (Vol. I). *What students know and can do*. https://read.oecd-ilibrary.org/education/pisa-2018-results-volume-i/summary/english_a9b5930a-en#page1

Oxfam. (2020). Half a billion people could be pushed into poverty by COVID-19: Dignity not destitution. https://oxfamilibrary.openrepository.com/bitstream/handle/10546/620976/mb-dignity%20not%20destitution-an-economic-rescue-plan-for-all-090420-en.pdf;jsessionid=9AA4AD252C0E6024E8A68E5A15BBC6C5?sequence=1

Phillips, T. (2016). China universities must become Communist Party 'strongholds', says Xi Jinping. https://www.theguardian.com/world/2016/dec/09/china-universities-must-become-communist-party-strongholds-says-xi-jinping

Prasad, V. S. (2009). Quality assurance in higher education: A developing country perspective and experience. In T. Bigalke & D. Neubauer (Eds.), *Higher education in Asia Pacific: quality and the public good* (pp. 121–131). Palgrave Macmillan.

PTI. (2014). One out of three young graduates unemployed in India: Labour Ministry. *Indian Express*. https://indianexpress.com/article/india/india-others/one-out-of-three-young-graduates-unemployed-in-india-labour-ministry/

Ravi, S., Gupta, N., & Nagaraj, P. (2019). *Reviving higher education in India*. Brookings Institute.

Reagan, T. (2018). Handed down from the ancestors. Indigenous educational thought and practice in Oceania. In Reagan (Ed.), *Non-Western Educational Traditions* (pp. 321–346). Routledge.

Robertson, S. (2008). "Europe/Asia" regionalism, higher education and the production of world order. *Policy Futures in Education*, 6(6), 718–729.

Rozman, G. (2005). Regionalization in Northeast Asia. In T. Satow & E. Li, *The possibility of an East Asian community: Rethinking the Sino-Japanese relationship*. Ochanomizu Shobo.

Schuman, M. (2019). The US can't make allies take sides over China. *The Atlantic*. https://www.theatlantic.com/international/archive/2019/04/us-allies-washington-china-belt-road/587902/

SCMP. (2020). Can ASEAN dance its way out of having to take sides in the US-China Conflict? https://www.scmp.com/comment/opinion/article/3101449/can-asean-dance-its-way-out-having-take-sides-us-china-conflict

Shameel, A. (2003). The new Asian realism: economics and politics of the Asia Cooperation dialogue. *Strategic Studies*, 23(4), 93–115.

Sharma, A. N., et al. (2014). Fiji; Evolution of education from colonial to modern times. In M. Crossley, G. Hancock, & T. Sprague (Eds.), *Education in Australia, New Zealand and the Pacific* (pp. 243–264). Bloomsbury.

Sharma, Y. (2018a). Ministry ends hundreds of Sino-foreign HE partnerships. *UWN*. https://www.universityworldnews.com/post.php?story=20180706154106269

Sharma Y. (2018b). Beijing Signals tighter control over dissenting scholars. https://www.universityworldnews.com/post.php?story=20181103144829874

Steger, M. (2009). *Globalization: A very short introduction*. Oxford University Press.

Stella, A. (2002). Institutional accreditation in India. *International Higher Education* (IHE).

Tan, E-c. (2011). Singapore National University's Mission to be a leading global university. Quality in higher education: Identifying developing and sustaining best practices in the APEC region. APEC Human Resources Development Working Group. https://www.apec.org/docs/default-source/Publications/2011/10/Quality-in-Higher-Education-Identifying-Developing-and-Sustaining-Best-Practices-in-the-APEC-Region/2011_hrd_quality_education.pdf

Thaman, K. H. (2014). Pacific Island countries: An overview. In M. Crossley, G. Hancock, & T. Sprague (Eds.), *Education in Australia, New Zealand and the Pacific* (pp. 199–217). Bloomsbury.

Tolley, H., & E. Coxon. (2014). Aid to Pacific education: From projects to SWAps. In M. Crossley, G. Hancock, & T. Sprague (Eds.), *Education in Australia, New Zealand and the Pacific* (pp. 177–197). Bloomsbury.

Transparency International. (2005). Stealing the Future. Corruption in the Classroom. https://www.transparency.org/en/publications/stealing-the-future-corruption-in-the-classroom-ten-real-world-experiences

Tsoi, G. & Wai, L-c. (2020). Hong Kong Security Law: What is it and is it worrying? https://www.bbc.com/news/world-asia-china-52765838

Underwood, R., Andreas, R., & Nabobo-Baba, U. (2014). Micronesia: An overview of the Federated States of Micronesia. In M. Crossley, G. Hancock, & T. Sprague (Eds.), *Education in Australia, New Zealand and the Pacific* (pp. 315–334). Bloomsbury.

UNESCO. (2014). *Education Systems in ASEAN+6 Countries: A Comparative Analysis of Selected Educational Issues*. UNESCO.

UNESCO. (2018). The Tokyo Convention: A new era for mobility and internationalisation of higher education in the Asia Pacific. https://bangkok.unesco.org/content/tokyo-convention-new-era-mobility-and-internationalisation-higher-education-asia-pacific

UNESCO. (2020). Education: From disruption to recovery. https://en.unesco.org/covid19/educationresponse

UN Human Rights Council. (2020). The parlous state of poverty eradication. https://chrgj.org/wp-content/uploads/2020/07/Alston-Poverty-Report-FINAL.pdf

University World News. (2013). China recognizes more higher educational institutions. https://www.universityworldnews.com/post.php?story=20130118143535690

Van Bruineissen, M. (2013). Contemporary Developments in Indonesian Islam: Explaining the "Conservative Tour" Singapore, *ISEAS*, 107, 194, 199, 215.

Vogel, E. (2010). Regionalism in Asia: Why we should stick with existing structures. *East Asia Forum*, https://www.eastasiaforum.org/2010/03/30/regionalism-in-asia-why-we-should-stick-with-existing-structures/

Volante, L., Klinger, D., & Bilgili, O. (Eds.). (2018). *Immigrant student achievement and education policy: Cross-cultural approaches* (Vol. 9). Springer.

Wang, L. (2014). Quality assurance in higher education in China: Control, accountability and freedom. *Policy and Society*, 33(3), 253–262.

Welch, A. (2008). Myths and modes of mobility: The changing face of academic mobility in the global era. In F. Dervin, *Students, staff and academic mobility in higher education* (pp. 291–311). Cambridge Scholars Press.

Welch, A. (2011). *Higher education in South East Asia. Blurring borders, changing balance*. Routledge.

Welch, A. (2014). Richer relations? Four decades of ASEAN-Australia relations in higher education. In B. He & S. Wood (Eds.), *The Australia-ASEAN Dialogue. Tracing 40 Years of Partnership* (pp. 185–203). Palgrave Macmillan.

Welch, A. (2015) Countering campus extremism. *University World News*. https://www.universityworldnews.com/post.php?story=20150914202706966

Welch, A. (2016). Audit culture and academic production. Re-shaping Australian social science research output 1993–2013. *Higher Education Policy*, 29(4), 511–538.

Welch, A. (2017). Immigrant student achievement and education policy in Australia. In L. L. Volante, L. Klinger, & O. Bilgili (Eds.), *Immigrant student achievement and education policy*. Springer.

Welch, A. (2018a). China's southern borderlands and ASEAN higher education: A cartography of connectivity. In P. Meusburger, M. Heffernan, & L. Suarsana (Eds.), *Geographies of the University* (pp. 567–602). Springer.

Welch, A. (2018b). Global ambitions: Internationalization and China's rise as knowledge hub. *Frontiers of Education in China*, 13(4), 513–531.

Welch, A. (2019). Higher education in Asia. In J. Rury & E. Tamura (Eds.), *The Oxford handbook in the history of education*. Oxford University Press.

Welch, A. (2020a). Australia: History v geography in an evolving national system. In D. Kapur, L. Kong, & D. Malone (Eds.), *The Oxford handbook on higher education in Asia*. Oxford University Press.

Welch, A. (2020b). Governance and corruption in East and Southeast Asian higher education: Close cousins, close encounters. In D. Jarvis & G. Capano (Eds.), *Convergence and diversity in the governance of higher education: Comparative perspectives*. Cambridge University Press.

Welch, A. (2021a). Neo-liberalism in comparative and international education. Theory, practice, paradox. In T. Jules, R. Shields, & M. Thomas (Eds.), *Handbook of theory in comparative and international education* (pp. 201–215). Bloomsbury.

Welch, A. (2021b). Private higher education in East and South East Asia. Growth, challenges, implications. *UNESCO GMER 2021 Non-State Actors in Education*.

Welch, A. (2022). A plague on higher education? COVID, campus and culture wars in Australian universities. *Higher Education Quarterly*. https://doi.org/10.1111/hequ.12377

Welch, A., & Cai, H-x. (2011). Enter the dragon: The Internationalization of China's higher education system. In J. Ryan (Ed.), *China's higher education reform and internationalization*. Routledge.

Welch, A., & Hao, J. (2016). Global argonauts: Returnees and diaspora as sources of innovation in China and Israel. *Globalisation, Societies and Education*, 14(2), 272–297.

Welch, A., & Wahidyar, A. (2012). Evolution, revolution, reconstruction: The interrupted development of higher education in Afghanistan. M-f Buck & M. Kabaum (Eds.), *Ideen und Realitäten der Universitäten*. Peter Lang.

Welch, A., & Wahidyar, A. (2019). Quality assurance in Afghan higher education: Achievements and challenges. *Asian Education and Development Studies*. https://doi.org/10.1108/AEDS-09-2018-0146

Welch, A., & Yang, R. (2010). Globalisation, transnational academic mobility and the Chinese knowledge diaspora: An Australian case study. *Discourse: Studies in the Cultural Politics of Education, 31*(5), 593–607.

Welch A., & Zhang, Z. (2008). Higher education and global talent flows: Brain drain, overseas Chinese intellectuals, and diasporic knowledge networks. *Higher Education Policy, 21*(4), 519–537.

Wen, W. (2016). China's approach towards HE regional cooperation with ASEAN. In C. Collins, M. Lee, J. Hawkins, & D. Neubauer et al. (Eds.), *Handbook on Asia Pacific higher education* (pp. 173–182). Palgrave Macmillan.

Wildavsky, B. (2010). *The great brain race: How global universities are reshaping the world*. Princeton University Press.

Wood, T. (2020, April 14). *COVID-19, and Australian and New Zealand aid to the Pacific*. DEVPolicy Blog. https://devpolicy.org/covid-19-and-australian-and-new-zealand-aid-to-the-pacific-20200414/

World Bank. (2020). *Enhancing government effectiveness and transparency: The fight against corruption*. World Bank. http://documents1.worldbank.org/curated/en/235541600116631094/pdf/Enhancing-Government-Effectiveness-and-Transparency-The-Fight-Against-Corruption.pdf

Xie, Y., & Zhou, X. (2014). Income inequality in today's China. *Proceedings of the National Academy of Sciences, 111*(19), 6928–6933. doi:10.1073/pnas.1403158111

Yang, R. (2020). Political culture and higher education governance in Chinese societies: Some reflections. *Frontiers of Chinese Higher Education, 15*(2), 187–221.

Yang, R., & Y. Gao, (2020). Innovating cultural competence education in the global era: Insights from Fei Xiaotong's theory of cultural self-awareness. *Frontiers of Chinese Education, 15*(4).

Yeom, M. (2013). Tensions between autonomy and accountability: Access, equity and capacity in Korean education. In D. Neubauer & Y. Tanaka (Eds.), *Access, equity and capacity in Asia-Pacific higher education*. Palgrave Macmillan.

Yepes, C. P. (2006). World regionalization of higher education: Policy proposals for international organizations. *Higher Education Policy, 19*, 111–128.

Yonezawa, A. (2015, Summer). The reintroduction of accreditation in Japan: A government initiative. *International Higher Education, 40*, 20–22. https://ejournals.bc.edu/index.php/ihe/article/view/7486

Zhou, H-w. (2011). Confucianism and legalism: A model of the national strategy of governance in ancient China. *Frontiers of Economics in China, 6*(4), 616–637.

15

Living Well Together in Our Oceanic "Sea of Islands"

Epistemology and Ontology in Comparative Education

Kabini Sanga
Victoria University of Wellington

David Fa'avae
University of Waikato

Martyn Reynolds
Victoria University of Wellington

ABSTRACT

By its nature, comparative education values diversity. Respectfully studying how different groups pursue education provides opportunities to learn about the variety of human experience, expand the boundaries of the field, and ultimately re-understand ourselves. At its core, the field leverages the dynamic space between life as culturally located and being human. This chapter contributes value to comparative education from an Oceanic viewpoint. Oceania is the world region with more water and languages than any other. Because of its diversity and colonial histories, Oceania is a site of creative tension between regionalism and self-determination. Unsurprisingly, conflict exists in the region. However, a key need in our "sea of islands" for sustainability is to live well together. Faced with the uncertainties of the future such as climate change, mutual understanding and support are at a premium. The collaboration of writers; Solomon Islander, Tongan, and Anglo-Welsh, embodies this, as does the chapter's woven mat-based structure. The thrust of this chapter is that through walking backward into the future and embracing solidarity through diversity, we can promote a sustainable educational journey that offers the hope of continuity in the face of the challenges ahead.

In his introduction to a previous edition of this book, Arnove (2013) describes the contribution of comparative and international education (CIE) to "international understanding and peace" as significant but "previously underemphasized." In his account, the relative diminution of this strand has been somewhat rectified as some have recognized "how forces from areas of the world previously considered distant and remote" (p. 17) have affected their lives. This chapter presents ideas from an area that some may consider far-flung, but which is home and the center of the world to those of us who live here. We offer ontological and epistemological gifts from what Hau'ofa (1994) called our "sea of islands" (p. 148) to those near and far who are interested in the dialectic of the local and global.

Ontology refers to the committed study of what might exist, embracing approaches that are substantialist hence, ontology as a substance or thing, and fluxist, ontology as occurrents, events, and processes. In this chapter, we assume ontology as subjective, intangible, "soft" and internal to a person's perception and experience. Epistemology refers to the grounds for knowledge, and epistemological debates center on how people know or understand their social reality (Sanga, 2004). That is, what is known, how, by whom, why and what can be passed on as "truth" to others. In the Pacific region social and cultural diversity implies multiple ontologies and epistemologies.

The organization of the chapter represents a woven mat. Such artifacts, often made from pandanus, are ubiquitous across Oceania. Separate strands are woven together from two directions to create a coherent and useful whole. Mats can be made by individuals, but often groups undertake the preparatory work as well as make contributions to weaving if the mat is large. Here, we weave sections organized around universal aspects of education together with strands that give salient accounts from specific locations. The final section attends to the wider context of such weaving. This mat is a cooperative effort, unrolled in Oceanic welcome to those from near and far.

The chapter starts by describing the dynamic diversity of Oceania. In a fractal of the global-local dynamic, both conflict and potentially creative tension between regionalism, nationhood, island-based societies, and specific language groups and clans (Bray, 1993) play out here. However, Oceanic relationalities, the state of being related, are ontologically unavoidable and always a matter of negotiation. Thus, we introduce ourselves as authors and friends who exercise mutual responsibility for our education and growth.

Next, colonial legacies are dealt with in relational terms. This does not deny the violence of the past (or present). However, the approach supports working for a future where relationships between knowledge systems are not made sense of through the metaphor of an eclipse (Turner et al., 2013), but through a *motutapu*, a sacred island space of negotiation (Johansson-Fua, 2016). Values, pedagogy, and curriculum are all areas of education where fruitful Oceanic negotiations can be seen.

Then, three diverse case studies are woven into the chapter. Two are island-based; one from the Solomon Islands in the area known as Melanesia, and the other from Tonga, a Polynesian kingdom. The third looks at education in the Pacific diaspora as it has developed in Aotearoa New Zealand, a space home to Indigenous Kaupapa Māori education. Having woven into the mat the strands of these case studies, we offer examples of Oceanic responses in the context of the ecocide of climate change.

A SKETCH OF OCEANIA

The ocean named Pacific by the Spanish-employed Portuguese-born navigator, Ferdinand Magellan, in 1519, was calm as he experienced it. He was lost in a vast body of nearly 165 million square kilometers that contains more than half the free water on the planet (NOAA, 2020). However, this vast reserve, this Moana (Ferris-Leary, 2013), had been a familiar home to many for generations. Crossing its vastness from at least the time of the Lapita people whose migrations began around 1500 BCE (Irwin, 2005), voyagers made their homes both on and off the water, spreading out in a series of migrations. Oceania is the term we chose to employ in this chapter for our region. The word focuses on the water that connects us all. For many, as Hau'ofa (2000) pointed out, the water of the "ocean in us" serves to trace Oceanic collectivity, both physical and imagined.

Oceania is home to around 25% of the world's languages (Tryon, 2009). Solomon Islands, for example, is home to approximately 80 language groups (Guy et al., 2000). On some maps, Oceania is conveniently divided into three: Melanesia, Polynesia, and Micronesia. However, this erases histories of exploration, migrations, alliances, and trade. There are "Polynesian" populations on so-called Melanesian islands such as Rennell and Bellona in Solomon Islands (Kuschel, 1988), and close trade and marriage links between Melanesian Fiji and Polynesian Tonga (Barnes & Hunt, 2005). Oceanic interactions have roots that go back in time and are evident in mythology (Ka'ili, 2005), concepts, and language (Wendt, 1999).

That said, any idyll of a totally pacific Oceania region is a construct of selective blindness. Regionalism can both support and obstruct self-determination (Bray, 1993). The region is no stranger to collisions between diversity and the homogeneity implied by the carving of nation-states; nor to the injustices of ongoing dominance based on colonial claims. Close examination reveals conflict in the region of many kinds: struggles between settler and indigenous peoples such as in West Papua (Mollet, 2007); histories of inter-island tensions within nation-states such as in Solomon Islands (Burnett & Dorovolomo, 2007); the need for conflict resolution, often an educative role of Oceanic women, in circumstances sharpened by successionist calls as in Bougainville/Papua New Guinea (Tankunani Sirivi & Taleo, 2017); and political activities that produce conflict as in Fiji (Halapua, 2008).

Conflicts also emerge at conceptual and philosophical levels as traditional thinking meets introduced perspectives. Such conflicts, however, are not uniform; the forces that are introduced may resemble each other across contexts, but the effects they have are singular. This is because points of both alignment and variation can be drawn between the way key concepts are understood and made significant in social life within multiple Oceania ontologies and epistemologies. Gender, for example, is always present but appreciated and represented in diverse, nuanced ways. Nanau (2017) describes the way gender, naming, and knowledge are connected in the matrilineal structure of the Tathimboko region of Guadalcanal, Solomon Islands; Taumoefalau (2017) shows the complexities of gendered relationships through the cultural-linguistic making of the Tongan female self, and Borja-Quichocho-Calvo (2017) presents the power of Chamoru women as leaders through traditional song narratives and their application in modern Guam as survivance. In all three contexts, introduced ideas and practices in the form of patriarchy or conceptualization of gender (Angoro, 2018) cut across long-standing thinking. The effect is the erosion or other alteration of the way gender plays out as the traditional conflicts with the introduced.

The actuality and aftereffects of various conflicts, political and philosophical, exist in the here and now. Thus, it is important to imagine the potential of cooperation and unity to shape the future. After all, education exists in the present but is valuable for its potential contribution to an imagined better world. Recent imaginers of the region include Crocombe (1976), whose *Pacific Way* speaks of collectivity as "a product of common environmental and cultural experience" (p. 38); and Hau'ofa (1994) who, when confronted by relational "belittlement" (p. 149) in a postcolonial world, says "[t]here is a gulf of difference between viewing the Pacific as *islands in a far sea* and as *a sea of islands*" (p. 152) in which one belongs. Bevacqua (2010), from Guam, reminds us that the idea of regional collectivity "can be a powerful force, but it is not a magic spell, it cannot alone be the goal or the hope, but rather we should focus on what it can promote or help push into being" (p. 87). Hope requires action and commitment, individual and collective. Despite and because of our diversity as authors, not hiding from but valuing our differences, this imperative for action inspires our relational ontological approach to weaving this chapter and to CIE more generally.

A further complicating factor in any conversation regarding Oceania is the way its nature and boundaries are understood. That space is not a simply held idea in this region can be exemplified in three ways. First, Gegeo (2001) from Mala'ita in Solomon Islands describes the Kwara'ae perspective of place as a matter of indigeneity that involves inhabiting a Kwara'ae ontology and epistemology. This is less a geographic and more a philosophical positioning. Understood differently, space is "the location a Kwara'ae person occupies while in motion or circulation" (pp. 494–495). When Kwara'ae shift in space, such as through migration, movement can be understood as an act that expands place through its portability. Gegeo (2001) continues, "because of the possibility of space, a person can be anywhere and still be inextricably tied to place" (p. 495). This has implications for the way Oceania is viewed, especially given the number of Oceanic people who spend their lives in territories such as Utah, California, and beyond.

Second, from a Tongan perspective Ka'ili (2005) describes space as relational. He discusses socio-spatial links across the distances between Hawai'i and Tonga, and across the time between generations. These relational links traverse temporal and physical space and maintain or renew connection through recognition, obligation and mutual assistance. Exchanges are a key aspect of renewal. These can be in the form of remittances, cultural knowledge, goods, or people. Relational space is not bound to physical location, not to the cartographic boundaries of Oceania.

Third, in a call supported by McHugh (2000), Lilomaiava-Doktor (2009) advocates for cultural ways of understanding migration to include cultural conceptions of movement, space, and time. Most literature embodies a Euro-American vision of space in diasporic migration (Lilomaiava-Doktor, 2009). The Euro-American view is negotiated through a dichotomy between local and global where movement is toward or away from the center. This vision is generally focused on an economic analysis using key concepts of development and remittance (e.g., Brown et al., 2014). It has the potential to portray remittances as a one-way economic support for certain economies by others.

However, in a way that relates to the observations of Gegeo (2001) and Ka'ili (2005), Lilomaiava-Doktor (2009) discusses the intersections between the concepts of *malaga* (movement back and forth; migration) and *va* (relational space between) to point to "the importance of thinking about migration more socially than territorially" (p. 22). Through this lens, the migration of people in Oceania is creative and circular. Migration as *malaga* is not focussed solely on destination. It has metaphysical dimensions and is part of a "moral economy" (p. 19), albeit partially achieved through economic means. In this economy, *malaga* implies an expansion of relationally defined space.

As Smith (1999) commented, framing research through the epistemology of research participants is an act of decolonization. It can also be an attempt to avoid the imposition of (outsider-) researcher or hegemonic paradigms, ontologies, and structures on research. These three perspectives suggest that migration from and to Oceania is more nuanced than might be seen at first by observers from distant shores whose thinking is cartographically framed. Ontologically speaking, many Oceania people understand the boundaries of the region to be less fixed and more fluid than the maps would have us believe. Relationality is the key to these viewpoints.

A RELATIONAL APPROACH

Positionality involves accounting for who one is; relational positionality (Crossa, 2012) accounts for who one is in relation to others (Fasavalu & Reynolds, 2019). This is consistent with the Oceanic idea of the relational self (Mila-Schaaf, 2006; Vaai & Nabobo-Baba, 2017). Thus, we offer brief statements about ourselves and our relationships as weavers and writers.

Kabini: At the time of writing, I am teaching at Victoria University of Wellington and living in Aotearoa New Zealand while I remain the principal *alafa* (leader) of the Gwailao tribe of East Mala'ita, Solomon Islands; a role I was socialized for since birth and while growing up in my indigenous tribal community. In theocratic indigenous tribal Mala'ita, my daily upbringing was within a theonomous or deity-centered culture. While attending schools in Solomon Islands and elsewhere, my socialization was influenced by an autonomous or locally self-regulating cultural worldview. As an adult working within formal organizations including schools and government departments, I also learned to live by the dictates of a more heteronomous culture. This meant adapting to patterns of behavior derived from multiple sources. In sum, throughout my life, I have been a straddler of value tensions and conflicts from multiple ontological-epistemological worlds and a student in building bridges in such worlds. Writing with my friends Martyn and David is therefore an absolute joy.

David: At this moment in time, my wife 'Elenoa, our son, Daniel, and I have returned to Aotearoa New Zealand after spending six years of educational and voluntary service in Tonga and other parts of Oceania. Although many Tongan people have journeyed into the diaspora, they maintain and continue their sense of service and provide provisions for their *kāinga* (extended family) back in their ancestral homeland. As a teacher-educator at a university in Aotearoa New

Zealand, I honor my ancestors by choosing to practice and share my Tongan ways of being and knowing through research engagement, publications, workshops, and mentoring of the next generation. It is my hope that through me, Daniel will be able to value and honor our *kāinga*'s legacy of love, service, leadership, hope, determination, and resilience. *Koe ngaahi taumu'a ia na'e tatala 'ehe fanga tamai moe fanga fa'ē mei he kuo hili. Tu'a 'ofa atu.* [These are our ancestral aspirations imparted and unfolded by our fathers and mothers from the past. With love and humility as a *tu'a* (commoner).]

Martyn: As an Anglo-Welsh person brought up in south London, I am a relatively recent arrival in the Oceanic region. However, taking the view that leadership is service, I seek to give where I can. In the recent past, I have extended my educational efforts beyond the secondary sector, my field for over three decades across the jurisdictions of the United Kingdom, Papua New Guinea, Tonga, and Aotearoa New Zealand. I now provide educative support and research services in Aotearoa New Zealand and across the Oceania region, including through coauthoring. I write as a learner in the field of education in Aotearoa New Zealand in order to honor developments in Māori and Pacific education with which I have engaged as a practitioner. I am happy to join with Kabini to contribute to this chapter and as a consequence to be reassociated with my friend and colleague of many years, David.

Together we represent elements of the diversity of those who reside in Oceania. We embrace the common purpose of CIE: living well together.

THE COLONIAL AS RELATIONAL

Oceania carries negative colonial legacies such as blackbirding (Summy, 2009) in which Pacific islanders were captured and taken as forced labor to plantations, and the depopulating effect of influenza (Tomkins, 1992). As Bevacqua (2010) reminds us, some Oceanic islands remain colonial territories. Here we approach colonialism with an educational focus centered on relationships.

Before Oceania was visited by Europeans, education existed here, both formal and informal. For example, there was a center of great learning at Taputapuatea Marae on Ra'iatea (Salmond, 2005). Clan knowledge was, and still is, transferred through pedagogic means such as storying and discussion (Sanga & Reynolds, 2020a). However, formal schooling arrived with missionaries and colonial administrations (Bray, 1993; Jensz, 2012) and remains as a testament to the longevity of prefabricated expressions of European thinking exported around the globe (Sanga & Reynolds, 2020b).

The nature of classroom space, seating arrangements, a competitive ethic, written examinations, and curriculum content are architectural features of colonial practice. Where Oceanic developments in formal education take place, they are negotiated within these parameters. Thus, the configuration of relationships between local and other traditions and knowledges is significant. Key questions for CIE include: Whose epistemology counts and how? In whose ontology should education make sense and why? What might it mean for traditions to live well together?

One initiative that seeks to reshape the relationships between knowledges is the Tree of Opportunity (Pene et al., 2002). This imagines education as a tree rooted in home soil producing locally valued fruits, but capable of receiving and nurturing grafted stems and their fruit from elsewhere. Embedded in the Rethinking Pacific Education Initiative (Nabobo-Baba, 2012), this image of forward-looking equitable relationships between knowledges and traditions has informed thinking across the region (e.g., McDonald, 2001; Otunuku, 2011) despite critiques (Moli, 1993, cited in McDonald, 2001; Burnett, 2013).

Other metaphors also reimagine relational configuration. For example, the *motutapu* (Johansson-Fua, 2016) is "a place for negotiations, a middle ground, a place for rejuvenation as well as a place to launch new journeys" (p. 36). The key to progress in renegotiating relationships in education is not to turn back the clock but to honor local pasts as a way to move forward. Values, pedagogy, and curriculum are all strands of education where fruitful Oceanic negotiations can be seen. Examples of each will be given.

(RE)NEGOTIATED RELATIONSHIPS

Values

Turning first to the strand of values, an indicative example of renegotiated relationships underpins the work of Solomon Islander Billy Fito'o (2016). He describes *kastom* (customary thinking) about values and citizenship and describes Kwara'ae rural villagers explaining "a good citizen was someone who can *saungailana kwaima'anga* (create a space for love and respect for everyone in the community), through creating *tuafiku'anga ani kwaima'anga ma aroaro'anga* (living together in love, peace, and harmony through mutual relationships)" (p. 177). Fito'o (2016) suggests that such values do not necessarily sit well with Citizenship Education as practiced in Solomon Islands, discussed later. He argues for a "*wantok*-centric citizenship framework" that embraces Melanesian ethics of relationality and obligation, and "recognizes . . . culture, spirituality, and modern institutions as complementary" (p. 62). This act of balance looks both forward to fast-changing aspects of life and backward to *kastom* values. It has potential to delineate a space in which to articulate the complexities that exist in Solomon Islands between nationhood, regionalism, and clan identity, significant in a state previously riven by ethnic tensions.

Pedagogy

Education is a relational activity in which knowledge is socially constructed (Brownlee, 2004). Social construction is significant in Oceania where groups hold the self to be social (Mila-Schaaf, 2006; Sanga, 2017; Vaai & Nabobo-Baba, 2017). The use of space can properly be viewed as an ontological expression of the significance of relationships in education. As an example, Naisilisili (2012) draws on the model of the Fijian *kava* or *yaqona* circle (Naisilisili, 1998) to organize classroom space. *Yaqona* consumption is a time of learning through conversation. *Yaqona* is traditionally consumed in a circle of distribution with a "top end" at one side. In the pedagogic model, this is the place for the teacher.

Naisilisili's (1998) classroom arrangement diverts power from the colonial structure of the dominant teacher through a pedagogy of exchange in the space of the circle. Understanding this arrangement has the potential to "encourage an exchange of views and ideas as everyone, including the teacher appears to operate from the same level [and because] the circular arrangement could denote respect for the teacher as well as between students" (Naisilisili, 1998, p. 210). As a space for exchange, the classroom circle expresses an ontology where learning is enhanced through collaboration and each person is recognized as part of the collective process. Similar processes practiced on a wider scale have reaped political benefits in conflict situations in the Oceania region (Brigg et al., 2015; Halapua, 2008).

Curriculum

Epistemology is central to developments in curriculum design and implementation; beliefs about knowledge structure are encoded in content, sequence, and values in the curriculum. Two examples are given of creative tension playing out in curriculum negotiation between putative universality and diversity. First, Panapa (2014) represents the concept of well-being as an octopus in Tuvaluan education. This avoids the narrowing of the concept to introduced ideas of physical health, hygiene, and diet. The octopus arms reference multiple aspects of traditional understandings of well-being such as relational and spiritual wellness. The image also references integration and interrelation between all aspects of the concept as it emphasizes holism. Second, the language of science and the practice of traditional agriculture are brought in a complementary relationship where Tonga science embraces the *ufi* or yam garden (Otunuku & Thaman, 2018). This notion can be extended by the inclusion of social ranking as an aspect of food beyond nutrition. It bridges science and social science through traditional knowledge that supports deep-level sense-making of Tongan food cultivation and consumption (Tu'inukuafe, 2019).

Harnessing and honoring Oceanic wisdom in education requires balanced relationships (Koya-Vaka'uta, 2017). These examples of (re-)negotiated relationships organized through the widely utilized strands of values, pedagogy, and curriculum show how the global and local can exist together productively in Oceanic education. However, much work remains to be done to realize the rich diet available from the Tree of Opportunity (Pene et al., 2002), or the full range of possibilities pregnant in a *motutapu* (Johansson-Fua, 2016).

CASE STUDIES

Having presented strands organized around universal aspects of education, we now cross-weave three place-based case studies to contextualize ways that ontological and epistemological considerations of value to CIE are developing in situ.

Solomon Islands

The modern state of Solomon Islands with its population of 680,809 people (Solomon Islands Government, 2020) comprises an estimated 1,000 tribal communities, the majority of whom continue to live on ancestral lands/islands in clan-tribal settlements throughout the archipelago of 900 islands. These tribal communities can be classified superficially as Melanesian, Polynesian, and Micronesian and anthropologically as patrilineal or matrilineal. A vast majority of Solomon Islanders follow their distinct clan *kastom* or customary land tenure systems outside of the confine of the land laws of the modern state of Solomon Islands, largely following a subsistence and semi-subsistence lifestyle. There is potential value to CIE in learning about these ways of living, understanding the similarities and dissimilarities of these tribal indigenous communities compared with others globally, and obtaining newer understandings that might enrich global CIE scholarship and methodologies.

According to Sanga (2009), Solomon Islanders' daily lives are influenced by three overlaying domains of relationships: *kastom* (Indigenous and multiple cultures/customs), the Christian church, and formal organizational/institutional life. While existing side-by-side for more than 100 years, these societal domains of influence in the modern-day Solomon Islands have not been fully explored or understood by researchers. CIE can benefit from exploring more relational models of community living based on deeper understandings of principles, storied expressions of living, straddling of ontological-epistemological worlds, and authentic adaptive CIE methodologies.

Represented by a closer look at the island of Mala'ita, this Solomon Islands case study offers a peek into the range of opportunities and challenges for CIE research in these new times. As an island in the Solomon Islands archipelago, Mala'ita is home to 160,000 indigenous Melanesian peoples, speaking 13 languages and members of an estimated 150 tribes. As explained by Sanga and Walker (2012), the Mala'ita mind sees the social world as socio-physical-spiritual; all existing together and in an integrated fashion (Sanga, 2019).

The Mala'ita tribal belief systems are theocratic, hence the societal indigenous cultures are theonomous. As such, the Mala'ita mind values a universe that is both physical and metaphysical and accepts living by rules which are vertical (spiritual, principles, and ordered) and horizontal (spatial, human, located, and other physical-environmental). Accordingly, when residents of the islets of Kwai and Ngongosila in East Mala'ita had to rebuild their houses closer to each other as a response to the environmental issue of sea-level rise, the act of proximal relocation resulted in newer challenges to the theocratic and anthropologic-axiological mind of the Mala'itans. Besides being ethnic and religious, the tribal communities are economic and political units as well. Moreover, the tribes are distinct epistemological communities and are governed by their morality systems.

Epistemologically, Mala'ita subscribes to different clan-based knowledge systems; all of which are part of what Gegeo (1998) sees as "part of the *kula* [place] system" (p. 297) or a pattern of cultural knowledge that includes the whole person, their family, and wider society. Mala'ita knowledge creators use indigenous systems of discourses and apply sophisticated knowledge-creation strategies in the three domains of knowledge; public, secret, and sacred (Sanga & Reynolds, 2020a). Even today, Mala'ita learners are still sensitive to their different sites of learning such as the *bisi*, a female-only private knowledge domain, or the *beu*, a men-boys-only private knowledge domain, or the *lalabata*, a shared communal teaching and learning public knowledge domain. Those involved honor the various forms of teaching and learning, and the rules of conduct and engagement in the different sites.

The Mala'ita Island example offers numerous implications, opportunities, and challenges for CIE research in these new times, as represented by the following research questions: What could be an authentic Mala'ita or Solomon Islands education? What are potential comparisons with other authentic education cases elsewhere? Based on a deeper understanding of the Solomon Islands situation, what insights might be used to enhance the authenticity of another case? How might a communal, theocratic Indigenous Mala'ita mind/thought enrich contemporary notions of education? How might CIE be more inclusive to embrace the diversities of the Indigenous Mala'ita mind? How does the Indigenous Mala'ita mind shift within and between knowledge domains? How does the Mala'ita mind negotiate ontological-epistemological tensions? What are the defining actions or approaches for negotiating ontological-epistemological competing worlds?

A Mala'ita education is potentially concerned with clan members, value systems, knowledge structures, properties, processes, and relationships, which in every way are more likely to capture and explain Mala'ita realities and educational visions. The potential of a Mala'ita authentic education is highlighted here only because the current Solomon Islands education (including for Mala'ita students on Mala'ita Island) does not include indigenous Mala'ita education ontologies, categorizations, and epistemologies. The questions posed point to the potential futures of CIE research that the Mala'ita case study offers. As yet, CIE research in Oceania has not explored these questions on Mala'ita or other islands in the Pacific region. Rather than offer preferences on the directionality of future CIE Oceanic research(ers) on authentic education, we leave these to Oceania researchers to explore such questions relationally.

Tonga

Dialectic reasoning questions "logic" and its place in the vast terrain that encompasses Indigenous knowledges and understandings in Oceania. From a Tongan perspective, like many indigenous Oceanic cultures, knowledge is fundamentally a relational concern that is intimately connected to *tu'ungava'e*, the land (place and space) in which one makes sense of their genealogical and diasporic groundings (Pulu, 2002). The continuous mobilities of Tongan *kāinga* (extended families) show us their fluid understandings and connections that are symbolic of shifting boundaries in which they make sense of their world including notions of "logic" and "tension" as Tongan.

CIE is not only a comparative analysis of intercultural educational relations, but also the intracultural education relations that shift across boundaries, take form, and are shaped transnationally. Such complexities and nuances in how indigenous Oceanic people make sense of education and learning are often missed in international literature and scholarship because quite often "logic" is already predetermined and predefined within Western notions of education, even across the diaspora.

What does leadership mean to Tongan people in all areas of life? This is a worthwhile question for comparative research. Yet, it does not always feature as being an important aspect of formal educational learning. 'Ana Maui Taufe'ulungaki (2014), a Tongan scholar and the first woman Minister of Education in Tonga, has exercised her *fua fatongia*, a sense of duty and service, by mentoring and inspiring many Tongan postgraduate students and leaders. Seu'ula Johansson-Fua has benefited from Taufe'ulungaki's mentorship and exercises her responsibilities in her role as director of the Institute of Education at the University of the South Pacific.

Similarly, Kabini Sanga, who values the *ivi moe mālohi* (potency and potentiality) of leadership and mentoring, has also shared much of his wisdom with Johansson-Fua's (2016) notions of leadership capacity. The result has been engagement in contexts in Oceania such as with local, regional, and international aid funders. These situations provide interest for CIE. Such leadership and mentoring practices are meaningful learnings that are expressed through *talanoa mālie* and *māfana* (Manu'atu, 2000), oral engagements that produce relational warmth, shared pleasure, and love. These are ways in which Oceania's indigenous knowledge and practices have been realized and operationalized in formal education contexts that are not always expressed in CIE scholarship. Education and schooling for Tongan people, therefore, is fundamentally a relational concern that takes into account the diversity and specificities in the contexts across the diaspora.

The "Pacific diversity" label itself misses the specificities that are inherent in how cultural knowledge and practices are utilized and realized within the diaspora of New Zealand, Australia, and the United States. Equally, so-called Pacific Education can be conceptualized and realized similarly. While Tongan communities take with them their cultural knowledge, practices, and aspirations, how they are operationalized in formal schooling in the diaspora varies (Fa'avae, 2018). At the same time, the "rural-urban," "small island–cosmopolitan island" contexts construct understandings of education that are becoming even more pressing with the growing population of Tongan people living outside of Tonga.

Konai Helu Thaman (1995), a Tongan scholar, educator, and poet, has articulated the benefits of culture and language in Tongan peoples' education across the diaspora. A key claim she makes is that education often ignores the informal learning that is a lifelong process for many Tongan *kāinga*. Education that includes such learning is for cultural continuity and survival (Thaman, 1995). *Fua fatongia* is embedded in how Tongan people exercise their *fakapotopoto*, learning to be wise and utilizing their knowledge to benefit the collective. This is more than just *'ilo*, the acquisition of knowledge and qualifications (Thaman, 1995).

In light of cultural continuity and survival, the intergenerational transmission of cultural knowledge through *koloa 'o e to'utangata Tonga* is a construct that encompasses the deep and layered cultural capital inherent in Tongan extended families; a point that is not always articulated in CIE scholarship (Fa'avae, 2019). Realizing the true potential in the cultural wisdom and learnings within *koloa 'o e to'utangata Tonga* requires an appreciation and affirmation of Tongan concepts and language, as constructed and contextualized through *tā* (time) and *vā* (space).

Hūfanga 'Okusitino Māhina (2010) utilizes *tā-vā* as a theoretical construct, grounded in Tongan language and philosophy, to make sense of the *ivi moe mālohi* (potency and potentiality) of our indigenous knowledge, ideas, and practices that transcend generations and spaces across the diaspora. It is how we understand the fluid and shifting nature of education and learning that is also aligned to *tu'ungava'e*, and how we negotiate and define our identities and pluralities across the diverse contexts within the diaspora. These and other lessons promise much for CIE as it negotiates with Oceanic realities.

Aotearoa New Zealand
The political structure of Aotearoa New Zealand is framed by the Treaty of Waitangi/Te Tiriti o Waitangi, an accord (or accords) signed in 1840 between the

representatives of some Indigenous Māori groups and the British Crown. Despite disputes over the interpretation and implementation of versions of the Treaty/Tiriti, recent years have seen moves toward a national vision of two peoples, Māori and non-Māori (Orange, 2012). This has had implications in education of relevance to those interested in CIE.

Historically, separate educational practices within formal education involved schools established under the Native Schools Act. More recently, Kaupapa Māori education, an education founded on Māori principles and developed by communities, has provided formal school-based Māori education aimed at sustaining language, culture, and other aspects of Māori life.

Among the understandings of the role of formal institutional education in Aotearoa New Zealand from Māori perspectives is that of Mason Durie (2003). He wrote of multiple educational aims: of Māori to live as Māori; to actively participate as citizens of the world; and, to enjoy good health and a high standard of living. He argued that since success for Māori involves a solid foundation in a Māori reality, "[e]ducation should be as much about that reality as it is about literacy and numeracy" (Durie, 2003, p. 200). Kaupapa Māori education can be seen as an answer to this call.

Kaupapa Māori educational research now forms a substantial corpus (Pihama et al., 2004) that examines education through Māori lenses and includes work on politics and knowledge (Royal, 2012), e-learning (Tiakiwai & Tiakiwai, 2010), leadership theory relevant to education (Barnes, 2019), sector-specific frameworks (Wilkie & Whakataukī, 2005), and professional development (Bishop, 2012; Bishop & Berryman, 2010). This body of work, resting on indigenous ontological and epistemological platforms, simultaneously provides contextual sense-making, challenges to hegemonic approaches to education in Aotearoa New Zealand, and a rich resource for CIE.

In Aotearoa New Zealand, Pacific people are among those groups whose relationship with the indigenous Māori population is subject to the Treaty of Waitangi (Orange, 2012). Pasifika or Pacific education is an umbrella term (Samu, 2006) used in Aotearoa New Zealand in many contexts such as Tapasā, community-informed documentation to support teachers of learners of Pacific origin (Ministry of Education, 2018). It is a term of convenience (Airini et al., 2010) although it remains a moot point as to whose convenience it serves (Reynolds, 2017). This field also offers value to CIE.

Research into the field of Pasifika/Pacific education has progressively embraced Oceania-origin frameworks. Many of these honor Samoan, Tongan, and other relevant cultural references. These thought traditions open education to scrutiny in ways that contrast with prior deficit approaches (Nakhid, 2003) by providing strengths-based alternatives that recognize community capital (Yosso, 2005). As observed by Refiti (2015), processes of construction and reconstruction are involved in the ways that ideas and concepts originally embedded in Oceania village life come to be enacted in other spaces to produce a result that is "interesting" (p. 18). While not lost in translation, the effect can be that for some concepts, meanings and nuances can shift or become muffled (Simati, 2011; Tuagalu, 2008). A brief consideration of the *va* (Samoan) or *vā* (Tongan) is offered as an example present in the literature of Pasifika/Pacific education.

The *va* or *vā* is a concept to be found in the literature of Samoa (Aiono-Le Tagaloa, 2003), Tonga (Koloto, 2017), and elsewhere (Hoem, 1993). It is a spatial, multidimensional understanding of relationships across the domains of the spiritual, social, and physical. The *va* has been described as "the space between, the betweenness, not empty space, not space that separates but space that relates, that holds separate entities and things together in the Unity-that-is-All, the space that is context, giving meaning to things" (Wendt, 1999, p. 402) and as emphasizing the space in between. "This is fundamentally different from the popular western notion of space as an expanse or an open area" (Ka'ili, 2005, p. 89). Every relationship involves a *va*. This connects and separates people (and/or other entities) and is conditional, affected by actions, words, and so on. In the literature of Pasifika/Pacific education, there are many references to *va* (e.g., Airini et al., 2010; Reynolds, 2016; Silipa, 2004; Tuagalu, 2008).

Central to those progressing the understanding of education by reference to the *va* is the New Zealand-based Samoan academic Melani Anae. In concert with others (Airini et al., 2010), she has provided sense-making in Pasifika/Pacific educational research from the stance of "native anthropology" (Anae, 2010b). Through the Samoan cultural reference of *teu le va*, to tidy/care for/make clean the sacred relational spaces, she has addressed relational ethics (Anae, 2016) in ways relevant to the enhancement of Pasifika/Pacific education (Anae, 2010a). This thinking, which supports a challenge to the conceptualization of success in education, has been developed to attend to the micro-environments of classrooms (Reynolds, 2017; 2018), educational research (Airini et al., 2010), digital education (Enari & Matapo, 2020), and beyond.

WEAVING THE STRANDS

An approach that unites diverse groups because some view them as the "distant and remote" does not do justice to what is available in the centers of our worlds. Variety in both the case studies and the approaches taken by each author indicates the centrality of context, an essential consideration if CIE is to gain from Oceanic wisdom. That said, a common aspect of the diverse material is relationality, albeit manifest in various ways.

One way of understanding identity is as a form of social representation which is a mediation between the individual and the social world (Chryssochoou, 2003). Identity involves negotiation in a journey that requires clarity, transparency, and reflexivity (Sanga & Reynolds, 2017). Individualism as an aspect of identity is not a significant element of the Solomon Islands case study. Clan and tribal positioning are the keys to the relational self in Mala'ita (Sanga & Reynolds, 2020a). The nation-state gains strength where the relational idea of being a *wantok* is drawn into its fabric and notions of communal identity at scale are woven into socialization through education (Fito'o, 2019). However, such developments have potential only to the extent that they are complementary to *kastom*, traditional thought and practice, and do not seek to replace long-held values. Where they occur, epistemological collisions (Gegeo & Watson-Gegeo, 2002) and intergroup tensions (Brigg et al., 2015) require strategic *kastom*-derived relationally negotiated solutions.

In the account of Tonga, relatedness and mobility are mediated by understandings based on the family. The case study traces the work of individuals whose leadership is modeled on the kinds of relational activity that have been practiced in Tongan families and communities across space and time (Ka'ili, 2005). In this way, mentoring practices provide family-framed pedagogical cultural transmission through the guiding influence that values collective and multifaceted wellbeing rather than the career paths of individuals.

The literature of Kaupapa Māori and Pasifika/Pacific education centers relationality and collectivism in ways that challenge the individualistic logic of colonial hegemonic understandings of education. Instead, education is a relational space that demands relational pedagogies (Bishop, 2008; Ministry of Education, 2018) akin to those advocated for by Naisilisili (2012), and the valuing of local lenses and knowledge that can also be referenced against, but need no justification from, globally sourced categories.

Perhaps future productive grounds for CIE might include investigating the revelatory potential of weaving *wantok*ism, a Melanesian expression of relationality, and other aspects of Solomon Island *kastom* into productive relationships with concepts at home further east in the Pacific such as *va* (relational space), *poto* (wisdom), *fua fatongia* (duty and service), and other Oceanic-origin relational understandings; and learning from the various ways transmission and adjustment of relationality are constructed in regional diasporic processes, particularly through the way relationships are configured in formal and informal education. Relevant too are the ways the major threat of our time, the ecocide of climate change, is understood and responded to through Oceanic wisdom and resources.

AN EXISTENTIAL THREAT

Higgins et al. (2013) discuss ecocide as a range of environmental crimes that "need to be responded to through both informal and formal means of resolution and restoration" (p. 252). In Oceania, the most evident results of ecocide are climate change generally and sea-level rise specifically. While some bodies advocate for education as a means of understanding and responding to the causes and effects of climate change (The Commonweath, 2016), practitioners at the edges of Oceania report pressure to maintain an as-you-were approach to curriculum and to downplay ecological problems to reduce the emotional burden on students (Reynolds, 2020; Stevenson et al., 2017). Meanwhile, Oceanic people continue to think and act in support of their sustainability. In this section, examples from Solomon Islands, Fiji, and Tuvalu suggest the significance of local ontologies and their transmission and narrativization in the face of globally generated but locally experienced threats.

An example of resilience in the face of pressures arising from ecocide centers on the relational structure of the *wantok* system by which obligations and responsibilities are mediated through kinship and other forms of connection Solomon Islands (Ha'apio et al., 2019). Following severe floods, villagers identified the strength of existing social structures embedded in the *wantok* system and pooled nonmonetary wealth as valuable to sustainability. The general advantages Fito'o (2016; 2019) identified for drawing the *wantok* system directly into the curriculum are made more salient if relational strength is understood as a significant resource for future sustainability and adaption (Ha'apio et al., 2019).

In Fiji, Lagi (2015) found the complex and long-standing environmental knowledge of Fijian elders to be a source of climate change knowledge, for example, through appreciating decreased harvests of pandanus, a staple used in mat weaving, and fish for consumption and sale. Gucake (2016) points to oracy as a main intergenerational transmission mode. However, Lagi (2015) notes that the transmission of traditional knowledge is becoming less effective, a finding echoed in Vanuatu (Hetzel & Pascht, 2017). Consequently, she recommended educators construct a database of community experts to assist the passing of valuable ecological knowledge. Through re-resourcing the school curriculum in this way, the ontologically founded wisdom of Indigenous Fijian knowledge may become increasingly apparent in classrooms.

Falefou (2017) shows how responses to climate change can be located in culturally framed narratives. He describes Tuvaluans' self-perceptions as incorporating ancestral voyagers and explorers. Tuvaluans are rooted to the *fenua*, the land, as coconut trees but are also the floating fruits of the coconut. However, as sea levels rise and reshape these ideas of rootedness and fluidity, uncertainty is produced. A Tuvaluan reinterpretation of the Biblical promise of the rainbow responds to this uncertainty by refocusing from the promise of no future flood to Tuvaluan awareness that an "ark" or solution must be constructed. However, as Falefou (2017) points out, the construction of a successful solution requires the support of the wider world to avoid Tuvaluan society and identity vanishing over time. While the ark must make sense locally, the resources required are more global. It is only when local actions are integrated into a wider mat of global change that Oceanic sustainability can be assured.

CONCLUSION: LIVING WELL TOGETHER

The mat of welcome, constructed by the weaving of globally defined strands and local case studies, has been unrolled throughout this chapter. Although the region of Oceania is as susceptible as any other to division and rancor, our deliberate focus has been on ways forward, a strengths-based approach. We have addressed the significance of naming through questions around who might be considered distant or remote, the origin of "Pacific," and by asking who is lost and at home in Oceania. We pointed to the significance of metaphors to guide the relational position of local and more global knowledge in education in pursuit of relevance, effective sense-making, and thus the usefulness of education. As we re-roll the mat, as authors and friends we offer the blessing that through walking backward into the future and embracing solidarity through diversity locally and globally, we can promote a sustainable educational journey that offers hope of continuity in the face of the challenges ahead.

The field of CIE can learn from Oceania to appreciate the context behind the context (Sanga, in Airini et al., 2010). Beneath the visible practices of the multiple peoples of Oceania sit the worldviews and knowledge systems of sense-making people. These are as unique and various as the languages, costumes, artifacts, and islands of those who live and love here. CIE research that honors the nonmaterial and the philosophical is that which can truly claim to promote international understanding and world peace. It goes beyond mere comparison by risking a journey into relational territories where the researcher is posed fundamental challenges regarding the nature and meaning of social life. As a consequence, engagement can change people, relationships, and ideas of a good life.

We leave the last substantive words to Selina Tusitala Marsh, Poet Laureate of Aotearoa New Zealand between 2017 and 2019. Of Samoan, Tuvaluan, English, Scottish, and French descent, she reminds us of our responsibilities to the past and to the future as we journey in the present.

> *What we leave behind, matters to those who go before*
> *we face the future with our backs, sailing shore to shore . . .*
> from "Unity," Selina Tusitala Marsh (2016)

In a world where the dialectic of the local and global is salient, the dialectic of the past and the future must also be part of our journeys. For without the local, the global has no constituents; and without the past, the future has no precedents. Our thinking about Oceania ontologies and epistemologies has taught us that we need to pay holistic, relational attention to our surroundings to live well together.

REFERENCES

Aiono-Le Tagaloa, F. (2003). *Tapua'i: Samoan worship*. Malua Printing Press.

Airini, Anae, M., Mila-Schaaf, K., Coxon, E., Mara, D., & Sanga, K. (2010). *Teu le va—Relationships across research and policy in Pasifika Education: A collective approach to knowledge generation and policy development for action towards Pasifika education success*. Ministry of Education.

Anae, M. (2010a). Research for better Pacific schooling in New Zealand: Teu le va–a Samoan perspective. *Mai Review*, *1*, 1–24. Retrieved from http://www.review.mai.ac.nz/index.php/MR/article/viewFile/298/395

Anae, M. (2010b). Teu le va: Toward a native anthropology. *Pacific Studies*, *33*(2), 222–240.

Anae, M. (2016). Teu le va: Samoan relational ethics. *Knowledge Cultures*, *4*(3), 117–130. Retrieved from http://go.galegroup.com/ps/i.do?p=AONE&sw=w&u=vuw&v=2.1&it=r&id=GALE%7CA458164605&asid=79728fe582dc9574894712b26dbb6a7e

Angoro, C. E. (2018). *The decentralisation of Australia's gender equality and women's empowerment strategy in Oro Province, Papua New Guinea* (MA). Victoria University of Wellington, Wellington, New Zealand.

Arnove, R. F. (2013). Introduction: Reframing comparative education: The dialectic of the global and the local. In R. F. Arnove, C. A. Torres, & S. Franz (Eds.), *Comparative education: The dialectic of the global and the local* (pp. 7–29). Rowman & Littlefield.

Barnes, A. (2019). Social justice theory and practice: Pākehā, Kaupapa Māori and educational leadership. *WINHEC Journal*, 23–39.

Barnes, S. S., & Hunt, T. L. (2005). Sāmoa's pre-contact connections in West Polynesia and beyond. *Journal of the Polynesian Society*, *114*(3), 227–266.

Bevacqua, M. L. (2010, December). Their/our sea of islands: Epeli Hau'ofa and Frantz Fanon. *LiNQ*, *37*, 80–92.

Bishop, R. (2008). A culturally responsive pedagogy of relations. In C. McGee & D. Fraser (Eds.), *The Professional Practice of Teaching* (Vol. 4, pp. 154–171). Cengage.

Bishop, R. (2012). Pretty difficult: Implementing kaupapa Maori theory in English-medium secondary schools. *New Zealand Journal of Educational Studies*, *47*(2), 38–50.

Bishop, R., & Berryman, M. (2010). Te Kotahitanga: Culturally responsive professional development for teachers. *Teacher Development, 14*(2), 173–187.

Borja-Quichocho-Calvo. (2017). "When you save a homeland and a culture, you save a people": How the Manmaha'haga Siha of the 21st century save Guahan. In U. L. Vaai & U. Nabobo-Baba (Eds.), *The relational self: Decolonising personhood in the Pacific* (pp. 43–60). University of the South Pacific; Pacific Theological College.

Bray, M. (1993). Education and the vestiges of colonialism: Self-determination, neocolonialism and dependency in the South Pacific. *Comparative education, 29*(3), 333–348.

Brigg, M., Chadwick, W., Griggers, C., Murdock, J., & Vienings, T. (2015). *Solomon Island National Peace Council: Inter-communal mediation.* Retrieved from https://espace.library.uq.edu.au/view/UQ:373816/brigg_et_al_2015_nat_peace_medn.pdf.

Brown, R. P., Connell, J., & Jimenez-Soto, E. V. (2014). Migrants' remittances, poverty and social protection in the South Pacific: Fiji and Tonga. *Population, Space and Place, 20*(5), 434–454.

Brownlee, J. (2004). Teacher education students' epistemological beliefs: Developing a relational model of teaching. *Research in Education, 72*(1), 1–17.

Burnett, G. (2013). Approaches to English literacy teaching in the Central Pacific Republic of Kiribati: Quality teaching, educational aid and curriculum reform, *Asia Pacific Journal of Education, 33*(3), 350–363. DOI: 10.1080/02188791.2013.787389

Burnett, G., & Dorovolomo, J. (2007). Teaching in difficult times: Solomon Island teachers' narratives of perseverance. *Journal of Peace, Conflict & Development, 12,* 1–34.

Chryssochoou, X. (2003). Studying identity in social psychology: Some thoughts on the definition of identity and its relation to action. *Journal of Language and Politics, 2*(2), 225–241.

The Commonweath. (2016). Climate change and education: A policy brief. Retrieved from https://www.thecommonwealth-educationhub.net/wp-content/uploads/2016/02/Climate-Change-Policy-Brief_Draft_140416_v4.pdf

Crocombe, R. G. (1976). *The Pacific way: An emerging identity.* Lotu Pasifika.

Crossa, V. (2012). Relational positionality: Conceptualizing research, power, and the everyday politics of neoliberalization in Mexico City. *ACME: An International E-Journal for Critical Geographies, 11*(1), 110–132.

Durie, M. (2003). *Launching Maori futures.* Huia.

Enari, D., & Matapo, J. (2020). The digital vā: Pasifika education during the COVID-19 pandemic. *Mai Journal, 9*(4), 7–11.

Fa'avae, D. (2018). Giving voice to the unheard in higher education: Critical autoethnography, Tongan males, and educational research. *MAI Journal, 7*(2), 1–24.

Fa'avae, D. (2019). Tatala 'a e koloa 'o e to'utangata Tonga: A way to disrupt and decolonise doctoral research. *MAI Journal, 1*(8), 3–15.

Falefou, T. (2017). *Toku Tia: Tuvalu and the impacts of climate change.* PhD dissertation. University of Waikato, Hamilton, New Zealand.

Fasavalu, T. I., & Reynolds, M. (2019). Relational positionality and a learning disposition: Shifting the conversation. *International Education Journal: Comparative Perspectives, 18*(2), 11–25.

Ferris-Leary, H. (2013). *An analytical perspective on Moana research and the case of Tongan faiva.* PhD dissertation. University of Auckland, Auckland, New Zealand.

Fito'o, B. (2016). *Citizenship education in a small island state: Exploring values for good citizenship in the Solomon Islands.* PhD dissertation. University of the South Pacific, Suva, Fiji.

Fito'o, B. (2019). Wantok-centred framework for developing citizenship. *International Education Journal: Comparative Perspectives, 18*(2), 55–67.

Gegeo, D. W. (1998). Indigenous knowledge and empowerment: Rural development examined from within. *The Contemporary Pacific, 10*(2), 289–315.

Gegeo, D. W. (2001). Cultural rupture and indigeneity: The challenge of (re)visioning "place" in the Pacific. *The Contemporary Pacific, 13*(2), 491–507.

Gegeo, D. W., & Watson-Gegeo, K. A. (2002). Whose knowledge? Epistemological collisions in Solomon Islands community development. *Contemporary Pacific, 14*(2), 377–409.

Gucake, R. N. (2016). *Itaukei (indigenous Fijian) oral narratives on climate change building adaptability and mitigation-a case study on University of the South Pacific students from the province of Nadroga, Viti Levu*. PhD dissertation. Royal Roads University, Colwood, Canada.

Guy, R., Kosuge, T., & Hayakawa, R. (2000). *Distance education in the South Pacific: Nets and voyages*. Institute of Pacific Studies, University of the South Pacific.

Ha'apio, M. O., Gonzalez, R., & Wairiu, M. (2019). Is there any chance for the poor to cope with extreme environmental events? Two case studies in the Solomon Islands. *World Development, 122*, 514–524. doi:https://doi.org/10.1016/j.worlddev.2019.06.023

Halapua, S. (2008). Talanoa process: The case of Fiji. Retrieved from http://unpan1.un.org/intradoc/groups/public/documents/un/unpan022610.pdf

Hau'ofa, E. (1994). Our sea of islands. *The Contemporary Pacific, 6*(1), 148–161.

Hau'ofa, E. (2000). The ocean in us. In A. Hooper (Ed.), *Culture and sustainable development in the Pacific* (pp. 32–43). ANU Press and Asia Pacific Press.

Hetzel, D., & Pascht, A. (2017). Young ni-Vanuatu encounter climate change: Reception of knowledge and new discourses. In E. Dürr & A. Pascht (Eds.), *Environmental transformations and cultural responses: Ontologies, discourses, and practices in Oceania* (pp. 103–124). Palgrave Macmillan.

Higgins, P., Short, D., & South, N. (2013). Protecting the planet: A proposal for a law of ecocide. *Crime, Law and Social Change, 59*(3), 251–266.

Hoem, I. (1993). Space and morality in Tokelau. *Pragmatics, 3*(2), 137–153.

Irwin, G. (2005). Pacific migrations—into remote Oceania: Lapita people. Retrieved from http://www.TeAra.govt.nz/en/pacific-migrations/page-3

Jensz, F. (2012). Missionaries and indigenous education in the 19th-century British Empire. Part II: Race, class, and gender. *History Compass, 10*(4), 306–317.

Johansson-Fua, S. (2016). The Oceanic researcher and the search for a space in comparative and international education. *International Education Journal: Comparative Perspectives, 15*(3), 30–41.

Ka'ili, T. O. (2005). Tauhi va: Nurturing Tongan sociospatial ties in Maui and beyond. *The Contemporary Pacific, 17*(1), 83–114.

Koloto, A. (2017). Va, tauhi va. *Encyclopedia of Educational Philosophy and Theory*. Retrieved from https://doi.org/10.1007/978-981-287-532-7_19-1

Koya-Vaka'uta, C. F. (2017). Rethinking research as relational space in the Pacific pedagogy and praxis. In U. Vaai & A. Casamira (Eds.), *Relational hermeneutics: Decolonising the mindset and the Pacific Itulagi* (pp. 65–84). University of the South Pacific; Pacific Theological College.

Kuschel, R. (1988). Early contacts between Bellona and Rennell Islands and the outside world. *Journal of Pacific History, 23*(2), 191–200.

Lagi, R. K. (2015). *Na bu: An explanatory study of Indigenous knowledge of climate change education in Ovalau, Fiji*. PhD dissertation. University of the South Pacific, Suva, Fiji.

Lilomaiava-Doktor, S. (2009). Beyond "migration": Samoan population movement (malaga) and the geography of social space (vā). *The Contemporary Pacific, 21*(1), 1–32.

Māhina, O. (2010). Tā, vā and moana: Temporality, spatiality and indigeneity. *Pacific Studies, 33*(2), 168–202.

Manu'atu, L. (2000). Tuli ke ma'u hono ngaahi mālie: Pedagogical possibilities for Tongan students in New Zealand secondary schooling. PhD dissertation. University of Auckland, New Zealand. https://researchspace.auckland.ac.nz/handle/2292/715

Marsh, S. T. (2016). Unity. Retrieved from https://poetryarchive.org/poem/unity/

McDonald, B. L. (2001). *Transfer of training in a cultural context: A Cook Islands study.* PhD dissertation. Victoria University of Wellington, New Zealand.

McHugh, K. E. (2000). Inside, outside, upside down, backward, forward, round and round: A case for ethnographic studies in migration. *Progress in Human Geography*, 24(1), 71–89.

Mila-Schaaf, K. (2006). Va-centred social work: Possibilities for a Pacific approach to social work practice. *Social Work Review*, 18(1), 8–13.

Ministry of Education. (2018). Tapasā. Retrieved from http://www.elearning.tki.org.nz/News/Tapasa-Cultural-Competencies-Framework-for-Teachers-of-Pacific-Learners

Mollet, J. A. (2007). Educational investment in conflict areas of Indonesia: The case of West Papua Province. *International Education Journal*, 8(2), 155–166.

Nabobo-Baba, U. (2012). Transformations from within: Rethinking Pacific Education Initiative. The development of a movement for social justice and equity. *International Education Journal: Comparative Perspective*, 11(2), 82–97. Retrieved from http://openjournals.library.usyd.edu.au/index.php/IEJ/article/viewFile/7439/7795

Naisilisili, S. (1998). *The effects of yaqona drinking on nutritional status in Fiji.* (MA Dev Studs.). University of the South Pacific, Suva, Fiji.

Naisilisili, S. (2012). *Iluvatu: An exploratory study of Cu'u Indigenous Knowledge and implications for Fijian education.* PhD dissertation. University of the South Pacific, Suva, Fiji.

Nakhid, C. (2003). "Intercultural" perceptions, academic achievement, and the identifying process of Pacific Islands students in New Zealand schools. *Journal of Negro Education*, 72(3), 297–317. doi:10.2307/3211249

Nanau, G. L. (2017). 'Na Vanuagu': Epistemology and personhood in Tathimboko, Guadalcanal. In U. L. Vaai & U. Nabobo-Baba (Eds.), *The relational self: Decolonising personhood in the Pacific* (pp. 177–203). University of the South Pacific; Pacific Theological College.

NOAA. (2020). How did the Pacific Ocean get its name? Retrieved from https://oceanservice.noaa.gov/facts/pacific.html

Orange, C. (2012). Treaty of Waitangi. *Te Ara: The Encyclopedia of New Zealand.* Retrieved from http://www.TeAra.govt.nz/en/treaty-of-waitangi

Otunuku, M. (2011). Talanoa: How can it be used effectively as an Indigenous research methodology with Tongan people? *Pacific-Asian Education Journal*, 23(2), 43–52.

Otunuku, M., & Thaman, R. (2018). *Toutu'u 'Ufi- The Tongan cooperative yam garden as educational paradigm on the frontline against global change.* Paper presented at the Vaka Pasifiki Education Conference: It takes an island and an ocean: Rethinking Pacific education for resilient, healthy communities., Suva, Fiji. https://www.usp.ac.fj/index.php?id=22825

Panapa, T. (2014). *Ola Lei: Developing healthy communities in Tuvalu.* PhD dissertation. University of Auckland, Auckland, New Zealand.

Pene, F., Taufe'ulungaki, A. M., & Benson, C. (Eds.). (2002). *Tree of opportunity: Re-thinking Pacific education.* University of the South Pacific, Institute of Education.

Pihama, L., Smith, K., Taki, M., & Lee, J. (2004). *A literature review on kaupapa Maori and Maori education pedagogy.* International Research Institute for Maori and Indigenous Education (IRI).

Pulu, B. T. J. (2002, September). Turangawaewae/Tu'ungava'e: Echoes of a place to stand and belong [online]. He Puna Korero: *Journal of Maori and Pacific Development*, 3(2), 14–30. https://search.informit.org/doi/10.3316/INFORMIT.884139579139228

Refiti, A. (2015). *Mavae and Tofiga: Spatial exposition of the Samoan cosmogony and architecture*. PhD dissertation. Auckland University of Technology, Auckland, New Zealand.

Reynolds, M. (2016). Relating to va. *AlterNative: An International Journal of Indigenous Peoples, 12*(2), 190–202. doi:10.20507/AlterNative.2016.12.2.7

Reynolds, M. (2017). *Together as brothers: A catalytic examination of Pasifika success as Pasifika to teu le va in boys' secondary education in Aotearoa New Zealand*. PhD dissertation. Victoria University of Wellington, Wellington, New Zealand. Retrieved from http://researcharchive.vuw.ac.nz/handle/10063/6487

Reynolds, M. (2018). Caring for classroom relationality in Pasifika education: A space-based understanding. *Waikato Journal of Education, 23*(1), 71–84.

Reynolds, S. (2020). Recycling as Seduction: Critiquing the practice of climate change education from a primary classroom. *Set-Research Information for Teachers*. Retrieved from https://www.nzcer.org.nz/nzcerpress/set/online-first

Royal, T. A. C. (2012). Politics and knowledge: Kaupapa Maori and matauranga Maori. *New Zealand Journal of Educational Studies, 47*(2), 30.

Salmond, A. (2005). Their body is different, our body is different: European and Tahitian navigators in the 18th century. *History and Anthropology, 16*(2), 167–186.

Samu, T. (2006). The "Pasifika Umbrella" and quality teaching: Understanding and responding to the diverse realities within. *Waikato Journal of Education, 12*, 35–50.

Sanga, K. (2004). Making philosophical sense of indigenous Pacific research. In T. Baba, O. Māhina, N. Williams, & U. Nabobo-Baba (Eds.), *Researching Pacific and indigenous peoples: Issues and perspectives* (pp. 41–52). Centre for Pacific Studies, University of Auckland.

Sanga, K. (2017). Leadership development through friendship and storytelling. In U. Vaai & A. Casamira (Eds.), *Relational hermeneutics: Decolonising the mindset and the Pacific Itulagi* (pp. 101–113). University of the South Pacific Press; Pacific Theological College.

Sanga, K. (2019). Ethics curriculum in Indigenous Pacific: A Solomon Islands study. *AlterNative: An International Journal of Indigenous Peoples, 15*(3), 243–252. https://doi.org/10.1177/1177180119874505

Sanga, K., & Reynolds, M. (2017). To know more of what it is and what it is not: Pacific research on the move. *Pacific Dynamics, 1*(2), 199–204.

Sanga, K., & Reynolds, M. (2020a). Knowledge guardianship, custodianship and ethics: a Melanesian perspective. *AlterNative*, 1177180120917481. Retrieved from https://doi.org/10.1177/1177180120917481

Sanga, K., & Reynolds, M. (2020b). A Review of the emerging indigenous Pacific research, 2000–2018. In A. W. Wiseman (Ed.), *Annual review of comparative and international education 2019* (Vol. 37, pp. 255–278). Emerald Publishing Limited.

Sanga, K., & Walker, K. (2012). The Malaitan mind and teamship: Implications of Indigenous knowledge for team development and performance. *International Journal of Knowledge, Culture & Change Management, 11*(6), 223–235.

Silipa, S. (2004). *"Fanaafi o fa'amalama": A light within the light: nurturing coolness & dignity in Samoan students' secondary school learning in Aotearoa/New Zealand*. PhD dissertation. University of Canterbury, Christchurch, New Zealand.

Simati, B. K. (2011). *The potential of Vā: an investigation of how 'Ie Tōga activate the spatial relationships of the Vā, for a Samoan diaspora community*. PhD dissertation. Auckland University of Technology, Auckland, New Zealand.

Smith, L. (1999). *Decolonizing methodologies: Research and Indigenous peoples*. Zed Books.

Solomon Islands Government. (2020). Projected population by province 2010–2025. Retrieved from https://www.statistics.gov.sb/statistics/social-statistics/population

Stevenson, R., Nicholls, J., & Whitehouse, H. (2017). What is climate change education? *Curriculum Perspectives*, 37(4), 67–71. doi:10.1007/s41297-017-0015-9

Summy, H. (2009). Fiji's forgotten people: The legatees of "blackbirding." *Social Alternatives*, 28(4), 39–44.

Tankunani Sirivi, J., & Taleo, M. (2017). *As mothers of the land: The birth of the Bougainville Women for peace and freedom*. Pandanus Books.

Taufe'ulungaki, A. M. (2014). Look back to look forward: A reflective Pacific journey. In U. Nabobo-Baba & S. Johannson-Fua (Eds.), *Of waves, winds and wonderful things: A decade of rethinking Pacific education* (pp. 1–15). University of the South Pacific Press.

Taumoefalau, M. (2017). The cultural-linguistic making of the Tongan female self. In U. Vaai & U. Nabobo-Baba (Eds.), *The relational self: Decolonising personhood in the Pacific* (pp. 137–152). University of the South Pacific; Pacific Theological College.

Thaman, K. H. (1995) Concepts of learning, knowledge and wisdom in Tonga, and their relevance to modern education. *Prospects: UNESCO Quarterly Review of Comparative Education*, 25(4), 723–735.

Tiakiwai, S., & Tiakiwai, H. (2010). *A literature review focused on virtual learning environments (VLEs) and e-learning in the context of te reo Maori and Kaupapa Māori education: Report to the Ministry of Education*. Ministry of Education.

Tomkins, S. M. (1992). The influenza epidemic of 1918–19 in Western Samoa. *Journal of Pacific History*, 27(2), 181–197.

Tryon, D. (2009). Linguistic Distribution in the Pacific. Retrieved from http://press-files.anu.edu.au/downloads/press/p60461/mobile/ch02s02.html

Tu'inukuafe, H.-T. (2019). *M-learning About Tongan food: A concept of a culture-specific App for learning About Tongan food culture*. (Master of Communication Science). Auckland University of Technology, Auckland, New Zealand.

Tuagalu, I. (2008). Heuristics of the va. *AlterNative: An International Journal of Indigenous Scholarship*, 4(1), 107–126.

Turner, N. J., Berkes, F., Stephenson, J., & Dick, J. (2013). Blundering intruders: Extraneous impacts on two indigenous food systems. *Human Ecology*, 41(4), 563–574.

Vaai, U. L., & Nabobo-Baba, U. (Eds.). (2017). *The Relational Self*. University of the South Pacific; Pacific Theological College.

Wendt, A. (1999). Afterword: Tatauing the post-colonial body. In V. Hereniko & R. Wilson (Eds.), *Inside out: Literature, cultural politics, and identity in the new Pacific* (pp. 399–412). Rowman & Littlefield.

Wilkie, M., & Whakataukī, H. (2005). Kaupapa Māori research, theory and frameworks in New Zealand tertiary education: A literature review. *Tihei Oreore: Monograph Series Intern Reports*, 1(3), 269–298.

Yosso, T. J. (2005). Whose culture has capital? A critical race theory discussion of community cultural wealth. *Race Ethnicity and Education*, 8(1), 69–91.

16

The Political Construction of European Education

António Teodoro
Lusofona University, Lisbon

ABSTRACT

The chapter takes a historical approach in exploring the process of constructing Europe and the Education Area, in seven sections. In the first section, we will briefly introduce the roots of the process of the political construction of Europe in the post–World War II period. In the second and third sections, we submit the arguments which made education shift from a marginal dimension of the process of European construction to the central issue of the 2000 Lisbon Strategy, reaffirmed in later documents, to make Europe "the most competitive and dynamic world economy," while at the same time maintaining the levels of well-being of the so-called European social model in its different regional varieties. In the fourth section, we will describe the governance method that underpinned the Europeanization process of education, and in the fifth section, we will highlight one of its most important policies: the Bologna Process and the construction of the European Higher Education Area. After recalling, in the sixth section, how education participates in the "fabrication of Europe," we present, in the seventh section, a summary of the six dimensions put forward for the 2019–2025 period by the European Commission (and adopted by the member states). To conclude, we will briefly present some of the contradictory trends (and feelings) present in the process of constructing Europe and the Education Area.

■ ■ ■

In recent decades, nation-states have responded in various ways to the challenges of the development process known as globalization.[1] One such way was the creation of regional blocs and entities, based on multilateral agreements between states. The European Union (EU) is one of the more advanced institutional forms in this area, implementing a wide range of interventions that involve an increasingly more active supra-national role in all political, economic, and social spheres.[2]

THE POLITICAL CONSTRUCTION OF EUROPE

Although the idea of a united Europe began to form in the early 20th century, when capitalist states transformed into liberal democracies, World War II ushered in new forms of relationships among European states. In 1949, the Council of Europe was founded with the aims of both (1) overcoming the difficulties caused by military conflicts and (2) uniting the European nations in common endeavors. The countries at the center of this united Europe, with the approval of their various constitutions, adopted the form of democratic and lawful states, based on Keynesian economic policies. The state acquired an interventionist character in the economic and social spheres, committed to ensuring the social rights of citizens—among them the right to education.

In the 1950s, Europe entered a phase of rapid economic development as well as extensive migratory movements. This situation favored cooperation with other sectors of society, notably education and culture. The importance of creating a European identity was closely tied to granting political rights to citizens at a European level. In the 1980s, integration of new member states involved not just mere cooperation but enhancing the interdependence of sovereign states. There were also initiatives to overcome the technocratic and bureaucratic image of a distant supranational governing body, which had hitherto prevailed. In addition to the free movement of individuals and goods, there were efforts to create a communal, European spirit, based on cooperation in the cultural and educational sectors.

With the approval of the Treaty of Maastricht in 1992, the evolution of the EU assumed sharp federalist contours.[3] This process of building the EU, from the Treaties in early 1951 to the Constitutional Treaty of Lisbon in 2007, corresponded to different, complex, and contradictory perspectives and interests. Implementation was done in a nonlinear way—with returns, drifts, adjustments, and abrupt spiking. The origin of the European Economic Community, as part of the post–World War II process, responded to the need to *normalize* relations among European nations, while at the same time strengthening the economies of European countries to be more competitive internationally.

Alongside the promotion of conditions that protected a lasting peace in Europe, the Union was also designed to contain the possibility of *instability* resulting from the increased participation and influence of the working classes in the political reality of postwar Europe. Efforts were also needed to counter the attractiveness of the Soviet model of development—all of this in the context of a cold war between the forces of capitalism and communism.

As designed by social democratic and Christian democratic elites, the European project first sought a compromise aimed at the general welfare: full employment and the creation of middle-class majorities. Such initiatives were based on private property and the operations of a free market—all within the framework of a welfare state.

At the same time, European resistance arose to contest the conditions in which capital was accumulated—particularly regarding the increasing benefits accruing to North American corporate interests. Both European capitalists and social democrats (advocates of the welfare state) sought to counterbalance an international economic framework in which the dollar was the primary reference point of financial transactions and in which North American products, businesses, and interests prevailed.

Treaties thus gave support to an essentially "neo-mercantilist" vision, one which defended the creation of a large domestic market, protected from external competition, and the strengthening of European companies in international markets.

> The neo-mercantilist vision, it is argued, underpinned the initial drive towards the creation of the European single market and Economic and Monetary Union (EMU). For neo-mercantilists, a European competitiveness gap vis-a-vis the rest of the world was attributed to fragmented markets, a related inability to fully exploit economies scale in production, and insufficient investment in research and technology. (For neoliberals, the problems were—and still are—more likely to be attributed to factors such as inflexible labor markets, and unsustainable and work-discouraging welfare states.) As van Appeldoorn documents, the neo-mercantilist project was closer to a "resistance" than "open" model of regionalism. (Storey, 2004)

However, the evolution of the global economic system and the substantial change in world conditions significantly influenced the development of the European process and its reconfiguration. As institutionalized, the EU of 27 countries has become more than just a regional body based on a specific model that combines articulated economic progress and social rights. This emergent model has been especially prominent since the late 1990s. It is an integral part of the global hegemonic neoliberal process. Despite the inherent tensions and contradictions, the EU presents itself as a disciplinary element, aiming at (1) accelerating the shaping of legislation and national practices to fit the guidelines of neoliberalism, (2) acting aggressively to liberalize international markets to accommodate the interests of dominant economic groups, and (3) facilitating European participation in education policies based on trends related to the creation of a "knowledge economy."

These developments do not mean that the EU works today in a monolithic way and according to a "pure" model of capital accumulation, without *nuances* or contradictions. Rather, neoliberalism has become the dominant paradigm in the EU, albeit in its ordoliberal version,[4] as highlighted by Michel Foucault (2004) in *Naissance de la biopolotique*. Thus, it is much more about tensions between this new regime of accumulation and the previous regimes centered in the so-called European social model, resulting from the social democratic project of the Keynesian era (Mitchell, 2004). Influential philosophers such as German Jürgen Habermas and French Jacques Derrida (Habermas & Derrida. 2003), and German sociologist Ulrich Beck (1992) emphasize that—despite neoliberal hegemony—the EU can still be a space where increased attention to the social model of welfare and solidarity prevails, with strong participation of citizens in defense of their rights and democratic politics. The European experience can perhaps be used as an exercise in federal union between democratic socialism and ordoliberalism, as suggested by Thomas Piketty (2020, pp. 482–485).

THE EUROPEAN DIMENSION OF EDUCATION

In the aforementioned decades, the development of the European economic-political area has been reflected in the way educational issues are addressed at supranational and national levels.

In the early 20th century, these functions were assigned to education systems: social control and reproduction, regime legitimation, human resources production, and citizenship formation. Simultaneously, education served as an agency for social mobility.[5] Within nation-states, education was also a fundamental mechanism for creating a national identity by making local and regional languages and cultures invisible, and downplaying overarching European as well as international loyalties and commitments. Furthermore, national educational systems were used to assimilate immigrant cultures, to encourage patriotic values, to promote established religious doctrines, to disseminate the standardized norm of the national language, to generalize new patterns and rational forms of thought, to inculcate moral discipline and, especially, to indoctrinate according to the creeds and economic policies of the ruling classes (Green, 1994).

After World War II, education was assigned new roles and functions, including the consolidation of a democratic political system, the reduction of social inequalities, and—more importantly—the formation of manpower needed for the economic reconstruction of Europe devastated by war (Starkie, 2006). Global reforms of educational systems were undertaken in practically all countries. Education reforms as well as those social and political related to citizenship rights, however, were not a principal focus of the European Treaty of Paris in 1951 and that of Rome in 1957. Education remained under the sole purview of each member state of the European Communities (Erlt, 2006).

Education as a European-wide subject of regulation did not emerge until the 1970s and then specifically concerning issues of vocational training. Community authorities recognized the existence of a "European dimension in education," but always preserved the diversity and traditions of the national educational systems of member states. The concern not to harmonize and interfere with the politics of education in each state contrasts markedly with the first proposals for supranational governance of European education (Starkie, 2006).

The 1990s heralded deliberate mechanisms of supranational regulation of education. The Treaty of Maastricht, which entered into effect in 1992, had profound implications for the process of European integration. In this treaty, educational issues received more explicit and detailed attention, assigning to the European Community (Articles 126 and 127) the role of contributing to the development of quality education. However, these articles excluded any process of restructuring the configuration of education systems of member states.

At the time, the European dimension in education was to be achieved through student, teacher, and researcher exchange programs as well as the increased mobility of workers from member states. All these efforts were aimed at building meaningful European citizenship. In 1997, the approval of the Treaty of Amsterdam—while maintaining the same articles on education—extended the rights of citizenship. Active citizenship was considered a key element for the construction of Europe.

The need for free movement of services, goods, and capital has reinforced the parallel need for the mobility of workers. As a consequence, the need to achieve comparability between qualifications and the education systems of member states increased. This led to the standardization and harmonization of qualifications in vocational training, as well as the creation of equivalent educational standards and European standards of occupational qualifications. As noted by Hirtt (2005), the rise of initiatives to "harmonize" education policies emerged as the progressive implementation of the recommendations made since 1989 by the European Round Table of Industrialists (ERT), a think tank composed of approximately 45 of the most powerful leaders of European industry.

Between 1997 and 2000, the EU intervention (based on Article 149 of the Treaty of Maastricht) sought to legitimize a common European education policy from a flexible and vague concept of "quality." The "sixteen quality indicators," published in 2000 (two months after the approval of the Lisbon Strategy), embodied further steps to evaluate the efficient functioning of national systems, while respecting supranational referents defined by the EU.

Over time, several structures, mechanisms, and processes have contributed to extending EU regulation on education and training. The development and impact of EU programs provide strong evidence of the "Europeanization" of national education systems.

EDUCATION AT THE CENTER OF THE LISBON STRATEGY

With the formalization of the Lisbon Strategy a new phase began.[6] As described earlier, the issues of education and training acquired centrality in EU policies. Priority areas of intervention were established, and an articulated program and strategy of action were defined. These processes intensified educational integration, beyond what had been expressly provided for in the treaty.

Roger Dale (2008) has identified different phases (or stages) of development of the European Education Area: the first phase refers to any period before the Lisbon summit in 2000, the second phase covers the time between 2000 and 2005, and the third phase, from that date on. In the period between 2000 and 2004, working groups of experts were created, the program "Education and Training 2010" started, and the "open method of coordination" (OMC) was implemented. This acceleration of the construction of the European education area had contradictory aspects and tensions that prevented the immediate achievement of the desired outcomes.

The "Education and Training 2010" program (preparations for which began in 1999) provided a set of objectives to be adopted by specific member states for their education and training systems. Detailed work programs were issued, with indicators and benchmarks for future monitoring of the implementation of the program. In November 2003, the European Commission published "Education and Training 2010: Success of Lisbon," in which strategy hinges on urgent reforms. This document was to have a strong impact on education policies throughout the EU. It analyzed national education policies and outcomes related to achieving knowledge economies, listed priorities for the following years, and proposed control mechanisms to ensure that each member state respected them (European Commission, 2004).

Although political community intervention in the educational area had been declared as early as the 1980s, with action programs set in motion in the 1990s (those with a delineation of national boundaries), it was not until the mid-2000s that something unprecedented occurred. As stated by Fátima Antunes (2005a):

> What we witness at this unprecedented moment is the establishment of a formal and explicit level of supranational governance as a locus of affiliation of the policies to develop in education and training systems. These initiatives thus represent an attempt to build a systematic process of articulation of national education and training policies around the common priorities and objectives agreed upon and congruent or convergent with goals and strategies defined at the EU level. It could be said that the previous stages, pursued in the three last decades, have allowed the slow gestation of the *Europeanization* process that now rehearses its maturity. (pp. 129–130, translated from the Portuguese original)

THE OPEN METHOD OF COORDINATION

The choice of the Open Method of Coordination (OMC) and the stated "reasons" are significant for understanding the political context that defines the guidelines adopted by the EU. The OMC—suggested by the European Council in Lisbon in 2000—initiated a new style of working relationship between the EU and member states, as well as among the member states, to achieve the objectives of the Lisbon Strategy (2000–2010). The OMC was applied in such diverse fields as economics, education and training, social protection, poverty, environment, technology, research, and the information society. This transnational form of work organization was based on guidelines expressed by benchmarks (reference values) and indicators created in response to the challenges of globalization. Such benchmarks were implemented so that national policies, within a process of "Europeanization," might contribute to making the EU the "most competitive and dynamic economy in the world."

The role of the member states, guided by national experts, involves sharing best practices, negotiating the benchmarks to be integrated into National Action Plans, and undertaking mutual training programs. The European Commission assumes responsibility for turning guidelines into indicators and evaluating the performance of member states.

The OMC introduced a rupture in the mechanisms that theretofore were used to manage the processes of transfer of powers to the EU. Certain fields, including social policy, involved the "Community Method" (CM). The CM was expressed in various forms: legislation, directives, and European regulations. Lack of clarity in the distribution of powers between member states and the EU created all types of implementation and management issues. Today, integration of policy is governed less through law than by coordination based on common political orientations and shared interests of member states.

As a case in point: In education, those responsible for changes in occupational training policies work together to share relevant knowledge. They are less concerned with laws than they are with various mechanisms and technologies that contribute to innovation, autonomy, flexibility, and entrepreneurship (Nóvoa, 2002).

At the same time, the OMC organizes and gives coherence to this form of governance in the form of political guidance and of monitoring at a supranational level, promoting the homogenization of European policies and their implementation. Monitoring, evaluation, and legal pressure—albeit not punitive—actually functions as a mechanism for convergence.

The Bologna Process and the Construction of the European Higher Education Area

In higher education, the so-called Bologna Process has developed in this context. Initially, it was the result of an intergovernmental agreement of cooperation between the ministers of higher education of four states (France, the United Kingdom, Italy, and Germany), worried about the loss of capacity of European universities to attract students in face of its U.S. counterparts. However, the Bologna Process soon opened to other states, not just from the EU, but also to other European countries as well as peripheral regions,[7] under the coordination of the European institutions that, rapidly, saw in this process the way to establish the necessary conditions for the emergence of a new sociopolitical space of higher education in Europe, the so-called European Higher Education Area (EHEA) (see Croché, 2009).

In the first decade of the 21st century in Europe, changes in higher education were fundamentally associated with the implementation of the Bologna Process. The goal was to establish the EHEA, which would give European higher education an increase in competitiveness, attractiveness, and comparability. To this end, various objectives were defined: the creation of a system of easy comparison and reading of the degrees of an education system; the establishment of a transferrable credit system; the promotion of student, teacher, and researcher mobility; and the construction of quality assurance systems according to European recommendations and guidelines. These changes were reinforced not only by the Lisbon Strategy but also by the European modernization agenda for universities.

The assessment of the results and the consequences of the Bologna Process depend on the perspective of those who oversee it. On a political level, it is easy to conclude that the Bologna Process has been a success since it allows for greater integration and harmonization among the different systems from the 46 participating states. However, on institutional and local levels, what prevails involves a cautious answer, coming from a wide diversity of contexts. On the one hand, the objective of achieving greater competitiveness and attractiveness for the European universities is yet to be empirically verified. On the other hand, different studies point to critical analyses of the processes and consequences observed in different national spaces.[8] The present dynamics of the EHEA (and for research) are characterized by a simultaneous tendency toward convergence and toward diversification, as well as by the tension between cooperation and competition.

Several authors have highlighted the neoliberal rationale underlying the Bologna Process, based on the decrease of the social responsibility of the state and on the idea of education as a private asset, favoring the constitution of a European higher education market. Amaral and Magalhães (2004) have pondered the possible contribution of the Bologna Process to the decrease in autonomy of higher education institutions, the marketing of education, the development of a centralized European bureaucracy, and a decrease in diversity of the higher education systems.

The importance of the social dimension, aiming at the equality of opportunities in access, participation, and completion of studies has been reinforced as regards educational policies for higher education within the scope of the Bologna Process. In 2012, at the Bucharest meeting, the ministers reiterated the objective of broadening access to higher education, increasing participation and approval rates for underrepresented or disadvantaged groups, to reflect the diversity of the population of member states. Also, the Europe 2020 Strategy defined as one of its objectives the completion of higher education for at least 40% of adults between the ages of 30 and 34 (European Commission, 2010).

Nevertheless, despite the policies aiming to promote participation, there subsist important inequalities in access, success, and results. Growing competitiveness in attracting candidates and financial resources has fostered stratification and inequality in higher education systems. Also, the neoliberal and meritocratic rationales which constitute the basis of the policies for broader participation do not seem to favor the development of an inclusive higher education system, committed to social justice (see Gairín et al., 2020).

Moreover, the end of the implementation of the Bologna Process and the first years of the 2010s coincided with the debt crisis in several southern European countries (Greece, Portugal, Spain, Italy; but also in Ireland, the United Kingdom, Slovakia, Holland, and even France). This crisis has led to strongly authoritarian policies, with profound consequences in higher education policies. In the United Kingdom, the conservative government implemented a strong rise in the fees paid by the students, with predictable consequences in the access to higher education by the social layers with lower incomes. In Greece, the external intervention of international creditors, represented by the troika, the European Commission, the European Central Bank, and the International Monetary Fund, resulted in thousands of teachers and researchers being fired from universities and led to a contingency budget, where many of the universities' basic functions all but disappeared. In Portugal and Spain, the radical cuts in universities' budgets led to a regression in such areas as research and scientific development.

FABRICATING EUROPE THROUGH EDUCATION

In the debate about "fabricating Europe," Ronald Sultana (2002) has drawn attention to the convergence between the main education agendas set by the EU guidelines and the recommendations produced by the European Round Table of Industrialists (ERT):

> In March 1995, [. . .] ERT published a report entitled *Education for Europeans: towards the learning society*. Two years later, the EU released a White Paper entitled *Teaching and Learning: towards the learning society*. In 1997, ERT published *Investing in Knowledge: the integration of technology in European education*. This was echoed by a document put out by the European Commission that very same year, with the title *Towards a Europe of Knowledge*. The similarity of agendas is more than skin-deep, indicating a tightly woven policy network that extends at all levels of education, higher levels included. (p. 122)

According to Dale (2008), changes to European educational policy based on goals and criteria of effectiveness with shared responsibilities—subject to strategies of economic policy—constituted a new understanding of "subsidiarity."[9] These changes also created a new "European Education Area" based on a division of labor in educational governance.

This European Area frames its vision of education on international standards, including those set by the Organization for Economic Cooperation and Development (OECD). For Martin Lawn (2002), this new transnational governance structure is the symbolic expression of the legitimization of the power of capital, free from the limits of the nation-state. It is not free, because the EU education agenda necessarily must be filtered through different sensitivities of member states. For policy analysts and comparative educators, Sultana's (2002) question is most relevant: Who wins and who loses in this new European area?

Which populations will benefit from shifts in education policy? Dale (2008) argues that in the third phase of education strategy development the focus of EU education policies will be on Lifelong Learning. This is understood as an integrative program of all education and training policies.

In February 2004, following the "Kok Report" on the implementation of the Lisbon Strategy, the European Council and Commission produced the document "The Success of Lisbon Strategy Hinges on Urgent Reforms." It states, "much remains to be done in such a short time," since all reports and indicators point to the same conclusion: "If we are to achieve the objectives in education and training, the pace of reform must be accelerated. There are still too many weaknesses that limit the potential of development of the EU." They also suggest there is a significant delay by the EU regarding its "competitors"—especially in higher education—and that "there are still many warning signs" (European Commission, 2004).

In this context, the council and the commission considered it necessary to pursue the Lisbon Strategy with much greater determination along three major axes: (1) focus on reform and investment in key areas, (2) make lifelong learning a reality, and (3) build a Europe of education and training.

The interim report was subsequently approved in 2006 under the title "Modernizing Education and Training: A Vital Contribution to Prosperity and Social Cohesion in Europe." This document analyzed the progress made in implementing the program "Education and Training 2010" and concluded there was a need to "accelerate the pace of reforms to ensure a more effective contribution to the achievement of the Lisbon Strategy and development of the European social model" (European Commission, 2006). In this context, member states and the commission agreed on a set of measures to increase the effectiveness of the implementation of the education and training program.

Despite the complexity of this issue and the tensions that it generates, the EU lacked a pressing need to change the legal framework that forms these integrative processes. Thus, the Treaty of Lisbon, adopted at the European Council in late 2007, provided an institutional framework identical to that already set by the previous treaties (Articles 149 and 150) related to education and training. The Treaty of Lisbon is a complicated legal puzzle that is difficult to understand. However, at least in terms of education, the treaty repeats the perspectives and formulations already present in the previous project of the European Constitution.

Despite the limited nature of the changes introduced by the Treaty of Lisbon in education, this document also created possibilities that were not available until then. As Louis Weber (2003) has warned, there may be greater concerns in the area of international trade, where formulations are less accurate and unanimity is no longer necessary for the adoption of trade rules, including social services, education, and health.

In fact, the new wording of the articles concerning common commercial policy facilitates the performance capacity of the EU in international trade. Of special concern is that the new wording changed trade rules concerning education. Until then, the EU could only establish international trade agreements on issues of education and training if there was unanimous approval of member states. However, the Treaty of Lisbon ushered in the possibility to conclude these agreements based on a majority decision of the council. Trade agreements pose serious problems for member states in the realm of education and social services. The ability to govern and organize their national education systems is constricted by EU agreements that turn education into a commodity traded in the international market. This is known as the "liberalization" of education, and it is a key component of the neoliberal agenda that accompanies the forces of globalization.

THE EDUCATION AND TRAINING EU TARGETS TO 2025

The end of the second decade of the 21st century was marked by two separate events, albeit both with deep implications in the European construction of the education space: the United Kingdom's departure from the EU on January 1, 2021, the so-called Brexit, and the response to the economic and social crisis brought on by the COVID-19 pandemic.

The United Kingdom's departure from the EU has immediate implications in the European Education Area in the field of student (and teacher) mobility as a result of the United Kingdom leaving the European Erasmus Project. Other implications, namely in the field of scientific and technological research and university cooperation have yet to be determined and fully ascertained.

To respond to the COVID-19 pandemic, the EU managed to approve, after long and taxing negotiations among the member States, the Recovery Plan for Europe (2021–2027), considered the largest stimulus package ever financed through the EU budget (a total of €1.8 trillion). The allocated funds are aimed, primarily, at three areas considered of strategic importance: (1) research and innovation, (2) fair climate and digital transitions, and (3) preparedness, recovery, and resilience, including a new health program. Additionally: (4) modernizing traditional policies such as social and economic cohesion and a common agricultural policy, (5) fighting climate change, and (6) fostering biodiversity protection and gender equality.[10]

The European Commission has systematically redefined the orientations and objectives considered in the Lisbon summit, by pointing toward a strategy for smart, sustainable, and inclusive growth. In the European Commission's communication to the European Parliament and Council, dated September 30, 2020, on achieving the European Education Area by 2025, President Ursula von der Leyen argues that "Education is at the heart of the European way of life, strengthening social market economy and democracy with freedom, diversity, human rights and social justice." To this end, "the right to quality and inclusive education, training and lifelong learning is proclaimed in the European Pillar of Social Rights as its first principle" (European Commission, 2020, p. 1).

From the assessment of the results achieved within the strategic framework for cooperation in education and training (European Commission, 2020), the European Commission put forward to the European institutions and the national governments the adoption of a new vision to achieve the European Area by 2025, grounded on six dimensions: (1) quality, (2) inclusion and gender equality, (3) green and digital transitions, (4) teachers and trainers, (5) higher education, and (6) geopolitical dimension (see Figure 16.1).

In each of these dimensions, steps are earmarked to deliver on these *ambitious goals*. Regarding the dimension of **quality**, the EC assumes the Programme International Students Assessment (PISA) to be the main indicator, with several priorities: mastering basic and transversal skills, including digital skills, critical thinking, entrepreneurship, creativity, and civic engagement; promoting learning mobility and cooperation across borders; fostering learning languages and multilingualism; supporting teachers in managing linguistic and cultural differences in schools; enhancing the European perspective in parallel with national and regional perspectives; and maintaining education and training institutions as safe environments, free of violence, harmful speech, disinformation and all forms of discrimination.

As for the dimension of **inclusion and gender equality**, after assuming that "Education is failing to reduce inequalities linked to socio-economic

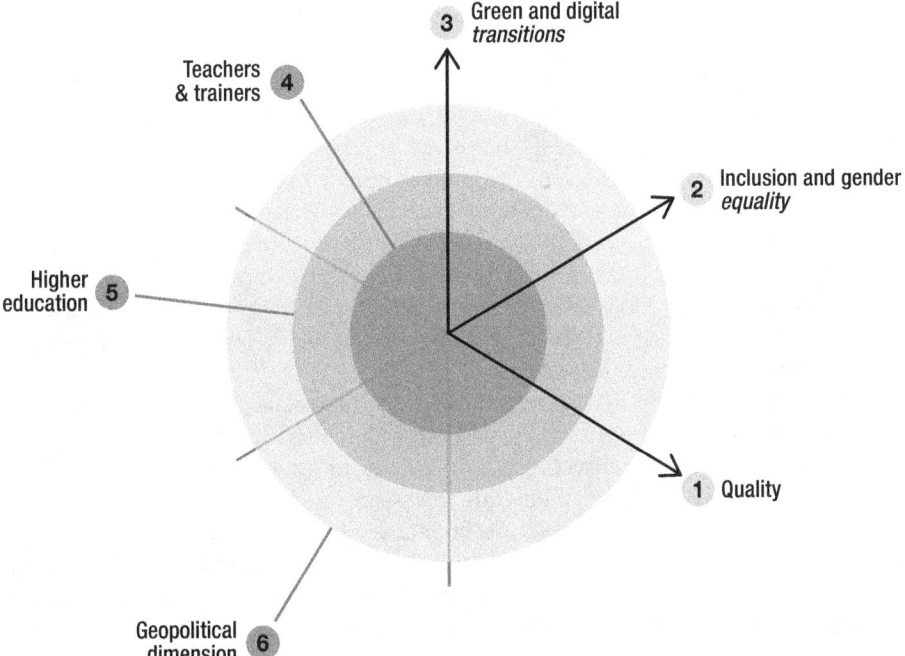

Figure 16.1. Dimensions of European Education Area (2019–2025)
Source: European Commission (2020, p. 5)

status"—although it is known that "the highest performing education systems are those that put a premium on equity" and that the COVID-19 pandemic "has highlighted even more starkly the importance of inclusion and fairness in education"—the EC document highlights directions and priorities: decoupling educational attainment and achievement from social, economic and cultural status, recognizing in early childhood education a critical element; integrating the UN Convention on the Rights of Persons with Disabilities in all education systems; developing Vocational Education Training (VET) systems and robust lifelong learning strategies; reinforcing cross-border cooperation; greater sensitivity toward the gender gap, with a clear bias in favor of young men in better-paid jobs; challenging and dissolving gender stereotypes, which constrain young women's access to engineering programs and Information and Communication Technologies (ICT) studies; and, working for a gender balance in leadership position, including higher education institutions.

The **green and digital transition** dimension is at the core of the discourse and priorities defined by the EU for the labor market and employment policies: "Digital literacy is a must, the more so in a post-COVID-19 world." Furthermore, "the transition to an environmentally sustainable, circular and climate-neutral economy has significant employment and social impacts." Thus, the defense of a transformative ambition involves changing people's behavior and skills—starting with schools setting the example, coupled with investments in the renovation of existing school equipment ("renovation wave") and in the formation of professionals who work toward a climate-neutral and resource-efficient economy, effectively supporting sustainability transitions by integrating environmental sustainability perspectives across natural and human sciences, and the omnipresent competences of "entrepreneurship and learning to learn."

The dimension **teachers and trainers** does not escape the repeated rhetorical declaration that they are at the "heart of education": "Without teachers and trainers, no innovation, no inclusion and no transformational education experiences for learners can take place." Acknowledging the role played by millions of teachers across Europe, who had to adapt rapidly to school closures due to the COVID-19 pandemic, the EC document advocates a valorization of the professions in education, of training programs, salaries, working conditions as well as the development of careers, to solve two of the most important bottlenecks in European education systems: a shortage of teachers in several countries as a result of low attractiveness of the teaching profession in some countries and regions, and very high age averages in others.

Regarding the **higher education** dimension, the focus is on internationalization and staff and student mobility, assuming that the Bologna Process played a driving role in these two directions. The document advocates closer and deeper cooperation between higher education institutions, fostering joint curriculum development and common courses, to facilitate mobility between different countries and allow for the development of a "pan-European talent pool," with a strong focus on advanced digital skills (artificial intelligence, cybersecurity, and high-performance computing). The point is that this cooperation may strengthen the attraction of students from other regions, in particular, Africa, the Western Balkans, and neighborhood countries. And that in these countries, education is instrumental for socioeconomic reforms and the consolidation of democracy.

As regards the sixth and last dimension, the **geopolitical,** it is assumed that cooperation in education has become a crucial instrument of the EU's external policy and an indispensable soft power tool. Given the rise of China and the retreat of the United States from the multilateral order (the document was submitted during the Trump administration), it is argued that the construction of a strong European Education Area is fundamental for the affirmation of the image of *Europa*, its values and way of life. Thus, internationalization must not only be reinforced in higher education, but also encompass other sectors, particularly VET and the sector of youth.

"Education is at the heart of the European way of life, strengthening a social market economy and democracy with freedom, diversity, human rights and social justice," is declared in a communication of the European Commission to the Parliament and other European institutions of September 2020 (p. 1). This is a powerful statement, which coexists, however, with many policies of the member states (and of the community institutions themselves) following in the opposite direction, which goes to show the ambiguity and contradictions of this process of building the European Education Area.

However, even such a powerful statement must not overlook other great challenges faced by the EU. The first is surely the issue of migrants and refugees. The Mediterranean has become an enormous graveyard, claiming the lives of several thousand human beings who continually seek in Europe better living conditions and a future for themselves and their families as a result of the misery and lack of employment in their countries of origin, but also as a way to escape conflicts, many of which created by the intervention of former European colonial powers. Finding a balance between the humanistic policy of including in the host societies these human beings who risk everything to reach Europe, the support to the development programs in the countries and regions where they come from, and a peace policy that will help solve the conflicts in the Middle East, in Northern Africa, and in Sub-Saharan Africa constitutes a considerable challenge that Europe as a whole is facing. Europe needs, at demographic and economic levels, this renovation of generations and this labor force. The question lies in the ability to embrace these new cultures in national societies of strong community traditions and, globally speaking, an aging population, who sees in the other a threat to its values and way of life.

A second challenge concerns the internal cohesion of the European space. Europe is a recent (and unfinished) political entity. There are several Europes in Europe. Its history comprehends internal colonialisms as well.[11] The enlargement processes of the EU relied on the assumption of economic cohesion policies, from which all could benefit and which would provide a common sense of belonging. The EU was not just constituted as a free market, despite the many efforts made to this end by such politicians as Margaret Thatcher. The challenge of overcoming national selfishness and stereotyped visions of the "other," even when "European," has been one of the most powerful challenges of the third decade of the 21st century. An even greater expansion of student mobility programs, like Erasmus, and the thrust to new multilingualism and interculturality programs will continue to be at the heart of European policies, besides, naturally, economic policies of territorial cohesion and policies to fight poverty and social exclusion.

The third and most decisive challenge is of a political nature. The European project was built based on a tense alliance between the Christian-democratic and the social-democratic traditions, which were joined by other political forces, such as the liberals and ecologists, but also the heirs to the communist and far-left tradition. On the whole, Europe was built by these political forces based on respect for a broad range of liberal democratic values and principles. The emergence and rise of far-right political forces in Western Europe (Italy, France, Spain, Denmark, Germany, Austria) and in Eastern Europe (Hungary, Poland, Slovakia, Czech Republic) surely constitute the greatest risk to the construction of a social Europe of solidarity, a space of peace and social justice. This risk derives from the programs of these political forces, with strong nationalistic sympathies and avowedly racist, patriarchal, and xenophobic nuances, but also because they call into question the liberal democratic principles which lay at the root of the construction of the EU: separation of powers and independence of the judicial power, freedom of the press and of belief, representative democracy and respect for the rights of minorities. How the peoples respond politically to this challenge will determine the future of Europe in the decades to come.

FINAL REMARKS

Neoliberal globalization has accentuated the competition between the different regions of the capitalist world system. Education (including higher education), training, and research have become, from the European side, privileged stages of this competition, within the frame of the perspective advocated in the 2000 Lisbon Strategy of turning the EU into the most competitive economy in the world. The definition of these targets has accentuated, in the EU, the dependency on education policies, training, and research of what's defined as "a social market economy," to which should be added the OECD's omnipresence in setting the agenda and problem definers.

Immediately before the 2008 international economic crisis, Europe could be considered an institutional space of experimentation—one that enjoyed enormous prestige around the world. For Goran Theborn (2002), Europe—a center of world commerce boasting 40% of the world exports—was widely considered pioneering in several fields, from law to politics. Throughout the process that Nóvoa and Lawn named "fabricating Europe," the EU was not only constructing a European Education Area, but also creating a new European model of education (Nóvoa & Lawn, 2002). This model has implications well beyond Europe itself. Suddenly, the state debts that exploded in 2010–2011 curtailed the assertiveness that Europe was expressing as a "normative area," and Europe entered a precipitous downward spiral leading to a global crisis of the EU itself. The ideal of European construction, of a united Europe of solidarity, constituted by different peoples, rich in their diversity and history, has suffered several setbacks; national egoisms and a directory of the strongest once again prevailed. Europe has become the world laboratory of the responses that neoliberalism, in its ordoliberal version, is giving the crisis it caused in 2008.

The European Education Area, as constituted at the beginning of this century, reflected a new political space strongly stimulated by European institutions (and generally accepted by national governments). It was run by experts and bureaucrats in a persuasive, gentle way, and depoliticized using standards and comparative statistics. The OECD agenda, which the EU accepted as its own, constructed a political space that facilitated the emergence of multiple networks. These networks range from schools and universities to research centers encompassing important and extensive transnational flows of people (students, teachers, researchers), ideas, and practices crisscrossing the borders of the member states. These networks also attracted (mostly) students from other regions.

This is a time when two strong feelings coexist regarding the future of the European project: skepticism and positive expectations. Some scholars insist that Europe needs to be more European: ideally, democratic, communitarian, able to balance successfully the unity and diversity of human expectations and experiences within the variety of cultures of free peoples. In this idealized context, what is the meaning of the evolution of educational issues in the EU? Contradictory tendencies coexist: on the one hand, there is the centralization and strengthening of the EU, involving the harmonization of education policies; but on the other hand, there are strong movements favoring deregulation and privatization of public social services, including education and health.

What policies will emerge from this tension? Will possible progressive agendas bring to the foreground the emancipatory dimensions of the educational process? Research in the area of public policy—and educational agendas as trendsetters in general—highlights the need for special attention to issues raised by this chapter and the various chapters in this volume.

NOTES

1. The chapter of the fourth edition followed closely the work carried out within the project "Educating the Global Citizen: Globalization, Educational Reform and the Politics of Equity and Inclusion in 12 Countries. The Portuguese case" (Ref POCI/CED/56992/2004 and PPCDT/CED/56992/2004) and the *Rede Iberoamericana de Investigação em Políticas de Educação—RIAIPE* (Ibero-American Network for Research in Education Policy). Thanks are due to Fatima Marques, Graça Anibal, and Vasco B. Graça, then my doctoral students, who—with their work and refined critical sense—have greatly contributed to the knowledge of these new modes of regulation of educational policies in Europe. Finally, I would like to thank Robert Arnove, Carlos A. Torres, and Rolf Straubhaar for their suggestions on a previous version of this chapter. The Portuguese original was translated into English by Maria Manuel Calvet Ricardo and revised by Robert Arnove. The present version (fifth edition) has been updated by the author and revised by Isabel Canhoto.

2. Present name. In 1951, in Paris, the treaty establishing the Economic Community for Coal and Steel Community was signed; in 1957, the Treaty of Rome designated this regional entity as European Economic Community, and, in 1992, the Treaty of Maastricht adopted the present name of EU.

3. Present name. In 1951, in Paris, the treaty establishing the Economic Community for Coal and Steel Community.

4. Ordoliberalism emerged in Germany in the 1930s, from the confluence between economists like Walter Eucken and jurists like Franz Böhm and Hans Grossman-Doerth. It is the German form of neoliberalism, which would assert itself in the post–World War II period in the German Democratic Republic, and in the process of building the EU. The word "ordoliberalism" derives from these theorists' insistence on the constitutional and procedural *order* which can be found in the foundation of a society and of a market economy. See Dardot and Laval (2009, Chap. 3).

5. The educational system was, up to that moment, based on a dual system: the lower classes received minimal training limited to primary education to be good subjects, while the upper classes had access to secondary education (high school) and the university, in order to effectively govern the State. See Starkie (2006).

6. During the Lisbon European Council in March 2000, the Heads of State and Government launched a strategy called "Lisbon," with the aim of making the EU the most competitive economy in the world while achieving the goal of full employment by 2010. Developed in several subsequent European Councils, this strategy rests on three pillars: (1) an economic pillar preparing the transition to a competitive and dynamic knowledge-based economy, (2) a social pillar which should facilitate the modernization of the Europe social model—investing in people and combating social exclusion, and (3) an environmental pillar, added at the European Council in Göteborg in June 2011.

7. In April 2012 the following were members of the Bologna Process—European Higher Education Area: Albania, Andorra, Armenia, Austria, Azerbaijan, Belgium (Flemish and French communities), Bosnia and Herzegovina, Bulgaria, Croatia, Cyprus, Czech Republic, Denmark, Estonia, Finland, France, Georgia, Germany, Greece, Holly See, Hungary, Iceland, Ireland, Italy, Kazakhstan, Latvia, Liechtenstein, Lithuania, Luxembourg, Malta, Moldova, Montenegro, Netherlands, Norway, Poland, Portugal, Romania, Russian Federation, Serbia, Slovak Republic, Slovenia, Spain, Sweden, Switzerland, the Former Yugoslav Republic of Macedonia, Turkey, Ukraine, and the United Kingdom.

8. For example, the *European Educational Research Journal* titles its special issue on the Bologna Process as "Help or Hindrance to the Development of European Higher Education?" (Vol. 9, 1, 2010), and in it its editor questions: "how much can we actually talk about a *European* higher education?" (Ursin et al., 2010, p. 30).

9. The principle of subsidiarity is defined in Article 5 of the Treaty on EU. It aims to ensure that decisions are taken as closely as possible to the citizen and that constant checks are made to verify that action at EU level is justified in light of the possibilities available at national, regional or local level. See https://eur-lex.europa.eu/summary/glossary/subsidiarity.html

10. See https://ec.europa.eu/info/strategy/recovery-plan-europe_en

11. See the interesting conference by Boaventura de Sousa Santos about the European colonial heritage (Santos, 2016).

REFERENCES

Amaral, A., & Magalhães, A. (2004). Epidemiology and the Bologna saga. *Higher Education*, 48, 79–100.

Antunes, F. (2005a). Globalização e europeização das políticas educativas. *Sociologia, Problemas e Práticas*, 47, 125–143.

Beck, U. (1992). *Risk society: Towards a new modernity*. Sage.

Croché, S. (2009). Bologna network: A new sociopolitical area in higher education. *Globalisation, Societies and Education*, 7(4), 489–503.

Dale, R. (2008). Construir a Europa através de um Espaço Europeu de Educação. *Revista Lusófona de Educação*, 11, 13–30.

Dardot, P., & Laval, C. (2009). *La nouvelle raison du monde. Essai sur la société néolibérale*, La Découverte.

Erlt, H. (2006, Spring). European Union programmes for education and vocational training: Development and impact. Skope Research Paper No. 42.

European Commission (2004). Education and Training 2010. The success of the Lisbon Strategy hinges on urgent reforms. Joint interim report of the Council and the Commission on the implementation of the detailed work programme on the follow-up of the objectives of education and training systems in Europe (2004/C 104/01), Official Journal of the European Union, April 30, 2004.

European Commission. (2006). Modernising education and training: a vital contribution to prosperity and social cohesion in Europe : Draft 2006 joint progress report of the Council and the Commission on the implementation of the Education & Training 2010 work programme {SEC(2005) 1415}. Brussels, 10.11.2005. COM(2005) 549 final.

European Commission. (2010). Europe 2020. A strategy for smart, sustainable and inclusive growth. Communication from the Commission. March 3, 2010, COM (2010) 2020 Final, Brussels.

European Commission. (2020). Communication from the Commission to the European Parliament, the Council, the European Economic and Social Committee and the Committee of the Regions on achieving the European Education Area by 2025. Brussels, September 30, 2020 COM(2020) 625 final.

Foucault, M. (2004). *Naissance de la biopolitique. Cours au Collège de France, 1978–1979*. EHESS/Gallimard/Seuil.

Gairín, J., Rodríguez-Gómez, D., & Dovigo, F. (Eds.). (2020). *The social dimension of higher education in Europe: Issues, strategies and good practices for Inclusion*. Brill Sense.

Green, A. (1994). Education and state formation revisited. *Historical Studies in Education*, 6(3), 1–17.

Habermas, J., & Derrida, J. (2003, Febuary 15). What binds Europeans together: A plea for a common foreign policy, beginning in a core of Europe. *Constellations*, 10(3), 291–297. Available at https://platypus1917.org/wp-content/uploads/archive/rgroups/2006-chicago/habermasderrida_europe.pdf

Hirtt, N. (2005). Marketisation of education in the global economy. Paper presented at the Worldwide Forum for Comparative Education, Globalisation of Education: Government, Market, and Society, Beijing.

Lawn, M. (2002). Borderless education: Imagining a European education space in a time of brands and networks. In A. Nóvoa & M. Lawn (Eds.), *Fabricating Europe: The formation of an education space* (pp. 19–31). Kluwer Academic Publishers.

Mitchell, K. (2004). Neoliberal governmentality in the European Union: Education, training and technologies of citizenship. *Environment and Planning Development: Society and Space*, 24(3), 389–407.

Nóvoa, A. (2002). Ways of thinking about education in Europe. In A. Nóvoa & M. Lawn (Eds.), *Fabricating Europe: The formation of an education space* (pp. 131–155). Kluwer Academic Publishers.

Nóvoa, A., & M. Lawn (Eds.) (2002). *Fabricating Europe: The formation of an Education Space* Kluwer Academic Publishers.

Piketty, T. (2020). *Capital and ideology*. Translated by Arthur Goldhammer. Belknap Press of Harvard University Press.

Starkie, E. G. (2006). El papel de la politica educativa europea en la formacion de los cidada- nos europeo, *Revista Ciencias de la Educacón*, 28(2), 105–118.

Storey, A. (2004). The European project: Dismantling social democracy, globalising neo-liberalism. Paper for presentation at the conference "Is Ireland a Democracy?" Sociology Department, National University of Ireland, Maynooth, April 2–3, 2004.

Sultana, R. G. (2002). Quality education and training for tomorrow's Europe. In A. Nóvoa & M. Lawn (Eds.), *Fabricating Europe: The formation of an Education Space* (pp. 109–130). Kluwer Academic Publishers.

Weber, L. (2003). *OMC, AGCS. Vers la privatisation de la société?* Éditions Nouveaux Regards/Éditions Syllep.

17

Education in Eastern and Central Europe

Rethinking Postsocialism in the Context of Globalization

Ben Eklof
Indiana University, Higher School of Economics

Iveta Silova
Arizona State University

ABSTRACT

This essay examines trajectories of educational reforms in the postsocialist countries, including the former 15 republics of the Soviet Union as well the former "satellite" states of South/East and Central Europe, a vast area encompassing more than a sixth of the earth's surface. After the fall of the Berlin Wall in 1989 and the revolutionary changes that shook the world in its aftermath, education moved into an unsettled state. Change occurred much more rapidly and profoundly in some areas than others. Internationalization left a mark but also varied from country to country in response and impact. While acknowledging the importance of global reform agendas, this chapter attempts to readjust our analytical gaze by taking difference and divergence as a starting point for theorizing postsocialist transformations in the globalization context. More specifically, it draws attention to the multiplicity of "socialisms" and "postsocialisms," and highlights diverse reform trajectories, for the three-decade-long interaction of socialist and postsocialist education institutions with Western reform projects—whether decentralization, privatization, or higher education reforms—has resulted in mixed, often contradictory outcomes. While freedom and opportunity beckoned, as time passed equity and egalitarianism declined while corruption remained rampant. Even today, 30 years later, resistance and lip service to reform can both be found, but so can remarkable dedication and a capacity for innovation, even in very difficult circumstances. A revival of national and imperial traditions proceeds, but a fascination with Western approaches persists at the same time. The postsocialist education space remains dynamic and diverse, while its reform trajectories remain inevitably open.

■ ■ ■

With the demise of the socialist bloc in 1989, the vast social and political landscape of Eastern/Central Europe and the former Soviet Union was fundamentally altered. The political monopoly exerted by the Communist Party was eliminated and state monopolies on the economy and the media were challenged. Even the political map of the region was redrawn as new (or newly reconstituted) states have emerged. The enormous energies released in this process produced major changes, setting the countries of Eastern/Central Europe and the former Soviet Union on distinctly different trajectories of postsocialist transformations. Approximately one-third of all countries experienced armed conflicts during the transformation period, resulting in devastating effects in all spheres of political, economic, and social life. Following the collapse of the socialist bloc, armed conflicts broke out in the Caucasus (including Armenia and Azerbaijan in 1988–1994 and 2020 and Georgia in 1990–1994), in Central Asia (including in the Ferghana Valley in 1989–1991 and Tajikistan in 1992–1993), the former Soviet republics (including the northern Caucasus of the Russian Federation in 1992–2001, and Moldova in 1992), and the former Yugoslav republic (including former Yugoslavia in 1991–1995, Federal Republic of Yugoslavia in 1997–1999, and FYR Macedonia in 2001). In 2022, the Russian military forces invaded Ukraine, escalating the Russo-Ukrainian conflict launched by Russia in 2014 into a war of aggression.

Meanwhile, 10 countries became new member states of the European Union (EU), including Bulgaria, the Czech Republic, Poland, Romania, the Slovak Republic, and Slovenia. While joining the EU has been generally associated with the emergence of open, liberal societies—at least partially rooted in respect for the rule of law, human rights, and economic freedom—some of the governments in these countries have moved toward authoritarianism as in the case of Hungary, Poland, and Slovenia. Many other countries—Azerbaijan, Belarus, Kazakhstan, Tajikistan, Turkmenistan, and Uzbekistan among others—seem to have more permanently settled into authoritarian or semi-authoritarian regimes.

Notwithstanding the diversity of postsocialist transformations, many observers at the time interpreted the collapse of the socialist bloc as an ultimate triumph of the West, pointing to the monumental replacement of the world socialist system by Western capitalism. In particular, world culture scholars argued that "contemporary economies seem to *all* adhere to capitalist models functionally and in most cases formally as well," suggesting that the collapse of the socialist bloc presented "*a complete example*" of a universal "adherence and conformance [of nation-states] to legitimate capitalist models of process and production" worldwide (Wiseman & Baker, 2006, p. 20, emphasis added). In this context, the West (particularly the United States) has been pronounced "a forerunner in global institutional trends," setting new global standards of education quality and achievement worldwide (Baker & LeTendre, 2005, p. 17). By implication, non-Western societies and those on the periphery of Europe have appeared as merely residual. At the same time, the "postsocialist" region has been conceptually portrayed to be "on a linear journey somewhere"—a predetermined movement toward the West, progress, and modernity:

> The transition recalls the earlier historical positioning of the region as "in between" east and west, a notion which not only redeploys the teleological construction of progress from east to west but also embeds the teleology (spatial and temporal) itself, focusing attention once again on the future and the west (then and there) rather than on the here and now of post-socialist Europe. In all of these ways, the diversity, depth and scale of the region's particular histories and geographies are erased as they become (just like) the west. (Stenning & Horschelmann, 2008, p. 321)

With few exceptions scholarship on postsocialist transformations in education has focused on examining the trajectories of "global" education reforms that have spread across different contexts, while overlooking existing alternatives in education policy and practice. Typically, the starting point is identifying a "global" reform—such as student-centered learning, outcomes-based education, curriculum standardization, privatization, or decentralization—and then tracing its complicated trajectory locally.[1] And although many studies highlight the complexity, plurality, and unpredictability of Western reform trajectories in the postsocialist education space, "the global" generally serves as the main reference point for understanding postsocialist transformations.

This is clearly problematic. As Burawoy (1999) explains, using "singular Western models" as a yardstick for postsocialist transformations inevitably results in losing "sight of alternatives, whether alternative capitalisms, alternative socialisms, or other utopias that offer novel lenses through which to interpret the present and the past, as well as future" (p. 309). This chapter attempts to readjust our analytical gaze by taking difference and divergence as a starting point for theorizing postsocialist transformations in the globalization context. More specifically, it draws attention to the multiplicity of "socialisms" and "postsocialisms," while highlighting diverse reform trajectories across different postsocialist contexts (Hann et al., 2003; Stenning & Hörschelmann, 2008). At the same time, writing in 2021, we must acknowledge that "difference" and "divergence" have become so marked in the region that many political scientists now call into question the utility of continued use of the terms "post-Soviet "or even postsocialist itself for understanding the trajectory of an enormous region encompassing more than one-sixth of the earth's land surface. Some even find discussion of a "post-Soviet reality" offensive in that it tends to lump together states and societies which, once the "veneer" of an imposed ideology had been stripped away, bore little resemblance to one another. While acknowledging the cogency of this point of view, we also agree with the editors of a collection of essays dedicated to "homo post-sovieticus" that one "cannot deny there is something idiosyncratic about the former socialist bloc, something which links its societies together, either through common experience or history (or both)" (Górecki, 2017).

Following the discussion of historical legacies, we turn to examine the complex interactions of resurgent, if altered or even imagined, national traditions, socialist and postsocialist histories, and subsequent (Western) reform projects. By focusing on the implementation—as well as a retraction in places—of decentralization and privatization reforms along with standardized testing across the region, we discuss how the "global" reform agenda has been received and redefined locally. Here the case of Russia merits special attention if only because of its size and preponderance in regional affairs; as the Prime Minister of Canada Pierre Trudeau once wryly said about his country's relationship with the United States: "When you sleep next to an elephant, you pay attention when it rolls over." Of necessity this chapter also focuses heavily on education policies; were we to take the approach of social history "from below," we would likely find far more evidence of diversity and less of commonality for all periods covered below.

DIVERSE HISTORICAL LEGACIES

Although a common 19th-century European [most often German] education tradition shaped pedagogy throughout the area, the Soviet-style governance introduced after World War II imposed a new and different layer of uniformity across state borders. At the same time, however, the underlying social and cultural diversity of the region was never fully eradicated in the schools. Beneath a weighty, if sometimes superficial, veneer of communist beliefs and practices, *Russian* traditions deeply embedded in the "Soviet" model vigorously vied with Baltic, Muslim, Turkic, and other influences:

> There is no way in which people can act, speak, create, come out from the margins and talk, or begin to reflect on their own experience unless they come from somewhere, unless they come from some history, unless they inherit certain cultural traditions. And in that sense, the past is not only a position from which to speak, but it is also an absolutely necessary resource in one's efforts to say something. (Pinkert, 2002, p. 24)

Before 1918 Southeastern and Central Europe was divided among three empires—the Hapsburg, Ottoman, and Russian—with very different outlooks on governance in general and education in particular. Since the middle of the 18th century, the rulers of the Hapsburg empire had shown interest in providing basic education for all subjects as a means of creating a cohesive empire. Primary education served to imbue children with feelings of loyalty toward the crown and the values for which it stood. Catholicism was an important element of this education, serving thus as an important counterforce against the threat of nationalism and ethnic challenges. Over the 19th century the Hapsburgs offered ambitious students of all nationalities the opportunity to study in its reputable schools (e.g., the Theresianum) or become part of the officer corps, another important educational institution in the empire. At the same time, authorities made it increasingly difficult for students who wanted to study in their own local language—be it Slovene, Croat, or Romanian—limiting their subventions only to schools that used German or (after 1867, especially) Hungarian as their primary language. Be that as it may, the empire offered many people (not just its German- and Hungarian-speaking populations) an opportunity to study in reputable Viennese universities and other schools abroad. The level of literacy and general education were higher here than elsewhere in Eastern Europe.

No such cohesive policy developed in the Ottoman Empire. The authorities were uninterested in the local administration and education of the non-Muslim populations. Instead, through the millet system (see *Encyclopedia of Modern Europe*, 2006) each religious community recognized under Islam—Orthodox Christian, Catholic, Protestant denominations, and Judaism—ruled over its respective flocks with little interference from the outside. The Orthodox Church, which came to dominate the lives of most Balkan Christians, had few educational goals beyond the training of parish priests. As the empire waned in the face of challenges from the growing nationalist movements, the various ethnic groups in the Balkans began building educational institutions that would ensure the creation of autonomous educated elites. Education reform proceeded from the top down, starting with the creation of elite schools and academies and only slowly spreading throughout the rest of the population. In addition, a small number of schools for vocational training appeared. The legacy of Ottoman rule for the development of education in the Balkans was meager, in part because the Orthodox Church lacked interest in education that was not strictly canonical. The various newly independent states tried to make up for these inadequacies but had a hard time catching up with the institutions, personnel, and other resources available in the Hapsburg lands. After 1918, the newly independent Balkan countries succeeded in passing legislation that made education compulsory to the fourth grade, although its implementation was rather haphazard. The illiteracy rate remained very high in this part of the world.

In the Russian empire, which at its zenith encompassed roughly one-sixth of the Earth's land surface, 18th-century rulers made education a state concern by establishing universities, an academy of science, and then secondary schools. The Orthodox Church also founded seminaries, many of whose graduates later became either prominent civil servants or revolutionaries. The Ministry of Education was created in 1802, and the Great Reforms of the 1860s included legislation enabling schooling for the newly liberated serfs and expanding opportunities for women at the secondary level. Trying to finance an army to support Russia's imperial and great power ambitions, the state had little left to spend on basic education. However, in the quarter-century before World War I, a combination of societal and state initiatives gave an enormous boost to public schooling for the lower classes, and educators hoped to achieve universally accessible elementary schooling in the European provinces by 1922. However, given a long tradition of arbitrary autocratic government, the notion of "compulsory education" found little traction with an educated society.

Russian pedagogy and classroom practices were derivative of European, especially Prussian, approaches. Universities, though plagued by issues of autonomy and political freedom, made substantial contributions to world science; at the secondary level, the atmosphere was formal, discipline often harsh, and the curriculum rigorous. At the primary level, however, Tolstoyan child-centered notions were influential, and after the turn of the century, progressivism made deep inroads into educational practice. Dewey's democratic classroom, in which redistributive justice was combined with decentralization and political freedom, became part of a powerful radical democratic and socialist movement against autocracy (Brickman, 1964). Indeed, self-government, or *samoupravlenie*, came to be seen by many as a panacea in education; yet such views found little favor with the autocratic state. Furthermore, religion and language presented problems for educators, whether loyal or oppositionist. Most progressives insisted on the right to use and teach local languages in the schools, yet many also believed in the civilizing mission of the empire and almost all agreed that the Russian language should also be taught. Reformers were overwhelmingly secular in orientation and believed that the Orthodox Church had no place in the schools. Yet believing in cultural autonomy, many argued that local populations should be allowed to establish private confessional schools, whether Catholic, Muslim, or (Orthodox) Old Belief. The practical problems involved in implementing such policies (e.g., teachers facing a classroom with children often from multiple minority groups) were never fully addressed, and tensions over ethnic and linguistic issues as well as general resentment against an arbitrary authoritarian state mounted in Russia's borderlands after 1900, making whatever school policies could be devised all but impossible to implement. As Radik Iskhakov (2011) has noted, all the paradoxes of the empire were compressed and contained within conflicts over educational policy and practice.

Institutionalizing Soviet-Style Socialism (1918–1989)

World War I led to the collapse of the Ottoman, Austro-Hungarian, and Russian empires and the emergence of numerous new states, many having ethnically and religiously diverse populations and sharply contrasting rural and urban cultures. After 1918, all Southeast and Central European countries focused on building a strong educational infrastructure. Education policies had been important in the nationalist debates in the 19th century, and political leaders recognized the power that such institutions had to create a loyal, mobilized community of citizens or to foster critical thinking. Furthermore, as these states had significant minority populations, education institutions and curriculum development became one of the main venues for constructing a homogeneous national identity. Policymakers favored highly centralized models over regional administrative and curricular autonomy since the latter appeared to be destabilizing, centrifugal forces.

The practical challenges had to do primarily with financial resources. Ambitions for creating a comprehensive primary and secondary education system with possibilities for vocational and theoretical education were high among most policymakers. They also encouraged the growth of higher education institutions, with increasing diversification among the liberal professions, from engineering to law and social sciences. Demography, anthropology, and sociology came to displace the central position held by philosophy and history among the humanities. These multiple agendas for developing various levels of education suffered especially after the Great Depression. Unfortunately for the bulk of the population, compulsory primary education suffered most. In Romania, for instance, the shrinking education budget prompted the minister of education to reduce the number of state-paid teachers by 2,000 in 1934, whereas university research institutes retained most of their state funding. This abatement of primary education was not as marked in places such as Bulgaria in which higher education was not as significant to the policymakers. Finally, Czechoslovakia was able to weather the 1930s better, since it already had a well-developed primary and higher education infrastructure, inherited from the Hapsburgs and an economy less vulnerable to a depression than that of other Eastern European countries.

By the end of the 1930s, all Southeast and Central European countries except Albania had an integrated education system that included universities and other higher education institutions. Czechoslovakia led the rest of the region in both institutional development and diversity. It also had the highest rate of literacy. Throughout the area, the state had become the most important agent for the dissemination of knowledge through schools at the expense especially of the Catholic and Orthodox churches. Independent education institutions did survive, especially those funded by religious denominations—Christian and Jewish. Efforts were also made by different nongovernmental organizations (NGOs) to develop vocational schools and schools for women. Access to education, especially at the postprimary levels, was still very difficult for women, and none of the Eastern European states made a very sustained effort to eliminate the institutional, economic, and cultural obstacles faced by women who wished to engage in education.

Meanwhile, the Russian Revolution of 1917 had swept away the old czarist order, and the new Bolshevik leaders, borrowing heavily from Western progressivism, set about creating a new, secular, and democratic school system without uniforms, grades, textbooks, or conventional disciplinary boundaries (Holmes 1991; Kirschenbaum, 2001). Open access to all levels of the school "ladder" was guaranteed for workers and peasants, and the walls separating school, work, and community were to be broken down. A major effort was launched to promote local languages through the indigenization (or *korenizatsiya*) policy.[2] Introduced on the borderlands in the early 1920s, the policy sought to foster indigenous elites and included the introduction of the local languages into all spheres of public life, including education, publishing, culture, and government. In particular, the Council of People's Commissars called for the establishment of native language schools for national minorities whenever there were at least 25 students at a given grade level who spoke that language (USSR, 1973). By the middle of the 1930s native language schools were operating in all regions of the Soviet Union, and in 1934 textbooks were printed in 104 languages (Sovetkin, 1958).

In the 1930s Stalin inaugurated a new era, often labeled a "Thermidor," referring to the authoritarian restoration of order in the aftermath of the French Revolution, in education as well as other spheres of society. The Stalinist school system now imposed a breathtaking uniformity and hierarchy across the vast territories and ethnically diversified populations of the Soviet Union (by now approximating the boundaries of the old czarist empire, less Finland, Poland, and the Baltic Region). Stalinist education was nominally egalitarian and "polytechnical,"[3] as well as strongly "collectivist" in that it discouraged individual initiative or choice. Textbooks were restored to their traditional place, the authority of the teacher was reinforced but the autonomy of the individual school or region was eliminated, uniforms were reintroduced, as were, briefly, separate schools for boys and girls; and rote learning once again reigned supreme. The rapid expansion of education did provide an opportunity for millions of peasants and workers, many of whom gained a secondary technical education and rose to positions of power and status then and later. But the *genuinely* emancipatory and redistributive aspects of socialism, not to mention the learner-based tenets of democratic education, were scarcely evident in this system. Instead, everyone—teacher, student, and administrator—was ascribed a place in a "command system" (a label critically applied in the perestroika era to describe the legacy of Stalinism as a whole). Individual choice was not prominent and students were assigned jobs by the state after graduation. In practice the system was far from foolproof, and millions of enterprising or well-connected individuals managed to beat the rules to get the education and careers they wanted, regardless of the state's plans for them. Still, for most the channels created by the state were those that directed their lives.

Stalinism also meant the ruthless suppression of local languages (and often those who spoke them) in an attempt to establish a "New Soviet Person" implicitly dominated by Russian culture. As Stalin (1934) proclaimed, national cultures had to be "national in form but socialist in content." This meant that national rights were merely matters of cultural "forms," distinct from the political and economic "content" strictly dictated by the Soviet government (Slezkine, 1994, p. 434). Accompanied by Russification policies, the status of the Russian language, schools, and (with immigration) students in the titular republics continued to grow, while the status of schools for titular nationalities rapidly declined (see Ewing, 2006). Between 1932 and 1988, for example, the number of languages of instruction in schools of the Soviet republics decreased from 102 in 1932 to 40 in 1988 (Zhdanova, 1989). Furthermore, nine of the 15 Soviet Union republics witnessed a steady decrease in the number of years of education in their native languages.[4] For the titular nationalities possessing an autonomous republic or region on the territory of the Russian Federation, the number of possible years of education in their native languages was halved between 1958 and 1972 (Dzyuba, 1970). Whether in Ukraine, Russia, Central Asia, or Moldova, all schools began to look alike, all textbooks were the same, and all teachers followed the same lesson plans. In this system, an insidious ideology of bombast, distortion, and untruth corrupted the teaching of history and literature, and it profoundly compromised the singular achievement of unprecedented educational expansion, the other hallmark of Stalinism.

Yet considerable diversity underlay the formal uniformity describing Soviet-style educational regimes Elsewhere in Southeast and Central Europe, the socialist regimes established after World War II did not completely do away with existing education legacies and institutions. To be sure, many qualified educators were purged between 1948 and 1956. Faculty in higher education institutions suffered the most. Taking their cue from the Soviet Union, the East European communists used education as a tool for legitimizing their control on ideological grounds. Studying Russian became compulsory for all students, and dialectical materialism became the basis for all social sciences. The applied sciences became a priority, and many of the new specialists from these countries received their training in the Soviet Union. Unlike the Soviet Union, however, education in the Yugoslavian system remained decentralized but fragmented. Following the adoption of the 1950 bill on "workers' self-management," the Yugoslav National Assembly introduced educational decentralization by increasing autonomy for both the federation's six republics and the educational authorities in districts and towns within these entities (Sobe, 2006). While the central authority kept responsibility for passing basic legislation, the Yugoslav republics were responsible for most education policies including those relating to teachers, curricula, and textbooks (Pantić et al., 2011). And although some American scholars interpreted Yugoslav decentralization as a pragmatic move toward Western "modernization," Yugoslav communists labeled it a "truer" form of communism than that of the Soviet Union, where strong political centralism "had strayed from Marx's call for the withering away of the state" and was seen to have achieved "not only internal unity but greater efficiency to centralized government" (Sobe, 2006, pp. 48–49). In other countries, the divergence from the Soviet model was subtler but still important, and too variegated to survey here. Across the former socialist region, childhood memories of everyday school life clearly indicate that learning experiences, including classroom instruction and extracurricular activities, depended considerably upon the local sociocultural contexts, as well as the personalities and convictions of individual teachers and school administrators (Silova et al., 2018).

Educational Achievements Under Soviet-Style Socialism

The achievements of the Soviet-type school were considerable. First and foremost, the Soviet system attempted to introduce a broad measure of social equality and mass educational opportunity, even if those measures were arguably compromised by episodes of repression, corruption that spread in the postwar era, and political favoritism (Johnson, 2008). In particular, the Soviet education system was effective in delivering universal literacy under Stalin and, under his successors, a complete secondary education to the population of a far-flung and linguistically diverse country. In higher education, strong state support and massive public investment meant that Soviet universities witnessed some of the most rapid and truly impressive quantitative and institutional growth in the world (Johnson, 2008). Russian, and then Soviet higher education grew from its modest domestic influence to become "one of the largest and most comprehensive systems of higher education and research in the postwar era" (Johnson, 2008, p. 162). By the 1980s access to higher education lagged only behind that of the United States. Vocational and technical schools, one network of special schools for the gifted and another for children with special needs, boarding schools, a vast network of preschool and extramural institutions—all were aimed at enhancing opportunity and recruiting talent. Indeed, relative to much of the Western world, Soviet inputs in the sphere of early childhood education as a proportion of the entire education budget were much higher; some argue this was a key to the success of the Soviet school.

The socialist regimes also opened up greater access to all levels of education for disadvantaged groups such as peasants, working-class people, women, and some national minorities. For example, female students comprised approximately half of undergraduate enrollments in the USSR by the 1980s (Rosen, 1980). Unlike women in other countries, Soviet women were strongly represented not only in the fields of education and art, but also at the professional level in the medical fields. Furthermore, state quotas were specifically granted for the political, economic, and social participation of women, including government, parliament, and even the Soviet Army. By the end of the Soviet period, women had a fairly strong representation in parliament, occupying approximately one-third of all government positions. And while it is justifiably argued that the number of women in key political positions was meager, perhaps only symbolic (Silova & Magno, 2004; Tadjbakhsh, 1998), the influence of Soviet policies on access to education for women and girls was powerful. Another major achievement of the Soviet-style educational complex was the vast network of extracurricular institutions (e.g., after-school programs, summer camps), which played a huge cultural role in identifying talent, promoting academic achievement, socialization, recreation, and, for many, compensating for limited cultural and financial family resources.

Notwithstanding these achievements, serious problems remained. Education was chronically underfunded: as a proportion of gross national income, investments in education steadily declined in the 1980s. For example, the Soviet Union spent 7% of its gross domestic product on education in the 1970s, but this declined to less than 4% by the late 1980s. Rural schools lacked in amenities; science laboratories were antiquated; underpaid and overworked teachers left in large numbers; and overcrowded and crumbling urban schools met in two and sometimes three shifts daily. According to official data, in 1988, 21% of all Soviet schoolchildren attended schools in buildings without central heating, 30% were in schools lacking indoor plumbing, and 40% studied in schools with no access to sports facilities (Yagodin, quoted in Eklof et al., 2005, p. 11). One might well argue that given the chronic inadequacies in funding and dismal infrastructure, it was remarkable what Soviet-era schools *did* achieve.

In Southeast and Central Europe and the Soviet Union, women were generally relegated to secondary positions in all branches of the economy and administration, despite academic performance equaling that of men (Silova & Magno, 2004). Schools for minorities were supported inconsistently. In most cases, special education remained limited to providing spaces for isolating individuals with physical and mental disabilities from the "able" population. Furthermore, strictly centralized control over curriculum had serious consequences for the quality of education. Although some graduates of Soviet schools often praise the education they received and speak of caring and highly competent teachers, more recent cross-national studies of student achievement revealed that students in Soviet-type schools, while excelling at the awareness of facts, fared less well in their application and did poorly at using knowledge in unanticipated settings (Eklof et al., 2005).

Some countries (e.g., Hungary, Czechoslovakia, and Poland) had attempted to address these problems as early as the 1970s. For example, the Gierek regime attempted to reduce the ideological content in all disciplines in Polish education. The Hungarian leadership also attempted such a change after Janos Kadar came to power, but it took another 13 years from the initial resolution in 1972 before any substantial change occurred. In 1985, the Education Act was passed, which finally decentralized administrative, budgetary, and, to some extent, curriculum matters. With this legislation, which transferred some responsibilities from the ministerial level to local administrators and teachers, Hungary became the first East European country to understand and grapple with the educational inadequacies of the communist regime (Gutsche, 1993). Another remarkable development occurred in Poland starting in 1980 when the Catholic church in collaboration with Solidarity established alternative education institutions such as primary and secondary schools under the administrative control of the church. This development was essential to fostering values, goals, and attitudes divorced from the communist order (Bartz & Kullas, 1993).

Yet these three countries were outliers. If stagnant economies were at the heart of growing difficulties in education, the structural rigidities of the entire command system in which education was embedded made it especially difficult to adapt schools to the changing needs of the economy. The area's limited communications infrastructure created daunting obstacles to participation in the information revolution by Soviet schools. An expensive network of research institutions under the various academies of science made only a limited contribution to economic growth. Furthermore, the intellectual brain drain to the West, which started in the 1970s and intensified in the 1980s, deprived Eastern Europe of much of its human capital.[5] The same strict, top-down control that fostered emigration also led to pedagogical restraints against creative and critical thinking among those who remained. By the early 1980s, the economic and administrative infrastructure in Eastern Europe was simply incapable of generating the type of creative, dynamic change needed to further development.

In short, the legacies of the Soviet period contained a mixture of both positive and negative elements, varying significantly across the countries of the socialist region. Notwithstanding the differences, the socialist regime established a solid infrastructure for educational provision with a manifest emphasis on equality, achievement, and self-sacrifice for the larger community—in theory, if not always in practice. With all the concerns about its quality, comprehensiveness, and the real degree of equity, the mass provision of Soviet education contributed to creating a *sense* of social cohesion as well as significant compensatory legitimacy for the socialist regime (Heyneman, 2000). Soviet education also established a widely shared public *expectation* for the continued provision of mass schooling at little or no individual cost and on a fundamentally egalitarian basis (Silova et al., 2007). It is these widely shared principles that have since then been most severely affected, revealing emerging tensions and contradictions between socialist legacies and Western-inspired educational reform projects.

POSTSOCIALIST TRANSFORMATIONS

The period following the collapse of the socialist bloc in 1989 was characterized by an acute sense of drift in educational policy, as various local actors and external (generally multilateral) institutions struggled to create "new" and autonomous educational systems out of what had earlier been a tightly integrated and highly standardized system. The reforms articulated in the Gorbachev era (1985–1991) and associated with *perestroika* (economic restructuring), *glasnost* (openness), and *demokratizatsiia* (democratization) had contradictory effects as they unfolded with variations across the entire region. On the one hand, these reforms gave rise to national movements that often advocated more autonomy, choice, and democracy at the local level. On the other hand, that period also witnessed the emergence of long-suppressed ethnic and religious conflicts in the former Soviet Union and elsewhere and prompted the party-state elites to begin expropriating or "privatizing" state property for their benefit and to grope for new forms of legitimacy through ethno-territorial nationalism (Jones-Luong, 2004; Silova et al., 2007).

An analysis of educational narratives throughout the 1990s and 2000s reveals that policy rhetoric across Southeast and Central Europe and the former Soviet Union increasingly appropriated Western "standards" and "norms." This was especially visible in the spread of a "postsocialist education reform package" across the region, reflecting a set of globally "traveling policies" such as student-centered learning, decentralization, privatization, standardization of student assessment, liberalization of textbook publishing, among others (see note 5). In some cases, "the postsocialist reform package" was imposed through the structural adjustment policies introduced by the World Bank and the Asian Development Bank in the 1990s. In other cases, however, it was voluntarily borrowed by policymakers in the former socialist states out of fear of "falling behind" internationally (Steiner-Khamsi & Stolpe, 2006, p. 189). Whatever the reasons for the adoption of the "postsocialist education reform package," its emergence and implementation highlight the complexity of postsocialist education transformation processes, revealing a variety of ways in which the "global" reform agenda has been integrated but also continuously contested and redefined in various postsocialist contexts. For this chapter, the discussion will be limited to selected elements of the "reform package": decentralization, curriculum, and higher education reforms.

The Meanings of Decentralization in Centralized States

In the early 1990s decentralization of education was a visceral reaction to the centralist administrative control setup under socialism. In particular, reforms were to be about "restoring the democratic political and professional legitimacy of decision-making" (Rado, 2010, p. 77). Decentralization reforms thus held the promise of promoting the administrative, technical, and pedagogical efficiency of educational systems while at the same time improving the quality of educational service providers. Such promised reforms also contained significant symbolic value as initiatives primarily associated with Western education ideals and signaling the adherence of postsocialist states to the principles of Western democratic governance. In Romania, for example, rationales for initiating decentralization reforms included references to quick policy fixes to enable countries to "rapidly pass through the primitive phase [of postsocialist reform]" and become "compatible with European standards" (Mincu & Horga, 2010, p. 96). More specifically:

> Decentralization was seen as a distinctive strategy to promote democracy, freedom, participation, and responsibility in education and, more generally, in society as a whole. . . . The pre-1989 pedagogical culture was [seen as] inadequate, since teachers were not autonomous in their classes and schools, and the individualization of education processes was unworkable in a centralized system. (Mincu & Horga, 2010, p. 102)

Given such a strong symbolic association with Western governance ideals, it is not surprising that most decentralization initiatives in Southeast and Central Europe and the former Soviet Union were funded by major international financial institutions (e.g., the World Bank and the Asian Development Bank). Reflecting foundational assumptions of economic neoliberalism, the general premise of these reforms was that private markets are inherently more efficient than central government bureaucracies. Furthermore, the assumption was that policymakers would readily choose to decentralize in order "to increase efficiency and to help decrease central government spending, as well as to deepen democracy by increasing sub-national control over resources and policy and thus presumably the quality of citizen participation at the local level" (Kubal & Kerlin, 2002, p. 3). At least theoretically, these initiatives would address decentralization comprehensively, incorporating finance, governance, professional development, and curriculum policy (see Rado, 2010, p. 44).

In practice, however, decentralization reforms across the region were rarely based on a comprehensive sector strategy resulting instead in only partial (and fragmented) reform implementation in different contexts. For example, Romania and Macedonia pursued partial fiscal decentralization, Macedonia and Croatia prioritized decentralization reforms in management, and Serbia focused on curriculum decentralization (Rado, 2010, p. 79). In Georgia, NGOs promoted decentralization of education governance, while the World Bank eventually replaced these participatory reforms with the decentralization of education finance (see Matiashvili, 2008). In Kazakhstan, the government decentralized in-service teacher education, while maintaining strict centralized control over curriculum policy (see Omoeva, 2011). In other words, there was little uniformity in how decentralization reforms were understood, let alone implemented, in different educational systems across the region.

The impact of decentralization reforms also varied. Rarely do we hear about significant democratization of education governance, increased efficiency of the educational systems, or improved quality of educational achievement among students. In particular, some studies highlight that shifting *financial* responsibility to the local levels occurred without empowering local communities to actually make decisions regarding school management (e.g., see Adam, 2011; Matiashvili, 2008). Other studies report that finance-driven decentralization reforms created inequalities between different subregions in many postsocialist countries (e.g., see Mertaugh, 2006; Mincu, 2009). Furthermore, decentralization reforms have compounded access to education for minorities, including Roma (UNICEF, 2011). Finally, there have been no conclusive results on whether and how decentralization reforms contributed to the improvement of educational quality or equity. As Mincu argues, the notion that educational decentralization could revitalize postsocialist educational systems has turned out to be largely a myth (Mincu, 2009, p. 72).

While creating new risks for the educational systems of Southeast and Central Europe and the former Soviet Union, decentralization reforms also opened new opportunities for local stakeholders to directly challenge (and perhaps even avoid) the introduction of Western reforms. In Kazakhstan, for example, the government has maintained strong control over curriculum policy to promote student-centered teaching and learning as one of the reforms symbolically associated with Western-style democratization of education. At the same time, however, fiscal pressures on the national government (along with the emphasis on neoliberal policymaking advocated by international donors) served as an impetus for shifting the burden of funding schooling to local communities. There, too, decentralization, to the degree it has been implemented, paradoxically worked against the goals of progressive reformers. In particular, the 2010–2020 National Education Strategy aimed to decentralize all in-service teacher training through the introduction of vouchers for professional development of teachers, leaving it up to local actors to decide upon the content of teacher training. As Omoeva (2011) skillfully illustrates, this new arrangement—whereby centralized policymaking has been combined with decentralized professional development teachers—has comfortably accommodated those Kazakh stakeholders who may not necessarily have endorsed the implementation of child-centered learning philosophy in practice. Some resisted implementation of such instruction because of uncertainty about learning theories underpinning such methods, while others exhibited their ongoing commitment to and "pride in the old Soviet [education] heritage" (Omoeva, 2011, p. 196). Thus, in this instance, a decentralized teacher training system has provided a perfect opportunity for local education stakeholders to evade "new" teaching methods and instead continue with the "old" Soviet education practices (e.g., teacher-centered instruction).

Similarly, education decentralization in Romania has reflected multiple "visions" of the reform. While the reform initially emerged in the context of a broader trend toward marketization and a "return to Europe," it was soon re-interpreted as freedom for teachers to implement their visions of reform "once the [classroom] doors are closed." Commenting on these contradictions, one teacher interviewed in Mincu and Horga's (2010) research draws clear parallels with the socialist education practices: "We arrived from where we came: we are talking about one thing and we are doing a completely different one!" (p. 118). In the Romanian case, then, decentralization reform has had little effect on what teachers do in their classrooms (Mincu & Horga, 2020, p. 119). Combined, both Kazakh and Romanian cases suggest that decentralization reforms have also failed to "cure" some of the educational problems associated with socialism, including inequities (in practice), inefficiency, and instructional quality issues. By granting some autonomy to teachers, schools, and communities, they have enabled local stakeholders to evade "new" (neoliberal) reforms, while providing enough freedom to articulate local visions of postsocialist futures in education, or to preserve much of the socialist legacy.

As for Russia, inertia, resistance, and economic collapse prevented any *systematic* deployment of innovative practices during the period lasting from the late 1980s to the late 1990s. Yet a mass revival of public interest in education also led to the establishment of a large number of experimental schools led by innovative professionals, the augmented presence of these professionals at different levels of government, and "the growing focus of academia and policy agencies on exploring . . . the ideas of innovative teachers" (Froumin & Remorenko, 2020). Additional freedom was provided by a decree that the federal government, regional authorities, and individual schools would each have control over one-third of the curriculum. Perhaps the culmination of this trend was the passage of the 1992 Education Law that embodied the principles of school autonomy, developmental psychology, diversity, and choice. However, soon afterward the public movement of educational innovators began to lose ground. As Safronov and Sidorova (2017) have argued, Russia lacked the infrastructure of a civil society needed to sustain such a public movement. Moreover, the institutional and regulatory foundations of the earlier national education system remained intact and statutory education standards reinforced the emphasis upon drill, repetition, and knowledge reproduction (Safronov & Sidoroba, 2017). Pedagogical innovators lacked the financial support needed to scale up their programs and little change was made in the national system for teacher training.

As for the role of the state, the distribution of control over curriculum was virtually the only state policy recorded in a decade marked by what observers labeled a "policy of no policies" in Russia. When at the turn of the millennium the state again reasserted itself in education it faced deteriorating facilities, outdated equipment, severe delays in salary payments and a shortage of young teachers, and rampant corruption in evaluating the quality of instruction and outcomes. It also bears noting that the dismantling after the collapse of communism of the massive and multifaceted network of extramural education institutions severely aggravated the economic woes and reduced the opportunities to thrive for millions of schoolchildren whose families were already terribly stressed by the economic collapse of shock therapy, mass unemployment, and loss of life savings.

Finally, beginning in the late 2000s, "improvements started to be felt in the regulatory domain of Russian education as greater levels of transparency, trust, and accountability were achieved" (Froumin & Remorenko, 2020, pp. 240–241). From that point on, according to experts, "one can see a consistent logic in how the Russian government proceeded to reform the sphere of national secondary general education. A holistic conception of a general action plan was first elaborated and then followed by all-around public discussions and the gradual implementation of its individual elements" (Froumin & Remorenko, 2020, p. 247). The system gradually shifted to competency-based approaches. In 2004, new state education standards were introduced and attempts made to move away from lists of topics by subject area to a "21st century skills agenda," including subject outcomes, meta-disciplinary outcomes, and personal [values, mindsets] outcomes. Considerable resources were allocated to bring teachers' skills in line with these goals as well as to enhance their financial status.

The process of implementing and harmonizing the regulatory framework with the new pedagogical one has been a painful and prolonged one. The fit between "competency-based" goals and regulatory guidelines remains imperfect and the reformed Ministry of Education and Science lacks adequate resources to implement fully its overall program. In recent years, fueled by nostalgia, a public backlash has set in, advocating a return to the conventional knowledge-based agenda following the fundamental model of Soviet school. Meanwhile, an authoritarian turn by the state (aided by the Orthodox Church) has largely erased school and regional curricular autonomy, and patriotic and religious elements have gained ground in school affairs. On the other hand, the return of authoritarian government and accompanying restoration of central control over education have been accompanied by marked advances in quality control measures, recent gains in teacher salaries and status in society, as well as in PISA scores of the country's students (Froumin & Remorenko, 2020). Moreover, most would agree that in ways both measurable and intangible the world of the Russian schoolchild and teacher has significantly changed since 1991.

The Meanings of Privatization in Public Education

As with decentralization, privatization added a new dimension to the debate over authority by introducing a market component of choice for the consumer. Although the establishment of religious schools and nonreligious private establishments (such as Montessori schools) considerably diversified educational systems across the region, the number of students enrolled in private schools has remained proportionally low in most countries during the last decade. According to UNESCO (2021), while the percentage of students enrolled in private primary schools in Hungary has doubled from 9% in 2009/2010 academic year to

18% in 2019/2020, it has slowly increased to 8% in Albania, Estonia, Slovakia, and Mongolia; fluctuated around 4–5% in Estonia and Mongolia; and remained below 1% in Azerbaijan, Belarus, Croatia, Kazakhstan, Russia, Serbia, Slovenia, Ukraine, and Uzbekistan. The private sector expanded more rapidly at the upper secondary and higher education levels, with private institutions accounting for approximately 90% enrollment in Latvia, 50% in Kazakhstan, 40% in Mongolia, and over 30 in Georgia in the 2019/2020 academic year. Private enrollments in higher education remained below 15% or more in Armenia, Azerbaijan, Belarus, Bulgaria, Croatia, Czech Republic, Estonia, Kyrgyzstan, Lithuania, Moldova, Romania, the Russian Federation, Serbia, Slovenia, and Tajikistan in the 2019/2020 academic year (UNESCO, 2021). The growth of private enrollments at the primary level has been limited primarily due to high tuition rates but also to a lack of trust in the quality of the schools by local education stakeholders (see Kitaev, 2007).

At a point, the pressure of EU accession led to stricter guidelines and enforcement of the regulations that govern the accreditation of private institutions. Government institutions have been more successful than private ones in moving toward compliance with EU accreditation, and they have thus situated themselves at a clear advantage vis-à-vis private institutions. In Russia, a law promulgated in 2001 subjects all state institutions engaging in for-profit activities to heavy taxation, and recently developed priorities make abundantly clear to rein in this private sector.

Privatization also spread informally in the form of "shadow education" or private tutoring. While being modest in scale until the early 1990s, private tutoring soon became a vast enterprise after the collapse of the socialist bloc. The findings of the cross-national studies of private tutoring in 12 countries of Southeast and Central Europe and the former Soviet Union (Silova et al., 2006; 2009) reveal that by 2006 private tutoring was widespread in all countries examined, with more than half of the student population (64%) receiving some type of private tutoring in the last year of secondary school. The scope of private tutoring has varied by country: over 80% of sampled students in the Caucasus (Azerbaijan and Georgia) had received tutoring; the figure was 60% in the Balkans (Bosnia and Herzegovina), Slovakia, and Kyrgyzstan. The unprecedented rise of private tutoring across the region has underscored the tension between socialist legacies (especially public expectation for fee-free mainstream education) and global forces (especially market-driven reforms in the education sector). Responding to students' needs in a more efficient, flexible, and prompt manner, private tutoring has been perceived as an important supplement to the rigid mainstream education system, which has been slow to embrace changes (Silova et al., 2006). In addition, a combination of increasing demand for higher education and a limited number of state-financed study places available in higher education institutions across the region has created an added pressure around school leaving or university entrance examinations. Many high school students often choose to invest in private tutoring to increase their chances of getting higher scores necessary for entering state-funded higher education groups and avoid having to pay for higher education for the following four years. On the other hand, private tutoring has brought many negative consequences such as exacerbating social inequities, distorting curricula, inviting corruption, and depriving the state of tax revenues (Silova et al., 2006; Silova, 2010).

The rise of private tutoring should be also examined in the context of the changing status of the teaching profession during the postsocialist transformations. Teachers were severely affected; their salaries plummeted and professional development opportunities shrank. In most of the former Soviet countries of the Caucasus and Central Asia, teacher salaries fell below the national wage average, accounting for only 53 to 70% of the national wage average (Steiner-Khamsi et al., 2008). In the Caucasus and elsewhere, teachers were surviving by engaging in petty trading, farming, teaching in more than one school, or taking other jobs in addition to mainstream schooling (UNICEF, 2001). In more economically developed countries in Eastern and Central Europe, the declining economic, social, and professional status of teachers led to increasing migration to better-paying jobs in other sectors of the economy. In particular, English language teachers fled the schools to enter the commercial sector. The poorly paid and demoralized teachers who stayed behind thus turned to private tutoring to gain economic advantage. In Russia and elsewhere, grossly underpaid university professors similarly relied on private tutoring as a major source of supplementary income.

For those who stayed, private tutoring served as a mechanism to raise a professional status undermined by increasing governmental pressures to change "traditional" school practices (teacher-centered learning) in favor of "new" teaching methods (child-centered learning). Combined with other neoliberal reforms—whether the increasing centralized control over school curriculum, a growing emphasis on academic testing, or mounting demands for accountability—teachers often felt stripped of their professional authority in the classroom. Private tutoring served as a mechanism to maintain control over what teachers themselves believed constitutes "best practice." Many teachers associated private tutoring with "the very notion of professionalism," including its "technical culture, a commitment to service ethic, and autonomy in planning and implementing their practice" (Popa & Acedo, 2006, p. 98; see also Kobakhidze, 2018; Šťastný & Kobakhidze, 2020). As such it offered a challenge to postsocialist education reforms (Popa & Acedo, 2006, p. 109).

Higher Education in Countries of the former Soviet Union[6]

Beginning in 1991 the Soviet model of higher education in 15 republics of the USSR, with its 5.1 million students and 946 higher educational institutions, underwent a fundamental transformation. Similar to reforms in the primary education sector, almost all newly independent states adopted a similar package of reforms, aiming to "normalize" their systems. Progress would be achieved through the establishment of a nonstate sector (i.e., private institutions), the introduction of tuition fees in the public sector, national standardized tests for admission exams to higher education, the decentralization of governance, and, in some countries, loans for students and performance-based funding. Reformers sought to exclude all remnants of official Soviet Marxism from the curriculum; the titular nation language became predominant in higher education instruction in each newly independent state, and courses on national history and culture were added to the curriculum. A new "consumerist" approach led initially to the large-scale introduction of courses in the humanities, business, law, from which for the first time students could choose freely. The overall institutional landscape of higher education underwent fundamental changes in nomenclature, structure, organization, and funding too elaborate to detail here, but included the upgrading of specialized institutes to general universities, the establishment of branch campuses [*filialy*], and in many cities the consolidation of several institutions.

According to a recent survey of higher education in the fifteen former republics of the Soviet Union, since 1991 developments in most of the post-Soviet states can be divided into two larger periods. Lasting more than a decade in many countries, the first period was characterized by chaotic or sporadic liberalization and expansion. At that time, change was largely driven by external factors: demand from students for places and demand from the labor market for graduates as well as many bottom-up processes within the states such as the role of private or academic entrepreneurs in the existing higher education institutions. The role of the respective governments was largely limited to general framing laws and accreditation regulations that were used to enable some institutional autonomy and the introduction of market mechanisms, particularly in the form of fee-charging in the public institutions. No longer-term visions of the shape and structure of the higher education systems were evident, apart from the transition to a bachelor-master degree system, and the introduction of national standardized admission tests. This first period was essentially an outcome of general liberalization after the breakdown of the Soviet sociopolitical, economic, and cultural system. It was hoped that a change from total state control to autonomy, from uniformity to diversity, from the engineering and vocational bias toward a greater role for the humanities and social sciences as well as an emphasis upon personal development would have a crucial impact on the economy, polity, culture, and society.

In Russia as in Poland, but unlike many other Central and Eastern European countries, this lack of political determination or a "policy of no policy" (Smolentseva et al., 2018, p. 36), was largely an outcome of the economic and political turbulence of the time rather than of ideological conviction. Higher education was not the only area in which necessary state action was weak or absent and governmental resources were very scarce. The perceived "solution" was to loosen governmental control and give institutions freedoms that would enable them to survive by raising their own money. The result was the displacement of the state in the early post-Soviet policy landscape along with a rapid expansion of higher education driven largely by consumer demand and marketization.

Accordingly, the earliest reform in most of the countries of the region was the introduction of a private sector in higher education and tuition fees in the public sector. "Creeping marketization" in the post-Soviet states was much more expansive than elsewhere in Eastern and Central Europe. In the period after 1991, non-state institutions experienced rapid growth, and in five countries (Armenia, Georgia, Kazakhstan, Latvia, Moldova) came to exceed the number of public institutions. However, in most areas, the private sector was unable to achieve the same level of prestige and demand as the traditional public sector, where enrollments continued to be concentrated. Instead, it was in that public sector where the most momentous change ensued; namely, the growing reliance on tuition fees to make up for declining state inputs. In public universities everywhere, except in Estonia and Turkmenistan, more than half of all students now pay fees. Moreover, the marketization of higher education had another important implication for most higher education systems of the region: as students and their families became an important source of revenue, higher education became more consumer-oriented. Accordingly, at the same time that the Soviet mechanism of regulating demand and supply through advanced planning of numbers of seats in about 300 specializations and mandatory job placing was abandoned, a rapid expansion of enrollments took place in the fields of business studies, economics, foreign language studies, and law. The nonstate or private sector was mostly built around these fields, as these types of programs were cheaper to provide and experienced high demand. Now, the public sector has also begun to offer degrees in such fields (whether with or without tuition fees).

Other "drivers" of policy also stepped in to reshape the structure and practices of higher education in the region; namely, the EU's Bologna Process and international agencies. Between 1999 and 2010 most of the countries of the region joined the Bologna Process; only four former republics, all in Central Asia, are outside of the Bologna group. Along Bologna lines, all 15 countries, including those outside the European Higher Education Area, have adopted a two-cycle degree system and introduced bachelor's and master's degree programs (3–4 plus 1–2 years). In some countries this system still coexists, at least in some fields, with the traditional Soviet five-year degree for specialists (e.g., in Russia and Turkmenistan). In terms of advanced qualifications, several countries, including Estonia, Latvia, Lithuania, Georgia, Kazakhstan, have abolished the second Soviet doctorate, so their third cycle now only consists of one doctoral degree (PhD). Bologna Process member states must formally comply with the agreed requirements and have introduced quality assurance bodies for program and/or institutional accreditation, established a system of credits, all measures to support increasing mobility within the European Higher Education Area (EHEA). This is indeed a momentous shift, and adoption of the new policies has created many tensions and uncertainties for higher education and employers, as the value and status of the degrees, especially at the bachelor's level, have been unclear. In many cases, traditional five-year curricula were simply shortened to meet the new length of studies requirements, which generated a lot of skepticism in terms of internal quality assurance about what seemed to many an "incomplete higher education" in the first cycle. In the case of countries with binary (private/public) systems, like Lithuania, there was a seeming disjunction between a bachelor's degree and access to further learning at the master's level (Smolentseva et al., 2018, pp. 26–27).

An important role in early post-Soviet developments was also played by international assistance, including from numerous Western government agencies, multilateral institutions (such as the World Bank, OECD, Council of Europe), private nonprofit foundations, and exchange organizations (the Open Society Institute, Ford Foundation, etc). International assistance promoted direct academic exchanges, the publication of international textbooks and literature and training programs, but also helped to support infrastructure development and academic staff. In Central Asia, international agencies largely supported structural reforms, such as establishing national test systems (Drummond, 2020).

The second period emerged in the mid-2000s and gained momentum after 2010. In that period a new balance between demand and supply was sought for—by governments, students, and higher education institutions—and demographic changes interacted with governmental policies (particularly accreditation). By the millennium, the low birth rates of the turbulent previous decade had produced decreasing enrolments in both public and private institutions. As the pool of applicants decreased and system retraction ensued, public institutions had a competitive advantage over private ones in that they could "sell" the most prestigious "commodity": a full-time degree in highly desirable fields stamped by established "brands." At the same time many countries switched to greater governmental intervention or supervision. Questions of quality, stimulated partly by the Bologna Process, but also by increasing pressure to make higher education demonstrably competitive globally, became impossible to ignore. Governments joined the worldwide trend toward new public management, endorsing policy goals such as efficiency, excellence, better matching higher education with the labor market, and striving for international visibility. In most countries, new accreditation and accountability procedures contributed to the declining number of private institutions and students. Ideologically, new conservative and authoritarian trends reinforced this trajectory as well as reversed the degree of autonomy of institutions in the public sphere itself—notably in Russia, Hungary, and Poland. In that respect, the Soviet legacy, albeit shaped by new trends, is on full display. Only in a few countries, such as Lithuania, have other actors—academic staff, rectors' unions—held some power over the direction of the changes to higher education. In Russia, national and international rankings, including competitive funding models, contributed to increased status differentiation as well as a government policy directing the lion's share of its funding to a limited number of designated "flagship" universities. By some accounts, the introduction of the national test and marketization have each led (the former inadvertently) to increased inequality of access to higher education. Those standardized tests, long in the making and introduced with both fanfare and skepticism to reduce inequality and provide transparency, are now encountering mounting criticism from some segments of society, including teachers, and calls to eliminate.

Many case studies report on the ongoing practices of corruption and fraud in public administration (e.g., Georgia, Kyrgyzstan, Kazakhstan, and Uzbekistan). According to Transparency International, only the Baltic states and Georgia are in the upper half of the ranking of 168 countries, and 11 countries, including Russia, appear in the bottom half (cited in Smolentseva et al., 2018, p. 29). Also the Democracy Index (composed by the Economist Intelligence Unit) reports major deficits in the level of democracy in the former Soviet states, with seven of these being qualified as "authoritarian." Undoubtedly, these features of the political climate affect the way policies in education are developed and implemented. In Russia, academics have been cautioned about collaboration with scholars abroad as well as warned that they could be held responsible for the political activities of their students.

Finally, despite the long-standing concern about the negative consequences of institutionally separating research and teaching, little has been achieved in the post-Soviet era to remedy that shortcoming. Only a few countries (e.g., Russia and Kazakhstan) made deliberate attempts to transform existing universities according to the model of global research universities or establish new research universities, and even there, the results have been uneven at best.

CONCLUSION

The three-decade-long interaction of socialist and postsocialist education institutions with Western reform projects—whether decentralization, privatization, or higher education reforms—has resulted in mixed, often contradictory outcomes. After a revolutionary change in Southeast and Central Europe and the former Soviet Union shook the world in 1989, education moved into an unsettled state. Change has occurred much more rapidly and profoundly in some areas than others. Internationalization left a mark, but much less so in, say, Kazan, than in Prague. While freedom and opportunity beckoned, equity and egalitarianism declined. Even today, 30 years later, resistance and lip service to reform can both be found, but so can remarkable dedication and a capacity for innovation, even in very difficult circumstances. A revival of national and imperial traditions proceeds, but a fascination with Western approaches persists at the same time. In this context, the postsocialist education space remains dynamic and diverse, while its reform trajectories remain inevitably open.

These "global" reforms appear to be simultaneously embraced and challenged here by local education stakeholders. In the case of decentralization reforms, policy rhetoric has been widely adopted across the region, while "only minor and cautious steps" were actually taken in terms of practical implementation (Rado, 2010, p. 13). Evoking the power and influence of "external" authorities or international "best practices," local policymakers enthusiastically embraced reform rhetoric to justify abdicating state responsibility for educational financing and social equity, while devolving much of the burden for educational finance and school maintenance onto weak municipal and local structures (Silova, 2005; Steiner-Khamsi, 2004). At the same time, in some instances, decentralization reforms served to sustain some of the socialist legacies in the educational systems of Southeast and Central Europe and the former Soviet Union. Granting some autonomy to teachers, schools, and communities, such reforms also enabled local stakeholders to evade "new" (neoliberal) policies and provided the necessary freedom to articulate local visions of postsocialist futures in education. And while these visions may appear contradictory and confusing, they nevertheless still present a serious challenge to the hegemony of so-called global reforms, precisely because of their irrepressible multiplicity.

Similarly, the emergence of market forces in the educational systems of Southeast/Central Europe and the former Soviet Union—whether reflected in privatization reforms of private tutoring practices—evinced contradictory effects. On the one hand, private tutoring reinforced the legitimacy of market forces in education by enabling teachers to become educational "entrepreneurs" outside of official school hours. While enabling teachers to generate the additional income necessary to supplement their meager salaries, private tutoring also generated corruption and contributed to educational inequities after the collapse of the Soviet-style regimes. On the other hand, teachers used private tutoring to avoid those "global" reforms that were increasingly encroaching on and negatively affecting their established practices. As Karpov and Lisovskaya (2001) observe, education privatization reforms in Russia and elsewhere thus "often bear misleadingly familiar Western names, but operate in distinctly non-Western ways" (p. 43). As public schools become increasingly focused on teaching to the test to increase students' academic competitiveness, private tutoring allowed teachers and students to pursue individualized learning through critical thinking and creative problem-solving. In a way, private tutoring restored teachers' professional legitimacy, social status, and even political influence by enabling them to make their own decisions about what constitutes quality education. And while private tutoring may not in itself be subversive, it has "a symbolic value which is not to be underestimated" during postsocialist transformations (Popa & Acedo, 2006, p. 109). Over time, however, market forces and privatization have declined in the region, at least in most of the former Soviet republics.

Given the complexity, plurality, and unpredictability of Western reform trajectories in the postsocialist education space, this chapter suggests that although the "global" reform agenda is visible, it is being continuously reconfigured into new (and often unexpected) arrangements across the region. More often than not, it is the rhetoric of the Western reform agenda that is being transferred, while a glance at practical implementation locally highlights the force of inertia or often resistance to the "new" reforms. Indeed, when socialist and postsocialist histories interact with Western reform projects, the outcomes are often contradictory. Western neoliberal reforms not only are modified in postsocialist contexts (often losing even superficial resemblance to their origins); they are also directly challenged. It is an open question whether these "deviations" from global patterns stem from deep-seated ideological convictions, the resurgence of tradition, or self-interest on the part of the "perpetrators." What is clear is that forces continue even now to restrain the hegemony of capitalist models in education. Postsocialist education space thus reveals a (re)reading of the global through the lens of pluralities, discontinuities, and uncertainties. Furthermore, it offers a (re)reading of the global that is free of its predetermined finality.

Thus, the experience of postsocialism becomes a site for studying a complex set of education alternatives in the early stage of their formation, rather than already formed (or forming) neoliberal policies and practices. We thus avoid focusing on what Bakhtin noted with regret as the "readymade and finalized" (Bakhtin, 1986, p. 139), and rather examine what is constantly in flux and shifting toward an open future. From this epistemological standpoint, postsocialism has the potential to open comparative education research to new theoretical and methodological possibilities. More specifically for the region itself, as one observer of recent events in Belarus commented (Rust, 2017): "Instead of portraying the remnants of the . . . Homo sovieticus as a problem, we should see it as a challenge and potential advantage: . . . collectivism as a chance to build a civil community; adaptability and opportunism as resourcefulness, and the multi-layered identity as an expression of a modern civil nation."

NOTES

1. The features of "the postsocialist education reform package" are unique in that they combine (1) elements common to any low-income, developing country that implements the structural adjustment programs recommended by the international financial institutions (e.g., decentralization and privatization), (2) education reform aspects specific to the entire former socialist region (e.g., market-driven textbook provision, increased educational choice, standardized assessment systems), and (3) country- or region-specific

components (e.g., conflict resolution in the former Yugoslavia and gender equity reforms in Central Asia). Although the features of this "postsocialist education reform package" vary from place to place, they do exist (at least discursively) in most countries of the region. See Iveta Silova and Steiner-Khamsi, *How NGOs React: Globalization and Education Reform in the Caucasus, Central Asia and Mongolia* (Kumarian Press, 2008), pp. 19–22.

2. The term *korenizatsiya*, which derives from the Russian "korennoe naselenie" ("root population") aimed at promoting representatives of titular nations of Soviet republics and national minorities on lower administrative levels of the local government, management, and bureaucracy in the corresponding national entities.

3. Polytechnical education was one of the central components of the Marxist-Leninist theory of education, as articulated by the 1919 Eighth Congress of the Communist Party of the Soviet Union. The mandate of polytechnical education included instruction in the basics of science and technology, focusing on practical application in industry and agriculture. It was introduced in general education schools through classroom instruction, visits to agricultural farms and industrial enterprises, as well as practical experiences in school workshops in an effort to establish a direct link between schools and workforce.

4. The Baltic republics (Estonia, Latvia, and Lithuania) and two of the Caucasus republics (Georgia and Azerbaijan) are the exception. These republics were treated preferentially in matters of language choice in education. Insisting that knowledge of both the Russian and the titular languages was necessary for living and working in these republics, these republics were successful in preserving the number of schools for titular nationalities, the original number of years of education in these schools, and the obligatory study of titular languages in Russian language schools (Bilinsky, 1962).

5. Although this phenomenon has been present in other developing countries with noncommunist regimes, such as India, Eastern Europe's patterns of emigration were particular in their one-way direction. The intelligentsia that has left Eastern Europe since the 1970s has not in most cases returned and has not maintained close professional relations with colleagues there, at least before 1989.

6. This section draws heavily from an excellent survey by Anna Smolentseva, Jeroen Huisman, and Isak Froumin, "Transformation of Higher Education Institutional Landscape in Post-Soviet Countries: From Soviet Model to Where," in J. Husiman et al. (Eds.), *25 Years of Transformations of Higher Education Systems in Post-Soviet Countries* (pp. 1–43). Palgrave Studies in Global Higher Education, https://doi.org/10.1007/978-3-319-52980-6_1

REFERENCES

Adam, Z. (2011). *Decentralizing education, managing the change: The case of Moldova.* Unpublished master's thesis. Central European University.

Bakhtin, M. (1986). *Speech genres and other late essays.* University of Texas Press.

Baker, D. P., & LeTendre, G. (Eds.). (2005). *National differences, global similarities: World culture and the future of schooling.* Stanford University Press.

Bartz, B., & Kullas, Z. (1993). The essential aspects of educational reform in Poland. *European Education, 25*(2), 15–26.

Bilinsky, Y. (1962). The Soviet education laws of 1958–59 and Soviet nationality policy. *Soviet Studies, 14,* 138–157.

Brickman, W. W. (1964). *John Dewey's impressions of Soviet Russia and the revolutionary world.* Teachers College Press.

Burawoy, M. (1999). *Uncertain transition: Ethnographies of change in the postsocialist world.* Rowman & Littlefield.

Drummond, T. (2020). Higher education admissions regimes in Kazakhstan and Kyrgyzstan: Difference makes a difference. In I. Silova & S. Niyozov (Eds.), *Globalization on the margins: Education and post-socialist transformations in Central Asia.* (pp. 95–124). Information Age Publishing.

Dzyuba, I. (1970). *Internationalism or Russification? A study in the Soviet nationalities problem*. Camelot Press.

Eklof, B., Holmes, L. E., & Kaplan, V. (Eds.). (2005). *Educational reform in post-Soviet Russia: Legacies and prospects* (Vol. 20). Psychology Press.

Encyclopedia of Modern Europe: Europe 1789–1914 (2006). Gale Group.

Ewing, E. T. (2006). Ethnicity at school: "Non-Russian" education in the Soviet Union during the 1930s. *History of Education*, 35(4–5), 499–519.

Froumin, I., & Remorenko, I. (2020). From the "best in the world" Soviet school to a modern globally competitive school system. In *Audacious education purposes: How governments transform the goals of education system* (pp. 238–249). Springer.

Górecki, W. (2017). Traces of the Soviet Union. *New Eastern Europe*, 28(5), 7–20.

Gutsche, M. (1993). The Hungarian education system in the throes of change. *European Education*, 25(2), 5–11.

Hann, C., Humphrey, C., & Verdery, K. (2003). Introduction: Postsocialism as a topic of anthropological investigation. In *Postsocialism* (pp. 13–40). Routledge.

Heyneman, S. P. (2000). From the party/state to multiethnic democracy: Education and social cohesion in Europe and Central Asia. *Educational evaluation and policy analysis*, 22(2), 173–191.

Holmes, L. (1991). *The Kremlin and the schoolhouse*. Indiana University Press.

Iskhakov, R. (2011). *Missionerstvo I Musul'manie Volgo-Kam'ia* [The Ministry and the Muslim of Volgo-Kami'ia] (pp. 194–213). Tatarskoe knizhnoe izdatel'stvo.

Kitaev, I. (2007). Education for all and private education in developing and transitioning countries. In P. Srivastava & G. Walford (Eds.), *Private schooling in less economically developed countries: Asian and African perspectives* (pp. 89–110). Symposium Books.

Jacoby, S. (1977). Inside Soviet schools. *Science and Society*, 41(2).

Johnson, M. S. (2008). Historical legacies of Soviet higher education and the transformation of higher education systems in post-Soviet Russia and Eurasia. In D. Baker & A. Wiseman (Eds.), *The worldwide transformation of higher education* (pp. 159–176). Emerald Group Publishing.

Jones-Luong, P. (2006). *The transformation of Central Asia: States and societies from Soviet rule to independence*. Cornell University.

Kirschenbaum, L. A. (2001). *Small comrades: Revolutionizing childhood in Soviet Russia, 1917–1932*. RoutledgeFalmer.

Kitaev, I. (2007). Education for all and private education in developing and transitioning countries. In P. Srivastava & G. Walford (Eds.), *Private schooling in less economically developed countries: Asian and African perspectives* (pp. 89–110). Symposium Books.

Kobakhidze, N. (2018). *Teachers as tutors: Shadow education market dynamics in Georgia*. Springer-CERC.

Kubal, M. R., & Kerlin, J. A. (2002, January). A neoliberal agenda for decentralization in transitioning countries? A comparative study of Chile and Poland. In *Annual Conference of Georgia Political Science Association, Savannah, Georgia*.

Matiashvili, A. (2008). On being first: The meaning of education decentralization reform in Georgia. In I. Silova & G. Steiner-Khamsi (Eds.), *How NGOs react: Globalization and educational change in the Caucasus, Central Asia, and Mongolia* (pp. 119–136). Kumarian Press.

Mertaugh, M. (2006). Education in Central Asia, with particular reference to Kyrguz Republic. In S. P. Heyneman & A. J. DeYoung (Eds.), *The challenges of education in Central Asia* (pp. 3–180). Information Age Publishing.

Mincu, M. E. (2009). Myth, rhetoric, and ideology in Eastern European education: Schools and citizenship in Hungary, Poland, and Romania. *European Education*, 41(1), 55–78.

Mincu, M., & Horga, I. (2010). Visions of reform in post-socialist Romania: Decentralization (through hybridization) and teacher autonomy. In I. Silova (Ed.), *Post-socialism is not dead: (Re)reading the global in comparative education*. Bingley.

Omoeva, C. (2011). *Student-centered Instruction and math and science achievement in the post-Soviet state: A mixed methods analysis*, unpublished doctoral dissertation. Teachers College, Columbia University.

Pantić, N., Wubbels, T., & Mainhard, T. (2011). Teacher competence as a basis for teacher education: Comparing views of teachers and teacher educators in five Western Balkan countries. *Comparative Education Review, 55*(2), 165–188.

Pinkert, A. (2002). Postcolonial legacies: The rhetoric of race in the East/West German national identity debate of the late 1990s. *Journal of the Midwest Modern Language Association, 35*(2), 13–32.

Popa, S., & Acedo, C. (2006). Redefining professionalism: Romanian secondary education teachers and the private tutoring system. *International Journal of Educational Development, 26*(1), 98–110.

Rado, P. (2010). *Governing decentralized educational systems: Systemic change in Southeastern Europe*. Open Society Foundations.

Rosen, S. M. (1980). *Education in the USSR: Current states of higher education*. US Government.

Rust, M. (2017). A 21st century Homo Sovieticus? *New Eastern Europe, 5*. https://neweasterneurope.eu/2017/10/04/21st-century-homo-sovieticus/

Safronov, P., & Sidorova, K. D. (2017). Sub'ektivnye innovatsii: pedagogicheskoe innovatsii v usloviiakh radikalnykh sotsialnykh izmenenii. *Voprosy obrazovaniia, 3*, 224–237.

Silova, I. (2005). Traveling policies: Hijacked in Central Asia. *European Educational Research Journal, 4*(1), 50–59.

Silova, I. (Ed.). (2009). *Private supplementary tutoring in Central Asia: New opportunities and burdens*. UNESCO Institute of International Educational Planning (IIEP).

Silova, I. (2010). Private tutoring in Eastern Europe and Central Asia: Policy choices and implications. *Compare, 40*(3), 327–344.

Silova, I., Budiene, V., & Bray, M. (Eds.). (2006). *Education in a hidden marketplace: Monitoring of private tutoring*. Open Society Institute.

Silova, I., Johnson, M. S., & Heyneman, S. P. (2007). Education and the crisis of social cohesion in Azerbaijan and Central Asia. *Comparative Education Review, 51*(2), 159–180.

Silova, I. & Magno, C. (2004). Gender equity unmasked: Revisiting democracy, gender, and education in post-socialist Central/Southeastern Europe and the Former Soviet Union. *Comparative Education Review, 48(4)*, 417–442.

Silova, I., Piattoeva, N., & Millei, Z. (2018). *Childhood and schooling in (post)socialist societies: Memories of everyday life*. Palgrave MacMillan.

Slezkine, Y. (1994). The USSR as a communal apartment, or how a socialist state promoted ethnic particularism. *Slavic Review, 53*(2), 414–452.

Smolentseva, A., Huisman, J., & Froumin, I. (2018). From Soviet model to where? In J. Huisman, A. Smolentseva, & I. Froumin (Eds.), *25 years of transformations of higher education systems in post-Soviet countries: Reform and continuity* (pp. 1–43). Palgrave Macmillan.

Sobe, N. W. (2006). US comparative education research on Yugoslav education in the 1950s and 1960s. *European Education, 38*(4), 44–64.

Sovetkin, F. F. (1958). *National schools in Russian Federation over the 40 years*. Academy of Science.

Stalin, J. (1934). *Marxism and the national and colonial question: A collection of articles and speeches*. International Publishers.

Šťastný, V., & Kobakhidze, M. N. (2020). Throwing light on shadow education. *Orbis Scholae, 14*(2), 5–12.

Steiner-Khamsi, G. (2004). *The global politics of educational borrowing and lending*. Teachers College Press.

Steiner-Khamsi, G., & Stolpe, I. (2006). *Educational import in Mongolia: Local encounters with global forces*. Palgrave Macmillan.

Stenning, A., & Hörschelmann, K. (2008). History, geography and difference in the post-socialist world: Or, do we still need post-socialism? *Antipode, 40*(2), 312–335.

Steiner-Khamsi, G., Harris-Van Keuren, C., Silova, I., & Chachkhiani, K. (2008). The pendulum of decentralization and recentralization reforms: Its impact on teacher salaries in the Caucasus, Central Asia, and Mongolia (Background Paper for UNESCO Global Monitoring Report 2009). UNESCO.

Tadjbakhsh, S. (1998). Between Allah and Lenin: Women and ideology in Tajikistan. In H. Bodman & N. Tawḥīdī (Eds.), *Women in Muslim societies: Diversity within unity* (pp. 163–185). Lynne Rienner.

UNICEF. (2001). *A decade of transition*. UNICEF Innocenti Research Center.

UNICEF. (2011). *The right of Roma children to education*. UNICEF.

UNESCO Institute of Statistics. (2021). http://uis.unesco.org

USSR. (1973). *Sovet narodniykh kommissarov* (Sovnarkom). *O shkolakh natsionalnykh menshinstv* [About minority schools]. In *Narodnoe obrazovanie v SSSR obscheobrazovatelnaia schola): Sbornik dokumentov, 1917–1973* [Public education in the USSR (secondary school): A Compilation of documents, 1917–1973]. Pedagogika.

Wiseman, A. W., & Baker, D. P. (2006). The symbiotic relationship between empirical comparative research on education and neo-institutional theory. In D. P. Baker & A. W. Wiseman (Eds.), *The impact of comparative education research on institutional theory* (pp. 1–26). Emerald Group Publishing.

Zhdanova, M. P. ed. (1989). *Narodnoye obrazovaniie i kultura v SSSR* [State education and culture in the USSR]. Finances and Statistics.

18

Technocracy, Uncertainty, Ethics

Contemporary Challenges Facing Comparative Education

Anthony Welch
University of Sydney

ABSTRACT

The 21st century reveals comparative education facing a set of key challenges to several of its taken-for-granted assumptions, especially internationalism. Its theoretical trajectory over the past century broadly parallels the social sciences in general. Initially based upon a faith in broadly modernist technocratic social science concepts, drawn largely from functionalism, this began fragmenting. Disputes arose around purpose, and arguably, a failure of vision. The current chapter traces key lines of that theoretical trajectory, beginning with an outline of the technocratic elements within a broadly modernist, positivist functionalism. This is followed by tracing the subsequent theoretical fragmentation and the associated collapse of certainty. In tracking this theoretical trajectory, I trace links between the literature of comparative education and that of the social and natural sciences. It is argued that the more recent failure of vision, and increasing fragmentation—in turn, a response to wider changes at national and regional levels, and perhaps the world system—is not inevitable. Alternatives, including non-Western sources, are advanced, based on arguments as to the urgent need to reassert ethical dimensions and responsibilities of comparative education, in an era of rising nativism, increasing neoliberal globalization, and retreat from internationalism.

■ ■ ■

FROM HISTORY TO SCIENCE?

Hindsight allows a distinct and more complete vantage point from which to evaluate competing theoretical perspectives, which protagonists of the time may have seen rather differently (Lakatos, 1974). From the perspective of the 21st century, then, it is easy to be somewhat skeptical as to the brash ebullience of comparative education of the 1960s, as new and more positivistic forms of comparative education were developed by an emerging generation of authors who eschewed the "factors and forces" traditions of more historically oriented predecessors, such as Nicholas Hans (1949), Isaac Kandel (1933), and Friedrich Schneider (1947; 1961). Despite substantial differences between such emerging figures of the 1960s as Brian Holmes (1965; 1981), Harold Eckstein and Harold Noah (1969), and George Bereday (1964; 1969), however, scientific methodology was generally held to ensure a more certain and precise future for comparative education. "Knowledge" and "facts" would play a major and determinate role in educational reform. Neither of these two concepts was yet much problematized, and it can be argued that debates in comparative education in the 1960s were mostly conducted within the parameters of a positivistically based modernism.

What is meant by positivism here? Briefly, the view that the methods of the social sciences were coextensive with, indeed drawn from, those of the natural sciences, whose methodological development was generally assumed to be more mature than the newly developing social sciences. Although the term "positivism" is widely debated (and much abused), it is nonetheless possible to distill several broad strands that underpin positivistic social science:

- the belief in monolithic methods of inquiry (the so-called unity of method);
- a belief in lawlike generalizations in the social sciences;
- a technical relation between theory and practice (which excludes any consideration of ethics in social theory); and
- the belief in a value-free science of social inquiry, in which "facts" and "knowledge" were the basis for progress and were rigidly separated from "values," which were not the concern of the (social) scientist.

This constricted sense of science and knowledge, which informed modernism, was inherited from the French Enlightenment (toward the end of the 18th century), and arguably earlier. While by no means the only theory of knowledge or science, its prominence restricted the development of alternatives, in both the natural and social sciences (see also Giddens, 1979; Habermas, 1970; Kincaid, n.d.; von Wright, 1971).

Methodological disputes among comparativists of the 1960s largely occurred *within* the bounds of that modernist faith in the capacity of science and technology to underpin social and intellectual progress, including in education. This was based on a belief in a positivist epistemology to root out errors in any arena of knowledge. Debates turned largely on the question of which particular position in the philosophy of the natural sciences was superior. Holmes's more explicit attempt to base claims for a new science of comparative education upon Popperian hypothetico-deductive foundations[1] was paralleled by the more or less explicitly inductive approaches of Bereday, and Noah and Eckstein. All ultimately fell victim to the principal tenets of the broad positivist tradition sketched earlier, and that underpinned much modernist social science. It was thought to herald the same golden age of progress and discovery that had been achieved in the natural sciences of the 17th and 18th centuries (Cowen, 1997).

It is in this sense, as Habermas (1984) has argued, that "the concept of enlightenment functions as a bridge between the idea of scientific progress and the conviction that the sciences also serve the moral perfection of human beings" (p. 147), a view that stems directly from figures such as Condorcet and other Enlightenment figures. From this perspective, false moral and political views were a product of false understandings of nature. Science itself was believed to be a form of enlightenment, which once perfected, would deliver the same rapid advances in knowledge to the "moral sciences" that had already been demonstrated in the natural sciences. In common with many social scientists of that era, major methodologists in comparative education of the 1960s were heirs to the Enlightenment belief that scientific reason was a secure foundation for the epistemological, and, by extension, the social and moral improvement of society.

Major theorists of the 1960s did not attempt to problematize scientific reason or to subject its social effects to critical scrutiny. This persisted despite powerful critiques of the social distortions caused by the uncritical adoption of scientific reason in the human sciences by largely German social theorists such as Herbert Marcuse (1968), Alfred Schutz (1964; 1967; 1953), Max Horkeimer and Theodor Adorno (1972), and in earlier eras, by Edmund Husserl (1960; 1965), and Wilhelm Dilthey (1926; 1934). In the philosophy of science too, at least by the 1970s, scholars such as Thomas Kuhn (1970; 1974), and Paul Feyerabend (1975; 1976; 1978) had developed a much more sociological profile of scientific change and development, from which none of the prevailing positivist models of the sciences had proved immune to criticism. Indeed, according to Feyerabend's (1978) withering critique of pretensions to a universal scientific methodology, the only rule is that there are no (final) rules: that is, "there is no 'scientific method,' no single procedure, or set of rules that underlies every piece of research and guarantees that it is 'scientific' and, therefore, trustworthy" (p. 98).

Despite these robust attacks on the adequacy of scientific reason, in its sphere, and even more so in the social sciences, the "modernists" in comparative education of the 1960s viewed science and scientific reason, in its various forms, as a beneficent force. Properly implemented, it would guarantee a more precise and certain science of comparative education. It is in this sense that the major figures of the 1960s were children of Enlightenment positivism and heirs to the rationalist ideology of perfectibility—the increasing subjection of the world to the dictates of technology of reason would promote a more rational and more morally perfect world. Despite vigorous disputes among several high priests of the scientific faith, such as Brian Holmes, Harold Noah, Max Eckstein, and George Bereday, the notion of the progressive rationalization of education, via the increasing methodological perfection of the science of comparative education, was common.

One of the better-known instances of the role of scientific reason in comparative education was functionalism (sometimes called structural functionalism),[2] arguably the most common form of scientism to hold sway in the postwar era, and for much of the 20th century. Not merely was it the most prominent of the range of grand theories that laid claim to the mantle of "social science," but a broadly functionalist ethos underpinned most major positions in comparative education of the 1960s, as indeed among the social sciences generally (Welch, 1985, p. 11; Woock, 1981; Karabel & Halsey, 1977).

Stemming from founding fathers like Auguste Comte in the 19th century and Emile Durkheim in the early 20th, functionalism held that "sociology," a term invented by Comte, should be modeled closely upon the methods of the natural sciences. A functionalist social science then, like its natural science forebears, should be lawlike and socially integrative (see the quote from Francis Bacon later in this chapter). Functionalism was influenced by other movements in the natural sciences too, however, notably the 19th-century scientific theory of evolution, from which was taken the view that social change should be, like biological change, slow and accretive rather than swift and/or large scale. In other words, the model of social change within functionalism was evolutionary rather than revolutionary. Lastly, functionalism asserted a supposedly value-free social science in which researchers should simply seek out and present the facts, eschewing questions of ethics or the moral dimensions of the knowledge they developed. (In practice, however, technicist values of efficiency and economy were dominant within functionalist forms of social science, if often implicitly.) Here, too, functionalism revealed its positivist heritage, drawn from the modernist presumptions of the Enlightenment and the beginnings of modern experimental science in the 17th century.

In comparative education, the functionalist tradition was arguably expressed most clearly in the substantial literature of the 1950s and 1960s. Much was applied to the theme of modernization, particularly to elaborating the role that education played in changing traditional societies. A common, broadly positivist agenda, based upon the technocratic values of efficiency and economy sketched earlier, and a strong system concept,[3] was often present in this literature. Also evident was a reified notion of social needs, evolutionary progress, social integration rather than social change, and reliance upon supposed laws of society. The basic aim mirrored Comte (1853; 1848), Durkheim (1964), Talcott Parsons (1949; 1951; 1966), and others: developing science of society modeled upon the natural sciences (Giddens, 1979). As with those theoretical fountainheads, functionalism embodied the aim of control. Just as the natural sciences had already brought nature under control, so too, it was argued, would the science of society, in the guise of functionalism, bring society under control. In this sense, functionalism was a direct heir to modernist presumptions; indeed it represented a modern form of sociological positivism.

Education plays a significant role within functionalist theories of modernization. It was given two principal roles. First, as a prime site for the inculcation of integrative, stabilizing values: education systems were seen as key in this sedative process, not merely in "modern" societies but also, crucially, in modernizing societies that were "developing." In this sense, too, as was argued earlier, functionalism was a direct heir to the positivist faith, in which the twin aims of the advancement of knowledge and an increase in social control were intertwined. Already in the 17th century, the scientist-philosopher Francis Bacon (1861) had compared science and learning to a harp that would quiet a mutinous crowd: "It is without all controversy that learning doth make the minds of men gentle, generous, maniable and pliant to government; whereas ignorance makes them churlish, thwart and mutinous" (p. 14).

The second key educational role within functionalism was the provision of adequate numbers of skilled personnel to service workforce needs. Both these functions worked to ensure the ongoing stability of society. The triumph of modernity was clearly expressed in the unilinear teleological process whereby societies became "modern." Third world, or developing, countries were always assumed to be at an early stage of progress toward the same inevitable end point: a technological, industrial, advanced bureaucratic, and pluralist society. When examined, this bore an uncanny resemblance to the United States, the United Kingdom, or other "advanced" Western societies. Modern capitalist societies were always the ultimate benchmark for former colonies, no matter how much this disrupted traditional cultures and values. Evolutionary assumptions, common to functionalist social science, were once again adopted from biological theory, via figures such as Durkheim. They implied a specific conception of historical development: advanced capitalist societies were seen as the ultimate destination, whereas the former colonies of Asia, Africa, or Latin America were, positioned at various earlier points on the same road. Clearly discernible, then, if not always stated, was "a teleological notion of history, in which the knowledge and ways of life in the colony were distorted or immature versions of 'normal' or Western society" (Niranjana, 1992, p. 11). Modernization was, in effect, Westernization. These unilinear evolutionary assumptions were part of modernization theory and embodied, as seen above, a distaste for swift or systematic social change, or political value systems inconsistent with modern, advanced capitalism. In this sense, modern functionalism is heir to Durkheim's goal of the establishment of integrative social science. Education had a particular role, as modern society's "civil religion" (Tiryakin, 1979, p. 188). But the evolution at the core of modernization theory was always a one-way street—toward Western capitalist structures and values—and presaged disruptions to traditional institutions and ideologies. The process of evolving toward modernity was based upon a foundation of modern science, which was assumed to be able to advance the rate of human progress significantly: As Harbison and Myers (1964; 1965) argued, "Man [sic] in this century of science can move forward in leaps instead of steps." Once again, this faith in the potential of science and technology to advance the perfectibility of humanity is a further echo of Enlightenment faith in the power of reason as *techne*—that is, the embodiment of modern, technocratic society, in which instrumental reason overwhelms ethical constraints and mores (Habermas, 1978; Marcuse, 1968).

Modernization theorists like McLelland, Coombs, Harbison, and Myers saw the process as an example of the Weberian rationalization of society, whereby traditional social mores and institutions such as kinship were replaced by a "coldly rational" modernist action orientation, more suited to complex, 20th-century bureaucratic societies (see McClelland, 1961, p. 174). Rationalization meant "a lessening of mystical or supernatural orientation towards life, an increase in striving, orderliness, rigidity, orientation to work without reward, and other such features which Weber saw (as) characteristic of modern capitalist orientations" (Welch, 1985, p. 11).

Indeed, David McClelland specifically adapted Talcott Parsons's reformulation of Weber's ideas to develop his "need achievement" index of modernization. The concept, as its name implied, comprised a composite index of modernization. It argued that to achieve an increase in economic growth and to become truly modern, developing nations needed to reform ideologies and institutions, while individuals needed to become more achievement-oriented. Suggested changes centered around implementing features like an increased division of labor and more contractual social relations. These were allied to reoriented values, such as the substitution of material for spiritual ethics. Here is more evidence of a means-ends style of rationality in which economic efficiency is, at least implicitly, accorded a prime value (for more, see Welch 1985; 1991). Little or no consideration was given to alternative value systems, least of all those held by people from the "modernizing" society. The end point of this process of evolution was always that of advanced capitalist society, a teleological element it shared with the more deterministic forms of Marxism, and that always led to the endpoint of a communist society.

DOMINANCE OF WESTERN CULTURE

Positivism, often including a broadly evolutionary perspective, has been only one common assumption underlying much modernist empirical and theoretical work in comparative education. But its influence is linked to (and helps to explain) others. The fact that modern science was associated with the rise of the West helps to explain another given within the traditions of mainstream, modernist comparative studies of education: Western culture as the apex of civilization. A common assumption of 19th and early 20th-century anthropology, it remained pervasive and influential in comparative education during at least the first half of the 20th century. Like many contemporaries in the social sciences, Coombs, McClelland, Harbison, and Myers, and others in the 1950s and 1960s, viewed "other" societies from a Western perspective. Modernization theorists situated non-Western nations at a point somewhere along the road culminating in "Westernization." The fact that the field of comparative education largely grew out of Western scholarly foundations (most founding figures were from Europe and America), made this teleology unsurprising. It helps explain the critique that modernization was coextensive with Westernization. But the devaluing of difference, and the rich and long-standing traditions associated with non-Western cultural traditions, was not a good base for a field of study that purported to analyze cultural difference (one such attempt was Reagan [2018]).

ALTERNATIVES TO WESTERN FRAMEWORKS

The spectacular rise of China and India and the broader shift of power from West to East in the 21st century has further challenged this assumption of Western dominance. In comparative education, the work of eminent Canadian comparativist Ruth Hayhoe (2007; 2008), together with work by Chinese scholars, has done much to open Western eyes to the rich world of Chinese and Eastern scholarship. Of a complex history, at least two major elements of traditional Chinese thought are relevant here. First is the complementary, relational quality of much traditional Chinese thought, originating in the Yin-Yang metaphysics of the Yi-Jin (I-Ching). Within such traditions, concepts as being and becoming, for example, are seen as contrary, yet complementary. This is very different from the traditional binaries of most Western thought, although has some affinities with more dialectical, relational qualities of some ancient Greek thought, and the work of Hegel.[4] The second element is the moral dimension of much traditional Chinese philosophy, evident in both Confucius's version of the Golden Rule ("Do not impose on others what you do not choose for yourself"), as well as the virtues of sympathy, benevolence, trustworthiness, and filial piety (see Mou, 2008).

Both elements challenge the basic assumptions of mainstream Western intellectual frameworks.

Indigenous research frameworks equally challenge mainstream Western assumptions. The relational and dialogical *Talanoa* research methodology stems from Pacific island nations such as Tonga, Fiji, and Samoa, and is based on very different underpinnings to mainstream Western principles of objectivism and value-free research. Taking its context from Pasifika cultures, *Talanoa*, by contrast, is "a personal encounter where people story their issues, their realities and aspirations" (Vaioleti, 2006, p. 21). Such personal encounters yield greater *mo'oni* (real, pure, authentic information) for Pasifika research. *Talanoa* ontology and epistemology begin from a context that recognizes the importance of face-to-face encounters, kinship systems, rank, age and gender regimes, spiritual order, church obligations, and other cultural concepts that are basic parts of the cultures of Pasifika peoples (Vaioleti, 2006, p. 5). In such settings, cultural protocols are critical: specialist knowledge, for example, is the domain of *tufunga* (learned people), who are its guardians. In practice, *Talanoa* is subjective, oral, and collaborative, and often begins as apparently aimless and irrelevant conversations, until trust is established and participants feel comfortable about sharing their stories. The reciprocal, open-ended nature of such dialogue offers "opportunities to probe, challenge, clarify and re-align" (Vaioleti, 2006, p. 25). The definition of issues stems from the encounter between researcher and participant, and the shared outcome is contextual. Ethics are grounded in good relationships among God(s), the land, and nature. The research relationship is equally based on ethical principles of respect that guard the dignity and interests of participants; researchers do not want to disappoint participants with whom they have developed a relationship.

Both the earlier approaches are much more relational in form than objectivist mainstream Western methodological frameworks. Both also embody ethical principles, rather than the value-free ethos of Western methodologies.

NATION-STATE AS UNIT OF ANALYSIS

A further assumption of traditional comparative education consisted of the nation-state as the prime unit of analysis. To some extent, this reflected the genesis of comparative education as social science that, like others, matured during the heyday of the growth and rivalry of the nation-state in the 19th and early 20th centuries. Major international organs such as United Nations Educational, Scientific, and Cultural Organization (UNESCO) and Organization for Economic Cooperation and Development, also collected statistics along national lines. Although some earlier comparativists analyzed the construction of political identity (Kandel, 1935) or the educative role and function of mission schools (Holmes, 1967), even these more thematic analyses were contained within one or another nation-state. Even Holmes's (1965) well-known problem approach did little to undermine the convention of the nation-state as the prime analytical unit.[5] The final section of his main work of 1965 was devoted to national case studies. Nor did Noah and Eckstein's (1969) programmatic statement that "a comparative study is essentially an attempt as far as possible to replace the names of systems (countries) by the names of concepts (variables)" succeed in checking the taken for granted status of the nation-state (p. 114).

Not all comparative education scholars of the time were trained as area specialists (Bereday was first and foremost a Soviet specialist, but neither Holmes nor Noah and Eckstein were), yet the nation-state still figured as the analytic unit in most comparative research. Now, however, the increasing globalization of economies and cultures is being paralleled by comparative research on diasporic knowledge networks, network theory, and regionalism (see Beech & Artopoulos, 2020; Pizmony-Levy, 2020). This includes the rise of regional bodies such as the European Union's flagship education and training program ERASMUS, the smaller University Mobility in Asia and the Pacific scheme and ASEAN's University Network, as well as trans-national university networks and consortia such as the Worldwide University Network, and journals such as *Globalisation, Societies and Education* (see also, Schneller et al., 2009; Vera & Schupp, 2006; Welch, 2010; Welch & Zhang, 2008; Yang & Welch, 2010). Together, these developments are reshaping our thinking, including problematizing the nation-state as the unit of analysis.

TRIBUTARIES

Although the elements characterized mainstream comparative education during the intense development of comparative methodologies from the 1960s, important tributaries diverged significantly. Some of these have since become significant currents. Not all comparative methodologies held that the further development of the field depended on debates in postrelativity physics, nor that Western culture was the apex of civilization.

Two developments challenging the ubiquitous emphasis upon scientism drew on more interpretive, anthropological traditions: ethnomethodology and ethnography. The first was largely seen in the work of Canadian American scholar Richard Heyman, who in the late 1970s and early 1980s developed an alternative tradition to the prevailing scientism. Like the ethnomethodologists upon whom he drew, Heyman (1979) decried the influence of the natural sciences upon the methodological development of the social sciences. Instead, he offered a "nonscience of comparative education."

For ethnomethodologists, context was vital and thus knowledge, and the language with which it was described, was "indexical," or situationally mediated. In stark contrast with scientifically based methodologies, there was no independent reality that each individual must accept according to a transcendental, abstract "method," and irrespective of individual background or interests. Indeed, the very assumption of a scientific method of detached observation that produced objective insights into social phenomena was simply false. Every observation was itself a construction, one of many possible constructions, each of which could be further deconstructed, or subjected to further interpretation (Heyman, 1979). Indeed, an interpretation of a social phenomenon was coextensive with accounting for a phenomenon. Observation equaled interpretation, and interpretation was, in principle, endless. Each account could, in principle, be subjected to yet another interpretation, and so on. Indeed, what Anthony Giddens (1976, p. 166) characterized as the hermeneutic vortex (an endless process of interpretation) at the core of ethnomethodology was embraced by its followers as a feature of social interpretation.

Heyman's application of such ideas led him to press for a focus on the microprocesses of school life via an intensive study of audio and videotaped interactions. This was a worthwhile corrective to the macro, systems-based traditions of comparative education. But to then argue that other forms of educational investigation should be postponed pending the provision by ethnomethodologists of "a reasonable picture of the essential processes of education" (Heyman, 1980, p. 46) was illogical and chimerical. Equally, although claiming to be strongly antipositivist and postulating an epistemology that celebrated concrete and different ways of constructing social reality, it nonetheless claimed to produce its facts, which were somehow ontologically before other interpretations. Claiming, at least implicitly, to provide an epistemic bedrock upon which other researchers could rely, it also fell victim to the self-same positivism it critiqued (Welch, 1986). The other problem was its field of vision. Focusing on the microcosm of classroom interaction, with its myriad small details, it often lost focus on the wider world (including the often powerful ways in which this macrocosm influenced the micro-world of the classroom). Indeed, a powerful critique of ethnomethodology was its failure to embrace or analyze power relations, particularly the important ways in which power structures in the larger world, including relations based on social class, shaped the microcosm of the classroom. In this sense, it could be argued that, in gaining one class, ethnomethodologists had lost another.

The Canadian connection was strengthened in Vandra Masemann's (1982; 1990) fruitful elaboration of critical ethnography, which avoided many of the pitfalls, and provided an important challenge to mainstream scientism of comparative research:

> Is it the task of social scientists to seek ever more diligently to define objective methods of researching the social world (or education), with possibilities for change seen as simply the result of "reading out the data" and making choices on the basis of some cost-efficient or technological rationale? (Masemann, 1982, p. 1)

For Masemann (1986), critical ethnography offered not merely a renewed emphasis on "participant observation of the small-scale . . . with an attempt to understand the culture and symbolic life of the actors involved" (p. 23) but also "insists upon a level of agency which is persistently overlooked or denied" (Willis, 1977, p. 194, cited in Masemann, 1982, p. 23). Masemann's ethnography cited the micro within the context of a macro-theory of social organization: she argued that "it should be possible to . . . investigate the lived life in schools while not necessarily limiting the analysis to the actors' perceptions of the situation" (Masemann, 1982, p. 23). Only in that way could the practices by which hegemonic rationality are imposed upon students be successfully revealed and analyzed. By connecting the macro to the micro, she avoided the problems of ethnomethodologists, whose bracketing (methodological exclusion) of larger structures and ideologies, made them unable to analyze power very successfully, if at all. (For further insights, see Chapter 4 in this volume.)

Other nonmainstream theories challenged the conventional Western-centric view of much research or proceeded from rather different political assumptions about the international political arena and the relationship between powerful and relatively disempowered groups in education. This included the role of philanthropic agencies in fostering dependency (Arnove, 1980a). Turning the functionalist assumption of a unilinear path to monolithic Western modernity on its head, several such scholars articulated a core-periphery model. This often drew on elements of the Marxist tradition, emphasizing the capacity of wealthy and powerful Western nations, as well as lending programs of agencies such as the International Monetary Fund a and World Bank, to deepen the dependency of third world nations (Carnoy, 1974; 1986). Too little has changed, it seems: in the aftermath of the Asian financial crisis of the late 1990s, the World Bank admitted that their interventions had deepened the crisis. Drawing upon scholars such as Andre Gunder Frank (1969; 1972), Immanuel Wallerstein (1979), and others, these comparative scholars cast a critical eye on the influence of colonialism and on relations between the first and third world. Martin Carnoy's important early book was succeeded by Philip Altbach and Gail Kelly's (1978) important work on colonialism, which critically examined the educational influence of Western colonial incursions in Africa, Latin America, and the Asia Pacific region, and included an important early study of internal colonialism in the education of indigenous minorities. This applied the work of figures such as Harold Wolpe (1975) to education among Native American peoples.

Robert Arnove's (1980b) application of world-systems analysis stemmed naturally from his work on the ideological penetration of philanthropic organizations, especially in the third world. His call for an international approach to understanding educational systems rather than the traditional reliance upon the nation-state, explored the benefits of setting educational analysis in the context of international economic, political, and social developments. The effects of colonial and neocolonial influences on Africa, Latin America, and Oceania were obvious instances of the necessity of such approaches. They emphasized the ongoing difficulties faced by these regions in overcoming an often-long-standing history of dependency, fostered by the colonial relationship and often only changing in form, postindependence. Arnove (1980) explained that the international ideological penetration of colonial and postcolonial nations also extended within nations of the third world:

> Dependency theory basically articulates a descending chain of exploitation from the hegemony of metropolitan countries over peripheral countries to the hegemony of the center of power in a Third World country over its own peripheral areas. Closely related to such notions of center and periphery are the concepts of Wallerstein concerning convergence and divergence in the global system. (p. 49)

Altbach's (1982) analysis of neocolonialism and dependency also articulated the processes that developed and sustained what he termed "servitude of the mind" both among and within nations, a process not merely fostered by disparities of economic wealth and power but also reflecting the fact that third world nations

> find themselves at the periphery of the world's educational and intellectual systems... The world's leading universities, research institutions, publishing houses, journals, and all the elements that constitute a modern technological society are concentrated in the industrialized nations of Europe and North America. (p. 470)

THINGS FALL APART

But these cracks in modernist scientism were not the only changes. By the late 20th century, the ebullience of the postwar decades was well and truly waning. The oil crisis of the 1970s, as well as subsequent periods of intermittent economic recession, led to mass unemployment, especially among youth, in many parts of the world. Widening gaps between rich and poor (both within and between countries) and the increasing deregulation of many economies paralleled a wider decline in government activity and intervention in social and economic affairs. Economically, politically and epistemologically, the *Zeitgeist* was much less certain and confident (Burns & Welch, 1992). In the social sciences, the confident certitudes of earlier decades were increasingly falling apart. The rise of poststructuralist thought, with its rejection of much modernist thinking, represented a considerable challenge; but not the only one.

GLOBALIZATION AND CHANGES IN THE STATE

By the 1990s, the assumed centrality of the nation-state as the unit of analysis in comparative education was under increasing challenge. This was reflected in the theoretical literature, the changing boundaries of both the nation-state, and our understanding (Giddens, 1994; Ohmae, 1991; 1995; Robertson, 1994). Diffuse international economic and political changes at the end of the century pushed older conventions aside. Centripetal and centrifugal forces substantially reshaped the boundaries of postcommunist Eastern Europe (Welch, 1993). New regional trading blocs, in part sustained by international trading and political agreements, challenged the traditional emphasis on the nation-state. The European Union, North American Free Trade Agreement (later the Free Trade Agreement of the Americas, including Latin America), and Asia Pacific Economic Community, often spawned regional educational architecture to support the internationalization of education (see also Wächter, 2009).

Despite considerable divergence about the meaning of globalization, and some hyperbole, definite trends were discernible: massive global movement of capital within a more deregulated international economic environment: huge growth in international communications; and increased labor mobility, including academic labor. Each had an impact on regional economic alliances, as well as on global manufacturing and financial enterprises (see, e.g., Meusburger et al., 2018; Saxenien, 2006; Welch & Cai, 2011; Yang & Welch, 2010). Internationalizing of previously more nationally based economies quickened, while the massive growth in information and communication technology further challenged national borders (including in education), despite the digital divide. China, for example, introduced strict regulations on the kinds of information that may legally be accessed on the internet (on regionalism in education, see Hawkins et al., 2012). (See Epstein [2023]). Despite rhetoric about developing broader forms of understanding not bounded by the nation-state (making "the world a central hermeneutic") (Robertson, 1994, p. 64), many argued that the effects were more economic than conceptual.

Analysts such as Huntington (1996) postulated a "clash of civilizations" between, for example, Islam, China, and the West, which had overtaken the preceding era of nationalist rivalries. Yet the clash of civilizations had more in common with theories of nationalist rivalries, or even earlier eras, than was usually supposed: both were predicated on mistaken essentialism, and orientalism.[6] In Huntington's case, neither "the USSR" nor "Islam" was a unitary entity:

> The key weakness of Huntington's analysis is that, like the early Cold Warriors, he has fallen into the trap of depicting the enemy as a monolith. . . . At the outset of the Cold War, the Communist countries were depicted as the vanguard of a movement dedicated to the triumph of an international communist utopia. . . . In like fashion, Huntington depicts the Islamic countries as part of a wider pan-Islamic movement, united in their hostility to the West and the United States. (Maswood, 1994, p. 19; Shahi, 2017)

Clearly, a more sophisticated analysis was needed. Scholars of comparative education must contribute to such clarification and analysis because, despite this rapidly changing scene, and the substantial implications of both globalization and the clash of civilizations thesis for comparative education, they have not gained sufficient critical appraisal. Approaches that reject essentialism and orientalism,[7] in favor of integrating political economy perspectives with education and social theory are more likely to be successful, particularly if combined with a multilevel approach (Bray & Thomas, 1995), that examines both the effects at an international, macro level but also local, small-scale effects. The story of globalization is ultimately written at the local level.

Equally, and notable exceptions notwithstanding (Arnove, 1997; Carnoy, 1984; Torres & Puiggros, 1995; Welch, 1993; 1996; 1997), theorizing the changing role of the state for education, and related issues like privatization, and deregulation, remained underdeveloped in comparative education literature, including access and equity in education (Mok, 1998; Tavassoli et al., 2000; Welch, 2011). Some comparative scholars highlighted the progressive erosion of the postwar democratic settlement in advanced capitalist states such as the United Kingdom, Europe, and Australia, including educational implications (see Yeatman, 1993). Others focused on the rise of a more neoliberal state model in Asia (Mok, 2006). Fewer cited such accounts within a systematic analysis of changes in the form of the state and in international economic patterns and relations (see Chapter 10 in this volume; Cerny, 1990; Habermas, 1976; Offe, 1984; 1993; Pusey, 1991). This included the tectonic shift from the postwar welfare state model (in which it was the state's responsibility to ensure that good-quality education, health, and welfare were available to all). The replacement, the competition state, (where the state intervenes only to heighten national or international economic competitiveness), devolved responsibility for success or failure to individuals or families) (Cerny, 1990; Yeatman, 1990). This analytical omission is troubling. Thorough analyses of this development have much to offer studies of educational change in the industrialized West, as well as former socialist nations, and various third world states. The rise of Asia (see Chapter 13), for example, particularly East Asia, has been associated with the so-called developmental state model, where the state plays an active role in every aspect of development, including education (see Welch, 2017).

But recently, there has been a significant rollback of globalization. The Global Financial Crisis (GFC) of 2007–2009 strengthened a revolt by those who felt marginalized and left behind (for different accounts of marginalization processes, see Standing, 2011; Vance, 2006). This included some working-class males, some rural dwellers, and those who felt their jobs and values were threatened by the "Other," either cosmopolitans or, often, migrants. In several systems, such sentiments fueled a retreat from international engagement and a turn to populist nativism and nationalism. The devastating COVID-19 pandemic of 2020 was also used by several regimes, such as the Philippines, Thailand, Turkey, Russia, parts of Eastern Europe, Africa, and Latin America, as well as in the United States and the Brexit movement in the United Kingdom, to stoke nationalist sentiments, retreat from international engagement, and in some cases, revert to more authoritarian rule (see Darius, n.d.; Hiebert, 2020). But once again, the effects were unequal: a combination of nationalism and dramatic economic decline hit poor countries hard, and poorer communities even harder. This included workers (often women) in the informal economy in third world nations, and manual, casual, or part-time workers in wealthier countries (the so-called Precariat) (Standing, 2011). In the case of the United States, rising nationalism accelerated a withdrawal from international organizations such as UNESCO, and the World Health Organization, as well as from international trade pacts such as the Trans-Pacific Partnership, and efforts to weaken the World Trade Organization.

Both the GFC and especially the COVID-19 pandemic reduced international trade, but also dramatically reduced student and staff mobility. But this was not just a result of travel restrictions introduced to curb the spread of the pandemic. The so-called Trade War between the United States and China was soon recognized as a technology war, and even a geostrategic struggle for dominance, especially in the South China Sea, and Asia-Pacific region. The Great Decoupling, as it was dubbed by the journal *Foreign Affairs*, was, by mid-2020, beginning to resemble an ideological cold war (Farrell & Newman, 2020; Lim & Ferguson, 2020; Walker, 2020). The impact on staff and student mobility was immediate, with the United States refusing numbers of visas to both Chinese faculty and research students in STEM (science, technology, engineering, and mathematics) areas. More broadly, rising nationalism and nativism, and the rancorous and rivalrous U.S.-China relations, threatened the values and institutions supporting international education.

FROM POSITIVISM TO POST-ISM

Many of the changes described here left major assumptions of modernism largely unchallenged. But the growth of poststructuralist thought in the West toward the end of the 20th century gave rise to challenging critiques in the social sciences and, somewhat later, in comparative education.

What does poststructuralist thought mean? Briefly, structuralist theories such as (structural) functionalism, as described earlier, and the more determinist forms of Marxism emphasized the central explanatory role of structure in determining societal outcomes (see Marques, 2020; Shields & Kameshwara, 2021; Welch, 1985; Welch, 1988). The central importance that such theories accorded to the social system viewed individuals as powerless, against a powerful, deterministic set of structures that shaped their social destinies. Such theories were akin to the religious doctrine of fatalism, which held that people were powerless to struggle against the fate that God had allocated them. Against such views, poststructuralist theories, including in education, held that people, and the diverse meanings they allocated to the worlds they inhabited, shaped social reality. According to such views, social reality was contingent, localized, and a matter of negotiation. It was not monolithic but constructed in different ways, according to how people and groups positioned themselves in the world. In principle, such views allocated more space to "agency" (people's ability to act upon the social world to change it) as compared with the more deterministic social theories described earlier, which emphasized "structure."

Poststructuralist theories reject the pretensions of large-scale "grand theory," which purport to explain how society works overall. Comparative scholars such as Paulston (1996), Paulston and Liebman (1994), Coulby (1995), Coulby and Jones (1996), Ninnes and Mehta (2004), and Cowen (1996) discarded many prior assumptions, such as the objectivity of knowledge or the centrality of scientific methodology, as the basis for research. Postcolonialism too exerted an influence, if perhaps more indirectly, and the joint insistence on heterogeneity and mistrust of grand theories informs poststructuralist thought generally: "The post-colonial distrust of the liberal-humanist rhetoric of progress and universalizing master narratives has obvious affinities with post-structuralism." Although postcolonialism insists on the centrality of the colonial experience, its implications, and aftermath (Niranjana, 1992, p. 9). But there are differences as H. Bhaba (1994) has indicated: "If the interest in Postmodernism is limited to a celebration of the fragmentation of the 'grand narratives' of post Enlightenment rationalism, then, for all its excitement, it remains a profoundly parochial enterprise" (p. 4).

Nonetheless, there are significant differences between postmodernism and postcolonialism. Postmodern critiques date from Rust's (1991) Comparative and International Education Society presidential address of 1991. This late onset of the debate within comparative education (and modest uptake since) is interesting, given the supposed insistence upon heterogeneity by postmodern critics, and the supposed centrality of cultural diversity to comparative education.

As with Winnie-the-Pooh, however, all was not what it seemed.[8] First, even Ninnes and Mehta's work of 2004 essentialized other theoretical traditions, refusing to acknowledge critical stances toward modernity, reason and rationalism, Westernization, science (as institution and ideology), and the rise and dominance of capitalism, evident in much critical scholarship. Second, just as the previous argument proposed that modernism represented, *inter alia*, the triumph of science over diversity (including cultural diversity), it will be argued that postmodernism was less about the celebration of differences than was commonly supposed.

This was for two reasons, arguably. An original aspiration of postmodernity was to put differences at the center stage of (social) theory, to overcome the universalizing, monolithic tendencies of modernist thought. In itself, this was a potentially valuable corrective to the tendency of modernism to carve out a unilinear path, and portray those who diverged from it as aberrations. The postmodern celebration of difference aimed to give voice to silenced ethnic and gender minorities. Both aims were reasonable, given modernism's record of intolerance to difference. Regrettably, however, these aims were rapidly overwhelmed by increasingly arcane terminology, in which language games/tropes (in which words gain variable meaning according to the rules of the game, and there is nothing outside the game) rendered the original intentions largely invisible and unintelligible. In practice, difference, like other social artifacts, became textualized and buried under an avalanche of discursive devices. It is one thing to underline the importance of language in describing social difference; quite another to argue there is nothing beyond language. Postmodernism falls into the latter camp and thus operates on an abstract (quasi-systemic) model of "opposition" and difference, where those terms are stripped of historical and experiential content, and treated, in effect, as linguistic artifacts (Norris, 1993).

> There is... a danger of textualising gender, denying sexual specificity, or treating difference as merely a formal category, rather than having an empirical and historical existence. (McLaren, 1991)

In other words, instead of confronting and opposing the oppression and marginalization of particular social groups, as certain forms of Marxism and feminism had tried to do, postmodernism increasingly consigned difference to a linguistic artifact, remote from the everyday world and concerns of marginal groups in which they professed to be interested.

Second, postmodernism's celebration of image(s) meant that it at times became more concerned with style rather than substance: how things looked, rather than their importance. Having rid itself of a solid standpoint from which to analyze events, postmodernism lacked a position from which to make ethical judgments. Knowledge was divorced from commitment (which was reduced to one value, among several others), and knowledge and meaning became devoid of ethics (Norris, 1993; see also Agger, 1991; O'Neill, 1995; Young, 1998). Thus even if differences were encompassed (and there were considerable doubts about this), there was no longer any basis to judge this difference. As an abstract category without a moral base, the "difference" expressed by white supremacists such as the American Nazi Party had the same inherent worth as the cultures they seek to oppress (such as African Americans, Jews, or indigenous minorities). Indeed, in some recent works, the only resort with which to complete the promise of postmodernity has been to connect it to some of the moral stances of feminism and African American literature, as in the work of Henry Giroux (1992). Some theorists of postmodernism make much of postmodernism's capacity to map the terrain (Paulston and Liebmann 1994, Paulston, 1996). By eschewing any moral compass, however, postmodern theories leave us unable to choose the direction of change.

Postmodern theories (there are now many) appear to offer substantial critiques of functionalist modernization theories. In particular, this included the supposed correspondence of modernization with Westernization, and the notion that third world social and economic progress depends on advanced science and technology, and scientific modes of rationality. Such critiques of the totalizing scientific rationality or other modes of universalistic reason seemed to offer space for alternative views of development and for marginalized groups to position themselves more centrally in development processes. Increasingly, however, the lived reality of oppressed rural peasantry was obscured by several layers of arcane and densely theoretic language that rendered the experience of those individuals unrecognizable to themselves, and invisible to others. Not only was the line between people's history and fictional accounts blurred, as Morrow and Torres (1995) argue, but the whole notion of domination and hegemony, by which forms of oppression were identified and opposed, was muted, if not abandoned. (See Chapter 3 in this volume.) Instead, according to theorists such as John O'Neill, Christopher Norris, and others, people are disattached from their history, floating free in a semiotic soup of images and signs. Equity and equality, according to postmodern theories, make up just one set of values, alongside many others. They may even have less importance than most, given the individualizing tendencies of postmodern theories, which tend to reject acting for the collective good. Ultimately, this offers little substantive critique of the concrete processes of modernity, which often destabilize long-standing cultural traditions (e.g., matriarchy) and oppress less powerful social groups (e.g., women, small landholders, and peasants). A more progressive resolution would ally postmodern critiques with forms of feminism and race: "Few theorists of race and gender would succumb to throwing out general theories of domination in the name of a pluralist celebration of difference" (Morrow & Torres, 1995, p. 421).

POSTMODERN, POSTCOLONIAL, AND THE "OTHER"?

As indicated earlier, postcolonial theories share with postmodern critiques an insistence on the centrality of difference. However, work by scholars such as Edward Said (1995), Gayatri Spivak (1999), Homi Bhaba (1991), and Tejaswini Niranjana (1992) forms a corrective to the moral vacuum at the heart of postmodernity by incorporating the political dimension into their understanding of difference (see also Schwartz & Ray, 2000). Central to this work is both a focus on, and critique of, hegemonic processes within colonialism and postcolonial experiences, and opposition to the domination by male, white, heterosexual, and Western forms of reason and practices associated with this form of logic. Hence, Braithwaite rather than Baudrillard, Fanon rather than Foucault.[9] Niranjana (1992), for example, reveals ways in which the medium of translation is used to create an exotic and uncivilized "other" in need of the fruits of Western civilization, including (like Francis Bacon, centuries earlier) the taming influence of education. In this sense she is an ally of Edward Said (1995), whose analysis of orientalism also showed how the process of translation was deployed in colonies such as India "to gather in, to rope off, to domesticate the Orient and thereby to turn it into a province of European learning" (p. 78).

Comparativists are familiar with the problems of translation. The experience of lawyer-novelist Louis Begley, who encountered some of his characters in a recent translation (in a language with which he was familiar), strikes a chord:

> Not so long ago, I came across some of my personages in a translation, who were standing on the sidewalk, outside their New York City hotel, in the hope that someone would bring them a lemonade with a great deal of water in it. "How strange," I said to myself, and checked the original, to find out that in English the poor chumps were waiting for their stretch limo. (Bilney, 1997, p. 18)

Confusing "lemo" for "limo" is one of the less serious problems of translation, which, as Niranjana (1992) indicates, can also reveal implicit or explicit strategies to portray the Other. Indeed, representations of the Other often reveal as much about the interests of the translator as they do about the translated, and highlight the need to be understood in the context of strategies of intercultural dialogue (see Chapter 5 in this volume) and the effects of colonialism and imperialism (Said, 1994). An illustration Niranjana (1992) provides of the work of 18th-century scholar and translator (Sir) William Jones is based not so much on his direct translations of key Indian classics, as on his prefaces, speeches, and poetry. Ultimately, Niranjana (1992) distills the most significant element of Jones's work into the following:

1. The need for translation by the European, since the natives are unreliable interpreters of their own laws and culture
2. The desire to be a lawgiver, to give the Indians their "own" laws
3. The desire to "purify" Indian culture and speak on its behalf. (p. 13)

Such strategies reveal key elements of colonialist discourse, in which the 'Other' is characterized as a "submissive, indolent nation, unable to appreciate the fruits of freedom, desirous of being ruled by an absolute power . . . (and) incapable of civil liberty" (Niranjana, 1992, p. 14). It is but a small step from here to justify the perpetuation of a paternalistic administration and governance that speaks for the colonial Other and keeps them in their place. By recognizing this power distortion as a key colonialist motif, such theories are better placed to oppose such paternalistic and oppressive practices.

NEW COMPARATIVE EDUCATION, NEW MILLENNIUM?

Given the argument about the failures of scientism, the absence of ethics in postmodernism, and the divisive social and economic effects of contemporary globalization, new foundations are needed for the new millennium (Welch, 2000a). As comparativists, we cannot stand by passively, faced with an ever more fractured social and economic world, characterized by privatization, "user pays" ideologies in education, and increasing gaps between the "haves" and "have-nots." As social scientists, we must recognize that theories are not neutral, and that a stance based on a specious pretense of objectivity is untenable. As comparativists, we either take the side of the marginalized and dispossessed or deepen their disadvantage.

What would such a renewed comparative education look like? Elsewhere, I have outlined the constituents of such a new vision (Welch, 2001). It is, first and foremost, a moral vision, in which the *telos* (purpose or goal) of the social good is still a key value, as it was in the West for the ancient Greeks, and during the Renaissance, and in the East for Confucianism, with its Golden Rule, and virtues of benevolence, sympathy, trustworthiness, and filial piety. Reasserting a more democratic ethos for comparative education, as some in the field have begun to do (see McGinn, 1996), should aim at more mutualist, reciprocal intercultural relations, resisting the technicism of earlier scientific accounts, and rejecting the moral hole at the center of postmodernity. This represents critical modernity—breaking free of much of its problematic legacy while retaining those elements that still have something to offer. This is very much in the spirit of Ruth Hayhoe (2000).

The model sketched here draws on both hermeneutics (a form of theory originally based around textual interpretation) and critical theory. Each resists any reduction to instrumentalist accounts of understanding. According to both hermeneutics and critical theory, no set of technical steps, no given formula, will guarantee the answer. Indeed, both schools of thought have shaped themselves, at least in part, in opposition to such a naïve belief. Within hermeneutics, "For Gadamer, hermeneutics does not provide a methodical procedure of understanding but instead clarifies the conditions which accompany any act of understanding" (Teigas, 1995, p. 41), while within critical theory, "We must remember that critique is always limited, fragmentary, and unsure" (Young, 1998, p. 70). Habermas, too, resists the simplistic self-understanding of science which reduces itself to a technical formula (Adorno, 1976).

Several methodological precepts are broadly common and can serve as the basis for a renewed comparative education, and perhaps intercultural relations more generally. The first of these principles is a refusal of *techne* (a means-ends form of rationality that eschews ethical considerations), and its instrumental account of knowledge, reason, and being, within the positivist tradition. There is a parallel here to the critiques of positivist understanding and its effects in the social sciences (Giddens, 1976; 1979). To some extent Gadamer's notion of "tradition" which preforms our understanding, parallels Kuhn's (1970) notion of "paradigm," in that both refer to socially concrete communities of understanding.

By contrast to the emphasis on control, mastery, and manipulation of knowledge and society, both hermeneutics and critical theory uphold respect for the Other. Unlike the positivist account of knowledge, where the other is regarded as an "object . . . of study" (Greene, 1994) both critical theory and hermeneutics, as well as Confucius's Golden Rule, uphold a principle of the Other as subject, with the same rights and privileges that one would expect for oneself. This openness to difference, is not merely of a textual kind, as in some forms of postmodernity, but a principled openness: to cultural differences of gender, race, and class.

Scientistic pretensions to objectivity and universal validity are rejected as ill-founded. Presuppositionlessness, of the kind advanced by both Descartes and the phenomenological tradition, is, on this account, illusory.[10] On the contrary, knowledge is informed by interest, and no initial understanding escapes the need for prejudgment:

> This is exactly the idea that Gadamer questions: could there ever be any understanding of tradition, of a text or a society, devoid of any preconception or fore-meaning. If this were true, reason would constitute the ultimate source of authority without any historical limit imposed upon it; reason would become Absolute Reason. (Teigas, 1995, p. 37)

Nor are the natural sciences immune from this critique, despite pretensions of some epistemologies to be objective and value-free: "Similarly, we can view as prejudice the way in which scientific programs and their technological implementation operate under old convictions of 'mastering' and 'exploiting' nature for the benefit of humanity" (Teigas, 1995, p. 39).

More than a century ago, the German theorist Dilthey railed against such pretensions, arguing that no universalistic science could answer real pedagogical questions. These questions were, by contrast, concrete and historical, and demanded to be answered in the same form. Indeed, Dilthey saw such universalistic pretensions of objectivist science, as evidence of the relative "wissenschaftliche Rückständigkeit" (scientific backwardness) of education, in comparison with other disciplines which had already recognized the historical articulation of thought.

Historicity then is a further key point in common: both critical theory and critical hermeneutics insist that the process of understanding is fundamentally historical, not abstract and idealist. Any understanding must begin with certain interests or prejudices, and is itself embedded in a specific historical context: "We share the prejudices of our tradition" (Teigas, 1995, p. 41). Both theoretical strains recognize a more mutual self-other relationship in the human sciences than that in the natural sciences:

> the "subject to object" epistemological relationship firmly established in the natural sciences could not do justice to the "subject to subject" relationship attained between the interpreter and the historical tradition in the human sciences. (Teigas, 1995, p. 32)

Another common building block for a renewed comparative education is the rejection of the binary poles that underpin mainstream Western epistemology: science or speculation, being or becoming, male or female, fact or value, mind or body. Both critical theory and hermeneutics espouse a more relational understanding, in which, for example, knowledge is related to social existence, a position far more in tune with contemporary sociology of knowledge, and Eastern thought traditions, than the fixed opposites of mainstream Western scientistic epistemologies.

But there are important differences between hermeneutics and critical theory. Critical hermeneutics, according to Habermas, is distinct in two ways, each of which has implications for understanding education, cultural difference, and relations between "self" and "other." Habermas argues that interpretation which is not critical will tend to reproduce the very social conditions which give rise to misunderstandings, and social distortions: "A non-critical understanding simply continues, reiterates, and reproduces tradition, cultural values, ideology and power structures" (Gallagher, 1992, p. 241).

The limits of language and its role in interpretation form the second point of difference. Critical hermeneutics holds that extra-linguistic forms of domination, in particular forces such as social class, and economic position, can significantly influence or condition interpretation and communication. Habermas "holds that language is dependent on social processes that cannot be reduced to language" (Gallagher, 1992, p. 242); therefore, interpretations may be *obstructed* by power structures and material relations in society. A key difference is a role ascribed to critical reflection in unmasking these social distortions, and perhaps overcoming them: Critical reflection "puts the interpreter in charge of those conditions which s/he had been passively and unconsciously suffering" (Gallagher, 1992, p. 243). This is indeed the role of ideology critique—for Habermas, it is possible to use self-reflection to break the bounds of tradition, whereas for Gadamer, tradition forms the limits to our understanding.

Here is the connection to reconstructed modernity: the purpose of critical reflection remains emancipation, hence existing, oppressive power structures need to be dismantled. This process of emancipation, however, presupposes mutuality and reciprocity: "In a process of enlightenment there can only be participants" (Gallagher, 1992, p. 245, citing Habermas, 1974). It is here that a critical theory of society, and critical hermeneutics, each display their Enlightenment heritage, and yet break free from it in important ways. Each acknowledges that in the Enlightenment, the "world was conceived as mathematicized and systematized, but the very linkage of an idea of reason as universal to an idea of reason as domination . . . gave rise to new myths and, in time, to new and ever more effective modes of domination" (Greene, 1994, p. 429). This recognition, however, does not necessitate abandoning the Enlightenment heritage altogether; on the contrary, the need to retain the connection between human *praxis* (forms of critically reflective action, containing a core of ethical concerns) and cognitive action is still important and is seen both in certain contemporary feminisms, and critical accounts of science, such as Feyerabend. Feyerabend (1975; 1976, 1978) critiqued pretensions to objective science and re-emphasized the connection between knowledge and emancipation.

The implications both for educational processes and relationships and for intercultural relations are clear. We cannot remain impartial and uncommitted observers, "who stand apart . . . unaffected, but rather, as . . . united by a specific bond with the other, (s)he thinks with the other and undergoes the situation with him (her)" (Greene, 1994, p. 438, citing Gadamer, 1975). This means that the "other," whether teacher, student, ethnic minority, or street child, must not have their language and needs filtered or translated by those who wish to interpret their reality for them. Preserving the "intersubjectivity of possible action-orienting mutual understanding" (Greene, 1994, p. 440, citing Habermas, 1978, p. 191) is central to this philosophy, which resists the domination of an instrumentalist code of reason and practice. Rather than Huntington's "clash of civilizations," such a renewed comparative education postulates a dialogue among civilizations.

It is in this sense that critical hermeneutics is, first and foremost, a normative theory, which proceeds dialogically, whether in education or intercultural relations. Comparative education based on such foundations will not be silenced in the face of the actively increasing social and economic differentiation and exclusion of recent decades. Insisting upon mutual and reciprocal relations, such a stance opposes "structural adjustment" policies in education and society, where these violate principles of justice and freedom. It stands with the "other," the dispossessed and marginalized (Snodgrass, 1992), rendered invisible by the untrammeled reign of modern science and its logic, the blasé stance of forms of postmodernity, and the widening influence of economic globalization (for more on this, see also Welch, 2001; 2003; 2018a; 2018b).

History can be a willing teacher—if we are willing to learn. The Enlightenment helped replace the older Christian religions, based on faith, with the revealed religion of science, based on a blend of empiricism and codified rationality. The priests of old were replaced with the new priesthood of science, thereby failing in many ways to fulfill the promise of the Enlighteners to free humanity from the constraints of a hidebound social order, and sclerotic epistemology, to better understand human relations and social institutions. Instead of heralding a new rational order of equality and human rights, science was often pressed into service to sustain existing stratified societies, at times helping make the existing social hierarchy more scientific. Nonetheless, the Enlightenment was the era in which the dignity and rights of man (Paine, 1791; 1793) (if not yet of women) (Wollstonecraft, 1929) were clearly asserted. Although modernity did not fulfill its early promise, much positive potential was available to help create a more just social order.

The contemporary rush by theorists of both left and right to jettison all features of modernity fails to appreciate its complex history and to some extent becomes captive to a naïve understanding of it. The simplistic critiques of the history of epistemology characterizing much poststructural thought are most clearly evident in postmodernism. Here modernist thought is routinely oversimplified and demonized as a field littered with grand, broken dreams, which were responsible for much of the problems and misdirection of late 20th-century humanity. The wholesale retreat from questions of social justice (dismissed as just another such dream) follows quite logically, if mistakenly, from such assumptions. But much can be salvaged from the detritus of modernity, and much from its agenda that urgently needs rearticulation when neoliberalism, xenophobic nationalism, fundamentalisms, and neoliberal globalization, are widening the already existing gap between rich and poor, white and black, rural and urban, male and female, both within and among nations and regions (Arnove, 1997; Boron & Torres, 1996; Welch, 2000b).

Yet too much poststructural thought, in particular postmodernity, leaves us rudderless in a sea of blasé ironic detachment. Drifting across the social world, we observe the rising tide of imagery but remain unable to distinguish stark images of third-world poverty from the star-studded funeral rites of Gianni Versace or the celebrity culture of Kim Kardashian, for example.

The methodological trajectory traced here reveals the preoccupation with developing a science of comparative education of the 1960s, largely fulfilling its modernist, positivist mandate, despite some oppositional crosscurrents. Although poststructuralist theories were slower to influence comparative education than other social sciences, the early decades of the 21st century confirmed their effects. But postmodernity is an unsatisfactory response to some of the shortcomings of modernist theories. Postcolonialism is, in many respects, a more solid starting point for comparative methodology—not just because it cites difference at center stage, but also because it rejects speaking for the other.

Postcolonial theories form one base from which such an ethical stance could be mounted. As argued previously (Snodgrass, 1992), another standpoint, based on substituting the values of mutuality and reciprocity, for paternalism and control, is found in social theorists such as Hans-Georg Gadamer (1989) and Jürgen Habermas, and could equally act as an important starting point for intercultural theories such as comparative education (see, e.g., Silverman, 1991).

Such values are all the more urgent, in the face of rising nationalism and nativism in many nations, the outlines of a rancorous new U.S.-China cold war that threatens to divide the world into two hostile camps, and the deepening fissures of neoliberal globalization. Faced with such developments, the need for more respectful, mutual, reciprocal forms of research and teaching in comparative education, that reject objectification of the Other in favor of a more inclusive dialogue of civilizations, could not be more urgent.

NOTES

1. Popper's hypothetico-deductive model of epistemology/scientific method begins with a problem, to which it then proposes a hypothetical solution, which is then tested rigorously by attempting to falsify it. If the hypothesis survives all attempts at falsification, we can have limited confidence in it, while acknowledging subsequent tests may yet falsify it. While a popular model, it has been criticized for failing to allow induction, as well as for its positivist assumptions.

2. Structural functional modes of sociology see society as a system, with interdependent parts, which each one contributing to the ongoing harmonious operation of the social system (society). The model of social change is slow and evolutionary.

3. In some versions, the sociological system was based on the model of a biological system, in which each interdependent part (or subsystem, such as the circulatory system, reproductive system, etc.) contributes to the ongoing health and operation of the overall system.

4. In the Western tradition, dialectal thought can be traced back to Plato and Aristotle, and is a process of seeking truth via a discourse between different points of view or perspectives. Hegelian dialectic is sometimes simply summarized in threefold form: thesis; antithesis; synthesis.

5. Holmes's problem approach is a mix of Deweyan stages of reflective thinking, and Popperian critical dualism, combined with his hypothetico-deductive method. Critical dualism distinguishes the realm of facts in the natural world, from decisions about norms, in the social world.

6. The notion of an uncivilized and monolithic "other" arguably provided the major rationale for the 12th-century Crusades, for example. In recent years, nativist impulses have begun to reappear in discourses around the Muslim and Chinese (more broadly Asian) Other.

7. The philosophical concept of essentialism holds that phenomena have certain properties that are essential to them. In sociology, the same assumption is made regarding issues of race and gender, for example. Orientalism, associated with the work of Edward Said, refers to the intellectual process of stereotyping Asia and its cultures and peoples. Such stereotyping was common during the colonial era, and persists to this day.

8. Winnie-the-Pooh, it will be recalled, lived under the name of Sanders: that is, he had the name Sanders above his door, and he lived under it.

9. Chris Braithwaite was an Afro-Caribbean seaman and labor activist, who fought for the rights of black and Asian seamen. Jean Baudrillard, was a French social critic and guru of postmodernism. Frantz Fanon, a psychiatrist and social critic from Martinique, is best known for his influential works *The Wretched of the Earth* (1961) and *Black Skin, White Masks* (1952). Michel Foucault, a French philosopher and social theorist concerned principally with the link between knowledge and power, is a key figure in poststructuralism.

10. René Descartes's philosophical presuppositionlessness rejected all prevailing forms of knowledge (mathematics, science, history, etc.) in favor of a rigorous epistemological path that he postulated would lead to secure truth. A similar stance was later taken up by the phenomenological school.

REFERENCES

Adorno, T. et al. (1976). *The positivist dispute in German sociology*. Heinemann.
Agger, B. (1991). *A critical theory of public life*. Falmer.
Altbach, P. (1982). Servitude of the mind? Education, dependency, and neocolonialism. In P. Altbach et al. (Eds.), *Comparative education*. Macmillan.
Altbach, P., & Kelly, G. (Eds.). (1978). *Education and colonialism*. Longmans.
Arnove, R. (1980a). *Philanthropy and cultural imperialism: The foundations at home and abroad*. Indiana University Press.
Arnove, R. (1980b). Comparative education and world systems analysis. *Comparative Education Review*, 24(1), 48–62.
Arnove, R. (1997). Neoliberal education policies in Latin America: Arguments in favour and against. In C. A. Torres & A. Puiggrás (Eds.), *Latin American education* (pp. 79–100). Westview.
Bacon, F. (1861). *Of the proficience and advancement of learning*. J. W. Parker.
Beech, J., & Artopoulos, A. (2020). Actor Network Theory and Comparative and International Education: addressing the complexity of socio-material foundations of power in education. In T. Jules et al. (Eds.), *The Bloomsbury handbook of theory in comparative and international education*. Bloomsbury.
Bereday, G. (1964). *Comparative method in education*. Holt, Rinehart, and Winston.
Bereday, G. (1969). Reflections on comparative method in education 1964–1966. In M. Eckstein & H. Noah (Eds.), *Scientific investigations in comparative education*. Macmillan.
Bhaba, H. (1991). *Nation and narration*. Routledge.
Bhaba, H. (1994). *The location of culture*. Routledge.
Bilney, G. (1997, May 24). Why do we got a problem with some words? *Sydney Morning Herald*.
Boron, A., & Torres, C. A. (1996). Education, poverty, and citizenship in Latin America: Poverty and democracy. *Alberta Journal of Educational Research*, 42(2), 102–114.
Bray, M, & Murray Thomas, R. (1995). Levels of comparison in educational studies: Different insights from different literatures and the value of multilevel analyses. *Harvard Educational Review*, 65(3), 472–490.
Burns, R., & Welch, A. (Eds.). (1992). *Contemporary perspectives in comparative education*. Garland.
Carnoy, M. (1974). *Education as cultural imperialism*. Longmans.
Carnoy, M. (1984). *The state and political theory*. Princeton University Press.
Carnoy, M. (1986). Education for alternative development. In P. Altbach & G. Kelly, *New approaches to comparative education* (pp. 73–90). University of Chicago Press.
Cerny, P. (1990). *The changing architecture of politics: Structure, agency, and the state*. Sage.
Comte, A. (1853). *The general philosophy of Auguste Comte*, 2 vols. (Trans., H. Harriet Martineau). Trübner, 1853.
Comte, A. (1848). *A general view of positivism* (Trans., J. Bridges.) 1848, Academic Reprints, n.d.
Coulby, D. (1995). Ethnocentricity, post modernity, and European curricular systems. *European Journal of Teacher Education*, 18(2–3), 143–153.
Coulby, D., & Jones, C. (1996). Post-modernity, education and European identities. *Comparative Education*, 32(2), 171–185.
Cowen, R. (1997). Last past the post: comparative education, modernity and perhaps post-modernity. *Comparative Education*, 32(2), 151–170.
Cowen, R. (1996). Last past the post: Comparative education, modernity, and perhaps Post-modernity. *Comparative Education*, 32(2), 151–170.

Darius, R. (n.d.) COVID has exacerbated anti-globalization sentiments, *Australian Institute of International Affairs* (AIIA) http://www.internationalaffairs.org.au/australianoutlook/covid-19-has-exacerbated-anti-globalisation-sentiments/.

Dilthey, W. (1926). Über die Möglichkeit einer allgemeingültigen pädagogischen Wissenschaft. In *Gesammelte Schriften* (Vol. 6). Teubner Verlag.

Dilthey, W. (1934). *Gesammelte Schriften* (Vol. 9). Teubner Verlag.

Durkheim, E. (1964). *The Rules of Sociological Method*. Collier Macmillan.

Epstein, I. (2023). Social media, technology, and protest movements. In L. I. Misiaszek et al. (Eds.), *Emergent trends in comparative education: The dialectic of the global and the local*. Rowman & Littlefield.

Farrell, H., & Newman, A. (2020, June 3). The folly of decoupling from China. *Foreign Affairs*. https://www.foreignaffairs.com/articles/china/2020-06-03/folly-decoupling-china

Feyerabend, P. (1975). *Against method*. New Left Books.

Feyerabend, P. (1976). On the critique of scientific reason. In C. Howson (Ed.), *Method and appraisal in the physical sciences*. Cambridge University Press.

Feyerabend, P. (1978). *Science in a free society*. New Left Books.

Frank, A. G. (1969). *Capitalism and underdevelopment in Latin America*. Monthly Review Press.

Frank, A. G. (1972). The development of underdevelopment. In J. Cockcroft, A. G. Frank, & D. Johnson et al. (Eds.), *Dependence and underdevelopment: Latin America's political economy* (pp. 3–18). Doubleday/Anchor.

Gadamer, H-G. (1975). Hermeneutics and social science. *Cultural Hermeneutics*, 2.

Gadamer, H-G. (1989). *Truth and method* (2nd ed.). Crossroad.

Gallagher, S. (1992). *Hermeneutics and education*. State University of New York Press.

Giddens, A. (1976). *New rules of sociological method*. Hutchinson.

Giddens, A. (1979). Positivism and its critics. In T. Bottomore & R. Nisbet (Ed.), *A history of sociological analysis* (pp. 237–286). Heinemann.

Giddens, A. (1994). *Beyond left and right: The future of radical politics*. Polity.

Giroux, H. A. (1992). *Border crossings: Cultural workers and the politics of education*. Routledge.

Greene, M. (1994). Epistemology and educational research: the influence of recent approaches to knowledge. *Review of Research in Education*, 20, 423–464.

Habermas, J. (1970). *Toward a rational society: Student protest, science, and politics*. Beacon.

Habermas, J. (1974). *Theory and practice*. Beacon.

Habermas, J. (1976). *Legitimation crisis*. Beacon.

Habermas. J. (1978). *Knowledge and human interests*. Heinemann.

Habermas, J. (1984). *A theory of communicative action*. Heinemann.

Hans, N. (1949). *Comparative education: A study of factors and traditions*. Routledge & Kegan Paul.

Harbison, F., & Myers, C. (1964). *Education, manpower, and economic growth*. McGraw-Hill.

Harbison, F., & Myers, C. (1965). *Education and manpower*. McGraw-Hill.

Hawkins, J., Ka-Ho, M., & Neubauer, D. (Eds.). (2012). *Higher education regionalization in Asia Pacific: Implications for governance, citizenship and university transformation*. Palgrave Macmillan.

Hayhoe, R. (2000). Redeeming modernity. *Comparative Education Review*, 44(4), 423–439.

Hayhoe, R. (2007). *Portraits of influential Chinese educators*. Comparative Education Research Centre/Springer.

Hayhoe, R. (2008). Philosophy and comparative education: What can we learn from East Asia? In K. Mundy et al. (Eds.), *Comparative and international education: Issues for teachers* (pp. 23–48). Canadian Scholars Press/Teachers College Press.

Heyman, R. (1979). Towards a non-science of comparative education. Paper presented at the annual conference of the *Comparative and International Education Society*, Ann Arbor, MI, 1–17.

Heyman, R. (1980). Ethnomethodology: Some suggestions for the sociology of education. *Journal of Educational Thought*, 14(1).

Hiebert, M. (2020, May 25). COVID-19 threatens democracy in Southeast Asia. *East Asia Forum*. https://www.eastasiaforum.org/2020/05/25/covid-19-threatens-democracy-in-southeast-asia/

Holmes, B. (1965). *Problems in education: A comparative approach*. Routledge.

Holmes, B. (Ed.). (1967). *Educational policy and the mission schools*. Routledge.

Holmes, B. (1981). *Comparative education: Some considerations of method*. Allen & Unwin.

Horkheimer, M., & Adorno, T. (1972). *The dialectic of enlightenment*. Continuum.

Huntington, S. (1996). *The clash of civilizations and the remaking of world order*. Simon & Schuster.

Husserl, E. (1960). *Cartesian meditations* (Trans., D. Cairns). Martinus Nijhoff.

Husserl, E. (1965). *Phenomenology and the crisis of European philosophy*. Harper.

Kandel, I. (1933). *Studies in comparative education*. George Harrap.

Kandel, I. (1935). *The making of Nazis*. Teachers College Press.

Karabel, J., & Halsey, A. H. (1977). Educational research: A review and interpretation. In *Power and ideology in education*. Oxford University Press.

Kincaid, H. (n.d.). Positivism in the social sciences. *Routledge encyclopedia of philosophy*. https://www.rep.routledge.com/articles/thematic/positivism-in-the-social-sciences/v-1/sections/influence-on-the-philosophy-and-practice-of-the-social-sciences

Kuhn, T. (1970). *The structure of scientific revolutions*. University of Chicago Press.

Kuhn, T. (1974). Reflections upon my critics. In I. Lakatos & A. Musgrave (Eds.), *Criticism and the growth of knowledge*. Cambridge University Press.

Lakatos, I. (1974). The methodology of scientific research programmes. In I. Lakatos, *Philosophical Papers* (Vol. 1). Cambridge University Press.

Lim, D., & Ferguson, V. (2020). Conscious decoupling: The technology security dilemma. China dreams. *China story yearbook: China dreams*. Australian Centre on China in the World (pp. 119–136). ANU Press.

Marcuse, H. (1968). *One-dimensional man*. Sphere.

Marques, M. (2020). Structural-functionalism in comparative international education: Antecedents, developments, and applications. In T. Jules et al. (Eds.), *The Bloomsbury handbook of theory in comparative and international education*. Bloomsbury.

Masemann, V. (1982). Critical ethnography in the study of comparative education. *Comparative Education Review*, 26(1), 1–14.

Masemann, V. (1986). Critical ethnography in the study of comparative education. In P. Altbach & Gail Kelly (Eds.), *New approaches to comparative education*. University of Chicago Press.

Masemann, V. (1990). Ways of knowing. *Comparative Education Review*, 34(4), 465–473.

Maswood, S. (1994). The new "mother of all clashes": Samuel Huntington and the clash of civilizations. *Asian Studies Review*, 18(1).

McClelland, D. (1961). *The achieving society*. Van Nostrand.

McGinn, N. (1996). Education, democratization, and globalization: A challenge for comparative education. *Comparative Education Review*, 40(4), 341–357.

McLaren, P. (1991). Schooling the postmodern body: Critical pedagogy and the politics of enfleshment. In H. Giroux (Ed.), *Postmodernism, feminism, and cultural politics* (pp. 144–173). State University of New York Press.

Meusburger, P., Heffernan, M., & Saursana, L. (Eds.) (2018). *Geographies of the university*. Springer.

Mok, K-H. (1998). Privatization or marketization: Educational developments in post-Mao China. *International Review of Education*, special double issue, Tradition, Modernity, and Post-modernity in Comparative Education, 43(5–6), 547–567.

Mok, K-H. (2006). *Education reform and education policy in East Asia*. Routledge.

Morrow, R., & Torres, C. A. (1995). *Social theory and education: A critique of theories of social and cultural reproduction*. State University of New York Press.

Mou, B. (2008). On some methodological issues concerning Chinese philosophy: An introduction. In *The Routledge history of Chinese philosophy* (pp. 13–52). Routledge.

Ninnes, P., & Mehta, S. (Eds.). (2004). *Re-imagining comparative education: Postfoundational ideas and applications for critical times*. Routledge Falmer.

Niranjana, T. (1992). *Siting translation: History, poststructuralism and the colonial context*. University of California Press.

Noah, H., & Eckstein, M. (1969). *Towards a science of comparative education*. Macmillan.

Norris, C. (1993). *The truth about postmodernism*. Basil Blackwell.

O'Neill, J. (1995). *The poverty of postmodernism*. Routledge.

Offe, C. (1984). Ungovernability: On the renaissance of conservative theories of crisis. In J. Habermas (Ed.), *Observations on the spiritual situation of the age*. MIT Press.

Offe, C. (1993). Interdependence, difference, and limited state capacity. In G. Drover et al. (Eds.), *New approaches to welfare theory*. Edward Elgar.

Ohmae, K. (1991). *The borderless world: Power and strategy in the interlinked economy*. Fontana.

Ohmae, K. (1995). *End of the nation state: The rise of regional economies*. HarperCollins.

Paine, T. (1791). *The rights of man*. J. S. Jordan.

Paine, T. (1793). *Common sense*. H. D. Symonds.

Parsons, T. (1949). *The structure of social action*. Free Press.

Parsons, T. (1951). *The social system*. Free Press.

Parsons, T. (1966). *Societies: Evolutionary and comparative perspectives*. Prentice-Hall.

Paulston, R. (1996). *Social cartography: Mapping social and educational change*. Garland.

Paulston, R., & Liebman, M. (1994). An invitation to postmodern social cartography. *Comparative Education Review*, 38(2), 215–252.

Pizmony-Levy, O. (2020). Social network theory and analysis in comparative and international education: Connecting the dots for better understanding of education. In T. Jules, R, Shields, & M. Thomas (Eds.), *The Bloomsbury handbook of theory in comparative and international education*. Bloomsbury.

Pusey, M. (1991). *Economic rationalism in Canberra: A nation building state changes its mind*. Cambridge University Press.

Reagan, T. (2018). *Non-Western educational traditions. Local approaches to thought and practice* (4th ed.). Routledge.

Robertson, R. (1994). Mapping the global condition: Globalization as a central concept. In R. Robertson (Ed.), *Global Culture* (pp. 15–30). Sage.

Rust, V. (1991). Postmodernism and its comparative education implications. *Comparative Education Review*, 35(1), 610–26.

Said, E. (1994). *Culture and imperialism*. Vantage.

Said, E. (1995). *Orientalism*. Penguin.

Saxenian, A. L. (2006). *The new argonauts: Regional advantage in a global economy*. Harvard University Press.

Schneider, F. (1947). *Triebkräfte der Pädagogik der Völker*. Otto Muller.

Schneider, F. (1961). *Vergleichende Erziehungswissenschaft*. Quelle and Meyer.

Schneller, C., Lungu, I., & Wächter, B. (2009). *Handbook of international associations in higher education: A practical guide to 100 academic networks world-wide*. ACA.

Schutz, A. (1964). *The problem of social reality* (Vol. 1, Collected Papers). Martinus Nijhoff.

Schutz, A. (1967). *The phenomenology of the social world*. Northwestern University Press.

Schutz, A. (1953). Commonsense and scientific interpretations of human action. *Philosophical and Phenomenological Research*, 14(3), 3–47.

Schwarz, H., & Ray, S. (Eds.). (2000). *A companion to post-colonial studies*. Wiley.

Shahi, D. (2017). The clash of civilizations thesis: A critical appraisal. In Understanding *post-9/11 Afghanistan: A critical insight* into Huntington's *civilizational approach*. E-IR.

Shields, R., & Kameshwara, K. (2021). Marxism in comparative and international education: Foundational political economy perspectives on education. In *The Bloomsbury handbook of theory in comparative and international education*. Bloomsbury.

Silverman, H. J. (Ed.). (1991). *Gadamer and hermeneutics*. Routledge, Chapman Hall.

Snodgrass, A. (1992). Asian studies and the fusion of horizons. *Asian Studies Review*, 15(3): 81–94.

Spivak, G. (1999). *A critique of postcolonial reason: Toward a history of the vanishing present*. Harvard University Press.

Standing, G. (2011). *The precariat: The new dangerous class*. Bloomsbury.

Tavassoli, G. A., Houshyar, K., & Welch, A. (2000). The struggle for quality and equality in Iranian education: Problems, progress and prospects. In A. Welch (Ed.), *Quality and equality in third world education*. Garland.

Teigas, S. (1995). *Knowledge and hermeneutic understanding*. Bucknell University Press.

Tiryakin, E. (1979). Emile Durkheim. In T. Bottomore & R. Nisbet, *A history of sociological analysis*. Heinemann.

Torres, C. A., & Puiggros, A. (1995). The state and public education in Latin America. *Comparative Education Review*, 35(1), 1–27.

Vaioleti, T. (2006). Talanoa research methodology: A developing position on Pacific research. *Waikato Journal of Education*, 12, 21–34.

Vance, J. D. (2006). *Hillbilly elegy: A memoir of a family and culture in crisis*. Harper.

Vera, E. R., & Schupp, T. (2006). Network analysis in comparative social sciences. *Comparative Education*, 42(3), 405–429.

Von Wright, G. H. (1971). *Explanation and understanding*. Cornell University Press.

Wächter, B. (2009). Increasing Europe's attractiveness for international students. What can we learn from the Bologna process? In R. Bhandari & S. Laughlin (Eds.), *Higher education on the move: New developments in global mobility*. IIE.

Walker, T. (2020, May 24). Beware the "cauldron of paranoia" as China and the US slide towards a new kind of Cold War. *The Conversation*, https://theconversation.com/beware-the-cauldron-of-paranoia-as-china-and-the-us-slide-towards-a-new-kind-of-cold-war-139023

Wallerstein, I. (1979). *The modern world system*. Academic Press.

Welch, A. (1985). The functionalist tradition in comparative education. *Comparative Education*, 21(1).

Welch, A. (1986). A critique of quotidian reason in comparative education. *Journal of International and Comparative Education*, 1, 37–62.

Welch, A. (1988). Marxism and the art of comparative education: Reflections and considerations. *Australian Education Researcher*, 15, 447–54.

Welch, A. (1991). La Ciencia Sedante: El Funcionalismo como Base para la Investigación en Educación Comparada. In J. Schriewer & F. Pedro (Eds.), *Educación Comparada: Teorías, Investigaciones, Perspectivas*. Herder.

Welch, A. (1993). Class, culture, and the state in comparative education. *Comparative Education*, 29(1), 7–28.

Welch, A. (1996). *Australian education: Reform or crisis?* Allen and Unwin.
Welch, A. (1997). *Class, culture, and the state in Australian Education: Reform or crisis?* Peter Lang.
Welch, A. (2000a). New times, hard times: Re-reading comparative education in a time of discontent. In J. Schriewer (Ed.), *Discourse formation in comparative education.* Peter Lang.
Welch, A. (2000b). Introduction: Quality and equality in third world education. In A. Welch (Ed.), *Quality and equality in third world education.* Garland.
Welch, A. (2001). Globalization, post-modernity and the state. Comparative education for a new millennium. *Comparative Education, 37*(4) (Special Issue on Comparative Education facing the New Millennium), 475–982.
Welch, A. (2003). Globalization, structural adjustment and contemporary educational reforms in Australia: The politics of reform, or the reform of politics? In K-H. Mok & A. Welch, *Globalization and educational restructuring in the Asia Pacific region* (pp. 1–31). Palgrave Macmillan.
Welch, A. (2010). Nation-state, diaspora and comparative education: The place of place. In D. Mattheou (Ed.), *Changing educational landscapes. Educational policies, schooling systems, and higher education—A comparative perspective* (pp. 285–308). Springer.
Welch, A. (2011). *Higher education in Southeast Asia: Blurring borders, changing balance.* Routledge.
Welch, A. (2017). Higher education and the developmental state: The view from East and Southeast Asia. In T. Carroll & D. Jarvis (Eds.), *Asia after the developmental state: Disinterring autonomy.* Cambridge University Press.
Welch, A. (2018a). Cultural difference and identity. In A. Welch et al., *Education, change and society* (pp. 176–178). Oxford University Press.
Welch, A. (2018b). Making education policy. In R. Connell et al. (Eds.), *Sociology, education and change* (pp. 264–303). Oxford University Press.
Welch, A., & Cai, H-X. (2011). Enter the dragon: The internationalisation of Chinese higher education. In J. Ryan (Ed.), *China's higher education and internationalisation* (pp. 9–33). Routledge.
Welch, A., & Zhang, Z. (2008). The Chinese knowledge diaspora: Communication networks among overseas Chinese intellectuals. In D. Epstein et al. (Eds.), *Geographies of knowledge, geometries of power: Framing the future of education, world yearbook of education 2008* (pp. 338–354). Routledge.
Willis, P. (1977). *Learning to labor: How working class kids get working class jobs.* Saxon House.
Wollstonecraft, M. (1929). *A vindication of the rights of woman.* J. M. Dent.
Wolpe, H. (1975). The theory of internal colonialism: The South African case. In I. Oxaal et al., *Beyond the sociology of development* (pp. 229–252). Routledge & Kegan Paul.
Woock, R. (1981). Integrated social theory and comparative education. *International Review of Education, 27*(4), 411–426.
Yang, R., & Welch, A. (2010). Globalisation, transnational academic mobility and the Chinese knowledge diaspora: An Australian case study. *Discourse. Australian Journal of Educational Studies* (Special Issue on Transnational academic mobility), 593–607.
Yeatman, A. (1990). *Bureaucrats, technocrats and femocrats: Essays on the contemporary Australian state.* Allen & Unwin.
Yeatman, A. (1993). Corporate managers and the shift from the welfare to the competition state. *Discourse, 13*(2), 3–9.
Young, R. (1998). Comparative education and postmodern relativism. *International Review of Education*, special double issue, Tradition, Modernity, and Post-Modernity in Comparative Education. *43*(5–6), 497–505.

19

Comparative Education

The Dialectics of Globalization and Its Discontents

Carlos Alberto Torres
UCLA

ABSTRACT

Each new edition Carlos Alberto Torres asks the following question: What has changed in comparative education since the previous edition? The fifth edition answers this question though the reader may find the same answers from the second edition onward. Taken together, this closing chapter of the fifth edition offers a historical analysis, from the perspective of one of the editors of this book, of the last quarter of a century in the dialectics of the global and the local and its impact on comparative education since the first edition of this book has been published. Nota bene: If the reader only wants to read the changes leading to the fifth edition, just skim the chapter until the last section.

■ ■ ■

> It takes more time and effort and delicacy to learn the silence of people than to learn its sounds. The learning of the grammar of silence is an art much more difficult to learn than the grammar of sounds.
>
> —Ivan Illich, *Celebration of Awareness* (1969, p. 46)

AFTERTHOUGHT FOR THE SECOND EDITION

It is relevant to ask what changes have taken place in the world since the publication of *Comparative Education* more than three years ago. What has changed in the global economy, in the global culture, in the global political systems, and how might those changes affect education? What follows is a description of some of the most important changes that we have witnessed in the world since the first edition. How to interpret those changes may deserve a different type of theoretical scrutiny and empirical analysis than the one permitted by the tenor of this chapter.

The most obvious change is the terrorist attack of September 11, 2001, which undermined the invincibility of the United States, never before attacked in its continental territories, and the implications of this attack for the global economy, politics, culture, and education. There is a heightened feeling that most salient among these transformations are the changes in the definition, enjoyment, and administration of freedom worldwide. The challenges to the liberal notion of freedom add to the growing fear of apocalypse resulting from an eventual world confrontation in an increasingly volatile world. After the demise of the former Soviet Union, there are journalistic reports of enriched uranium and even nuclear bombs unaccounted for, and a growing threat of biological and chemical weapons of mass destruction.

An ongoing debate centers on how the terrorist attacks have played into the hands of a Republican administration in the United States that has displayed a narrow view of international politics, a complete sense of political intransigence and disrespect for human rights, and a determined interest in enforcing narrow U.S. interests on a global scale, including the ignoring of Mexico's request for an immigration agreement. According to Human Rights Watch, "The U.S. government's willingness to compromise on human rights to fight terrorism sets a dangerous precedent and drives some nations away from joining that war. Washington has so much power that when it flouts human rights standards, it damages the human right causes worldwide" ("Group Says Bending on Rights Risky," 2003). Many analysts consider that this is partly the reason why Jorge G. Castañeda resigned as Mexico's foreign minister at the beginning of 2003 (Kellner, 2003). Many observers, including Nobel Peace laureate Jimmy Carter, have warned of the potential dangers of U.S. unilateralism in international affairs. The U.S. refusal to participate in the Kyoto Accords is symptomatic of how energy security increasingly drives U.S. policy. Energy politics is seen as the key reason why the Bush administration—an administration closely connected with U.S. energy corporations like Enron—went to war against Iraq, the fourth-largest oil producer in the world, holding the second-largest crude oil reserves. Iraq is the second-largest OPEC (Organization of the Petroleum Exporting Countries) member in terms of proven crude oil reserves (112,500 million barrels) after Saudi Arabia (262,697 million barrels). Another country that President Bush named as part of the triple evil axis, Iran, is the third-largest country in terms of proven crude oil reserves (99,080 million barrels), followed by the United Arab Emirates (97,800), and Venezuela (77,685 million barrels). In terms of crude output exports, Iraq, even under severe restrictions after the Gulf War, is the fourth-largest producer of crude (2,593.7 million oil barrels), with Saudi Arabia as the first (7,888.9 million oil barrels), and Iran ranks third in volume (3.572 million oil barrels). This combination of oil reserves with crude oil output makes Iran and Iraq targets for the U.S. policy in the Middle East. Energy policy concerns are shown also in the uneasiness of the United States in dealing with the conflicts with the government of Hugo Chavez since Venezuela possesses the fifth-largest crude oil reserves in the world and ranks third in terms of crude oil output (2,791.9 million oil barrels) (see www.opec.org/).

Allegations of the existence of weapons of mass destruction were the putative reason given by the Bush administration for the U.S. invasion of Iraq in March 2003. These allegations have yet to be substantiated. A preliminary analysis of the political-educational implications of the terrorist attacks of September 11 has been done elsewhere and need not be repeated here (Torres, 2002). Nevertheless, we have not yet seen in the United States or elsewhere how these changes are provoking a new understanding of patriotism in the schools. In concluding his assessment of his personal feelings and his professional responsibility as a teacher in dealing with the attacks, cultural critic Michael Apple (2002) warns us of unintended, and perhaps still unobservable, consequences of the events:

> In any real situation there are multiple relations of power. Any serious understanding of the actual results of September 11 on education needs to widen its gaze beyond what we usually look for. As I have shown, in the aftermath of 9/11 the politicization of local school governance occurred in ways that were quite powerful. Yet, without an understanding of "other" kinds of politics, in this case race, we would miss one of the most important results of the struggle over the meaning of "freedom" in this site. September 11 has had even broader effects than we recognize.

The war in Afghanistan, the immediate U.S. and allied response to the September 11 attacks, showed the difficulties of combating global terrorism. Despite the massive bombardment and deployment of personnel, and after heralding the war as one low in allied casualties and high in military results, the majority of the objectives have not been fully achieved. Sheikh Osama bin Laden and the leader of the Students of Islamic Knowledge Movement (Taliban), Mullah Mohammad Omar, have not been found. The majority of their lieutenants and hundreds of war-hardened al Qaeda fighters are still at large. The government of Afghanistan remains shaky, plagued by political assassinations of its leadership, and under considerable pressure from the different ethnic tribal groups and warlords reasserting their independence from the central government and even protecting representatives of the old deposed regime.

Terror has a logic of its own. Common citizens discover the dimensions of this logic only when a particularly spectacular attack is orchestrated, or when new developments prompt attention in terms of personal security. In the United States, the creation of the Homeland Security Office, including 22 government agencies, the most important reorganization of the federal government since the New Deal, is an indication of the realignment of priorities. And these administrative changes take place in an administration that inherited a fiscal surplus and in less than two years in office has managed to reach US$600 billion in fiscal deficit. With the tax cuts enacted in 2003, the deficit of the federal government may continue to grow substantially. The tax cuts and fiscal deficit may also deeply affect the budgets of the states, which are nearly bankrupt given the transfer of responsibilities since the Reagan administration and simultaneous diminishing revenues.

In regional terms, Latin America is changing in ways that were virtually unimaginable just a few years ago. The formidable economic failure of Argentina, the model country for the application to the letter of the law of neoliberal prescriptions of the International Monetary Fund (IMF) and the World Bank in the region, calls the neoliberal development model seriously into question. Yet, at the level of human tragedy, Argentina offers an even more somber note, enduring high levels of poverty and the tragic documented death of starving children in a country historically known as a producer of food staples. The Nobel laureate economist George Stiglitz has written provocative ideas about these questions,[1] and a debate has been initiated with powerful effects on different fronts, including renewed severe criticism of neoliberal bilateral organizations and their implications in development, particularly in education The World Bank has the rare privilege of being criticized by representatives of the right, of liberalism, and the left. Hence, there is an abundant critical bibliography that could be used to illustrate the critique of the implications of the World Bank's neoliberal expert knowledge and policy orientations (see, for instance, Bandow & Vasquez, 1994; Harriss, 2002; Torres, 1994).

Responses to neoliberalism have also reached other fronts, with a new interest for democratic socialism in the region. The rise to power of Hugo Chavez in Venezuela is one such anti-neoliberal response. Under the combined mantle of populism and nationalism, the attempt of former paratrooper and elected President Hugo Chavez to dismantle the old democratic system, and his erratic policies and behavior, have generated a great deal of resistance from many different quarters, and have destabilized one of the world's largest oil-exporting countries.

There is no question that the arrival of Ignacio "Lula" da Silva, a metallurgical union leader and founder of the Workers' Party, or PT, to the presidency of Brazil is an unexpected political novelty in Latin America. The importance of education in Lula's success is highlighted in the remarks of his spiritual adviser, Frei Betto: "Lula arrives to the presidency of Brazil thanks to a social movement articulated in the past forty years, in which the pedagogy of Paulo Freire carried more weight than the theories of Marx" (Betto, 2002, author's translation).

The truth is that the PT has won the presidency twice with the support of a great majority of Brazilians and on the shoulders of the political activism of many social movements in the country, most prominently the agrarian reform movement, *Sem Terra*, so well portrayed in the photography of Sebastian Salgado. It is also known that most of the organizational meetings of the *Sem Terra* movement start with an invocation to Paulo Freire's name and his role in community organization and popular education (For a graphic description of the movement see Salgado, 1997).

The Asian economies, not long ago considered a central engine of economic development in the world system, continue to revolve and struggle around the continuing economic stagnation of Japan. The paradoxical situation of economic stagnation and deflation in Japan has reached certain surrealism when the *Financial Times* of London reports that "Japan's interest rates fall below zero." This means a negative rate of 0.01. "The negative rate means that Société Générale and BNP are, in effect, being paid to borrow funds as they find themselves in the fortunate situation of having to pay back less than they were lent" (*Financial Times*, January 25–26, 2003, p. 3). The same article concludes that the policy of the Bank of Japan in keeping rates "virtually zero and flooding the money market with liquidity has largely been ineffective in stimulating the economy, which is set to contract in the fourth quarter." Yet the growing economic and political power of China, which continues to show surprising rates of economic growth, solidifies its position as a major regional and world player. China's power is also evident in the recent confrontation over North Korea's nuclear program, technology transfer.

The ongoing confrontation between India and Pakistan, two countries with atomic bombs, is perhaps one of the most destabilizing conflicts in the world. In addition to the religious hatred between Muslim and Hindu activists, there is the thorny issue of India's administration of Kashmir and growing militaristic and religious movements on both sides of the border that contributed to the development of the atomic bomb. The fact that both countries possess nuclear weapons and that they have already waged a bloody war (in December 1971) adds to the danger. The triumph of India in the 1971 war led to the separation of East Pakistan from West Pakistan and the creation of Bangladesh, one of the poorest countries on Earth. Unfortunately, as some scientists claim, the Indian subcontinent is the most likely place on the planet for nuclear war (Ramana & Nayyar, 2001). Despite all sorts of political gestures from the United States and European governments, Sub-Saharan Africa continues its downward spiral, and growing political unrest in several nations (Zimbabwe, Ivory Coast, Nigeria) indicate that political instability and economic crises continue to go hand in hand in the region. The hoped-for ends of the Angola and Sierra Leone wars offer a window of hope, yet the same hope for democratization and economic development represented by postapartheid South Africa will be crushed by its population's AIDS epidemic.

The success that the antiglobalization movement has had since 1999 in Seattle in constructing a more proactive alternative globalization agenda has already—though not well represented in the hegemonic mass media—impacted economic summit meetings. Even the deliberations of the multilateral and bilateral economic organizations have lost the "privacy" of their discussions of how to prime the economic engines of the world or how to salvage the countries in economic distress.

In the last few years, the creation of the European Community and the euro seems to be the success story of globalization, with the entry of new members and the rise of the euro as the strongest exchange currency in the world. The resulting harmonization of European higher education in this process will have a long-term impact in the region, a model that is being contemplated in several other common markets. There is a growing interest in the North American Free Trade Agreement countries to reach similar agreements across the board for accreditation models (as described in the document produced by the American Council on Education, with the support of a grant from the Fund for the U.S. Department of Education—Improvement of Post-Secondary Education) (Turlington et al., 2002).

HOW MIGHT THESE CHANGES AFFECT EDUCATIONAL PRIORITIES?

To those of you who received honors, awards and distinctions, I say, well done. And to the C students, I say, you, too, can be president of the United States.

—U.S. President George W. Bush, addressing the graduates at his alma mater, Yale University, at its 2001 commencement (cited in Gerstenzang, 2003).

The epigraph from George W. Bush that opens this section may sound shocking to educators who believe in meritocracy and the selection role of education. It bespeaks opportunity and chance beyond tenacity and study. The unspoken truth of this statement by President Bush is that education not only reproduces inequality, as theories of social reproduction have amply demonstrated, but it also legitimizes privilege (see Morrow & Torres, 1995). That education could indeed foster social mobility within certain limits is a subject that has been well documented in the economics of education. Yet the implication in this apparent joke by the president of the United States is the subtle indication that race, class, and gender matter in achieving the highest echelons of the political system in a bureaucratic rational society like that of the United States.

As the epigraph indicates, the holder of the highest political office in the United States is proud to underscore how political and business success is often more related to whom you know, and what kind of network you are a member of, than of academic achievement. The statement is even more telling because it was made at the commencement of one of the most distinguished private universities in the United States, justifying Vilfredo Paretos's view of reproduction and the circulation of elites.

In George W. Bush's views, politics has nothing to do with education. This seems perhaps reasonable, coming from somebody of patrician origins who attended a fine private university, obviously receiving what Ronald Reagan, referring to his own educational experience, called "Gentleman Cs" (cited in Gerstenzang, 2003). Though Bush's comments are telling, they should not be considered an *aphorismus*. He replaced President Bill Clinton who, though from humble origins, managed to be a Rhodes Scholar, the governor of Arkansas, and president of the United States.

In the realm of education, the United States is often cited as a model for private higher education. Yet, per-student expenditures in four-year public colleges and universities in the United States have increased by roughly 20% over the past decade or so, whereas in Canada and other countries they have decreased by about the same amount. So it is strange that neoliberal policy advisers, many of them trained in U.S. universities, suggest decreasing support of public universities elsewhere, even though the great success of the United States in research and development is based on the public system, as is indicated by the growing number of Nobel Prize recipients teaching in U.S. public universities.

The continuing expansion of the use of the internet for the globalization of higher education is prompting several studies to focus on the transformation of the university systems given the political economy of globalization and the new role of languages. By *globalization* here, I refer to the "increasing interdependent and sophisticated relationships between economies, cultures, institutions, and nation states. Such relations challenge higher education leaders and policy-makers in ways heretofore difficult to imagine as the autonomy of the nation-state becomes compromised and the role of the university is increasingly aligned with market-driven interests" (Rhoads & Torres, 2006b). The decision of literary publisher Alfred A. Knopf to publish in the United States the first book of Colombian Nobel laureate Gabriel Garcia Marquez's memoirs in Spanish, *Vivir para Contarla*, has been heralded as a sea change in the U.S. publication markets, with its first printing of 50,000 copies sold out in a matter of weeks and a second printing of 5,000 ordered immediately (see Rutten, 2003).

A casualty of September 11 in the United States, and a factor that presumably could affect other industrialized countries given changes in visa requirements and process, is the availability of international education for foreign students—not a minor source of income for the countries involved. The United States is the biggest exporter of international education, which had 547,867 "foreign students" studying in American institutions in 2000–2001. This represents earnings of US$11 billion to its national economy. After the United States, the largest producer of international education is the United Kingdom. In 1999–2000, the United Kingdom enrolled 277,000 international students of which 129,180 were university students. Earnings from the international education exports and consumption of goods and services by students were estimated then at 8 billion British pounds (Sidhu, n.d., p. 12).

What is happening in the world, as de Souza Santos has indicated, is a paradigmatic transition (see de Sousa Santos, 1995). Hence, it is important to explore the connections between social changes and theoretical analysis. When we ask what, if anything, may result from the impacts of September 11 in educational settings, Michael Apple's remarks discussing the question of schooling and patriotism are a fitting conclusion for this section:

No analysis of the effects of 9/11 on schools can go on without an understanding of how the global is dynamically linked to the local. Such an analysis must more fully understand the larger ideological work and history of the neoliberal and neoconservative project and its effects on the discourses that circulate and become common sense in our society. And no analysis can afford to ignore the contradictory needs and contradictory outcomes that this project has created at multiple levels and along multiple axes of power. Thus, I argue that educators—whether teaching a university class or participating in local school board decision-making—must first recognize our contradictory responses to the events of September 11. We must also understand that these responses, although partly understandable in the context of tragic events, may create dynamics that have long-lasting consequences. And many of these consequences may themselves undercut the very democracy we believe that we are upholding and defending. This more complicated political understanding may well be a first step in finding appropriate and socially critical pedagogic strategies to work within our classes and communities to interrupt the larger hegemonic projects—including the redefinition of democracy as "patriotic fervor"—that we will continue to face in the future (Apple, 2002).

THE OUTSTANDING DEBTS OF COMPARATIVE EDUCATION

I am the wound and yet the knife. The torturer and yet he who is flayed.

—From Baudelaire's poem *Héautontimoroumenos*, Charles Baudelaire, "L'héautontimorouménos," in *Les Fleurs du Mal* (1861)

By looking ahead, it is perhaps wise to outline some of the still "outstanding theoretical debts" of comparative education. What are some of the enigmatic theoretical relationships still unsolved? What elusive analytical dimensions still lack understanding? What theoretical connections have been missed? Unquestionably, from the pragmatic perspective I have chosen to outline changes and challenges, limited space mandates that my analysis of the outstanding debts be subjectively selective and purposeful.

The connections between politics and education remain an unresolved theoretical enigma in comparative education. In this debate, the analytical and normative positions of the establishment (liberals, conservative, neoconservative, and neoliberals) remain comfortably close but in startling contrast to the New Left positions.

The view of the establishment is that politics and education are two separate sets of practices, which do not, and should not, interconnect. Education remains *objective*, in theoretical terms (because the truth could be told objectively); *neutral*, in political terms (because educators don't take sides); and above all, *apolitical*, considering normative and political choices (politics usually embodies the praxis of fighting for ideological positions defending social or particular interests, while education is a noble practice that seeks the public good for everyone involved).

The establishment view sees scholars, practitioners, and policymakers leaving their political clothes—be they a political affiliation, doctrine, or ideology—outside the classroom or some distance from their research or policy cabinets. Otherwise, the merging of politics and education necessarily results in the manipulation and ideologization of the subject matter. Good, decent educators practice a value-neutral education in their teaching, policy-making, and research. Education is thus a practice that should be devoid of ideology and political interests. Though the establishment's normative view recognizes that there are inequities and disparities in the world, the differences in this assessment, in the naming of the victims as well as in assessing the magnitude of the problem, depend on the ideology of the analyst. Moreover, the view of the establishment is that in many instances, even in rational-legal societies, processes of discrimination are taking place, processes that need to be prevented through social engineering and the application of the law.

Therefore, a quality education (one documented through testing and accountability), when it is understood and practiced scientifically, as well as informed by rigorous empirical research, will be the most important asset in the social engineering of a more efficient and equitable society.

For the New Left, there is a very different and much more complex story. Politics is intimately linked to power and is concerned with the control of means of producing, distributing, consuming, reproducing, and accumulating material and symbolic resources. Politics and the political should not be restricted to political parties, the activities of the governments and its critics, or voting. Political activities take place in private and public spheres, and they are related to all aspects of human experience that involve power. It is from this vantage point, of politics as a set of relations of force in a given society, that the relationships between education and politics need to be examined (see Ginsburg, 1995; Torres, 1995).

Freire (1970) developed a *Pedagogy of the Oppressed*. His analysis of the relationships between politics and education (Freire, 1998), speaking in the code of class analysis, indicates that politics, power, and education are indissolubly united. His analysis deserves to be quoted at length:

> The comprehension of the limits of educational practice requires political clarity on the part of educators in relation to their project. It demands that the educator

> assume the political nature of her practice. It is not enough to say that education is a political act, just as it is not enough to say that political acts are also educative. It is necessary to truly assume the political nature of education. I cannot consider myself progressive if I understand school space as something neutral, with limited or no relations to class struggle, where students are seen only as learners of limited domains of knowledge which I will imbue with magic power. I cannot recognize the limits of the political-educative practice in which I am involved if I don't know, if I am not clear about, on whose behalf I work. Clarifying the question of in whose favor I practice puts me in a position, which is related to class, in which I see against whom I practice and, necessarily, for what reason I practice. (Freire, 1998, p. 46; see also Freire, 2000)

This book, the first one published by Freire after leaving his post of secretary of public education of the city of São Paulo, is exemplary of the position of the New Left regarding politics and education (O'Cadiz et al., 1998; Torres, 1998).

Despite Freire's immensely rich analyses and insights, coined in the phrase "the politicity of education," a neologism that he popularized in English, the nature of the relationship between politics and education is far from being clearly understood. Freire's positions have been the subject of important debates also in his native Brazil and elsewhere (de Mello, 1990; Saviani, 1982).

If one considers Freire's analysis, many questions remain regarding the connection between politics and education at a theoretical level. Besides the criticism to grand narratives, or the charge of idealism in Freire's views of oppression, or the question of how can we empirically construct indicators of oppression, other pressing questions need to be addressed. If there is a relative autonomy of education and relative autonomy of politics in the context of the dialect's agency and structure, are these two independent domains that intersect only at some point? Or, as Freire seems to indicate, do they overlap completely? As Illich's dictum on the atmosphere of "monastic" studies seems to indicate, is there any autonomy of knowledge production independent of politics?

The question of dependence/independence between politics and education begs the question of the real nature of both human domains, their goals and purposes, and their similarities and differences in practice—in short, a whole gamut of questions that may require, following the insightful analysis of Freire, a much more developed, refined, and completed theoretical solution.

In searching for a more complete theoretical answer, we cannot forget that as sites of confrontations of public and private interests, politics and education are also mediated by state actions, tools, regulations, codes, controls, and resources.

Another key unresolved theoretical challenge is the postmortem analysis of postmodernism in education. In theoretical terms, the extreme forms of postmodernism have lost their momentum, and the shift of some postmodernists to Marxist revolutionary perspectives and other forms of structuralist traditions is perhaps symptomatic. These changes deserve to be discussed in light of the utility of postmodernism for educational studies.

In one of the most recent attempts to unthink postmodernism while rethinking modernism from a critical perspective, Greg Dimitriadis and Dennis Carlson (2003), offer an excellent summary of the new cultural terrain of the postmodern age:

> Inequalities are increasing between the haves and the have-nots within the United States, and between economically elite nations and the "developing" world. It is an age of hyper-consumerism in which one's sense of self and identity is defined by what one consumes in popular culture icons and styles marketed in the new shopping mall public. It is an age of backlash and resentment against the gains made by people of color, women, gays and lesbians, and other marginalized identity groups, and a time of the rise of religious fundamentalism in both America and around the world. And it is an age in which conservatives use the democratic language of equity to oppose affirmative action and "special rights" for gay people. In public education, it is an age of a corporate state discourse of high-stakes testing, "accountability," "standards," and "efficiency," an age of preparing America's young people to be more competitive and productive in the new global labor market. Meanwhile, commercialized popular culture is busy blurring the lines between "reality" and "hyperreality," the material world and the virtual world. It is an age in which identity is constructed around performance, style, and image, and hybrid, border-crossing identities subvert the naturalness of race, gender, and sexual identity categories.
>
> The aim of postmodernism is thus to push modernism to supersede itself and become something new. Postmodernism is not, in itself, a sufficient basis for forging a new progressivism in American education and public life. But it does play an important role in establishing the conditions for the emergence of a new progressivism, for allowing us to unthink modernism and rethink it in new ways. (pp. 16–17)

In the same vein, Foucault's acknowledgment of his myopic analysis having missed the connection to the established tradition of critical theory (in itself tributary of Marxist theory) stands out as a sobering reminder of the honesty of one of the most important theoreticians of the last century, so influential in the development of critical pedagogy (Morrow & Torres, 2002). Foucault muses, in celebrating Kant's essay "What Is Enlightenment?":

> Now, obviously, if I had been familiar with the Frankfurt School, if I had been aware of it at the same time, I would not have said a number of stupid things that I did say, and I would have avoided many of the detours I made while trying to pursue my own humble path—when, meanwhile, avenues had been opened up by the Frankfurt School. It is a strange case of nonpenetration between two very similar types of thinking which is explained, perhaps, by that very similarity. Nothing hides the fact of a problem in common better than two similar ways of approaching it. (See Foucault, 1998, pp. 440–441)

While these theoretical challenges should be at the top of our theoretical agendas, inspiring our empirical research, since the publication of the first edition of this book, we have seen the death of three giants in the study of education who deserve to be mentioned here: Basil Bernard Bernstein, Pierre Bourdieu, and Ivan Illich. Counting the death of Freire in 1997, or, a bit more removed from the field of comparative education, the death of political philosopher John Rawls (1921–2002), we have witnessed the passing of some of the most important theorists in education, a generation that will be very difficult to replace. Standing on the shoulders of giants is certainly easier than filling their shoes.

Basil Bernard Bernstein (1924–2000) passed away after a long illness. From 1979 until his retirement in 1991, he was the holder of the most prestigious chair in sociology of education in the world, the Karl Mannheim Professor in the Sociology of Education at the University of London Institute of Education.

Bernstein leaves behind a legacy of more than 40 years of rigorous research and a new understanding of the connections between class, codes, and control. His published works, in particular the three-volume series on *Class, Codes and Control*, have become classics in the field. Bernstein's theory has shown how people use language in everyday conversation, reflecting but at the same time shaping assumptions of certain social groups; hence, private and public codes matter, and play an enormous role in the curriculum of public education.

With the death of the multifaceted and prolific Pierre Bourdieu (1930–2002), professor of sociology at the Collège de France and also director of studies at the École des Hautes Études en Sciences Sociales in Paris, we have lost, without any question, one of the most important sociologists in the history of the discipline. Jointly with Basil Bernstein one of the founders and past president of the Research Committee of Sociology of Education of the International Sociological Association, Bourdieu inspired our studies in education (where *Reproduction* stands out as a landmark that impacted a whole generation of intellectuals), aesthetics, in social theory, popular culture, mass media, French intellectual thought, and literature.

In the last years of his life, Bourdieu single-handedly constituted himself in one of the most severe and intransigent European critics of globalization and one of the most uncompromising critics of the Americanization of the global world. His criticism of globalization in the intellectual and cultural spheres is coupled with his questions about the depoliticization of the academic world and the role of intellectuals. One of his last books, *Counterfire: Against the Tyranny of the Market* (Bourdieu, 2002), is an eloquent testament to his analytical abilities and to his personal and political commitments.

Ivan Illich (1926–2002)—characterized by Eric Fromm in his famous preface to *Celebration of Awareness* as a radical humanist—was also an emblematic thinker of possibilities. Illich leaves behind a legacy of a genial man, as Freire described him, but one who, being ahead of his time, described himself as an "Errant Pilgrim," as "one that was caught between the contesting powers of Byzantium and Venice" (Illich, 1998, p. 3).

Perhaps there is no better tribute to the geniality of Illich than to remember that he considered himself a disciple of a 12th-century monk Hugh of St. Victor. This association with the monastic life explains why he always considered the hospitality of monastic asceticism, coupled with rigorous disciplinary training and jovial friendship, indispensable conditions for nurturing an environment where meaningful scholarship could flourish:

Learned and leisurely hospitality is the only antidote to the stance of deadly cleverness that is acquired in the professional pursuit of objectively secured knowledge. I remain certain that the quest for truth cannot thrive outside the nourishment of mutual trust flowering into a commitment to friendship. Therefore I have tried to identify the climate that fosters and the "conditioned air" that hinders the growth of friendship. Of course, I can remember the taste of strong atmospheres from other epochs in my life: I have never doubted that—today, more than ever—a "monastic" ambiance is the prerequisite to the independence needed for a historically based indictment of society (Illich, 1998, p. 4).

The deaths of Freire, Bernstein, Bourdieu, and Illich have deprived comparative education of powerful intellectual voices amid a very perilous epoch in human history. Though their deaths will not help in settling the many theoretical debts of comparative education, the theoretical paths they have opened remain an invitation to continue the journey.

The pedagogical challenges for comparative education are enormous. There is a profound crisis in the understanding of who is to be educated. What could be considered an endemic crisis of the educational systems is reflected in the real and symbolic dislocation between the discourses of the teachers and the students, which is reflected also in the dislocation, also marked, between the discourses of the new generation (which has been denominated the Nintendo generation) and adult generations. This cultural dislocation in school settings adds to the proverbial issues of equality and relevance of education, equity, equality, and social mobility as well as discrimination in the school curriculum. In addition, we confront now a crisis of legitimacy in the educational systems in terms of their effectiveness—that is, the effectiveness of the educational agents per se, including the teachers, parents, and private and public educational institutions. However, with the rupture of the public link between generations, this perhaps may give rise to a crisis that supersedes the secular deficiencies of the system. The presence of massive systems of communication and new technologies creates new combinations between popular traditional cultures, a popular transnational culture, and the political cultures developed by the state institutions, occasionally drastically confronted by the institutions of civil society, social movements, and unions.

In short, obsolete school rituals, opposing discourses, problems in the definition of the cultural capital of the schools and the incorporation of diverse populations, crisis in the concepts of citizenship and democracy, growing disparity between the educational models and the job market, now accentuated with the impact of neoliberalism, provide all sorts of challenges to comparative education. Not surprisingly, many of these challenges need to be addressed, in understanding the connection between education, power, politics, and the culture of modernity (Torres, 2003).

In solving this enigmatic connection between politics and education, analyzing the crisis of legitimacy of public education, or assessing the role of postmodernism in comparative education, there is no question that the years ahead will demand a clearer and more compelling theorizing in the field. Comparative education is still in debt for having failed to produce a definitive understanding of the role and theories of area studies and ethnic studies in the development of the discipline. Similarly, discussions about minority education concerning issues of multiculturalism in the United States, or interculturalism in Europe, will continue to besiege the field many years from now, igniting the theoretical imagination of scholars. I hope that the second edition of this book will contribute to this rethinking of the field and to the profession in solving the dilemmas of contemporary education and, in the words of Freire (2005), "in the creation of a world in which it will be easier to love" (p. 40).

AFTERTHOUGHT FOR THE THIRD EDITION: THE FUTURE OF COMPARATIVE EDUCATION

In the second edition, I queried what had changed in the world since the first edition of *Comparative Education*.[2] In working toward the third edition of this book, several questions about the future of comparative education remain. Perhaps they should be nested in the context of a highly aggregated and succinct description of the historical process of comparative education since its establishment as a discipline.

First stage: From my perspective, the first generation of comparative educators came to the fore approximately 90 years ago as an intellectual exploration with a strong positivistic overtone of the possibilities of educational development outside the confines of national or domestic processes. Indeed a valuable tool, but simply complementary to discussions in educational foundations (e.g., John Dewey, without having had a title, spent significant time studying education and revolutionary change in Mexico, the Soviet Union, and China).

Second stage: 50 to 60 years ago, comparative education began to ride the wave of educational expansion in the world (fueled by theories such as human capital theory), becoming increasingly important to the growing network and communities of the nascent international system. This is the second generation of comparativists whose writing must be set against the context of the Cold War, the struggle between Western and Eastern bloc countries over whether capitalism or communism would triumph in the newly independent nations of Africa, Asia, and Oceania. While there were strong international influences on the goals, forms, and contents of education in the so-called third world, national educational systems also displayed a substantial degree of autonomy. This autonomy fueled the growth of national educational systems to unprecedented levels—sometimes to that extent there may have been overbuilding of schools in some societies, and generating an abundance of teachers. During this period, comparativists not only promoted school expansion but also identified and promoted the importance of teacher unions in collective bargaining while laying the foundations of systematic policy planning and educational budgeting.

Third stage: 35 to 40 years ago, the next generation of comparative scholars, in the spirit of the 1960s, attempted to create alternative visions of education. The contributions of Illich and Freire were central to this rethinking. A new school of scholars considered comparative education as the key to understanding not only development but also liberation. They pushed the envelope by critiquing dominant paradigms, such as rate-of-return analyses of education (the obsession of the previous generation), while advocating nonformal education, revolutionary education, incipient multiculturalist policies, and the like. As such, this generation may be responsible for the most "social democratic" development in the field.

By the first decade of the 21st century, this generation is beginning to retire. Their vision and ideas must face the challenge of the economic crisis of the eighties, and the consolidation of the neoliberal state as the model guiding educational reform worldwide, as detailed in various chapters in this book. This generation has coexisted with several streams of scholars, including socialists, libertarians, business-minded people (e.g., the World Bank experts), and social democrats. The

Comparative and International Education Society, as the premier society of its kind in the world, reflects with rare clarity this cohabitation.

Fourth stage: The current generation of scholars, which entered the field approximately 25 years ago, is well established within the academy today. In attempting to preserve the achievements of previous generations in contributing to progressive educational policy and practice, they necessarily must take corrective action against strong negative policy trends. To mention just two: diminished support for social science research and social welfare programs as unlimited funds go to support military operations; in the academy, erosion of tenure and replacement of full-time faculty with part-time and contractual labor. To counter these trends, as Raymond Morrow and Carlos Alberto Torres have argued in this book, activists in our field need to link up with social movements that are directed at achieving more democratic and just societies.

I would argue that more than ever, we are needed and can contribute to better-informed and more enlightened educational policy—linking theory with action, the type of praxis that Freire called for. As comparativists are hired in educational policy, teacher education, and foundation fields we can impact the future generation of teachers and policymakers; and, given the increasing importance of nongovernmental organizations (NGOs), many of our graduates will work with them and are likely to have a significant positive impact on the lives of the people with whom they work at the grassroots. Perhaps, in a Socratic way, it is useful to end these reflections with some questions: How relevant are comparative education theories to dialogue across fields and cultures? How different is European education, with new models of educational and scholarly exchange and standardized educational programs across borders, from the rest of the world? What can be learned from the Middle East, with the crisis of "radical Islam" and the rejection of the modernizing West? What can be learned from Africa, with the failure of development, the growing AIDS crisis, and the power of self-enriching elites, many of them duly educated in Europe or the United States? What role does comparative education play in the academies of the emerging 21st-century powers of China and India?

We need statistical data, historical analysis, and a political economy discussion of the new trends in academia and societies, not vignettes, human stories, nor simply hunches. Here is where comparative theories, scholarly analyses, systematic research, and insights can contribute to an improved understanding of the workings of education systems and their evolving national and transnational contexts. Here is where our field can contribute to unmasking failed policies while contributing to progressive social and educational change.

AFTERTHOUGHT FOR THE FOURTH EDITION: ANOTHER GLOBALIZATION IS POSSIBLE

It is relevant to ask what changes have taken place in the world since the publication of *Comparative Education* third edition more than three years ago. What has changed in the global economy, in the global culture, in the global political systems, and how might those changes affect education? What follows is a description of some of the most important changes that we have witnessed in the world since the first edition.

Writing an afterword to a new edition of this book, and trying to account for what has happened in the world in the years that have elapsed between the third and fourth editions, is not an easy undertaking. But I must confess that writing this afterword, given the world financial meltdown and socioeconomic crises after 2007, has been particularly difficult, both intellectually and personally.

There is no question that we face several intellectual and personal challenges. While we are debating the nature of a knowledge society we are suffering from an over-information society—it has been projected by IBM that the world's information base will be doubling in size every 11 hours (cited in Gregorian, 2010, p. 27). There are hyper-specializations in knowledge, but in the end, we lack analysis, comprehension, and understanding. "We have more scientists, scholars, and professionals than ever before, but fewer cultivated ones. To put the dilemma in twenty-first-century terms, I might describe this as everybody doing their own thing, but nobody really understanding what anybody else's thing really is" (Gregorian, 2010, p. 29). The "grand" narratives are more suspect than ever, and the "small" narratives are collections of stories, which while very important—particularly for those who "lived" the experiences—remain disconnected and ambiguous, adding to the fragmentation of knowledge and making it ever more difficult to discern the nature of problems, and the nature of possible solutions. To make matters worse, one of the main culprits of this state of affairs, neoliberalism, has produced a new narrative form: "One of the distinctive features of neo-liberalism then is the development of a new form of newspeak which allows narrative control of events" (Meeting in Cuba, 2012).

The financial meltdown, which has not yet reached its end point, is not only deeply affecting the workings of global capitalism in the central countries—so far the emerging economies and the Brazil, Russia, India, China, and South Africa (BRICS) countries have fared quite well compared with Europe and the European Union—but also adds fuel to the terrible conditions of the poorest of the poor: "After the collapse of Lehman Brothers in September 2008, in a matter of weeks an additional 90 million people were added to the approximately 1.5 billion people in low-income countries already living on less than 1.5 dollars a day" (World Bank figures cited in Suárez-Orozco & Sattin-Bajaj, 2010, p. 195).

The crises that have emerged after the publication of the third edition affect the social, moral, economic, and cognitive fabric of our civilizations; they undermine the nature and workings of our democratic systems, unveiling growing inequalities by any scientific measure and marking the dilemmas of education at this time (Torres, 2010). In the next section, I will outline the specific educational dilemmas.

WILL THE ECONOMIC CRISIS HERALD THE END OF THE MARKET DEMOCRACY?

... a balanced treatment of an unbalanced phenomenon distorts reality.

—Thomas Mann and Norman Ornstein (2012)

Economic inequality is no longer a buzzword about capitalist economics, it is a palpable reality that has been reported in many books, journal articles, and research reports and can be observed in a short walk through the urban environments of the most affluent societies on Earth, not to mention the less affluent. Most analysts document that the gap between the U.S. rich (1% of the population) has been growing markedly by any measure for the last three decades. There are several "teach ins" on the matter. The press has also indicated several reasons for this growing disparity (see Gibson & Perot, 2011). The crisis of 2008 has made even more evident the importance of the growing inequality that has deeply affected market democracies.

A casualty of these crises in the global economy has been the loss of jobs, which has, in turn, increased inequality and poverty. In a recent book, Jim Clifton (2011), Chairman of Gallup Corporation, argues that of the seven billion people in the world, five billion are over 15 years old. Three billion said they currently worked or wanted to work, yet only 1.2 billion have full-time formal jobs. Hence there is a shortfall of 1.8 billion jobs worldwide. What is the educational response? I am afraid we are enmeshed in a set of educational dilemmas difficult to address. Just to identify some, let me suggest that the schooling model of the industrial society is exhausted; but while there are few notable local experiences with alternative schooling models, no new national or worldwide model has been designed to replace it. A second situation, magnified by the current crises, is that we continue to extend educational opportunity and access, which demands more and more resources from individuals, families, and societies. However, the system of production and consumption is unable to produce sufficient job opportunities for a highly qualified population—for instance, the unemployment rate for youth in Europe is twice as high as the rate for the overall population, and in some countries like Spain, the discrepancy is even greater. Culture and identity have become central elements in the discussion of citizenship building, and hence arguments about diversity continue to be at the top of the reformer's agenda, though one cannot but think that much of the conversations pay lip service to the real dilemmas that are very difficult to tackle, both in schools and society. Early school learning, reading, writing, and arithmetic continue to be serious challenges for children and youth who come from nonschooled cultures and find an alienated and alienating curriculum, even more so when there is high-stakes testing in place. Learning theories and practices need to be revisited particularly when the majority of the theories that have informed our understanding in the 20th century have not yet benefited from the discoveries of neurosciences and the knowledge about the working of the brain.

The production of knowledge and school curricula is another crucial element facing the transformation of digital cultures. Educational systems continue to be critical in the process of knowledge transfer, but many critics argue that what schooling does is completely insufficient to address the needs of the new buzzword of the day, a *knowledge society*. Streaming and tracking continue to exist as long as the school system performs its traditional general functions of training, selection allocation, and expected regulation. How does this fare compare to Durkheim's thesis that schooling was a mechanism to create social cohesion? The paradox is that educational systems are simultaneously "sorting machines" but through mechanisms of social selection produce some sort of structural change. In doing so, school policy pendulums have swung between goals of *performance*—a requirement of middle classes for their children to access the upper echelon of the occupational and educational ladders—and *inclusion*—the product of democratic pressure requiring that all children and youth regardless of their physical, cultural, class, race, gender, or any other condition, have access to quality education without any type of discrimination. But the dilemmas of schooling do not end there. They affect and are reproduced in other areas of the systems and learning domains. Adult education lives in the duality of goals that are not easily combined—both a model of lifelong learning for all citizens, and economic colonization that serves the goals of a knowledge society requiring specific dexterities, skills, and knowledge, and affirming the idea of possessive individualism. Teachers are by and large under attack in many countries, with their status diminished, the teaching profession badly paid, and teachers blamed for the low-quality output of schools. Teachers are disillusioned, disheartened, and distressed about all of these issues and many are leaving the profession before they are laid off. Teacher training, while recognized as a major factor for the improvement of educational systems, lacks integration of theory and practice; few if any of the multiple research findings in educational research about teachers are ever disseminated let alone implemented; and teaching and learning methodologies continue to be implemented as top-down models in schools, very often lacking the basic institutional foundations, particularly in the developing world. Findings and recommendations of evidence-based research work only when they reach the right person at the right time and in the right position. Otherwise, tons of pages (and now tons of megabytes) are shelved in real and imaginary archives with the hope of impacting practice someday.

The issue of educational reform and transnational regulation has emerged as the last conundrum. There is a "talk" that education is in crisis, which has led many governments to attempt a series of reforms, becoming cyclical episodes. Teachers, many parents, and public opinion alike feel a serious mistrust about political action (and politicians in general) and the credible processes of change in schools. International comparability of performance, which has serious technical and epistemological limitations for implementation in national societies, has emerged as a tool of transnational regulation, defining the priorities for change, the terms of the debate, the concepts that need to be implemented (testing, accountability, quality of education) and eventually alienating several segments within educational systems—teachers, teachers' unions, and eventually professional organizations and parent organizations. These ideas have emerged in conversation with Antonio Teodoro (see also Teodoro, 2012).

Educational dilemmas of educational reform and policy get magnified if we focus on educational finances. The worldwide expenditure on educational systems exceeds two trillion dollars and the cost of public health exceeds three-and-a half-trillion dollars. Therefore, it is not surprising that global corporations are trying to privatize both services (Cavanaugh et al., 2003, p. 99). Looking at the United States, Hank Levin (2011) tell us why the field of education is second only to healthcare in terms of a new frontier for capital to colonize and profit from:

> The United States and most other countries devote a huge share of their resources to education. In 2008–09 the U.S. spent considerably more than one billion dollars in institutional expenditures on education from kindergarten through higher education (Levin, 2011). What is notable is that this figure does not include preschool or spending on education and training by businesses or the military. Nor

does it include private tutoring or the types of specialized lessons provided to children and adults by public and private entities such as the YMCA, Boys and Girls Clubs, and after-school academies. Even so, the official spending statistics accounted for almost 8 percent of Gross Domestic Product, a percentage that would surely rise to over 10 percent if all educational spending were included, more than one of every ten dollars of national income. This amount exceeds considerably the spending on the military and is second only to the health care sector. Moreover, this spending has doubled in real terms (adjusted for price level inflation) between 1986–87 and 2008–09. (NCES, 2010, Table 26)

Moreover, the problem of inequality of unemployment and lack of jobs is not lack of education. There is a staggering economic disparity between the income of a corporation CEO, a hedge fund manager, or a New York stock trader's income and that of a worker with a similar level of education, say a high school teacher. Thus, inequality is growing not only among people with different levels of education but also among those with similar education levels.

Productivity is not declining, but the share of profits of improved corporate productivity is going to high-earning CEOs rather than to income wage earners. Large segments of the U.S. workforce (and certainly of the European workforce) are at a disadvantage in the global competition with countries and workers willing to earn lower salaries. Temporal labor market dislocations may have resulted in a permanent situation. Some have predicted that one in six displaced workers in the United States will never regain full employment (Edsall, 2012; see also Byrne, 2012; Krugman, 2012; Levin-Waidman, 2011).

Growing inequality has a price for democracy. Is it possible that the top 0.1% has the political leverage to influence the political systems in ways that market democracy represents the ruling power of a plutocracy rather than a struggle among diverse interests of political representation? Is it possible that capitalism no longer provides benefits to a majority of workers? For example, will it be possible that the concentration of wealth in the United States and Western Europe, and the diminishing middle class, indicates the end of market democracies? Will the financial sector's unfettered capitalism, unchecked greed, and rampant behavior bring the capitalist world system to an irremediable collapse? (See Fukuyama, 2012.)

The "global" has become a meta-narrative, and neoliberalism has developed a "common sense," which has become an ideology that plays a major role in the process of constructing hegemony as moral and intellectual leadership in contemporary societies. Although neoliberalism has utterly failed as a viable model of economic development, the politics of culture associated with neoliberalism is still in force and remains quite strong, becoming the new common sense in shaping modern concepts of the role of government and education (Torres, 2011).

The university has been also deeply affected by these changes and crises. Neoliberal globalization, the most prominent model of globalization predicated on the dominance of the market over the state and on deregulatory models of governance, has deeply affected the university in the context of "academic capitalism." The resulting reforms, rationalized as advancing international competitiveness, are also known as "competition-based reforms," and public universities have been particularly affected.

The increasing penetration of market forces into higher education and the reorganization of university governance around "playing the game" of academic capitalism mark the influence of neoliberalism on universities in four primary areas: efficiency and accountability, accreditation and universalization, international competitiveness, and privatization. By introducing managerialism as a new form of institutional governance, however, universities have deepened and magnified their crises (for further discussion, see Chapter 10 in this volume).

While these reforms are implemented and adopted, there is also growing resistance to globalization as top-down-imposed reforms through policies and priorities taking place in diverse domains, including curriculum and instruction, teacher training, and school governance, and this growing resistance is also reflected in the public debates about schooling reform. Likewise, many people question whether these reforms attempt to limit the effectiveness of universities as sites of contestation of the national and global order and thus undermine the broader goals of education. In many cases, neoliberal reforms have limited access and opportunity along class and racial lines, including restricting access to higher education through the imposition of higher tuition and reduced government support to institutions and individuals (Darling-Hammond, 1993, p. xi).

HOW CAN WE FACE THE CHALLENGES AHEAD TO COMPARATIVE EDUCATION: WHAT CAN BE DONE?

Freire's notion of generative themes may provide us with a reasonable set of guiding principles for action against neoliberalism, based on a rereading of globalization that focuses on issues central to critical theory, including the dialectical nature of reality, the use of science to reduce suffering and increase happiness, and an ethical imperative to challenge systems of domination and oppression. Included next are themes that I believe best capture the challenges and possibilities of alternative globalizations.

ANTI-HEGEMONIC GLOBALIZATION

The need for universities, social movements, scholars, intellectuals, and communities to confront the dilemmas of the global and the local should not distract us from a most pressing concern: to challenge authoritarian neoliberal globalization and its hegemonic discourse of inevitability through networks, institutions, and practices that can change the intensity and dynamics of social interaction, and the actual lives of people in impoverished societies. This involves challenging the narratives of neoliberal globalization, particularly the fatalistic idea of *un pensamiento único* (the only possible thinking) so prevalent among economists and policymakers who, following rational choice models and game theory, have come to conclude that in a post-Fordist society the only possible theoretical model and social order is neoliberal economics and liberal democracy.

This consensus has been ratified and consolidated by a diverse group on the left and right, including neoconservative governments that have implemented neoliberal reforms, as explicated by Michael Apple in many of his books and articles. Challenging defying, and demystifying this technocratic approach to social sciences (particularly economics) and public policy is the most important generative theme of contemporary struggles. These struggles in the form of social movements forge the sort of decentered unity Apple has advocated in recent years that brings together—a unity the diverse groups forming the fragmented left and challenges the commonsensical idea that globalization and neoliberal reform are inevitable (see Apple, 1999; 2001; 2004; 2006).

Freedom Is Emancipation, Not Tutelage

One of the most important insights of a critical analysis of educational policy is that the attempt to highlight representative democracy as the only viable model is also an attempt to create freedom that is controlled and circumscribed; it is essentially used as a device of elites to dominate and control the masses. What we have come to see is that representative democracy often represents a dictatorship of capital, or at least the dictatorship of the economic elites. There are other alternatives, starting with a liberal notion of participatory democracy that will expand the limitations of representative democracy and enhance the quality and texture of democratic life. In a more radical vein, there is the model of radical democracy as practiced in the implementation of participatory budgeting for more than a decade in Porto Alegre, Brazil.

A renaissance of democracy emerges as a central concern in the context of education and the larger society. Movements toward reforming campaign finance and elections to increase transparency and accountability, as well as attempts to create better ways to increase the connections between education and citizenship, or between citizenship and the practice of democracy, are essential to this work. We must also work to link the university with social movements opposing hegemonic globalization and schooling with the broader debates on globalization and the roles, purposes, and goals of education in general.

Defense of Public Education

The defense of public education is one of the central concerns of innumerable social movements and public declarations, including the World Social Forum, the World Educational Forum, student strikes in Chile or Egypt, student protests over tuition around the world, and teachers' union protests. For those who still view participatory democracy as viable, a robust defense of the importance of public support and public goods must be waged. We must also defend the achievements of some of the most cherished ideals of a democratic pact that includes equality, freedom, and solidarity, and that does not allow the hegemony of neoliberalism to erode these essential ideals by redefining the citizen as merely a consumer.

Defense of the Democratic State

Given the intense dynamics between the local and the global, the nation-state takes on even greater importance within the context of globalization. Yet, it is clear that without resorting to a serious defense of the principles of representation and participation in the democratic state, we may not be able to implement the generative themes outlined earlier.

The state plays an important role in altering the nature of public education and cannot be subsumed by discourses of individual or small group autonomy. This is not to undermine these movements or the importance of the local, just to recognize the essential role the democratic state will play in the realization of a more holistic, just, and emancipatory education for all.

A Planetarian Multicultural Citizenship

This is perhaps the most important action to be undertaken by schools and universities as part of their responsibility to serve the public good. With increased immigration, and the slippage of cultures and languages in local communities and national societies, it is imperative to work toward a cosmopolitan democracy based on a planetarian multicultural citizenship. Indeed, as utopian as this model may sound—and remembering that many of the most astute and critical social scientists like Immanuel Wallerstein (1998) have called for a science of "utopistics"—there are really few options but to create new social and human horizons.

We need to seek these new trajectories through pedagogical models that facilitate novel encounters between humans and nature. We need a new model of relationships between the mind and body, one that moves beyond the logocentric characteristic of European and North American white cultures into a biocentric model. We need a new model for building and sustaining global relationships, one not based on the threat of a nuclear holocaust, but rooted in ideals anchored to a more peaceful world.

The responsibilities of educational institutions to the survival of the planet, to social justice and democracy, and to peace and solidarity among individuals and communities cannot simply be a subject of study within ivory tower walls. The knowledge and ideals advanced by our greatest minds must impact our societies, our social policies, and indeed our global practices.

We, therefore, call for a transformation of education across the globe with schooling becoming a source of social action that can transcend economic rationality and reengage with the long, hard struggle for the good life and a good society. This involves a new vision of education and the will and collective action necessary to struggle toward its realization.

In closing, I will emphasize that critical theory offers a way to better understand and work toward the implementation of these generative themes. Critical theory provides powerful analytical tools to go beyond the generally accepted assumptions of globalization and neoliberalism to the forces that are shaping and leading radical transformations in societies worldwide. In rereading globalization in this vein, we see how the interests served by its dynamics undermine social justice and democracy, as well as the opportunities and quality of life of large proportions of the globe. Critical theory also reminds us of the power people have to intervene in the world and the ways the ideology of inevitability becomes a profound tool of the economic and social elite in their pursuit of global domination and control. In this sense, critical theory can serve as the inspiration for progressive education policy and social and educational movements that challenge globalization from above and reaffirm the global struggle for social justice, democratization, and a common good outside the instrumental rationality of markets and consumption (Misiaszek et al., 2011; Rhoads & Torres, 2006b; Torres, 2010; van Heertum & Torres, 2009a; 2009b; 2011).

AFTERTHOUGHT TO THE FIFTH EDITION: THE END OF GLOBALIZATION AND THE CRISES OF DEMOCRACY AND CITIZENSHIP

Writing this concluding chapter has become a ritual. Every time I ask a question: What has changed since the publication of the previous edition?

In the following sections I explore the connections between globalization, the crisis of democracy and citizenship, and the implications for comparative education (first and second section). Next, I explore the need for introspection in comparative education (third section), new actors, new concepts, and new challenges (fourth section), and a Conclusion: COVID-19 and Our Circumstances.

THE END OF GLOBALIZATION? THE CRISES OF DEMOCRACY AND CITIZENSHIP

In the fourth edition I asked: Will the economic crisis herald the end of the market democracy? Today, one of the major global trends is the decline of democratic participation in many countries reflected in low participation rates in elections and trade union, the rise of populist movements, and the role of social media in this issue. In addition, migration and the rise of multicultural societies pose innumerable challenges to democratic societies. There are tensions, not only between developed and developing countries, but also strong threats to liberal democratic societies, fueled by nationalism, isolationism, and racism. These factors, jointly with growing inequality are threatening social cohesion.

Let us consider a central measuring concept for democracy: voting participation or voter turnout. Higher voter turnout is an indicator of democratic vitality, while lower voter turnout is an indicator of apathy and mistrust in the voting political process (Pintor et al., 2002; 2004). The International Institute for Democracy and Electoral Assistance (IDEA), measuring democratic participation as voters turn out, IDEA indicates that voter turnout has been declining across the globe since the beginning of the 1990s. Higher voter turnout would be an indicator of democratic vitality, while lower voter turnout is an indicator of apathy and mistrust in the voting political process. Voter turnout is the extent to which eligible voters use their vote on election day.

IDEA's data generate many questions. Does lower turnout mean that the population doesn't consider elections the method to give legitimacy to parties controlling decision-making? Will that mean that political parties are no longer the key actors of democratic representation? Does lower participation mean that citizens are no longer interested in politics? Or instead, there are other forms of citizens participation as suggested in many places (Isin & Nielson, 2008).

One of the conclusions of the report is that "the number of countries that hold direct national elections has increased substantially since the beginning of the 1990s. However, the global average voter turnout has decreased significantly over the same period. The decline in Europe is the most visible and is a result mainly of the sharp decline in postcommunist states (established European democracies (countries and territories): Andorra, Austria, Belgium, Cyprus, Denmark, Faroe Islands, Finland, France, Germany, Gibraltar, Greece, Iceland, Ireland, Italy,

Liechtenstein, Luxembourg, Malta, Monaco, the Netherlands, Norway, Portugal, San Marino, Spain, Sweden, Switzerland, United Kingdom).

The explanation seems to focus on people's disenchantment with democracy and disappointment over the transitional hardships. It seems that the data indicate further decline for the period under analysis (2011–2015) (established European democracies (countries and territories): Andorra, Austria, Belgium, Cyprus, Denmark, Faroe Islands, Finland, France, Germany, Gibraltar, Greece, Iceland, Ireland, Italy, Liechtenstein, Luxembourg, Malta, Monaco, the Netherlands, Norway, Portugal, San Marino, Spain, Sweden, Switzerland, United Kingdom). Also voters may have been coerced under an authoritarian system into voting.

Asia and the Americas' voter turnout has been more stable but much lower than most of the decades since 1940 with exception of the last election which shows an incredible display of democratic voting. The 2020 election in the United States was an outlier. The population had to choose between a return to a normal democratic process with the election of the Biden-Harris ticket, or the continuation of an authoritarian norm-bashing administration led by the charismatic personality of Mr. Trump. Because the result was not accepted by the loser, the conclusion of this episode was an attempt of insurrection on January 6, 2021, which is being investigated. Over 400 cases of potential crimes committed by a crowd incited by a conspiratorial discourse from the still sitting and election loser President Trump are investigated by the FBI. At the moment of writing this chapter, a second impeachment of former President Trump is about to take place in the U.S. Senate.

Further evidence of democracy decline is evident in several indicators, including electoral process and pluralism, the functioning of government, political participation, democratic political culture, and civil liberties. Recent research finds that just 8.4% of the world's population live in a full democracy while more than a third live under authoritarian rule. The global score of 5.37 out of 10 is the lowest recorded since the index began in 2006 ("Global Democracy," 2021).

Will the disenchantment with democracy be connected with neoliberal globalization? Multiple globalizations, or what can be called different faces of globalization, had a heavy impact on the field and its orientation. Globalization takes different forms and we really should talk about globalization processes in the plural. There is not one all-encompassing globalization but multiple globalizations with multiple faces.

Let's call attention to the predominant forms of globalization. One form, often seen as "globalization from above," is framed by an ideology of neoliberalism and calls for an opening of borders, the creation of multiple regional markets, the proliferation of fast-paced economic and financial exchanges, and the presence of governing systems other than nation-states. Without any doubt, the dominant form of neoliberal globalization has affected "competition-based reforms," transforming educational policy in K–12 and higher education.

Another form represents the antithesis of the first. This form of globalization is often described as "globalization from below," or antiglobalization. Globalization from below is largely manifested in individuals, institutions, and social movements actively opposed to what is perceived as corporate globalization. For these individuals and groups, "no globalization without representation" is the motto.

There is a third form of globalization that pertains more to rights than to markets—the globalization of human rights. There is the fourth manifestation of globalization. This form extends beyond markets, and to some extent is against human rights. It is the globalization of the international war against terrorism.

There is a fifth form of globalization that is the growing cultural hybridity.[3] These plural forms of globalization created hybrid spaces, which are full of differences, including racial and migratory status, and hence affect the way citizenship is being played out and negotiated in communities.

There is a sixth form of globalization: The Global Media. Political polarization in the United States has reached historic levels, not only in the form of competing ideologies but, increasingly, competing perceived realities, with broadcast and social media platforms creating filter bubbles that reflect, reinforce, and consequently intensify beliefs and enable the viral spread of misinformation. Collectively, these developments have created a crisis of citizenship, including increased disregard for democratic rules and norms, which in turn has created a crisis of democracy and of constitutional patriotism, in which political attachment centers on norms, values, and procedures of a liberal democratic constitution.

There is finally another form of globalization connected with the principles of the knowledge society and the network society (Pintor et al., 2002; Pintor et al., 2004). Let's explore the implications for comparative education.

Globalization, the Crisis of Democracy and Citizenship: Implications for Comparative and International Education

All these forms of globalization are deeply affecting our discipline. Likewise, the crises of democracy and citizenship are affecting the educational systems in ways that have not yet been experienced.

Forces unleashed by globalization and the counter-globalization movement can be seen as a threat to education involving the following: socialization function whether it is from a top-down or bottom-up approach; the potential for advancing moral and social progress by imbuing values such as tolerance, respect, compassion, empathy, and understanding toward the Other; the capacity to enable individuals to develop foresight that transcends narrow self-interests or world views; and, the possibility of enhancing individuals understanding of themselves and the world they inhabit.

Therefore, not surprisingly, comparative international education is facing what could be perceived as a perpetual identity crisis. What is comparative international education in actuality? Is it a field of expertise with a scientific comparative method like the one that some of our predecessors from the early decades tried to establish from a positivist orientation? Or a field concerned with the practical implications of the loaning and borrowing of innovations among educational systems? Or a field concerned with the internationalization of education and the implications of global education for world citizenry?[4] Is comparative education an oscillating directionless metronome depending on the music played in societies?

The field has evolved from its precarious beginnings, by most standards, to have progressed internationally with a reasonable degree of academic institutionalization and respectability. Despite progress, perpetual questions about identity continue to besiege the field and many of its practitioners. Reading these situations through the lenses of Marx, many discussions in comparative education show "the poverty of theory" in the field.

Debates on theory and method in comparative education, ultimately underscore the need for a better intellectual definition of the field and, particularly, for what could be termed as better ways of teaching, research, and policy-making in the field and the art of comparative international education.

Globalizations will not provide us with answers for these questions; more so, when in the middle of a pandemic that highlights the role of globalization in the life of societies, the whole globalization model is being challenged by new populist nationalisms, some of them borderline fascism for the 21st century.

Since the publication of the fourth edition and until very recently, what seemed the naturalization of unstoppable globalization was a given factor to parlay the process of growth for the world economic system—one may consider the concept of globalization as the contemporary counterpart of or perhaps even a substitute for the traditional concept of development (Wallerstein, 2005).

We are facing a great paradox at the moment. On the one hand, the pervasive presence of the globalization phenomena challenges the field to answer the question of what is the relative advantage of CIE in understanding the changing social contexts of education, and some of the proverbial dilemmas of equity, equality, and quality of education throughout the world. On the other hand, the growing rejection of globalization as a process that benefits the world elites, calls for local interventions as a response. Hence growing nativism and nationalism are emerging worldwide, and moving more often than not on differential forms of authoritarianism, reaching neo-Nazism in its most extreme configuration.

Will the premises of this new nationalism erase the contributions of comparative education, seen as a cosmopolitan field and by implication refractory to this new nationalistic impetus? It has been incumbent on scholars in our field for decades to question these national tendencies from comparative and international perspectives. A new nationalism will question not only comparative education but also take to task the contributions of the United Nations, its specialized agency of UNESCO, or multilateral institutions such as OECD, or the World Bank as regulatory nodes of the global economic, political, and sociocultural systems.

The first part of the paradox seems to hint at a renewed importance of CIE as a field of scholarship and inquiry with the increasing interconnectedness of all societies. This in no way implies that globalization has brought to us a more homogeneous world in terms of living standards and political regimes. The opposite could also be true in several domains.

In short, if globalization is mostly an expression of global capitalism and a neoliberal economic agenda ruling the world, there is still enough room for dissent. Moreover, there is a diasporic process of people's movements and cultural renewal that cannot be easily coerced into a neoliberal one-size-fits-all lifestyle, particularly when neoliberal globalization, rather than incorporating the majority of the world's population on equal terms, marginalizes and impoverishes it.

Today, the contestation to globalization processes, as a benefit to elites, is the growing nationalist and nativist authoritarian populism, borderline occasionally with fascism. From a strong local nativist perspective, a provocateur might ask, is CIE as a field losing relevance nowadays if globalization is under attack? If so, are comparativists, ready to leave that cozy niche of being a possibly residual category in scholarship that incorporates scholars and technocrats coming from several disciplines with an international and comparative orientation?

If we scratch a theory, we find a biography (Torres, 1998). The biographies of our predecessors made comparative education an established profession and field of inquiry, research, and teaching. No matter how uncomfortable they might be, the difficulty to handle and to answer them in policy terms, questions of equality, equity and quality of education are perennial challenges for comparative education as are questions of identity as recognition and distribution of resources, which will never go away. We should remain oriented and sensible to the new historical realities of our time (Tully, 2000).

Interdisciplinarity in education and social sciences has reached a level never seen before. The contributions of comparative and international education appear as a precondition for any rigorous analysis of democracy, citizenship, and multiculturalism, just to mention three classic themes that should be part not only of our theoretical and methodological toolbox but of our individual passions if we want a better, caring, just, ethical, and sustainable development world.

Considering what we are confronting now in the third decade of the new century with COVID-19, we need a renewed dialogue in the field. The effort to know what the multiple globalizations are, what are their origins and their implications for education, just to speak about our field, reveals a multitude of answers, approaches, and analyses. However, this effort for understanding hitherto lacks sufficient concrete empirical and comparative research products. In an academic world where there is less and less money for research, and less institutional investments, this is worrisome.

We may have come full circle. To the extent that theory and empirical research do not adequately comprehend and address the issues raised by changing transnational trends, we defeat the purpose of comparative education as an intellectual field for the analysis of globalization and anti-globalization movements. More so, if technocratic or institutional comparativist educators ignore the movements for global social justice and equality.

I use technocratic to simplify what is a mixture of technocracy and bureaucratic rationality prevalent in certain hard spaces or institutional spaces. Many of these comparativists are usually located in bilateral and multilateral institutions, lacking the almost unlimited autonomy that scholars in academia have—though autonomy is necessary but not a sufficient precondition for good thinking, theorizing, or analysis. Though these institutional comparativists accept a technocratic approach devoid of serious critical theorizing, they follow the dominant precepts and orientations of their institutions of employment.

Let's go back to the conversation on globalization. While globalization is heralded by neoliberalism as a new model of social relationships throughout the world, not all the regions in the world, or localities in all countries, are being globalized in the same manner, intensity, and direction. Furthermore, some regions (and some educational systems) are not being globalized at all, or revert to a growing nationalistic discourse, often sprinkled with nativism and isolationism postures.

The answer to the implications of globalization and antiglobalization movements—or what we have called the dialectic of the local and the global in this book—will always depend on the framework that we use to analyze them.

We need to imagine how different an expert of the World Bank or Organisation for Economic Co-operation and Development (OECD), or a poor yet politicized peasant of the *Movimento dos Sem Terra* (Landless Peasant Movement) in Brazil will view globalization processes with different lenses and have radically different expectations and policy orientations.

Macro-narratives, for instance, the Enlightenment, democracy, or Marxism have been damaged by the postmodernist storm with its critique of master narratives, and, according to some, are beyond repair? Will, however, practitioners of comparative education agree that reality is a social construction and that every social construction is as good as the next one? Will comparativists conclude that all we are, do, and struggle for evidence-based research, are simply constructed narratives marinated in a linguistic turn? If the answer to these questions is yes, it means that this interdisciplinary field has accepted the defeat of Reason in the search for reasonable explanations of social phenomena or at least the search for dialogue across different paradigms or logics in use.

Multiple globalization and its discontents, bring with its baggage not only a new challenge but also a crisis for comparative education as a field (Safranski, 2004). The debate about globalization and the presence of antiglobalization movements present us with new opportunities to conduct serious cross-cultural and comparative investigations about globalization in education and sharpen our methodologies and theories.

In facing these challenges, we will be able to provide a better answer to our perpetual question of who we are, and what our contributions can be. The *diferentia specifica* so to speak, in the scholarship that comparative educators provide to better the world.

It is not only a matter of learning the trade of research and teaching skills. A consistent answer to these questions requires, above all, vision, wisdom, generosity, and compassion. Unfortunately, colonial thinking remains in our midst. We require a critical perspective, or what philosophers like Paulo Freire or Paul Ricoeur called a hermeneutic of suspicion about the subtexts of many scholars who despite good intentions, are still embedded within colonialist and imperialist traditions.

In the present dilemmas of the dialectics of the global and the local, should comparative educators speak as public intellectuals, learning from a critical theory of society in the spirit of Paulo Freire? That is, should comparativists follow the epistemological principles of theories built in the struggles for liberation or rather adopt the **hegemonic positions** of the establishment?

The main challenge for comparativists approaching the toolkit of critical theory is: scholars in this tradition epistemologically shall not fully separate the analytical from the normative. Therefore, academics in these critical traditions cannot be *voyeurs* observing reality with sarcasm and irony while enjoying their privileges. They cannot be technocrats who implacably implement their models of social engineering without considering the damage that they can do to countries, communities, and individuals.

For instance, many of the proposals of OECD have been accused of being culturally insensitive, ignoring scientific criticism, and pursuing a hegemonic leadership policy affecting local traditions and autonomy (Zhao, 2020). Many of the projects supported by the World Bank have been deemed highly costly for the lives of communities (Torres, 2009), or case in point, is the lending logic of the IMF that is heavily confronted by many of the most indebted countries for their authoritarian fiscal tradition (Pettinger, 2021).

Let me say that for critical theorists of society, the contradictions of reality hurt us very intimately, and this is the reason we teach, conduct research, and accept responsibilities in administration to change the world for the better, not to reproduce it.

The next section confronts us with an important question that invites serious introspection in the field. Is it possible that a field of study like comparative education has no originators outside of the West and Global North intellectuals? Many truly founders outside the Western hemisphere are omitted, ignored, or simply unknown to the field.

The Need for Introspection in the Field of Comparative and International Education

Let me draw from the case of Latin America. While still there is no systematic study of the contributions of Domingo Faustino Sarmiento to this discipline, it is worth knowing that already in the first half of the 19th century, Sarmiento had developed contributions that could well qualify him as one of the precursors of CIE in the entire world.

Sarmiento was a man as genial as controversial. With the publication of "Facundo" in 1845 (Fishburn, 1979; Sarmiento, 1845), Sarmiento inaugurated a controversial but important literary tradition that, I dare say, is foundational not only of gauchoesque literature (reflecting the mentality of the gaucho, an equivalent to the American cowboy) that comes partly in response to his argument about the tensions between civilization or barbarism but as well as within Argentinean literature.[5]

Sarmiento was an exiled and inveterate traveler who learned from others, activities that once the Greeks defined as the role of the philosopher—the one who travels and learns represents the essence of philosophy.

Between 1845 and 1848 Sarmiento visited Europe—in the middle of the social revolutions that Marx studied in the "18 Brumaire of Napoleon Bonaparte"—and the United States, where he traveled to 21 states, and discovered, in Boston, Horace Mann, then Superintendent of Public Instruction of the State of Massachusetts.

Mann's theories and practices offered Sarmiento the principles of the model of public education he was searching for. Sarmiento, who eventually became seventh president of Argentina, was a self-made man and an autodidact who was searching for the proper model of education for the emerging new nation-state of postcolonial Argentina.

Sarmiento visited the United States again in 1865 as Minister Plenipotentiary and Extraordinary Ambassador to the United States coinciding with the end of the Civil War and Lincoln's assassination. He learned in the United States that slavery was an atrocity that needed to be eliminated from the Earth, and that education was indispensable to achieving gender equality essential to citizenship building. He invited a large number of women teachers to come to Argentine to teach, despite that they were all Protestant and most likely would not be well received in the nascent Catholic country (Christenson, 2011). Sarmiento's political and pedagogical travels were in the eye of the social and political storm of his time.

When Sarmiento published the fruits of his trips in a book titled *Popular Education* in 1849 and helped establish a foundation for public education in Latin America, he became an unknowing practitioner of a nonexistent discipline: CIE.

For Sarmiento, public education is the ideal path to educate citizens who will build the nation-state, and conversely, the nation-state would become responsible in promoting and financing public education.

In *Popular Education* Sarmiento (1849) wrote that the adoption of a policy of equality is the basis of social organization. Moreover, as has been noted by several commentators, Sarmiento along the lines of the democratic revolutions of the 19th century states that it is "the duty of every government to provide education to future generations because we cannot compel all individuals in the present generation to receive the intellectual preparation which involves the exercise of the rights that are attributed to citizenship." Having suffered and observed the hegemonic anti-intellectual moment in his country unequivocally, he states that "not educating new generations, all the flaws that our current organization suffers will continue to exist" (Sarmiento, 1849, p. 26).

Ricardo Piglia, in a beautiful text titled *Notes on Facundo* (Sarlos, 1980), canonized Sarmiento as one of the early pioneer intellectuals in comparative education. For Sarmiento, "to know it is to compare. Everything makes sense if it is possible to reconstruct the analogies between what you want to explain and something else that is already judged and written" (Piglia, 1980, p. 17). Sarmiento is virtually unknown by the specialists in CIE because a great deal of the history of comparative education has been told from the perspective of the Global North, not the Global South.

A call to introspection requires us to understand that knowledge is not unidirectional. There were and are important influences from the third world in these discussions, particularly what later came to be known as the epistemology of the Global South (de Souza Santos, 2018).

Without a doubt, the insights and lessons provided by *Pedagogy of the Oppressed* (1970) the corpus of contributions of Paulo Freire—became universal. *Pedagogy of the Oppressed* was classified as the third book most cited in Google in the publication of the London School of Economics and Political Science. The book of Freire is listed as the third most cited after the book of Thomas Kuhn *The Structure of Scientific Revolutions,* and the second most cited, from Everett Rogers's *Diffusion of Innovations*. It is important to mention that *Pedagogy of the Oppressed* is the only book on education in the 25 most cited (Green, 2016).

Julius Nyerere from Tanzania, one of Africa's most celebrated independence figures, was a politician of great intelligence and even more solid principles. His work inspired generations of scholars attentive to the process of postcolonialism in Africa.

He was known as Mwalimu, or teacher, who has a vision of education as the logic and practice of possibility. Africa gave the world iconic figures of education and social liberation such as Nelson Mandela and Amilcar Cabral. Mandela spent more than two decades imprisoned as a "terrorist." Yet upon his liberation was the architect of reconciliation in South Africa; or Amilcar Cabral, whose contributions, particularly his powerful article the "Weapon of Theory," (Cabral,

1979; 2016; Noyoo, 2014) influenced a whole generation of educators, political militants and social activists in Africa and elsewhere.

From the bully pulpit of politicians such as Evita Perón, one of the most noted fighters for women's equality in Latin America, conditions were created for new perspectives in the social sciences, which should percolate in comparative education.

But also, countless practitioners made contributions that have not been sufficiently studied in the field or remain simply unknown. Let me use as an example a rural teacher in Argentina whom I had the honor to meet and break bread with Rosita Weinschebaum Ziperovich.

Rosita Ziperovich worked as a rural teacher and trade union militant for more than 70 years. She was fired many times from her work as a teacher and administrator, either because she was a socialist or did not agree with the Peronist government in the 1950s, or simply because she was a Jew. At 81 years of age, in 1994, despite her failing health, she worked as Federal Representative in the Reform of the Argentinean Constitution with special interest in the changes in education law.

The list of people who have contributed to the educational adventure and enriched comparative education is very long. Particularly people who fought for social transformation and were assassinated by the true forces of terror, state terrorism. Comparative education should honor in our writings and teach the names of the invisible and anonymous educators murdered for their convictions or their pedagogical practice. The invisible teacher who works in the trenches in the most remote and most dangerous places of the Earth are making this world a better place and their students better citizens.

In addition to extraordinary leaders, the third world has offered educational systems that are beginning to show signs of autonomy constituting mass national education systems at unprecedented levels. The convergence or institutional isomorphism in organizational terms has led to several theoretical frameworks, especially those linked to neo-institutionalism to talk about a global culture (Boxenbaum & Jonsson, 2017).

Looking back, while CIE is well established in international organizations and academia, the question that requires further exploration is if it is truly a discipline. From our perspective comparative and international education should be defined as an interdisciplinary quilt, an interdisciplinary field.

Yet, what the critical studies in comparative education seem to have in common is to share with Paulo Freire and Paul Ricoeur, our concern with an epistemology of suspicion—at times Ricoeur used the term hermeneutics of suspicion. The epistemology of suspicion is to always suspect that any social relationship involves instances of domination as taught us by Freire in *Pedagogy of the Oppressed* but also Albert Memmi (1965), Franz Fanon (1961), the Black Consciousness Movement with the unique thought of Steve Biko (2020), and of course the indispensable French philosopher Paul Ricoeur who taught for many years at the University of Chicago (Pellauer, 2020).

With the fall of the Berlin Wall neoliberal technocracy won a privileged place in the academies of science and education. It is a model that favors systematically a movement of privatization and standardized testing with a corollary movement of "accountability" and the evaluation state.

The first two decades of the new century offer to us a very complex picture. CIE is installed within the academies, especially in the advanced industrial world, and there are many more societies of comparative education than in the beginning. But it is not growing in universities as represented by new academic positions, and the duly replacement of scholars retiring who belong to this interdisciplinary field.

The employment growth in this interdisciplinary field is not in academia but other institutions, including the global institutional system of bilateral and multilateral institutions, local and regional state management agencies in charge of educational research and planning, transnational social movements, and national and transnational NGOs.

NEW ACTORS, NEW CONCEPTS, NEW CHALLENGES

We shall assume our commitment remains firm for equity transformational projects aimed at disrupting inequalities. For instance, revisiting or promoting analyses following Amartya Sen's (1990) capability approach or the many recommendations emanating from Thomas Piketty in *Capital in the Twenty-First Century* (2014) and particularly in his latest book *Capital and Ideology* (2020).

We should pay special attention to the proposal of Laudato Si (Praise be to you—On Care for our Common Home) pronounced by Pope Francis in defense of the environment (Francisco, 2015). In this spirit, comparative and international education should understand, learn, practice, research, and teach the paradigm of ecopedagogy related to the work of critical pedagogues, and the concept of education for sustainable development as a framework for action in protecting the environment.

How to understand the transformations of multipolarity in the world system in the context of a new model of globalization where immigration becomes a transformative character of social realities? CIE should pay attention to the new narratives that are emerging in the context of the global system to challenge hegemonic narratives, especially the powerful idea of global citizenship education discussed by Tarozzi and Torres in this book. In the context of the current crisis of humanity, is imperative to generate more courses in universities fostering a comprehensive global conversation about education for peace.

The UN Assembly in 2015 formulated a consensus built by all nations of the globe. For comparative and international education, the UN sustainable development goals are fertile grounds for research, teaching, and learning, especially on peace education, education for sustainable development, and global citizenship education.

The global system recognizes the importance of the 2030 Sustainable Development Agenda with 17 goals and 169 targets and implements its symbolic five dimensions including people, planet, prosperity, peace, and partnership.

Comparative education should contribute to the Sustainable Development Agenda. Having served from 2013–2016 as president of the World Council of Comparative Education Societies, I made several proposals to the field and its representative societies *tout court*. I take the liberty to briefly list them here.

1. We must not repeat failures of the past. We must use this opportunity for a better world with alternative approaches to conflict resolution and peace. Though war might sometimes be inevitable (it is after all one of the responsibilities of the nation-states as defined by Western political philosophy), we must organize against war, and stop the perpetual visions of foreign policy and economies that thrive on war. We must pressure governments to seek political and diplomatic solutions to global problems. But if ideologies like Nazism and Fascism cannot be persuaded to give up their global ambitions, the world democracies should organize a reasonable response avoiding as much as possible civilian casualties.
2. We must support and guide the building of global solidarity movements that are founded on premises that counter racism, Islamophobia and extremist ideologies. Groups need to be established to educate communities about mutual respect, empathy, various privileges, histories of marginalized groups, and community and socially responsible entrepreneurship.
3. We should find ways to bring together various religious scholars, civil society organizations, youth leaders and activists, international and multilateral institutions, and other people to address and organically and inclusively create new peaceful ideologies and social policies that resonate with indigenous structures and beliefs that challenge violence.
4. As scholars and members of academic societies we should pressure all governments and the U.N. to prosecute war crimes for those responsible for atrocities on all sides of the political spectrum.
5. As scholars and members of academic societies we should support and build spaces for disenfranchised and marginalized youth throughout the world to listen to their grievances, empower them to participate in society, provide tools for conflict resolution, and have them contributing to addressing social issues.
6. Let us make sure that we use the power of reason and education to prevent further radicalization of youth following extremist religious and nationalistic perspectives giving meaning to lives that find no meaning otherwise. But most importantly, intense conversations about violent interpretations of Islam should take place throughout the world, conducted by Islamic scholars who should answer these radical interpretations responsible as well for the internecine wars between Islamic faith groups.
7. Scholars of Comparative and International Education should counter governments' adoption of neoliberal based policies to seek out economic alternatives that are more inclusive and less socially and environmentally destructive.
8. As scholars and members of academic societies we must convey to UNESCO that they need to double its efforts to bring dialogue about conflict and peace in the world system inside our governments, community organizations, social movements, political parties, and world citizens. WCCES needs to feature in our mass media more dialogue about peace, global citizenship, and education for sustainable development. We should offer our services to promote peace at any cost. Only this way we may be able to promote life, liberty and the pursuit of happiness. Peace is a treasure of humanity and we should preserve it at any cost.

9. As members of the WCCES community, it is our duty to help educators complicate their understanding of diversity, and subsequently create a more inclusive learning environment for all students. Helping educators to expand student perspectives toward a more global and interconnected framework, which is essential in deconstructing the marginalizing discourses that often permeate our educational institutions.

Writing in 2021 I would be remiss if I do not focus on the most significant event that has brought to our life existence, our families, communities, regions, and nations, a most powerful challenge with COVID-19, the 21st-century plague. COVID-19 put the global economies in check, reduced the sociability engagements of the population, undermined the education of whole generations during 2019–2021, and killed a large number of people worldwide.

CONCLUSION: COVID-19 AND OUR CIRCUMSTANCES

One of the lessons of the COVID-19 crisis is that the social network of solidarity is limited and insufficient to help people who are unemployed, part-time employed, who work two or three jobs a week to make ends meet, or who lives paycheck to paycheck. This is population unable to save, heavily indebted, and unable to confront catastrophic health care crises. In short, the recognition that inequality needs to be confronted and solved is an indication of many of the demands for the near future.

In this time of uncertainty, health care and economic crises, a new, and yet, old theme emerges as important for research and teaching in comparative education. Adult learning education may play a unique role in dealing with these crises. A reinvigoration of adult learning education, as it happened in the 1960s may renew initiatives about nonformal education and alternative forms of education and production. This is the time to have a renewed approach to adult education, heading to the goals proposed in the 1970s by UNESCO's "Learning to Be." More important now that UNESCO Institute for Lifelong Learning is preparing the new CONFITEA 7, and the Global Report on Adult Learning Education.

A desirable outcome to implement the scientific humanist model that has emerged from UNESCO is that governments and places of worship stop using adult education merely as a tool of franchising individuals or as a method of acquiring social legitimation of political and institutional regimes. At the same time, they should make sure that there is a fundamental role for adult and lifelong learning to play in the reconstruction of the future world and national economies, public spheres, and national cultures.

Social movements and NGOs will proliferate even more demanding actions for participatory democracy, one of the key elements of adult education in progressive quarters. The future will show also the growth of new social movements to confront racism, the politics of hate, and white supremacy normativity. There will also be a demand, from the United Nations and particularly UNESCO for taking global citizenship education as a global phenomenon more seriously by all governments, and for nations to take it local.

Like the Greeks' "eternal return law," the questions of civic culture may be again, as it was in the 1960s, a central concern for democracy. Gabriel Almond and Sidney Verba's (1963) book centered on how political attitudes anchored in political cultures may help expand or undermine liberal democracy.

The recent experience in the United States of an authoritarian yet democratically elected leader like President Trump, obtained more than 70 million votes in the recent election. While he fell short of votes to be reelected, because the Democratic ticket Biden-Harris surpassed 80 million votes, winning both the popular vote and the votes in the electoral college, the question remains: how is it possible that in the older democracy on Earth, so many people have voted for someone who ostensibly was destroying democratic norms, practices, and undermining the rule of law?

Corollary: There is a need to promote a new civic culture in the United States, and other places in the globe, where neo-authoritarian populism, are promoting an alt-right perspective, white supremacy, and even neo-Nazi perspective.

There is no question that better international communications and a network of international solidarity movements created by global citizenship education practices in schooling, higher education institutions, literacy, and nonformal education programs will help to avoid the prevalence of a post-truth society, conspiracies theories, or the lack of evidence-based research. Comparative and international education is responsible for the renewal of education in the post-pandemic new normal.

NOTES

1. Nobel laureate economist Joseph E. Stiglitz spent seven years in Washington as chair of President Clinton's Council of Economic Advisors and Chief Economist of the World Bank. His views have been popularized in his best seller, titled—as an economic paraphrasing Sigmund Freud's book about Western civilization—*Globalization and Its Discontents* (2002).

2. Bob Arnove read in great detail and commented critically to this afterthought. I am deeply grateful to him for his contributions to this book, for his many contributions to my academic work, and particularly for his emblematic work in comparative education, from which so many of us have benefited over the years.

3. Cultural critic Néstor García Canclini discussed this in the context of Latin America: Undoubtedly, urban expansion is one of the causes that intensified cultural hybridization. What does it mean for Latin American cultures that countries that had about 10% of their population in the cities at the beginning of the century now concentrate 60 to 70% in urban agglomerations? We have gone from societies dispersed in thousands of peasant communities with traditional, local, and homogeneous cultures—in some regions, with strong indigenous roots, with little communication with the rest of each nation—to a largely urban scheme with a heterogeneous symbolic offering renewed by a constant interaction of the local with national and transnational networks of communication. https://azargh.farhang.gov.ir/ershad_content/Media/image/2012/01/175362_orig.pdf#page=461.

4. This section includes a revised material from C. A. Torres (2018, November), "The State of the Art in Comparative Education and WCCES at a Crossroads in the 21st Century," *Revista Lusófona de Educação*, 41(1), 107–124.

5. In a private conversation Ricardo Piglia, one of the noted Argentinean literary critics and the Walter S. Carpenter Professor of Language, Literature, and Civilization of Spain, Department of Spanish and Portuguese Languages and Cultures at Princeton told me that in his expert opinion the lineage of the Argentine literature will pass from Domingo F. Sarmiento to Jorge Luis Borges and to Roberto Arlt.

REFERENCES

Almond, G. A., & Verba, S. (1963). *The civic culture: Political attitudes and democracy in five nations*. Princeton University Press.

Apple, M. (1999). Between neoliberalism and neoconservatism: Education and conservatism in a global context. In N. Burbules & C. A. Torres (Eds.), *Globalization and education: Critical perspectives*. Routledge.

Apple, M. (2001). Comparing neo-liberal projects and inequality in education. *Comparative Education, 37*(4), 409–423.

Apple, M. (2002). Patriotism, pedagogy, and freedom: On the educational meanings of September 11th. *Teachers College Record, 104*(8), 1770–1771.

Apple, M. (2004). *Ideology and curriculum* (3rd ed.). Routledge.

Apple, M. (2006). *Educating the "right" way: Markets, Standards, God, and Inequality* (2nd ed.). Routledge.

Bandow, D., & Vásquez, I. (Eds.) (1994). *Perpetuating Poverty: The World Bank, the IMF, and the Developing World*. CATO Institute.

Betto, F. (2002, November 2). El amigo de Lula. *La Jornada* [Author's translation].

Boxenbaum, E., & Jonsson, S. (2017). Isomorphism, diffusion and decoupling: Concept evolution and theoretical challenges. In R. Greenwood, C. Oliver, T. B. Lawrence & R. E. Meyer et al. (Eds.), *The SAGE handbook of organizational institutionalism* (pp. 79–104). Sage.

Bourdieu, P. (2002). *Counterfire: Against the tyranny of the market*. Verso.

Byrne, J. (Ed.). (2012). *The occupy handbook*. Back Bay Books.

Cabral, A. (1979). *Unity and struggle: Speeches and writings of Amilcar Cabral*. Monthly Review Press.

Cabral, A. (2016). *Resistance and decolonization* (Trans., D. Wood). Rowman & Littlefield International.

Cavanaugh, J. et al. (2003). *Alternatives to economic globalization, a better world is possible*. Berrett-Koehler Publishers.

Christenson, J. (2011, May 7). Teaching Argentina: WSU teachers played major role in 1800s. *Winona Daily News*, https://www.winonadailynews.com/news/local/teaching-argentina-wsu-teachers-played-major-role-in-1800s/article_eabda930-7864-11e0-ac7f-001cc4c03286.html

Clifton, J. (2011). *The coming jobs war*. Gallup Press.

Darling-Hammond, L. (1993). Introduction. In *Review of research in education*. American Educational Research Association 19.

de Sousa Santos, B. (1995). *Toward a new common sense: Law, science and politics in the paradigmatic transition*. Routledge.

de Souza Santos, B. (2018). *The end of the cognitive empire*. Duke University Press.

de Mello, G. (1990). *Social Democracia e Educação: Teses para Discussão*. Cortez-Autores.

Dimitriadis, G., & Carlson, D. (2003). Introduction. In G. Dimitriadis & D. Carlson (Eds.), *Promises to keep: Cultural studies, democratic education, and public life*. Routledge Falmer.

Edsall, T. B. (2012). *The age of austerity: How scarcity will remake American politics*. Double Day, Random House.

Fanon, F. (1961). *The wretched of the earth*. Penguin.

Financial Times, January 25–26, 2003, 3. *Financial Times*, January 25–26, 2003, 3.

Fishburn, E. (1979). The concept of "civilization and barbarism" in Sarmiento's "Facundo": A reappraisal. *Ibero-amerikanisches Archiv, 5*(4), 301–308.

Foucault, M. (1998). *Essential works of Foucault 1954–1984: Aesthetics, method, and epistemology* (Vol. 2). New Press.

Francisco, P. (2015). *Carta Encíclica Laudato Si' Del Santo Padre Francisco Sobre El Cuidado De La Casa Común*. Vervo Divino.

Freire, P. (1970). *Pedagogy of the oppressed*. Translated by M. Bergman Ramos. Continuum.
Freire, P. (1998). *Politics and education*. Translated by P. Wong. UCLA Latin American Center Publications.
Freire, P. (2000). *Pedagogy of freedom: Ethics, democracy and civic courage*. Rowman & Littlefield.
Freire, P. (2005). *Pedagogy of the oppressed*. Continuum International Publishing.
Fukuyama, F. (2012, January/February). The future of history: Can liberal democracy survive the decline of the middle class? *Foreign Affairs, 91*(1).
Gerstenzang, J. (2003, January 12). That retro feel to Bush's style: It's Reaganesque. *Los Angeles Times*, A18.
Gibson, D., & Perot, C. (2011, March/April). *It's the inequality, stupid: Eleven charts that explain what's wrong with America*. Mother Jones. http://www.motherjones.com/politics/2011/02/income-inequality-in-america-chart-graph.
Ginsburg, M. (1995). A personal introduction to the politics of educators' work and lives. In M. Ginsburg (Ed.), *The politics of educators' work and lives* (pp. xxv–xxxviii). Garland.
Green, E. (2016, May 12). What are the most-cited publications in the social sciences (according to Google Scholar)? *LSE Blogs*. https://blogs.lse.ac.uk/impactofsocialsciences/2016/05/12/what-are-the-most-cited-publications-in-the-social-sciences-according-to-google-scholar/
Gregorian, V. (2010). *Education in an era of specialized knowledge*. In M. M. Suárez-Orozco & C. Sattin-Bajaj (Eds.), *Educating the whole child for the whole world: The Ross School model and education for the global era* (pp. 27–41). New York University Press.
Group says bending on rights risky. (2003, January 15). *Los Angeles Times/Associated Press*, A20.
Harriss, J. (2002). *Depoliticizing development: The World Bank and social capital*. Anthem-Wimbledom.
Illich, I. (1969). *Celebration of awareness: A call for institutional revolution*. Introduction by Erich Fromm. Doubleday.
Illich, I. (1998, March 14). The cultivation of conspiracy. Translated, edited, and expanded version of an address given by Ivan Illich at the Villa Inchon, in Bremen, Germany, on the occasion of receiving the Culture and Peace Prize of Bremen, p. 3, available at www.paulofreireinstitute.com
Isin, E. F., & Nielsen, G. M. (Eds.). (2008). *Acts of citizenship*. Zed Books.
"Global democracy has a very bad year." (2021, February 2). *The Economist*. https://www.economist.com/graphic-detail/2021/02/02/global-democracy-has-a-very-bad-year
Kellner, K. (2003). *From 9/11 to terror war: The dangers of the Bush legacy*. Rowman & Littlefield.
Krugman, P. (2012, May 3). Plutocracy, paralysis, perplexity. *New York Times*.
Levin, H. (2011). Economics of education. *Albany Law Review, 4*(2), 395–426.
Levin-Waidman, O. M. (2011). *Wage, policy, income distribution, and democratic theory*. Routledge.
Mann T., & Ornstein, N. (2012, April 27). Let's just say it: The Republicans are the problem. *Washington Post*.
Meeting in Cuba (2012). Riaipe, Working Papers, Habana, Cuba, Xerox.
Memmi, A. (1965). *The colonizer and the colonized*. Beacon Press.
Misiaszek, G. W., Jones, L. I., & Torres, C. A. (2011). *Selling out academia? Higher education, economic crises and Freire's generative themes*. In B. Pusser et al. (Eds.), *The University and the public sphere: Knowledge creation and state building in the era of globalization*. Routledge.

Morrow, R., & Torres, C. A. (1995). *Social theory and education: A critique of theories of social and cultural reproduction*. State University of New York Press.

Morrow, R., & Torres, C. A. (2002). *Reading Freire and Habermas: Critical pedagogy and transformative social change*. Teachers College Press.

National Center for Educational Statistics (NCES). (2010). U.S. Department of Education, *Digest of Education Statistics*: 2009. U.S. Government Printing Office.

Noyoo, N. (2014, January 22). Revisiting Cabral's "weapon of theory." *Pambazuka News*. https://www.pambazuka.org/governance/revisiting-cabral%E2%80%99s-weapon-theory.

O'Cadiz, P., Wong, P. L., & Torres, C. A. (1998). *Education and democracy: Paulo Freire, educational reform and social movements in São Paulo*. Westview.

Pellauer, D. (2020). Paul Ricoeur. *Stanford Encyclopedia of Philosophy*. https://plato.stanford.edu/entries/ricoeur/

Pettinger, T. (2021). Criticisms of IMF. *Economics Help*. https://www.economicshelp.org/blog/glossary/imf-criticism/

Piglia, R. (1980). Notes on Facundo. In B. Sarlos, *La literature de America Latina Unidad y conflict*. http://www.bazaramericano.com/media/punto/coleccion/revistasPDF/08.pdf

Piketty, T. (2014). *Capital in the twenty-first century* (Trans., A. Goldhammer). Belknap Press of Harvard University Press.

Piketty, T. (2020). *Capital and ideology* (Trans., A. Goldhammer). Belknap Press of Harvard University Press.

Pintor, R. L., Gratschew, M., & Adimi, J. (2002). *Voter turnout since 1945: A global report*. International IDEA.

Pintor, R. L., Gratschew, M., & Bittiger, T. (2004). *Voter turnout in Western Europe since 1945: A regional report*. International IDEA.

Ramana, M. V., & Nayyar, A. H. (2001). India, Pakistan and the bomb: The Indian subcontinent Is the most likely place in the world for a nuclear war. *Scientific American*, 72–83.

Rhoads, R., & Torres, C. A. (Eds.). (2006a). *The political economy of higher education in America*. Stanford University Press.

Rhoads, R., & Torres, C. A. (Eds.). (2006b). *The university, state, and market: The political economy of globalization in the Americas*. Stanford University Press.

Rutten, T. (2003, January 15). Nobel laureate's memoir is a success in any language. *Los Angeles Times*, 1, 16.

Safranski, R. (2004). *Cuanta Globalizacion Podemos Soportar?* Tusquets.

Salgado, S. (1997). *Terra: Struggle of the landless*. Phaidon.

Sarlos, B. (1980). *La literature de America Latina Unidad y conflict*. http://www.bazaramericano.com/media/punto/coleccion/revistasPDF/08.pdf

Sarmiento, D. F. (1845). *Civilizacion I Barbarie. Vida de Juan Facundo Quiroga*. Imprenta del Progreso.

Sarmiento, D. F. (1849). *De la educación popular*. Imprenta del Progreso.

Saviani, D. (1982). *Escola e democracia*. Cortez-Autores.

Sen, A. (1990). Development as capability expansion. In J. DeFilippis & S. Saegert (Eds), *The community development reader* (pp. 41–58). Routledge.

Sidhu, R. (n.d.). Selling futures to foreign students: Global education markets. Unpublished manuscript, University of Queensland, Australia.

"Steve Biko." (2020). *Britannica*. https://www.britannica.com/biography/Steve-Biko

Suárez-Orozco, M. M., & Sattin-Bajaj, C. (Eds.). (2010). *Educating the whole child for the whole world: The Ross School model and education for the global era*. New York University Press.

Teodoro, A. (2012). Challenges EU education systems for the 21st century. Manuscript, Universidade Lusófona de Humanidades e Tecnologías. Lisbon, Portugal.

Torres, C. A. (1994). The state, privatization and educational policy: A critique of neoliberalism in Latin America and some ethical and political implications. *Comparative Education, 38*(4), 365–385.

Torres, C. A. (1995). Fictional dialogues on teachers, politics, and power in Latin America. M. Ginsburg (Ed.), *The politics of educators' work and lives* (pp. 133–168). Garland.

Torres, C. A. (1998). *Education, power, and personal biography: Dialogues with critical educators*. Routledge.

Torres, C. A. (2002). Requiem for liberalism? Editorial. *Comparative Education Review, 46*(4).

Torres, C. A. (2003). Education, power and the state: Successes and failures of Latin American education in the twentieth century. In C. A. Torres & A. Antikainen, *The international handbook on the sociology of education: An international assessment of new research and theory* (pp. 256–284). Rowman & Littlefield.

Torres, C. A. (2009). *Education and neoliberal globalization*. Routledge.

Torres, C. A. (2010). Neoliberal globalization and human rights: Crises and opportunities. In V. Masseman, S. Majhanovich, N. Truong, & K. Janigan et al. (Eds.), *A tribute to David N. Wilson: Clamouring for a better world* (pp. 239–246). Sense Publishers.

Torres, C. A. (2011). Public universities and the neoliberal common sense: Seven iconoclastic theses. *International Studies in Sociology of Education, 21*(3), 177–197.

Torres, C. A. (2018, November). The state of the art in comparative education and WCCES at a crossroads in the 21st century. *Revista Lusófona de Educação, 41*(1), 107–124.

Tully, J. (2000). Struggles over recognition and distribution. *Constellations, 7*(4), 469–482.

Turlington, B., Collins, N., & Porcelli, M. (2002). *Where credit is due: Approaches to course and credit recognition across borders in U.S. higher education institutions*. American Council on Education.

Wallerstein, I. (1998). *Utopistics: Or historical choices of the twenty-first century*. New Press.

Wallerstein, I. (2005). After developmentalism and globalization, what? *Social Forces, 83*(3), 1263–1278.

van Heertum, R., & Torres, C. A. (2009a). Education and domination: Reforming policy and practice through critical theory. In G. Sykes, B. Schneider, & D. Plank (Eds.), *Handbook on education policy and research, American Educational Research Association and Routledge* (pp. 221–239). Routledge.

van Heertum, R., & Torres, C. A. (2009b). Globalization and neoliberalism: The challenges and possibilities of radical pedagogy. In M. Simons, M. Olsen, & M. Peters (Eds.), *Re-reading education policies: Studying the policy agenda of the 21st century* (pp. 143–163). Sense Publishers.

van Heertum, R., & Torres, C. A. (2011). Educational reform in the U.S. over the last 25 years: Great expectations and the fading American dream. In L. Olmos, R. Van Heertum, & C. A. Torres (Eds.), In *In the shadows of neoliberalism: Educational reform in the last 25 years in comparative perspective*. Bentham E-Books.

Zhao, Y. (2020). Two decades of havoc: A synthesis of criticism against PISA. *Journal of Educational Change, 21*(2), 245–266.

Index

Pages in italics indicate figures and tables.

Abhiyan, Samagra Shiksa, 198
Abu-Lughod, Lila, 382
Abzug, Bella, 215–16
Academic Ranking of World Universities (ARWU), 397
access
  in Africa, 300–305, *301, 302, 304,* 312–13, 314, 334
  in Asia-Pacific region, 401–4
  in developing countries, 165
  equality of, 171, 173–74
  feminism and, 191
  to higher education, 276, 290, 402–3
  of indigenous peoples in Latin America, 351–53
  for refugees in EU, 388–90
  in Syria, 382–84
  for women, 195–96, 202, 204
Accord on Indigenous Peoples' Identity and Rights, 352
accreditation, for higher education, 405, 406, 409–12, 414
acculturation, definition of, 127
accumulation, in Africa, 330–32
achievement
  in Asia-Pacific region, 398
  curriculum for, 542
  development and, 177–79
  in Latin America, 365
  responsibility for, 170
  socialism and, 481–83
  socioeconomic status and, 7
ActionAid, 323
Adams, Don, 166
ADEA (Association for the Development of Education in Africa), 37, 41, 323
ADHR (Arab Human Development Report), 382
Adichie, Chimamanda Ngosi, 154–55
Adorno, Theodor, 99, 501
adult education
  curriculum issues with, 251–55
  definition of, 248
  economic reconstruction through, 559
  in Grenada, 251–55, 262–66
  modern technology for, 265
  NGOs and, 264–65

  social mobility and, 249–50
  structural issues with, 251–55
  as system-maintaining, 249
  for women, 204–6
ADVANCE, US, 203
Afghanistan, 529
Africa. *See also* conflict-ridden regions of the Middle East; *specific countries*
  access in, 300–305, *301, 302, 304,* 312–13, 314, 334
  accumulation in, 330–32
  assessments of educational programs in, 329–30, 338n24
  authoritarianism in, 331
  categorization of, 336n3
  colonialism in, 334, 335
  conflict and education in, 318–20
  contested policies in, 313–25
  COVID-19 in, 319
  data problems in, 300–301, 337n5
  decolonization in, 298–99
  development in, 326–28
  Ebola epidemic in, 319, 320
  education as production in, 333–36
  education as social transformation in, 333–36
  education spending in, 306–8, *307*
  emergencies and education in, 318–20
  enrollment in, *301,* 301–5, *302, 304,* 314
  equality in, 313–18, *318,* 337n16
  equity in, 313–18, 337n16
  experimentation in, 305–6
  female enrollment in, *195*
  foreign aid in, 42–43, 299, 308–11, *309,* 335
  Forum of African Women Educationalists in, 199, 206
  global goals and, 328–30
  higher education in, 302
  initiatives in, 313–25
  innovation in, 305–6
  Learning for All in, 311–13
  legitimacy in, 330–32
  literacy in, 301, *302,* 315–16, *316*
  NGOs in, 322–23
  pessimism about, 303–4
  planned dependence in, 309–11
  policy and agenda-setting in, 323–25
  postcolonialism in, 313

primary enrollment in, *301,* 301–3, *302, 304,* 314
privatization in, 214, 320–22, *321*
promise of education in, 297–98
research in, 51–52
secondary enrollment in, 301, *301, 302,* 303, 304, 314
segregation in, 313–14
social mobility in, 333
state and education in, 330–34
structural adjustment in, 307–8
women in, *315,* 315–17
African Association of Political Science, 306
African Economic Research Consortium, 37, 306
African Virtual University, 37, 306
Aga Khan Foundation, Pakistan, 38, 183
agency
  feminism and, 192
  poststructuralism and, 512
Agency for Rural Transformation, Grenada, 262
ALBA (Alianza Bolivariana de los Pueblos de América, Bolivarian Alliance of the Peoples of America), 3, 358–59
Albania, 478–79, 488
Albert, Michael, 81
Alger, Chadwick, 11
Alianza Bolivariana de los Pueblos de América (ALBA), 3, 358–59
ALICE project, 364
Almond, Gabriel, 559–60
Alperovitz, Gar, 81
Altbach, Philip, 5, 8, 30–31, 132, 409, 508
Althusser, Louis, 98, 191
Amin, Samir, 31, 60
Anae, Melani, 445
analytical Marxism, 96
anarchism, social movements and, 113–14
Anderson-Levitt, Kathryn, 139
Angola, 531
anthropological theory, comparative education and, 125–26
Anthropologies of Education (Anderson-Levitt), 139
anthropology, functionalism and, 134–36
Anthropology and Education Quarterly (journal), 139, 153
anti-hegemonic globalization, 545–47
antisexist textbook approach, 199
Antunes, Fátima, 460
Anyon, Jean, 96, 110
Aotearoa New Zealand, 226, 415, 437–38, 443–45
APEC (Asian Pacific Economic Cooperation), 400
Apple, Michael, 96, 533, 545–46
Arab Human Development Report (ADHR), 382
Arab Spring, 377, 380, 385
Archer, Margaret, 106
Argentina, 350
  Catholic Church in, 200
  decentralization in, 357
  enrollment patterns in, 348
  female enrollment in, 194
  neoliberalism in, 529
  PRIOM in, 200
  privatization in, 355
Arnove, Robert, 20, 32–33, 360, 508
ARWU (Academic Ranking of World Universities), 397
ASAIHL (Association of Southeast Asian Institutions of Higher Learning), 419
ASEAN (Association of Southeast Asian Nations), 398, 419–21
Asian Development Bank, 420, 484
Asian Pacific Economic Cooperation (APEC), 400
Asian Pacific Quality Network, 404–5
Asian University Network (AUN), 420
Asia-Pacific region. *See also specific countries*
  access and equity in, 401–4
  aging population in, 397, 401
  corruption in, 424, *424*
  COVID-19 and, 396, 398–99
  decentralization in, 405
  diversity of, 395, 402
  educational achievement in, 398
  employment challenges in, 400
  foreign aid and, 395–96
  higher education in, 397–98, 402–3, 414–15
  higher education in, regionalism and, 417–23
  inequality in, 398
  knowledge society in, 400, 423
  middle class in, 398
  migration and, 414–17
  nationalism in, 417–18
  neoliberalism in, 403, 404, 418
  population growth in, 416, *416*
  quality assurance in, 400, 404–14
  regionalism and higher education in, 417–23
  religion in, 423
  social mobility and, 414–17
  SSCI syndrome in, 405
Assaad, R., 384–85
Assié-Lumumba, N'Dri Thérèse, 5, 11
Association for the Development of Education in Africa (ADEA), 37, 41, 323
Association of Southeast Asian Institutions of Higher Learning (ASAIHL), 419
Association of Southeast Asian Nations (ASEAN), 398, 419–21
Athena SWAN, UK, 203
ATLAS.ti software, 141
AUN (Asian University Network), 420
austerity measures, 11–12, 214
Australia
  centralization/decentralization in, *228,* 234
  colonialism in, 150–51
  identity in, 153–54
  international students in, 398–99, 415
  LBOTE students in, 155–56
Austria, *228*
authentic communication, 152–53
authoritarianism
  in Africa, 331
  in Eastern/Central Europe, 474, 492
  globalization and, 551–52

US and threats of, 560
autoethnography, 141
autonomy
  Bologna process decreasing, 461–62
  decentralization and, 412–13
  development and, 208
  Global South national education and, 539
  Latin America, development and, 368–69
  multilateral organizations and, 552
  QA and, 409–11
  in Russian Empire, 477–78
Ávalos, B., 355
Azerbaijan, 226, 488

Bachelet, Michelle, 355, 356
Baker, David, 7
Bangladesh, 531
  BRAC in, 60, 201–2, 265
  female education stipends in, 197
  nonformal education in, 201–2
  Nonformal Primary Education in, 183
  population growth in, *416*
  primary school enrollment in, 173
banking model of education, 50, 312
Bartlett, Lesley, 16, 139
Bashir, B., 152
Basset, César August, 4
Baudelaire, Charles, 533
Baudrillard, Jean, 520n9
Bauman, Zygmunt, 96
Baytiyeh, H., 385–86
Beck, Ulrich, 87, 96–97, 117, 457
Beckford, George, 267
Begley, Louis, 514
Belafonte, Harry, 256
Belarus, 488
Bellei, C., 355
Bellino, M. J., 352
Benhabib, Seyla, 153, 156
Bereday, George, 500
Berman, E. H., 32–33
Bernstein, Basil, 130, 137, 536–37
Betto, Frei, 530
Bevacqua, M. L., 436, 438
Bhabha, Homi, 151–52, 512, 514
Biden, Joe, 549, 560
Biko, Steve, 556
bilingual education, social movements and, 104
bin Laden, Osama, 529
Bishop, Maurice, 244
Biza, Najah El, 156
Black Lives Matter movement, 149
Blaug, Mark, 63n18
Böhm, Franz, 469n4
Boli, J., 32
Bolivarian Alliance of the Peoples of America (ALBA), 3, 358–59
Bolivia, 347, 351, 358, 368
Bologna, University of, 282, 284, 289
Bologna process, 461–62, 491–92
La Bolsa program, Brazil, 362
Bolshevik Revolution, 31–32, 479
Bolsonaro, Jairo, 351, 367
borrowing, of educational practices, 8–10

Botswana, 194, 305
Bouazizi, Mohamed, 380
Bourdieu, Pierre, 96, 97, 99, 536–37
Bowles, Samuel, 32, 98
BRAC, Bangladesh, 60, 201–2, 265
Bradshaw, York, 17
Braithwaite, Chris, 520n9
Bray, Mark, 5, 16, 181
Brazil, 74, 196, 203, 344, 347, 350
  La Bolsa program in, 362
  Cajamar Institute in, 264
  Citizen School movement in, 80
  enrollment patterns in, 349
  indigenous peoples in, 351
  Landless Workers Movement in, 80, 112, 264, 359–60, 530, 553
  popular education in, 110–11
  UNILAB in, 363
Brembeck, Cole, 12
Brexit, 285–86
Brissett, N. O. M., 141
Brookfield, Stephen, 94–95
Bulgaria, 478
Bull, B. L., 360
Burawoy, M., 475
Burde, D., 19
Burkina Faso, 179
Burns, James, 99
Bush, George W., 528–29, 531–32

Cabral, Amilar, 113, 555
CAFTA (Central American Free Trade Area), 369
Cajamar Institute, Brazil, 264
Cambodia, 414
Cameroon, 179
Canada, 532
  decentralization in, 225
  dropout rates in, 175
  Robarts Plan in, 164
  university buffer funding bodies in, *233*
Canadian International Development Agency (CIDA), 3, 37
Canadian Journal of Education, 140
Canales, A., 351–52
Capacity Building Foundation, 37
capital, human, 39, 47–48, 72–73, 76–78, 80, 164
Capital and Ideology (Piketty), 557
Capital in the Twenty-First Century (Piketty), 557
capitalism, 34–35
  Keynes on, 81
  social movements and, 93, 97
  welfare state, 101
Cardoso, F. H., 345–46
Carew, Jan, 256
Caribbean Vocational Qualification, 253
Carlson, Dennis, 535–36
Carnegie Corporation, 38
Carnoy, Martin, 6, 80, 106, 346, 365
Carter, Jimmy, 528
Carter, Martin, 256
case studies. *See also specific case studies*

limitations of, 18
as most common research approach, 16
vertical, 16
Castañeda, Jorge G., 528
Castells, Manual, 116
Catholic Church
  in Argentina, 200
  in Eastern/Central Europe, 476
  feminism and, 200–201, 212
  in Mexico, 200, 350–51
  in Poland, 482
Cayuela, J. W., 355
Celebration of Awareness (Illich), 527, 537
Center for Popular Education (CPE), Grenada, 251–54, 256, 258, 260, 266, 267n3
center-periphery theory, 132–33
Central African Republic, 310
Central American Free Trade Area (CAFTA), 369
Central American University (UCA), 365
Central Europe. *See* Eastern/Central Europe
centralization
  administrative reform and, 236–37
  culture and, 224
  deconcentration and, 223
  definition of, 222–23
  delegation and, 223
  devolution and, 223
  for efficiency, 224, 234–35
  functional, 222
  government structure and, 225–26
  higher education and, 231–32, *233*
  inequality and, 235–36, *236*
  measurements of, 226–28, *228*
  models of, 225–26
  motives for, 223–25, 237–38
  school-leaving qualifications and, 228–30, *229*
  territorial, 223
  textbooks and, 230–31
charter schools, 115. *See also* privatization
Chavez, Hugo, 528, 530
cheerful eclecticism, 101
Chicago School, 92
Chile, 74, 107, 344, 347
  decentralization in, 357
  enrollment patterns in, 348–49
  MECE Rural Program in, 183
  privatization in, 354–56, 366
  student movements in, 114
China
  aging population in, 397, 401
  centralization in, 225–26, 230
  decentralization in, 230
  economic growth of, 396, 401, 530
  globalization and, 509–10
  higher education in, 283, 402–3
  Hong Kong and, 226–27, 413
  inequality in, 398
  Internet use growth and, 14
  Macao and, 230–31
  middle class in, 398
  National Security Law in, 413
  philosophy in, 504, 515–16
  population growth in, 416, *416*
  quality assurance in, 406–8
  textbooks in, 230–31
  US relations with, 398–99, 511
China Academic Degrees and Graduate Education Development Center, 407
CIDA (Canadian International Development Agency), 3, 37
CIE. *See* comparative and international education
CIES (Comparative and International Education Society), 6, 19, 140–41
Citizen School movement, Brazil, 80
citizenship
  globalization and crisis of, 550–54
  planetarian multicultural, 547
civil society
  decentralization and, 357, 358
  NGOs and, 351
  popular education and, 255, 360–62
  social movements in, 90
  state collaboration with, 360–62
  women and, 209, 351
civil society organizations (CSOs), 112
Clark, B. R., 282
class
  in Asia-Pacific region, 398
  differentiation by, 169
  gender and, 189–90
  literacy and, 249
  pedagogy and, 130
  social movements and, 96, 99
  status, power and, 98–99
Class, Codes and Control (Bernstein), 537
Clifton, Jim, 542
climate change
  EU and, 466
  Oceania and, 446–47
  student movements against, 107, 149
Clinton, Bill, 532
CM (Community Method), 460
Coard, Bernard, 261
CODESRIA (Council for the Development of Economic and Social Research in Africa), 60, 306
Cogan, John J., 9
Cohen, Jean, 93
Cohen, Yehudi, 127
Colclough, Christopher, 192, 214–15
collective agency, feminism and, 192
collective/collaborative ethnography, 141
collective learning, social movements and, 103
colleges. *See* higher education
Collins, Randall, 106
Colombia, 350
  decentralization in, 224, 357
  enrollment patterns in, 348
  Escuela Nueva in, 60, 183, 360–61
  female enrollment in, 194
  literacy rates in, 178–79
  privatization in, 355
colonialism. *See also* postcolonialism
  in Africa, 334, 335
  in Australia, 150–51

center-periphery theory and, 132–33
CRME and, 381
culture and, 131–34
fixity and, 152
intercultural interaction and, 150–53
internal, 132
mental, 134
in Oceania, 438–39
colonial rule, education and influence of, 31
colonial schools, 132
Comenius, John Amos, 129
commissioned research, 57–59
Committee on the Elimination of Racial Discrimination, 352
communication
authentic, 152–53
distorted, 148–49
globalization and, 2–3
miscommunication, 148
in postcolonialism, 152
successful, 148
communicative action theory, 89, 100, 103, 152
Community Method (CM), 460
Community Schools Program, Egypt, 183
A Companion to Anthropology and Education (Levinson and Pollock), 140
comparative and international education (CIE)
globalization under attack by nationalism and, 551–52
introspection for, 554–57
in Oceania, 434, 438, 441–47
Comparative and International Education Society (CIES), 6, 19, 140–41
comparative education
anthropological theory and, 125–26
challenges of, 538
changing nature of, 19–21
COVID-19 and, 1–2, 6
culture and, 141–42
current trends in, 14–19
dimensions of, 5–13
eclecticism and, 15–16
evolution of, 4–5
future of, 14–19, 539–40
global dimension of, 10–13
historical stages of, 539–40
identity and, 147–50, 153–59, 550–51
new concepts and challenges in, 557–59
for new millennium, 515–20
politics and, 534–35
postmodernism and, 535–36
pragmatic dimension of, 8–10
scientific dimension of, 5–10
theoretical debts of, 533–38
complexity theory, 17–18
Compton, Mary, 369
computer data sets, for research, 141
Comte, Auguste, 501–2
"conditioned" states, in Latin America, 346–54
conferences, international, 45
conflict-ridden regions of the Middle East (CRME), 377
access to education in Syria, 382–84
colonialism and, 381

education access in EU for refugees from, 388–90
foreign aid and, 379
global factors in, 381–82
globalization and, 378–79
Israel/Palestine right to education, 386–88
local factors in, 380–81
quality of education in, 384–86
women in, 382, 390–91
youth in, 390–91
conflict theories, educational reform and, 97–98
Confucius, 504, 516–17
Congo. *See* Democratic Republic of Congo
Connell, Raewyn, 150, 191
conscientization, 384
conservatism
high education and, 105–6
neoclassical economics and, 71–72
consulting, research as, 57–58
contemporary educational reform, 31–32
control, higher education for, 282–84
Coombs, Philip H., 165
Córdoba Reform, 285
Corruption Perceptions Index (CPI), 424, *424*
Cortina, Regina, 111–12
cosmopolitanization, 116, 117
Costa Rica, 44
Côte d'Ivoire, 179
Council for the Development of Economic and Social Research in Africa (CODESRIA), 60, 306
Council of Europe, 456
Count, George, 167
COVID-19
in Africa, 319
Asia-Pacific region and, 396, 398–99
austerity measures and, 214
comparative education and, 1–2, 6
disruption of, 149, 318–19
in EU, 464, 466
inequality and, 35, 159, 559
international students and, 398–99, 415
international trade reduced by, 511
in Latin America, 345, 357, 362, 367
online instruction in higher education and, 274
opportunities of, 116
social movements and, 116–18
vaccines for, 13
Cowen, Robert, 17
CPE (Center for Popular Education), Grenada, 251–54, 256, 258, 260, 266, 267n3
CPI (Corruption Perceptions Index), 424, *424*
cram-schools, 287
credentialism, higher education and, 404
critical ethnography, 138
critical hermeneutics, 517–18
critical inquiry, methodological orthodoxy and, 58–59
critical literacy, 113, 155
critical pedagogy. *See also* pedagogy
literacy and, 108
social movements and, 109–10
critical race theory, 140

critical theory
  feminism and, 190
  hermeneutics and, 516–18
  positivism compared to, 516
  social movements and, 94–95, 99–103
CRME. *See* conflict-ridden regions of the Middle East
Croatia, 485, 488
Crocombe, R. G., 436
Crossley, Michael, 10
cross-national studies, 6–7, 16–17
CSOs (civil society organizations), 112
Cuba, 254, 345–46, 350, 358, 370n2
cultural class theory, 140
cultural hybridity, globalization of, 550
cultural reproduction, Marxism and, 97–99
cultural values, 128–29
culture, 125
  centralization/decentralization and, 224
  colonialism and, 131–34
  comparative education and, 141–42
  concept of, 126–28
  definition of, 126
  educational philosophy and, 129–31
  evolutionism and, 131–34
  identity and, 159
  of indigenous peoples, 505
  of positivism, 136
  school ethnography and, 136–41
  values of, 128–29
  Western, dominance of, 504
curriculum
  for achievement, 542
  in adult education, 251–55
  in higher education, 285
  labor market linked to, 327
  in Oceania, 440
Czechoslovakia, 478–79, 482
Czech Republic, 228, 488

DAC (Development Assistance Committee), 309
DAE (Donors to African Education), 37, 41
Dakar conference, 45, 52, 173, 175, 210
Dale, Roger, 459, 463
Dare the School Build a New Social Order? (Count), 167
Darwin, Charles, 131
Davis, Angela, 256
debt relief, 43
decentralization
  administrative reform and, 236–37
  in Asia-Pacific region, 405
  autonomy and, 412–13
  civil society and, 357, 358
  culture and, 224
  deconcentration and, 223
  definition of, 222–23
  delegation and, 223
  devolution and, 223
  in Eastern/Central Europe, 484–87
  for efficiency, 224, 234–35
  functional, 222
  government structure and, 225–26
  higher education and, 231–32, 233
  inequality and, 235–36, *236*
  in Kazakhstan, 485–86
  language and, 225
  in Latin America, 236–37, 344, 357–58
  measurements of, 226–28, *228*
  models of, 225–26
  motives for, 223–25, 237–38
  in Romania, 484, 486
  school-leaving qualifications and, 228–30, *229*
  territorial, 223
  textbooks and, 230–31
  in Yugoslavia, 480–81
decision-making, research and, 53–54
decolonization. *See also* postcolonialism
  in Africa, 298–99
  social movements and, 110–12
deconcentration
  control and, 227, 237
  definition of, 223
delegation, definition of, 223
delivery system, education as, 50
democracy
  defense of state in, 546–47
  deliberative, 118, 152
  erosion of, 93, 103
  for freedom, 546
  globalization and crisis of, 550–54
  inequality and, 544
  market, end of, 541–45
  voter turnout and, 548–49
Democratic Republic of Congo, 226, 319
Denmark, 228
Depelchin, Jacques, 33
dependence
  on foreign aid, 42–45, 61
  planned, in Africa, 309–11
dependency theory, 508
Derrida, Jacques, 457
Descartes, René, 516, 520n20
development
  achievement and, 177–79
  in Africa, 326–28
  autonomy and, 208
  education and, progress in, 60–62
  foreign aid and, 33–34
  frameworks, difficulty of, 50–51
  GDP as metric of, 55
  Latin America, autonomy and, 368–69
  neoliberalism and, 35
  social movements and, 134
  social stratification and, 177
Development Assistance Committee (DAC), 309
devolution, definition of, 223
Devonish, H., 267
Dewey, John, 129, 477
Diffusion of Innovations (Rogers), 555
digital literacy, in EU, 466
Dilthey, Wilhelm, 501, 517
Dimitriadis, Greg, 535–36
distorted communication, 148–49
District Primary Education Program (DPEP), India, 197–98
division of labor, 130, 197–98, 335

Dobreau, Robin, 256
Dominican Republic, 348
Donors to African Education (DAE), 37, 41
DPEP (District Primary Education Program), India, 197–98
dropout rates, 175
Du Bois, W. E. B., 105
Durie, Mason, 444
Durkheim, Emile, 99, 130, 501–3

Eastern/Central Europe. *See also specific countries*
  armed conflict in, 474
  authoritarianism in, 474, 492
  Bologna process and, 491–92
  Catholic Church in, 476
  corruption in, 492
  decentralization in, 484–87
  in EU, 474
  higher education in, 489–92
  historical background of, 476–83
  marketization in, 490
  postsocialism in, 474–75, 483–92, 494
  private tutoring in, 488–89, 493–94
  privatization in, 487–89
  socialism in, 474, 478–83
  Soviet Union and, 478–83
  teachers in, 489
  transformation period of, 474–75, 483–84, 493
Ebola epidemic, 319, 320
Eckstein, Harold, 500, 505–6
eclecticism, comparative education and, 15–16
economic redistribution, social movements and, 100
economics. *See also* neoclassical economics; socioeconomic status
  adult education and reconstruction of, 559
  free markets for economic growth and development in, 73–74
  free markets for efficiency and organization of, myth of, 74–75
  human agency and, 80
  inequality and, 80, 541–42
  political economy and, 72
  regional, globalization and, 2–3
  as social science, 56–57
Ecuador, 344, 347, 348, 351, 358–59, 368
Eddo-Lodge, R., 149
Eder, Klaus, 103
"educated person," in Sri Lanka, 158–59
educated unemployment, 326
Education and Training 2010 program, 459, 463
education finance, 77–78
Education for All (EFA), 29, 43–44, 61, 62n6, 78, 207, 303–4, 308, 328–30
Education for Self-Reliance (Nyerere), 305
Education International, 323
EFA (Education for All), 29, 43–44, 61, 62n6, 78, 207, 303–4, 308, 328–30
efficiency
  centralization/decentralization for, 224, 234–35

  educational production and, 48–49
  free markets for economic organization and, myth of, 74–75
  internal/external, 49
Egypt
  Arab Spring and, 377, 380, 385
  Community Schools Program in, 183
  quality of education in, 384–85
EHEA (European Higher Education Area), 286, 461, 491
Eisenhart, M., 191
Elmore, Richard F., 238
El Salvador, 344, 345, 347–50, 353
EMANCIPA project, 364
emancipation, higher education for, 284–85
empowerment
  literacy and, 248
  of women, 197, 206, 210
enculturation, definition of, 127
energy politics, US and, 528
English
  as dominant language, 14, 275, 286
  in higher education, 275, 286, 288
  language backgrounds other than, in Australia, 155–56
enlightenment, science and, 500–501
environmental social movements, 104–5, 117
epistemic literacy, 248
epistemology, definition of, 434
Equal Education, South Africa, 60
equality
  of access, 171, 173–74
  in Africa, 313–18, 318, 337n16
  in Asia-Pacific region, 398
  centralization/decentralization and, 235–36, 236
  changing meanings of educational, 168–71
  COVID-19 and, 35, 159, 559
  democracy and, 544
  economics and, 80, 541–42
  equity compared to, 170–71
  in EU, 465–66
  higher education and, 287
  identity and, 154
  in Latin America, 344–48, 362
  model of, 171–72
  opportunity and, 169–70
  of outcome, 172, 179–80
  of output, 171, 176–79
  as similarity, 170
  social mobility and, 179
  of survival, 171, 174–76
  as valuation of difference, 170
equity
  in Africa, 313–18, 337n16
  in Asia-Pacific region, 401–4
  equality compared to, 170–71
  in Latin America, 346–48
ERA (European Research Area), 286
ERASMUS program, 506
ERT (European Round Table of Industrialists), 459, 462
Escobar, Arturo, 133–34
Escuela Nueva, Colombia, 60, 183, 360–61

essentialism, 510, 520n7
Esteva, Gustavo, 81–82
Estonia, 228, 488, 490
ethics, global higher education challenges of, 287, 288
Ethiopia, 175–76, 223, 310
ethnicity, in Latin America, 351–53
ethnography, 507
  auto-, 141
  collective/collaborative, 141
  critical, 138
  school, 136–41
Ethnography and Education (journal), 139
ethnomethodology, 506–7
EU. *See* European Union
Eucken, Walter, 469n4
European Economic Community, 456
European Education Area, 464–68, 465
European Higher Education Area (EHEA), 286, 461, 491
European Research Area (ERA), 286
European Round Table of Industrialists (ERT), 459, 462
European Union (EU). *See also* Eastern/Central Europe; *specific countries*
  Bologna process in, 461–62, 491–92
  Brexit and, 285–86
  climate change and, 466
  Community Method in, 460
  COVID-19 in, 464, 466
  digital literacy in, 466
  Eastern/Central European nations in, 474
  Education and Training 2010 program and, 459, 463
  education dimension in, 458–59
  equality in, 465–66
  fabricating, through education, 462–64
  future of, 469
  gender in, 465–66
  geopolitics and, 467
  globalization and, 4, 456
  higher education in, 285–86, 466
  Lisbon Strategy in, 459–60, 463, 470n6
  nationalism in, 468
  neoliberalism and, 457
  neo-mercantilism in formation of, 457
  Open Method of Coordination in, 460–62
  political construction of, 456–57
  privatization and states joining, 488
  quality of education in, 465
  refugee education access in, 388–90
  social mobility in, 458, 467
  social movement theories in, 90–97
  teachers in, 466
  2025 targets for education and training in, 464–68, 465
Evangelicals, 212
evidence-based policy, for education improvement, myth of, 75–76
evolutionism, 131–34
expansion, educational, social movements and, 106
external efficiency, 49

extra-territoriality units, 4
Eyerman, Ron, 93–94, 96

Falefou, T., 447
family background, focus on, 6
Fanon, Frantz, 331, 520n9, 556
Farrell, Josh, 179, 180, 403
Fast Track Initiative (FTI), 43
FAWE (Forum of African Women Educationalists), 199, 206, 323
feasibility, 49
feminism, 105. *See also* women
  access and, 191
  Catholic Church and, 200–201, 212
  concept of, 190
  critical theory and, 190
  educational institutions and, 189–93
  gender identity and, 212
  higher education and, 192
  primary education and, 192
  racism and, 149
  social justice and, 211–12
Feyerabend, Paul, 501, 518
Fiji, 435, 439, 447
financial crisis of 2008
  austerity measures and, 11–12
  international trade reduced by, 511
  Latin America and, 353–54
Finland, 9
Fiske, Edward, 7
Fito'o, Billy, 439
fixity, colonialism and, 152
Foley, Douglas, 138, 139, 155
Ford Foundation, 38
foreign aid
  in Africa, 42–43, 299, 308–11, 309, 335
  Asia-Pacific region and, 395–96
  conditions of, 44–45
  critiques of, 42, 61
  CRME and, 379
  dependence on, 42–45, 61
  development and, 33–34
  expenditures covered by, 43
  influence pathways, 45–51
  organizations, 36–41
  research and, 36–37, 51–60
  resource transfer in, 61
  women's education and, 207–10
Forum of African Women Educationalists (FAWE), 199, 323
Foster, Philip, 176–77
Foucault, Michel, 97, 99, 102, 457, 520n9, 536
foundations, 38
Fox, Christine, 133
framing processes, 92–93
France, 232, 276–77, 284
Frank, Andre Gunder, 508
Frankfurt School, 99–100, 117
freedom, democracy for, 546
free markets, myths of
  for economic growth, 73–74
  for efficient economic organization, 74–75
Free Trade Area of the Americas (FTAA), 369

Freire, Paulo, 117, 267
  on banking model of education, 50, 312
  Cajamar Institute and, 264
  critical literacy and, 113
  critical theory and, 94–95
  Giroux and, 108–10
  impact of, 359, 530
  on mental colonialism, 134
  on pedagogy of oppressed, 129–30, 534–35, 555
  popular education and, 110
Freud, Sigmund, 92
Friedman, Milton, 80
Fröbel, Friedrich, 108, 129
Fromm, Eric, 537
FTAA (Free Trade Area of the Americas), 369
FTI (Fast Track Initiative), 43
functional centralization, 222
functional decentralization, 222
functionalism
  anthropology and, 134–36
  cultural reproduction and, 98
  educational reform and, 97
  modernization and, 502–4
  positivism and, 501–3
  postmodern critiques of, 513–14
  research and, 135
The Future Is Asian (Khanna), 399

Gadamer, Hans-Georg, 153, 516, 519
Galtung, Johann, 132–34
García Canclini, Néstor, 560n3
GCE. *See* global citizenship education
GDP. *See* gross domestic product
Geertz, Clifford, 126, 154
GEFI (Global Education First Initiative), UN, 378–79
Gegeo, D. W., 436–37, 441
GEM (Gender Empowerment Measure), 196
gender. *See also* women
  class and, 189–90
  differentiation by, 169, 189
  education and, studies on, 188–89
  equality of survival and, 175
  in EU, 465–66
  higher education participation by, 279
  identity, 190, 212, 256–57
  in Latin America, 349–51
  migration in Mexico and, 366
  pedagogy and, 199–200
  textbooks and neutral approach to, 199
Gender Empowerment Measure (GEM), 196
Gender Inequality Index (GII), 196
gender parity index (GPI), 194, *195*
Georgia, 226, 485
GERM (Global Educational Reform Movement), 115
Germany, 283, 389
Ghana, 44, 223, 306, 317
  Schools for Life program in, 183
Giddens, Anthony, 96, 117, 506
GII (Gender Inequality Index), 196
Gingrich, Newt, 62n3
Gini index, 347

Gintis, Herbert, 32, 98
Giroux, Henry, 108–10
Global Campaign for Education, 323
global citizenship education (GCE), 109, 116, 378
  school ethnography and, 140
global dimension, of comparative education, 10–13
global education, international education compared to, 11
Global Educational Reform Movement (GERM), 115
Global Education First Initiative (GEFI), UN, 378–79
globalization
  from above, 549
  anti-hegemonic, 545–47
  authoritarianism and, 551–52
  from below, 549
  changes in state and, 509–11
  China and, 509–10
  communication and, 2–3
  by conference, 45
  CRME and, 378–79
  of cultural hybridity, 550
  definition of, 2
  democracy/citizenship crisis and, 550–54
  educational standards and, 46, 115
  EU and, 4, 456
  extra-territoriality units and, 4
  higher education and, 285–87
  of human rights, 381, 550
  of international war against terrorism, 550
  Internet and, 532
  of media, 550
  nationalism and, 551–52
  neoliberalism and, 102, 510, 544–45, 552
  regional economies and, 2–3
  roll-back of, 511, 531
  women and, 213
Global March Against Child Labour, 323
Global Partnership for Education, 43
global risk society, 89
Global South. *See also specific countries*
  education in, 36
  higher education in, 285
  national education and autonomy in, 539
  social media in, 263
  subaltern social movements, southern theory and, 110–12
  Third World terminology compared to, 62n2
Golden Rule, of Confucius, 504, 516–17
Gómez Vera, G. G., 365–66
Gorostiaga, Xabier, 285, 365
GPI (gender parity index), 194, *195*
Gramsci, Antonio, 94–95, 96
Great Recession
  austerity measures and, 11–12
  international trade reduced by, 511
  Latin America and, 353–54
Grenada
  adult education issues in, 251–55, 262–66
  Agency for Rural Transformation in, 262
  Center for Popular Education in, 251–54, 256, 258, 260, 266, 267n3

574 ■ Index

community associations in, 257–58, 260–62
electoral processes in, 262
gender identity in, 256–57
language in, 260
Marxism in, 261–62
National In-Service Teacher Education Programme in, 244, 246, 259
National Women's Organization in, 257, 267n3
National Youth Organization in, 258, 267n3
neoliberalism and, 247
New Jewel Movement in, 246, 255, 258, 261
People's Budget in, 259, 260
popular education in, 255–56
postcolonial context of, 245–47
Productive Farmers Union in, 258
public literacy in, 257–62
revolution in, 244–45, 264
socialism in, 246
T.A. Marryshow Community College in, 252
women in, 256–57
Workers' Parish Councils in, 256
Zonal Councils in, 256
gross domestic product (GDP)
as development metric, 55
for economic growth measurement, 74
education impact on, 77
Grossman-Doerth, Hans, 469n4
Guam, 436
Guatemala, 344, 347–49, 351–53
Guatemala Literacy Project, 353
Guinea, 183
Gulbenkian Foundation, 38

Habermas, Jürgen, 148, 457, 519
communicative action theory of, 89, 100, 103, 152
on critical hermeneutics, 517–18
critical theory of, 99–103
on incomplete modernity, 117
legitimation crisis theory of, 89, 100–103
on science and enlightenment, 500–501
on welfare state capitalism, 101
Hahnel, Robin, 81
Haiti, 347
HakiElimu, Tanzania, 60
Hamann, E., 140
Hans, Nicholas, 500
Hanseatic League, 284
Hapsburg Empire, 476
Harf, James, 11
Harris, Kamala, 549, 560
Hau'ofa, Epeli, 434–36
Hayhoe, Ruth, 15, 504, 516
Heavily Indebted Poor Countries (HIPC), 43
Hechinger, Fred, 7
HEEACT (Higher Education Evaluation and Accreditation Council), 411–12
HEEC (Higher Education Evaluation Centre), 407
hermeneutics, 516–18
Heyman, Richard, 506–7
Heyneman, Stephen, 6, 12
Hickling-Hudson, Anne, 154, 251, 265

higher education
access to, 276, 290, 402–3
accreditation for, 405, 406, 409–12, 414
in Africa, 302
in Asia-Pacific region, 397–98, 402–3, 414–15
in Asia-Pacific region, regionalism and, 417–23
centralization and, 231–32, 233
contemporary debates over, 273–74
for control, 282–84
credentialism and, 404
curriculum in, 285
decentralization and, 231–32, 233
in Eastern/Central Europe, 489–92
for emancipation, 284–85
English in, 275, 286, 288
ethical challenges of global, 287, 288
in EU, 285–86, 466
expansion of, 31
female enrollment in, 193–94, 195
feminism and, 192
gender and participation in, 279
globalization and, 285–87
in Global South, 285
Human Capital Index and participation in, 280–81, 281
inequality and, 287
international policy framework for, 276–77
language and, 288
in Latin America, 356, 362–65
lifelong learning and, 288–89
neoliberalism and, 283–84, 288
online instruction and, 274
participation rates in, comparative data on, 277–81, 278, 279, 281
popular education and, 362–65
quality control for, 289–90
research and, 30–31, 290–91
roles of, 274–75, 281–87
rural and urban participation in, 279, 279
socialism and, 481–83
social rate of return of, 6–7
Socratic method in, 30
state and, 274, 281–84
UN and, 277
in US, 283, 532
women and, 202–4
Higher Education Evaluation and Accreditation Council (HEEACT), 411–12
Higher Education Evaluation Centre (HEEC), 407
HIPC (Heavily Indebted Poor Countries), 43
Hirsch, E. D., 115
Hoff, Lutz, 265
Holland, Dorothy, 139, 158, 191
Holmes, Brian, 500, 505–6
Holst, John, 95
Honduras, 194, 344, 347–49, 353
Hong Kong, 226–27, 230–31, 233
quality assurance in, 412–14
Honneth, Axel, 363
Horga, Irina, 486
Horkheimer, Max, 99, 501

human agency, economics and, 80
Human Capital Index, 280–81, *281*
human capital theory, 39, 47–48, 72–73, 76–78, 80, 164
Human Development Report, UNDP, 196, 208
humanist literacy, 249, 256–57
human rights
  globalization of, 381, 550
  US and, 528
Hungary, 348, 482, 487–88, 492
Huntington, Samuel, 509–10, 518
Husén, T., 18
Husserl, Edmund, 501
hybridity, identity and, 152

Iceland, *228*
IDEA (International Institute for Democracy and Electoral Assistance), 548
identity
  authentic communication and, 152–53
  comparative education and, 147–50, 153–59, 550–51
  culture and, 159
  fluidity of, 147–48
  gender, 190, 212, 256–57
  humanist literacy and, 256–57
  hybridity and, 152
  indigenous peoples and, 150–51
  inequality and, 154
  intercultural interaction and, 150–53
  intersectionality of, 149, 153–59
  LGBTQ+, 150, 159, 212
  in Oceania, 445
  "single stories" and, 154–55
  social justice and, 159–60
  sociocultural, 147
ideology, of World Bank, 78–79
IEA (International Evaluation of Educational Achievement), 18, 63n15, 178, 338n24
Illich, Ivan, 527, 536–38
Ilon, Lynn, 192
IMF (International Monetary Fund), 3, 34, 82n4, 207, 213, 554
Incheon conference, 41, 45, 52
incomplete modernity, 117
index of modernization, 503–4
India, 60, 203, 396
  aging population in, 397
  decentralization in, 226
  District Primary Education Program in, 197–98
  economic growth of, 401
  enrollment in, 408
  female educational attainment in, 196
  higher education access in, 402
  Mahila Samakhya program in, 204–5
  middle class in, 398
  nonformal education in, 202
  Pakistan relations with, 531
  population growth in, 416, *416*
  primary school enrollment in, 173
  quality assurance in, 408–9
  university buffer funding bodies in, *233*
indigenous peoples
  culture and philosophy of, 505
  education of, school ethnography and, 140
  identity and, 150–51
  in Latin America, 351–53
  social movements of, 111–12
  stereotypes of, 155
individual agency, feminism and, 192
Indonesia, 225–26, 263–64, 401, 416, *416*
inequality. *See* equality
influence
  conceptions and, 47–51
  constructs and frameworks of, 50–51
  education as delivery system and, 50
  education as production and, 48–50
  knowledge management and, 46–47
  pathways of, 45–51
  standards and, 46
Institute for Lifelong Learning, UNESCO, 262
institutions of education
  feminist theory and, 189–93
  as social movement target and resource, 104–6
Inter-American Development Bank, 347
intercultural, definition of, 127
intercultural interaction, 150–53
Interface (journal), 111
internal colonialism, 132
internal efficiency, 49
International Bank for Reconstruction and Development, 34
international education
  global education compared to, 11
  overview of, 10–13
  US and, 533
International Evaluation of Educational Achievement (IEA), 18, 63n15, 178, 338n24
International Institute for Democracy and Electoral Assistance (IDEA), 548
International Labor Organization, 37
International Monetary Fund (IMF), 3, 34, 82n4, 207, 213, 554
International Political Science Association, 38
international students, COVID-19 and, 398–99, 415
international war against terrorism, globalization of, 550
Internet
  China language use on, 14
  globalization and, 532
intersectionality, of identity, 149, 153–59
intervention, educational, as term, 50
investment, education as, 6, 47–48, 76–78
invisible pedagogy, 130
Iraq, 528
Ireland, *228*
Iskhakov, Radik, 478
Israel, 378
  Nation State Law in, 381, 388
  right to education in, 386–88
Italy, *228,* 348
Ivory Coast, 74

Jamaica, 194, 258
James, C. L. R., 267
Jamison, Andrew, 93–94, 96
Japan, 396
    aging population in, 397, 401
    borrowing of educational practices in history of, 8
    centralization in, 226, 228
    decentralization in, 228
    economic stagnation in, 530
    middle class in, 398
    population growth in, 416, 416
    quality assurance in, 409–11
    School Education Act in, 410
Japan International Cooperation Agency (JICA), 3
Japan University Accreditation Association (JUAA), 409–11
Jatoi, Haroona, 198
Jerven, M., 55, 300
JICA (Japan International Cooperation Agency), 3
Johansson-Fua, Seu'ula, 442
Jomtien conference, 40–41, 45, 52, 173, 210
Jones, William, 515
Jordan, 194
JUAA (Japan University Accreditation Association), 409–11
Jullien, Marc-Antoine, 4, 10

Kadar, Janos, 482
Ka'ili, T. O., 436–37
Kandel, Isaac, 10, 500
Kardashian, Kim, 519
Kazakhstan, 485–86, 488
Kelly, Donald, 139
Kelly, Gail, 20, 132, 141, 188–89, 508
Kenya, 44, 233, 321
Kerr, Clark, 418
Keynes, John Maynard, 81
Khanna, Parag, 399
Kim, Young Yun, 151
kindergarten movement, 108
Klein, Naomi, 82, 117–18, 149
Kluckhohn, Florence, 128–29
Knopf, Alfred A., 532
"Knowledge Bank," World Bank as, 79
knowledge management, 46–47
knowledge mystification, research and, 59
knowledge society, 400, 423, 541–43
Kobayashi, T., 8
Korea, 194, 228, 229, 396–98, 416
Krafft, C., 384–85
Kuhn, Thomas, 501, 516, 555
Kyoto Accords, 528
Kyrgyzstan, 488

labor
    curriculum linked to, 327
    division of, 130, 197–98, 335
Laclau, Ernest, 96
Ladd, Helen F., 7
Lamming, George, 256

Landless Workers Movement, Brazil, 80, 112, 264, 359–60, 530, 553
language backgrounds other than English (LBOTE) students, in Australia, 155–56
language(s)
    Chinese, growth of, on Internet, 14
    decentralization and, 225
    English as dominant, 14
    in Grenada, 260
    higher education and, 288
    indigenous peoples in Latin America and, 351–53
    of Oceania, 435
    refugee education access in EU and, 389
    in Soviet Union, 479
    translanguaging, 389
    translation and, 514–15
Laos, 153
large-scale research, 18
Latin America, 343. *See also specific countries*
    achievement in, 365
    "conditioned" states in, 346–54
    Córdoba Reform in, 285
    counter-hegemonic initiatives in, 358–59
    COVID-19 in, 345, 357, 362, 367
    CSOs in, 112
    debt crisis and, 353–54
    decentralization in, 236–37, 344, 357–58
    development and autonomy in, 368–69
    educational equity in, 346–48
    enrollment patterns in, 348–49
    equality in, 362
    ethnicity/race in, 351–53
    female enrollment in, 195
    gender in, 349–51
    Gini index in, 347
    higher education in, 356, 362–65
    income inequality in, 346–48, 362
    indigenous peoples in, 351–53
    inequality in, 344–48
    literacy rates in, 179
    nationalism in, 344, 369
    neoliberalism in, 344, 353–54, 363, 368, 529–30
    popular education in, 359–65
    Popular Education Network of Women in, 206, 360
    privatization in, 344, 354–57, 366
    research in, 365–67
    rural and urban enrollment patterns in, 349
    structural adjustment in, 367–68
    subaltern social movements, southern theory and, 110–12
    urban expansion in, 560n3
    women in, 349–51
Latin American Laboratory for Assessment of the Quality of Education (LLECE), 63n15
Latvia, 226, 488
Lawn, Martin, 463
LBOTE (language backgrounds other than English) students, in Australia, 155–56
learning, social movement, 112–13
Learning for All, 311–13

leaving qualifications, 228–30, *229*
Lebanon, 377, 380–81
  quality of education in, 385–86
Le Bon, Gustave, 91
legitimacy, in Africa, 330–32
legitimation crisis theory, social movements and, 89, 100–103
lending, of educational practices, 8–10
Lesotho, 194, 320
Levin, Benjamin, 180
Levin, Henry, 106, 298, 543–44
Levinson, Bradley, 139, 140, 153, 199–200
von der Leyen, Ursula, 464
LGBTQ+ identity, 150, 159, 212
liberalism. *See also* neoliberalism
  education finance and, 78
  neoclassical economics and, 72
Liberia, 319, 321
lifelong learning, higher education and, 288–89
Lilomaiava-Doktor, S., 436–37
Lipman, Pauline, 153
Lisbon Strategy, 459–60, 463, 470n6
literacy
  adult rates of, 165–66
  in Africa, 301, *302*, 315–16, *316*
  class and, 249
  critical, 113, 155
  critical pedagogy and, 108
  empowerment and, 248
  epistemic, 248
  humanist, 249, 256–57
  identity and, 256–57
  of indigenous peoples in Latin America, 351–53
  political participation and, 257–62
  of primary students, 178–79
  public, 249, 257–62
  social stratification and, 249–50, 260
  technical, 248–49
  universal, 165
Lithuania, 488, 492
Liu, Judith, 139
LLECE (Latin American Laboratory for Assessment of the Quality of Education), 63n15
The Location of Culture (Bhabha), 151–52
longitudinal data, 6–7
Longwe, S., 210
Lula Da Silva, Luiz Inácio, 351, 530
Luschei, T. F., 349
Luxembourg, 227–28, *228*

Macao, 230–31
MacArthur Foundation, 38
Macedonia, 485
Machel, Samora, 256
Macron, Emmanuel, 277
Madagascar, 179, 310
Mafeje, Archie, 134–36
Magellan, Ferdinand, 435
Magnani, J. G. C., 346
Mahila Samakhya program, India, 204–5
Māhina, Hūfanga 'Okusitino, 443
Mahoney, J., 344–45

Malawi, 178, 197, 310
Malaysia, 227, 399, 401, 416
Mali, 175, 310
Malinowski, Bronislaw, 134
Malta, 226
Mandela, Nelson, 555
Manley, Michael, 256
Mann, Horace, 554
Mann, Thomas, 541
"manpower planning," 305, 326
Marcuse, Herbert, 99, 501
marketing, 44
marketization, 358, 486, 490, 492. *See also* privatization
Marquez, Gabriel Garcia, 532
Marsh, Selina Tusitala, 448
Marshall, Alfred, 72
Marxism
  analytical, 96
  in Grenada, 261–62
  social and cultural reproduction and, 97–99
  social change in, 177
  social movements and, 93–97
  women and, 214
Masemann, Vandra, 507
mass education
  social movements and, 106
  Westernization and, 32–33
mass mobilization, social movements and, 90–91
mass psychology, 92
Mauritius, 178, 194, 321
Mbembe, Achille, 33
McCain, John, 62n3
McClelland, David, 503
McCormack, Rob, 248–49, 257
McHugh, K. E., 436
McLaren, Peter, 95
Mead, George Herbert, 91
Mead, Margaret, 127
MECE Rural Program, Chile, 183
media
  in developing countries, women in, 215
  globalization of, 550
  participatory, 391
Mehta, S., 512
Melanesia, 435
Melucci, Alberto, 97
Memmi, Albert, 556
mental colonialism, 134
methodological orthodoxy, critical inquiry and, 58–59
Mexico, 344. *See also* Latin America
  Catholic Church in, 200, 350–51
  centralization in, *228*
  decentralization in, 224, *228*, 357
  female education stipends in, 197
  gender and pedagogy in, 199–200
  indigenous peoples in, 351–52
  migration and gender in, 366
  Prospera program in, 362
  Revolution in, 114
  urban and rural enrollment in, 349
  Zapatistas in, 112

Meyer, John W., 7, 32, 106
Micronesia, 435
Middle East. *See* conflict-ridden regions of the Middle East
migration
   Asia-Pacific region and, 414–17
   gender and, in Mexico, 366
   Oceania and, 436–37
   school ethnography and, 140
Millennium Development Goals, UN, 45, 207
Mills, Charles, 261
Mincu, Monica, 485, 486
miscommunication, 148
Mitchell, Thomas, 151
MLA (Monitoring Learning Achievement), 63n15, 338n24
MOB (Monopoly Opinion Bank), World Bank as, 79
"mob hysteria," 92
mobilizing structures, 92
modern, traditional compared to, 33–34
modernization, functionalism and, 502–4
modernization theory, resuscitation of, 36
Moldova, 488
Mongolia, 194, 488
Monitoring Learning Achievement (MLA), 63n15, 338n24
Monopoly Opinion Bank (MOB), World Bank as, 79
Monro, Surya, 159
Montessori, Maria, 129
Morgan, Lewis Henry, 131
Morocco, 179
Morrow, Raymond, 540
Mouffe, Chantal, 96
movements. *See* social movements
Mozambique, 303, 310
Mudimbe, Valentin Y., 33
multicultural, definition of, 127
multicultural citizenship, planetarian, 547
multilateral organizations, 37, 552. *See also* nongovernmental organizations
Murillo, E. G., Jr., 140
Muslims, stereotypes of, 155
Myanmar, 402

Naisilisili, S., 439–40, 446
Naissance de la biopolotique (Foucault), 457
Namibia, 178, 194
National In-Service Teacher Education Programme (NISTEP), Grenada, 244, 246, 259
National Institute for Academic Degrees and University Evaluation (NIAD-EU), 410
nationalism
   in Asia-Pacific region, 417–18
   in EU, 468
   globalization and, 551–52
   in Latin America, 344, 369
National Program for the Promotion of Women's Equal Opportunities in Education (PRIOM), Argentina, 200
National Security Law, China, 413

National Women's Organization (NWO), Grenada, 257, 267n3
National Youth Organization, Grenada, 258, 267n3
Nation State Law, in Israel, 381, 388
nation-states. *See* state(s)
Native Americans, stereotypes of, 155
neoclassical economics
   alternatives for, 80–82
   conservative perspective of, 71–72
   education finance and, 77–78
   education production in, 77
   evidence-based policy for education improvement myth of, 75–76
   free markets for economic growth and development myth of, 73–74
   free markets for efficient economic organization myth of, 74–75
   historical development of, 72–73
   human capital theory and, 72–73, 76–78, 80
   liberal perspective of, 72
   myths of, 71
   progressive perspective of, 72, 80–81
   World Bank ideology and, 78–79
neoclassical synthesis, 72
neocolonialism, 508
neoliberalism
   in Asia-Pacific region, 403, 404, 418
   development and, 35
   educational reform and, 88, 102–3, 115
   educational standards and, 115
   education finance and, 78
   EU and, 457
   on free markets for economic growth, myth of, 73–74
   globalization and, 102, 510, 544–45, 552
   Grenada and, 247
   higher education and, 283–84, 288
   in Latin America, 344, 353–54, 363, 368, 529–30
   student movements against, 107
   women and, 213–14
neo-Marxism, 95, 136–38
neo-mercantilism, 457
Nepal, 158
New Jewel Movement (NJM), Grenada, 246, 255, 258, 261
New Left, 534–35
new public management, 288
New Zealand, 226, 415, 437–38, 443–45
Next System Project, 81
NFE (nonformal education), 201–2, 204, 359. *See also* popular education
NGOs. *See* nongovernmental organizations
Nguyen, A. T., 421–22
NIAD-EU (National Institute for Academic Degrees and University Evaluation), 410
Nicaragua, 344–50, 355, 358, 365, 368
Niesz, Tricia, 88–90, 94, 108, 113
Nigeria, 155, 223–24, 317, 319
Ninnes, P., 512
Niranjana, Tejaswini, 514, 515
NISTEP (National In-Service Teacher Education Programme), Grenada, 244, 246, 259

NJM (New Jewel Movement), Grenada, 246, 255, 258, 261
Nkrumah, Kwame, 134
Noah, Harold, 500, 505–6
nonformal education (NFE), 201–2, 204, 359. *See also* popular education
Nonformal Primary Education, Bangladesh, 183
nongovernmental organizations (NGOs)
    adult education and, 264–65
    in Africa, 322–23
    civil society and, 351
    scope of term, 37
    women and, 204–5, 209, 211
nonsexist textbook approach, 199
Nordtveit, Bjorn H., 17–18
normative rationality, 100
Norris, Christopher, 514
Notes on Facundo (Piglia), 555
NVivo software, 141
NWO (National Women's Organization), Grenada, 257, 267n3
Nyerere, Julius, 298, 300, 305, 324, 555

Obama, Barack, 62n3
Occupied Palestinian Territory. *See* Palestine
Oceania, 433. *See also specific countries*
    case studies in, 440–45
    CIE in, 434, 438, 441–47
    climate change and, 446–47
    colonialism in, 438–39
    curriculum in, 440
    diversity of, 434, 437–38
    identity in, 445
    languages of, 435
    migration and, 436–37
    overview of, 435–37
    pedagogy in, 439–40
    Tree of Opportunity in, 438–39
    values in, 439
    women in, 435–36
OECD (Organization for Economic Cooperation and Development), 3, 178, 309, 463, 553
Offe, Claus, 87, 100–102
official statements, policy compared to, 325
Omar, Mohammad, 529
OMC (Open Method of Coordination), 460–62
O'Neill, John, 514
online instruction, higher education and, 274
ontology, definition of, 434
Open Method of Coordination (OMC), 460–62
opportunity, equality and, 169–70
oppressed, pedagogy of, 129–30, 534–35, 555
order, social, 48
ordoliberalism, 469n4
Organization for Economic Cooperation and Development (OECD), 3, 178, 309, 463, 553
orientalism, 510, 520n7
Orientalism (Said), 151
Ornstein, Norman, 541
Ottoman Empire, 476–77
outcome, equality of, 172, 179–80
output, equality of, 171, 176–79
over-information society, 541
Oxfam, 109, 323
Oxford, University of, 282, 284, 289

Pacific Education Development Framework, 396
Pacific Way (Crocombe), 436
Pakistan, 416
    Aga Khan Foundation in, 38, 183
    female education in, 198
    India relations with, 531
    nonformal education in, 201
    primary school enrollment in, 173
Palestine, 378, 381
    participatory media and, 391
    right to education in, 386–88
Pan, Julia, 15
Panama, 350
Papua New Guinea, 153
    decentralization in, 225, 234, 235
    literacy rates in, 179
    women in, 156–58, 160n2
Paquette, Jerome, 180
Pareto, Vilfredo, 532
Paris, University of, 282, 284, 289
Parsons, Talcott, 33, 502, 503
participation rates, in higher education, comparative data on, 277–81, *278, 279, 281*
participatory media, 391
Pascoe, Bruce, 150–51
PASEC (Programme d'Analyse des Systèmes Éducatifs de la CONFEMEN), 63n15, 338n24
patriarchy, schools and, 190
pedagogy
    class and, 130
    gender and, 199–200
    invisible, 130
    literacy and critical, 108
    in Oceania, 439–40
    of oppressed, 129–30, 534–35, 555
    in popular education, 359
    social movements and critical, 109–10
    student-centered, 130
Pedagogy of the Oppressed (Freire), 534–35, 555
People's Budget, Grenada, 259, 260
Perez Gonzalez, Laura, 252–53
performance-based funding, 288
Perón, Evita, 556
perspective consciousness, 11
Peru, 344, 345, 347, 349, 351–52
Pestalozzi, Johann Heinrich, 129
Phelps, Stephen, 155
Philippines, 223, 238, 401, 414, 415
Piglia, Ricardo, 555
Piketty, Thomas, 457, 557
Pinar, William, 99
Piñera, Sebastian, 356
Pinochet, Augusto, 355
PIRLS (Progress in International Reading Literacy Skills), 63n15, 338n24

PISA (Program for International Student Assessment), 7, 18, 63n15, 338n24, 397, 465
Piscitelli, Barbara, 11
planetarian multicultural citizenship, 547
Plaza-Coral, David, 155–56
Pleyers, Geoffrey, 112–13
Poland, 482, 490, 492
policy
　in Africa, agenda-setting and, 323–25
　Africa and contested, 313–25
　for higher education, international framework of, 276–77
　official statements compared to, 325
　research and, 53–54
　women and, 211–12
political economy, 72
political movements, student movements as, 107. *See also* social movements
political opportunities, 92
politics, comparative education and, 534–35
Pollock, Mica, 140
Polynesia, 435
polytechnical education, 495n3
popular education
　civil society and, 255, 360–62
　development of, 110
　in Grenada, 255–56
　higher education and, 362–65
　in Latin America, 359–65
　NFE compared to, 359
　pedagogy in, 359
　subaltern social movements and, 110–11
Popular Education (Sarmiento), 555
Popular Education Network of Women (REPEM), 206, 360
Portugal, 348
positivism
　concept of, 500
　critical theory compared to, 516
　culture of, 136
　functionalism and, 501–3
　hermeneutics and, 516
　hermeneutics compared to, 516
　poststructuralism and, 511–14
　science and, 500–501
　Western culture and, 504
postcolonialism. *See also* colonialism
　in Africa, 313
　communication in, 152
　Grenada from context of, 245–47
　intercultural interaction in, 151–52
　methodology and, 519–20
　"Other" and, 514–15
post-Fordism, 102
Post-Foundational Special Interest Group, 140–41
post-Marxism, social movements and, 93–97
postmodernism, 116–17, 151
　comparative education and, 535–36
　diversity and, 512–13
　functionalism and, 513–14
　images and, 513
　"Other" and, 514–15
post-secondary education. *See* higher education

postsocialism, in Eastern/Central Europe, 474–75, 483–92, 494
poststructuralism, 151
　agency and, 512
　definition of, 511–12
　positivism and, 511–14
Poverty Reduction Strategy Papers, World Bank and, 207, 324
power relations
　class, status and, 98–99
　research and, 59
PPPs (public-private partnerships), 18
practicality, 49
pragmatic dimension, of comparative education, 8–10
Pratham, India, 60
Prawda, J., 236–37
precision, in research, 54–56
primary education
　in Africa, 301, 301–3, 302, 304, 314
　completion of, 174–75
　female enrollment in, 193–94, 195
　feminism and, 192
　in Hapsburg Empire, 476
　on Indian subcontinent, 173
　as investment, 6
　literacy rates in, 178–79
　nonformal education and, 201–2
　US funding of, 235, 236
　women and, 197–98
PRIOM (National Program for the Promotion of Women's Equal Opportunities in Education), Argentina, 200
private tuition, 287
private tutoring, 488–89, 493–94
privatization
　in Africa, 214, 320–22, 321
　in Eastern/Central Europe, 487–89
　EU joining and, 488
　in Latin America, 344, 354–57, 366
　of research, 58
　of school, women and, 214
privilege, 174, 258
production, education as, 48–50, 77, 333–36
Productive Farmers Union, Grenada, 258
professionalization, of teachers, 9
professional movements, teacher activism as, 108–9
Program for International Student Assessment (PISA), 7, 18, 63n15, 338n24, 397, 465
Programme d'Analyse des Systèmes Éducatifs de la CONFEMEN (PASEC), 63n15, 338n24
Progress in International Reading Literacy Skills (PIRLS), 63n15, 338n24
Progressive International, 81
progressive perspective, of neoclassical economics, 72, 80–81
Prospera program, Mexico, 362
Przeworski, A., 35
Psacharopoulos, George, 6
psychology, mass, 92
public literacy, 249, 257–62
public-private partnerships (PPPs), 18
Puri, Shalin, 247

al Qaeda, 529. *See also* September 11 attacks
quality assurance (QA), 400, 404–14
quantification, research and, 54–56
Quebec, 107, 114
"Quiet Revolution," in Quebec, 114

race
 differentiation by, 169
 in Latin America, 351–53
racism, feminism and, 149
Radcliffe-Brown, A. R., 134–35
radical pluralism, 81–82
radical-pluralism, social movements and, 95–96
Ragin, C. C., 16–17
Ramirez, F. O., 32
randomized controlled trials (RCTs), 76
Rappleye, J., 15
rate of return (ROR), 47–48, 77
rational choice theory, 288
rationality, social movements and, 100
rationalization, of society, 503–4
Rawls, John, 536
RCTs (randomized controlled trials), 76
Reagan, Ronald, 532
reflexive modernity, 117
reform, educational. *See also* centralization; decentralization
 centralization/decentralization and administrative, 236–37
 challenge of, 180–81, 543–44
 conflict theories and, 97–98
 contemporary, 31–32
 CSOs and, 112
 elite-driven, 114–15
 fads in, 181–82
 functionalism and, 97
 Global Educational Reform Movement and, 115
 local stakeholders in, 61–62
 neoliberalism and, 88, 102–3, 115
 in 1960s, 163–65
 in 1970s, 165–67
 "one size fits all" approach to, 168
 profiting from, 543–44
 social and cultural reproduction and, 97–99
 social mobility and, 166
 social movements and, 88–89, 97–103, 113–15
 social order and, 167–68
 theoretical accounts of, 167–68
refugee education access, in EU, 388–90
Regional Centre for Higher Education and Development (RIHED), 419–20, 422
regional economies, globalization and, 2–3
regional higher education, in Asia-Pacific region, 417–23
Reimagining Japanese Education (Willis, D. B., and Rappleye), 15
relationships, valued modalities of, 128–29
religion, in Asia-Pacific region, 423
REPEM (Popular Education Network of Women), 206, 360
"repertoires of contention," 92

research
 in Africa, 51–52
 case studies as most common approach to, 16
 commissioned, 57–59
 computer data sets for, 141
 as consulting, 57–58
 decision-making and, 53–54
 in developing countries, women, 214–15
 economics as social science and, 56–57
 evidence-based policy for education improvement myth of, 75–76
 foreign aid and, 36–37, 51–60
 functionalism and, 135
 higher education and, 30–31, 290–91
 knowledge mystification and, 59
 large-scale, 18
 in Latin America, 365–67
 methodological orthodoxy and critical inquiry in, 58–59
 policy and, 53–54
 power relations and, 59
 precision in, 54–56
 privatization of, 58
 quantification and, 54–56
 RCTs and, 76
 roles of, 51–59
 World Bank on primacy of, 53
resource mobilization theory, 92
Rethinking Pacific Education Initiative, 439
Revisiting Education in the New Latino Diaspora (Hamann, Wortham, Murillo), 140
revolution, educational, social movements and, 113–15
revolutionary left, high education and, 106
Rhea, Zane Ma, 139
RIAIPE project, 364
Ricardo, David, 353
Ricoeur, Paul, 556
RIHED (Regional Centre for Higher Education and Development), 419–20, 422
Rincón-Gallardo, Santiago, 109
risk society, 117–18
Robarts Plan, Canada, 164
Rockefeller Foundation, 38, 323
Rodney, Walter, 267
Rodrik, Dani, 82n2
Rogers, Everett, 555
Romania, 348, 478, 484, 486, 488
Roma people, 485
ROR (rate of return), 47–48, 77
Rosemberg, Fulvia, 196
Ross, Heidi, 17, 139
Rousseau, Jean-Jacques, 129
Rousseff, Dilma, 351
rural participation
 in higher education, 279, 279
 in Latin America, 349
Russian Empire, 477–78
Russian Federation, 487, 488, 490, 492
Russian Revolution of 1917, 31–32, 479
Rwanda, 310, 317

SACMEQ (Southern African Consortium for Monitoring Educational Quality), 63n15, 338n24
Sadler, Michael, 10
Sahlberg, Pasi, 115
Said, Edward, 151, 381, 514
Salgado, Sebastian, 530
Sanders, Bernie, 82
Sanders, Jane, 81
Sanga, Kabini, 443
Sao Tome, 321
Sarmiento, Domingo Faustino, 554–55
Sarup, Madan, 136
Saudi Arabia, 154
Schiefelbein, Ernesto, 179, 180
Schneider, Friedrich, 500
School Education Act, Japan, 410
school ethnography, 136–41
schooling, education compared to, 188
school-leaving qualifications, 228–30, 229
schools
    colonial, 132
    patriarchy and, 190
    social order and, 48
Schools for Life program, Ghana, 183
School Strikes for Climate, 149
Schutz, Alfred, 501
science
    enlightenment and, 500–501
    functionalism and, 501–3
    methodology of, 501
    modernization and, 502–4
    positivism and, 500–501
scientific dimension, of comparative education
    overview of, 5–8
    pragmatic compared to, 9–10
scientism, 134–36, 507, 515
Scotland, 228
SDGs (Sustainable Development Goals), 187–88, 207–9, 211, 276, 364
SEAMEO (Southeast Asian Ministers of Education Organizations), 419, 422
secondary education
    in Africa, 301, *301, 302,* 303, *304,* 314
    as best education investment, 6
    dropout rates in, 175
    female enrollment in, 193–95, *195*
    increased access to, 165
    US funding of, 235, *236*
    women and, 197–98
second modernity, 117
segregation
    in Africa, 313–14
    charter schools and, 115
    refugee education access in EU and, 388–89
    in US, 164–65
self-reliance, 305, 324, 328
Sem Terra movement, Brazil. *See* Landless Workers Movement, Brazil
Sen, Amartya, 557
Senegal, 44, 179. *See also* Dakar conference
September 11 attacks, 381, 528–29, 532–33
Serbia, 488

sexual orientation, gender identity, and expression (SOGIE), 150
shadow education, 287, 488–89
Sierra Leone, 303, 319, 531
"silent Indian" stereotype, 155
similarities, in education worldwide, 32–33
Singapore, 397
    quality assurance in, 412–14
Singh, M., 408–9
"single stories," identity and, 154–55
Skinner, Debra, 158
Slovenia, 488
Smith, Adam, 72, 82n2, 353
Smith, Angus, 260
Smith, L., 437
Smock, Audrey, 198
Sobe, Noah, 141
social-conflict theory, 106
social crisis theory, 100–101
social engineering, 56–57
socialism
    defeat of, 34–35
    in Eastern/Central Europe, 474, 478–83
    educational achievements under, 481–83
    in Grenada, 246
    higher education and, 481–83
    social movements and, 95
socialization, definition of, 127
social justice
    feminism and, 211–12
    identity and, 159–60
social media, in Global South, 263
social mobility
    adult education and, 249–50
    in Africa, 333
    Asia-Pacific region and, 414–17
    equality and, 179
    in EU, 458, 467
    gender transformation and, 190
    reform and, 166
    in US, 532
    women and, 190
social movements
    activity levels of, 91
    anarchism and, 113–14
    bilingual education and, 104
    Black Lives Matter, 149
    capitalism and, 93, 97
    charter schools and, 115
    in civil society, 90
    class and, 96, 99
    cognitive approach to, 93–94
    collective learning and, 103
    COVID-19 and, 116–18
    critical pedagogy and, 109–10
    critical theory and, 94–95, 99–103
    crowds to collective behavior in, 92–93
    decolonization and, 110–12
    definition of, 90–91
    development and, 134
    economic redistribution and, 100
    educational institutions as target of and resource for, 104–6

educational reform and, 88–89, 97–103, 113–15
educational revolution and, 113–15
environmental, 104–5, 117
framing processes and, 92–93
indigenous, 111–12
kindergarten movement, 108
legitimation crisis theory and, 100–103
Marxism, post-Marxism and, 93–97
mass education, educational expansion and, 106
mass mobilization and, 90–91
mobilizing structures and, 92
political opportunities and, 92
radical-pluralism and, 95–96
rationality and, 100
as sites of learning, 112–13
socialism and, 95
spectrum of educational transformation and, 113–15
state and, 92–93
student-led, 107, 114, 149
subaltern, 110–12
teacher activism and, 108–9
theories of, US and EU, 90–97
transnational, 109
united field of scholarship on, 88–89, 94
social order
educational reform and, 167–68
schools and, 48
social rationality, 100
social reproduction, Marxism and, 97–99
social science, economics as, 56–57
Social Science Citation Index (SSCI) syndrome, 405
social stratification
development and, 177
literacy and, 249–50, 260
sociocultural identity, 147
socioeconomic status. *See also* economics
achievement and, 7
industrialization and, 7
sociology, 501–2
Socratic method, 30
SOGIE (sexual orientation, gender identity, and expression), 150
Solomon Islands, 435, 436, 440–42
de Sousa Santos, B., 533
South Africa, 107, 114, 233, 313–14, 321
Equal Education in, 60
female enrollment in, 194
Southeast Asian Ministers of Education Organizations (SEAMEO), 419, 422
Southern African Consortium for Monitoring Educational Quality (SACMEQ), 63n15, 338n24
southern theory, 110–12
Soviet Union, 478–83
Spain, 223, 226, 228, 229
spectrum of educational transformation, social movements and, 113–15
Spencer, Herbert, 131
Speth, Gus, 81
Spindler, George, 136

Spindler, Louise, 136
Spivak, Gayatri, 151, 381, 514
Sri Lanka, 153–54, 233
"educated person" in, 158–59
SSCI (Social Science Citation Index) syndrome, 405
Stalin, Josef, 479–81
standards, educational, globalization of, 46, 115
state(s), 87–89
African education and, 330–34
civil society collaboration with, 360–62
"conditioned," 346–54
defense of democratic, 546–47
definition of, 345–46
globalization and changes in, 509–11
higher education and, 274, 281–84
schooling as ideological apparatus of, 191
social-conflict theory of, 106
social movements and, 92–93
structural adjustment and, 39, 207
as unit of analysis, 505–6
welfare state capitalism, 101
women's education and, 206–7
Steiner, Rudolf, 129
stereotypes, 154–55
Stiglitz, George, 530, 560n1
St. Lucia, 265
strategic rationality, 100
Stromquist, Nelly, 350
structural adjustment, 39, 207, 307–8, 367–68
structural functionalism. *See* functionalism
The Structure of Scientific Revolutions (Kuhn), 555
Stuardo, G. M., 355
student-centered pedagogy, 130
student movements, 107, 114, 149. *See also* social movements
subaltern social movements, 110–12
subject-object relations, 135
successful communication, 148
Sultana, Ronald, 462
survival, equality of, 171, 174–76
Sustainable Development Goals (SDGs), UN, 187–88, 207–9, 211, 276, 364
Sweden
centralization/decentralization in, 228, 229
higher education in, 282–83
Switzerland, 225
Syria, 175
access to education in, 382–84
civil war in, 380
women in, 390

Taif Accord, 385
Taiwan, 230–31, 396, 401
quality assurance in, 411–12
Taiwan Assessment and Evaluation Association (TWAEA), 411
Tajikistan, 488
T.A. Marryshow Community College, Grenada, 252
Tamir, Yuli, 156
Tan, Eng, 5
Tanzania, 44, 60, 178, 300, 305, 321, 324–25

Tarlau, Rebecca, 359–61
Tatto, M. T., 12
Taufe'ulungaki, 'Ana Maui, 442
Taylor, Edward, 131
teachers
  activism of, 108–9
  challenges facing, 543
  in developing countries, women as, 215
  in Eastern/Central Europe, 489
  in EU, 466
  foreign aid in payment of, 43
  private tutoring and, 488–89, 493–94
  professionalization of, in Finland, 9
  training, 543
Teasdale, Bob, 139
technical literacy, 249
territorial centralization, 223
territorial decentralization, 223
terrorism, 155, 381, 528–29, 532–33, 550
tertiary education. *See* higher education
textbooks
  antisexist approach to, 199
  centralization/decentralization and, 230–31
  in China, 230–31
  gender-neutral approach to, 199
  nonsexist approach to, 199
  provision of, 177
  in Soviet Union, 479
  women in, 198–201
Thailand, 173, 401, 414
Thaman, Konai Helu, 443
Thatcher, Margaret, 81, 467
Theborn, Goran, 468
Theisen, Gary, 12
Third World, Global South terminology compared to, 62n2
Thomas, R. M., 5, 16
Thunberg, Greta, 107, 149
Tilly, Charles, 92, 93, 104
time, institutionalization of, 133
TIMSS (Trends in International Mathematics and Science Study), 63n15, 338n24
Togo, 179
Tomasevski, Katarina, 329
Tonga, 226, 436, 442–43, 446
Torres, Carlos Alberto, 359, 367, 381, 540
Touraine, Alain, 97
traditional, modern compared to, 33–34
transitology, 17
translanguaging, 389
translation, 514–15
transnationalism
  school ethnography and, 140
  social movements and, 109
Treaty of Amsterdam, 458
Treaty of Lisbon, 456, 463–64
Treaty of Maastricht, 456, 458
Treaty of Paris, 458
Treaty of Rome, 458
Treaty of Waitangi, 443–44
Tree of Opportunity, in Oceania, 438–39
Trends in International Mathematics and Science Study (TIMSS), 63n15, 338n24
Trinidad and Tobago, 265

triumphalism, of US, 34–36
Trudeau, Pierre, 476
Trump, Donald, 82, 549, 560
Tunisia, 380
Turkmenistan, 490
tutoring, private, 488–89, 493–94
TWAEA (Taiwan Assessment and Evaluation Association), 411

UCA (Central American University), 365
Uganda, 303, 319, 321
UK. *See* United Kingdom
Ukraine, 488
UMAP (University Mobility in Asia-Pacific), 420
UN. *See* United Nations
UNDP (United Nations Development Programme), 40, 196, 208
unemployment, educated, 326
UNESCO (United Nations Educational Scientific and Cultural Organization), 20n1, 37, 39–40, 78, 178, 262, 364, 399, 505, 559
UNICEF (United Nations Children Fund), 12–13, 20n1, 40
UNILAB (University for International Integration of the Afro-Brazilian Lusophony), 363
unions, teacher activism and, 108–9
United Kingdom (UK)
  Athena SWAN in, 203
  Brexit and, 285–86
  centralization in, 227, 228
  decentralization in, 225, 228
  higher education in, 283, 285–86
  school-leaving qualifications in, 228–29
  university buffer funding bodies in, 232, 233
  University Funding Council in, 232
United Nations (UN)
  education system of, 38–41
  Global Education First Initiative of, 378–79
  higher education and, 277
  Millennium Development Goals of, 45, 207
  Sustainable Development Goals of, 187–88, 207–9, 211, 276, 364
United Nations Children Fund (UNICEF), 12–13, 20n1, 40
United Nations Development Programme (UNDP), 40, 196, 208
United Nations Educational Scientific and Cultural Organization (UNESCO), 20n1, 37, 39–40, 78, 178, 262, 364, 399, 505, 559
United States (US)
  ADVANCE in, 203
  Afghanistan war and, 529
  Asian educational systems and, 8–9
  authoritarian threats in, 560
  borrowing/lending of educational practices in history of, 8
  centralization in, 224, 238
  China relations with, 398–99, 511
  decentralization in, 238
  educational reform in, 1960s, 164–65

energy politics and, 528
higher education in, 283, 532
human rights and, 528
international education and, 533
primary/secondary school funding in, 235, 236
segregation in, 164–65
social mobility in, 532
social movement theories in, 90–97
terrorism and, 381, 528–29, 532–33
triumphalism of, 34–36
voter turnout in, 549
United States Agency for International Aid (USAID), 3, 37
universal primary education, 165
universities. *See* higher education
University for International Integration of the Afro-Brazilian Lusophony (UNILAB), 363
University Mobility in Asia-Pacific (UMAP), 420
Unterhalter, E., 149
urban participation
in higher education, 279, *279*
in Latin America, 349
Uruguay, 179, 348–50
US. *See* United States
USAID (United States Agency for International Aid), 3, 37
utilitarianism, 58
Uwezo, East Africa, 60
Uzbekistan, 488

vaccines, for COVID-19, 13
values
cultural, 128–29
education, 11
in Oceania, 439
Varoufakis, Yanis, 81
Vavrus, Frances, 16, 139
Venezuela, 344, 348–50, 358–59, 528, 530
Verba, Sidney, 560
Verger, Antoni, 18, 355, 366
Versace, Gianni, 519
vertical case studies, 16
Vietnam, 396–98, 401, 414
Villa, Pancho, 114
Vogel, Ezra, 419
voter turnout, democracy and, 548–49
vouchers, charter schools and, 115
Vulliamy, Graham, 10

Waghid, Yusef, 5, 11
Wallace, Michael, 17
Wallerstein, Immanuel, 508, 547
Warwick, Donald, 198
Washington education consensus, 36, 51, 52
Watson, Keith, 5
WCCES (World Council of Comparative Education Societies), 14, 557
The Wealth of Nations (Smith, Adam), 72
Webb, A., 351–52
Webber, J. R., 344–45
Weber, Louis, 464
Weber, Max, 17, 96, 98–99, 101

Weiler, H. N., 224
welfare state capitalism, 101
West Bank. *See* Palestine
Western culture, dominance of, 504
Westernization, mass education and, 32–33
Western Samoa, 153
"white man's burden," 34
Willis, D. B., 15
Willis, Paul, 98
Wolfensohn, James, 6, 209
Wolpe, Harold, 508
women. *See also* feminism
access for, 195–96, 202, 204
adult education for, 204–6
in Africa, 315, 315–17
civil society and, 209, 351
conditions of schooling of, 193–97, *195*
conferences and, 207–8
content of schooling and, 198–201
in CRME, 382, 390–91
in developing countries, 213–316
education stipends for, 197
empowerment of, 197, 206, 210
enrollment numbers for, 193–95, *195*
experience of schooling and, 198–201
feminist theory and, 189–93
foreign aid and education of, 207–10
gender parity index for, 194, *195*
globalization and, 213
in Grenada, 256–57
higher education and, 202–4
in Latin America, 349–51
Marxism and, 214
in media in developing countries, 215
neoliberalism and, 213–14
NGOs and, 204–5, 209, 211
nonformal education and, 201–2, 204
in Oceania, 435–36
in Papua New Guinea, 156–58, 160n2
policy and, 211–12
practical needs of, 205
primary education and, 197–98
privatization of school and, 214
secondary education and, 197–98
social mobility and, 190
in Soviet Union, 481–82
state and education of, 206–7
as teachers in developing countries, 215
in textbooks, 198–201
World Bank and, 209–10
Women's Eyes on the World Bank, 209–10
Workers' Parish Councils, in Grenada, 256
World Bank, 3, 34, 37, 553
advice from, 299
Africa categorization of, 336n3
Donors to African Education and, 41
EFA and, 78
governance and anticorruption focus of, 338n26
Human Capital Index and, 280–81, *281*
human capital theory and, 47–48
ideology of, neoclassical economics and, 78–79
as "Knowledge Bank," 79

Learning for All and, 311–13
as MOB, 79
Poverty Reduction Strategy Paper and, 207, 324
on research primacy, 53
UNESCO and, 39–40
women and, 209–10
World Conference on Education for All, 40, 173
World Council of Comparative Education Societies (WCCES), 14, 557
world culture theory, 106
The World Educational Crisis (Coombs), 165
World Education Forum, 40–41, 173, 210, 546
World Social Forum (WSF), 82, 546
World Trade Organization (WTO), 410, 420

Worldwide University Network, 506
Wortham, S., 140
WSF (World Social Forum), 82, 546
WTO (World Trade Organization), 410, 420

Yang, Shen-Keng, 133
Yemen, 179
Yonezawa, A., 410
Young, Michael, 136
Yugoslavia, 480–81

Zapata, Emiliano, 114
Zapatistas, Mexico, 112
Zimbabwe, *233*, 305
Ziperovich, Rosita, 556
Zonal Councils, in Grenada, 256

About the Contributors

■ ■ ■

Robert F. Arnove, lead coeditor of the previous four editions of *Comparative Education: The Dialectic of the Global and the Local,* is Chancellor's Professor Emeritus of Educational Leadership & Policy Studies at Indiana University, Bloomington. He is a past president and Honorary Fellow of the Comparative and International Education Society. A visiting scholar at universities ranging from Argentina to Australia, he has published extensively on the contours, dimensions, and major trends in the field of comparative education with a focus on education and sociopolitical exchange. His latest book, *Talent Abounds*, examines teaching and mentoring interactions and societal policies that can foster peak performance in various domains of the arts and athletics for all students. He has been a teachers' union president, a third-party candidate for the U.S. Congress, and the president of an experimental theater company in Bloomington, Indiana.

Muzna Awayed-Bishara has a PhD from the Department of English Language and Literature at the University of Haifa. Her main research interests are critical discourse studies and language (specifically English) and intercultural communication in conflict-ridden contexts. She is a senior faculty member in the Program for Multilingual Education, School of Education at Tel Aviv University. She is the author of *EFL Pedagogy as Cultural Discourse: Textbooks, Practice, and Policy for Arabs and Jews in Israel* (Routledge, 2020).

Mark Bray is Distinguished Chair Professor in the Faculty of Education at East China Normal University (ECNU), and also holds the UNESCO Chair in Comparative Education at the University of Hong Kong He is a past president of the U.S.-based Comparative & International Education Society, and of the Comparative Education Society of Hong Kong. He began his career as a teacher in Kenya and Nigeria before teaching at the Universities of Edinburgh, Papua New Guinea, and London. He moved to Hong Kong in 1986 and took leave from 2006 to 2010 to work in Paris as director of UNESCO's International Institute for Educational Planning. He joined ECNU in 2018. Email: mbray@hku.hk

Bidemi Carrol is Senior Research Education Analyst in the International Education Division of RTI International. She is an international education specialist with more than 15 years of experience in education policy and programs in sub-Saharan Africa. In her work she provides technical assistance and policy support to education programs and governments in Sub-Saharan Africa, most recently in

Malawi, Sierra Leone, and Liberia. Her research interests include education system strengthening, education leadership, and the role international agencies play in Africa's education. Dr. Carrol holds a master's degree in economics and a PhD in International Comparative Education from Stanford University.

Ben Eklof, Emeritus Professor of History and Education at Indiana University and Senior Researcher at the Higher School of Economics in Moscow, Russia, is a specialist in late Imperial Russia as well as the Gorbachev and post-Soviet era educational regimes. He has spent more than eight years of his career in residence in Moscow and Russia's regions and has published extensively on education, politics, society, daily life, as well as Russian populism and local governance.

David Taufui Mikato Fa'avae, PhD, is the son of Sio Milemoti Fa'avae and Fatai Onevai Fa'avae. His ancestral links are to Ma'ufanga i Tongatapu, Taunga i Vava'u, Niuafo'ou, Angahā i 'Eua in Tonga. Through his paternal great grandfather, David has heritage links to Satalo in Samoa. David is a lecturer in Pacific education at the University of Waikato (Kirikiriroa Hamilton, Aotearoa New Zealand). He supports the mentoring of new and emerging Oceania researchers through the auspices of the Oceania Comparative and International Education Society.

Joseph P. Farrell was professor emeritus in the Comparative, International and Development Education Centre of the Ontario Institute for Studies in Education, University of Toronto. He was an Honorary Fellow and past president of the Comparative and International Education Society.

Christine Fox is a comparative and international education consultant, researcher, writer, and former senior academic at the University of Wollongong in Australia. She has an MA in educational planning from the University of London's Institute of Education and a PhD in Education and Intercultural Communication from the University of Sydney. She was twice president of the Australian and New Zealand Comparative and International Education Society, and is past secretary-general of the World Council of Comparative Education Societies (2005–2012).

Stephen Franz has a doctorate in education policy studies from Indiana University and is an education consultant and research analyst focusing on topics related to equality of educational opportunities and outcomes. He has written extensively on education in Latin America.

John Hawkins was Professor Emeritus of Comparative and International Education at the UCLA Graduate School of Education & Information Studies. He was also co-director of the Center for International and Development Education at UCLA and Senior Advisor to the International Forum on Education 2020 at the East West Center in Honolulu, Hawaii.

Anne Hickling-Hudson, born and raised in Jamaica, has wide experience as an educator in the Caribbean, the United Kingdom, and Australia, where she is now a retired professor of teacher education at the Queensland University of

Technology. Anne's degrees are from the University of the West Indies and the University of Hong Kong, with a PhD from the University of Queensland, Australia. A Rockefeller Fellow and winner of several Australian national research awards, she is a pioneer in the analysis of postcolonial issues and decolonization strategies in education. She is a past president of the World Council of Comparative Education Societies, the Australia and New Zealand Comparative and International Education Society, and the British Association for International and Comparative Education. She coedits a postcolonial education journal and book series and has numerous publications including a landmark edited book on Cuban internationalism in education.

Steven J. Klees is professor of International Education Policy and Distinguished Scholar-Teacher at the University of Maryland. He completed his PhD at Stanford University and has been a faculty member at Cornell University, Stanford University, Florida State University, and the Federal University of Rio Grande do Norte in Brazil. He was a Fulbright Scholar on two occasions at the Federal University of Bahia in Brazil and has taught many short courses at universities around the world. He has worked on evaluations of education programs and policies in dozens of countries for a wide array of international agencies, ministries, and nongovernmental organizations. Recent books include: *The World Bank and Education: Critiques and Alternatives*; *Women Teachers in Africa: Challenges and Possibilities*; and *The Conscience of a Progressive*. He is a former president and Honorary Fellow of the Comparative and International Education Society.

Vandra Lea Masemann is an adjunct professor in the Leadership, Higher and Adult Education Department at the Ontario Institute for Studies in Education at the University of Toronto. She is a past President of the World Council of Comparative Education Societies, the Comparative and International Education Society (United States), and the Comparative and International Education Society of Canada.

Lauren Ila Misiaszek (PhD, UCLA) has been associate professor in the Institute of International and Comparative Education at Beijing Normal University since 2013. Lauren is immediate past secretary general of the World Council of Comparative Education Societies (2016–2019), an associate Director of the Paulo Freire Institute, UCLA, and a co-founder and Fellow of the International Network on Gender Social Justice, and Praxis. Some of the other positions she has held have included as a UK Fulbright Scholar, a national program manager for the U.S. Veterans Administration, a sustainable development fellow in Nicaragua, and a free clinic worker and translator in the United States. Lauren works across various linguistic and geographic contexts at the intersection of the humanities and social sciences on a wide range of intersectional social justice issues, including social movements and nonformal education, critical sociology of higher education, and postfoundational comparative education.

Raymond A. Morrow earned a PhD in sociology at York University in Toronto in 1981 and subsequently taught sociology at the University of Alberta from 1984 until his retirement as an emeritus professor in 2010, serving also as an adjunct professor in educational policy studies. His books include *Critical Theory and Methodology* (1994; Choice Magazine Academic Book Award); *Social Theory and Education: A Critique of Theories of Social and Cultural Reproduction* (with C. A. Torres, 1995); *Reading Freire and Habermas: Critical Pedagogy and Transformative Change* (with C. A. Torres, 2002).

Carlos Ornelas is a professor of education and communications at the Metropolitan Autonomous University in Mexico City. He earned a PhD in education at Stanford University. His most recent edited book is *Politics of Education in Latin America: Reforms, resistance, and persistence* (Brill-Sense Publishers, 2019). Siglo XXI Editores published the Spanish version in 2020.

Martyn Reynolds, PhD, was born near London of Anglo-Welsh parentage. He has been an educator for over 30 years and has worked in the United Kingdom, Papua New Guinea, Tonga, and Aotearoa New Zealand. His interests include understanding the place of culture in education. Currently, he is a postdoctoral fellow in Pacific Education at Victoria University of Wellington. Martyn and his wife, Sylvia, have two children. He is the secretary of the Oceania Comparative and International Education Society.

Joel Samoff is an educator, researcher, and evaluator who combines the scholar's critical approach and extensive experience in international development. He studies the links among research, public policy, and foreign aid. At Stanford University since 1980, and research associate, University of Johannesburg, he holds honorary doctorates from the University of Pretoria and the University of the Free State in South Africa. Recent publications include *Capturing Complexity and Context: Evaluating Aid to Education* (with Jane Leer and Michelle Reddy) and *Higher Education for Self-Reliance: Tanzania and Africa*.

Kabini Sanga, PhD, is a Solomon Islander and currently an associate professor in education at Victoria University of Wellington, New Zealand. A two-time Commonwealth scholar, he obtained his graduate degrees from Canadian universities. He advises, speaks, and writes on topics relating to leadership, education, and international development in the Pacific region. He is the co-president of the Oceania Comparative and International Education Society.

Daniel Schugurensky is a professor at Arizona State University, where he is the director of the Graduate Program in Social and Cultural Pedagogy and the Participatory Governance Initiative. His current interests include citizenship education, higher education, civic engagement, participatory democracy, and school-community relations. His most recent book is *Global Citizenship Education and Teacher Education: International Perspectives and Practices* (Routledge, 2020).

Iveta Silova is professor and director of the Center for Advanced Studies in Global Education at Mary Lou Fulton Teachers College at Arizona State University. She holds a PhD in comparative education and political sociology from Teachers College, Columbia University. Her research focuses on globalization and postsocialist education transformations, including intersections between postcolonialism and postsocialism after the Cold War. Silova's most recent research engages with the decoloniality of knowledge production and being, childhood memories, ecofeminism, and environmental sustainability. Her latest books include *Globalization on the Margins: Education and Postsocialist Transformations in Central Asia* (2020), coedited with Sarfaroz Niyozov; *Childhood and Schooling in (Post)Socialist Societies: Memories of Everyday Life* (2018, coedited with Millei & Piattoeva); and *Reimagining Utopias* (2017, coedited with Sobe, Korzh, & Kovalchuk). She is a coeditor of *European Education: Issues and Studies* and an associate editor of *Education Policy Analysis Archives*.

Nelly P. Stromquist is emerita professor and former H. R. W. Benjamin Chair of International Education at the College of Education, University of Maryland. Her research focuses on the dynamics of educational policies and practices, gender relations and social justice, adult literacy, and the impact of globalization on education, particularly the professoriate. She is the author of numerous articles and several books. In 2017, she was appointed honorary fellow in the U.S. Comparative and International Education Society.

António Teodoro is professor of sociology of education and comparative education in Lusofona University, Lisbon, and director of the Interdisciplinary Research Centre for Education and Development. Founder of free teacher trade unionism in Portugal after the Portuguese Revolution in April 1974, he was the first general-secretary of National Teachers Federation, the most representative Portuguese teacher union (1983–1994). He is founder and chair of the Portuguese Society of Comparative Education, and member-at-large of the Executive Committee and chair of the Constitutional Standing Committee of World Council of Comparative Education Societies.

Carlos Alberto Torres is Distinguished Professor of Education, Director of the UCLA Paulo Freire Institute, and former UNESCO-UCLA Chair in *Global Learning and Global Citizenship Education*. Dr. Torres is a political sociologist of education educated in Argentina, Mexico, the United States, and Canada. He is also founding director of the Paulo Freire Institute in São Paulo, Brazil; Buenos Aires, Argentina; and UCLA. Past President of the World Council of Comparative Education Societies, Past President of the Research Committee of Sociology of Education, International Sociological Association, and Past President of the Comparative and International Society. He is a Fellow of the Royal Society of Canada and Corresponding Member of the Mexican Academy of Sciences. Has published over 60 books and more than 300 peer research articles, and received three Fulbright grants.

Anthony Welch is professor of education, University of Sydney. Numerous publications address education reforms, principally within Australia and the Asia-Pacific. A consultant to state, national and international agencies, governments, institutions, and foundations, particularly in higher education, his project experience largely includes East and Southeast Asia. His work has been translated into a dozen languages, and he has been visiting professor in the United States, the United Kingdom, Germany, France, Japan, Malaysia, Turkey, China, and Hong Kong, China.

Susan Wiksten serves as associate editor to the *European Journal of Education*. She is affiliated with the European Institute of Education and Social Policy and the Paulo Freire Institute at UCLA. In recent work, she has served as a research consultant for UNESCO; developing guidelines for a curriculum of Global Citizenship Education (2019); and by contributing to a background paper for the UNESCO Futures of Education agenda (2020). Her most recent book, which is the outcome of a collaboration with several authors from the Global South and the Global North, is titled *Centering Global Citizenship Education in the Public Sphere: International Enactments of GCED for Social Justice and Common Good* (Routledge, 2021).

CPSIA information can be obtained
at www.ICGtesting.com
Printed in the USA
BVHW061033240722
642751BV00002B/8